ACCELERATING

INDIA'S

DEVELOPMENT

ADVANCE PRAISE FOR THE BOOK

'The 1991 economic reforms were all about dismantling a highly dysfunctional system of government interference with what was much better done by the market. This needed to be accompanied by the government playing a much stronger role in critical areas, notably the delivery of high-quality public services such as education and health, and also the rule of law. These are areas where our performance needs to be greatly improved if we are to achieve the objective of inclusive growth leading to high-income status. In this magisterial book, Karthik Muralidharan draws on extensive research and practice to tell us how this is best done. Since these issues are constitutionally state subjects, the book highlights the importance of state-level actions. Since much of what needs to be done in the years ahead lies primarily in the realm of the states, the book also recommends much greater decentralization from Centre to state, and from state to local governments. It sets an ambitious national agenda for evolving a well-considered programme of Centre–state cooperation, which will be essential if we are to make progress in these areas'—**Montek Singh Ahluwalia**, former deputy chairman, Planning Commission of India, and former Finance Secretary, Government of India

'In a context where rapid technological change, global crises, and international capital markets have captured the headlines about the world economy, Karthik Muralidharan reminds us that at the heart of economic growth and welfare of nations is *state capacity*. Karthik's message is not simply a rediscovery of the role of the state in economic development. It is a comprehensive reimagination and recrafting of the concept of state capacity, and why and how it affects the welfare of nations. For political leaders and policymakers, this book is a clear guide to what drives national development. For students researching the economic growth paths of nations, Karthik's treatise offers a powerful analytical framework, based on decades of meticulous research. To his credit, Karthik has intelligently drawn from beyond the usual narrow boundaries of randomized controlled trial (RCT) analysis to reflect on the larger story of national development. For those interested in the transformation of nations and those who follow the global footprint of India, this book is a must-read'—**Junaid Kamal Ahmad**, vice president, Multilateral Investment Guarantee Agency (MIGA), and former country director for India, World Bank

'Karthik Muralidharan's wonderful empirical work has helped us understand the provision of public goods better, especially in social sectors. He brings that wealth of research experience and his incisive lens to bear in crafting this ambitious book on India's future development trajectory, with an emphasis on state capacity, and ideas for improvement. This is a major contribution in an area often neglected, and will make us think about reinventing the Indian state, as we embark on our journey towards a developed India'—**Bibek Debroy**, chairman, Economic Advisory Council to the Prime Minister

'There is a trove of simple policy reforms in India that could go a long way in improving people's lives. However, they are not easy to find, let alone initiate. Karthik Muralidharan's sustained quest for evidence-based reforms is an important contribution to this effort. This book presents a rich application of an approach to policymaking that cannot be ignored even when we differ'— **Jean Drèze**, honorary professor, Delhi School of Economics; and co-author of *Hunger and Public Action*, and *An Uncertain Glory: India and Its Contradictions*

'A well-written and enjoyable read for both laypeople and experts. The solutions to building stronger state capacity are practical, recognizing that ours is a highly stratified society, and within that, making suggestions that would work in everyone's interest. For me, an important part is understanding the role for civil society and the ways in which a broad social coalition can be built to accomplish this goal'—**Renana Jhabvala**, chairperson, SEWA Bharat

'This wonderful book by Professor Muralidharan is a seminal contribution to the theory and praxis of economic transformation of a large country. Every country is, of course, unique in its own way, but the sheer size of India makes the tasks facing policymakers rather daunting. In the coming years, these challenges will get more complex while the urgency to meet them is becoming greater as the growth accelerator, called the "demographic dividend", is slowing down with every passing day. Fortunately, this is precisely where Professor Muralidharan's policy insights offered in this book are almost heaven-sent for our policymakers. I hope they will "just do it"'—**Vijay Kelkar**, chairman, Thirteenth Finance Commission; former Finance Secretary, Government of India; and co-author of *In Service of the Republic: The Art and Science of Economic Policy*

'After decades of excessive state control of the economy and slow growth, India broke out of its earlier development paradigm in the early 1990s and began to increase and improve the role of markets in the economy. Paradoxically, over the next three decades, it turns out that the binding constraint on greater growth is "state capacity". Karthik Muralidharan comprehensively addresses this quest for a better and smarter state in this master volume. The definitive work on the subject, which needs to be read by everyone connected with and interested in development'—**K.P. Krishnan**, chairman, Shriram Capital, and former Secretary (Skills), Government of India

'This book addresses India's critical challenges in education, health, safety, justice, welfare, and jobs, and offers an actionable roadmap for better governance and improved public service delivery. Every chapter blends academic rigour with practical relevance in highly accessible writing. Essential reading for anyone interested in India's development, it is an invaluable guide for India's leaders and policymakers to drive national progress'—**Nandan Nilekani**, chairman and co-founder, Infosys, and founding chairman, UIDAI (Aadhaar)

'This is an excellent book with enormous data, research findings, and astonishing insights into what ails our system. I have yet to see anything so exhaustive, which covers almost every gamut of governance. Researchers and practitioners have written on specific issues or sectors, but this book covers everything! It is highly accessible to non-experts but is also packed with new insights and actionable reform ideas even for lifelong veterans of governance and policy. As a former chief secretary, I am also delighted to see a book focused on state-level actions to accelerate India's development. This book can be of immense help in setting a national agenda for governance reforms'—**Rajiv Sharma**, former Chief Secretary, Government of Telangana

'This book features a potent combination of academic rigour and practical realism, offering both diagnosis and prescription. It has outstanding conceptual frameworks and many valuable insights, but one is of particular import: a focus on budget allocation may be a distraction from the more important issue of improving the *quality* of expenditure. It will be of high value to academics, practitioners, and any reader interested in governance, policy, and India's future'—**T.V. Somanathan**, Finance Secretary, Government of India, and co-author of *State Capability in India*

ACCELERATING
INDIA'S
DEVELOPMENT

A STATE-LED ROADMAP for
EFFECTIVE GOVERNANCE

KARTHIK
MURALIDHARAN

PENGUIN
VIKING
An imprint of Penguin Random House

VIKING

USA | Canada | UK | Ireland | Australia
New Zealand | India | South Africa | China | Singapore

Viking is part of the Penguin Random House group of companies
whose addresses can be found at global.penguinrandomhouse.com

Published by Penguin Random House India Pvt. Ltd
4th Floor, Capital Tower 1, MG Road,
Gurugram 122 002, Haryana, India

First published in Viking by Penguin Random House India 2024

Copyright © Karthik Muralidharan 2024

All rights reserved

10 9 8 7 6 5 4 3 2

ISBN 9780670095940

Typeset in Minion Pro by MAP Systems, Bengaluru, India
Printed at Thomson Press India Ltd, New Delhi

www.penguin.co.in

To the people of India

Contents

Preface   xi

Chapter 1: India@75: The Imperative of State Capacity   1

Section I: The Key Actors

Chapter 2: The Politicians' Predicament   39
Chapter 3: The Bureaucracy's Burden   69

Section II: Building an Effective State

Chapter 4: Data and Outcome Measurement   105
Chapter 5: Personnel Management   129
Chapter 6: Public Finance—Expenditure   165
Chapter 7: Public Finance—Revenue   199
Chapter 8: Federalism and Decentralization   229
Chapter 9: The State and the Market   267

Section III: Accelerating India's Development

Chapter 10: Shifting the Preston Curve for Development   301
Chapter 11: Education and Skills   325
Chapter 12: Health and Nutrition   361
Chapter 13: Police and Public Safety   403
Chapter 14: Courts and Justice   431
Chapter 15: Social Protection and Welfare   453
Chapter 16: Jobs, Productivity, and Economic Growth   483

Section IV: Making It Happen

Chapter 17: Reimagining Institutions   523
Chapter 18: State, Citizen, and Society   557

Notes   601
References   729
Acknowledgements   783
Additional Resources   791
    Expanded Table of Contents   793
Index   807

Preface

My main goal of writing this book is to contribute to accelerating India's development and thereby improve the lives of over 1.4 billion people in the coming years.

This book is based on over twenty years of studying, discussing, researching, thinking, writing, teaching, and advising on how governments can improve citizens' lives through better policymaking and governance. It aims to contribute to: (a) academic and intellectual discourse on development, (b) public communication and education on critical topics that affect public welfare, and (c) more effective governance in India.

Its main academic contribution is to synthesize research insights over the last twenty years to argue that investing in 'state capacity' for better policymaking, implementation, and public service delivery should be a top priority for India. This view reflects years of work across public finance, education, health, early childhood development, and welfare programmes—spanning nearly every Indian state. A recurring theme in this work is that weak state capacity is a *critical binding constraint* to achieving national development goals. So, the first half of this book focuses on how we can build a more effective Indian state, and the second half on how we can accelerate India's development. This sequencing reflects my assessment that the first is essential for the second.

While the book is rooted in economics, it includes insights and perspectives from ethics, politics, sociology, psychology, and management. Further, the empirical evidence it draws on is mainly from the last two decades. So, while some ideas in this book may be familiar to those trained in the corresponding fields, the synthesis is new and original. I therefore hope that it will be useful to scholars, practitioners, teachers, and students across social science disciplines, development studies, and public policy. It also includes extensive notes, references, a link to a book website with data and code, and an expanded table of contents (at the end of the book) for those who may seek to delve deeper, and use the book as a long-term reference.

Beyond its intellectual contributions, a primary goal of this book is to make research insights and key concepts widely accessible. Well-informed and engaged citizens are essential for effective democracy. Further, governance and policy are too important for public welfare to be shrouded in mystery and jargon. So, the book is written at a level that a general reader, who is a college student or graduate in *any* field, can easily comprehend and relate to. It aims to present complex and interconnected ideas in clearly written and accessible language, while being mindful of Einstein's advice that: 'Everything should be as simple as possible, but no simpler.'

This advice explains the length of this book, which is needed to do justice to the task it takes on. Each chapter offers a concise synthesis of complex issues that could easily warrant a full book. Further, splitting the book into two volumes would not work, as the two halves are deeply interconnected. So, I urge readers not to be deterred by the book's length, but to approach it as an engaging novel that takes you on a journey to understand the functioning of the Indian state, and offers insights on how to make it more effective, and thereby accelerate both growth and human development.

Finally, a key feature of this book is that it provides both a conceptual and a *practical* roadmap for India's next twenty-five years with several implementable ideas that policymakers can act on. It discusses not just *what* we need to do, but also *how* we can do it, while considering political, bureaucratic, social, judicial, and fiscal constraints. This practical focus aligns with the fact that the primary goal for my research and policy engagement over the years has been to improve government functioning. This motivation reflects the complexity, importance, and wide-ranging impact of government actions, especially for the poor and marginalized. So, the book's approach combines that of a scholarly 'scientist' seeking to better understand the world, and a practical 'engineer' aiming to apply scientific understanding to solve real-world problems, while also using ethical reasoning to identify *what* problems we should focus on.

The practical ideas in this book have been shaped and honed by over a decade of interactions with officials at the Planning Commission, NITI Aayog, and in finance and line departments in both Central and state governments. They also reflect the iterative learning enabled by my role as co-founder and scientific director of the Centre for Effective Governance of Indian States (CEGIS), a non-profit organization that has been working with multiple state governments across India since late 2019 to improve governance and service delivery. They also focus on *state-level* reform ideas, which increases the chances that at least some of them will be tried, following which they can be rapidly replicated if successful, and fine-tuned or dropped if not.

Overall, this book reflects a lifelong intellectual and practical journey that combines ethics, economics, and politics. It uses ethics to inform the moral goals we should aim to achieve as a society. It uses economic reasoning and evidence to suggest ideas that can accelerate our ability to achieve these moral goals *within* our resource constraints, and can relax these constraints over time by promoting faster economic growth. Finally, it pays careful attention to political incentives and the distributional consequences of policies, and tries to present reform ideas that can obtain broad coalitions of political support. Thus, the book aims to provide a roadmap that combines idealism and pragmatism to build a brighter future for all Indians.

To conclude on a personal note, I feel privileged to be an academic whose main *job* is to think, write, and teach; and to have been able to spend around half my time on this project for nearly five years. This book is my attempt to pay it forward by contributing ideas to accelerate India's development journey. The writing process has been exhausting and overwhelming at times, but has mostly been joyful and rewarding. I hope readers will mainly experience the latter feeling as they engage with the book!

Chapter 1

India@75: The Imperative of State Capacity

1. Framing the Problem

Taking stock of India as we reflect on over seventy-five years of Independence, we have much to be proud of spanning political, economic, and administrative fronts.

Politically, at the time of our Independence, many outsiders were doubtful that India would even remain united for long, let alone do so while maintaining a democracy.[1] Yet, seventy-five years later, the political project that is modern India has been an astounding success: India has remained united, its basic Constitutional structure has been maintained, and electoral democracy has mostly endured.[2]

This political success has been accompanied by economic success—especially starting in the 1980s, and accelerating after the 1991 economic reforms. Very few countries, and even fewer democracies, have surpassed the pace, duration and stability of India's economic growth.[3] This growth has helped lift hundreds of millions of people out of poverty: India's poverty rate fell from 70 per cent in 1947 to 21.9 per cent in 2011.[4]

Turning to administration, the Indian state is also impressive in many ways. For example, it successfully conducts the world's largest elections and vaccination campaigns, and has recently completed the world's most cost-effective Moon-landing mission. It also does well in conducting relief operations during natural disasters and managing the logistics associated with globally unique events, such

1

as the Kumbh Mela, where tens of millions of people gather in the same location on a single day!

Yet, as scholars like Devesh Kapur have noted, the same Indian state that does well in 'mission mode' when tasks, outputs, and deadlines are well defined, does a much poorer job in delivering basic public services—including education, health, security, justice, and welfare—to all citizens.[5] These issues are not only essential components of citizen well-being, but are *also* key contributors to productivity and economic growth. Thus, the weak performance of the Indian state in delivering basic services is a critical constraint to India's development, and the scale of the problem is staggering.

Consider education: despite spending over Rs 7.5 lakh crore (around 3 per cent of GDP) on education annually, half the fifth-grade children in rural India cannot read at a second-grade level. Thus, around 10 million Indian children finish their schooling *every year* without even the basic skills needed to participate in a modern economy.[6] This is both a moral tragedy for the children and an economic tragedy for the country since we are wasting a demographic dividend that occurs only once in a nation's history.[7]

Similarly, the Indian state struggles to keep its children healthy and well-nourished. Nearly 35 per cent of India's children are stunted, and India has more malnourished children than any other country: over 60 million children under five are stunted or underweight. However, government programmes that aim to improve child nutrition are inadequately resourced and plagued by critical implementation weaknesses.

Healthcare for adults is not much better. Public hospitals are understaffed and under-resourced, staff are often absent, and exert limited effort even when present. As a result, over 70 per cent of Indians use fee-charging private providers for primary care, many of whom are *unqualified*, despite the existence of a 'free' public healthcare system. Further, poor environmental quality hurts population health every day—with India having thirteen out of the fifteen cities with the most polluted air in the world.[8]

The challenges extend to public safety, a core function of the government. Nationwide, police forces are understaffed, undertrained, underequipped, and overworked. The low capacity of the police system contributes to low public confidence, and only 10–15 per cent of crimes are even reported. On one hand, unreported crimes allow many criminals to get away scot-free. On the other hand, police often resort to violent treatment of suspected criminals, many of whom may be innocent. Such behaviour, in turn, partly reflects weak systemic capacity for forensics and investigation, and a painfully slow justice system.

Speaking of justice, the Indian state does an unacceptably poor job of delivering it in a timely manner, which is a core function of any society that aims to follow the rule of law. The Indian court system has accumulated a backlog of nearly 30 million cases, which have been pending for over a year. As a result, securing justice for citizens can be a long and arduous slog, and the process itself feels like a punishment.

Turning to economic well-being, India faces twin challenges of an inadequate welfare system on one hand, and inadequate creation of good-quality jobs on the other. One stark reminder of the limitations of our welfare system is the tragedy of millions of migrant workers walking hundreds of kilometres to reach their villages during the pandemic-induced lockdown in 2020. A striking indicator of our jobs crisis is the fact that there are hundreds of applicants for *every* public sector job. As we will see in Chapters 5, 11, 15, and 16, these challenges reflect weaknesses in policies and programmes to support skilling, welfare, and job creation.

The scale of these problems, and the number of people affected, is so large that economist Lant Pritchett has described the poor performance of the Indian state in delivering basic services as one of the ten biggest challenges facing humanity![9] Further, weak public services disproportionately hurt the poor and vulnerable. They are the most dependent on public services, have the least influence in improving their quality, and pay a higher fraction of their income in seeking private solutions to state weaknesses.

A core argument of this book is that India's weaknesses in basic service delivery reflect inadequate investments in the capacity of the Indian state to deliver these goals. However, investing in state capacity does *not* imply that we just need to increase public spending on health, education, law, or the police. As shown throughout this book, a large body of research evidence has documented the very poor *quality* of expenditure under the status quo. In other words, the translation of public spending into desired outcomes is highly inefficient. In addition, our tight fiscal situation and relatively low tax-to-GDP ratio imply that large increases in public expenditure are often just not feasible.

Thus, what we need is not just higher public spending to solve our massive social and developmental problems. Rather, what we need is to *reimagine* governance to focus on improving the *effectiveness* of the Indian state, and to do this in a way that reflects data and evidence, and pays much more attention to efficiency and cost-effectiveness. Such a reimagination will require us to not just do 'more of the same', but to redesign, rebuild, and reinvest in key structures of the Indian state.

One way to characterize our situation is to imagine the Indian state as a vehicle in which we are all travelling towards a higher- quality life. Unfortunately, at present, the vehicle is like a slow-moving, overworked car from the 1950s. Political parties compete to determine who gets to drive the car and where to steer it. But the car itself can barely move!

Increasing budgets on programmes without improving the efficiency of the Indian state is like spending money on more fuel for that worn-out car. The additional fuel can help move the car a little bit, but the translation of the fuel budget into distance travelled will be very limited in such an antiquated car. Policy discussions focus on where the car should go, but much less attention is paid to the functioning of the car itself.

Comparing the Indian state to a 1950s car is a deliberate analogy because the 1950s was the last time we made systematic investments in the institutional foundations of the Indian state. Since then, we have continuously added expectations on the state, without commensurate investments in the state itself. Just like the 1950s Ambassador—which was still the main car available in India till the mid-1980s—was the symbol of India's economic underperformance in the pre-liberalization era, the metaphor of the 1950s car applies equally well to the Indian state itself.

While the economic reforms of 1991 helped kickstart private sector-led economic growth in India, we have failed to improve the functioning of the state itself, which is now *the* major binding constraint to national progress. As noted by economist Rakesh Mohan in his 2018 essay reviewing twenty-five years of economic reforms: 'The way forward for accelerated growth in India is being held back by major governance deficits in all areas connected with the delivery of public goods and services.'[10]

Therefore, as we enter our seventy-fifth year as a sovereign Republic, there is almost no other endeavour more important for our collective future than building a more effective Indian state. This will require us to understand:

- Why does the Indian state do poorly in delivering basic services?
- What will it take to improve the effectiveness of the Indian state?
- How can we use this understanding to create politically feasible and practically implementable reform roadmaps for key sectors to sharply improve outcomes?
- How can each of us—individually and collectively— contribute towards building a more effective Indian state, and thereby help accelerate India's development?

The goal of this book is to provide answers to these questions. Most importantly, it aims to offer tangible, evidence-based ideas that can improve the functioning of the Indian state, and help accelerate India's development. The book is addressed to *all* Indians—political and business leaders, officials, students, citizens, and civil society—

and aims to provide a clear understanding of how the Indian state functions, why things are the way they are, and how we can build a more effective Indian state and, thereby, a better India.

It is a book deeply informed by research—including a lot of my own work over the past two decades. But it is also informed by my extensive interactions with practitioners—in and outside government—working on solving these problems daily. Thus, the book aims to combine perspectives of both 'social science' and 'systems engineering'. It aims to illustrate key facts, principles, and evidence to help readers better understand complex issues of governance (social science), and to then use this understanding to suggest practical ways of building more effective public systems (systems engineering).[11] It also pays careful attention to the motivations and constraints of key actors and aims to propose politically, administratively, and fiscally realistic reform ideas.

Finally, this book focuses on ideas to improve governance at the *state* level, which is a topic that has mostly been neglected in our Delhi-centred public discourse. Yet, we cannot build a better India without sharply improving state-level governance. This is because several key areas of service delivery, including school education, health, the police, district courts, implementation of welfare programmes, and policies regarding the use of land and labour that are central to job creation, are primarily the responsibility of states. Indian states are more populous than most countries, and states collectively spend 50 per cent more than the Centre.[12] It is time for states to get the attention they need and deserve in our policy discourse, and this book hopes to contribute to that goal.

2. Characterizing India's Crisis of State Capacity

A key premise of this book is that India is struggling to deliver better development outcomes because we have a crisis of weak state capacity. But what do we mean by state capacity, and in what ways does India have weak state capacity?

A useful framework for thinking about these questions is to consider both the *scope* of a state, which refers to the range of goals it takes on, and the *strength* of a state, which refers to its ability to achieve these goals.[13] The scope of modern states is determined by their political process and has steadily expanded over time. Historically, states focused primarily on providing external security and internal order. Over time, their scope has expanded to include development and welfare functions (see Chapter 2).

Correspondingly, the amount of state capacity needed to deliver against this expanded scope has also increased. Historically, states were considered effective if they were able to defend their borders, maintain internal security, enforce their laws, and raise enough revenue to perform these functions. Over time, the definition of state effectiveness has expanded to include the state's ability to build infrastructure, promote economic growth, regulate firms and economic activity, deliver public services, improve human development, and promote normative goals such as equity and social justice.[14]

So, we can think about state capacity in both *absolute* and *relative* terms, and this distinction helps clarify how the Indian state is both effective and weak at the same time. The Indian state has done a good job when measured by its absolute performance in delivering on core goals such as defence, law and order, macroeconomic stability, and above average economic growth. These are laudable achievements. However, it has done less well when measured by its effectiveness in delivering on several key aspirations of its citizens—including education, health, safety, justice, social protection, and jobs. Thus, India can be considered to have weak state capacity in the sense that the Indian state has not delivered *relative* to the democratic aspirations of its people.[15]

However, while poor development outcomes are an indicator of weak state capacity, they do not tell us *how* to improve it. A core contribution of this book is to get into the 'black box' of state effectiveness and examine the state as an *organization*, and not just as an institution.[16] Doing so is essential to better understand the innards of how the Indian state functions, and why it does not deliver more for citizens. Such an understanding can, in turn, guide reforms to enable the state to deliver better.

In analysing the state as an organization, I identify six key *systemic* elements of state capacity, explain their importance, document weaknesses in the status quo, and provide a roadmap for improvement. These include systems and processes for (i) collecting, analysing, and acting on data; (ii) recruiting, training, and managing public personnel; (iii) ensuring quality of public expenditure; (iv) collecting adequate revenue and doing so efficiently; (v) optimizing tasks across layers of our federal governance structure; and (vi) effectively leveraging non-state actors, including the private sector and civil society.

These systems play a critical role in state effectiveness. They affect both the quality of policymaking, and the quality of programme implementation and delivery. Thus, the deeper and more fundamental way in which India has a crisis of state capacity is that we do poorly on *all* six of these systemic elements of state capacity, as seen below.

Data

The centrality of good data to governance is seen in the very term 'statistics', which originates from the fact that the most important use case for statistics was for analysing and managing the affairs 'of the state'. Unreliable data *corrodes the very foundation of governance* by depriving decision makers of an accurate understanding of reality. Such understanding is the basis for goal setting, resource allocation, progress tracking, and performance management. However, India suffers from severe limitations in the frequency, granularity, and reliability of data. This contributes to a system of governance that often relies more on anecdotes, personal experience, intuition, and seniority rather than data and evidence (see Chapter 4).

Personnel

From a citizens' perspective, public employees are the main embodiment of the state. However, contrary to popular belief, India has too few of them, with only 16 public employees per 1000 people, compared to 57 in China, 77 in the US, 111 in Brazil and 159 in Norway (see Chapter 3). The motivation and accountability of existing staff is also weak. Frequent transfers of senior officials and district and block-level officers contribute to poor management of public systems. Government employees are also poorly trained and have limited opportunity and incentives to upgrade their skills. These weaknesses have contributed to a gradual atrophy in the core capabilities of both Central and state governments (see Chapters 3 and 5 for further details).[17]

Quality of public expenditure

Why do we not have the money to invest in these core functions of the state? One reason is that the *quality* of public expenditure in India is poor on many dimensions, including low social returns on public investments, poor targeting and delivery of welfare spending, large time and cost overruns on capital projects, and subsidies that *reduce* economic efficiency and citizen welfare. For instance, free electricity to farmers to run borewells costs tens of thousands of crores every year but generates low (or even *negative*) return on investment, mainly benefits richer farmers with more land who use more water, and has accelerated our water crisis by encouraging suboptimal water-intensive agriculture. The point is not to criticize spending on farmer welfare, but to highlight that we can deliver the *same* amount of benefits much more efficiently through alternate policies (see Chapters 6, 15, and 16).

When we hear about waste of public money, the first thought that occurs is usually to blame corruption. However, while corruption is part of the problem, a well-known study of public-sector inefficiency found that corruption likely accounts for only 17 per cent of the waste in government and the remaining 83 per cent is due to inefficiency resulting from poor management and governance.[18] Thus, while it is common to complain about inadequate funds for key development expenditures, we can achieve a *lot* more if we improve the quality and efficiency of existing spending.

Tax revenue

The Indian state is also hampered by limited revenue. India's tax-to-GDP ratio of 18 per cent is around half that of higher income countries, such as the US or the UK. This partly reflects the fact that it is more difficult to collect taxes on informal activity, which is much more prevalent in poorer countries.[19] Thus, when the people are poor, the government is *also* poor. This magnifies the importance of improving the *quality* of public expenditure. Revenue collection in India is also hampered by weak analytical and enforcement capacity.

But the vicious cycle of low state capacity is seen here as well, with cash-strapped governments often being unable to invest in analytical and staff capacity to improve the quality of tax administration (see Chapter 7).

Federalism and decentralization

Large countries also need to optimize roles and responsibilities across tiers of a federal governance architecture. An effective federal system will allocate responsibility for service delivery to *local* governments, which can better respond to local conditions and hold employees accountable (see Chapter 8). India, however, is one of the most over-centralized countries in the world. For instance, India spends only 3 per cent of its budget at the local government level compared to over 50 per cent in China. While outsiders often think of China as highly centralized, in practice its budgets are nearly seventeen times more decentralized than India's!

Leveraging non-state actors

Effective states also leverage the private sector and civil society to enhance public welfare. However, doing this well requires state capacity for functions such as procurement and regulation. In practice, government procurement in India is rife with corruption and inefficiency. Further, attempts to reduce corruption have resulted in such complicated procedures that many officials prefer to not even attempt projects that require complex procurement. Thus, not only is the Indian state weak in direct provision of goods and services, it also struggles to contract those who can deliver these. Even worse, the Indian state often hurts public welfare through its distrust of markets and the private sector, which leads it to routinely stifle their activities and thereby *reduce* national capacity for service delivery (see Chapters 9 and 16).

3. Why Is the Indian State Ineffective at Core Service Delivery?

Improving India's public systems will require strengthening each of these six sub-systems that together determine overall state effectiveness. But, before delving into potential solutions, it is useful to understand *why* these systems are so weak.

3.1 From nation-building to election-winning

When India began our unique experiment with democracy, the agenda for the political leadership was clear: nation-building. They focused on building an industrial base, institutes of higher education and technical excellence, and major institutions of the state. They also retained the structure of the British colonial administration—including the apex administrative and police services—which provided a strong initial base of administrative capacity, at least for basic functions such as preserving law and order.

Political conditions also enabled longer-term investments. As the party that drove the Independence movement, the Indian National Congress enjoyed widespread popularity and did not face much electoral opposition at the national level. Further, the founding generation of leaders, many of whom were jailed and endured considerable hardship under British rule, were motivated more by sacrifice and the common good and less by the material trappings of office. This gave them the motivation and public trust to focus on nation-building investments because electoral success was virtually guaranteed.[20]

Over time, the broad-tent Independence-era coalition of the Congress splintered into distinct parties who often appealed to voters on narrower lines of caste, region, and religion.[21] Greater electoral competition also increased political incentives to cater to narrower 'vote banks', rather than invest in broad-based development (see Chapter 2). Politicians have also found it easier to appeal to voters based on short-term palliative interventions such as loan waivers and subsidies, rather than longer-term development.

Even when politicians pay attention to sectors such as education and health, electoral incentives induce them to focus on providing *visible* benefits that they can take credit for. This can come at the cost of investments in governance, which may take a longer time to yield meaningful results. Put simply, it is easier to build new schools and advertise pictures of opening ceremonies than it is to ensure that children are learning.

Overall, the underinvestment in India's public systems and state capacity reflects in large part the perceived lack of political benefits of doing so, relative to alternative uses of public funds. As discussed further in Chapter 2, democracy in India has expanded the ability of citizens to *make claims on the state*, but it has not provided adequate political incentives to invest in building the state's capacity to deliver against these claims.

3.2 Systemic overload

One consequence of the political pressure to announce schemes and programmes is the steady addition of tasks to the bureaucracy without commensurate investments in its capacity to deliver. As a result, the 'scope' of the state has expanded faster than its 'strength'. Thus, the Indian state can function well in 'mission mode' when its attention and resources are focused on solving a well-defined, time-bound problem—such as running elections or vaccination campaigns. However, it is simply *overwhelmed* when it functions in 'regular mode' because the demands on the state far exceed its capacity.

Trying to do too much can further weaken the state. When a government makes more commitments than it has resources for, it is forced to ration public services. This can *reduce* state capacity because time and resources spent on deciding *who* gets benefits, and arbitrating conflicts over access, are diverted from actually delivering benefits (see Chapter 3). Rationing also disproportionately hurts the vulnerable, who are often not equipped to complete the paperwork needed to access benefits. A bigger cost may be the loss of focus that comes from being chronically overcommitted, which contributes to officials constantly operating in a 'firefighting' mode, where time and attention are allocated based on immediate urgency rather than long-term importance.

This discussion illustrates the costs of 'premature load-bearing'— a term coined by Lant Pritchett and co-authors.[22] Weightlifters train by gradually increasing the load they lift and allowing their muscles to build the strength to handle progressively greater loads. However, if a novice weightlifter were to attempt to lift too heavy a load, he would hurt himself badly and be able to lift even less. Similarly, by trying to do too much, the Indian state has further weakened its ability to deliver even its core functions. Thus, we can *increase* state effectiveness by *reducing* the scope of what the Indian state tries to do, so that it can better perform its core functions.[23]

3.3 Trust deficits

When the state promises more than it can deliver, it is often forced to break some promises, which contributes to a trust deficit between citizens and the government. Trust deficits *further* weaken state effectiveness by limiting the state's ability to negotiate policy changes with stakeholders. For instance, most experts agree that our current farming practices are fiscally and ecologically unsustainable, and that reforms are needed. Yet, designing and negotiating these reforms is a complex economic and political problem that requires trust on all sides. The impasse between the government and farmers during the 2021 farm protests reflected, in part, this trust deficit.[24]

The Indian state has a history of broken promises, affecting Indians of all classes. For the elite, examples include reneging on a *constitutional* commitment of a privy purse to rulers of princely states who peacefully acceded to India, and more recently, changing tax laws to apply retrospectively. Middle classes are hurt when governments delay payments to small and medium vendors, and sometimes even to their own employees when liabilities exceed revenues.[25] Promises to the poor are broken when the state legislates rights without corresponding fiscal or staff allocations to implement them well, and when they are asked to pay bribes to obtain the public services they are entitled to.

In a memorable essay reflecting on his decades of public service when he turned 100 years old, former US secretary of state and treasury George Shultz noted that the most important thing he had learnt in his career was the centrality of trust in any collective situation. In his words: '*Trust is the coin of the realm*.' When trust was in the room, whatever that room was—the family room, the schoolroom, the locker room, the office room, the government room or the military room—good things happened. When trust was not in the room, good things did not happen. Everything else is details.[26]

An effective state keeps its promises, and a state that cannot be trusted is less effective in every arena. Its laws and declarations will be taken less seriously by its own citizens and officials; it will struggle to attract investors; and even its global commitments may be discounted. As Kaushik Basu notes in his book *The Republic of Beliefs*, 'The most important ingredients of a republic, including its power and might, reside in nothing more than the beliefs and expectations of ordinary people going about their daily lives.'[27]

3.4 An ineffective bureaucracy

Building trust with citizens requires a state that can deliver on its commitments. The ability to deliver is primarily determined by the bureaucracy, which is ineffective in many ways. This ineffectiveness partly reflects the bureaucracy being overburdened and understaffed. But it also reflects several structural weaknesses including (a) short tenures and frequent transfers of managerial personnel, (b) limited connection of public employees with the communities they serve, (c) limited incentives and opportunities for upgrading their skills, (d) inadequate autonomy and empowerment to deliver, and (e) inadequate and misdirected accountability.

Bureaucratic processes are also riddled with excessive and often pointless paperwork, which diverts staff effort towards maintaining records rather than delivering services. The focus on paperwork also creates incentives to depict 'alternative realities' on paper that bear little resemblance to facts on the ground. In many cases, I have seen officials seek to brush aside independent data that contradict more rosy internal reports. While some of the decline in bureaucratic capacity over time can be attributed to increasing political interference, much of the weakness reflects inertia and poor management, which can be fixed within the bureaucracy itself (see Chapters 3 and 5).

3.5 Elite exit

Why have we, as a society, not paid more attention to addressing the fundamental problem of weak state capacity? One reason is that Indian elites and middle classes have mostly seceded from being recipients of public services. The policy- and opinion-making classes primarily use private education, health, water, and even security.[28] However, while this elite exit may be individually rational, it has further weakened the impetus and political pressure for improving the functioning of the state, with studies showing that the quality of public services is higher when they are used by elites.[29]

The greater accountability of private service providers combined with the difficulty of improving public systems has also contributed to a view that it may make sense to shrink the public sector over time by letting private providers gradually increase their market share in service delivery. After all, in sectors where this has happened, such as telephones and airlines, consumers have benefited from better quality at lower prices. Public providers such as Air India and VSNL continued to exist, but they mattered less for citizen welfare since their market share shrunk over time.

However, this is a myopic view. While a private sector-led approach makes sense for many sectors, it will not work for core state activities. Despite the growth of private solutions, the government is by far the largest service provider and often the only option for the poor. The state also has a legal monopoly in functions such as policing and justice, and has a crucial role in providing public goods such as infectious disease control and environmental quality. Further, improving state effectiveness will also benefit elites and middle classes, and should therefore be a priority for *all* Indians (see Section 4.3).

3.6 A highly stratified, fragmented, and unequal society

At some level, it is inevitable that governments, and the state more broadly, will reflect the nature of society itself. Governments are more likely to deliver public goods and services well if voters and society demand it. However, India may be particularly hampered in this regard by the nature of the caste system and its long-lasting legacy. As Dr Ambedkar has memorably pointed out, every society has group-based identities and inequality, but the caste system is unique in being a system of *graded* inequality that has been transmitted and sustained over several generations.[30] This structure has created three fundamental social challenges for effective public service delivery.

First, it may have delayed public demand for *broad-based* service delivery because of limited solidarity across castes. Further, since politics reflects society, political parties have had incentives to convert social cleavages into political cleavages, and keep the polity divided.[31] Thus, a fragmented society is more likely to demand 'vote bank' politics where the focus of political activity is on directing the resources of the state to preferred voter groups rather than providing broader public services (see Chapter 2). Consistent with this point, it is worth noting that Indian states with better public services such as Tamil Nadu, Kerala, and Maharashtra have also seen broad-based *social* reform movements that *demanded* better public services from *all* political parties.[32]

Second, even when governments create programmes to deliver better services for the poor, their implementation is often *thwarted* by entrenched caste and economic elites who want to preserve their relative position of power in their communities—especially in rural areas with a stronger feudal past.[33] Thus, another reason for the Indian state's weakness in service delivery is that it has had to contend with social power structures that often try to undermine the state's ability to better serve marginalized groups.[34]

Third, these social factors have also *indirectly* hurt state effectiveness by contributing to over-centralization of governance in India. Progressive policymakers, starting from Dr Ambedkar, have not trusted local elites to deliver services such as education that could empower marginalized groups. This is partly why our founders concentrated powers in higher-level officials rather than local governments, and this over-centralization has also hurt the quality and accountability of public service delivery in India (see Chapter 8).

Beyond caste, India's long history of patriarchy and gender discrimination may have also contributed to weak public service delivery.[35] Since women are typically more directly affected by the quality of public services, their limited representation in positions of power may have also contributed to the underinvestment in public goods. For instance, a highly cited study shows that reserving leadership positions in panchayats for women led to significantly greater investment in public goods such as better drinking water— which women would otherwise have to travel several hours to obtain.[36]

This is primarily a book about governance that aims to present implementable ideas for building a more effective Indian state, holding society as *given*. It is not a book on social structure or social reform. But it is important to recognize that the functioning of the state will also reflect social forces and norms, rules of political representation, and the nature of the demands made on the state by citizens and society. Chapters 17 and 18 discuss ideas for reforms to improve representation, and citizen and civil society actions that can contribute to improving state effectiveness and public service delivery.

3.7 Institutional stasis

Building and maintaining state capacity itself requires state capacity! This is why we have independent institutions for specific roles related to state functioning. For instance, the Union Public Service Commission (UPSC) is designed to maintain the quality of recruitment into the civil service; the Comptroller and Auditor General (CAG) of India is meant to hold government departments and officials accountable for how they spend public money; and the National Statistical Commission (NSC) is meant to ensure quality data collection, and accurate and timely reporting of key statistics in the public domain.

Many of these institutions were established after Independence, during our period of nation-building, and reflected global best practices of that time. However, these institutions have not kept pace with the times.[37] This institutional stasis reflects both underinvestment and a lack of imagination and initiative with regard to how these institutions should evolve to continuously strengthen state capacity.

For instance, the UPSC maintains the integrity of public recruitment, but this is not enough to ensure that public employees continue to be effective *after* they are hired. The National Capacity Building Commission set up in 2020 under Mission Karmayogi is a good, but belated, effort to fill this gap by improving the skills and competencies of public employees. Similarly, CAG audits focus on procedural compliance but have not been effective in ensuring the quality of public expenditure. Finally, the NSC has not been effective at even maintaining the quality of India's statistics, let alone improving it.

This book presents several ideas for strengthening public systems. However, even if adopted, they need to be institutionalized for sustained impact. I therefore suggest institutional homes and structures for implementing reforms in specific chapters as relevant, and discuss ideas for reimagining institutions more broadly in Chapter 17.

3.8 Fixing the problem is really difficult

Finally, an important but underappreciated factor behind India's weak state capacity is that fixing the problem is really difficult. Even when there is conceptual clarity on what needs to be done, making it happen is challenging because of the need for coordination and sustained engagement between different actors who often work in silos.

For instance, reforming public-sector personnel policies requires coordination across ministries of finance, planning, personnel, general administration, law, and concerned line ministries. Even if there is consensus within the government, reforms may be challenged by other stakeholders, including frontline employees, civil society, and even the judiciary. The challenge for reformers is well captured by the anecdote of an Indian lobbyist who reportedly told his client: 'However much you pay me, I cannot guarantee that I can get your job done. What I can guarantee is stopping your rival's project!'

This anecdote aptly reflects the existence of multiple veto points for action. It illustrates why it is much harder to implement reforms in the Indian system than it is to stop them. This problem is magnified in the case of administrative reforms. Unlike the economic reforms in the 1990s where many losers from reforms were outside the government, reforms to public systems are more likely to be opposed within the government, by those who benefit from the status quo or are simply nervous about changes.

4. Why Should Investing in State Capacity Be a Top Priority for India?

Improving state effectiveness is a long-term project that will require continuity across political parties and governments. This will be facilitated by reaching a broad consensus on the way forward. The first step towards such a consensus is to make the case for *why* investing in state capacity needs to be a top national priority in the coming years.

4.1 It offers a 10x+ Return on Investment (RoI) opportunity

Consider a policymaker who wants to deliver more benefits to citizens. The default approach is to increase department and programme budgets. However, evidence from multiple studies across sectors shows that investing in better governance can be *over ten times* more cost effective than increasing spending in a government as usual way.[38]

In 2018, the Government of Telangana launched the Rythu Bandhu Scheme, a flagship cash transfer programme for farmers, with an annual budget of over Rs 10,000 crore. Working with the state government, my colleagues and I helped set up an outbound call centre that contacted over 25,000 randomly selected farmers to verify payment receipts. We found that simply informing block-level officials that their performance was being measured by directly contacting farmers, improved their performance significantly. Most importantly, the intervention was highly cost effective, with each rupee spent on the call centre leading to over twenty-five more rupees delivered to farmers, and over hundred rupees delivered on time, for a 25–100x return on investment *within a few months*.[39]

In another large-scale study, we evaluated a new payment system that used biometric authentication and local business correspondents to transfer National Rural Employment Guarantee Scheme (NREGS) wage payments and social security pensions in (undivided) Andhra Pradesh. We found that the new system sharply reduced corruption and inefficiency. Beneficiaries received more money, and also collected their payments with fewer delays. The savings from the reduced leakage of funds in NREGS (~Rs 200 crore) and the value of time saved in collecting payments (~Rs 25 crore) was over ten times greater than the cost of the intervention.[40]

Similar patterns are seen in school education. In a nationwide study in 2010, my colleagues and I found that 23.6 per cent of teachers in rural public schools were absent on any given day, and we estimated the fiscal cost of teacher absence to be over Rs 10,000 crore per year.[41] We also found that regularly monitored schools have 25 to 40 per cent lower rates of teacher absence. Yet, large numbers of supervisory positions remain vacant. We calculate that investing in filling supervisory positions (and thereby reducing teacher absence) would be over ten times more cost-effective at reducing *effective* student–teacher ratio than spending on hiring more teachers.[42]

Similarly, multiple studies show that increasing government school teacher salaries does not improve student learning. In contrast, linking even 3 to 5 per cent of teacher pay to performance has led to large gains in student learning.[43] Thus, even modest amounts of performance-linked pay for teachers can boost education-system effectiveness many times more than the default of unconditional salary increases.

In other cases, state capacity is weak because there are not enough frontline staff. India's Integrated Child Development Services (ICDS) programme serves over 80 million children under six years of age. Yet ICDS *anganwadi* centres are staffed with just one worker who (along with a helper for cooking and cleaning) is responsible for early childhood nutrition, education, home visitation and copious administrative work. In a recent large-scale study in Tamil Nadu, my colleagues and I found that adding a half-time worker to anganwadis to focus on early childhood education led to large gains in learning outcomes, and also reduced child malnutrition and stunting. We estimate that the present discounted lifetime value of these benefits would be thirteen to twenty-one times more than the cost of hiring the extra worker.[44]

Similarly, another recent study finds that filling judge vacancies in Indian district courts both sped up case resolution and boosted economic activity by unlocking assets for productive use, which would otherwise be unused while under legal dispute. Further, the study estimates that the aggregate economic benefit of filling these vacancies would be over *thirty times* the cost, and that the increase in tax revenue from the increase in economic activity would more than cover the cost of additional judges.[45]

Any private investor who is offered a chance to earn a 10x+ return on investment would scramble to invest as much as possible in that opportunity. Yet, as a country, we are forgoing these large returns by chronically underinvesting in state capacity. A prime motivation for writing this book is to synthesize twenty years of research on service delivery in India, and to make a broad public case for prioritizing data and evidence-based investments in governance and state capacity. The public returns to doing so will be enormous and it will lay the foundation for accelerating India's development.

4.2 An effective state is essential for accelerating India's development

It is easy to get overwhelmed and pessimistic by the scale of India's development challenges. However, when considered in a global perspective, India has not done badly. In fact, India's performance on key human development indicators is exactly in line with our GDP/capita (see Chapter 10). Overall, the cross-country comparisons suggest that India's grade over the past seventy-five years is a solid B+, capturing our above-average performance on some metrics and average performance on others.[46]

Yet, India has the potential to perform at an A or even A+ level, and there is reason to be optimistic that we *can* do much better. A key reason for optimism is that, in the 20th century, poor countries have attained lower infant mortality and higher life expectancy, than high-income countries had at similar income levels. This phenomenon is referred to as 'shifting the Preston Curve' (see Chapter 10). A key enabler of this shift has been the availability of newer medical research and technologies, and their widespread use.

Similarly, a key reason for optimism is that we now also have access to much better data, evidence, and technologies in other crucial development areas beyond health, compared to what rich countries had when they were poor. This allows us to deliver better development outcomes even at lower levels of GDP/capita *if* we act on this evidence, and reallocate funds from less to more cost-effective public interventions. Specifically, as highlighted in the previous section, evidence-based investments in governance and state capacity can significantly accelerate India's development.

4.3 *All Indians* will benefit from a more effective state

One reason for underinvestment in state capacity is its low priority among tax-paying elites and middle classes who have seceded from using public services. Yet, the returns from such investments will not only be large but also broad-based. For instance, during the COVID-19 crisis, all Indians were hurt by the state's inadequate response. Similarly, elites can use air filters indoors, but they cannot escape poor air quality outdoors. This is why *all* Indians should care about getting the state to work better.

Improving public service delivery will benefit elites and middle classes even if they do not use public services themselves. Studies show that the quality of public and private services is highly correlated within a market (see Chapter 9). Thus, improving public service delivery has a double benefit. It will directly benefit the users of public services, who tend to be poor and vulnerable, and also indirectly benefit the better-off users of private services since private providers will have to increase their price-adjusted quality to compete with an improved free public option.

Politicians and bureaucrats will also benefit from investing in state capacity. Evidence suggests that the returns from doing so are not only large but can also be quick and create visible positive impact for citizens. In other words, such investments can be both good policy and good politics (see Chapter 2). Similarly, such investments should also be supported by the bureaucracy because they will improve the autonomy, capability, and effectiveness of public officials; improve their public perception and respect; and also enhance officials' own feelings of self-worth (see Chapters 3 and 5).

4.4 We also need state capacity to secure democratic freedoms for individuals

Beyond apathy, many Indians even have a hostile attitude towards the state. Reasons include: (a) arbitrary actions by the state (or its agents) that hurt firms and individuals without due process, (b) an overbearing state that often impedes voluntary actions of citizens and civil society, and (c) the perception that the state collects taxes but does not deliver commensurate services in return. In many ways, the Indian state and its agents can seem like an extortion racket that collects money both legally (taxes) and illegally (bribes) to benefit those who belong to or are closely connected to the state.

In such a milieu, reasonable people may worry that building state capacity can backfire if it allows the state's agents to exercise even more arbitrary power over citizens.[47] For those who are suspicious of the state, a weak state may be seen as a benefit because it limits its overreach. While there is some merit in this view, it is a self-limiting one. This is because even the state's ability to follow legal processes to protect citizen rights and freedoms is critically constrained by our underinvestment in state capacity.

For instance, our laws proclaim that citizens suspected of a crime are 'innocent until proven guilty' and entitled to a legal due process. But these laws are often ignored in practice because the police and courts *do not have the resources to follow the law* (see Chapters 13 and 14). One extreme example is the use of 'encounter' killings of suspected criminals by the police. Senior police officers have noted that they find the practice distasteful but have had to condone it because of strong *public demand*, which creates political demand as well. The public demand in turn reflects the reality that the alternative would be for many serious criminals to walk away scot-free given the lack of investigative resources and judicial capacity to complete trials in a timely manner.

Thus, investing in staff, training, forensics, intelligence, and analytical capabilities of the police, courts, and tax authorities will not only improve crime detection and compliance with laws but also help state agencies work *smarter* and *reduce* the harassment of ordinary citizens. Over time, such investments can also enhance the protection of legal rights by boosting the *ability* of the police and courts to ensure prudence and due process in the use of the coercive powers of the state. Thus, protecting democratic freedoms requires us to both strengthen legal guardrails on state actions, and to strengthen the institutional capacity of the entities meant to enforce these guardrails in practice. Chapters 13, 14, and 17 discuss these issues further.

4.5 The COVID-19 crisis highlights the importance of state capacity

I started writing this book in 2019 to make the public case for investing in state capacity. Since then, the COVID-19 crisis of 2020 and 2021 has starkly exposed the weaknesses of the Indian state. These include a weak public health infrastructure, poor regard for data quality and transparency, ambiguous and often hostile relationships with the private sector, and poor coordination across multiple levels of a federal governance structure. Together, these weaknesses hampered the ability of both Central and state governments to respond to the pandemic.

The COVID-19 crisis also showed that we *all* have a stake in building a more effective Indian state. To extend the transport analogy from cars to planes, the elites and middle classes in India are like the first and business class passengers on the plane that is India. They have created islands of comfort that obscure the dysfunction of the plane itself. However, as the COVID-19 crisis has shown, a crashing plane will take down all passengers regardless of what class they are travelling in. Clearly, all passengers (citizens) will be better off if they are travelling in a better-functioning car or plane.[48]

The good news is that the government's strong performance in procuring and administering over a billion vaccines between June and November 2021 shows that the Indian state is capable of being effective, especially when prompted to do so by a crisis. The problem of governments focusing on short-term priorities at the cost of longer-term investments during normal times is not unique to India. Historically, investments in state capacity have mainly happened during times of national crisis, like wars and pandemics.

Thus, one silver lining of the devastating COVID-19 pandemic may be the creation of a shared understanding among citizens, civil society, politicians, and officials that it is critical to invest in core state functions, such as public health, and capacities for real-time data collection, analysis, and action. As we reflect on India at seventy-five, the pandemic has been a rude wake-up call. It reminds us of the costs of a weak state and highlights the urgency of building a more effective Indian state.

5. How Do We Build a More Effective State and Accelerate India's Development?

While reforms often happen during a crisis, a crisis alone is not enough. As accounts of India's 1991 economic reforms have described, the background work for the reforms had been conducted over several years by economic advisers and senior officials, yielding policy notes that were ready to be acted on by the political leadership. Thus, the process of reimagining the Indian economy as needing to move from the old state-led licence-permit raj to a new market-led model with better incentives and accountability had already started.[49] The balance of payments crisis, the political leadership of Prime Minister P.V. Narasimha Rao and technical leadership of Finance Minister Manmohan Singh helped make the reforms happen, but the ideas were already in place.

Similarly, while the COVID-19 crisis may help create some national consensus on the importance of improving state capacity, the crisis by itself does not provide either the reimagination of what a capable Indian state should look like or a roadmap to get there. The goal of this book is to provide such a roadmap for the reforms that can help to have a transformative impact on the effectiveness of the Indian state in the coming years.

It is *not enough* to just say that we will spend more on health, education, the police, or courts because even when additional budgets are sanctioned for these sectors, they are often spent ineffectively. For instance, even if healthcare budgets are increased in light of COVID-19, additional funds may be spent on visible curative care even though the public return on investment will be much higher if we spend more on disease surveillance and preventive *public* health rather than on curative *private* health (see Chapter 12).

The importance of data and evidence to guide public spending is especially high because political and bureaucratic incentives often reward the *appearance of activity* rather than the effectiveness of that activity.[50] Companies face 'market tests' that keep them accountable. If they do not create more value for customers than their costs of production, they will go out of business. In contrast, governments can spend taxpayer money ineffectively for a very long time without facing any consequences.

Most of this book is dedicated to answering the question of *how* we can build a more effective Indian state, and thereby accelerate India's development. It is structured in four sections.

5.1 The key actors

Before discussing *what* we need to do and *how* to do it, it is useful to examine *why* things are the way they are. In particular, we need to understand the incentives and constraints of the two key actors of the state—politicians and bureaucrats. Both are much derided by many Indians. Politicians are considered corrupt and power-hungry, while bureaucrats are considered officious, risk-averse, and lazy. While there is some truth to this view, I believe that it is often wrong and unfair. Being a politician or a bureaucrat can be an incredibly difficult, stressful, and often thankless job; and much of their failures can be explained by the systemic constraints within which they operate.

Chapter 2, 'The Politicians' Predicament', explains how India's unique experiment of 'democracy before development' has led to greater voter demands on the Indian state *relative* to its fiscal and administrative capacity than today's high-income countries had at similar stages of development. Further, the practical realities of what it takes to win elections have created political incentives to focus more on cultivating narrower groups of base voters and directing public resources to politically powerful interest groups, rather than investing in broad-based service delivery. Together, these factors have contributed to inadequate funds and political incentives for investing in state capacity. However, it argues that one reason for optimism is that governance is increasingly important for politicians' re-election prospects. Thus, improving state effectiveness and service delivery will not only be good policy but can also be good politics.

Chapter 3, 'The Bureaucracy's Burden', summarizes key structural challenges of the bureaucracy. It explains how, despite the presence of several outstanding officers and highly motivated individuals, the *system* as a whole under-delivers. Understanding these systemic issues is essential to outline a reform roadmap. The chapter highlights key steps that India's political leadership needs to take to strengthen state capacity to deliver better for citizens. Once the political leadership takes these steps, the bureaucratic leadership can drive implementation of many other ideas in the book.

5.2 Building an effective state

If political and bureaucratic leaders want to improve the functioning of the state, *how* should they do so in practice? Section II addresses this question, and is the conceptual core of the book. It devotes a full chapter to each of the six systemic components of state capacity identified in Section 2. These include data and measurement (Chapter 4); public personnel management (Chapter 5); quality of public expenditure (Chapter 6); quantity and quality of revenue (Chapter 7); federalism and decentralization (Chapter 8);

and leveraging non-state and market actors to better serve public interests (Chapter 9).

The chapters follow a similar structure: they first explain concepts, present key facts, and discuss relevant research and evidence. They then present a list of implementable reform ideas based on first principles and evidence. These lists are not meant to be exhaustive. Rather, they reflect ideas that in my assessment are likely to (a) have a large public return on investment, (b) be practically implementable, and (c) be able to draw support from the broader public, and hence be politically feasible.

These chapters are the conceptual core of the book, and are also interconnected. For instance, better outcome data can improve both personnel management and quality of expenditure; more local control over funds and functionaries can help improve quality of public spending and public personnel management; and conceptual clarity on the optimal relationship between the state and markets followed by appropriate policy and regulatory actions can improve the quality of both public and private providers.

The interconnectedness of these themes also highlights the value of taking a 'whole systems' approach to augmenting state capacity. While senior officials are aware of many of the issues discussed in this book, the siloed nature of government functioning impedes system-level reforms. Understanding these systemic themes, and designing a coordinated reform agenda to improve all of them, will likely have a greater impact than piecemeal actions. This is analogous to the 1991 economic reforms, where a set of coordinated reforms helped to alleviate multiple binding constraints in the economy.

A key cross-cutting theme is the transformative potential of technology. Many of the book's reform ideas rely on technology for quality, standardization, speed, and scale. However, technology is integrated into all chapters and does not get a chapter of its own. This is because technology is an *enabler*, but by itself is not a panacea. Using it effectively requires us to first understand the key challenges in the status quo and use technology thoughtfully to alleviate binding constraints.[51] It is also important to note that technological divides can *increase* inequity, and mitigate this to the extent possible.

Another cross-cutting theme is equity. Poor and marginalized groups disproportionately depend on the state for accessing basic rights and services. Thus, a reform agenda of improving the state's effectiveness in delivering basic services will be the most effective *systemic* way of improving outcomes *at scale* for citizens who are disadvantaged for a variety of reasons, including gender, income, education, and caste. Implementing such an agenda will improve outcomes for *all* Indians and also improve equity by design.

5.3 Accelerating India's development

The ideas in Section II apply broadly to improving state effectiveness across the government. Section III discusses how these ideas should be applied in key sectors to accelerate India's development, and is the core policy section of the book.

Chapter 10 is a key conceptual chapter that bridges Sections II to III. It takes a big picture look at our national development priorities, projects future scenarios, and shows that staying on our current trajectory will yield unacceptably poor development outcomes when we turn 100 in 2047. It explains why investing in a more effective Indian state and improving the *quality* of public expenditure should be a top national priority. It shows that doing so will accelerate both 'development' and 'growth', and thereby deliver substantially better development outcomes for hundreds of millions of Indians.

Section III spends a full chapter on each of six key areas: education and skills (Chapter 11); health and nutrition (Chapter 12); police and public safety (Chapter 13); courts and justice (Chapter 14); social protection and welfare (Chapter 15); and jobs, productivity and economic growth (Chapter 16). These chapters can be read individually by those with sector-specific interests, but readers will benefit from having read prior chapters first. Three other key areas— agriculture, urbanization, and environment—do not have dedicated chapters, but are discussed in some detail in other relevant chapters.[52]

The choice of sectors is driven both by their importance to public welfare and by the scale of public resources (budgets and employees) allocated to them. These chapters aim to provide a summary of the key facts and main insights from sector-specific research. They also outline implementable sector-specific reforms that integrate the themes discussed in Section II. They aim to provide an actionable roadmap for reforms that any minister, secretary, or commissioner can act on.

Improving education, health, public safety, justice, social protection, and job creation are all *intrinsically* important for improving citizen capabilities and freedoms. But, they are also *instrumentally* important since they provide a foundation for boosting productivity, economic growth, and incomes. Thus, acting on the roadmap in Section III to improve outcomes in these key areas will lay the foundation for accelerating both broad-based individual human development and aggregate economic growth.

5.4 Making it happen

Chapter 17, on 'Reimagining Institutions', discusses how states can build new institutions to help strengthen public systems, and to institutionalize more effective ways of functioning into the daily routines of the government. To increase the chances that these reforms actually happen, it also discusses ideas for reforming the institutional rules of our democracy to better align the private interests of politicians with the public interest, to reduce the role of money in politics, to improve representation, and to increase citizen participation in governance.

Chapter 18, on 'State, Citizen, and Society', concludes the book with a discussion of why citizens across classes should come together in a broad-based social coalition, and actively engage in improving governance. It then presents ideas for how different social actors can each contribute towards our shared goal of building a more effective Indian state. Finally, it shows how acting on this roadmap will not only strengthen India, but also help us lead the world in accelerating global development.

6. Why States and Chief Ministers Should Lead the Way

Improving state functioning will require actions at all levels of government. However, this book focuses on ideas that can be implemented at the state level, for several reasons.

First, states are constitutionally responsible for primary education, health, and law enforcement; and control budgets and personnel for these sectors. State governments also determine laws and policies that influence investments and job creation, such as labour laws, land acquisition rules, and awarding of various permits. Finally, even if the Central government funds programmes, it is states who implement them. So, improving the effectiveness of state governments is vital for improving governance in India.

Second, India is simply too big for service delivery to be effectively governed at the national level. The ten largest Indian states all have over 50 million people, and would *each* rank in the top thirty countries of the world (or top 15 per cent of countries) by population. So, Indian states are large enough to be meaningful in their own right but small enough to be more manageable units for reforms, relative to India as a whole.

Third, there is large variation in state capacity and development outcomes across Indian states. Examining *why* there are differences across Indian states is beyond the scope of this book because it involves a combination of historical, social, cultural, political and economic factors.[53] However, there is a lot to learn from *what* the better-performing states have done. Focusing reform efforts at the state level can help accelerate the adoption of effective practices of high-performing states in other states as well.

Fourth, and related, this variation implies that governance reforms will have to be customized to state contexts. While the principles outlined in this book apply broadly across Indian states (and even to other countries), translating them into specific action plans will require customization. This need for customization makes it important for states to be the main drivers of appropriate reforms in their context.

Fifth, political priorities will vary across states. Given the complexities of governance reforms, sectors prioritized by the political leadership are more likely to see changes. Since chief ministers are likely to have varying priorities based on their own experiences and state contexts, making the case for reforms at the state level substantially increases the chances that at least some states will adopt at least some of these ideas.

Sixth, for India as a whole, states are valuable laboratories for policy experimentation, because they may try different ideas. This can enable diffusion of successful ideas and dropping of less effective ones. Overall, state-led innovation and experimentation in policy reforms can increase India's chances of trying out at least some reforms, reduce the risk of failure, and increase the chances of rapid replication of successful ideas.

Seventh, political accountability may be stronger at the state level. Analysis of election results shows that chief ministers who deliver better economic growth are more likely to get re-elected. In contrast, national elections can be more complex and reflect the sum of different state-level factors. Thus, the political rewards for implementing the ideas in this book may be more salient at the state level.

Finally, focusing on state-level governance reforms may help to make our national political discourse more constructive. While opposition parties will naturally criticize the government, they can earn more credibility if they demonstrate better alternatives. This is especially feasible in India because national opposition parties often run state-level governments. Conversely, the Central government will be able to sell its ideas better by first implementing them in states where their party is running the state government.

Overall, the majority of policy discourse and writing in India has been targeted at the national level, even though Indian states are larger than most countries. This book aims to correct this imbalance by giving Indian states the attention they deserve—especially in core service delivery sectors, that are constitutionally in their domain.[54]

India's landmark 1991 economic reforms could be done relatively quickly because they were mainly about scrapping and removing ineffective policies. In contrast, *building* a more effective state is a long-term task that will require steady and continuous effort. A state-led roadmap provides us with twenty-eight more opportunities to make progress than a centrally led one! Chief ministers who lead on this journey will not only deliver meaningful improvements in the lives of their citizens but will also have the opportunity to leave a broader national legacy by serving as positive role models for the country.

7. Conclusion

Improving state capacity and public service delivery is a goal that should be prioritized by all Indians across the political and ideological spectrum. Strengthening India's public systems by making cost-effective investments will enable us to deliver basic services and welfare more effectively to the poor and vulnerable, which should be welcomed by those on the economic left who prioritize equity and justice. But it will also improve the efficiency of public spending and lay the foundations for sustainably higher long-term growth, which should be welcomed by those on the economic right. Thus, beyond providing a conceptual and practical roadmap for how we can build a more effective Indian state, a key goal of this book is to unite all Indians around this agenda.

By highlighting the importance of state capacity, I also hope to redirect the intellectual, ideological, and policy discourse on development. One central debate has focused on whether governments should prioritize spending on physical infrastructure or on social sectors and welfare. In this debate, economists like Jagdish Bhagwati and Arvind Panagariya have argued that economic growth is the key driver of better long-term development outcomes and that we should therefore prioritize growth-enhancing investments, such as infrastructure. But another influential view, put forth by economists like Amartya Sen and Jean Drèze, argues that the goal of development is not boosting per capita income per se but improving human capabilities and quality of life, including through better education and health. They argue, therefore, that we should prioritize spending on human development, which will also improve longer-term growth.

Both views have merits, as discussed in Chapter 10. However, the point of departure in this book is to argue that this focus on budget *allocation* may be distracting us from the more important issue, which is to improve the *quality* of public expenditure—*regardless* of what we spend on. Arguments over the budget are zero sum because increased allocations for any sector must come at the cost of reductions for other sectors (or greater debt). However, investing in better public systems to improve governance will enable us to improve outcomes in *all* sectors, and deliver much greater improvement in citizens' lives than simply expanding budgets for more 'government as usual' spending.

The traditional debate focuses more on the 'top line' of budgetary allocation across sectors and less on the 'bottom line' of how allocations actually improve service delivery and citizens' lives. This focus on the top line is easier because budgets and allocations are easily visible. However, the bottom line of how budgets are translated into last-mile service delivery and outcomes is what actually matters, though it is less visible.

Interpreted broadly, 'state capacity' is the intermediating factor that determines how the top line of budget allocations translate into the bottom line of development impact for citizens.[55] Thus, we would do well as a country to focus much more on the critical long-term task of building a more effective Indian state, because this will help *all* our development goals. This book hopes to contribute towards this goal and provide a practical roadmap for actions that can accelerate our collective progress as a nation.

Acting on this roadmap is not only important for boosting government efficiency, but is also a *moral imperative*. India's constitution enshrines equality among citizens through universal voting rights. Yet, weak public service delivery limits the ability of the poor and marginalized to translate political equality into equality of opportunities through better education, health, and essential public services. This is why building a more effective Indian state is the *great unfinished task of Indian democracy itself* (see Chapter 2).

However, even though a key goal of this book is to promote equity and justice, it spends more time discussing issues such as data, evidence, cost-effectiveness, and efficiency of public spending. This is because improving government effectiveness in providing basic services for all Indians is the most practical way to improve equity at scale and better *deliver* on the promise of democracy for marginalized groups.

Finally, this book aims to strike a balance between appreciating India's many impressive achievements on one hand, and also acknowledging the scale of our challenges and not sugar-coating realities on the other.[56] Further, while it is easy to criticize leaders and governments, it is harder to figure out how to make progress *within* the constraints we face. This is why the discussion of India's challenges in this book is factual rather than critical; and focuses more on systems, incentives, and constraints than on people and personalities. It aims to highlight the importance of these systemic issues and to sketch out a practical roadmap that will allow us to significantly accelerate national progress.

Reforming the Indian state is an enormous task, and it can be easy to just give up. But building a more effective Indian state is so essential to our collective future that we have no choice but to be optimistic and try. This book is driven by optimism that 'we can do this'—with a combination of conceptual clarity on what needs to be done, and sustained hard work to act on this roadmap over the coming years. This spirit of cautious optimism is partly inspired by the closing words of David Landes's *Wealth and Poverty of Nations*:

> In this world, the optimists have it, not because they are always right, but because they are positive. Even when wrong, they are positive, and that is the way of achievement, correction, improvement, and success. Educated, eyes-open optimism pays; pessimism can only offer the empty consolation of being right.[57]

Section I

The Key Actors

Chapter 2

The Politicians' Predicament

Why does the Indian state not do better at basic service delivery despite being a democracy? In theory, electoral accountability should provide political leaders with incentives to deliver better for citizens. In practice, the facts on weak service delivery outlined in Chapter 1 seem to be an indictment of Indian democracy.

However, in assessing Indian democracy, it is important to note that India is historically unique, by being a country that adopted democracy based on *universal* adult franchise from the outset—at a much lower level of per capita income and state capacity than most other modern democracies. India's choice of 'democracy before development' has in turn created a unique set of political incentives and constraints.

First, it has created voter demand for and political supply of welfare and subsidy programmes at a *much* lower level of fiscal and administrative capacity than other modern welfare states. The problem is not welfare spending per se. In fact, well-designed and implemented welfare programmes can often improve both equity *and* productivity (see Chapter 15). Rather, the problem is the low *quality* of much of our welfare spending (see Chapter 6 and 15). Combined with India's low tax-to-GDP ratio, this has squeezed funds for making productivity-enhancing investments, including investing in the capacity of the state itself.

Second, the practical realities of what it takes to win elections create political incentives to prioritize allocation of public resources towards concentrated, politically influential interest groups. These tend to be elite groups that can make financial contributions to parties, shape public opinion, or mobilize large numbers of voters. The skewed allocation of public resources to elite interests further reduces funds for investing in state capacity. While elite capture of public resources is seen in many countries, the social costs are higher at low levels of per capita income and government revenue.[1]

Third, when the state is unable to effectively deliver for *all* citizens, it often makes political sense to direct the state's limited resources to narrow groups of base voters as opposed to investing in state capacity to better serve all citizens. This phenomenon is commonly known in India as *vote-bank* politics. As we'll see in this chapter, weak state capacity contributes to vote-bank politics, and vote-bank politics further weakens state capacity, reinforcing each other in a vicious cycle.

These deep structural challenges capture the core of the politicians' predicament in India. They are under pressure to deliver on a wide variety of voter demands. However, the state they govern lacks the fiscal and administrative capacity to do so effectively for *all* citizens. This creates incentives for both voters and politicians to focus on vote-bank politics. However, vote-bank politics is often *zero sum* in nature because state benefits that go to one group cannot go to another. In contrast, a politics of investing in state capacity and service delivery can make *everyone* better off. But making this transition is difficult because of the nature of political incentives described further in this chapter.

Thus, the core challenge for Indian democracy is: How do we move from a politics that rewards cultivating vote banks to a politics that rewards leaders who deliver better growth and public services for *all* Indians? There are reasons to believe that India is ready for such a transition, as explained in this chapter. But this transition itself is constrained by weak state capacity because politicians cannot credibly promise broad-based growth and service delivery if the state they lead cannot effectively deliver on this promise. We therefore need to make the *political* case for investing in state capacity to break out of the vicious cycle discussed above and accelerate this transition.

This chapter has three sections. First, it situates Indian democracy in a global context and highlights India's unique challenges resulting from choosing 'democracy before development'. Second, it clarifies the constraints and incentives that Indian politicians function under, and shows how these can often lead their actions to deviate from the public interest. Third, it explains why it should be politically attractive and feasible to invest in state capacity and implement the reform agenda outlined in this book.

1. Indian Democracy in a Global Historical Perspective

1.1 The evolution of the modern state

The role of the state has evolved over time and can be categorized into three broad phases.[2] First, for most of their history, modern states have functioned primarily as 'security' states, whose focus was on external defence and internal law and order. This was a natural response to the existential threat faced by civilizations throughout history: risk of invasion, plunder, and slaughter or enslavement. Correspondingly, the primary function that early and medieval states focused on was to protect their inhabitants.

One striking way of seeing this is that military spending often accounted for 70–90 per cent of spending in national budgets (excluding interest and major capital projects) of several European countries in the seventeenth century.[3] Correspondingly, the capacity of the state to raise tax revenue was also augmented before and during wars.[4] As noted by historian Charles Tilly, 'War made the state, and the state made War.'[5]

Next, the Industrial Revolution in the nineteenth century heralded a gradual shift in the state's role, moving beyond fighting wars to supporting economic growth. In this phase, 'industrial' states started investing more in infrastructure like roads, railways, ports, and sanitation and sewage systems. The rise of mass production in this era sharply increased the productivity benefits of these investments,[6] and enabled a virtuous cycle whereby the state used tax revenues (and borrowing) to build productivity-enhancing infrastructure, which drove increases in both output and future tax revenues. These revenues could then be used to strengthen the military further and repay the debt issued to fund capital expenditure. This shift in state focus first took place in Britain but spread to other Western countries along with the diffusion of the Industrial Revolution.[7]

Until the emergence of industrial states, the world was mostly stuck in a 'Malthusian trap' where productivity gains were primarily absorbed by population growth, with GDP *per capita* mostly remaining stagnant.[8] The Industrial Revolution, combined with public investment in infrastructure and school education, changed this, resulting in growing GDP per capita and *average* living standards for the first time in history. However, this phase also saw increasing inequality as the gains from growth disproportionately accrued to the classes who possessed land, capital, and/or education.[9]

It is only in the last hundred years that we see the emergence of the third phase of the state, which is the 'welfare' state. During this phase, governments raised taxes and launched programmes to share the gains from productivity growth more broadly and protect citizens from various risks and vulnerabilities. Examples include social security or pensions for the elderly, food security for the poor, government-provided health insurance or healthcare, and unemployment or disability insurance. These programmes took root in Western democracies in the 1930s after the Great Depression and expanded sharply in the 1950s and 1960s after World War II (see Figure 2.1).

Figure 2.1: Welfare Spending Post World War 2

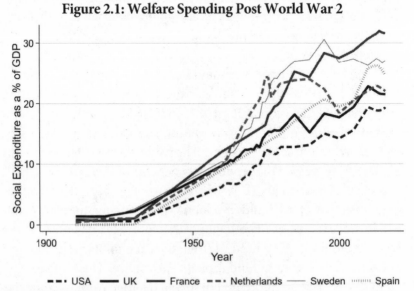

Note(s): Data from the Organization of Economic Cooperation and Development (OECD); graph produced by author.

Of course, these three functions of the state (security, infrastructure and welfare) are not mutually exclusive. Security states also built roads and occasionally had welfare programmes, and welfare states also spend on the military. So, the three phases of the state are best seen as representing the *relative* importance given to these three functions, measured by the share of national income and budgets allocated to security, productivity-enhancing public goods, and welfare or redistribution, respectively.

A key point to note is that welfare states are expensive and were historically built only *after* countries had grown rich or at least achieved middle-income status.[10] Western democracies also developed the fiscal capacity to run a welfare state during World War II when the tax-to-GDP ratio increased sharply to finance the war effort.[11] At the end of the war, they kept taxes high and used the 'peace dividend' to spend on welfare.[12] Once they started the shift to a welfare state, their share of budgets devoted to welfare has steadily increased over time. Welfare spending now accounts for 20–30 per cent of GDP and over 50 per cent of the national budget in many Western democracies.

A second key insight is that this historical evolution of the state across three phases is strongly correlated with the extent of democracy, measured by the fraction and composition of the population who have a vote. Thus, security states had no provision for voting by average citizens. They primarily served the interests of kings, nobles and the ruling classes, and are strongly correlated with non-democratic governments even today. Individuals had very few rights or protections from arbitrary actions of the state, and the government typically did little for public welfare other than provide security.[13]

The industrial state served more people but disproportionately benefited landowners, capitalists, and the professional classes. For instance, building roads and railways helps the poor in the long run through greater market integration and lower prices, but in the short run, it mainly benefits owners of capital and land, whose value appreciates sharply when infrastructure is built. It is therefore not a coincidence that industrial states emerged in an era of *limited* democracy. While the US and the UK were 'democracies' in the nineteenth century, voting rights were restricted, and concentrated among those who were educated and owned land or property. These voters would be more inclined to support infrastructure investments that they would benefit disproportionately from.

It was only after years of struggle that women, minorities, and the working classes won the right to vote in Western democracies, and it is only in the last hundred years (or *less*) that these countries adopted universal adult franchise.[14] A large body of research shows that expanding the franchise to marginalized groups is correlated with greater welfare spending. These groups typically have below-average incomes and therefore benefit from greater welfare and redistribution. This naturally makes them more likely to vote in favour of parties and candidates that prioritize spending on welfare.[15] Thus, it is not surprising that the modern welfare state has mainly emerged in the last hundred years, at a time when voting rights have expanded both within and across countries.

1.2 Indian exceptionalism and its consequences

A key challenge for state effectiveness in India is the compression of all three phases above into the seventy-five-year period since Independence, whereas most high-income democracies took much longer to build states that could effectively perform all three roles. In particular, we have tried to deliver large-scale welfare programmes at a *much lower level* of national income, tax-to-GDP ratio, and administrative capacity than today's developed countries had when they launched their welfare states.

There are two key reasons for this—one related to ideas and one to incentives. First, many Indian elites—who disproportionately influence the public discourse—have been educated in or at least exposed to the West. This was true of several leading figures of the independence movement, including Gandhi, Nehru, and Ambedkar, and continues to be true among Indian elites today. This exposure builds awareness of the benefits of a modern welfare state and a desire to replicate these ideas in India.[16]

A second and more important reason is India's decision to adopt democracy based on universal adult franchise. Most countries became more democratic as they grew richer. India, however, started highly democratic and has stayed that way throughout its post-Independence history. This is a unique historic exception, a phenomenon that Arvind Subramanian has referred to as India's 'precocious democracy' (see Figure 2.2).

Figure 2.2: At Comparable Levels of Income, Other Democracies Were Far Less Democratic than India

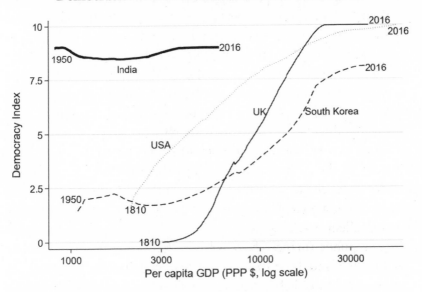

Note(s): Data from Lamba and Subramanian (2020), graph recreated by author.

India's choice of universal adult franchise democracy at the very outset *is a great moral triumph.* Despite being 'democracies', countries like the US and the UK excluded large fractions of their population from voting in the eighteenth and nineteenth centuries, with voting rights essentially restricted to land-owning white men.[17] Further, the wealth of these nations was built at least in part on the back of extreme exploitation of either slaves (in the US) or the colonies (in the case of the UK). This is why India's democracy, which empowers even the most marginalized groups in society, is a signature achievement that we should all be proud of.

Consistent with the global patterns discussed above, this democratic empowerment of the poor has created political incentives for welfare spending in India as well. However, this has taken place at a *much* earlier point in our development trajectory. For example, the US launched food stamps for the poor in the 1930s at a GDP per capita of ~$20,000 (in 2011 dollars). In contrast, India launched the public distribution system (PDS) for food security for the poor in the 1960s at a GDP per capita of ~$1250, which is less than *a tenth* of the analogous US figure.[18] Similarly, India introduced free midday meals in government schools at lower levels of income than most other countries. These are again laudable moral achievements, which were facilitated by India's universal-franchise democracy.[19]

At the same time, 'democracy before development' in India has created political pressure to expand the scope of the Indian state before building its strength to meet this expanded scope.[20] This pressure, in turn, has made it more difficult to invest in building the capacity of the state to deliver against these goals by creating two fundamental challenges. The first is a public finance challenge and the second is a political incentives challenge. While they are distinct, these challenges also reinforce each other.

The public finance challenge is as following: given India's low GDP/capita and tax-to-GDP ratio, the pressure for spending on welfare and subsidies has limited the resources available to invest in productivity-enhancing public goods—which was the primary focus of today's developed countries as they went about becoming industrial states. In India, the squeezing of funds for public goods is seen both in the underinvestment in infrastructure and in the chronic underinvestment in the capacity of the state itself.

This tension is well illustrated by the case of Indian Railways. For several decades after Independence, politicians across parties prioritized keeping passenger fares far below costs to enable the poor to access rail travel. However, this came at the cost of not investing in infrastructure and overcharging for freight traffic to cross-subsidize low passenger fares. Over time, these choices have contributed to high logistics costs for Indian industry, which hurts the poor both in the form of higher prices and fewer better-paying jobs because of the reduced competitiveness of Indian firms (see Chapter 16). Similar examples are seen in the case of water and electricity, which are often provided for free, which contributes to underinvestment and poorer quality of services over time.

Of course, it is a democratic imperative to provide essential services to *all* citizens. However, India's low resource base makes it imperative to design *cost-effective* policies and *implement* them well. However, as discussed throughout this book, this is a key area where we have fallen short. In turn, poor programme design and implementation itself reflects weak state capacity, exacerbating a vicious cycle between weak state capacity, poor quality of spending, and lack of funds to invest in state capacity. It is this chronic underinvestment that partly explains why there is so much 'low-hanging fruit' in the domain of governance reforms and why the rate of return from investing in governance and state capacity is often *ten times* greater than the cost (as shown in Chapter 1).[21]

The question then is, why have politicians not prioritized making these investments despite the returns to public welfare from doing so being so high? We now turn to understanding the challenge of political incentives better.

2. Understanding Political Incentives and Constraints

2.1 The status quo incentivizes vote-bank politics and polarization

A key mechanism by which democracy should deliver for citizens is elections. If parties and leaders serve them well, citizen satisfaction should translate to electoral success. However, the mechanics of electoral rules can significantly affect how voter preferences are reflected in a government and its policy priorities.

India uses a *first past the post* (FPTP) election system, where the candidate with the most votes wins, regardless of the percentage of votes won. If an election has several contestants, candidates can often win with less than 50 per cent of votes cast. Further, since voter turnout ranges from 50 to 70 per cent, candidates can often win with the support of under 25 per cent of registered voters.[22] For example, from 1991–2002 in Uttar Pradesh, an average of twenty candidates contested each seat, average voter turnout was 50 per cent, and the average winning candidate got 37 per cent of votes cast. Thus, many candidates won with support from *less than 20 per cent* of the electorate.[23]

This electoral calculus profoundly affects political incentives. Consider a politician with a public budget of Rs 1000 for 100 voters. They can invest in a public good that *increases* the total value to Rs 1500, benefiting each voter by Rs 15. Or they can redistribute Rs 750 (with 25 per cent lost to administration and corruption) to twenty-five 'base' voters, providing them Rs 30 each, and zero to the other seventy-five. The first option generates greater social value (Rs 1500 vs Rs 750). However, if only 20–25 per cent of registered voters are needed to win, the second strategy is politically more attractive—especially because Rs 30 is double of Rs 15, and hence, more likely to motivate base voters to turn out to vote.

Thus, FPTP, especially in multi-contestant settings, creates incentives for candidates and parties to cultivate a dedicated group of base voters, rather than serving a broad set of voters. The latter results in smaller improvements for all, while targeting base voters leads to larger improvements for a few that are more easily attributable to the politicians in question. These beneficiaries then vote for politicians they perceive as having contributed to these changes.[24] In political science terminology, this results in politics based on clientelism—defined as targeting public benefits towards preferred voter groups in return for their votes—rather than broad-based service delivery.

In India, clientelism is known as vote-bank politics, where parties and leaders cultivate and focus on serving demographic subgroups—often based on caste, region, or religion—rather than the broader public interest. Vote-bank politics has been so common in India that many politicians are remembered by their coalition acronyms rather than their policies. Examples include Charan Singh's AJGAR (Ahir, Jat, Gurjar, Rajput) in the 1970s in Uttar Pradesh, Madhav Singh Solanki's KHAM (Kshatriya, Harijan, Adivasi, Muslim) in Gujarat in the 1980s, and the MY+ (Muslims, Yadavs, plus small groups) strategy of Mulayam Singh Yadav in UP and Lalu Prasad Yadav in Bihar in the 1990s.

Weak state capacity and vote-bank politics can reinforce each other in a vicious cycle. Because weak states cannot credibly deliver services well to *all* citizens, voters often support politicians who can direct public resources to their group. Politicians, in turn, build their power base by representing the interests of specific groups— typically those with whom they share an identity—rather than the population at large. Reflecting the expectations of their voters, they use their time in office to reward their base voters rather than invest in improving broad-based governance. This underinvestment then perpetuates the cycle of weak state capacity and vote-bank politics.

A good example of such a vicious cycle is seen in Lalu Prasad Yadav's tenure as chief minister of Bihar in the 1990s. Multiple studies have documented widespread atrophy in governance during this period.[25] Yet, what is perhaps less well-known is that programmes targeting the welfare of Yadavs and Muslims—his two main vote banks—functioned relatively well.[26] Thus, by directing the limited resources of the state towards his loyal base voters, he could still get re-elected, despite poor overall performance.[27]

The central role of FPTP elections in making vote-bank politics a viable strategy is seen by noting that in the 1995 state elections, Lalu Prasad Yadav's party won with just 34.3 per cent of votes cast. Since the turnout was 59 per cent, he won with the support of just 20.2 per cent of registered voters. Thus, under FPTP, it is possible for politicians to win with intense support from smaller groups, who are more likely to vote, than with diffused support among more people, which is often not strong enough to get them out to vote.[28]

The value of intense support among base voters also creates political incentives for polarization. Citizens are more likely to make the effort to vote if they believe that only 'their' party will serve their interests. This is even more true if they believe that other parties are a threat to their well-being. Politicians, therefore, have incentives to increase the intensity of voters' preferences for their own religion, caste, or region, and make them regard other groups and parties as enemies. While this may yield short-run electoral dividends, it weakens trust among citizens, and makes it much more difficult to get groups to work together in the broader public interest.

This dynamic is exacerbated by India's diversity across multiple dimensions, including religion, caste, region, and language. A large body of research has shown that places with greater ethno-linguistic diversity have found it more difficult to build the broad-based coalitions and trust that are conducive to a politics of 'public goods'.[29] Such settings of low trust across groups are more likely to encourage clientelistic politics, where groups try to capture public resources for themselves when they are in power. This can happen in many ways, including targeting government policies and programmes to groups in power, favouring group members in hiring for government jobs, and through corruption.[30] However, all of them hurt state capacity for general service delivery.

Given India's enormous diversity, our initial social conditions already made it difficult to build broad coalitions to demand better public good provision. But political incentives and the short-run electoral benefits of increasing polarization and entrenching identities can exacerbate social cleavages and make it even more difficult to build broad social coalitions for prioritizing public goods and services that benefit all citizens.[31]

2.2 Concentrated benefits and diffused costs of bad policies

There is also a more general problem in *all* democracies that the private incentives of politicians can deviate from the public good because of the concentrated benefits and diffused costs of bad policies.[32] Consider the case of import tariffs—say on steel. Such tariffs usually hurt public welfare, but are often implemented because they generate small, diffused costs for many consumers through higher prices on products that use steel, whereas they generate large, concentrated benefits for a small number of domestic steel producers. This can profoundly affect political incentives.

For instance, if the tariff costs Rs 50/year per consumer, then its total cost for 140 crore Indians would be Rs 7000 crore/year. If it raises producer profits by Rs 30 crore/year on average for 100 steel producers, the total benefits would be Rs 3000 crore/year. In this example, the tariff results in a *national loss* of Rs 4000 crore/year.[33] Yet, people are unlikely to protest against tariffs since the costs are diffused and are only Rs 50/year on average. In contrast, concentrated benefits make it worthwhile for steel producers to lobby for tariffs. They could each make political contributions of Rs 10 crore in return for tariffs, and be better off by Rs 20 crore each on average. This can create political incentives to implement the tariffs despite their negative impact on public welfare.

The same idea holds in reverse. Good policies often create concentrated costs and diffused benefits, which can explain weak political incentives for implementing them. For instance, demanding accountability from public-sector workers may result in protests and strikes from unions. Further, resulting benefits to the quality of service delivery may take time, be less visible to voters, and be spread across millions of citizens. As a result, reforming public service delivery is politically risky because the costs are certain, immediate, and concentrated while the benefits are uncertain, distant, and diffused.

The political reluctance to take on concentrated interest groups is magnified by the highly non-linear relationship between votes and seats in the FPTP election system. For instance, in the 2016 Tamil Nadu state elections, the DMK won 98 seats out of 234 with 39.9 per cent of votes cast, whereas the AIADMK won 136 seats with 41.9 per cent of votes cast. Thus, a slight 2 per cent advantage in vote share translated into a striking 39 per cent advantage in seats and a significant legislative majority! Hence, even small vote-share differences can lead to dramatic differences in political outcomes.

This highly non-linear relationship between votes and seats can magnify political reluctance to implement public interest reforms that generate concentrated costs. For instance, it would be in the public interest to sell many of our loss-making public sector enterprises. This would both save scarce taxpayer money, *and* improve economic efficiency. However, such a move would generate large, concentrated costs among worker unions and be strongly opposed by them. Hence, politicians are often too nervous to antagonize them, because losing the votes of just public employees and their families could mean the difference between victory and loss in an election.

2.3 Strategic underinvestment in state capacity

Weak state capacity can also shape politics in ways that *reduce* political incentives for investing in such capacity. Specifically, the limited capacity of the Indian state means that there is almost always excess demand for public goods and services. This creates the conditions for a *politics of scarcity* where citizens see political participation as a way to access basic rights and services from a state with limited capacity to deliver them.[34]

This puts local politicians and intermediaries (or 'brokers') in a critical role in helping citizens access the scarce resources of the state. This role of politicians can also help explain the widespread prevalence of criminally accused candidates becoming elected representatives! In the 2019 general elections, 43 per cent of elected MPs had pending criminal cases against them. State-level figures are even worse. In the 2021 assembly elections in Assam, Kerala, Tamil Nadu, and West Bengal, over half the winning MLAs across these states had pending criminal cases against them.[35]

While political parties may give tickets to such candidates because of their ability to self-finance their campaigns, the bigger puzzle is: why do voters *choose* to elect them?

One compelling explanation provided by political scientist Milan Vaishnav is that voters often care less about their representative's ability to deliver broad-based development or draft good laws, and more about their effectiveness at helping them access limited state resources. So, a corrupt or crime-accused politician may be seen as effective because he can deliver benefits for his community by making state officials work for them. When the state is unresponsive, voters may want 'their' leader to be powerful enough to get agents of the state to respond to them—which can make a reputation for being 'tough' a positive feature! Colloquially, voters are known to say: '*Haan, goonda hai, magar hamara goonda hai* (Yes, he is a gangster, but he is *our* gangster).'[36]

When crime-accused candidates are elected, it is not surprising that they will not be interested in expanding state capacity, because such an expansion could undermine their own power. For instance, the last thing they would want is an effective and professional police force because they draw their local power from a weak police force.

Even when politicians are only middlemen and facilitators and not criminals, they may still prefer a weak state. IAS officer-turned-political scientist Anirudh Krishna has noted that politicians often assess their own importance through the concepts of *poochh* (ask) and *pahunch* (reach). *Poochh* refers to the favours people ask them for, and *pahunch* refers to their ability to fulfil them. Thus, a politician's value and respect is determined by the perceived and actual benefits they can provide for potential voters. Yet, this fact can limit their incentives to bolster systematic state capacity, as doing so may diminish the importance of the politician as an intermediary between voters and the state. Krishna recounts an instance where his efforts to automate government processes and deliver benefits more smoothly were obstructed by local leaders fearing a loss of relevance, with one remarking: '*Hamari kya poochh rahegi* (Who will ask after us)?'[37]

2.4 Politicians value visible and short-term measures of effectiveness

Many politicians genuinely wish to improve citizens' well-being. Yet, political incentives push them to prioritize *visible, short-term* measures that voters can see and give them credit for.[38] Hence, even politicians who care about education and health focus more on visible actions like building a school or hospital and being photographed at the opening ceremony, or distributing laptops with their pictures on them, than on less visible but more important issues like staff quality, management, and performance.

Visible, short-term investments can win votes by yielding demonstrable outputs within an election cycle. In contrast, systematic investments in governance and state capacity may only yield results in the future beyond the next election. These benefits also accrue gradually, making them more difficult for voters to discern. A large body of research in psychology has documented that people often do not notice gradual changes, which makes it less likely that they will give credit for these changes to a politician.[39]

The focus on providing visible, rapid, and concentrated benefits can also explain why politicians often see public-sector employment more through the lens of 'providing jobs' rather than that of improving service delivery. A public-sector job provides an immediate and dramatic improvement in life prospects, which can ensure votes of job recipients and their families. In contrast, the benefits of improved services are diffused across citizens, accrue over time, and may be less visible to voters. This reasoning may also explain why politicians representing disadvantaged groups often focus on securing reservations in government jobs for their groups, rather than on improving the quality of public services, though the latter will help *many more* disadvantaged citizens over time.

2.5 Political financing and the 'democracy tax'

A fundamental challenge for democracy in India and around the world is that contesting elections is expensive and requires significant funding. For instance, the total spending across parties in the 2014 Indian national election was estimated at Rs 35,000 crore, far exceeding Election Commission limits.[40] This amount has been increasing rapidly over time, with expenses in the 2019 national election estimated at Rs 55,000 crore.[41] These are only figures for national elections. State and municipal elections also cost money to contest, adding substantially to political fundraising requirements.

Thus, political leaders spend considerable amounts of time and attention on political fundraising. The pressures of election financing also contribute to politicians often using state power for political fundraising rather in the public interest. These actions impose a large 'democracy tax' on the quality of governance in India.

The need for political fundraising by elected leaders hurts public welfare both directly and indirectly. The direct costs include diversion of taxpayer funds through corruption in public contracts and procurement; policies and laws that benefit political funders rather than the public; and overlooking legal violations in return for financial considerations.[42] These costs are magnified by the opacity of election financing, which has increased in recent years due to the introduction of electoral bonds.[43] Such opacity makes it easier for policies to reflect the interests of political funders rather than the public interest.[44]

The indirect cost is that politicians may not pay enough attention to core functions of the state, such as management and training of public personnel because there is no money to be made in doing so. A memorable example of this point was when a senior official recounted to me that the Department of Personnel and Training (DoPT) in his state was informally called the Department of Postings and Transfers, since this is what the department mainly focused on. In turn, this reflected the fact that there was money to be made in postings and transfers of officials but not in training.

The widespread perception and reality of corruption in public life has contributed to the low public regard for politicians.[45] However, even personally honest politicians are often forced to condone corruption to raise money for their parties. The need to raise large sums of electoral financing is a *root cause* of many of the pathologies of Indian democracy, and is a fundamental challenge for democracies globally. There are no easy solutions. However, recognizing the political constraints imposed by the 'democracy tax' can help craft more realistic and effective approaches to reforms to improve state capacity and service delivery, as discussed in Chapters 3, 17, and 18.

2.6 Disproportionate influence of elites on politics and the state

The factors above help to explain how, even in a democracy, small groups of well-organized elites can disproportionately influence politics and direct state resources towards themselves. In his classic book, *The Political Economy of Development in India*, economist Pranab Bardhan identified three sets of politically-influential elites as having captured a lion's share of India's public resources: big business groups, large landholders, and government employees.[46]

The outsized influence of these groups reflects their ability to (a) fund parties and elections, (b) directly influence large numbers of voters through their social and economic position,[47] and (c) organize to mobilize and protest if the government tries reforms that would threaten their interests.[48]

Thus, despite universal franchise, Indian democracy in practice has catered much more to these elite groups. The skewed allocation of public funds to these groups, which we will see evidence of throughout this book (see Chapter 18 for a summary), has reduced funds for investing in core state capacity for service delivery. Further, since these elites have largely exited from using public services, their political activity has focused more on preserving their privileges than on improving public service delivery. Thus, they may not only be indifferent to weak state capacity, they may also actively *thwart* reforms that threaten their positions. These factors create challenges even for political leaders who want to invest in better governance.

3. Making the political case for investment in state capacity

In a democracy, the legitimacy to take action to improve public welfare lies with the political leadership. However, as seen above, the electoral incentives of politicians often diverge from the public interest. At one level, the problem seems almost hopeless. The challenge is that even if politicians intuitively understand that investing in long-term governance will be better for the country than practising vote-bank politics, they also need to win elections. This politicians' predicament is nicely captured in the words of Jean-Claude Juncker, former prime minister of Luxembourg and President of the European Commission, who memorably noted that:

'We all know what to do, we just don't know how to get re-elected after we've done it!'

Yet, there are reasons to be cautiously optimistic that India is ready to transition from an older politics that rewarded patronage and clientelism to a newer politics that rewards governance and broader service delivery. The key insight is that vote-bank politics is a 'zero sum' game because public resources that go to one group cannot go to another.

In contrast, a politics that focuses on improving governance, state capacity, and service delivery can substantially *increase* the size of the pie and deliver improved outcomes to many more people. Further, as voters get more educated, it becomes more difficult for local strongmen and influencers to control and deliver a large number of votes. Finally, advances in technology also make it possible to deliver services directly to citizens without relying on intermediaries. These trends favour politicians who can deliver better services to citizens at scale over those who focus on providing patronage to a few local elite intermediaries who, in turn, mobilize voters for the concerned politician.

Crafting a new political settlement for India

In other words, India is ready for a new 'political settlement' that is more inclusive than the status quo. Scholars of development studies use the term 'political settlement' to describe an arrangement between key groups of elites in a society, whereby they agree to maintain peace and social order, and not destabilize the government, in return for a set of 'rules of the game' (that are often tacit and not explicit) by which these elite groups obtain a level of benefits that they find preferable to disrupting the status quo.[49]

Thus, India's status quo of weak public service delivery partly reflects the political settlement among elites in the post-Independence era, as identified by Bardhan—big businesses, large landowners, and government employees. Their dominant share of India's public resources, in turn, reflects their disproportionate political influence. India's political settlement has evolved over time to include the interests of professional elites, especially in globally competitive sectors, in economic policymaking. However, none of these elite groups have exerted pressure for improving public services because they have found it easier to exit to private solutions.

Yet, this elite-biased political settlement is under pressure from rising democratic expectations of non-elite groups that are now more educated, have access to better information, and intuitively understand the limitations of vote-bank politics in improving their lives. However, they are frustrated by their inability to access better basic services, and improve their quality of life.[50] This status quo also limits India's economic growth because we simply cannot function at our full potential if half our children complete primary school without being able to read, and if a third are malnourished. Improving state capacity and service delivery is therefore essential for both inclusion and growth.

Thus, politicians who can grasp these facts and trends, invest in governance and state capacity to benefit many more people, and thereby craft a new and more inclusive political settlement are also likely to be rewarded electorally. Indeed, there is evidence that this is already happening as discussed below.

3.1 Voters increasingly reward good governance

For much of India's post-Independence history, politicians have prioritized vote bank politics because they believed this was a better way to win elections than focusing on development. Evidence suggests that this may no longer be the case, and that over time, voters appear to be rewarding better-performing governments with more votes.

One study found that between 2000 and 2012, Indian governments that delivered higher economic growth obtained more votes and seats, which was a break from 1980–2000 when such a correlation was not present.[51] Another study, of the 2009 elections, found that state-level economic growth was significantly correlated with the success of incumbent party candidates.[52] These studies suggest that Indian voters are growing sophisticated over time, probably reflecting increasing education and better information.

There is evidence that politicians are also recognizing the benefits of investing in governance reforms to improve citizens' lives even though they may forgo some 'revenue' and 'control' by doing so. A study found that leaders invest in information technology (IT) reforms when their perceived electoral benefits from improved governance outweigh the costs of reduced 'revenue' from corruption.[53]

Based on personal interviews, the author quotes officials as saying that: 'Politicians supported [the service centre policy] . . . Anything that provides convenience to the people, politicians know will be good for them', and, 'MLAs didn't resist [an e-service centre initiative] because they saw this as citizen-friendly . . . They know that this can be sold politically.'

I have seen examples of this first-hand in my own research. In 2010, the Government of (undivided) Andhra Pradesh introduced biometric smartcards to better deliver payments in its NREGS and pension system. My colleagues and I evaluated this reform and found that it significantly reduced leakage and improved beneficiary experiences in collecting payments.[54] However, it also reduced the ability of intermediate functionaries to siphon off public funds. Unsurprisingly, they opposed this reform and tried to subvert the programme. However, the chief minister went ahead with the reforms, suggesting that he believed there was greater political benefit from effectively delivering services to a much larger number of people, even at the cost of antagonizing intermediaries.[55]

An insightful comment we received on this study came from senior IAS officer Dr Santhosh Mathew, who noted that, 'The miracle here is not that the technology itself was effective, but rather that it was *allowed* to be effective.'[56] In other words, implementing governance reforms can be politically challenging because allowing corruption in public welfare programmes is an important source of revenue and reward for lower-level officials and politicians in return for their political support during elections. Thus, reforms to reduce leakage can cost political support in the old model of patronage-based politics. However, the chief minister's backing of the reform suggested that the political incentives were changing towards rewarding better service delivery.[57]

3.2 Winning political narratives increasingly rely on a record of good governance

The combination of voter education and easier access to information has made it increasingly necessary for politicians to pay at least some attention to their governance record when facing re-election. Election campaigns around the world are fought on narratives, and in recent years, winning parties have increasingly included their track record of governance and service delivery in their political narratives.

The best example of this is probably the BJP's winning campaign of 2014, which combined the traditional politics of identity (that aimed to consolidate Hindu voters) and the modern politics of emphasizing good governance and broad-based development. Campaign slogans like 'sabka saath, sabka vikaas' (with everyone, for everyone's progress) spoke to voters' desire to elect a leader who would embody shared national progress as opposed to catering to narrow vote banks.

Some analysts have observed that despite these slogans, the BJP's political strategy relies mainly on the old politics of identity and polarization. They argue that the BJP's electoral success is built on consolidating the Hindu majority by broadening their caste coalition under the umbrella of a Hindu identity, and that the RSS's organizational field strength ensures that BJP voters turn out to vote.[58] However, while these factors have clearly contributed to the BJP's electoral success, it is noteworthy that the party saw the need to frame their pitch to voters in terms of good governance to win elections.

Consistent with this view, several political analysts have noted the importance of the good governance image of then Gujarat Chief Minister Narendra Modi in explaining his popularity in the 2014 elections.[59] Similarly, the BJP/NDA government's success in improving delivery of welfare schemes and cutting out corrupt middlemen is believed to have played an important role in the re-election of Prime Minister Narendra Modi in 2019.[60] More recently, many political analysts have noted that the re-election of Yogi Adityanath in UP in 2022 was at least partly due to improved delivery of law and order and welfare benefits (also referred to as the labharthi or beneficiary vote).

Parsing reasons for electoral outcomes is a complex problem, but one notable metric suggests that the BJP's re-election in UP was at least partly driven by better public service delivery. Historically, the BJP had a lower female vote share, but this changed in the 2022 UP elections. Since women put a greater weight on welfare globally, this switch is consistent with improved delivery of welfare schemes.[61] Conversely, the BJP's 2023 Karnataka election loss was widely attributed to poor governance, strengthening the argument that polarization without delivery may not be enough to win elections.[62]

Another good example of political success enabled by focusing on better public services is the Aam Aadmi Party (AAP) in Delhi. They campaigned primarily on issues of good governance and improved service delivery. After getting elected in 2015, they focused on core development sectors, such as health, and education with visible investments in neighbourhood (*mohalla*) clinics, and improving government schools. Consistent with my argument that there are political rewards to improving service delivery, the AAP was voted back to office in 2020 with nearly *90 per cent* of Assembly seats.

Many re-elected chief ministers in recent decades, across states and parties, have had signature schemes or accomplishments that delivered *broad* benefits, and these achievements have played a key role in their re-election narratives. Examples include Narendra Modi in Gujarat (industrial development), Chandrababu Naidu (information technology) and Y.S. Rajashekhar Reddy (health insurance) in Andhra Pradesh, Shivraj Singh Chouhan in MP (agriculture), Raman Singh in Chhattisgarh (PDS reforms), Sheila Dikshit in Delhi (public transport), Nitish Kumar in Bihar (law and order, education), K. Chandrashekhar Rao in Telangana (farmer welfare), Naveen Patnaik in Odisha (several welfare programmes), and Mamata Banerjee in West Bengal (schemes for women).[63]

It is *not* my contention that the traditional axes of political mobilization such as caste, region, and religion do not matter for winning elections. Rather, the point is that these are unlikely to be enough *on their own* to win elections. Even for parties for whom identity politics provides a solid base of voters, delivering better *general* welfare is becoming essential for getting the additional votes needed to win elections.

3.3 Data-driven governance reforms can work—and work fast

Successful political leaders in India are increasingly targeting programmes towards broad groups, such as farmers and women, rather than narrow groups based on caste and community. Yet, even welfare-minded politicians focus on delivering *visible* schemes that they can take credit for with voters. The main limitation of this approach is that the government soon runs out of public funds to give away in exchange for votes.

Thus, the big opportunity for chief ministers is to grasp the fact that making data- and evidence-driven investments in governance can often be ten times more cost effective at delivering benefits to citizens than simply spending more money in a 'government as usual' way. Making this mindset shift and acting on it will allow the Indian state to become much more effective, and thereby enable politicians to sharply 'expand the pie' and deliver much more for citizens and voters.

Further, there is evidence that governance reforms can improve service delivery *fast enough* to demonstrate visible impact to voters within a five-year term. For instance, setting up outbound call centres to conduct high-frequency monitoring of beneficiary experiences, and using this data for performance management of block-level officials delivered meaningful increases in beneficiary welfare within just a few months.[64] Such systems can not only improve service delivery quickly but also help politicians by reaching a much broader set of citizens than officials normally hear from, and enable them to *listen* to citizens between elections (see Chapter 4). Similarly, hiring additional anganwadi workers would generate large long-term returns from improved education and nutrition, and be immediately visible to communities.

Chief ministers can also lay the foundations for better governance by investing in better data. Improving the quality, reliability, speed, and disaggregation of data will provide political leaders with tools to hold the bureaucracy accountable. This is an agenda that politicians should strongly support because *they* are accountable to voters and can be removed from office in five years. In contrast, public employees enjoy lifetime jobs with limited accountability. Investing in data-driven governance will boost the ability of political leaders to get the state machinery to deliver services to citizens more effectively, for which they can get credit and votes from citizens (see Chapter 4).

3.4 A politics of service delivery can *reduce* the need for political fundraising

The practical reality of politicians' lives is that they spend considerable time and effort on raising funds to support party operations and contest elections. Even personally honest leaders grudgingly accept that some corruption in government is inevitable in order to meet their political financing requirements. However, many leaders do not like having to raise money, because they know that the process compromises them and reduces their ability to function in the public interest.

Thus, politicians themselves will benefit from reduced election spending. However, they are trapped in a *zero-sum* game, where they cannot unilaterally disarm from the spending race because doing so would put them at a disadvantage against opponents who spend more. This is why attempts to impose legal limits on election spending have not been very effective. The spending simply goes off the books and makes a mockery of the law, which no serious party or candidate follows.[65] Thus, the best way to reduce the role of money in politics is to help to create the conditions whereby money becomes less important for parties' electoral prospects. How can we facilitate such a shift?

Studies of election financing in India show that political parties spend heavily on direct payments or handouts to voters before elections, to secure their support. One reason why politicians compete with direct handouts to voters is that they are not able to deliver broad-based services effectively, which makes these handouts a more feasible way of credibly delivering at least some benefit to voters.[66] This creates a chicken-and-egg problem, where the need to finance handouts requires even more political fundraising, which, in turn, requires additional corruption, leading to underinvestment in the state capacity that could have improved broad-based service delivery. Once again, we see how weak state capacity and inefficient politics reinforce each other in a vicious cycle.

The discussion above suggests that it may be politically feasible for a chief minister, at the start of a five-year term, to commit to an agenda of improving governance and to go back to the voters after five years with a credible track record of improved service delivery. Importantly, doing this may *reduce* the need for financing voter handouts before elections and thereby lessen the pressure to seek illicit political financing. If quality of service delivery has truly improved, then a chief minister can point to it and publicly note that this has been enabled by reducing corruption.

Some evidence that such an approach can be a feasible political strategy comes from the re-election of leaders like Narendra Modi, Naveen Patnaik, Yogi Adityanath, Sheila Dixit, and Arvind Kejriwal, which can at least partly be attributed to their public image as not being personally corrupt, and having improved service delivery.[67] Such successes highlight that Indian voters are ready to reward politicians who transition from a politics of vote banks to a politics of performance. Improving governance can reduce the need for pre-election handouts, thereby lowering the corruption needed to finance them and increasing funds available to invest in state capacity. This will enable even better service delivery, and kickstart a virtuous cycle that can accelerate India's development.

3.5 Intrinsic and legacy motivations

In addition to caring about re-election, most politicians have areas of intrinsic motivation, and care about their reputation and legacy. A senior official who has worked with chief ministers across parties nicely captured this sentiment by telling me that politicians care about 'vote', 'note', and '*dil*' (heart). In other words, politicians do care about getting elected and raising money for their parties and themselves; but they also care about doing good, especially in areas close to their heart where they can leave a legacy.

Many Indian chief ministers have made notable contributions to the development of their states that they are well remembered for.

Examples include K. Kamaraj in Tamil Nadu (education), Narendra Modi in Gujarat (infrastructure and industrialization), Shivraj Singh Chouhan in Madhya Pradesh (agriculture), Chandrababu Naidu, and Y.S. Rajasekhar Reddy in unified Andhra Pradesh (for information technology and welfare, respectively) and Nitish Kumar's first term in Bihar (law and order, and girls' education).

Leaders matter greatly for the course of states and nations. In India, leaders who care about development have often increased budget allocations and created new schemes in their preferred sectors. However, this approach is limited by tight budgets and by the weak translation of spending into outcomes. Thus, chief ministers who make data and evidence-based investments to strengthen public systems and service delivery will be able to sharply improve *all* development outcomes and not just in some focus areas, increase their chances of getting re-elected, and also secure their legacy.

3.6 Preserving faith in democracy itself

Beyond their individual legacies, political leaders should pay attention to citizens' growing disenchantment with democracy itself. A recent book by data journalist S. Rukmini uses data from multiple surveys to show that Indians' faith in democracy is eroding.[68] She also notes that more Indians express support for a 'strong' leader than in any country, including Russia, and quotes a (not atypical) urban tax-paying professional who says that 'elections are a waste of time' and expresses a desire for a strong leader who can run the country in the right direction (with the army).[69]

At a superficial level, this argument seems appealing. Many successful East Asian economies in the last fifty years, including South Korea, Taiwan, Singapore, and China, have had limited or no democracy, contributing to the not uncommon view (noted above) that India needs a 'strong leader' and less democracy to develop faster.

However, this comparison is misleading because it cherry-picks a few cases where less democratic governments have delivered strong economic growth and development. For every effective autocrat or strongman, there have been *many more* ineffective and even disastrous ones. Overall, studies across large samples of countries and time periods suggest that democracies deliver higher growth on average.[70] There is even stronger evidence that democracies experience lower volatility in growth.[71]

The value of checks and balances is also seen *within* countries over time. While it is tempting to attribute China's economic success to having a 'strong' state, this would be a mistake. Some of the world's greatest man-made disasters in the second half of the twentieth century—including the Great Leap Forward and the Cultural Revolution—happened in China under the 'strong' leadership of Mao Zedong. China started thriving only after Deng Xiaoping introduced checks and balances in the Chinese Communist Party. The significance of these changes is seen in the backsliding of China's economic performance and global standing in the past decade, which coincides with Xi Jinping's moves to undo the Deng Xiaoping reforms and concentrate and centralize power.[72]

Even within India, the growth rate in the fifty-year period from 1969 to 2019 was higher under coalition national governments than single-party ones.[73] This non-intuitive fact points to the great practical virtues of democracy, distribution of powers, and checks and balances. It promotes moderation and accommodation of diverse viewpoints, and reduces the chances of big policy mistakes.[74] However, while data and evidence point to the benefits of democracy, declining faith in democracy among citizens can create the conditions for a weakening and backsliding of India's democratic experiment itself.

The risk of citizens' getting disenchanted with democracy if it did not deliver economic and social progress was pointed out early by Dr Ambedkar, who noted before the Constituent Assembly in 1949 that:

> On the 26th of January 1950, we are going to enter into a life of contradictions. In politics we will have equality and in social and economic life we have inequality. In politics we will be recognizing the principle of one man one vote and one vote one value. In our social and economic life, we shall, by reason of our social and economic structure, continue to deny the principle of one man

one value . . . We must remove this contradiction at the earliest possible moment or else those who suffer from inequality will blow up the structure of political democracy which this Assembly has so laboriously built up.[75]

India's Constitution recognizes all citizens as equal through equal voting rights. But the main instrument that the poor and marginalized have for translating political equality into greater economic and social equality is the state itself. Thus, the weak capacity of the Indian state to effectively deliver for all citizens is a key binding constraint in translating the political equality of our democracy into greater equality of opportunity.

This is why investing in building a more effective Indian state that can deliver against democratic aspirations is *the great unfinished task of Indian democracy.* Doing so will not only accelerate India's development and growth but also contribute to preserving citizens' faith in Indian democracy itself.

4. Conclusion

India's historically unique experiment of 'democracy before development' is a great moral triumph that we should all be proud of. However, it has created more demands of the state than the state has the capacity to deliver, which has given rise to a 'politics of scarcity'. Hence, citizens' political participation has focused on obtaining access to supply-constrained public benefits and politicians have correspondingly focused on directing rationed state resources to preferred political constituencies.[76]

Thus, a key insight of this chapter is that, while Indian democracy has enabled citizens to make claims on the state, it has not provided enough political incentives to invest in the state's capacity to meet those claims. A second insight is that weak state capacity contributes to vote-bank politics, and they reinforce each other in a vicious cycle. The need to raise large amounts of money for funding elections further vitiates the problem, and skews the allocation of public resources towards concentrated elite groups.

Going forward, a central question for India's politics is: How do we transition from zero-sum vote-bank politics to a positive-sum politics of broad-based service delivery? A different but related way of framing the question is: How do we transition from our elite-biased political settlement that is not working well for a large number of Indians, to a new and more inclusive political settlement?

Data suggests that Indian voters and society may be ready for these transitions, and that politicians who can cater to this voter demand will reap electoral rewards. Yet, to translate the promises of better governance into reality, politicians need to recognize that they need to invest in upgrading the 1950s car that is the Indian state. Even when politicians want to deliver better services for voters, the car simply won't move much even with more fuel (budgets) and pressure (accelerator), without strengthening the car itself. Investing in state capacity to strengthen and revamp the car will have large and rapid returns, and should therefore be a top priority for any newly elected chief minister.

Political will is a prerequisite for meaningful action, and this chapter, correspondingly, aims to make the political case for prioritizing investments in state effectiveness. Once the political will is there, the rest of this book can provide a roadmap for specific cost-effective, evidence-backed ideas that can help translate that will into meaningful results.

Finally, while this chapter has argued that it is in the self-interest of politicians to act on the roadmap in this book, it is also true that many of the Indian state's weaknesses reflect the divergence between the private interests of politicians and the broader public interest. Chapters 17 and 18 discuss how leaders, citizens, and civil society can help to reduce this divergence, and make the government work better for *all* citizens.

Chapter 3

The Bureaucracy's Burden

In India, as in most democracies, the elected political leadership decides *what* the government should do, by drafting legislation and heading the executive branch. These intentions are then translated into practice through the bureaucracy—including senior officials at the policymaking level, mid-level managerial staff, and frontline workers. Therefore, the challenge of strengthening state capacity is primarily one of improving the effectiveness of all levels of our bureaucracy.

At one level, the Indian bureaucracy is impressive. The top rung of the civil service—the Indian Administrative Service (IAS)— is selected through a rigorous, transparent, exam-based process, and the best IAS officers are among the most capable public officials anywhere in the world. Further, as a collective, the Indian bureaucracy delivers many impressive administrative achievements, including successfully running the world's largest census, elections, and vaccination campaigns. Yet, the same bureaucracy struggles with effective ongoing delivery of basic services—as seen by the facts on education, health, nutrition, public safety, and justice highlighted in Chapter 1.

How can we make sense of this contradiction? One way is to recognize that we have simply not invested enough in the capacity of the Indian state to effectively deliver basic public services. Thus, the India bureaucracy is able to succeed in 'mission mode' when its resources and attention are directed at solving specific problems with well-defined and monitored goals and deadlines. However, it does poorly in its routine tasks mainly because we have not equipped the bureaucracy with the adequate staff strength, skills, autonomy, processes, and management to do these tasks well.[1]

The strong performance of the Indian bureaucracy in 'mission mode' projects suggests that the ingredients for success do exist in our public systems. However, even well-intentioned, dedicated, and talented officials are constrained by the systemic realities within which they function. Over time, the 'bureaucracy's burden' has steadily grown as we have added increasing expectations on the bureaucracy without a commensurate investment in increasing its capacity to meet these expectations.

This underinvestment reflects two distinct sets of political pressures. First, politicians have prioritized spending public funds on immediately visible subsidies and palliative measures rather than longer-term investments in state capacity. Second, politicians across parties have undermined the professionalism and capacity of the bureaucracy to make it easier to control and use it for narrow personal and political goals. Over time, the combination of these two factors has led to an increasing mismatch between public expectations from the state on one hand and its capacity to deliver on the other.

The good news for India is that, as voters get more educated and aware, politicians are increasingly under pressure to deliver better. However, even political leaders who want to deliver better governance are constrained by the weak bureaucracy, which, in turn, is the cumulative result of decades of neglect. This is why investing in strengthening the capabilities and effectiveness of our bureaucracy needs to be a top political priority for reaching our potential as a nation in the coming years.

The second piece of good news is that we now have a lot of research and evidence to guide *specific* interventions that will be effective, cost-effective, and yield rapid returns. As noted in Chapter 1, even if there is political will to invest in state capacity, it does *not* imply that we should implement a 'government as usual' expansion of the bureaucracy. This is because, there are massive inefficiencies in the status quo.

The status quo is well described by the tragicomic story of two people discussing the food in a restaurant. The first one says: 'The food here is terrible' and the second one says: 'And the portions are too small!'[2] Similarly, our bureaucracy is both too small and highly inefficient. Thus, we need to increase staffing and capacity. However, we also need to do so in cost-effective ways alongside reforms to improve bureaucratic efficiency.

This chapter has three main goals. First, it presents key facts on the Indian bureaucracy and its systemic challenges. Second, it explains the key reasons for why things are the way they are, and have been difficult to improve. Third, it aims to make the *political* case for investing in the bureaucracy, and outlines key actions that political leaders should take to alleviate the bureaucracy's burden and improve its functioning. Once this becomes a political priority, the rest of the book outlines specific ideas for strengthening public systems and service delivery that leaders and senior officials can act on.

1. The Indian Bureaucracy: Key Facts and Challenges

The Indian bureaucracy is a massive and complex labyrinth, with around 10 million employees across the Central and state governments. Of these, roughly 75 per cent are state government employees and 25 per cent are Central government employees.[3] This ratio is in line with state governments being responsible for the functions with the largest numbers of public employees, such as school education, health, and the police.

At the top of this structure are officers of the apex All India Services, such as the IAS and the Indian Police Service (IPS). The IAS, in particular, is the backbone of the country's administration and was referred to by India's first Home Minister, Sardar Vallabhbhai Patel, as the 'steel frame' of India. IAS officers are assigned to a state as their home cadre, but are also deputed to the Central government, and occupy senior policymaking and administrative roles in both Central and state governments.

The state-level bureaucracy typically comprises three broad levels. At the top are senior IAS officers based in the state capital, who work with political leaders to make policy, and are also the administrative heads of various departments. In the middle are district and block-level officials, usually recruited as part of a state civil-service cadre, responsible for management of frontline employees and for implementing government policies and programmes. Finally, there are frontline workers who are responsible for delivering services like education, health, and public safety to citizens.

These frontline workers—such as teachers, health workers, and police constables—account for 80–90 per cent of public employees. IAS and other officials in policymaking and senior administrative roles comprise less than 1 per cent of the workforce. The rest are mid-level officials and supervisors at the state, district, and block levels. At each level, the Indian bureaucracy is afflicted with systemic, often interrelated, challenges that compromise service delivery. The most important of these are discussed below.

1.1 Severe staff shortages

A common misconception is that the inefficiencies of the Indian state stem from its large size—that there are too many workers doing too few things. In practice, the opposite is true, and the Indian state is highly *understaffed*. As Figure 3.1 shows, India has only 16 public employees per 1000 people. For comparison, China has over three times as many (57) and Norway has nearly ten times as many (159). Even the US, often viewed as a leading example of a market-driven economy with limited government, has 77 public employees per 1000 people—nearly five times as many as India!

Shortage of staff afflicts every service delivery sector in India. For instance, the number of qualified doctors, nurses, and midwives per 1000 people in India is about a *quarter* of the World Health Organization (WHO) benchmark. The effective number of civilian police per population is around *one-third* of UN benchmarks. A 2021 UNESCO report noted that over 11 lakh teaching positions were vacant, and that 19 per cent of schools had teacher vacancies—with this figure increasing to 33, 40, and 56 per cent in the states of UP,

Jharkhand, and Bihar.[4] Similarly, anganwadi centres responsible for early childhood health, nutrition, and education are also understaffed. There are striking shortages at the managerial level too. In a 2010 study, we found that 19 per cent of district-education officer (DEO) positions across India were vacant, leaving a critical role—overseeing over 1000 schools on average—vacant nearly one-fifth of the time.[5] In 2011, a government report noted that over 50 per cent of district-level financial management positions were vacant.[6] In more recent work, we have found vacancy rates of over 40 per cent at the *mandal* (block) education officer level in Telangana, and similar rates for ICDS supervisor positions in Tamil Nadu. The situation in northern states with fewer public employees per capita is likely to be even worse.

Figure 3.1: Per Capita Public Employees across Countries

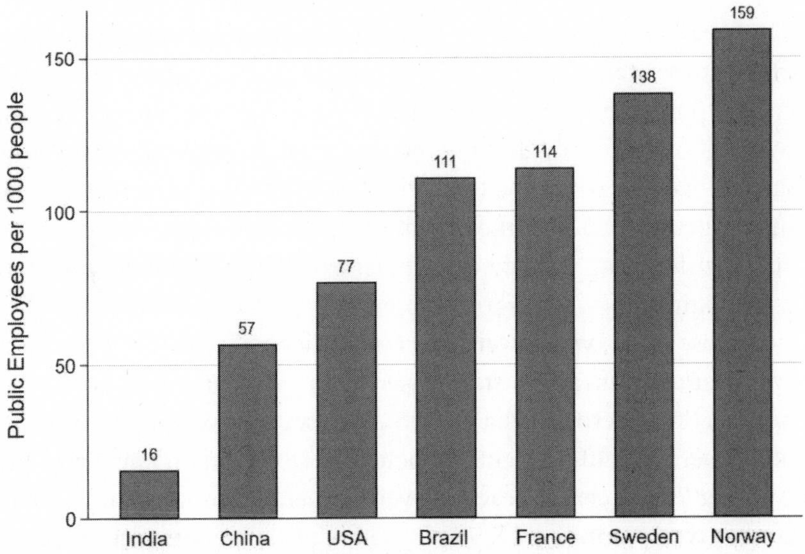

Note(s): Data from Chandrasekhar and Ghosh (2019), graph recreated by author.

Staff shortages directly compromise the quality of service delivery. A study by political scientists Devesh Kapur and Aditya Dasgupta surveyed block development officers (BDOs) across India and found that (a) 42 per cent of full-time positions were vacant, (b) staffing rates are strongly correlated with quality of service delivery as measured by days of NREGS employment provided and NREGS expenditure per capita, and (c) understaffing is correlated with BDOs spending more time on transactional ('firefighting') tasks rather than on planning and oversight of programme implementation.[7]

Simply put, it is not possible to effectively deliver public services without enough frontline workers and supervisors to manage them well. The all-India figures also mask enormous variation across states. Staffing ranges from fewer than 3 public employees per 1000 people in Bihar, to roughly 6 per 1000 in Uttar Pradesh and West Bengal, to nearly 13 per 1000 in Tamil Nadu.[8] Unsurprisingly, governance and service delivery outcomes are much poorer in the states with lower levels of government staffing.

1.2 Limited and misdirected accountability

The problem of low staffing is exacerbated by poor accountability of existing staff—exemplified by high rates of absence. Across critical public services, such as education and health, many frontline workers often simply don't show up for work. I saw this first-hand during my field work as a PhD student in 2002. I would visit schools in villages at 11 a.m.—the middle of the school day—only to find children loitering outside closed classrooms and teachers nowhere to be found.

These field visits were part of a larger research project to systematically measure staff absence in government schools and health clinics across India. We found that, on average, 25 per cent of teachers and 40 per cent of doctors were absent on any given day. Another 25 per cent of teachers were present but not teaching. Thus, at any given point in time, 50 per cent of government teachers across India were not teaching.[9]

The numbers have not improved much since then. In a follow-up nationwide study in 2010 where we revisited the same villages we visited in 2002–03, we found teacher absence rates of 24 per cent in rural India.[10] More recently, in 2015–16, we found that 33 per cent of government school teachers were absent in Madhya Pradesh.[11]

Based on 2010 salaries, we estimated that the all-India fiscal cost of teacher absence was over Rs 10,000 crore *per year*, which is likely greater now since salaries are even higher.

These high absence rates are directly correlated with weakness in management and supervision. Our study found that teacher absence was significantly higher if the school had not had a supervisory visit in the past three months. However, such visits are much less likely to happen when there are vacancies in supervisory roles. Thus, the 30–40 per cent vacancy rate in block-level supervisory positions directly hurts governance.

In contrast, teacher absence rates are much lower in private schools, driven by better governance. In our all-India data, there was a 175 times greater chance of being held accountable for teacher absence in private as opposed to government schools![12] In another study where we directly measured school management practices in (unified) Andhra Pradesh, my colleagues and I found that the quality of personnel management was orders of magnitude higher in private schools compared to government schools.[13]

More generally, employee performance management is a key weakness in the public sector across all departments. In theory, the system of annual confidential reports (ACRs) feeding into employee service records should be an effective tool to motivate performance. However, in practice, both employee recognition for performance and accountability for non-performance are weak. Consistent with this, in a 2010 survey, less than 16 per cent of civil servants believed that the appraisal system was effective.[14]

It is not that there is no accountability in the public system. However, it is directed towards compliance rather than service delivery. Supervisors mainly check paperwork, and worry more about fraud than about improving service delivery. Consistent with this, I have seen several cases where schools were provided books and computers that teachers kept locked up and did not allow students to use! This is because teachers were mainly concerned about not damaging or losing the books or computers rather than whether they were used effectively by students to improve learning.

This reality of public employees' lives was nicely captured in the TV series *Panchayat*, which depicted the travails of a junior government official who is investigated as a suspect when a computer monitor gets stolen.[15] Few cared if the computer was not used, but there was a price to pay if it got stolen! Thus, bureaucratic accountability in India prioritizes paperwork and compliance over performance (also see Section 1.6).

1.3 Inadequate autonomy

This focus on compliance also constrains officials' autonomy—defined as having the freedom and ability to exercise judgement in one's daily professional functioning. Autonomy can improve performance for several reasons. First, it increases intrinsic motivation by boosting employees' sense of agency over their daily functioning. Second, it improves staff effectiveness by enabling them to better respond to local conditions. Third, it nurtures a culture of taking initiative rather than passively carrying out orders.

Several studies in India have found significant benefits of increasing bureaucratic autonomy in sectors spanning education, environmental regulation, and public-sector enterprises.[16] Recent studies from other developing countries reinforce this point. For instance, a study of public procurement in Pakistan found that increasing autonomy by moving decision-making authority closer to the field and away from 'headquarters' made procurement more efficient by reducing both time taken, and prices paid.[17]

The importance of autonomy for bureaucratic effectiveness is reinforced by officials themselves. A 2010 survey of Indian civil servants found that the 'opportunity to make a useful contribution' and 'autonomy in the job' were the top two factors contributing to job satisfaction.[18] Yet, in practice, India's bureaucracy has very little autonomy, which contributes to low intrinsic motivation. In the same survey, the most frequent reasons cited for dissatisfaction on the job were lack of autonomy and lack of opportunity to make a useful contribution—with nearly 50 per cent of dissatisfied officers citing these two factors as an important reason for their dissatisfaction.

This lack of autonomy reflects a combination of political, judicial, and administrative factors (see Section 2).

1.4 Lack of local embeddedness of government employees

Government employees in India also have limited connections to the communities they are meant to serve. This is seen in multiple dimensions.

On the spatial dimension, government employees rarely live in the communities they serve. Qualified personnel are often most needed in rural areas, but they prefer to live in urban areas with better amenities, including private schools for their own children. In contrast, locally hired contract teachers and community health workers typically live in the villages they serve. For instance, in one of my studies, we found that contract teachers on average lived 1 km away from the school, compared to over 12 km for regular teachers.[19] This distance increases the likelihood of provider absence, and weakens their ties to the community.

On the sociological dimension, despite reservations, government employees are more likely to belong to advantaged communities, due to large backlogs in filling reserved positions.[20] Further, women are significantly under-represented in government jobs—especially in northern states. These structural features of government employment also reduce the connection between public employees and the communities they serve.[21]

The third, and perhaps most striking, metric of disconnectedness is how government employees mostly avoid public services that *they* provide. In our all-India study of teacher absence, under 20 per cent of government school teachers sent their own child to any government school, including the one they taught in. Similarly, for healthcare, officials and politicians typically use private options or top-tier public facilities like the All India Institute of Medical Sciences (AIIMS), where they can obtain special attention.

Taken together, these weak connections between government employees and the communities they are meant to serve contribute to weak public service delivery in India. In particular, the secession of Indian elites—including most government employees—from using public services may partly explain the low priority placed on improving them.[22]

1.5 Limited opportunities and incentives for skill upgradation

Both classic and contemporary texts on bureaucracy emphasize the importance of government employees having adequate professional training, domain expertise, and technical capacity to do their jobs well.[23] However, the Indian bureaucracy is severely constrained on these fronts, as noted in several government reports and commissions.

There are problems on both the supply and demand side. On the supply side, there is a shortage of good training institutes and faculty. Further, content quality is highly varied, and there are few systematic methods for assessing the quality or impact of training programmes. Training is considered a low priority and low status function, and the position of the director of state-level training institutions is often considered a 'parking lot' for senior officers. On the demand side, there are limited incentives for public employees to upgrade their skills since salary increments and promotions are mostly determined by seniority and not even by competence, let alone performance. Further, given staff shortages, departments are often unwilling to let staff go on training leave.

One striking indicator of weak technical capacity in the government is the proliferation of external consultants at both Central and state levels. While I have not been able to find systematic data on the use of such consultants, I have encountered them in practically every government department I have interacted with. There are certainly advantages of the consultant model, including flexibility and accountability due to renewable contracts. However, since senior officials are under pressure to deliver projects quickly, they prefer to use consultants rather than improve the capacity of their own staff, which is a longer-term project. Thus, the widespread reliance on external consultants both reflects and contributes to the long-term atrophy of core state capacity in India.

1.6 A paperwork state

The problem of limited staff is compounded by poor prioritization and use of their time. In particular, multiple studies have noted that officials at all levels spend large amounts of time on (often pointless) paperwork. Paperwork pervades the Indian bureaucracy to such an extent that scholarly books on the Indian state have titles such as *Paper Tiger* and *Red Tape*. The obsession with paperwork imposes several costs on governance.

First, it diverts staff *time* away from actual service delivery. For instance, anganwadi workers maintain up to fourteen paper registers, and multiple time-use studies show that 20–30 per cent of their time is spent on administrative tasks.[24] Since many of these records are never used, the time spent on them directly impedes service delivery. This problem has been documented across sectors. For instance, Nayanika Mathur's aptly named book *Paper Tiger* shows how the demands of paperwork in NREGS severely impeded officials' ability to plan and implement the programme itself.[25]

Second, the system's focus on paperwork shifts supervisor and staff *attention* to compliance and record-keeping rather than service delivery or outcomes. I saw a striking example of this in my work evaluating a school governance improvement programme in Madhya Pradesh. The programme design reflected several global 'best practices' and was implemented at scale. However, our independent evaluation found that it *had no impact on any outcome that mattered* (student or teacher attendance, effort or learning outcomes). Based on qualitative interviews, we learnt that teachers primarily treated the programme as requiring them to fill a bunch of forms. So, the programme was a great success on paper, but nothing actually changed in practice![26]

Third, the focus on paperwork provides strong incentives for creating a facade of performance on paper that is often divorced from reality. As anthropologist Akhil Gupta has noted, the culture within the Indian government is to create administrative records or report data for its own sake. He memorably recounts one meeting where a secretary is asked to file a report, even when he has nothing to report. He is told: '*Aur kuch to nahi, gaadi ko kagaz par hee dodaa do*' (If nothing else, let the train at least run on paper).[27] The perception that the 'system' mainly cares about appearances rather than reality can also breed cynicism and erode employee motivation over time.[28]

Fourth, the onerous paperwork requirements to establish eligibility for public benefits can result in disproportionate exclusion of illiterate and vulnerable populations. For instance, a recent study shows that the Right to Education (RTE) Act's provision to reserve 25 per cent of seats in private schools for economically weaker sections (EWS) mostly benefits *better-off* households whose children would have enrolled in a private school anyway. This was partly because the most disadvantaged households were unable to fill the forms and submit documents needed to access programme benefits.[29]

Lastly, a preoccupation with paperwork can erode the autonomy and initiative of frontline staff to solve local problems. An influential study by Yamini Aiyar and Shrayana Bhattacharya found that lower-level officials report a sense of powerlessness and view their roles as operating a 'post office' where they deliver directives from senior officials and simply gather data to report back.[30] The study quotes a block education officer (BEO) who says that 'as long as you keep sending data and as many forms as possible, you are a good worker here', and another official who laments, 'Our job is focused on filling forms well, we don't honestly know what happens after we collect this information.'

Despite these costs, we should recognize that *all* bureaucracies require paperwork to document decisions and their rationales. Such records are essential for preserving institutional memory and continuity within the government, which has to function even after the individuals involved in a decision have moved on. Thus, the goal should not be to eliminate paperwork, but to streamline it, use technology to make it more efficient and reduce redundancies, and focus on collecting information that can directly help improve governance and outcomes (see Chapters 4 and 5).

1.7 Lack of tenure and managerial stability

The issues above largely concern frontline staff. At the policymaking level, a critical challenge for governance is the short tenure and frequent transfers of senior officials. Analysis by *Mint* noted that the average tenure of IAS officers in their post in the twenty years prior to 2019 was just fifteen months.[31] This itself was an improvement over an average of twelve and a half months in the previous twenty years! As a result, principal secretaries and commissioners, who lead entire departments, are typically in their role for only around eighteen months (and often even less). This creates several problems.

First, frequent transfers make it difficult for officers to build relevant domain expertise. IAS officers are justifiably proud of their 'generalist' skills and their ability to function in any government role. However, while general administrative skills may transfer across departments, policymaking requires deeper domain knowledge—including an understanding of the direct and indirect ways in which government actions can shape sectoral ecosystems (see Chapter 9). Even highly capable officers require time to get up to speed with the complexities of new sectors, and I have frequently seen decision-making slow down for weeks and even months after transfers of senior officials.

Second, even if frequent transfers do not affect domain expertise per se (say because of good technical advisers and staff in the department), short leadership tenures reduce incentives to initiate any substantial reforms. Such reforms require time even to design and implement, let alone show results. So, it often makes sense for senior officers to continue the status quo rather than attempt any meaningful systemic reforms because they will most likely not be around in the role long enough to see them through.

Third, even when senior officials attempt reforms, their subordinates may not take these efforts seriously and prefer to 'wait out' the 'over-enthusiastic' reformer. This is because they know that the reforms may not be pursued by the next occupant of the post, who may have different priorities. Short tenures also contribute to frequent shifts in priorities, weakened institutional memory, and inefficient replication of effort.[32] Put together, short and unpredictable tenures of senior officials is a key reason why the bureaucracy as a 'system' underperforms, despite having outstanding individuals in it.

A senior IAS officer, who averaged a typical fifteen months per post in his career, said to me that frequent transfers were wonderful for his own learning by giving him exposure to many parts of the government. But he also noted that it was *terrible* for governance because by the time he had understood a department and started trying to improve things there, he was transferred out. In his words, he was mainly 'holding the fort' and 'firefighting' to ensure that there were no disasters on his watch, but frequent transfers made it nearly impossible to deliver sustained improvements in governance.

Using a cricket analogy, he noted that in each new posting, he felt like a T20 batsman who had to hit out from the first ball because time was so short. In contrast, doing deep high-quality work in governance requires the skills and temperament of a test-match batsman, and the corresponding duration at the crease or in the post. Just like good cricketers adjust across formats, our top officers are also able to do at least some good despite short tenures. The problem is that the 'system' is making them play the wrong game (T20), as opposed to giving them the stability and tenure needed to play the long game (test match) of building a more effective Indian state.

2. Understanding the Status Quo

These systemic weaknesses reflect a combination of historical, political, economic, judicial, and institutional factors. This section aims to explain why things are the way they are, since such an understanding can help in crafting a practical reform agenda.

2.1 Colonial legacy

Many of the weaknesses above reflect the fact that the modern Indian state has been built on the same structure as the British colonial state. While the colonial state did undertake some development projects like the railways, its main goal was not the welfare of the population but rather to *extract surplus* from India's land and its people to finance the colonial army and the opulent lifestyle of its rulers.[33] Hence, the British colonial state was primarily a security state, whose main administrative goals were preservation of law and order, and collecting revenue by taxing economic activity.

The legacy of these structures is felt even today. The head of the colonial district administration was called the Collector, highlighting that revenue *collection* was the primary goal of the colonial state. The other key official was the Superintendent of Police (SP) who was responsible for law and order, which was an essential prerequisite for economic activity and taxation. Though their roles have evolved over time—with the Collector in particular having many more development-related responsibilities—the colonial legacy is seen in how we still use the same titles for these positions even today.

Beyond titles, a substantive relic of the colonial era that persists is the frequent transfers of public officials. The original purpose of such transfers was to prevent colonial officials from becoming too close or sympathetic to local populations, and to thereby reduce their chances of 'going native'. The system was designed to keep administrators *distant* from the population and correspondingly feel less guilt about their extractive roles.[34]

For modern India, it makes little sense to continue this system. However, it remains popular among both employees and politicians. For employees, transfers to better postings are a way to reward seniority, and to get new experiences. Frequent transfers also makes it easier for officials to escape accountability for performance.[35] Politicians value transfers as a tool for controlling the bureaucracy and a lucrative source of bribes. However, while the system serves the interests of the ruling classes, frequent transfers hurt citizens and service delivery by disrupting both staffing and management.[36]

Similarly, insisting on copious and immaculate paperwork may have made sense when the state only focused on revenue collection and maintaining law and order. However, the cost of paperwork is greater when the functions of the state have grown faster than the growth in staffing. The opportunity cost of time and the moral costs of exclusion are both higher. A colonial state would not care if people were excluded from benefits for being illiterate and unable to fill a form. But, a democratic state should.

Overall, the Indian state has not yet fully completed the transition from being an extractive colonial state to becoming a modern, democratic state whose primary goal is to *serve* citizens rather than *rule* them as subjects. On the positive side, we have passed many rights and laws to reflect the democratic aspirations of a citizen-centred state. On the other hand, our administrative structure and processes that are a relic of the colonial state hinder the translation of legislative intent into reality.

2.2 Political factors

There are several political factors that contribute to the weakness of the bureaucracy. The first is the low political priority placed on investing in stronger public systems, for the reasons explained in Chapter 2. Over time, the cumulative underinvestment in bureaucratic capacity has severely limited its ability to effectively deliver for citizens.

A second political factor is corruption in personnel matters. Government jobs are highly valuable and sought after due to higher-than-market compensation (especially at lower levels), lifetime job security, and the potential for additional 'unofficial' income in many positions. As a result, corruption in recruitment and postings can be very lucrative for politicians as seen in the several public recruitment scams over the years.[37] Over time, such corruption erodes both the quality of candidates and the culture of organizations.

Third, even without corruption, politicians across parties have sought to 'control' the bureaucracy. For instance, UPSC hiring is clean and free from political interference, and civil-service rules protect officials from arbitrary dismissal. But, politicians use transfers as a tool to control officials. This trend started under Prime Minister Indira Gandhi, and has now become widespread. Honest officials who refuse to condone corruption are harassed by frequent transfers till they 'fall in line'.[38] Thus, though frequent transfers hurt governance, the practice has persisted partly because politicians value their ability to control the bureaucracy more than they value its ability to better serve people.

A fourth and related factor is that politicians often prioritize loyalty over competence in public hiring. A senior IAS officer once shared a striking example of a case where a politician was presented with a candidate shortlist for an important district-level position. Unsurprisingly, he preferred a candidate from his own caste and party. However, what was surprising was that even among two candidates of his own caste and party, he selected the *less* capable one. His reasoning was that the more capable candidate may start thinking that he actually deserved the position, and work independently after being appointed. In contrast, the less capable one would know that he only had the position due to political backing and be more 'reliable' in carrying out the politician's wishes.

Thus, a combination of political indifference to the long-term health of the bureaucracy, and political interference for short-term benefits have played a key role in weakening India's bureaucracy. These political actions are a natural *consequence* of the electoral and financial pressures that politicians face (as noted in Chapter 2). Politicians seek to control the bureaucracy because it enables them to direct public resources to their vote banks and funders. However, the long-term costs of these actions have been enormous, and deeply weakened state capacity to serve the broader public.

2.3 Economic factors

Economic factors also contribute to weak bureaucratic performance. Governments operate without a 'market test', which limits their incentives to improve efficiency. While companies will go out of business if they do not provide adequate value for the price charged, governments can spend taxpayer money badly for a long time without facing consequences. In the classic terminology of Janos Kornai, a pre-eminent scholar of the economics of socialism, governments face a 'soft budget constraint' because public funds can be used to bail out inefficient operations.

Consider the case of India's public sector undertakings (PSUs), such as state road transport corporations and the recently privatized Air India. These PSUs are often poorly managed, pay above-market salaries and benefits, and also used to siphon off funds for political interests—all of which contribute to large losses. For instance, Air India is estimated to have had cumulative losses of over Rs 1 lakh crore prior to privatization, which were ultimately borne by the taxpayer.[39]

Inefficiencies and losses in PSUs are at least visible in the accounts. In government departments, the inefficiency is hidden because there is no profit and loss statement. But even here, high salaries and poor management contribute to much higher costs per unit compared with private provision of comparable quality in sectors such as education and health (see Chapters 5 and 9). No private enterprise would survive with such a high cost structure relative to the quality of services provided. Yet these enormous inefficiencies have continued for decades because they are hidden in the budget.[40]

Overall, while there are conscientious officers—especially in finance departments—who scrutinize department budgets and care about efficiency, there are very few systematic incentives for efficiency in most parts of the government (see Chapter 6). The resulting low quality of public expenditure both starves us of funds to invest in state capacity and reduces the effectiveness of additional public spending on service delivery.

2.4 Judicial factors

The judiciary is increasingly involved in government personnel matters. Parties who are dissatisfied with a government personnel policy or decision often appeal to the courts to stay or overturn them. In principle, judicial review should provide an independent check against administrative or political violations of rules and procedures. In practice, courts are also severely understaffed, leading to long delays in judgments. As a result, judicial backlogs contribute to administrative paralysis and reduced government effectiveness.

I have personally seen this play out. Candidates are often recruited into government service through multiple channels, and so creating an integrated seniority list across all candidates is a non-trivial challenge. This process is often contested and ends up in the courts.[41] In one state I worked in, over 60 per cent of the positions of BEO remained *vacant for several years*, and the main reason was that the court decision on seniority lists, which would determine who would get promoted, was pending during this period.

The judiciary often intervenes in personnel matters that should be in the domain of the executive. For instance, courts have often retrospectively ruled against government decisions to prioritize hiring local, albeit less qualified, candidates over more qualified candidates from further afield. These rulings fly in the face of evidence from multiple studies that local candidates are often more effective at local service delivery—even if less qualified. In any case, this is a policy decision that should lie in the domain of the executive as long as it is consistently and transparently applied. The risk of ex-post legal challenges often makes bureaucrats wary of recruitment in the first place, and partly explains the large number of vacancies in government positions.

Judicial interventions, though well-intentioned, can *hurt* state capacity. They contribute to important positions remaining vacant, recruitments not being conducted, and eat into already overburdened senior officials' time. Many state education secretaries have told me that they spend 20–40 per cent of their time responding to litigation on personnel matters. One of them even mentioned to me that his greatest wish was to have a legal representative in his office to handle the cases and endless summons from the courts, so that he would have the time to actually focus on education!

These points have been corroborated by senior IAS officers T.V. Somanathan and Gulzar Natarajan in their recent book on state capability in India. They note plaintively that: 'Personnel litigation takes up a huge share of administrative bandwidth. In some ways, cases involving service matters are like a *tapeworm inside the administrative system*, continuously enfeebling it. The growing pile of cases takes up inordinate time and effort of officials, detracting attention from their substantive activities.'[42]

2.5 Institutionalized risk aversion

The bureaucracy also has institutional incentives for risk-aversion because rewards for success are limited, while the costs of failure are high. Rewards for success are limited because pay and promotions are mostly determined by seniority and not performance. Even at important junctures in officers' careers—such as when they are empanelled for senior positions—it is often enough to be above average as opposed to outstanding.

In contrast, even one adverse action—such as an inquiry for a decision taken in the past—can jeopardize an officer's career. Even if officers make a good-faith error, their reputation can be adversely affected during an inquiry, which can be a long-drawn-out process because investigating agencies and courts are also understaffed. Thus, the process itself is often a punishment. Paraphrasing a senior official, this dynamic deters innovation and creativity because officials often believe that 'the best way to survive in the system is to not try to innovate or deviate from established norms and procedures'.

Such risk aversion runs deep in the bureaucracy, and creates a strong bias towards inaction. When faced with a problem, risk-averse bureaucrats may procrastinate, pass the problem to another entity, cite rules and procedures that prevent action, or simply deny the problem's existence! A recent study on risk aversion in the Indian bureaucracy confirms this point and notes in its abstract that 'we argue that bureaucratic indecision, in a large part, is a form of rational self-preservation exercised by bureaucrats from the various legal and extra-legal risks to their person, careers, and reputation'.[43]

Risk aversion also contributes to poor quality of public expenditure. For example, in procurement, officials often prefer a tender process that awards contracts to the vendor with the lowest price quote (L1) rather than undertake quality-based procurement, because L1 procurement is easier to justify than paying extra for better quality.[44]

Using a football analogy, India needs strikers who score goals and move us forward, but our bureaucrats function as goalkeepers, focused on avoiding errors. Goalkeepers' incentives reflect the problem that 'few remember the many goals they save, but few forget the occasional goals they let through'.[45] Similarly, Indian officials are mostly unappreciated for their heroic efforts at juggling the many balls they have in the air at the same time, but face considerable risk of being penalized for any mistake they make.

Of course, *all* bureaucracies are bound by procedures and paperwork, and bureaucratic risk aversion is common globally. But the cost of risk aversion and inaction is higher for a low-middle-income country like India. Playing defence and avoiding mistakes can make sense if a team is leading in a football game, but not when it is trailing. Similarly, given the scale of India's development challenges, the Indian government needs more innovation and initiative from its officials, but its systems encourage risk aversion.

2.6 The bureaucracy's work can be inherently more challenging

One subtle and underappreciated point is that the 'inefficiency' of the bureaucracy can be partly explained by the much more complex nature of government work. As Nobel Prize-winning economist Abhijit Banerjee has explained in his classic paper, 'A Theory of Misgovernance', bureaucracies can look less efficient than their private-sector counterparts in part because the public sector takes on much more challenging tasks.[46]

An example of this 'selection bias' is that unlike the private sector, the government has the mandate of serving *all* citizens. Private companies can focus on well-defined market segments where they have a competitive advantage. However, the government needs to accommodate different goals for different segments of the population. This makes it more challenging to deliver services, and to measure and manage staff performance.

Consider education. Private schools routinely screen students for admission, and often reject academically weaker students or those with special learning needs. In contrast, public schools cannot exclude any student. This makes it much more challenging to deliver quality education to *all* their students. Similarly, private companies will often not bother catering to the poor because the profit margins are thin. However, governments have to serve the most marginalized citizens—including those who are illiterate and need more support to access public benefits. This is a much more complex task.

Of course, this is not the only reason for bureaucratic inefficiency—as seen by weaker government management of public-sector enterprises in the *same sector* as their private counterparts. However, it is important to recognize and acknowledge that the tasks that we expect the bureaucracy to take on are often much more complex and difficult than those in the private sector. These are magnified by the understaffing and low resourcing of the Indian bureaucracy relative to the tasks it is expected to handle.

2.7 Premature load bearing: Trying to do much with too little

The combination of high voter expectations due to universal franchise democracy, global norms and ideas on what states *should* do (which often reflect standards of richer countries with higher state capacity), and chronic underinvestment in state capacity—have created demands on the Indian state that are significantly greater than its administrative and fiscal capacity to deliver. However, what is less appreciated is that this excess load can *further reduce* state capacity. Policy scholars Matt Andrews, Lant Pritchett and Michael Woolcock have coined the term 'premature load-bearing' to refer to the problem of weak states getting further weakened by taking on more 'load' than they can bear.[47]

Trying to do too much has several costs. First, it forces the government to ration public benefits resulting in cumbersome procedures to access them, which disproportionately hurt the vulnerable. Second, rationing can weaken service delivery because resources spent on deciding *who* should get benefits are diverted from actual service delivery. Third, and related, excess demand can lead to time wasted in adjudicating contesting claims *after* an allocation is made. Fourth, overcommitting relative to capacity results in unkept promises that can undermine public trust in the state. This can further weaken the state, by limiting its ability to negotiate policy changes with stakeholders who are less likely to trust the government's commitments. Fifth, it can reduce bureaucratic effectiveness by diverting focus from tasks that are 'important' to those that are 'urgent'. Finally, it can demoralize the bureaucracy by increasing its feeling of inadequacy to deliver against expectations, which can further weaken its ability to function effectively.

In conversations, I have characterized how overcommitment can reduce state effectiveness as follows: 'In India, the legislature makes laws and commitments that are beyond the capacity of the executive to deliver. This can then lead to the third branch of government (the judiciary) holding the second branch (executive) in contempt of the first one (legislature)! The time spent by the executive in responding to judicial efforts to hold them accountable, further reduces their time to actually deliver services. In this way, the three branches of the government are each doing their job as they see it, but end up tying the system in knots and further reducing overall capacity to deliver!'[48]

2.8 Bureaucratic self-interest

While there are many external reasons for its weaknesses, the bureaucracy itself should share some of the blame because employee lobbies often put their self-interest ahead of the needs of governance, as illustrated by the three examples below.

First, government employees have lobbied for and obtained such generous pay and benefits, that their total compensation for most jobs is *several times higher* than market rates for the same job. As a result, India's ratio of public employee salaries to GDP is among the highest in the world (see Chapter 5). Given such high salaries, it is easy to see why the government is so understaffed: there simply is not enough money to hire the required number of public workers. Thus, India's public employee shortage largely reflects insiders using their political clout to reward themselves through higher pay and benefits, at the cost of the government not having funds to hire more staff.

Second, the bureaucracy is also partly to blame for short tenures of officials in important posts. The norm of seniority-based promotions implies that when a senior official retires, their successor is often the next in line by seniority, regardless of how close they are to retirement. While this system is bad for governance, officials like it because it allows many more of them to retire at a higher rank, and thereby get the benefits of higher pensions, post-retirement benefits, and social prestige.

For instance, in one state, the revenue officers' union lobbied to not allow anyone to hold the position of *taluk tahsildar* (a key post in the revenue administration) for more than a year. While this was bad for governance, unions wanted to allow more staff members to occupy this prestigious post.[49] In another state, officials were upset when a chief minister ignored the seniority norm to appoint a chief secretary who would have a longer tenure in office and thereby provide greater stability in governance. The priority placed on personal ambitions over effective governance is seen in the words of a disgruntled officer who noted to a journalist that, 'The chief secretary post is the dream of every IAS officer recruited directly. We would like to sit in that chair even for a day.'[50]

Third, senior officers are partly responsible for the over-centralization of governance. While the 73rd and 74th Constitutional Amendments aimed to substantially increase the decentralization of funds, functions, and functionaries to rural and urban local bodies, in practice, senior officials have resisted doing so because that would reduce their own power and authority.[51] This resistance to decentralization is seen both from Central to state governments, and from state to local governments (see Chapter 8).

In a hard-hitting 2019 book, N.C. Saxena, a distinguished retired civil servant, has blamed the IAS for many of the problems outlined in Chapter 1. He has observed that: 'The system seemed to be running for the convenience, first and foremost, of civil servants themselves.'[52] While there is some merit in his arguments, I believe that it is unfair to blame *all* of our governance travails on the beleaguered bureaucracy, given the many structural constraints it faces—as outlined in this section. However, it is fair to note that the bureaucracy often places the interests of insiders over the broader public interest, and has partly contributed to its own institutional weakening as a result.[53]

3. How Can We Ease the Bureaucracy's Burden and Make It More Effective?

Among the factors above, the political reasons for bureaucratic weakness are the most critical. I therefore divide the discussion of how to improve bureaucratic effectiveness into two parts. The first, covered here, highlights *political* actions that are needed to improve bureaucratic functioning. The second, discussed in Chapter 5, on 'Personnel Management', delves deeper and presents specific evidence-based ideas, which can be implemented by bureaucratic leaders themselves with adequate political backing.

3.1 Make it a political priority to invest in strengthening the bureaucracy

As voter demand for governance is growing, politicians increasingly need narratives and substantive records of better governance and delivery to get re-elected. Yet, they face a key challenge: even when politicians *want* to deliver better, the bureaucracy is often not able to do so. I have heard multiple politicians across states and parties complain that they are frustrated with the bureaucracy, its inertia, and its inability to deliver better for citizens.

However, such complaints are unfair because the weakness of the bureaucracy reflects decades of *political* neglect, which cannot be fixed overnight. Further, the cynicism and corruption in many parts of the bureaucracy partly reflects officials' own experience of seeing politicians prioritize personal gains and narrow political goals over public interest. In an environment where corruption is institutionalized, and honesty and competence do not seem to be rewarded, it is not surprising that many public officials become corrupt themselves, or content themselves with enjoying the benefits of a government job.[54]

This is why it will take years of sustained effort to build more effective public systems. However, rising voter demands for governance make such investments politically sensible. Continuing the car analogy, politicians are like the race-car drivers who get the public attention for the performance of the car. However, just like driver performance is limited by the quality of their car, politicians can only be as effective as the state they lead. Thus, politicians who want to be successful leaders cannot do so without also investing in upgrading the systems of the car that is the Indian state.

This is why politicians should make it a top priority to invest in strengthening the bureaucracy. Further, many of the specific, evidence-based, reform ideas discussed in this book are likely to be effective, cost-effective, yield results within five years, benefit large numbers of people, and also be easy to communicate to voters. Thus, if chief ministers undertake this reform agenda at the beginning of a five-year term, it is likely that the results can be seen in time to take to the voters before the next election.

3.2 Eliminate corruption in hiring, postings, and transfers

As discussed in Chapter 2, political corruption in India often stems from the need to raise funds for party and election expenses. However, a subtle and underappreciated point about political corruption is that it can take different forms, and that these can have very different consequences for public welfare. While a long-term solution for this problem has to involve reducing the role of money in politics, in the short-term, we will do better as a country even if politicians avoid the most harmful forms of corruption.

In particular, corruption in appointments, postings, and transfers is especially harmful for public welfare. Such corruption can corrode the very foundations of the state by making it more likely that we: (i) select the wrong type of public employees, (ii) provide perverse incentives to those who are selected, (iii) promote the wrong type of officials, and (iv) create organizational cultures of weak performance.

First, corruption in hiring increases the chances of selecting less honest and public-spirited individuals. High-integrity candidates are not only less likely to offer a bribe, but they would also expect less 'side' income from the job, and would hence offer a lower bribe, even if they were willing to do so—which puts them at a double disadvantage.

Second, employees who have paid for their position will seek to recover this cost by demanding bribes from citizens whom they interact with—thereby strengthening incentives for extortion, and weakening incentives for service delivery.

Third, corruption in promotions has both the problems above! In addition, officers who are known to have obtained their senior positions by paying for them will find it more difficult to command respect among their own staff, which can further reduce organizational effectiveness. Also, the belief that career prospects depend more on corruption and connections than on competence and performance can be deeply demoralizing to the culture of entire government departments.

Finally, if many employees have paid for their jobs and expect to receive bribes, it can vitiate the entire culture of the concerned organization. Such cultures make it difficult for honest and competent officials to function, because they are viewed as threats to the existing arrangement. In well-functioning professional organizations, employees take pride in their collective identity and reputation, and quickly eject 'bad apples' from the system. However, corruption in appointments and promotions can create a culture where the 'good apple' is the outlier and made to feel unwelcome. Reforming such organizations is incredibly difficult and often requires a wholesale clean-up.

For fans of Hindi cinema, many of these issues are captured in the film *Gangaajal*. The social cost of corruption in hiring is made clear by the example of a corrupt junior police officer who is caught by an honest SP, and pleads for mercy by explaining that he had to extort citizens for extra income to repay the loan he had taken to pay the bribes to get his job. Similarly, the cost of a corroded organizational culture is seen in the various attempts made by his own colleagues to get the honest SP transferred. Throughout the movie, we see how it is citizens who bear the cost of this atrophy in police functioning.

This is why my most important recommendation to political leaders who want to improve the effectiveness of their government is to eliminate corruption in public-sector hiring, postings, transfers, and promotions. Corruption in personnel matters weakens the very foundations of the state and has long-lasting negative consequences.

A politician who takes a bribe to facilitate the hiring of an incompetent or corrupt official may be out of office in five years, but that official will remain in the system for over thirty years!

Of course, the key question is why should politicians forgo the substantial income from corruption in personnel matters? The answer lies in the changing political calculus. As discussed in Chapter 2, many senior leaders have realized that the electoral benefits of improved voter satisfaction enabled by using technology in service delivery exceed the costs of losing political support by reducing corruption revenue for party functionaries. Similarly, senior leaders should recognize that the electoral benefits of better service delivery that will be enabled by boosting the quality and integrity of public personnel management is likely to exceed the costs of forgone revenue from lower corruption.

In other words, political corruption often reflects politicians seeking 'notes' to buy 'votes'. Historically, this approach worked when less-informed voters could be influenced by local elites, who would 'deliver' large numbers of votes in return for notes.[55] But as voters get more sophisticated, it makes sense for politicians to improve governance as a direct route to mass appeal, because this is the best way to improve people's lives *at scale*. Reducing corruption in public administration is a key enabler of this transition.

There is some evidence that this transition is already happening. My discussions with electoral finance experts in India suggest that effective politicians are using more 'strategic' approaches to political fundraising by targeting select high-value sectors and funders, while directing the rest of the government to prioritize service delivery and public welfare. To enable this goal, they have embraced the use of technology to curb corruption in welfare programmes, and also reduced corruption in personnel matters.

Eliminating or at least sharply reducing corruption in public-sector staffing will play a critical role in helping pivot Indian democracy from a politics of patronage to one of governance and service delivery. The challenges of the Indian bureaucracy largely stem from politicians shaping it over the years to serve the needs of patronage politics. But the resulting reduction in bureaucratic effectiveness is now hindering politicians who want to deliver for citizens. Effective politicians in India have realized this and are reducing corruption in personnel matters. Others will hopefully follow suit.

3.3 Ensure stability of tenure of government staff

One straightforward reform to boost bureaucratic effectiveness is to institute a minimum tenure of three years in most government roles. The importance of stability of tenure for effective policymaking is well understood, and reflected in the policy of five-year tenures for joint secretaries in the Central government. Chief ministers would do well to institute similar norms of at least a three-year tenure for principal secretaries, and department heads at the state level, and for collectors and other district-level department heads.

Stability is crucial for service delivery roles too. As discussed earlier, the practice of frequent staff transfers is a colonial relic that has outlived its utility. While some transfers due to retirements and promotions are inevitable, states should create policy guidelines to minimize transfers of frontline staff and supervisors. This will deepen their ties to the communities they serve, make it easier to hold them accountable for quality of service delivery, and reduce the administrative burden of frequent transfers. It will also reduce the favour-seeking and corruption associated with the 'transfers and postings' industry.

In my years of interacting with state governments, nearly all notable achievements in governance I have seen have come when the concerned department heads have had stable tenures of over three years. Conversely, officers with short tenures rarely do anything noteworthy other than 'mind the store'. Thus, ensuring a minimum three-year term for key roles is one of the easiest ways to increase bureaucratic effectiveness.

3.4 Increase autonomy on process and accountability for outcomes

As seen in Sections 1.1 and 1.2, the Indian state gets both autonomy and accountability wrong. High-performing organizations provide autonomy on process to frontline employees, combined with accountability for delivering outcomes. In contrast, the Indian government *does exactly the opposite*! On the one hand, it micro-manages employees, restricts their autonomy, and squeezes the initiative out of them through various means. On the other, it does not hold anyone accountable for poor outcomes.

The biggest cultural shift that is needed to improve the bureaucracy's effectiveness is to reverse this pattern and increase employee autonomy on processes, while holding them accountable for outcomes. So, political leaders who want to deliver better for citizens, should set departmental goals, and empower top officials with operational autonomy on how they hire, motivate, and manage their staff, and how they spend their budgets. It means that political leaders should defend officials for honest mistakes and encourage them to be goal-scorers who solve problems rather than just goalkeepers focused on avoiding mistakes.[56] Greater autonomy also needs to percolate down to districts and blocks within departments to empower local staff to better serve their communities.

The importance of setting clear goals for leaders of organizations or business units, and giving them autonomy on *how* to achieve them is a well-known management principle. Even within our government, better performing institutions, such as the Indian Space Research Organisation, the Atomic Energy Commission, the Reserve Bank of India, the UPSC, the CAG, and the Election Commission, have considerable autonomy.[57] Even at the state level, periods of effective governance have featured chief ministers providing senior officials both stable tenure and autonomy to deliver better outcomes. What we need therefore is to implement this approach *throughout* the government.

Increasing autonomy on processes will be more effective if accompanied by greater accountability for improving outcomes. A key challenge for bureaucratic accountability and performance management is the lack of rapid, real-time data. Advances in technology now make it possible to rapidly collect and analyse such data (see Chapter 4). Such data can be a powerful tool for political leaders to hold officials at different levels more accountable for delivering better outcomes (see Chapters 4 and 5).

This is an area where we can learn a lot from China. The Chinese governance system places great emphasis on measuring, monitoring, and rewarding performance at all levels. Pay and promotion of public employees *and* party officials are linked to performance. This is combined with more autonomy to local officials and *much* greater decentralization of budgets (see Chapter 8). This blend of autonomy and accountability improves both the ability and the incentives for officials to perform at all levels of the government, and leads to higher-performing officials getting promoted.[58]

This package of governance reforms was one of Deng Xiaoping's key contributions to China's economic success.[59] As noted in Chapter 2, outsiders often mistakenly attribute China's success to having a 'strong' state. Rather, the main lesson to learn from the Chinese experience is that it performed better after Deng Xiaoping's *administrative reforms*, which introduced more checks and balances at senior levels of government and increased accountability at junior levels. Thus, the key to China's success was not a 'strong' state but a more 'accountable' state.

In India, while politicians are accountable to voters, government employees with jobs for life have no such accountability. This is why politicians should strongly support a reform agenda that improves bureaucratic performance and accountability at all levels.

3.5 Invest in data-driven governance at all levels of the government

To realize this goal, politicians will need to invest in tools that make agents of the state both more capable, and more accountable for performance. In particular, collecting, analysing, and acting on the right data on outcomes, personnel, and budgets—an approach that I broadly refer to as data-driven governance—can boost bureaucratic effectiveness at all levels. These ideas are expanded on in Sections II and III.

The main point to highlight here is the importance of *political support* for such an agenda of data-driven governance. Ironically, politicians deeply understand the importance of data for the decisions that really *matter to them* as seen by the growing use of data in planning and managing election campaigns.[60] Unfortunately, they do not seem to apply the same rigour to improving the performance of the government itself.

The core skills of politicians are campaigning and winning elections. These are different from the skills needed to *run* a government well, which are different from those needed to *design* a better functioning state! However, just as champion race-car drivers depend on top engineers and mechanics to design and maintain their car, effective politicians understand the importance of data and technical expertise for their success. They have shown that they value such expertise in contesting elections. So, it is a logical next step for them to bring the same approach to designing and building a more effective state.

3.6 Communicate the rationale for reforms both internally and externally

A final point that will require political leadership is effective communication—both to government employees and to the public. Past attempts at administrative reforms have often failed due to the resistance of public-sector employees. It is therefore important to be sensitive to concerns from government employees, gain their trust, and obtain broad buy-in from the bureaucracy itself that the reform agenda is *in their interest.*

Many reform ideas for improving the effectiveness of public personnel in this book—such as increasing hiring, improving training and skilling, stabilizing tenure, reducing paperwork, using data and technology for better service delivery, and increasing staff autonomy—should appeal to the bureaucracy. Of course, this will have to be accompanied by better performance management, which may be resisted by unions. However, research has shown that government employees are quite open to performance-linked pay if the criteria are transparent and fair.[61] This is why it is essential for political leaders to communicate the rationale and details of reforms clearly to employees and the public, to *build broad support* for such reforms.

Overall, a grand bargain that boosts the capacity and autonomy of the bureaucracy to deliver, and combines this with greater accountability for delivery should be appealing to *all* Indians, including government employees. Besides enhancing service delivery for citizens, such a grand bargain will improve government effectiveness, boost public perception of officials, and enhance their feeling of self-worth and satisfaction.

4. Conclusion

The previous chapter discussed how being a politician in India is an incredibly difficult job. The same applies to our public officials. While it is easy to blame them for many of the travails that India faces, they deserve greater appreciation and understanding. They are often good people in a weak system, doing difficult work under severe constraints.

The weakness of the 'system', in turn, reflects the actions of various stakeholders—including politicians, officials, courts, citizens, and civil society—who are each acting in rational ways that reflect their incentives and constraints. However, the critical issue that we have not addressed as a society is that most of our development challenges stem from a chronic underinvestment in the capacity of the Indian state to deliver better.

Investing in building stronger public systems will bring enormous benefits for citizens, politicians, and the bureaucracy itself. Citizens will experience better governance and service delivery. Politicians will benefit from a more capable bureaucracy that is able to deliver on their vision and thereby increase their electoral success, and help them leave a lasting legacy. Finally, the bureaucracy will benefit from a better working environment where they can be more productive and focus on truly contributing to society—which is an important reason for why many join the government in the first place.

Yet, despite the large and broad-based benefits of investing in state capacity, it has been highly neglected by our leaders. This reflects the complexity of the issue, and the fact that it is critically important but rarely urgent enough to command focused political attention. Yet, as we enter our seventy-fifth year as a sovereign Republic, there are few tasks more essential for reaching our potential as a nation than building a more effective Indian state. The rest of the book mostly focuses on how exactly we can do this.

Section II

Building an Effective State

Chapter 4

Data and Outcome Measurement

How does a government know how fast its economy is growing? How healthy are its citizens? Do they feel safe? Are they learning in school? Are they finding good quality jobs? Are outcomes for marginalized groups improving? Answering these fundamental questions regarding citizen well-being requires data. Good data provides governments and citizens with a shared understanding of reality and is essential for effective governance. The centrality of data for governance is seen by noting that the very origin of the word *statistics* comes from its crucial role in managing the affairs of the *state*![1]

Yet, despite the centrality of good data for effective governance, India's data systems are outdated and function far below their full potential. The Indian statistical system put in place in the 1950s was considered one of the world's best in a low-income country at that time. However, it has not kept pace with the possibilities enabled by the dramatic advances in technology for collecting rapid, real-time, high-quality data. Over time, we have underinvested in and even undermined our statistical systems, for a combination of financial, technical, and political reasons.

As a result, the data we have are often inaccurate, unreliable, not granular enough, or too delayed to be useful. Even when data are credible, they are used mainly to describe how we are doing, and not used to improve government functioning. The lack of investment and resulting weaknesses in our measurement infrastructure contribute to weak governance in several ways, including poor quality of public expenditure; a focus on more easily measured inputs, as opposed to less measured outcomes; and lack of timely and actionable feedback on policies and programmes.

Just like pilots need real-time data to safely fly a modern aircraft, India's leaders' ability to govern effectively is severely constrained by the lack of good data. The problem of reliable data is so severe that a senior government official once told me that 'we are mostly flying blind' and confessed that officials mostly rely on experience, anecdotes, intuition, and informed guesswork—as opposed to systematic data and analysis—in making decisions that affect hundreds of millions of people. If even the pilots of the Indian state acknowledge that they are flying blind, it is clearly time for us to take our data challenges seriously and invest in strengthening our measurement systems.

The good news is that the dramatic advances in data collection methods—especially aided by digital technologies—have now made it possible for us to not only reimagine a new data and measurement architecture for India but also to make this happen rapidly. As explained further in this chapter, we can achieve a step-function improvement in our statistical systems at a cost of less than 0.1 per cent of state budgets. This will, in turn, sharply improve the effectiveness of the remaining 99.9 per cent of the budget.

Setting up systems to generate consistent, accurate, and timely data on key parameters will enable governments to manage personnel better, spend money more effectively, obtain rapid citizen feedback, track if public benefits are reaching the most marginalized populations, and refine policies and programmes to work better with rapid course corrections based on data on both processes and outcomes. This makes improving our measurement systems a *foundational* investment in state capacity.

This chapter has two sections. The first summarizes key challenges under the status quo and explains why things are the way they are. The second outlines a reimagined measurement architecture for India, explains how this can transform governance, and lays out a set of implementable and cost-effective ideas.

1. Understanding the Status Quo and Its Limitations

1.1 A snapshot of the Indian statistical system

India has a comprehensive structure for collecting, analysing, and disseminating key economic statistics, overseen by the National Statistical Office (NSO). The NSO has two main divisions: the Central Statistics Office (CSO) and the National Sample Survey Office (NSSO). The CSO is responsible for key macroeconomic statistics such as national income and GDP, and consumer prices and inflation. The NSSO is responsible for the National Sample Survey (NSS), which uses household surveys to estimate microeconomic development indicators such as consumption, poverty, and employment.

Established in the 1950s under the leadership of P.C. Mahalanobis, India's statistical systems were globally acclaimed.[2] Notably, the NSS template shaped the World Bank's Living Standards Measurement Survey (LSMS) and thereby influenced global standards for measurement of consumption and poverty. However, over time, a combination of technical and political challenges have contributed to a weakening of the NSS to the point that even the data for the 2016–17 round were not released. Thus, as of 2022, the last large-sample NSS data we have is from 2011–12, which has dealt a severe blow to our ability to understand trends in consumption and poverty in the past decade.[3]

However, even when NSS data is released, it has limitations. While the NSS provides a useful barometer of national progress on key development outcomes, it was not designed—and hence not very useful—for day-to-day governance. There are several reasons for this. First, large-sample NSS rounds are conducted only every five years, which limits its use for decision-making since the feedback cycle from government actions to data on changes is too slow. Second, results are usually not spatially disaggregated enough to support localized government actions. Finally, the NSS does not measure the quality of service delivery or outcomes: for instance, it asks if children go to school but does not check if teachers are in classrooms or if children are learning.

Simply put, India's statistical systems were designed to track national progress, but not for supporting day-to-day governance. An effective measurement infrastructure *for governance* should allow governments to track—and act on—growth and development outcomes such as employment, education, and health; understand beneficiary receipt and experiences of key public programmes; and ensure that administrative data recorded by government staff are reliable. India struggles on all three fronts.

1.2 There is little actionable data on fundamental development *outcomes*

In 2000, India set out to enrol all six- to fourteen-year-old children in school. Today, that goal is nearly met: over 98 per cent of these children are now enrolled in schools.[4]

This is an impressive achievement. However, while enrolment is a necessary first step for learning, it is far from sufficient. In practice, many millions of 'enrolled' children do not attend school regularly and millions more attend school without learning very much. In 2018, only *half* of rural government school students enrolled in Class 5 could read even a Class 2 level text.[5] Overall, despite large increases in public expenditure on school inputs over the last two decades, the conversion of these inputs into the ultimate goal of learning has been weak (see Chapter 11 for details).

One reason is that the government focuses more on measuring inputs than outcomes. As one indicator, the most widely used data on learning outcomes in India does *not* come from the government, but from the non-governmental organization, Pratham, through the Annual Status of Education Report (ASER). The focus on measuring visible inputs over less visible—but far more important—outcomes is seen across sectors and departments, and deeply hinders the effectiveness of government policies and programmes.

1.3 The government lacks visibility on citizen experiences with public services

Governments' also have limited visibility on how public programmes are truly performing on the ground. Are the poor getting their PDS food-security benefits? Are they able to get work under the NREGS? Are they getting paid on time? Can they access funds in their bank accounts? This is an age-old problem. Historically, emperors from Ashoka to Akbar were known to travel in disguise to observe the true state of affairs in their kingdoms. Yet, despite dramatic advances in technological possibilities, systematic measurement of last-mile service delivery continues to be almost non-existent.

For instance, in 2015, the Central government introduced direct benefit transfers (DBT) to beneficiary bank accounts instead of providing subsidized food through the PDS in the union territories of Chandigarh, Puducherry, and Dadra and Nagar Haveli. Working with NITI Aayog, my colleagues and I monitored these pilots. While government officials proudly pointed to bank records showing that 99 per cent of funds had been transferred successfully, our field-based surveys of nearly 5000 beneficiaries revealed that over 30 per cent reported either not receiving funds or not knowing if they had![6]

Often, beneficiaries were unaware of fund transfers because they had not updated their passbooks, and there was no mechanism to notify them when funds were transferred. In some cases, funds were sent to inactive bank accounts. Without data on beneficiary experiences, the government was unaware of these problems. While governments do have grievance redressal phone helplines, these are used mainly to solve *individual* issues, and not to understand systemic issues.[7] Across sectors, the lack of systematic data on beneficiary experiences hinders effective programme design and delivery.

1.4 The government's own administrative data is often unreliable

Given limited data on outcomes and beneficiary experiences, governments in India mostly rely on official administrative data, reported by government employees as a part of their jobs. This is how the government 'system' measures everything from agricultural yields and productivity to children's nutrition status in ICDS centres. Indeed, the majority of data within the government comes from such internal sources. The problem is that there is growing evidence that there are substantial inaccuracies in such data.

Consider the experience of the Madhya Pradesh government in education. To take on the challenge of low student learning, the state's education department began testing every government school student each year and recording child-level learning levels. This impressive annual exercise, called *Pratibha Parv*, involved the entire education department and was hailed as a 'best practice' in education reform by NITI Aayog.

But when a research team led by economist Abhijeet Singh carried out an independent retest a few weeks after Pratibha Parv—using a sample of the *same* questions and retesting a sample of the *same* students—they found that official learning data were highly inflated. As we see in Figure 4.1, in the official data, *all* students were reported as scoring over 65 per cent in Hindi. In the independent retest, *no one* scored over 65 per cent. The inflation is even more striking in maths: in the official data all students scored over 60 per cent, whereas in the retest no one scored even above 40 per cent.[8]

Figure 4.1: Inflation of Learning Outcomes in Official Data

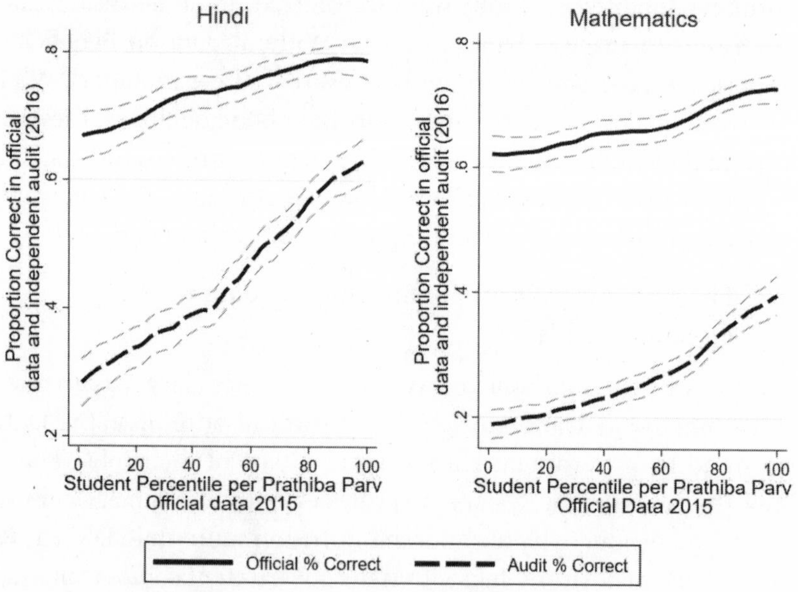

Note(s): Data from Singh (2020), graph recreated by author.

Thus, as per the official data, there was no learning crisis at all—in sharp contrast with multiple independent studies! The same pattern was found in Andhra Pradesh, suggesting that the problem of unreliable administrative data is widespread.[9] Figure 4.1 also illustrates how we have wasted over fifteen years as a country, as a result of governments across nearly *all* political parties being in denial about the learning crisis.[10] The cost of this denial is that over 150 million Indians have entered adulthood and the labour market without even primary school levels of literacy and numeracy.

Such discrepancies in administrative data are widespread. For instance, in Tamil Nadu, official data showed rates of severe and moderate malnutrition of 1 and 8 per cent respectively in ICDS centres. However, both our independent data and data from the National Family Health Survey (NFHS) found these to be around 8 per cent and 25–35 per cent respectively. Thus, the true rates of moderate/severe malnutrition were four to eight times higher than reported in official data.[11] Similarly, true crime rates in India are estimated to be five to ten times higher than that reported in official data (Chapter 13), and even agricultural statistics have been found to be highly inaccurate (Chapter 5).

The problem of systematic over-reporting of outcomes in official data is well-known to researchers studying development in India.[12] This reflects several substantive and incentive problems faced by staff including: (a) lack of tools or training to conduct accurate measurements, (b) wanting to avoid looking bad to, or getting pulled up by, their supervisors, (c) wanting to avoid the risk of being asked to do extra work to address the issue,[13] and (d) pressure from senior officials and leaders to not present data that would paint the department or government in an unfavourable light.

Taken together, the lack of data on outcomes and beneficiary experience combined with poor administrative data quality severely hinder the state's effectiveness. Many senior officials are aware of these data issues. One school education commissioner looked at data on sudden learning improvements in a disadvantaged district and said: 'Of course, they have made up the data.' In addition to the senior government adviser who once remarked to me that, 'We are usually flying blind' (without good data), I recall the memorable words of a state chief secretary who reacted to the problem of administrative data quality by telling me that 'our systems are built on a house of cards'.

1.5 Why is there no systematic, actionable measurement system in India?

If top officials understand the importance of actionable, credible data for improving governance, then why are we not collecting it? There are at least four reasons for this.

First, data collection is seen as expensive even though it need not be so. Further, data collection usually does not have a dedicated budget, and is therefore considered discretionary spending, which has to compete with other political priorities. In practice, governments often prefer to spend on immediately visible and politically more rewarding items, rather than on long-term investments in better measurement systems.

Second, most government departments lack the technical capacity to conduct or even procure high-quality measurement. Technical issues include sampling, non-response bias, and representativeness of data; designing good survey questions and field testing them; managing field operations; analysing and presenting the data; and interpreting the data and analysis with suitable caveats.[14] As a result, measurement often relies on external donor-funded initiatives and technical support. This results in an approach to measurement that is often sporadic and inconsistent, as opposed to one that is consistent and institutionalized within the government to inform policymaking.

Third, even with adequate budgets and technical capacity, data collection typically does not yield timely returns. A principal secretary or department head aiming for tangible achievements in their two-year (and often shorter) tenure will often see investing in measurement as a low-return activity because the data will often come in only after they leave their role. Further, if their successor is not interested in continuing the measurement or has different views on what to measure, their efforts will be wasted.

Finally, for politicians and officials, ignorance can often be bliss. In a culture of headline-driven media, there is little nuance in public discourse about the complexity of India's problems. Thus, data on the reality of India's poor development outcomes often puts officials and leaders on the defensive. Even though good data and measurement are the foundation for better governance, the short-term consequences for officials can be negative. As a secretary to a chief minister once told me when I recommended high-frequency measurement of service delivery quality: 'It is a very good idea; but if the data makes us look bad, we will waste a lot of time dealing with negative press coverage.'

The 'ignorance is bliss' attitude of officials is powerfully illustrated in an anecdote narrated by Rukmini Banerji, the CEO of Pratham. In a field visit, she asked a village leader why his village had such poor learning levels among children. The leader and an accompanying education department official insisted that the students were doing fine and pointed to their administrative records which said just that. Rukmini then took them to ask children in the village basic questions and demonstrated that, contrary to the official records, many students struggled with basic literacy and numeracy. When confronted with this inconvenient fact, the official got upset and asked her, 'Madam, *aapko asliyat se itna lagaav kyun hai?* (Why are you so attached to reality?)'!

2. Building a New Measurement Architecture for Better Governance

The good news is that several top government officials understand the importance of high-frequency and high-quality data for governance. However, to be effective and deliver to full potential, measurement should not be a sporadic effort driven by the initiative of individual officers. Rather, improved measurement should be seen as the first step in a broader set of systematic investments in state capacity.

The key to effectively using data for governance is to *institutionalize* the collection, analysis, and reporting of data so that decision-makers and managers within the government can *rely* on having the data available to guide their actions and it becomes standard operating procedure to do so. I now turn to a practical discussion of how a state government may institutionalize and implement such a measurement architecture.

2.1 Who should lead measurement?

It may seem logical and cost-effective to rely on departments themselves to collect the relevant data for their work. After all, the education or health department is best placed to collect data on education or health outcomes. But this is unlikely to be good enough. As Figure 4.1 shows, internal measurement by department staff is often not credible. This is why researchers often collect data themselves or rely on credible independent surveys, such as the NSS, the NFHS, or the India Human Development Survey (IHDS).

An alternative approach may be for governments to outsource data collection. However, this can also be problematic because officials tend to be wary of numbers put out by non-government actors. For instance, since 2005, Pratham has carried out an annual survey of *hundreds of thousands* of households as part of the ASER to yield district-level estimates of learning across India. Data from this survey has become the reference point for everyone in the education sector—except the government!

The official reaction of the Ministry of Human Resource Development (recently renamed the Ministry of Education) for many years was to ignore the learning crisis highlighted by the ASER data. The Ministry preferred its own data source, the National Assessment Survey (NAS), which painted a rosier picture, but has several serious limitations.[15] These actions reflected both the preference of officials to ignore inconvenient data (at least in public), and the fact that governments are often institutionally required to base their actions on 'official' data. Thus, even though many senior officials would, *in private*, accept that the ASER data provided valuable insights, the 'official' response of the government was to mostly disregard it, and to even question the quality of ASER data.

The point of this example is not to dwell on the technical aspects of the NAS versus ASER debate.[16] Rather, it is to highlight that even high-quality independent data may not lead to follow-up actions by the government because data needs to be 'official' for governments to accept the data and findings. If data collection has to be independent of line departments to be credible but still be considered 'official', who should do it?

The ideal solution would be state planning departments, which have the mandate to collect, analyse, and report data. Unfortunately, in practice, they often simply *collate*, and report data provided by departments themselves. But what they should be doing is to lead efforts to *collect* independent, high-quality data and become the primary hub of credible data within the government, to support better governance across departments.

State planning departments should therefore spearhead the creation and management of a multisector outcome measurement system, and finance departments should fund this as a strategic priority. Even under conservative assumptions, doing so would cost less than 0.1 per cent of a state government's budget. Crucially, anchoring this exercise in the planning department separates measurement from the line departments. This structure will ensure independence and data quality, and also ensure that the data is considered 'official' and therefore taken seriously and acted upon.

While planning departments should lead on the agenda of improving measurement systems, they need not collect all the data themselves. Given their own capacity and staff constraints, they can empanel high-quality external agencies to collect the data. Department staff can oversee and quality control the process. The external agencies are likely to be able to deploy technological innovations and quality control faster than the government itself. However, planning department officials should randomly recheck some of the data collected by third-party agencies to verify and validate the data.[17] This way, external agencies can provide speed, technical support, and implementation, whereas the planning department can conduct the validation and quality control.

I now discuss three specific ideas for improving measurement and data collection, and also describe how each kind of data can improve governance and service delivery.

2.2 Conduct regular field-based surveys to measure key development outcomes

The first and most important gap we need to fill in our measurement systems is to be able to generate annual district-level outcomes on key development indicators. Districts are the most important administrative units in India at the implementation level. Thus, having annual data on key indicators at the district level is essential for planning, goal setting, resource allocation, and progress tracking.

Such data can be obtained through annual district-level household surveys. Given survey time constraints, states should focus on measuring a few essential indicators such as the main outcomes in the United Nations' Sustainable Development Goals (SDGs) framework, which covers both development issues and overall economic conditions. Further, conducting a single multisector survey is *much more cost effective* than each department trying to carry out its own surveys for sectoral outcomes.

Such an exercise will provide states with regular data on district-level outcomes on child health and nutrition; education and learning outcomes; crime and perceptions of safety; household receipts of public welfare schemes; their access to and use of public and private services; and key measures of economic well-being and opportunity such as employment, livelihoods, volatility in income, financial inclusion, and credit access. Importantly, it will cover outcomes for *all* citizens regardless of whether they use public or private services (or neither), thereby providing an accurate picture of *population-level* well-being and how these indicators are changing annually.

In practice, a survey that covers around 2000 households per district will provide enough precision on district-level estimates to be usable for management purposes.[18] Just a decade ago, the prospect of conducting 2000 surveys in every district every six to twelve months, would have been considered wildly unrealistic and prohibitively expensive. But thanks to advances in technology, large-scale *annual* or *biannual* district surveys are not only feasible but also highly affordable.

Before these technological advances, data collection was an arduous, time-consuming, and error-prone process. Surveyors would capture responses on paper forms, which had to be entered into statistical software, leading to large delays due to the need to correct errors in data recording and entry. The emergence of tablet- and smartphone-based data collection has transformed this process. Data collection is now quicker, cheaper, *and* more accurate. For instance, using tablets with pre-coded questions that automatically skip non-applicable questions sharply reduces surveyor errors, compared to manually skipping questions.[19] Similarly, geotagged data collection and analysis of keystrokes makes it easy to verify that enumerators actually visited the household and administered the survey and did not just make up the data! Overall, technology has dramatically reduced the cost and increased the speed and reliability of data collection.

This vision of annual district-level surveys is not a pipe dream. A similar survey has already been carried out in several districts by IDinsight, an advisory and research organization, as part of NITI Aayog's Aspirational Districts Programme (ADP). While the ADP has many positive features, it covers only a few districts in each state. As a result, the ADP's rich district-level data has *not yet been institutionalized* for planning and decision-making within state governments. Thus, the opportunity is ripe for state governments to take this template, roll it out to all districts, and make such data an integral part of state-level planning, resource allocation, and management.[20]

Conducting such a measurement exercise (with around 2000 households per district surveyed twice a year for two hours in each round) will cost at most Rs 1 crore per district per year. Even for a large lower-income state, such as UP, which has seventy-five districts, the annual cost would be under Rs 75 crore, or just over 0.01 per cent of the state's total expenditure of Rs 6.5 lakh crore in the 2023–24 Budget.[21] Once the viability of this approach has been demonstrated, it will be easy to obtain estimates that are precise enough for *block-level* decision-making by increasing the sample size. Even with such an increase, the total cost will still be under 0.1 per cent of the state budget. It will also be possible to add a rotating set of survey modules to a subset of the sample to generate more detailed understanding of key phenomena at the *state* level.[22]

Having annual district-level data on key development outcomes can transform Indian governance. It will enable better goal setting, progress monitoring, and performance management of staff and departments (see Chapters 5, 10, and the sector chapters). It will facilitate improved allocation and use of public funds to better reflect principles of equality, equity, and effectiveness (see Chapter 6). It will enable a sharper focus on equity goals by making it possible to track the extent to which outcomes of women and marginalized groups are improving over time (see Chapter 10). By measuring outcomes for all citizens regardless of whether they use public or private services, such data will help to focus policy attention on the need to improve both public service delivery and the functioning of private markets (see Chapter 9).

Most importantly, it will enable a change in the culture of government from focusing on inputs and schemes to outcomes. Consider the case of education, where three key policy goals are access, equity, and quality. In practice, governments often convert each of these laudable goals into input targets: the access goal is 'met' by meeting targets for school construction; the equity goal is 'met' by creating schemes and programmes for girls and disadvantaged groups, though outcome gaps may still be growing; and quality goals are 'met' by programmes for upgrading infrastructure and teacher training.[23]

These are all important inputs in an education system, but evidence consistently shows that most of these inputs are poorly correlated with learning outcomes, or are not as cost-effective as other interventions (see Chapter 11). Thus, despite good intentions, large budgets, and considerable effort, these inputs have not yielded the desired outcomes. This example highlights a fundamental challenge for governance: bureaucracies often convert outcome goals into programmes and schemes, and make the latter an end in themselves, thereby losing sight of whether the ultimate objectives are being achieved.

With annual district-level outcome data, this changes. It will enable senior officials and political leaders to focus their review meetings with district-level staff on monitoring improvements in a few key development *outcomes* as opposed to just 'scheme implementation'. In the education example above, school access can now be tracked not just by enrolment, but by actual attendance.[24] Equity goals can be monitored by tracking if outcomes are improving for girls and marginalized groups, and if outcome gaps are falling. Finally, quality can be assessed by tracking learning outcomes.

Data on outcomes will also enable the cultural shift in the bureaucracy of increasing 'autonomy on processes' and 'accountability for outcomes' described in Chapter 3. Since districts can now be assessed on their effectiveness in improving outcomes, the energy and creativity of local staff can be unleashed by providing them more flexible untied funds to spend on items that they think will work best for improving outcomes given local needs and conditions. Annual outcome data will also make it possible to tie some of the annual discretionary funds to performance in improving district-level outcomes. Such a structure can be highly effective at improving both autonomy and accountability for better outcomes (see Chapter 5).

When I wrote the first draft of this chapter in 2019, the idea of such a state-wide survey may have seemed wildly optimistic. Yet, since then, the Telangana government has implemented such a multi-sector household survey reaching nearly 50,000 households across 33 districts. Thus, the idea is practically feasible, and the templates from Telangana are available for any state that would like to replicate it.[25]

2.3 Use phone-based surveys to capture real-time beneficiary experience

While annual field surveys will generate outcome data, they may still not be timely enough to inform real-time improvements of government service delivery. For this, there is a simple alternative. The government could call beneficiaries directly, which is now feasible due to the proliferation of mobile phones across India. Regular phone calls that capture beneficiary experiences can provide real-time feedback that can be rapidly used to improve the design and delivery of government programmes, and also be used to improve the motivation and accountability of frontline staff.

For instance, in 2018, my colleagues and I worked with the Government of Telangana (GoTS) to measure and improve implementation quality of the state's flagship *Rythu Bandhu* programme, which provided income transfers to farmers via cheque. Our team helped GoTS contract a call centre that made 25,000 calls to farmers over a period of two weeks and asked basic questions on last-mile programme delivery and beneficiary experience such as: Have you received your money? When did you receive it? Have you been able to cash your cheque? Delivering money *on time* was a key success metric for GoTS since a major goal of the programme was to get money to farmers before the monsoons so that they could avoid taking on debt to pay for seeds and fertilizers.

We found, using a large-scale randomized control trial, that simply informing lower-level officials that their performance was being measured this way led to significant increases in total funds delivered and funds delivered on time to farmers. The approach was also highly cost-effective, resulting in farmers receiving over Rs 25 in total, and over Rs 100 *on time* for every one rupee spent on the call centre. Thus, the benefit to farmers was *25 to 100 times greater* than the call-centre cost.[26]

These results highlight the power of investing in better data and measurement and tying it to performance measurement and management of government staff. It shows how spending one rupee more on governance can deliver the same amount of benefits to farmers as increasing the programme budget by Rs 25. Further, the benefits of the phone-based monitoring were broad-based, with everyone being better off; but they were *also* progressive, since there were larger gains for farmers with the smallest landholdings. The example highlights how better governance can benefit *everyone* and be especially important for poor and vulnerable groups.

A key attraction of this approach is that it is easy and inexpensive to scale. India is already a world leader in call-centre services, and this expertise can be leveraged to improve governance at home. On average, a phone survey costs only 5 per cent as much as a field survey. Of course, the limitation is that phone surveys are much shorter. Still, it is a powerful tool for senior officials and middle-level managers to get real-time feedback on beneficiary experience with a wide variety of programmes, including the PDS, NREGS, and other welfare programmes (see Chapter 15).

States should therefore invest in phone-based measurement alongside field-based measurement. States such as Andhra Pradesh and Odisha have already invested in such outbound call centres, which may provide a template for other states to follow. The planning department, with support from the IT department if needed, can coordinate the procurement of the call centres and ensure adequate technical support for issues such as sampling, analysis, and creation of dashboards, while line departments can use this infrastructure to improve their day-to-day functioning.[27]

High-frequency phone survey data can provide rapid feedback on ground-level programme effectiveness. It will also enable better performance measurement and management of government staff. While outcomes can take time to improve, staff can be held immediately accountable for programme implementation quality. Short phone surveys can also be used to get *citizen inputs* into the design of programmes based on their experiences in accessing them. Governments in India rarely *listen* to citizens. Regular phone surveys can transform citizens from being passive recipients of government initiatives, to becoming active participants in improving programme design and delivery.

Such data can also help to protect the vulnerable from exclusion in public programmes. For example, in my work on evaluating the impact of using Aadhaar-based biometric authentication (ABBA) in the delivery of PDS benefits in Jharkhand, my colleagues and I found significant reductions in leakage. But we also found an increase in exclusion errors, especially during the transition to the new system, with nearly two million beneficiaries losing access to PDS benefits for a few months during the transition.[28]

The public debate on the desirability of ABBA was polarized, with proponents pointing to reduced leakage to justify it and opponents pointing to increased exclusion to argue for scrapping

ABBA. However, this binary debate was not very productive because *both sides were right*: there was a reduction in leakage, but also an increase in exclusion. While it is a moral imperative to minimize exclusion, especially since it often affects the vulnerable, it is also morally important to reduce leakage. This is because funds saved from corrupt intermediaries can expand the fiscal capacity of the state to provide other public goods and services that disproportionately benefit the poor.[29]

Thus, a better approach would have been to improve ABBA implementation to get the benefits of reduced leakage, while also minimizing the risk of exclusion. However, though officials and courts were sensitive to the costs of exclusion, they were limited in their ability to act because there was *no systematic real-time data to monitor exclusion*. High-frequency phone-based monitoring can directly address this challenge. Since the most vulnerable may not have phones, respondents can be asked for both their own programme experiences, and if they are aware of cases of exclusion in their locality. Such an approach can quickly identify problem areas, and facilitate targeted remedial actions.

Collecting and publicly sharing anonymized data from such representative phone-based surveys can also improve public trust in the government. One reason for the polarized debate on ABBA was the lack of trust between the government and activists. Officials believed that complaints of exclusion were based on a few exceptional cases and 'motivated' by activists' political antipathy towards the government. Conversely, activists felt that the government was in denial about exclusion and hence pushed for scrapping ABBA altogether as opposed to finding ways to improve it.

This discussion also illustrates how there can be genuine disagreement on policies and reforms because people experience them in different ways. Reforms often benefit some people while adversely affecting others. Assessing their overall impact and mitigating negative effects requires us to understand how different groups are affected, and by how much. Collecting and sharing data on citizen experiences with public services before and after reforms, and acting on the data to mitigate negative effects, can therefore play a key role not just in improving governance but also in boosting public trust in the government that will help both the state and society (see Chapter 18).

2.4 Implement nested supervision to improve administrative data integrity

The final pillar we need to strengthen is the quality and reliability of administrative data. Currently, departmental staff who collect and report such data often inflate outcomes and under-report problems because the data reflects on their performance, and they know there is no way to verify their claims. A simple way to fix this problem is to digitize frontline data reporting so that the same quality control standards used in high-quality survey operations can be implemented in the government system. Digital records can then be randomly audited by department supervisors and also by independent staff from the planning department, social audit unit, or the district collector's office.

Such random audits can be used to generate 'truth scores' for officials, based on the frequency and extent of discrepancies between reported data and the data captured in independent rechecks.[30] These truth scores can then become a key metric on which staff performance is assessed. Crucially, the person recording data is also attesting to its veracity and the identity of this person is recorded in the system. This enables *any superior officer* to conduct random data audits and hold the person who entered the data accountable if there is a large discrepancy. The default supervision and verification will happen within the department itself by block- or district-level officials. However, the system allows for independent audits from officials *outside* the department to reduce the risk of collusion within a department between staff and supervisors.[31]

This approach of 'nested supervision' accounts for supervisory capacity constraints.[32] Consider the school education system, where cluster resource coordinators (CRCs), block education officers (BEOs) and district education officers (DEOs) oversee 20–40, 200–300, and

1500–2500 schools respectively. Thus, in a year, CRCs can make two to three random visits to *every* school in their area of responsibility and verify the data reported on student learning. BEOs can visit some schools in *every* cluster, and DEOs can visit some schools in *every* block. This allows a DEO to generate truth scores for BEOs, BEOs to do so for CRCs, and CRCs to do so for headteachers. Such a structure can incentivize the entire system to tell the truth because any case of a school found to be fudging data in an *external* data audit will reflect negatively not only on the headteacher, but also on the concerned CRC, BEO, and DEO.[33]

This approach can be deployed across departments ranging from education, ICDS, health, agriculture, and rural/urban development. It should be limited to the *few most critical indicators* for each department such as learning outcomes (education), child malnutrition (ICDS), vaccinations (health), crop yields (agriculture), and key measures of local service delivery such as clean streets and garbage collection, working streetlights, and running water (for rural and urban development departments). The planning or IT department can provide technical support in designing software systems for nested supervision including data capture, reporting, dashboards, and calculation of truth scores. Planning department field staff, overseen by the Collector's office, can also conduct random audits to ensure data quality and integrity at the district level.

Improving data integrity through nested supervision and 'truth scores' can profoundly change the culture of governance by making it harder to deny reality. Given the widespread prevalence and scale of administrative data fudging (see Figure 4.1 again) the deep cultural shift needed within the government is that improvements will have to come from 'real' gains and not simply by making up data to show gains when there is pressure to do so. Governments should therefore start by recognizing and rewarding employees just for telling the truth even if outcomes are poor. Thus, the truth score by itself should become a key input for staff performance evaluation.

Once a culture of truth-telling is established, supervision can evolve from 'nested' to 'supportive' supervision, where supervisors are not just 'monitoring' data quality, but also coaching and supporting staff to improve performance. However, forcing the system to report the truth will be a critical first step in getting government employees to focus on solving problems as opposed to hiding them by fudging data. It will also make it possible to recognize and reward strong performance based on *true* results (see Chapter 5).

2.5 Institutional safeguards for data quality, privacy, and transparency

While building new systems of technology-enabled measurement can significantly improve governance and service delivery, such efforts need to be accompanied by suitable institutional safeguards for privacy. Government actions in India have often prioritized transparency over privacy. For instance, information on beneficiaries of programmes such as NREGS and PDS is publicly available online and often includes personal details. With the Supreme Court declaring privacy as a fundamental right, India will have to shift the balance towards privacy and confidentiality.

So, it will be critical that data collected from individuals is not traceable back to them but is only available at a level of aggregation relevant for better governance, such as at the district or block level. To ensure this, data should be de-identified, using standard protocols.[34] Such anonymization will also facilitate whistle-blower protection. A citizen complaining about a government service should not fear reprisal from local officials.

The issue of anonymity can be subtle. In my work supporting governments with phone-based monitoring of public service delivery, officials have often asked for the identity of people who report problems, so that they can address them promptly. However, there is a difference between grievance redressal, where citizens themselves call to ask for help and *willingly* share their identity, and a government-initiated measurement system for obtaining systemic feedback on service delivery, where citizens' anonymity should be respected. Thus, the right way to respond in cases where respondents to an outbound call report problems is to provide them with a number they can call for help, if they want to do so. However, their identities should not be revealed by the outbound call centre.

While safeguarding individual data is essential, summary statistics of key indicators, such as district- and block-level averages, *should* be released to the public. Using the data within the government can improve 'top-down' administrative accountability of officials, but sharing it can also boost 'bottom-up' public accountability from citizens.

Releasing summary statistics can also boost democratic effectiveness by providing political incentives to focus on the things that actually matter.[35] As noted in Chapters 2 and 3, the Indian state will work better for citizens if the private incentives of politicians and officials are better aligned with the public interest. Publicly sharing key data on outcomes and on citizen experiences with receiving public services can promote this goal by making these traditionally 'unseen' aspects of governance become more 'seen', and thereby increase their political salience.[36] One way to institutionalize such data sharing may be to include key statistics from *independent* measurement exercises of the kind outlined in this chapter in the annual state economic surveys that are presented in the legislative assembly along with the annual budget.

Such public disclosure signals that the government is acknowledging reality. While politicians may worry that data on the reality of key development indicators will make them look bad, effective politicians should be able to share the data publicly, and then focus public attention on the *improvements* rather than poor initial outcomes. It can also help politicians hold officials accountable for delivering improved outcomes (Chapter 5), and help justify resource allocation based on both need and performance (Chapter 6). Releasing data on annual district- and block-level improvements can also stimulate broader public engagement with the effectiveness of policies, and provide political rewards for leaders who deliver meaningful improvements during their time in office.

Of course, data is inherently political and there will likely be pressure from governments to highlight favourable data and conceal unfavourable ones. One way to mitigate this challenge may be for states to constitute their own statistical commissions with technical experts as members to review the methods of data collection, and sign off on the annual publicly released data. Political discourse can and should focus on the extent of *improvement* or lack thereof in key development indicators, but the data itself should not be politicized to the extent possible. See Chapter 17 for a more detailed discussion of the role and importance of a state-level statistical commission in enabling this goal.

3. Conclusion

Throughout human history, better measurement has been the foundation for improving management and productivity. For instance, the widespread adoption of clocks played a critical role in boosting productivity by facilitating coordination of employee schedules, and enabling managers to track and improve output per unit of time. Similarly, the use of on-board GPS devices revolutionized fleet management and efficiency in logistics, by making it easier to monitor the productivity of trucks and drivers.[37]

Reflecting the value of data and analysis for boosting productivity, world-leading companies invest heavily in these areas to improve performance. For instance, *just one company*, Amazon, is estimated to employ over *one thousand PhD holders* working on data analytics, which likely exceeds the total number in Indian state and Central governments put together![38] Given the scale of Indian governments, and their impact on the lives of 1.4 billion people, it is imperative that we start making similar investments in data and analytics to improve productivity and efficiency in government functioning.

This section of the book correspondingly starts with a focus on improving our public systems for measurement as the first step towards building a more effective Indian state. Over the years, I have discussed many of the ideas in later chapters of this book with senior officials and received the response that 'these are great ideas, but *we do not have the data to act on them*'. This chapter is therefore a foundational one, since many of the ideas in the later chapters depend on the existence of the right data to inform improvements in all other aspects of state functioning.

This chapter outlines a feasible redesign of our measurement architecture to enable states to collect high-quality data on outcomes and processes quickly and cost effectively. Implementing this vision would cost under 0.1 per cent of state budgets. But, it will sharply improve the effectiveness of the remaining 99.9 per cent of the budget, by getting the government machinery to focus on what actually matters and by helping to align public personnel and budgets towards these goals (see Chapters 5 and 6).

Politicians already understand the importance of data in planning election campaigns. It is time to bring the same approach to governance itself. Further, doing so is likely to have political payoffs as well. Chief ministers who embark on this vision at the start of a five-year term will be able to drive a step-function improvement in state performance during their term, and showcase tangible improvements in governance to voters at the end of five years. Beyond re-election, chief ministers who execute this vision are likely to leave a lasting legacy by strengthening public systems for long-term positive impact.

Chapter 5

Personnel Management

Any organization, including the government, is only as effective as its employees and their management. However, as we will see in this chapter, public-sector personnel management in India suffers from substantial inefficiencies in how we hire, train, assign, support, evaluate, pay, promote, motivate, and manage public employees.

Simply put, we cannot build a more effective Indian state without improving the quantity, quality, autonomy, and accountability of public employees. Yet, this is one of the most neglected areas of our public discourse and attention. There are at least five reasons why improving public personnel management needs to be a top policy priority for India.

First, studies show that personnel management *is the most important* component of management that matters for organizational effectiveness.[1] Second, public employees are citizens' main point of contact with the state, and improving their motivation and effectiveness will directly translate into better service delivery and citizen experiences. Third, as India's largest employer with nearly 10 million public employees, it is the government's duty to create a professional work environment that helps employees reach their full potential. Fourth, salaries and benefits account for the largest fraction of public spending in service delivery sectors, and improving the efficiency of public-payroll spending is critical for delivering better public services *within* any given budget. Fifth, a growing body of research has identified several promising and implementable ideas for improving public sector personnel management. It is now time to act on these.

This chapter comprises two main sections. First, it presents key facts and evidence on public sector personnel management in India and explains how weaknesses in this area hurt state effectiveness, and public welfare. Second, it outlines a series of evidence-based ideas to sharply improve personnel management in the public sector, presents a case study, and discusses principles for implementing these ideas.

1. Key Facts on Public Sector Personnel Management in India

Chapter 3 discussed challenges affecting the bureaucracy as a whole. These include: (a) severe staff shortages at all levels, (b) short and unstable tenures of supervisory staff, (c) limited autonomy, (d) weak and misplaced accountability, and (e) poor time use of existing staff. This section dives into the details of public personnel management and highlights key facts and challenges. The discussion of reform ideas will aim to address both these challenges and those covered in Chapter 3.

1.1 Government salaries (on average) are too high

For India's urban professionals, government salaries may appear modest compared to private sector pay. However, while top government officials are underpaid relative to the complexity and importance of their roles, most public employees are *paid much more* than their private-sector equivalents.[2] Averaged across all employees, public employee salaries in India are among the *highest* in the world.

A 2017 study of public sector pay across thirty-two countries by economist Rohini Pande and colleagues finds that India has among the highest 'public-sector pay premiums' in the world.[3] In their 2013 book, Amartya Sen and Jean Drèze noted that relative to GDP per capita, public school teachers in India are paid *three times more* than in China.[4] While the data is older, a 2003 World Bank report also noted that in India, the average public employee pay was 7.2 times

GDP per capita. In comparison, this ratio was 5.7 in Africa, 3 in Asia, and only 1.6 in the OECD.[5]

Another way to see this fact is to directly compare pay for the *same* jobs across the public and private sector. For instance, multiple studies on Indian education show that government schoolteachers earn *five to ten times more* than private-school teachers.[6] Data from one of my studies in (undivided) Andhra Pradesh in 2012 show that government teachers earn around six times more on average than those in the private sector (see Figure 5.1). Remarkably, even a top 5 per cent earner among private-school teachers earns less than a bottom 5 per cent government teacher![7]

Figure 5.1: Distribution of Private and Government Teacher Salary in Andhra Pradesh

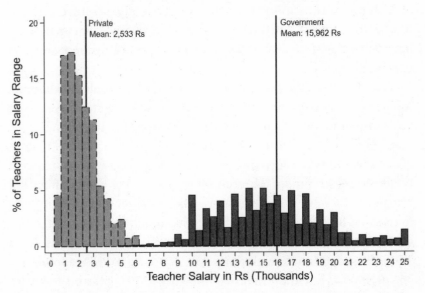

Note(s): Data from Muralidharan and Sundararaman (2015), graph created by author.

The high costs of salaries and benefits of public employees *directly* contribute to staff shortages and weak state capacity. With our current tax revenues, we simply cannot afford to hire enough staff at these compensation levels. This status quo partly reflects 'insiders' with government jobs, leveraging their influence to make their own terms more generous over time, at the cost of public funds that could be used to hire more staff to better serve citizens. The recent lobbying by public employees to revert to the much more expensive old pension scheme (OPS), and the yielding of some state governments to this pressure despite high long-term costs is a good example of this phenomenon.[8]

1.2 High public-sector pay may *hurt* recruitment quality, and the broader economy

In theory, high public-sector pay and a large candidate pool for government jobs can be beneficial. If high pay attracts top talent for public jobs that affect the common good, the expense might be justified. Unfortunately, this does not seem to be the case in practice. In fact, if government jobs are *too* lucrative and disconnected from market realities, it can create perverse incentives that may even *hurt* recruitment quality, state capacity, and the entire economy as explained below.

The key point is that the combination of high salaries, lifetime job security, and potential for unofficial 'side income' have made government jobs extremely attractive to India's educated youth. For many of them, a *sarkari naukri* (government job) is the dream job. A 2016 survey of youth aged fifteen to thirty-four found that 65 per cent preferred a government job, compared to just 7 per cent preferring a private-sector job.[9] A 2022 survey of Class 10 students in Tamil Nadu found that *88 per cent* aspired for a government job.[10] Hence, every government job is fiercely contested. A striking example was when 2.3 *million* applicants, including over 250 with a PhD, applied for 368 *peon* posts in Uttar Pradesh—implying 6250 applicants for every single job![11] Given these vast numbers, applying for a government job is often like *playing a lottery*. This creates several problems.

First, the large disparity between government and market compensation creates a fertile ground for corruption in public-sector hiring. Given the sizeable lifetime value of winning the government job lottery, candidates are often willing to pay to increase their chances of success, and politicians and officials cash in on this.

While UPSC hiring is clean, other areas of public-sector hiring are often compromised, as seen in recruitment scams over the years in hiring for positions ranging from teachers to railway employees.[12] Such corruption in hiring can negate the potential benefits of offering higher wages to attract top talent.[13] It may even draw more intrinsically corrupt candidates to public jobs. For instance, a study of job preferences among Indian college students found that students who were more likely to cheat on lab games were *more* likely to want to enter the government.[14]

Second, the logistical challenge of conducting recruitments with such large numbers of candidates and the high risk of cheating greatly increases the administrative fixed costs of hiring. The elevated risk of corruption in recruitment, and the costs of being accused of it can also act as a deterrent to officials from taking on the burden of recruitment. These high fixed costs of recruitment partly explain why many government departments do not hire annually, and instead prefer to recruit only every few years.[15] This sporadic, as opposed to regular, hiring partly explains why even many sanctioned government positions lie vacant, which contributes to weak state capacity.

Third, even when recruitment takes place and is not corrupt, our exam-based selection system does poorly in identifying candidates who will be effective on the job. While the exams may be fair, the lure of a government job often leads candidates to apply for *any* such job they are eligible for—in departments as varied as rural development, railways, police, and forests—regardless of their own strengths and interests, and how these align with the needs of the specific job they are applying for. As a result, candidates selected for a *lifetime* job often have little or no interest in the specific area of work. The obsession with government jobs, regardless of the actual job, was seen in a BBC news story that profiled one such job candidate and noted that '(he) is not fussy—he has previously applied to be a teacher and a forest guard, but both ended in failure.'[16]

While it is rational for candidates to apply for every possible government job regardless of their interests, thereby buying more tickets for the government job lottery, it is citizens who pay the price for public employees' lack of interest in their actual jobs. I have seen this problem first-hand during field visits to government schools. Speaking to teachers, I learnt that many of them had obtained teaching credentials in courses with minimal requirements, often by correspondence, so that they could also apply for *other* government jobs. Thus, they were primarily interested in a government job, and only secondarily in teaching. The resulting lack of interest in their job was evident in their attitude: they often appeared indifferent to poor student learning outcomes.[17]

Fourth, the fixation with government jobs is a leading cause of unemployment among India's educated youth. Many spend several years unemployed or under-employed, preparing for various government job exams. The problem of educated unemployed youth 'waiting' and 'hoping' for a government job is so widespread that a scholarly book on this topic, set in western UP, is titled *Timepass*.[18] The scale of the problem is seen in a recent study in Tamil Nadu, which estimates that *80 per cent* of *all* unemployed people in the state were preparing for state public-service commission exams.[19]

Fifth, the attraction of government jobs also contributes to the low demand for skills among India's youth. Studies show that a third of the candidates of skilling programmes either turn down job offers or leave their jobs within one month of placement.[20] Exit interviews suggest that a key reason is that many youth prefer to attempt government job exams. While preparing for these exams, candidates rely on family support and part-time jobs, but typically do not build skills or secure any certification. Thus, India's crisis of low skills and high unemployment among educated youth can partly be attributed to the structure of public-sector labour markets. It results in the main 'skill' that millions of youth develop in their prime years being how to 'crack' government exams, as opposed to learning actual skills that make them productive in the *real* economy outside the government.

Given the large private benefits of obtaining a government job, it may be rational for the youth to keep on trying to do so instead of getting skilled and working in the competitive real economy. However, this is *highly wasteful for society*. The chances of winning this lottery are very low, resulting in millions of Indian youth wasting several prime years of their lives, which could be used to obtain real skills and be productively employed.[21] Thus, while it may seem counter-intuitive, we will likely be much better off as a society by *reducing* the value of the government job lottery (see ideas in Section 2).

1.3 There is no link between pay and productivity in the public sector

A different but related question is whether pay variation within the government is in any way correlated with productivity. However, multiple studies across key sectors such as education and health find no link between pay and productivity in the public sector.

In a series of studies, economist Venkatesh Sundararaman and I tracked learning outcomes of tens of thousands of students in 500 primary schools across five districts of (undivided) Andhra Pradesh over multiple years.[22] Annual data on learning progress combined with data on assignment of students to teachers each year allows us to estimate each teacher's effectiveness at improving learning outcomes of their students, and correlate their effectiveness with their pay and other professional characteristics.[23]

Across multiple samples and time periods, we found no correlation between teachers' effectiveness and their salary in the public sector.[24] If anything, better-paid teachers were *less* effective. This may reflect the fact that pay increases with seniority, and more senior teachers have been found to have higher absence rates.[25]

In another study, we found that locally hired contract teachers were at least as effective as regular teachers at improving learning outcomes for primary school students, despite being less educated, not having formal teacher training credentials, and being *paid less than one-fifth* the salary of regular government teachers. Contract teachers made up for their lower education, training, and experience with higher levels of effort, as seen by their significantly lower 18 per cent absence rates compared to 27 per cent for regular teachers. Thus, higher salaries and qualifications did not ensure better performance. But, locally hired staff who were more *accountable* and connected to their communities performed as well as regular employees who were more qualified *and* paid much more.

Turning to health, in a study in rural Madhya Pradesh, my colleagues and I found no link between salary and effort or quality among public health providers, but found a strong positive correlation among private health providers.[26] Similarly, in education, while there is no correlation between pay and productivity in public schools, there is a strong positive correlation in private schools.[27] Overall, private markets reward effective service providers with higher pay, whereas there is no such correlation in the public sector.

While there is no evidence that better-paid public employees are more productive, a related but distinct question is whether pay increases for existing staff can boost their motivation and increase productivity. Again, evidence suggests that this is not the case. In studies based on randomized controlled trials (RCTs), my colleagues and I found very little effect of unconditional pay increases to ICDS workers in Tamil Nadu on child development outcomes.[28] In a different RCT in Indonesia with other colleagues, we found that even *doubling* teacher pay had no impact on learning outcomes.[29]

Overall, a growing body of evidence suggests that unconditional salary increases for current public employees have *no impact* on their performance. This is a key point for Central and state government Pay Commissions to consider, because such pay increases absorb large fractions of the increases in tax revenue and increases in sectoral budgets over time, but do not yield much benefit to citizens at large.

In contrast, multiple studies have found that augmenting staffing, especially with locally hired staff on renewable contracts, can significantly improve development outcomes. In Tamil Nadu, we found using a large-scale RCT that adding even a half-time extra worker to ICDS centres focused on preschool education led to large and significant gains in learning outcomes. Strikingly, it *also* reduced child malnutrition and stunting, likely reflecting the freeing up of time of the existing ICDS worker to focus on health- and nutrition-related tasks. Similarly, in Andhra Pradesh, we found that adding an extra locally hired contract teacher to primary schools significantly improved learning outcomes.[30]

A simple summary of the evidence is that we overpay existing public employees, but do not hire enough of them. While cutting pay is politically unrealistic, even slowing down pay increases for existing staff and using saved funds to hire more staff would improve state capacity for service delivery within existing budgets.[31] Alternatively, designing systems for adding staff at closer to market salaries, rather than inflated government salaries, will allow us to augment staffing for better service delivery (see Section 2.3).

1.4 Credentialing and training systems for public employees are weak

Public-sector recruitment in India heavily emphasizes qualifications. For instance, norms for teacher selection require candidates to have a diploma or degree in education. Yet, several high-quality studies in India find no positive correlation between teachers having such a credential and their classroom effectiveness in the public sector.[32]

Why might this be the case? There are at least three plausible reasons.

First, since credentials are needed to apply for government jobs, many low-quality institutions have emerged to meet this demand. In many cases, credentials are provided through low-quality courses with little faculty engagement. In other instances, teacher training certificates *can even be purchased*.[33] So, it is not surprising that having such a credential does not improve teaching quality.

Second, even when credentials are genuine, the training content can be too theoretical. Analysis of teacher training curricula reveals that they mostly focus on theoretical topics such as the history, theory, philosophy, and sociology of education with very little attention to effective pedagogy. Such training may not adequately prepare teachers for the practice of effectively managing and teaching an actual classroom full of children.

Third, even if the training has useful content, it may not translate to better performance if employees lack motivation. Quality depends on *both knowledge and effort*, and the benefits of greater knowledge are higher when effort is also higher.[34] We found direct evidence of this in our Andhra Pradesh research. Trained teachers were not more effective on average, but they were when they were also rewarded for their output. In other words, being trained gave them the 'ability' to teach better, but this only translated into better outcomes when they were also 'motivated' to do so.[35]

Similar weaknesses are seen with in-service training for existing employees, and studies suggest that such training is either non-existent or ineffective.[36] The challenges include a lack of standardized, high-quality training content; insufficient skilled trainers; departments not providing time for staff to attend trainings due to understaffing; and a lack of professional incentives for upgrading skills. Since promotions and even postings are rarely linked to competence and skills, it is not surprising that many public employees show limited interest in upgrading their skills.

A recent study of Class 5 and 6 municipal school teachers in Maharashtra highlights the challenge of weak skills among public employees.[37] Teachers scored only 29 per cent on a test of effective instructional practices, 52 per cent on a test of identifying student errors, and 83 per cent on a test of the *same* questions that their students were tested on. Thus, qualified government teachers could not answer one in six questions that they had to *teach* their own Class 5 and 6 students, and got nearly half the questions on identifying student errors wrong.

The evidence above mainly comes from primary education because this is the sector with the most high-quality research. However, similar patterns are seen in health, where studies show that medical knowledge is low among both public and private health practitioners (see Chapter 12). More generally, the crisis of low skills, capacity, and motivation among public employees pervades almost every department in both state and Central governments. One measure of the scale of the crisis is the widespread use of external consultants throughout the government (as noted in Chapter 3).

1.5 Public-sector personnel management is also weak

Beyond staff strength and capacities, the government's ability to deliver also depends on how well staff are managed. Global research shows that (a) management quality is crucial for organizational effectiveness, (b) management quality is considerably lower in the public sector than in the private sector, and (c) the biggest driver of this difference is weak to non-existent systems for *personnel* management in the public sector.[38] My colleagues and I have found very similar results in our own research in India.[39]

Public-sector personnel management in India is weak for several reasons. First, many block- and district-level supervisory positions are often vacant, with block-level vacancy rates as high as 50 per cent in some states and sectors.[40] Second, supervisors' tenures are often short and unpredictable, hindering effective management. Third, supervisors receive very little training on how to be effective managers. Fourth, they have limited tools to motivate their staff since pay, promotions, and postings are mainly based on seniority and not performance; and taking actions against staff for non-performance is also administratively difficult. Thus, both carrots and sticks are limited. Fifth, existing accountability frameworks prioritize procedural compliance over outcomes.

Of course, implementing a full menu of private sector personnel management practices in the government may not be practical.[41] However, given the importance of personnel management to organizational effectiveness, and the large weaknesses in the status quo, even basic improvements in this area are likely to yield significant benefits.

1.6 Lifetime employment

Many challenges in public personnel management stem from lifetime employment. In principle, permanent employment is meant to protect civil-service employees from arbitrary dismissal and ensure independence from the political executive. In practice, it has become a key contributor to government inefficiency for several reasons.

First, it reduces accountability for performance and incentives for upgrading skills since jobs are guaranteed for life. Second, it burdens public finances with salary costs for jobs that have been made obsolete by technology.[42] Third, it limits governments' ability to hire staff with current skills because budgets are used on staff with obsolete skills. Fourth, having employees with outdated skills and weak incentives to upgrade them can slow down governments' ability to adopt newer technologies and improve productivity.

Consider the case of revenue collection, where most current staff used to focus on doing 'assessments' of how much tax is owed. But this role is less relevant after India's shift to the Goods and Services Tax (GST). Rather, what we need now is capacity for data analysis to derive insights from vast amounts of GST data, which matters much more for revenue collection than the old field-based assessments. But most government staff do not have these skills, resulting in governments either not analysing GST data adequately, or relying on external consulting firms to do so (see Chapter 7).

In another example, I recall visiting a government department in Bihar in 2012 with a large open office with sixty employees, thousands of files, and no computers (the only computer was in the principal secretary's office). The department had been sanctioned funds for computers and digitizing records, but the project had not started because most department staff could not operate a computer, and few showed any inclination to learn.

Similarly, employees of public-sector banks opposed the introduction of computers in the 1980s and 1990s reflecting resistance to adapting to new ways of working, and worries that their jobs would be at risk. Eventually, many public-sector banks could only modernize after offering generous voluntary retirement packages to the existing staff, highlighting how lifetime employment can impede organizational renewal. In this case, modernization was not delayed too much because private banks were using technology to offer customers a better experience, forcing public banks to respond. In government departments, with much less competition and pressure to boost productivity, such modernization may be delayed much longer, as seen in the Bihar example above.[43]

Of course, there are key roles in the government that benefit from employees having extensive experience in multiple roles in that department over a full career. Yet, in many roles, lifetime employment is a significant barrier to state effectiveness. So we should aim to achieve a better balance between employee rights and the benefits of longevity and institutional memory on the one hand, and better accountability and flexibility on the other.

1.7 Geographic mismatch

Another personnel management challenge is the geographic mismatch between where posts exist and where providers want to live. Our current systems prioritize hiring the most credentialed candidates at the district level. However, since highly qualified candidates either come from urban areas or aim to move there, it is common to find staff vacancies in rural areas. Even if staff allocations are rationalized across locations, many employees prefer to live in urban areas and commute long distances to work.

These long commutes are a key reason for the higher absence rates of regular teachers and health workers compared to contract teachers and community health workers who live in the villages they are serving.[44] When service providers choose to live far away, it also reduces their connection to the communities they serve. Further, the problem of corruption in transfers and postings also reflects the geographic mismatch between posts and employee preferences on where they want to live.[45] As discussed further in Chapter 8, a key reason for this spatial mismatch is that we have over-centralized many service delivery functions, which should ideally sit at the local level.

2. Some Implementable Ideas for Improving Public Personnel Management

The challenges above are daunting, but addressing them is crucial for improving state effectiveness. The ideas in this section aim to provide a practical roadmap for addressing these challenges and improving public personnel management.

2.1 Invest in a digital human resource management information system (HRMIS)

One indication of weak public personnel management in India is that most states do not even have a digital record of every government employee and their employment history. I have often tried to obtain data on the average tenure of staff and supervisors in key district- and block-level posts to analyse stability in governance, but have found that this data typically does not exist in a systematic way even in better-governed states.

Finance departments typically have electronic records of all employee salary payments. However, this employee database typically has no information on their posting and transfer history, their skills and competencies, or any indicator of performance. While some departments do have such electronic personnel records, there is wide variation in the quality of personnel data even across departments in the same state.

Thus, a basic first step for improving public personnel management is to build an integrated finance and human resources management information system (HRMIS) that has electronic records of every government employee, their employment history, skills, competencies, and performance evaluations. The system should also have a record of every sanctioned *post* in the government and the history of the occupant of the post. Thus, the system can be queried and analysed both by person and by post.

Such a system can enable a significant improvement in personnel management, by facilitating analysis followed by action. Examples include: (a) analysing vacancies and tenure in all block- and district-level posts and ensuring that managerial vacancies are filled with a stable tenure, (b) analysing spatial variation in staffing and rationalizing staff allocation, and (c) anticipating vacancies due to retirements and putting a succession plan in place to minimize gaps in leadership. It will enable transfers to be implemented online, boosting transparency and reducing corruption.[46] Over time, it will also allow employee career trajectories, including postings and promotions, to better reflect their skills, interests, performance, and fit for specific jobs (see next sub-section).

A comprehensive HRMIS will be a foundational investment for better human resource planning and management, and provide top political and bureaucratic leadership with visibility on key staffing metrics. It could be hosted by the finance department because they maintain the payroll database, and shared with other departments for improving personnel management.[47] Tamil Nadu has recently built such a system, and is adding analytical capabilities to use the HRMIS for improved personnel management. Other states could easily replicate this approach.

2.2 Institutionalize capacity-building and competence-based career progression

A typical government employee serves for over thirty years after recruitment. Hence, ensuring that public employees continuously upgrade their skills should be a top priority for augmenting state capacity. However, while in-service training requirements are often stipulated on paper, training programmes are inconsistently provided, of variable quality even when provided, and typically ineffective as a result.[48] So, the challenge is less about intent and more about execution, *within* our fiscal and capacity constraints. This requires improvements in design, delivery, and motivation.

The *design* of in-service training can be improved by following a few key principles. Modules must be short, focused, and practical, since evidence suggests that this is the most effective way to absorb content. They should emphasize practice more than theory, and integrate theory with practice, such as by using role plays and simulations. They should emphasize soft skills for effective interaction with the public, especially for frontline staff who are the interface between citizens and the state. For instance, a study in Rajasthan showed that basic soft skills training for the police improved both their performance and public perception.[49] Further, peer learning can often be more effective than lectures. Thus, facilitating the generation and sharing of training content by employees themselves can be an effective way of encouraging peer learning.

The *delivery* of training can be sharply improved by using technology. For instance, in-service training for teachers, health workers, the police, and almost every government official can be improved by developing portals that can host modules comprising a combination of reading materials, videos, role-playing, and practice exercises—with translations in all major Indian languages.

Such a portal could effectively incorporate all the design principles outlined above. Modules would be standardized, and can be absorbed in short segments whenever staff have free time. Practical knowledge and soft skills can be taught through role-playing various situations that public employees routinely face, and demonstrating a range of appropriate and inappropriate responses. Employees could upload user-created content, and rate the quality of content shared by others, enabling a crowdsourced approach to identifying high-quality training content. Over time, the modules can be organized into officially sanctioned courses, and the government could offer credentials based on completion of in-service training, which is currently uncommon.

The third critical piece is improved *motivation* for training, which can be done by assessing and certifying staff on absorption and mastery of the training content. This is a key gap in the status quo, which limits the incentives and motivation to learn. A simple solution is to require employees to log in to the training portal with their HRMIS unique ID, and have a personal 'competency passbook' that records their completion, mastery, and certifications of various training modules and competencies.[50] This is exactly the approach envisaged by the Capacity Building Commission under Mission Karmayogi, and is one that can be easily adopted by states.[51]

Similarly, every government role should map out the competencies required to do it well. Over time, demonstrated skills and the fit of candidates' competencies to job requirements should play a key role in postings and promotions, rather than just seniority, or an exam rank from many years ago. Candidates can assess their own skills against the requirement of roles they aspire to and work to fill their competency gaps. Hiring panels can also use HRMIS data to identify candidate shortlists for posts.

Such an approach can also help in enhancing diversity, and improving representation of women and underprivileged groups in leadership positions. The HRMIS can help to identify a larger pool of qualified candidates from these groups, who may not be as visible due to a lack of networks or mentors. It can help to improve the leadership pipeline of such candidates by early detection of skill gaps for leadership positions and offering customized training and mentoring programmes to bridge these gaps in advance.[52]

Using data on demonstrated skills, and role-specific competencies for postings and promotions can significantly boost long-term state capacity. It would motivate public employees for lifelong learning and skilling, and improve leadership quality by promoting candidates who have shown that they possess relevant skills. While performance-based pay and promotions are difficult in the public sector, it is more feasible to implement a system of competence-based promotions.[53] Implementing such an approach can not only improve employee skills, and identify better leaders; it can also help shift bureaucratic culture to value and reward competence and not just seniority.

As a society, we often require that people serving in roles that provide critical services to *other* citizens stay current in their knowledge. Doctors are expected to get re-certified every ten years, and armed forces officers cannot get promoted to leadership roles without advanced training. Given the vast impact of public employees on the lives of thousands of citizens, it is equally, if not more, crucial to institutionalize a system of continuous learning and capacity-building for them, and reward those who do so.

2.3 Design and implement apprenticeship-based models for skilling and hiring

One of the most important ideas in this book is to institute an apprenticeship-based model for skilling and hiring into government jobs. Such a model could mitigate many of the problems identified in Section 1, have a transformative impact on state capacity and service delivery without large budget increases, and also deliver other social benefits.

The essence of the idea is that governments should institute a two- to four-year-long practicum-based training course in sectors such as education, health, and public safety. Open to any candidate who has passed Class 12, the training would intersperse theory modules (three to four months/year) with hands-on practicum-based modules (eight to nine months/year). The course would be run at the district level, and would admit the most qualified applicant from each panchayat or ward, giving preference to those from understaffed areas.[54] Funded by the government, the training would be free to selected candidates. During the practicum, trainees would be placed in their local government school, clinic, or police station; receive a modest stipend; support senior staff in service delivery; learn practical skills under their supervision; continue receiving digital training modules; and interact with their peers and teachers in online or phone-based groups.[55]

Upon completing their two- to four-year course, candidates would earn a professional credential (diploma or degree based on duration and content covered), while also having *done the actual* job for a few years as part of their practicum. These credentials would be recognized by the government and also be valuable in the private sector, which employs a large number of teachers, health workers, and security staff.

A key innovation is that regular government recruitment should award applicants extra points for the practicum, say 5 per cent for each year of practicum-based experience, capped at 20 per cent. So, an applicant with 70 marks out of 100 and two or four years of practical experience would score 80 or 90 marks. Thus, the practicum-based training would not guarantee a government job, but it would increase the chances of getting one *in the area* of demonstrated experience.

This approach to training and hiring is informed by Indian and global evidence, and would address several challenges identified in Section 1 and Chapter 3.

First, it would significantly boost training quality. Global evidence suggests that training content, especially for service-delivery roles, is better absorbed by interspersing theory and practice as opposed to the default of lecture-based instruction.[56] Introducing young cohorts of service-delivery professionals to digital training modules and peer learning groups at the start of their careers will also help foster lifelong learning. Crucially, in an age of increasing automation, the future of jobs lies in the service sectors that require human interactions and cannot be automated away. Thus, strengthening investments in training using this approach will improve the skills and employability of young service-sector professionals—across the public and private sector, in India and abroad.

Second, since apprentices will obtain their practical training in public facilities, and support regular government employees in actual service delivery tasks during their practicum, it would augment frontline staffing capacity for public service delivery. Several studies find that adding locally hired staff in service delivery roles, even with limited qualifications and in part-time roles, can significantly improve outcomes. The apprentices would serve a similar function. The details of how this approach can be deployed in key sectors to improve service delivery are laid out in Chapters 11–13.

Third, this approach offers a fiscally feasible way to expand frontline staffing, since the stipends, which may range from Rs 2500–Rs 5000/month, will be much lower than regular government salaries, which range from Rs 20,000–Rs 50,000/month. Yet, this is still a very attractive proposition for trainees. As per the 2017–18 NSS, the average Indian had a monthly consumption of Rs 2500. Thus, the stipend would be a considerable income—especially in rural areas. Combined with the preference of youth for non-manual 'white collar' jobs, the *free* training and credentialing, and social and community respect, the apprenticeship would be appealing and even aspirational to youth completing Class 12.

Fourth, it would reduce geographic mismatch in staffing by placing apprentices in their home areas for their practicum, thereby improving services in remote and underserved areas. Rather than hiring the most qualified candidates in a district and expecting them to serve in remote areas—which they do not want to do—this approach would identify and invest in *local* talent. This mirrors the approach used by Drs Abhay and Rani Bang for training community health workers in Gadchiroli district in Maharashtra, which inspired the nationally scaled up ASHA worker programme.[57] ASHA workers are among the most effective components of our health system (see Chapter 12), and the proposed approach would build on this model by investing in the skills of locally-hired staff.

Fifth, it will improve the long-term fit of employees to government jobs. At present, candidates often apply for every possible government job even without genuine interest in many of the jobs they apply for. As a result, many candidates who obtain *permanent* government jobs may be a poor fit for the actual job. By providing points in selection for practicum-based experience, the new approach to public-sector recruitment will favour candidates who show *interest in a specific sector* by obtaining a practicum-based credential, over those who simply take every possible government job exam and hope to win the public sector job lottery. This will improve match quality over time.

Of course, *all* the graduates of practicum-based training programmes cannot obtain a government job when the applicant-to-position ratio often exceeds 100:1.[58] This is why the practicum-based training should primarily be seen as a *skilling programme* for the youth in sectors with high employment potential in *both* the private and public sectors. The key innovation here is to use the government's position as the largest service provider, the largest employer of service-delivery professionals, and a funder of skilling programmes to *shape and improve the quality of training for the entire sector*. The proposed approach would create a win-win arrangement whereby trainees obtain publicly funded free training, credentials, and increased job prospects, while paying it forward by supporting actual service delivery in their communities during their practicum-based stints.

Beyond improving their prospects of obtaining a government job in their chosen area, such practicum-based training will also boost candidates' appeal to the *private* sector, which is also a major provider of education, health, and security services. The service sector is the largest source of employment in India. So, improving the skills of service-delivery professionals should be a cornerstone of a national skilling and employment strategy. If the training is good enough, programme graduates may even find jobs abroad, potentially earning even more than in a government job.[59]

Beyond these direct benefits to skilling and service delivery, the apprenticeship programme can generate indirect economic and social benefits by reducing youth unemployment and misallocation of talent. Instead of wasting several years attempting entrance exams to various government jobs, candidates can now acquire valuable skills through the practicum training, earn a stipend, and increase their chances of getting a job in their area of interest across the government and private sector.

Such programmes can also increase female labour force participation (FLFP), and thereby boost female empowerment. A major barrier to FLFP is the unwillingness or inability of young educated rural women who have completed Class 10 or 12 to travel outside their village to work. This could reflect both social norms and safety concerns, especially in rural north India. An emphasis on local hiring for apprenticeship positions as teaching assistants, early-childhood caregivers, public health workers, and police personnel can significantly improve female labour force participation and empowerment.

Such a scheme can also improve the quality of services delivered to women. Studies show that female teachers have additional positive effects on female students,[60] and female police staff may be especially important for improving women's public safety. Yet, women are under-represented in government jobs, especially in northern states. Improving job opportunities for young women who have completed Class 10 or 12 will also raise both the real and perceived benefits of education for girls, which has been shown to positively affect schooling for younger girls and delay the age of marriage and fertility.[61] These, in turn, are correlated with better child human development outcomes.

A testament to the aspirational nature of such roles for young women can be seen in Tamil Nadu's recent *Illam Thedi Kalvi* (Education at Doorstep) initiative to offset COVID-19 learning loss. The programme engaged over 2 lakh young women who had passed Class 12 to provide supplemental after-school lessons for sixty to ninety minutes daily, and paid a modest monthly stipend of Rs 1000. Remarkably, there were about four applicants per position even at such a modest stipend.[62] Qualitative interviews suggest that, beyond the stipend, the candidates greatly valued the dignity, community respect, and empowerment from being able to leave home to engage with the community that the position afforded. These benefits are likely to be even stronger in northern states with lower rates of female education and empowerment.

Some elements of this idea have been tried before with mixed success, making it important to learn from prior experiences. For instance, several states have used locally hired contract teachers in lieu of regular civil-service teachers. As noted earlier, studies show that such locally-hired contract teachers are at least as effective, if not more, at improving primary school learning outcomes as regular teachers who are more qualified, and paid much higher salaries. But this 'contract teacher' model faced multiple concerns and challenges, spanning professional, legal, and political realms.

The professional concern is that using untrained staff can dilute standards and lower staff quality over time, and professional bodies opposed the use of 'para' teachers.[63] Legally, having contract employees do the same job as regular staff at much lower pay violates the principle of 'equal pay for equal work', and invites lawsuits from contract employees.[64] Finally, there is the political risk of mass regularization of contract employees prior to elections to obtain their electoral support. This can defeat the entire purpose of having more accountable local staff on renewable contracts, and can even worsen staff quality if less-qualified candidates obtain permanent positions.

The proposed approach addresses all three concerns. Professionally, it not only values training, but makes improved training a core goal of the proposal. As noted above, research suggests that theoretical constructs taught in standard training programmes are better absorbed when combined with practice. So, rather than diluting professional standards, the new approach would considerably *strengthen* training, skilling, and long-term capacity building of service-delivery professionals (see details in Chapters 11–13).

The legal concern is addressed by explicitly defining the practicum as a part of training, where the practical work is supervised by a senior regular staff member. Further, unlike para-teachers who faced indefinite lower pay while being employed, the apprenticeship is situated within the context of a *time-bound* practicum-based training. Paying apprentices a modest stipend during a time-bound practical training is much more legally tenable than paying staff lower wages indefinitely while doing the same job.

Finally, the political concern of 'regularization' pressure is addressed by clarifying that this is a *skilling* programme rather than a contractual job that can be 'regularized'.[65] The key benefit to candidates is receiving free high-quality training, with the practicum based in public facilities serving to strengthen their training in the practical aspects of service delivery, while also contributing to actual service delivery during this period. Thus, the core purpose of this programme would be to improve training and skilling, with the default job being a private-sector job since the private sector *employs many more people* in service-delivery roles such as education, health, and public safety than the public sector. The increased probability of getting a government job through extra points for practicum experience at the time of regular recruitment would be a bonus.

Overall, this approach to training and recruitment can transform service delivery in India. It would provide additional staffing to improve service delivery in a fiscally feasible way while also improving the skills, training, and match quality of employees in the long run. The approach can be deployed in several key sectors, including education, health, and public safety, as discussed further in Chapters 11–13.[66]

Such a scheme should also be politically popular because it will provide skills, jobs, improved service delivery, and *visible* changes in communities where the apprentices would be working. It can be especially transformative for women, and it may make sense to reserve 50 per cent of apprenticeship positions for women, to accelerate their representation and empowerment. Given the increasing importance of women voters, it may be a political winner to launch a scheme whereby every gram panchayat is provided with at least one female apprentice, who gets progressively skilled and empowered, in the three key sectors of education, health, and public safety.

2.4   Augment state capacity by hiring staff on fixed-term renewable contracts

The apprentice-based training approach offers a way to mitigate staffing shortages in government, but applies best to frontline workers. In practice, governments are short-staffed in almost every department—especially in technical roles. However, while they need to hire more, the productivity of permanent government employees is quite low.

One way of addressing this challenge is to hire staff on three- to five-year contracts with competitive pay and benefits but *no guarantee* of contract renewal. This structure allows governments to boost staffing *and* productivity, since the lack of guaranteed renewal incentivizes employee skill acquisition and performance. It also gives governments flexibility to match their workforce to evolving needs over time, and avoid the costs of lifetime employment noted in Section 1.6. At the same time, three to five years is long enough for employees to understand the department and master their roles.

At present, governments typically address staff shortages by hiring consulting firms and young professionals under various fellowships. However, though they can be useful, excessive dependence on consultants and short-term staff hurts governance and state capacity. As consultants rotate out of their roles, institutional memory is lost. They also have limited legitimacy and authority in interactions with counterparts inside and outside the government. Core state capacity will gradually atrophy through excess reliance on external consulting firms who can help execute well-defined projects but cannot be asked to think and act in the public interest, which is an essential government function.[67]

The proposed approach of hiring government staff on renewable medium-term contracts offers the flexibility and accountability benefits of using consulting firms, while mitigating the weaknesses. Their selection and appointment would go through a well-designed institutional process (see below). Thus, these staff members would be government employees, undergo relevant training and induction, and be able to represent the government, unlike consultants. However, the renewable nature of their employment contract will increase accountability and motivation for staff, and provide flexibility on personnel planning to the government. Over time, strong performers would have their contracts renewed, and top performers could be offered full-time government positions.

To ensure objective selection, and reduce recruitment costs, the current exam-based selection system for government jobs can also be used to create an empanelled list of candidates for contractual positions. So, instead of hiring only 'x' candidates for 'x' open positions, the UPSC exam process can be used to identify 5x or 10x more candidates. This approach would identify the top 1 or 2 per cent of candidates for an 'empanelled' shortlist instead of just the top 0.2 per cent who get selected at present. While the top 0.2 per cent can continue to be hired into full-time roles, the next 0.8 or 1.8 per cent would be invited to undergo a foundation course on government and its procedures,[68] and then be eligible for contractual appointments in any government department.

While exams are objective, they only screen for general aptitude and may not predict actual job performance accurately. The proposed approach retains the objectivity and selectivity of exam-based selection, ensuring only the top 1 or 2 per cent of applicants are selected. But it offers several advantages over the status quo.

First, and most important, it allows central and state governments to use the rigorous UPSC-based selection process to efficiently identify a much larger pool of high-quality candidates for public service roles. These candidates can be deployed in a wide range of government roles, especially at the district and block levels, where their presence can meaningfully increase state capacity.

One key role would be to improve implementation of top policy priorities. For instance, the Swachh Bharat Mission (SBM) used a team of young professionals to support district collectors. Param Iyer, the then head of SBM, notes that they played a crucial role in SBM implementation.[69] Yet, as Iyer himself observes, the government did not have the capacity to hire these professionals fast enough, and could only deploy them because they were hired and paid by the Tata

Trusts. Formalizing a system where collectors are supported by a few outstanding young professionals, selected and trained as outlined above, can sharply improve field-level implementation capacity.

Another key role is in data analytics and management. There is a serious shortage of technically skilled staff at district and block levels. Collectors often handle over fifty departments and it is nearly impossible to monitor them all effectively. Having a pool of 'empanelled' staff from the top 1 to 2 per cent of UPSC aspirants allows governments to support collectors with a few highly qualified assistant collectors to help oversee and coordinate specific domains, such as social sectors, economic sectors, etc.[70] Since these staff would be hired on contract for specific positions, they can also have longer tenures of three to five years and provide stability in district administration.

Second, it will improve incentives of public sector personnel to upgrade their skills and deliver results. Currently, these incentives fall sharply after getting hired since the job is guaranteed for life. In the new system, empanelment makes candidates eligible for a job but does not guarantee it, thereby motivating both skill acquisition and strong performance. Empanelled candidates could also be encouraged to work and gain experience in the private and non-profit sectors, and apply for government positions when there is a suitable contractual opening for their skills, experience, and interests.

Third, this model offers a structured approach for lateral entry of professionals into government. Many civil-service reform proposals have recommended such lateral entry. Yet, two key concerns are that such hiring can be politicized, and that lateral entrants may not understand the government well enough.[71] This approach addresses both concerns. Lateral entrants in this model will have gone through an objective UPSC-based selection process, and will also understand the government and its processes through the empanelment, training, and field postings early in their careers. But, their external work experience for part of their careers would enable them to bring a diversity of skills, perspectives, and professional experience to government, and thereby enrich its functioning.

Fourth, it will improve 'match quality' between candidates and roles across government. At present, many UPSC aspirants aim for the IAS, but 'settle' for the best service they can get, often leading to a lifelong mismatch between their interests and their roles.[72] Under the new approach, departments can better identify empanelled candidates whose skills and interests are aligned with the functions of that department (using information such as college subjects, role-specific experience, or a department or role-specific test), and offer them contractual positions. Over time, strong performers can be renewed on longer-term contracts, and top performers can even be offered permanent positions.[73]

Finally, empanelling five to ten times as many candidates as the status quo makes the process of preparing for UPSC exams less wasteful for candidates, by increasing their chances of obtaining meaningful jobs in the government. It would be fairer to the aspirants who put in immense effort to prepare for the UPSC exams, and could also attract many more talented and motivated youth to public service, who might otherwise be dissuaded from pursuing a recruitment process with very low odds of success.

The UPSC hiring process entails enormous efforts from candidates, exam-setters, and examiners, and it is incredibly inefficient to use it to select only the top 0.2 per cent of applicants and discard the remaining 99.8 per cent. Given that candidates prepare for around two years (many take more), the social cost of every selected candidate is over *1000 years of time* of unsuccessful candidates! Many of them have great potential to serve the country, with the best being of comparable quality to those who are selected. By using the same system to identify the top 2 per cent, we can generate a ten times larger pool of talent for roles in government (after a foundation course).[74] Combined with a competence-based framework for appointments, building such a pool of candidates for contractual positions can be a transformative way to boost staffing and state capacity, while maintaining flexibility for government, and accountability for staff.

2.5 Improve time use and task allocation of staff

Beyond augmenting staffing, state capacity can also be increased by improving the efficiency of how existing staff *use* their time. Two specific ideas for doing so include: (a) reducing and streamlining paperwork, and (b) doing a staff time use audit to help prioritize and redesign workflows based on the findings.

While some documentation is essential, government employees in India waste too much valuable time on onerous record-keeping and producing reports with little broader purpose. This comes at considerable cost to both employees and citizens.[75] Simplifying paperwork and workflows can meaningfully improve government effectiveness and should be a high reform priority.

Technological advances make it possible to simplify data collection and record-keeping, and streamline workflows. With smartphones being widespread, frontline workers can easily capture and record essential information digitally. Doing so will have several benefits, including (a) reducing time needed for manual record-keeping, (b) improving data quality with automated checks and audits, including geocoding and timestamping of data recording, (c) enabling real-time data summaries available to higher-level officials, and (d) enabling analytical software to be built on top of this data to provide guidance to frontline staff and supervisors on optimal allocation of time and effort.

In other cases, we can be much smarter about task design. A striking example from my own work is the case of agricultural output and yield estimation. Government staff around India collect data on area sown, crop sown, and yields. Yet, field-level audits suggest that *this data is often simply made up*: one field study found that in over 25 per cent of plots, even the crop sown had been recorded incorrectly![76] However, on closer examination, it became clear that it was unfair to just blame officials because they were expected to conduct a *census* of agricultural plots, which would take over two years to complete at current staffing levels, even assuming that they did no other work! So, the only way for them to 'do' what they are expected to do is to 'guesstimate' the plot level data.

This is a case that would benefit from thoughtfully redesigning the task. For instance, collecting data from a 10–20 per cent stratified random sample would generate *more accurate* estimates than a census because of the higher quality of the underlying data. This idea was also suggested by the Vaidyanathan Committee on agricultural statistics in 2011. Yet, over a decade later, not much has changed. This is an example of the kind of mundane technical issue that the public rarely pays attention to, but acting on it would meaningfully improve the time use and productivity of overburdened frontline staff.

Overall, government departments can significantly improve productivity by conducting periodic time use audits, say every ten years. These audits will clarify where staff are spending time and if their time use correctly reflects the most important priorities. Often, non-essential tasks can be eliminated, simplified, or made more efficient through better use of technology. In addition, cost-benefit analysis of various paperwork requirements may help to eliminate those that do not add value, and reduce the growth of paperwork.

Bureaucracies, whether public or private, often value money but not time, adversely affecting both staff and citizens. As former Intel CEO Andy Grove memorably noted: 'If you need to spend 500 dollars, you will need multiple levels of authorization and scrutiny. But you can easily call a meeting of twenty people and waste thousands of dollars in time with no accountability.'[77] Similarly, while the CAG dedicates enormous efforts to auditing public fund use, we spend almost no time on auditing and improving employee time use. However, salaries comprise 20–25 per cent of public spending and over Rs 12 lakh crore annually. Thus, improving time use of all public employees by even 5 per cent could generate *annual* efficiency gains of Rs 60,000 crore![78]

2.6 Implement data-driven performance measurement and management

Several high-quality studies in sectors such as education, health, and tax collection show that linking career outcomes such as pay, postings, or promotions to independent measures of performance can significantly improve the effort and performance of government employees.[79] Further, even small amounts of performance-linked pay have been found to be highly effective, whereas much more expensive unconditional pay increases to all employees have been shown to have no impact on performance. However, while these studies provide a useful proof of concept, the key operational challenge is: How do we implement performance-based career management at scale? Is it even feasible?

At the outset, it is important to recognize that performance measurement can be highly complex. Challenges include defining and measuring the correct outcomes, attributing outcomes to individuals in team-based settings, and accounting for factors outside the control of individuals. Thus, the appropriate metrics for measuring performance will vary by department and level of the employee, and should be designed in a customized way with suitable sectoral inputs. However, there are a few key principles for designing effective performance management systems that apply broadly.

First, it is essential to invest in data quality and integrity before using it to evaluate performance. As noted in Chapter 4, data manipulation happens even when it is *not* used for formal performance assessments, and this problem will be magnified when the data is used this way.[80] Thus, implementing the ideas in Chapter 4 is an essential prerequisite for a performance-management system. Over time, as data is used to assess performance, employees themselves may monitor data quality, as data manipulation by their peers will affect them directly. This can gradually shift institutional norms and culture to the point where data manipulation becomes professionally unacceptable—unlike in the status quo, where it is widespread and not penalized.

Second, it is important to identify just a *few* key performance indicators (KPIs) for departments, to provide clear goals for all staff. These could include a few measures of quality of public service delivery (measured by independent citizen phone surveys), a few district-level population outcomes (measured by independent outcome surveys), and a measure of administrative data integrity. While processes and compliance do matter, the approach above will help focus departmental attention on the critical points of reporting the truth, ensuring citizen satisfaction with public services, and promoting improved outcomes for the entire population.[81]

Third, counter-intuitively, weak incentives may work better than strong ones. The reason is that people often derive intrinsic value from being honest. However, if the incentives tied to outcomes are too strong, they can exceed the moral costs of cheating, and lead to unintended negative consequences. However, when incentives are modest, they can boost effort without crossing the threshold where cheating is preferred. The problem in the status quo is that there is typically *no reward* for performance. Thus, even a modest amount of performance-based recognition and professional rewards can positively affect organizational culture and employee motivation.

Fourth, annual performance evaluations should be captured in the HRMIS to create a cumulative record of employee performance across roles and over time. The measures of performance can get more sophisticated over time as data quality improves, but it is important to institutionalize annual performance evaluations in the HRMIS even with basic metrics to begin with, to inculcate a culture that performance does matter.

For most employees, it may be enough to start by just assessing them on their level of skills and competencies, accumulation of skills and bridging of competency gaps, and on truthful data reporting. For higher-ranked officials, the performance review could include some weightage on the average improvement in critical, independently measured outcomes at the district or block level. Finally, it may be both feasible and effective to implement a group performance-based bonus system for all department staff in a district based on the extent of improvement in key outcomes (see Chapter 6).[82]

Implementing performance-based career management in the public sector is not easy. But evidence suggests that the potential boost in organizational effectiveness from doing so can be substantial, thereby justifying the effort and resources invested. One measure of the importance of implementing such systems is the amount of time and resources private companies, who are more accountable for overall performance, spend on this problem. Thus, even modest improvements over the status quo are likely to yield large benefits to the public and even to government employees themselves.

2.7 Case Study: Junior Panchayat secretaries in Telangana

Many concepts from this and the previous chapter have been implemented in a recent Government of Telangana (GoTS) initiative to improve rural service delivery. Specifically, the Department of Panchayati Raj and Rural Development appointed around 10,000 new junior Panchayat secretaries (JPSs) on three-year contracts, with a stipulation that they would be regularized on the basis of their performance.

To develop a performance management system, the department created a smartphone app for JPSs to record key indicators of local quality of life, such as functioning of street lights, garbage clearance, and availability of water. Additionally, they examined over 160 records maintained by JPSs, and streamlined them to around eighty essential ones, thereby saving considerable time and enabling JPSs to focus on core service delivery.

Another critical step was the creation of a 'nested supervision' system whereby mandal (block) level supervisors would independently verify the data reported by JPSs on their own supervisory app. The supervisory app randomly selects villages to be audited, and randomly selects indicators to be cross verified. If there is a significant discrepancy between the JPS's report, and the supervisors' findings, it is flagged for further scrutiny. The evaluation system assesses JPSs not only on their reported performance but *also* on their truth-telling. A final layer of verification was built-in through random audits by department staff from outside the concerned blocks.

This case illustrates the feasibility of implementing several ideas from this section such as: augmenting state capacity by large-scale hiring of staff on fixed-term contracts, streamlining paperwork, using technology to improve real-time field data collection, building a technology-enabled nested supervision system, and introducing a culture of performance measurement and management in a government department at scale.

This case study also illustrates how political incentives are changing to prioritize not only the concentrated interests of government employees, but also the more diffused interests of citizens at large. For instance, in April 2023, the JPSs agitated to get regularized, but GoTS held firm that the principle of performance evaluation will be maintained.[83] Thus, even if GoTS decides to regularize all the JPSs at the end of their probationary period, the performance measurement system developed as part of this pilot can continue being used for ongoing performance management.[84]

One measure of the effectiveness of such initiatives is that Telangana received thirteen national awards for Panchayati Raj in 2023. Gram panchayats (GPs) from Telangana were ranked in the top three in India in eight out of nine categories, and ranked first in four of the nine categories.[85] This was by far the highest among all states.

Every state and sector can learn from this experience. A core challenge for India's state capacity is that we do not have enough frontline government employees, but the ones we have are not accountable for performance. This makes it fiscally risky to hire more permanent staff in a 'government as usual' mode, and so we are stuck without enough government employees. The Telangana experience provides a useful template and confirms a core proposition in this chapter: public welfare can be meaningfully improved by hiring more government employees to augment state capacity for service delivery, but it is essential to do so in ways that promote performance and accountability.

2.8 Key implementation principles

The JPS case study shows that the ideas in this and prior chapters are not just theoretical possibilities, but that they can also be successfully implemented within the government. Yet, we need to do a lot more to *institutionalize* practices to improve public personnel management. I now discuss four practical considerations for doing so.

First, as the JPS case study shows, it is essential to have political commitment to boost public personnel management. This commitment should start by implementing the ideas in Chapter 3 including (a) prioritizing investing in bureaucratic capacity, (b) avoiding corruption in postings and transfers, (c) ensuring stability of tenure of officials, and (d) investing in data-driven governance, including by using the ideas in Chapter 4. Once these political decisions are taken, the ideas in this chapter can be implemented by the bureaucratic leadership itself. Further, if initiated at the beginning of a five-year term, these ideas can deliver meaningful improvements in the lives of both employees and citizens, enabling political leaders to take credit for these while seeking re-election.

Second, implementing personnel reforms successfully will require convergence and coordination across several government departments. These include finance (budgets and forecasting), planning (data and measurement), general administration, personnel or human resources (personnel policy and training), law (service rules and labour laws), and the concerned line departments (who actually employ the staff). This siloing of roles has thwarted many reform attempts. Over the years, several principal secretaries have told me that they agreed on the pressing need for reforms to personnel management and policy, but lacked the power and coordination authority to make them happen.

So, a government wanting to improve public personnel management should constitute an empowered task force led by a senior political leader, such as the finance minister or even the chief minister, with ministers and secretaries of concerned departments for effective coordination. This task force can also draw on technical expertise as relevant. Some of the tasks related to revamping public personnel management can also be delegated to a state-level public human resources commission (see Chapter 17).

Third, personnel reforms should have engagement with and buy-in from government employees themselves. Many 'top-down' reform efforts face resistance from employees, because they are seen as an imposition. Further, such efforts can make things worse if they do not engage with practical daily challenges of employees and managers.

One approach could be to create *departmental* task forces with members at various staff levels (state, district, block, and field levels) to engage with specific ideas in this chapter such as training, time use optimization, and performance management. Supported with technical expertise, these groups could be made responsible for (a) consultation, (b) design of reforms, (c) communication of reforms and their rationale, (d) training and capacity-building, (e) conducting small-scale pilots to test and refine ideas, and (f) monitoring implementation and fine-tuning reforms as needed. While the high-level task force would ensure timely progress of personnel management reforms and approve department-level proposals, the departmental task forces would be in charge of details as appropriate to their sectoral context and needs.

Finally, effective communication, both internally and externally, is vital for successful reforms. For instance, framing personnel reforms as aiming to improve 'accountability' may be counterproductive since it is an adversarial framing that will be resisted by employees and unions. Rather, it may be better for political leadership to emphasize the importance of reforms for boosting the government's capacity, professionalism, and effectiveness—which will benefit both citizens *and* boost the self-esteem and image of government staff. Many employees join the government with high intrinsic motivation, but their enthusiasm and idealism is stifled over time by the 'system'. Successful reforms should seek to kindle and harness the intrinsic motivation of public employees, acknowledge them and their understanding of field-level constraints and reality with respect, and make them allies in a long-term process to improve state effectiveness.

3. Conclusion

Public employees are the core of the state, and it is almost impossible to improve state effectiveness without better public-sector personnel management. Successful private companies invest heavily in personnel management because effective hiring, training, motivation, and promotion of employees is essential for organizational effectiveness. Yet, this is a severely neglected topic in India's policy discourse, attention, and practice. In many ways, weak state capacity in India largely reflects inadequate attention to the management of public employees, and thereby to the state itself.

In theory, departments of personnel or general administration should be leaders in this area. In practice, they often focus more on postings and transfers, reflecting the power and control associated with this role. In a memorable anecdote shared by a senior IAS officer, he recalled once asking staff of the department of personnel in his state: '*Aap log idhar karte kya hain?*' (What do you people do here) and promptly received the response: '*Hum logon ka tabaadla karaate hain*' (We get people transferred)!

The anecdote aptly illustrates the sorry state of public-sector personnel management in India. It also exemplifies why there is so much low-hanging fruit in this area. Simply introducing an HRMIS and institutionalizing capacity-building can yield a meaningful improvement over the status quo. Implementing some of the other ideas in this chapter, such as practicum-based training and hiring, can yield transformative gains in state capacity, job, and skill creation, female empowerment, and service delivery.

Of course, while these ideas reflect research evidence and practical considerations, they will need to be piloted, tested, and iterated based on ground-level feedback. This increases the value of state-level experimentation and learning across states. The good news is that these actions can also be politically rewarding and acting on this agenda can be both good policy and good politics (see Chapters 2 and 3). It only takes one chief minister and state to show the way!

Chapter 6

Public Finance—Expenditure

Globally, governments collect taxes and decide how to spend these funds. These taxing and spending decisions can either help or hurt public welfare. They can improve welfare when government spending delivers greater public benefits compared to what taxpayers would do with the same money. Examples include the provision of 'public goods' such as defence, law and order, infrastructure, and infectious disease control that would not be adequately provided by markets and individuals.[1] Conversely, public spending that delivers less value than the cost of funds detracts from citizens' overall well-being.

While some government agencies in India deliver high value at low cost,[2] Central and state governments as a whole waste lakhs of crores of rupees annually. Further, while it is common to blame wastage of public funds on corruption, the bigger problem may be inefficiency.[3] This inefficiency largely reflects underinvestment in systems to analyse and improve the *quality* of public spending. In turn, this underinvestment reflects a lack of public, political, and bureaucratic attention to the importance of doing so.

While we do pay attention to budgets in India, the media and commentators mainly focus on the *allocation* of public funds across sectors, rather than how these allocations are translated into intended outcomes. Similarly, sectoral advocates often measure success by the amount of budget increases they secure for their cause, but spend less effort on ensuring the *effectiveness* of these funds. This is partly because budget allocations are visible and easily measured, whereas their efficacy is much harder to measure. Yet, this is a critical weakness in our discourse because what finally matters for citizen welfare is not just the amount of public spending, but its effectiveness.

For a low-middle income country like India, the large inefficiencies in public spending documented in this chapter are a national tragedy. With constrained resources, and several urgent demands on them, optimizing the use of public funds is not just an economic imperative, but also a *moral* one. We often waste money on low-value activities and, as a result, miss opportunities to invest in high-return projects that would improve the lives of hundreds of millions of Indians. Thus, one of the most important ways in which we can boost the effectiveness of the Indian state is to improve the *quality* of public expenditure. Doing so will allow us to deliver substantially better outcomes for citizens at any given level of income and budgets (see Chapter 10).

This core thematic chapter is organized in four sections. The first presents key facts on public spending in India. The second explains how and why the quality of expenditure in India is poor. The third section outlines key principles for improving the quality of public expenditure, and the last one presents ideas for implementing these principles.

1. Key Facts and Themes on Public Spending in India

1.1 Expenditure by level of government and sectors

Table 6.1 breaks down public spending in India by major categories, and by Central and state government spending. It presents figures for 2019–20, which is the last pre-COVID-19 year, and better represents typical public expenditure patterns in India.[4]

Beyond illustrating the sectoral priorities of Indian governments, there are two key insights in Table 6.1. First, the combined spending of Central and state governments in 2019–20 was Rs 55.5 lakh crore, amounting to 27.6 per cent of India's nominal GDP of Rs 201 lakh crore that year. The scale of public spending highlights the importance of improving its quality. Even a 2 per cent efficiency gain

Table 6.1: 2019–20 Actual Expenditure, in Rs '000 crore[5]

Item	Central Spending	State Spending	Total Spending	Per cent of total spending	Per cent of item-level spending at state level
Defence	319	0	319	5.7	0.0
Fertilizer subsidies	82	0	82	1.5	0.0
Food subsidies	109	0	109	2.0	0.0
Agriculture	106	203	309	5.6	65.7
Energy	44	197	241	4.3	81.7
Education	69	508	576	10.4	88.1
Health	36	149	185	3.3	80.5
Police	117	137	254	4.6	53.9
Rural Development	82	109	191	3.4	57.1
Social Security and Welfare	27	114	141	2.5	80.9
Transport	154	166	320	5.8	51.9
Urban Development	34	81	115	2.1	70.4
Interest	613	352	965	17.4	36.5
Pension	302	346	648	11.7	53.4
Others	115	979	1102	19.9	88.8
Total Expenditure	**2209**	**3341**	**5550**	**100.0**	**60.2**

Note(s): Central government data from Bag 6 (Expenditure), Ministry of Finance; state government data from the Study of State Finances, Reserve Bank of India (RBI); some states augment Central government food subsidies, but this line item is not reported separately in a standardized way across states and is hence set to zero, and included in the 'Others' category.

in public spending is worth over Rs 1.1 lakh crore *annually*. This is why boosting the effectiveness of public spending will be among the most impactful ways of improving development outcomes at scale.

Second, states account for over 60 per cent of India's public spending. The role of states is even larger in service-delivery sectors: they account for nearly 90 per cent of spending in education, and over 80 per cent in health, and social security and welfare. In policing, the Central government's 46 per cent share reflects spending on paramilitary forces for countering insurgency and protecting national assets.[6] But states still spend more (54 per cent) and play the leading role in *civil* policing and public safety.

A conceptual challenge in creating Table 6.1 is that the Central government transferred Rs 6.3 lakh crore to state governments, in addition to directly spending Rs 20.6 lakh crore. These transfers have to be apportioned to avoid double counting.[7] Some of these transfers are untied, implying that states can mostly spend them as they like. However, nearly half the transfers were tied to centrally sponsored schemes (CSSs) that are *designed* by the Central government, but *delivered* by state governments (see Chapter 8 for details on CSSs). Since the quality of expenditure depends on both design and delivery of spending programmes, the figures in Table 6.1 allocate tied transfers equally between the Centre and the states, but classify untied transfers as state spending.[8]

Overall, these figures highlight the centrality of state-level actions to improve expenditure quality in India, especially in service-delivery sectors. While the Central government can help by supporting reforms to improve quality of expenditure across government, much of the actual work will need to be done at the state level.

1.2 Expenditure by major spending categories

Table 6.2 takes the same total spending as Table 6.1, but organizes it by spending categories, rather than by sector. Doing so yields several key insights.

First, *over 50 per cent* of public spending is tied up in committed expenses of salaries, pensions, and interest payments. Interest and pensions alone consume 29 per cent of spending. These are *current*

Table 6.2: 2019–20 Actual Expenditure, in Rs '000 crore[9]

Spending Category	Central Spending	State Spending	Total Spending	Per cent of total spending	State share of total spending
Salaries	486	728	1214	21.9	60.0
Pensions	302	346	648	11.7	53.4
Interest	612	351	963	17.3	36.4
Capital Outlay	388	418	806	14.5	51.9
Other Expenses	422	1498	1920	34.6	78.0
Total Expenditure	2209	3341	5550	100.0	60.2
Net Additional Debt	994	564	1558	28.07	36.20

Note(s): Central government data from Bag 6 (Expenditure), Ministry of Finance; state government data from the Study of State Finances, Reserve Bank of India (RBI); Central government funds transferred to states are apportioned as in Table 6.1 and included under 'Other Expenses'.

expenses to honour *past* commitments, to lenders and government employees, respectively. These large costs highlight the long-term impact of current spending decisions, and how they limit funds available for other essential public spending. For instance, reverting to the old pension system, as some states have done recently, will exact a heavy toll on future public finances, especially since the total number of government pensioners now exceeds the number of active employees.[10]

Second, total public spending considerably exceeds revenues. As a result, Central and state governments issued Rs 15.6 lakh crore *of additional debt* in 2019–20. Thus, 28 per cent of total public spending is financed by borrowing. Further, this figure only includes debt taken on directly by governments, and does not include liabilities of legally distinct public entities such as state electricity distribution companies, or public sector banks. However, since these are public entities with government guarantees, they often require a taxpayer-funded bailout to cover their liabilities, implying that the true level of public liabilities is often higher than what is reported in government budgets.[11]

Note that debt itself is not problematic, if it is used to make public investments with a high rate of return. In this case, the resulting growth in the economy and in tax revenues will typically be enough to cover the interest cost. This is analogous to companies borrowing to invest in opportunities that will yield a higher return than the interest cost of debt. However, it is crucial that debt be primarily used to finance *productive* investments rather than current consumption or past inefficiencies. In the latter case, the interest burden on unproductive borrowing can severely squeeze public finances over time.

Third, and related, net capital outlay was only 14.5 per cent of total public spending (Rs 8.1 lakh crore). One way of seeing that this is probably too low is that only 51 per cent of India's additional borrowing was used for investment. This implies that we not only do not invest anything from current tax revenues, but nearly half of our borrowings are used to finance current consumption and not investment.[12] Consistent with this, the majority of the 'other' expenses listed above, amounting to nearly 35 per cent of total spending, is accounted for by various welfare schemes and subsidies.

1.3 Investment versus welfare spending

A central challenge for governments is to balance spending on investments to boost future productivity and economic growth, and spending on subsidies and welfare to support the present needs of the population.

Examples of productive investments include infrastructure for transportation and market integration—such as roads, railways, ports, and airports; investments in electricity and communications grids; public health—anti-vector campaigns, water and sanitation; and basic research that is the foundation of innovation and long-term productivity growth.

In contrast, welfare spending aims to improve the *current* quality of life of citizens, especially the poor. These include items such as subsidies to make essential items such as food and fuel cheaper for the poor, and direct income support such as pensions for the elderly and disabled, and farmer support payments.

Some spending serves a dual purpose. For instance, the NREGS has elements of both investment—by constructing productive rural assets, and welfare—by creating jobs for the rural poor. Similarly, publicly funded schools and early-childhood care centres not only promote investment in human capital for future productivity growth but also aid the poor, who may not be able to afford them otherwise.

Crucially, markets will typically underinvest in public goods such as infrastructure, public health, and contract enforcement. Likewise, they will not address issues like poverty. Historically, social, religious, and community organizations provided some welfare; and commercial organizations contributed to contract enforcement norms. However, they had neither the resources nor the authority to predictably and effectively perform these functions at scale. This is why governments can *increase* public welfare if they collect taxes from citizens, and focus on the functions that the government is better at doing *relative* to individuals, markets, and society.[13] But it is critical to achieve a good balance between welfare and investing for long-term growth, and to spend public funds well.

In practice, public expenditure in India is skewed towards short-term subsidies rather than longer-term investments that can boost productivity. As noted in Chapter 2, these choices reflect the political pressures created by 'democracy before development' with examples in several sectors, including railways, banking, utilities, and agriculture. In all of these cases, the cost of short-term subsidies has been lower long-term productivity.[14]

Consider agriculture: In the 2019–20 Budget, the Central government spent nearly *twenty times more* on fertilizer, interest, and income subsidies than on agricultural research and extension (which refers to the process of 'extending' knowledge on new agricultural technologies to farmers and facilitating their adoption). Fertilizer subsidies alone accounted for over Rs 81,000 crore, which was over ten times the budget for the Department of Agriculture Research and Education of around Rs 7500 crore. Another Rs 65,000 crore went to interest and income subsidies.[15] These patterns are repeated at the state level. For instance, in 2019–20, Punjab spent over Rs 6000 crore on farm electricity subsidies, compared to only Rs 380 crore on agricultural research.[16]

The cumulative underinvestment in public goods, research, and extension along with inefficiencies induced by many of our agricultural policies has had a profound negative effect on India's agriculture productivity. For instance, agricultural output per worker in high-income countries like the US is *fifty times higher* than in India (see Chapter 16). This ultimately hurts workers the most because productivity, measured as output *per worker*, is the most long-term determinant of workers' earnings.

This discussion should *not* be interpreted as privileging capital investment over welfare spending. In settings with high rates of poverty, the ethical case for welfare spending to alleviate immediate suffering is strong. The poor often cannot just wait for the long run. As John Maynard Keynes famously said, 'In the long run, we are all dead.' Rather, our main problem is that the quality of public spending in India is low *regardless* of whether we spend on welfare or on capital investments, as explained further below.

2. Quality of Expenditure Is Weak across All Categories of Spending

2.1 Quality of welfare spending

Unlike 'development' spending that is amenable to 'return on investment' calculations, welfare spending aims to support vulnerable citizens. How should we assess the quality of such spending? I propose three metrics to do so: targeting, delivery, and broader economic impact. In other words, is welfare spending directed to the right beneficiaries? Does it actually reach them? How does it affect the broader economy?

Targeting

The quality of targeting can be assessed by considering exclusion and inclusion errors at the individual and geographic levels.

Exclusion errors occur when intended beneficiaries are excluded from welfare benefits. For instance, the PDS, which is India's largest welfare programme, was estimated to have exclusion error rates over 50 per cent in some states as recently as a decade ago.[17] Though these rates have come down in recent years, concerns remain. A 2019 study found average PDS exclusion errors of 11 per cent across Bihar, Jharkhand, Madhya Pradesh, Chhattisgarh, Odisha and West Bengal, peaking at 24 per cent in Jharkhand.[18] Reasons include beneficiaries not having adequate documentation of eligibility, not being able to access benefits while migrating for work, and PDS shops not having adequate stocks of grain due to diversion by corrupt intermediaries.

Inclusion errors occur when benefits are claimed by those who are not eligible for them. A good example is cases where the non-poor obtain 'below poverty line' (BPL) cards, and use these to access benefits meant for the poor.

A broader definition of inclusion errors, which I use in this chapter, is when programmes spend scarce public resources on the relatively better-off. India's fertilizer and electricity subsidies for farmers exemplify such inclusion errors and poor targeting. Since there are no quantity caps, most of the subsidy spending goes to rich farmers with larger landholdings, who consume the most fertilizer or electricity.

The extent of this targeting problem is seen in Figure 6.1, which uses 2011–12 SECC data, and categorizes rural households in Maharashtra by size of landholdings. It shows that 53 per cent of them own no land, 18 per cent own under 2 acres, 16 per cent own 2–5 acres, 8 per cent own 5–10 acres, and the top 5 per cent own above 10 acres, with this top group owning 17.3 acres of land on average.[19] If we assume that fertilizer and electricity use is proportional to landholdings, 49 per cent of the total subsidy spending goes to the top 5 per cent of rural landowning households, with over 10 acres of land.

Thus, the top 5 per cent of rural landowning households in Maharashtra receive nearly 50 per cent of power and fertilizer subsidies, while the landless bottom 50 per cent get nothing![20] This skewed distribution is also seen in (undivided) Andhra Pradesh,

Figure 6.1: Landholding Distribution in Maharashtra

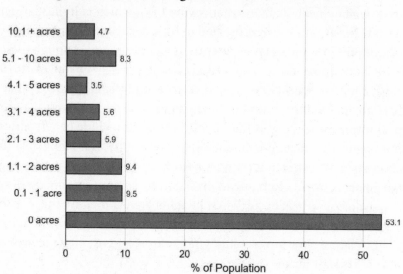

Note(s): Data from the Socio-Economic Caste Census, 2011; graph created by author; the SECC landholding measurement does not include land on which respondent homes are located (homesteads) or homestead cultivation

where the top 4 per cent get 46 per cent of subsidies, and in Punjab, where the top 6 per cent garner 50 per cent.[21] These three states are from different regions of the country, but they all provide free electricity to farmers, and a similar pattern holds across them.

Another example of inclusion and exclusion errors is seen in education. To promote equity, the Right to Education (RTE) Act reserves 25 per cent of seats in private schools for socio-economically disadvantaged students, with governments reimbursing private schools for these seats. Yet, studies show that this provision mainly benefits better-off students who would have attended private schools anyway (inclusion error). In contrast, poor households who were the intended beneficiaries, struggle to access programme benefits due to challenges like not having the needed documents and being unable to fill the necessary forms (exclusion error).[22]

Similar paperwork-induced targeting problems are seen in the geographic allocation of funds. Many Central government welfare schemes require extensive documentation by states to receive funds.

However, richer states have more administrative capacity for such paperwork, enabling them to receive a disproportionate share of Central funds. For instance, Bihar has 19 per cent of India's poor households, but received only 4.7 per cent of Central NREGS funds in 2019–20. In contrast, Kerala with just 0.1 per cent of India's poor households received 3 per cent of these funds.[23] Similar disparities are seen in fund allocation across states in the Ayushman Bharat programme.[24]

Overall, large fractions of India's social sector and welfare spending are poorly targeted. The better-off often obtain a disproportionate share of public spending in these areas, and the neediest often struggle to access their fair share of benefits.

Delivery

Even if the right beneficiaries are targeted, they may not receive all their benefits due to leakage in delivery. Leakage is defined as the difference between benefits disbursed under a programme and those received by beneficiaries, and often reflects corruption.[25]

In several studies over the past decade, my colleagues and I estimated leakage rates of 20–30 per cent in major welfare programmes, such as NREGS and PDS.[26] One channel of leakage is over-invoicing the government for welfare payments, say by over-reporting NREGS work done or creating fake beneficiaries. Another is under-payment, say by providing a lower quantity of PDS grains or lower payments for NREGS work done to programme beneficiaries, than they are entitled to.[27]

Taken together, targeting errors and leakage limit the extent to which public welfare spending reaches the truly needy. The Government of India's own 2016–17 Economic Survey estimated that only 28 per cent of the PDS outlay reaches the poorest 40 per cent of the population, with the corresponding figure for the NREGS being 37 per cent.

However, this is an area where substantial improvements have been made in the past decade. In particular, the combination of Jan-Dhan bank accounts, Aadhaar-based identification, and mobile-phone-based access to payment systems (or the JAM trilogy), have sharply augmented state capacity for welfare delivery and enabled governments to bypass intermediaries, deliver benefits directly to beneficiaries, and reduce corruption.[28]

Leakage is also a problem in public education and health. In particular, teacher and health worker absence implies public expenditure on salaries that did not reach citizens as intended, which is equivalent to leakage. As mentioned before, nationwide studies have estimated the rates of teacher and doctor absence in public facilities in India to be around 25 per cent and 40 per cent respectively, and the fiscal cost of teacher absence alone was estimated at around Rs 10,000 crore/year (at 2011 salaries).[29]

Design

A third crucial weakness in India's welfare spending is poor design, which contributes to inefficiency in *other* parts of the economy. Specifically, welfare programmes often try to support the poor by modifying prices instead of providing direct income support. This violates a core principle of economics: it is usually more effective to mitigate poverty by augmenting the incomes of the poor rather than subsidizing specific goods or services.

This is because competitive market prices play a critical role in efficient resource allocation, by providing socially beneficial incentives to both producers and consumers. On the producer side, higher prices encourage market entry by new players. On the consumer side, they incentivize more frugal use. Both sets of actions will reduce prices over time. Yet, since the poor cannot afford goods at high prices, governments often try to lower prices through subsidies or directly setting prices. However, global and Indian evidence suggests that government attempts to reduce prices for *some* users may not always help the poor, and can lead to several adverse long-term effects.[30]

Two examples from India illustrate the inefficiencies of price subsidies. One is the PDS, which creates a *dual price system* for commodities: subsidized prices inside the PDS, and much higher market prices outside. This creates strong incentives for diversion of goods from the PDS supply chain into the open market. Thus, even with monitoring, the *design* of the PDS is inherently conducive to leakage and corruption. In contrast, an approach of income-based support that provided the same subsidy value to beneficiary bank accounts, to enable them to buy desired items at market prices, would both boost flexibility, and also be likely to reduce leakage by eliminating the dual-price system.[31]

A second and more striking example is the case of electricity subsidies to farmers to run borewells to draw groundwater for irrigation. This free or heavily subsidized electricity significantly under-prices water relative to its true social cost, contributing to farmers growing water-intensive crops like paddy, sugarcane, and cotton even in water-scarce areas. Over time, the overuse of water has pushed Indian agriculture to the brink and made it ecologically unsustainable in many regions. With over 80 per cent of India's water being used for agriculture, our water crisis is a direct consequence of supporting farmers through electricity subsidies.[32] Further, while these subsidies are presented as supporting 'poor' farmers, they mainly benefit the better-off (Figure 6.1), and the costs of the water crisis will be borne disproportionately by women and vulnerable populations.

Note that the *design* costs of subsidies are different from their *fiscal costs*. The latter would be incurred even in an income support programme. Rather, the design costs refer to the broader economic distortions caused by decoupling prices from the true social costs of producing a good or service. In some cases, the costs of these distortions can be even greater than the direct cost of the subsidy itself. But these design costs are rarely considered or understood by policymakers, who focus mainly on the fiscal cost.

2.2 Quality of capital spending

Economic analysts and commentators often view increases in public capital spending as a signal of improving quality of expenditure. In principle, this makes sense because such investments can boost productivity. In practice, our quality of capital spending is also poor. Numerous CAG reports have noted problems across various capital projects. The discussion below highlights key issues using the example of irrigation projects.

Since Independence, major irrigation projects have been a national priority, as seen in Prime Minister Nehru's declaration that dams were the 'temples of modern India', and the First Five-Year Plan allocating 25 per cent of its budget to water resource management. The political focus on water continues to the present day, as seen in the recent formation of the Ministry of Jalshakti by the Central government. It is also a high priority for many state governments.[33]

India's irrigation strategy has historically emphasized major and medium irrigation (MMI) projects. From the First to the Eleventh Five-Year Plan periods, MMI projects accounted for around 60 per cent of all water resources management expenditure, with over 60 per cent being capital expenditure. Between 2008–09 and 2016–17, capital expenditure on MMI projects accounted for 8 to 15 per cent of the Government of India's total capital expenditure across *all* sectors.[34] However, the quality of this spending is low on multiple dimensions including project selection, execution, and maintenance.

Project choice and location

MMI projects are mainly executed at the state level, but receive substantial funding from the Central government, notably through the Accelerated Irrigation Benefits Programme (AIBP).[35] Since states compete for AIBP funds, projects tend to be concentrated in larger, politically powerful states. In 2011, the Planning Commission estimated that 94 per cent of all MMI investment went to just fourteen states, home to only 60 per cent of India's population. The same pattern is seen within states. For instance, in Maharashtra, irrigation investments have been concentrated in plantation-rich and politically powerful western Maharashtra, at the cost of other regions.[36]

Further, MMI projects are often undertaken in locations with neither the most irrigation potential nor the greatest requirement. In other cases, inadequate planning for land acquisition, resettlement, and clearances leads to stalled projects.[37] These inefficiencies reflect strong incentives for politicians to announce and set up big projects in their areas of influence as visible markers of achievement, and the large potential for corruption through using politically favoured contractors in these projects.[38]

Project execution

A good metric of poor spending quality in capital projects is time and cost overruns relative to initial commitments. A 2018 CAG audit of 115 MMI projects prioritized under the AIBP revealed significant delays (Table 6.3).[39] Out of thirty completed projects, 60 per cent were delayed by over two years. Among the 85 ongoing ones, *only 3 per cent* were on time: 31 per cent were delayed by two to five years, 32 per cent were delayed by five to ten years, and 34 per cent were delayed by over ten years!

Table 6.3: Time Delays in Irrigation Projects (based on Sample Audited by CAG)

Delay	Completed Projects	Ongoing Projects
0 years (on time)	7 (23 per cent)	3 (3 per cent)
<2 years	5 (17 per cent)	0
2–5 years	11 (37 per cent)	26 (31 per cent)
5–10 years	6 (20 per cent)	27 (32 per cent)
>10 years	1 (3 per cent)	29 (34 per cent)
Total*	30	85

Note(s): Data from the Accelerated Irrigation Benefit Program report, published by the Comptroller Auditor General (CAG) of India in 2019.

The time delays also increase project costs. These audited projects had cost overruns of over Rs 1,20,000 crore, averaging 294 per cent or nearly triple the original budget. Several projects had overruns beyond 1000 per cent, and some even exceeded 5000 per cent, implying final costs were *ten to fifty times higher* than originally budgeted![40]

Project maintenance

Finally, even when projects are completed, poor maintenance hinders their use. For instance, the Irrigation Potential Created on a set of audited MMI projects was only 68 per cent and Irrigation Potential

Utilized was only 44 per cent of total potential.[41] This partly reflects the higher priority placed on new projects, with greater potential for bribes and kickbacks, than on maintaining existing projects.

This pattern is not unique to big dams. Most residents of urban India will be familiar with the sight of roads developing potholes in every monsoon, and needing to be built again! Overall, capital works in India often follow a 'Build-Neglect-Rebuild' model, and the CAG has repeatedly called out the poor standard of public works in multiple audit reports.

To summarize, there are large inefficiencies in capital expenditure in India, which have been documented in multiple CAG audit reports. Yet, the public is hardly aware of such waste of taxpayer money, and these issues are rarely discussed in Parliament or state assemblies. Further, CAG audit reports are used more to score political points than to *improve the processes* that contribute to poor spending in the first place. Since the CAG can only submit its reports to the legislature for action, the weakening of the legislature relative to the executive has also reduced the CAG's effectiveness (see Chapter 17).

2.3 Quality of salary spending

Table 6.2 shows that public employee salaries account for 21 per cent of government spending, and cost over Rs 12 lakh crore in 2019–20. As noted in Chapter 5, there are large inefficiencies in payroll spending due to (a) excessively high salaries, (b) no correlation between pay and productivity, (c) provider absence and low effort, (d) poor management of staff and processes, and (e) poor time use of existing staff. Thus, implementing the ideas in Chapter 5 can both boost state capacity for service delivery, and also improve public expenditure quality by making payroll spending more efficient.

2.4 Weak fund flow processes hurt quality of expenditure

Quality of expenditure is also hurt by an outdated public finance management system (PFMS) and the many layers through which funds have to pass before reaching the end user. This leads to large delays in getting funds from the disbursing authority to the spending entity. For instance, the Accountability Initiative's PAISA report traced fund flows in education and found that annual grants for teaching and learning materials often reach schools only near the end of the academic year. At this point, the value of these materials is sharply reduced relative to having them at the start of the year.[42]

The same problem is seen in health. A study by the National Institute for Public Finance and Policy (NIPFP) found that only 55 per cent of National Health Mission (NHM) funds were utilized between 2015 and 2017, and attributes this in large part to 'significant delays in release of funds from State treasuries to implementing agencies'.[43] The study noted that in Bihar a file has to pass through thirty-two desks before funds reach the field, with a corresponding number of twenty-five in Maharashtra![44]

The problem of late arrival of funds is compounded by 'use it or lose it' norms whereby departments with unspent funds at the fiscal year-end risk having their budget cut the next year. This pressures them to spend hastily towards the fiscal year-end, often sacrificing expenditure quality. For instance, the PAISA report notes that 60 per cent of the schools in their sample whitewashed their walls *every* year, likely reflecting the need to find projects that are easy to spend money on at the end of the fiscal year.[45]

Overall, weaknesses in India's PFMS lead to both delays in sanctioned funds reaching where they are supposed to go, and poor quality of spending once the funds get there. These are not just abstract problems but have real and painful consequences. A recent book on the travails of the PFMS starts by noting that sixty children died in a Gorakhpur government hospital in 2017, due to a lack of oxygen cylinders. The shortage arose because the government had not paid the oxygen vendor for over six months, resulting in the vendor stopping further supplies till payment was made.[46]

3. Improving Quality of Expenditure—Key Principles

The discussion above highlights the vast inefficiencies in how we spend public funds. Since the details of how to improve expenditure quality will vary by sector, this section focuses on the *principles* for doing so, whereas more specific ideas are presented in Chapters 11–16. Three key ways to improve the effectiveness of public spending are to improve processes for budget allocation, budget utilization, and fund flows.

3.1 Improving effectiveness of budget allocation

Public spending decisions are ultimately political. Yet, even holding political goals constant, budget allocation can be improved to boost both efficiency and equity by following the principles below.

Estimate and present RoI calculations for major spending items

First, we should analyse the public return on investment, or RoI, on different kinds of spending. Such RoI analysis is a basic first step in prudent financial management and one that any well-run company undertakes before spending even, say, Rs 10 crore.

Yet, governments in India often spend thousands of crores of taxpayer money without analysing its public RoI. While these calculations will need assumptions and pressure-testing, simply conducting them can improve clarity in making budgetary trade-offs amidst resource constraints. Even if RoI estimates are not always used in policy, just having them available as an input into policymaking can profoundly improve public expenditure quality, by helping decision-makers consider alternative uses for scarce public funds and better assess their relative strengths and weaknesses.

The ultimate goal should be to rank every major public spending proposal from highest to lowest RoI. Governments could then undertake projects in descending order of RoI up to their fiscal limits. If there are unfunded high RoI projects, it could make sense to borrow for them if the RoI exceeds the cost of borrowing.[47] Projects with RoI below borrowing costs should be de-prioritized, and ongoing spending with a negative RoI should be phased out over time. While equity goals may justify some low RoI projects, it is often possible to meet equity goals more efficiently as outlined later in this section.

Of course, the data needed for such RoI calculations may not always be available, and most state governments in India lack the technical capacity to conduct such analysis. However, given the vast sums of taxpayer money involved, it is critical to invest in the technical capacity and data systems needed for such analysis (see Section 4).

Consider the broader economic effects of proposed policies and expenditure

Beyond the direct RoI of public spending, it is essential to also consider the indirect ripple effects of policies on the broader economy. For instance, finance departments assess the *affordability* of subsidies, but they spend much less time on analysing their indirect costs. Yet, these costs can be substantial, and decrease the efficiency of how we use land, labour, and capital, across the *entire economy* (see Chapter 16).

Again, the case of farm electricity subsidies illustrates the distortions and indirect costs of subsidies. These include: (a) rapid groundwater depletion, and a growing national water crisis, (b) increased air pollution in north India due to the burning of paddy stubble by farmers in Punjab and Haryana, who would not be growing paddy without the subsidies, (c) insolvency of electricity distribution companies, which hurts investment in power generation,[48] and (d) adverse effects on industrial development and creation of higher-quality jobs due to the practice of increasing industrial power tariffs to cross-subsidize free agricultural power (see Chapter 16). Over time, these indirect costs are likely to far exceed the direct fiscal cost of the electricity subsidies themselves, and it is essential to account for these costs in policymaking and budget allocation.

Estimate and present the distributional impacts of major spending items

Third, we should also analyse the distributional effects of major spending items. In public finance terms, this is called 'incidence analysis'. Two insightful ways to do this are to analyse where programme beneficiaries fall in the income distribution (economic incidence) and where they are located (spatial incidence).

Figure 6.1 provides a good example of analysing the economic incidence of spending. It shows that fertilizer and electricity subsidies in agriculture mainly go to rich farmers, who are least in need of the subsidy. In multiple states, the top 5 per cent of households by landholding receive nearly 50 per cent of the subsidy! Yet, the public justification for free electricity is that it supports farmers, who are perceived to be poor. So, presenting such incidence analysis publicly can help build public and political support for pro-poor subsidy reforms of the kind described in Chapters 15 and 16.

Turning to spatial incidence, there are large regional inequalities in public spending and access to services even within states. For instance, an NIPFP study of Bihar and Tamil Nadu found large variations in per capita primary health spending across districts within the same state, with some districts receiving 2.5 to 3 times as much as others.[49] Interestingly, the within-state variation across districts was progressive (pro-poor) in Tamil Nadu, whereas it was regressive (pro-rich) in Bihar. Thus, while it is well known that there is variation *across* states in resources for health and education (especially because the Finance Commission focuses on this issue), we should also pay more attention to spatial inequalities *within* states.

Analysing the distributional effects of policies is important both ethically and politically. Ethically, it allows us to clearly see who benefits from a policy, and examine if it meets the Mahatma Gandhi test of benefiting the most marginalized members of society.[50] Politically, identifying groups adversely affected by a policy can help in identifying ways to compensate them to obtain their buy-in for a positive-sum reform. It can also help to build public support for pro-poor reforms, by showing that the beneficiaries of India's most inefficient policies (like farm electricity subsidies) are disproportionately better off.

Putting it together: Evaluate budget allocations based on both equity and efficiency

Integrating the concepts above, we can analyse the quality of expenditure for any major proposed spending by assessing its impacts on *both* equity and efficiency, using the 2x2 framework in Figure 6.2. To locate policy ideas on this chart, we could use the estimated RoI (including indirect effects) for the 'efficiency' axis. For the 'equity' axis, we could use simple measures such as the fraction of spending that reaches the poorest 10, 20, or 50 per cent of the population, or more statistically sophisticated measures.[51]

Figure 6.2: Conceptualizing Efficiency and Equity

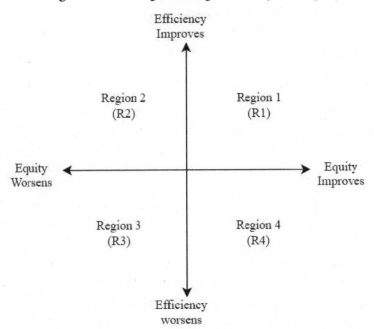

Figure 6.2 provides a *foundational framework* for this book, and offers a unified way to think about the quality of public expenditure. It includes viewpoints of economics, ethics, and politics by considering the efficiency, equity, and distributional impacts of policies.

Throughout this book, we will see vast differences in the equity and efficiency impacts of policies and programmes. There are some in Region 1 (R1) that improve *both* equity and efficiency; some in Region 3 (R3) that hurt both; some in Region 2 (R2) that boost efficiency but may increase inequality; and others in Region 4 (R4) that promote equity but may hurt efficiency.[52] A key goal of this book is to use data and evidence to identify R1 ideas that we should invest more in, and highlight R3 items that we should spend less on. Later chapters will analyse and locate specific policies in the four regions. Here, I briefly illustrate examples of R1 and R3 policies from current and previous chapters.

For instance, free electricity for farmers is an excellent example of an R3 'welfare' policy that hurts both equity and efficiency, for reasons explained in this chapter. Thus, replacing it with income transfers to farmers up to a landholding cap will improve both equity and efficiency and therefore be an R1 reform idea (see Chapters 15 and 16).

Drawing from Chapter 5, other examples of R3 spending are large unconditional pay increases for government employees, or reverting them to the old pension scheme. Spending scarce taxpayer funds this way hurts equity since public employees are already in the top 5 to 10 per cent of India's income distribution, and it does not improve productivity as shown in Chapter 5. In contrast, slowing the growth of public-sector pay and using these funds to hire more public employees on fixed-term contracts, which are renewable based on performance, is an R1 idea. It would increase efficiency by improving service delivery. It would also boost equity by creating more jobs, and by directly benefiting the poor, who disproportionately use public services.

Stakeholders may prioritize R2 or R4 policies based on the relative weight they place on equity and efficiency, and on current versus future welfare. Yet, a balance between R2 and R4 is essential. The risk of prioritizing R4 is that improving current equity may come at the cost of economic stagnation and lower future welfare, as was the case under our failed socialist policies. The risk of just focusing on R2 is that faster economic growth is often accompanied by growing inequality and will not by itself deliver benefits for all citizens without active policy intervention. So, we should think of R2 and R4 spending as making up a *portfolio* of public investments, where R2 items promote growth and higher future welfare, and R4 spending ensures that the benefits of growth improve current welfare for more people. Such a balanced portfolio will enable inclusive growth.

However, a key message of this book is that there is often *no trade-off* between equity and efficiency, because we spend *lakhs of crores* of taxpayer funds every year on R3 items. If we identify these items and reduce the amount spent on them, we can find the money to invest in the many R1 ideas identified in this book. Pivoting public expenditure from R3 to R1 will allow us to accelerate India's development, deliver better outcomes at any level of GDP per capita, and also improve equity. At a minimum, if cutting funds to R3 items is politically difficult, we should aim to build a broad national consensus to at least slow the growth of R3 spending, and allocate those funds to R1 items.

3.2 Improving effectiveness of expenditure

The first step in improving expenditure quality is to improve budget allocation, which is led by the finance department. But once allocations are made, the spending is done by individual departments. While these expenditures are subject to procedural audits by the CAG, we pay much less attention to whether budgets are used effectively to deliver outcomes. Three principles can help improve effectiveness of departmental spending: prioritizing cost effectiveness, improving autonomy and rewarding performance, and improving post-contract management and accountability of vendors and contractors.

Institutionalize a focus on cost effectiveness

Post-budget discussions focus on the size of sectoral allocations, with an implicit assumption that higher sectoral spending will result in better outcomes. Yet, several studies show that spending more does not necessarily result in better outcomes. As documented throughout this book, we often spend sector-specific funds quite badly.

Why are we in this situation? A key reason is the lack of incentives in government for cost effectiveness. Departments often aim to maximize their budgets, and this goal is also supported by sector-level advocates, who often measure their success by getting higher budget allocations for their sector. This mindset was vividly illustrated by a formative experience I had many years ago: a senior official in the Ministry of Human Resource Development (now Ministry of Education) told me: 'I am not interested in cost effectiveness because if you show that we can deliver quality education with less money, the Finance Department will use it to cut our budget!'

My younger, naive self was stunned to hear a senior official say this and be oblivious to fiscal pressures, and the *moral imperative* of cost effectiveness given the need for funds in several *other* key development sectors. For instance, India spends much less on health than comparable countries (see Chapter 12), and we spend three times more on education than on health (see Table 6.1). Yet, over time, I have come to recognize that this behaviour was quite typical, and reflected the institutional incentives of every department to maximize its budget.[53] It can make sense for departments to ask for more money, even when they *know* that they will not get it due to fiscal constraints. This is because it helps them evade accountability: poor outcomes can be blamed on lack of funding, as opposed to lack of departmental initiative for finding cost-effective solutions.

So, if we want government departments to pay attention to cost effectiveness, we will need to incentivize it. This agenda should be led by state finance departments (with inputs from the planning department), because they are the main advocates for cost effectiveness within government. Finance departments should assure line departments and sectoral advocates that emphasizing cost effectiveness does not signal a lower commitment to a sector. Rather, the goal is to achieve better value for money and outcomes in *all* sectors. A practical approach to doing this is outlined in the next section.

Improving autonomy and rewarding performance

As noted in Chapter 5, high-performing organizations grant frontline staff autonomy over processes, while holding them accountable for outcomes. Yet, the Indian state does the exact opposite: it micro-manages employees on process, but does not hold anyone accountable for outcomes. We do the same with budgets. Even district-level officials, let alone staff at block or facility levels, often lack spending autonomy to meet key local needs, which limits their effectiveness. On the other hand, they are mostly held accountable for paperwork and procedural compliance, and rarely for outcomes.

So, to improve expenditure quality, we must increase both autonomy and accountability over public spending. Increasing autonomy will allow local officials to better use funds for local needs without waiting for multiple approvals, and increasing accountability for outcomes will incentivize them to use the funds in ways that deliver better outcomes.

One way to practically implement this idea is to use a 70:20:10 funding formula across districts based on equality, equity, and effectiveness. So, 70 per cent of sectoral funds could be allocated equally across all citizens in the state, reflecting an equality principle. 20 per cent could be allocated on a sliding scale of need to reflect the equity principle, and 10 per cent on a sliding scale of improvement to reward effectiveness. To begin, departments can allocate annual untied funds to districts, blocks, and facilities using 70:20 weights on equality and equity. The 10 per cent effectiveness component can be introduced in later years, and augment local budgets for discretionary expenditure. Both equity and effectiveness can be calculated using annual data on levels and changes in key district-level development indicators from the KPI survey discussed in Chapter 4.

A similar principle can be used for staff allocation and pay. They can be allocated across locations in ways that reflect a 70:20 weight on equality and equity.[54] Over time, 10 per cent of the total salary budget can be allocated to a performance-based bonus pool, and be used to pay staff bonuses at the district or block levels.[55] This approach is consistent with evidence that rewarding staff based on performance can be a force multiplier that improves the effectiveness of other inputs.[56]

The discussion also highlights the synergies between the ideas in Chapters 4, 5, and 6, and the value of taking a 'systems' approach to state capacity because strengthening one component (data systems) allows us to improve other components like personnel management, which in turn is key to improving quality of public expenditure.

Improving post-contract accountability for vendors and contractors

The principles above apply not only to government departments but also to private vendors and contractors. As we saw earlier, the quality of capital spending in India is quite poor. In practice, governments use private contractors to carry out most of the work for capital projects, and the volume of such public procurement in India likely exceeds Rs 5 lakh crore every year.[57] Thus, a key component of improving the quality of capital expenditure in India is to improve the performance of private contractors.

However, while government systems pay a lot of attention to the process of contracting and tendering up to the point of awarding contracts, they pay a lot less attention to how contractors perform *after* being awarded their contracts. One measure of this inattention is the large number of time and cost overruns documented in Section 2.2.

This problem partly reflects power asymmetry at different points in time. Before contract awarding, the government has the upper hand since multiple vendors are competing for the project. However, after a contract is awarded, vendors often have the upper hand because the project needs to be completed, and the government cannot afford the time and cost delays of re-awarding the contract midway through execution. Hence, vendors often underbid during tendering to increase their chance of winning the contract, and seek more funds later, when their bargaining position is stronger. Another frequent outcome is the production of sub-standard output reflecting the lower bid amounts.

Thus, to improve the quality of capital expenditure, we need to strengthen systems for post-contract accountability. A starting point can be to build a Management Information System (MIS) of all contracts above a certain value, and start recording post-contract quality metrics in the MIS. Starting with simple metrics such as cost and time overruns, the MIS can eventually include quality ratings from random sample-based audits. Over time, vendor reputations based on these measures of post-contract quality appraisal can be given greater weight in contract-awarding decisions. Building a dynamic procurement system that awards greater market share over time to high-performing contractors can significantly improve the quality of capital spending over time.[58]

3.3 Improving timing and process of fund flows

In addition to allocating public money better, and incentivizing departments to spend their allocations more effectively, a third key principle is to improve the process and timing of fund flows. Fund flow issues mainly reflect the multiple levels of government that funds have to pass through to reach their final recipient. Funds get stuck at each level due to the need for approvals to allow funds to flow to the next level. For many programmes, the multiple levels of approvals also engender corruption.

A practical solution to reduce these delays is to directly transfer funds to end users. Thanks to technological advances, this can now happen almost instantly. This is why direct benefit transfers (DBT) have become a popular way for governments to transfer funds to beneficiaries, and research studies have shown that doing so can reduce leakage as well as payment delays. The DBT approach can also be institutionalized for transferring funds to government offices and facilities at the beginning of the fiscal year itself. If a 70:20:10 principle is adopted at the time of making the budget with a quantum of discretionary funds identified for different levels of government, 90 per cent of these funds can be directly disbursed to the entity that has to spend it shortly after the budget.

We can also reduce delays in fund flows by creating digital records of every transfer combined with dashboards for real-time visibility on where money is stuck. These dashboards will enable senior officials to make speed of fund flows a salient metric for performance management and evaluation. This can be done by monitoring if the intended recipients (individuals or entities) are receiving funds promptly, and making this a key performance indicator for departments.

Improving the speed of fund flows will also reduce the problem of rushed, low-quality expenditure at the fiscal year-end. It will enable more thoughtful and useful expenditure at the start of the fiscal year. Of course, it will be necessary for spending units to preserve some funds for unexpected uses. One way to reduce the risk that this money is spent poorly at fiscal year-end is to soften the 'use it or lose it' norms of budget allocation and allow a rollover of at least some unspent funds to the next fiscal year. This will also help with ensuring availability of funds at the start of the new fiscal year, when fund allocations may not have reached the spending entity.[59]

4. Improving Quality of Expenditure—an Action Roadmap

As mentioned earlier, the sector chapters will discuss specific ideas for improving value for money. This section focuses on ideas that finance departments can implement to improve the quality of expenditure throughout the government.

4.1 Invest in technical and analytical capacity in state finance departments

The principles in Section 3 are conceptually straightforward, but applying them in practice requires dedicated technical capacity to conduct and validate the analysis to feed into budget decisions. Currently, key considerations such as return on investment on major spending items, economic and spatial incidence of expenditure, incentive effects of tax and subsidy policies, or cost effectiveness of proposed spending versus alternative options rarely feature in budget decisions or in public discourse on budgets.

One way forward is to create a specialized unit within state finance departments to focus on 'strategic budgeting'. This unit would conduct analysis of the kind outlined in Section 3 on major current and proposed future spending items and provide these as inputs into the budgeting process. It would also stay connected with the latest research to better incorporate evidence into policy and budgeting. The benefits of investing in such a unit are likely to far exceed the costs, since this kind of analysis can improve the effectiveness of hundreds of thousands of crores of public spending every year.

In a public discussion with the then chief economic adviser (CEA) to the Government of India (Dr Arvind Subramanian) in 2015, I had made a case for each state to have its own CEA, noting that Indian states had populations larger than many countries, and that it was imperative that states have the technical capacity to conduct the analysis needed to improve their quality of expenditure.[60] Dr Subramanian agreed and noted that some states had, on their own, expressed interest in such an idea. So, the creation of such a 'strategic budgeting' unit should be welcomed by state finance departments and should be a *top priority* for improving India's public expenditure quality.[61]

The specific institutional form may vary across states. Options include one or more of: (a) an in-house CEA leading a team of economic analysts; (b) an economic advisory council of external experts, who provide inputs on specific areas of their interest and expertise, which is a model announced by Tamil Nadu in 2021; (c) building close partnerships with local research institutes focused on state-level fiscal analysis such as the Gulati Institute in Kerala, the Asian Development Research Institute (ADRI) in Bihar, or the Centre for Budget and Policy Studies in Karnataka; (d) hiring teams of external professionals on medium-term contracts, a model that Andhra Pradesh has initiated in 2023.[62] States can also seek technical assistance from institutions such as NIPFP or the state finances research unit within the RBI, and request (and pay for) a few dedicated staff in these institutions to conduct state-specific research and analysis.[63]

4.2 Institutionalize a focus on quality of expenditure in budget processes

The analysis above is a key starting point, but will remain an academic exercise unless its outputs are institutionalized in the budget process. Concretely, finance and line departments should jointly review the analysis, and use it to guide a conversation on how various budget expenditure items are contributing to the development goals of the state. These discussions should aim to identify ideas in R1 in Figure 6.2 to prioritize for more funding, and also identify areas in R3 to prioritize for cutting spending.

A practical way of doing this is for the finance department to ask line departments to list their top new spending priorities each year, and ideas for saving money by reducing fraud, waste, and ineffective spending. The key innovation is that finance departments should encourage line departments to implement the proposed cost savings and *commit* that the saved funds can be used to finance the desired new programmes. At present, line departments have few incentives to save money since the finance department will often just take the money back.[64] This simple change can promote a culture of cost effectiveness, by allowing departments to use saved funds for new priorities.

Of course, in practice, it is politically difficult to cut existing spending, around which interest groups would have already coalesced. So, a more realistic approach may be to apply the budgeting principles outlined above to *new* spending. In practice, this would imply slowing the growth of spending on R3 items and allocating more of the annual budget increase due to revenue growth to R1 activities. Consistently implementing a process like this for a decade or more will meaningfully improve the quality of public expenditure, and help to accelerate India's development (see Chapter 10).

4.3 Use strategic budgeting analysis for better public communication

Budget making is an inherently political process and a central way in which the democratic aspirations of people are reflected. Governments should therefore invest not just in economic analysis but also in better public communication of the key insights from the analysis to facilitate more informed discourse on how public funds are spent.

One way to institutionalize 'strategic budgeting' in public communications is for state governments to present key insights in their state economic surveys. Just like the national economic survey, state-level surveys are meant to provide an overview of state performance across different sectors, justify public spending, and present policy ideas. Since these surveys are presented in the state legislative assembly alongside the budget, they are the right platform to present analysis on RoI, incidence of expenditure, and the rationale for proposed budget allocations.

Strategic budgeting analysis can help political leaders make more informed decisions, and also communicate them better. For instance, voters may want the government to support farmers but may not be aware of the true economic costs of current subsidies, or the extent to which they mainly benefit large landowners. Thus, politicians should welcome a strategic budgeting unit that can provide them with a well-analysed menu of ideas for achieving development goals. With such analysis, political leaders can make better decisions, and also use the data and analysis for public communication, stakeholder engagement, and consensus-building around specific reforms.

Finally, voters are sophisticated and often willing to make short-term sacrifices if they can trust that these will pay off in the future. For instance, in our research on Aadhaar-authenticated transfers in the PDS, we found that despite facing personal hassles, many survey respondents supported the reform because they felt it would reduce corruption. Thus, providing political leaders with analysis and visual materials can help them better communicate policy choices and trade-offs to voters and build public support for policies that will deliver better medium- and long-term outcomes.

4.4 Pay Commission reforms

Table 6.2 shows that one of the biggest line items in government budgets is salaries. Similar to the Central government, state government employee salaries and raises are also set by periodic Pay Commissions. These raises take up a substantial portion of the budget, often leaving little money for many R1 ideas. But as we have seen, large raises for incumbent employees are an R3 idea that hurts both equity and efficiency.

One evidence-backed way of paying government employees well, but also benefiting public welfare is to move from unconditional pay raises to linking at least some pay to performance. This is not a new idea and has been recommended by several past Pay Commissions. However, it has not been implemented due to the difficulty of measuring performance. So, the challenge is not the acceptability of the idea of performance-linked pay, but the feasibility of implementation. How then should we proceed?

One practically feasible way of introducing variable pay in government even without a performance measurement system is to link pay growth to the growth of state revenues. So governments can earmark some of the recommended Pay Commission increases for variable pay that is linked to state revenues.[65] Doing so has several benefits.

First, it will improve macro-fiscal stability since salary expenses will adjust with state revenues. Currently, when there is an economic downturn, development expenditure gets squeezed because salary payments are fixed.[66] With variable pay, salaries rise when the state does well and fall when it does not, providing an 'automatic stabilizer' for states' macroeconomic management. Second, such a reform can boost employee motivation: linking the states' performance to their own well-being makes them direct stakeholders in the state's growth. Third, if states improve outcome measurement or build an HRMIS to track employee competencies, as outlined in Chapters 4 and 5, the variable pay component can start including some weight on department, district, block, and individual performance. Thus, setting aside funds for variable pay at the time of Pay Commission increases makes it possible to introduce performance-linked pay when the measurement infrastructure is ready without an *additional* financial burden.[67]

Crucially, implementing such a variable pay system will be cost-neutral. It will neither increase payroll costs, which will hurt public finances; nor decrease total pay, which will be resisted by employees. The key difference is that instead of being used fully for an across-the-board pay increase, the same salary budget will be used to provide some unconditional increases (say, for inflation) and some variable pay that can be linked to performance once performance measurement systems are in place.[68] So, average pay will stay the same, but stronger performers will be recognized with higher pay. Over time, such a reform can change the entire culture of government departments and be a force multiplier to improve the quality of *all* other public spending.

4.5 An innovation fund for improving expenditure quality

Despite limited resources, many Indian government officials devise ingenious solutions to local problems. Yet, many of these innovations are not scaled up and often do not even persist locally, as successor officers might have different priorities. Conversely, the spread of an innovation often depends more on effective marketing of the idea than credible evidence on its actual impact. In some cases, this can lead to scaling up of ideas that look excellent on paper and in presentations but have little real impact.[69]

Strategic budgeting should result in scaling up cost-effective ideas and programmes, and reducing spending on ineffective ones. So, we should encourage innovations, and also generate evidence on their impacts. One way to meet both goals is for finance departments to create an innovation fund for pilots and evaluations. Departments could seek funds for testing promising new ideas, and would commit to an independent evaluation of impact and cost effectiveness. Funding can grow in stages: a Phase I for a proof of concept and prototyping ideas, a Phase II for testing and evaluating Phase I successes at a moderate scale, and a Phase III to scale up proven solutions.

Such an approach is already used by agencies such as USAID's Development Innovation Ventures (DIV) and the Global Innovation Fund (GIF), who provide funds to test and scale cost-effective new ideas. The government of Tamil Nadu has adopted a similar approach, setting a precedent for other states. Even with modest allocations, such an innovation fund can improve quality of expenditure by stimulating innovation within the government, and also introducing robust evidentiary standards on impact and cost effectiveness prior to scaling potentially expensive programmes.

5. Conclusion

Using taxpayer funds effectively is a central function of governments. Given the sheer size of government spending, improving its quality is perhaps *the* most leveraged way of accelerating India's development at scale. For a low-middle income country like India, cost-effective public expenditure is not just an economic virtue but a moral imperative.[70]

This chapter highlights core public finance ideas that are often overlooked in India's policy discourse. One reason for this neglect is our underinvestment in technical capacity to better analyse the quality of public expenditure, and to communicate these insights to political leaders and the public. This chapter aims to highlight the importance of doing so by documenting key facts on public finance and expenditure in India, explaining how and why our quality of expenditure is poor, providing principles for improving the quality of expenditure, and sketching out an implementation road map.

With recent advances in data availability and analytical techniques, these ideas are not just a conceptual pipe dream but are quite practical to implement. Consistently implementing them will enable states to significantly improve the quality of public expenditure, deliver better development outcomes for any given level of GDP/capita, and thereby accelerate India's development.

Chapter 7

Public Finance—Revenue

Raising revenue is an essential enabler for a state to perform its functions. Historians have noted that modern states only became possible with the advent of agriculture, because the immovable and visible nature of crop production made it easy to collect a fraction of agricultural output as taxes.[1] In India, historical treatises like the *Arthashastra* recognize the centrality of revenue for state functioning and outline principles for effective taxation. Thus, raising adequate revenue while minimizing inconvenience to citizens, and disincentives for productive effort is a crucial component of state capacity.[2]

Yet, state and Central governments in India face several challenges in raising revenues. This partly reflects our stage of development. As countries get richer, there is more formalization of economic activity, which makes it easier to collect taxes, leading to higher tax-to-GDP ratios. However, India's inadequate revenue collection also reflects inefficiencies in tax design and administration. Low revenue, in turn, limits our ability to invest in several critical areas, including revenue collection itself!

The good news is that there is a growing body of high-quality global evidence on how to cost-effectively improve tax administration and compliance. Further, advances in data analytics combined with large volumes of data, especially from the GST, enable us to significantly improve tax collection. Yet, much of this potential remains untapped. Implementing reforms based on both first principles and evidence can: (a) improve the design of revenue collection instruments; (b) reduce compliance costs and simplify the taxpayer experience;

(c) improve both the quantity and *quality* of revenue collection, and (d) minimize collateral damage to the economy from the process of taxation itself.

Beyond the economics of effective taxation, this chapter also discusses its politics. In particular, a key challenge for revenue collection is the eroded fiscal compact between the state and taxpayers in India. Many tax-paying citizens see little connection between taxes paid and public services received. This, in turn, legitimizes tax evasion in their minds. Thus, improving this fiscal compact by tightening the link between taxes paid and public services received will also increase public willingness to pay their taxes.

This chapter comprises three sections. The first overviews key facts on revenue collection in India, places them in a global perspective, and briefly summarizes challenges in the status quo. The second discusses economic and political principles of revenue collection, and summarizes recent evidence on improving tax administration and compliance. The final section presents implementable ideas to increase both the quantity and quality of revenue collected, with a focus on state-level actions.

1. Key Facts on Government Revenue in India

1.1 India's tax-to-GDP ratio in global perspective

India's tax-to-GDP ratio is low relative to higher-income countries. As of 2018–19, the total tax revenue across Central and state governments was Rs 32.8 lakh crore, or 17.4 per cent of India's nominal GDP of Rs 189 lakh crore in 2018–19.[3] In contrast, the average for OECD country national governments was 34.1 per cent, nearly double that of India.

However, once we adjust for GDP per capita, India's tax-to-GDP ratio is no longer a global outlier as seen in Figures 7.1 and 7.2. Figure 7.1 shows that richer countries have a higher tax-to-GDP ratio, and Figure 7.2 shows that this ratio increases over time. These patterns reflect greater formalization of the economy in richer countries, and in poorer countries as they grow. Formalization of economic activity boosts productivity and the GDP, and also generates better official records that facilitate tax collection.[4]

Increasing tax-to-GDP ratio over time reflects growth in both the administrative *ability* to tax and political *willingness* to tax and be taxed. Both factors grew in Europe and the US in the 1930s and 1940s to mobilize the economy to fight and finance the Second World War, consistent with Charles Tilly's view that 'War made the state.'[5] After the war, higher tax rates were maintained, and the proceeds of the 'peace dividend' were used to finance the modern welfare state, as noted in Chapter 2.[6] The higher tax collections in Sweden and France, relative to the US and the UK, reflect political support for a more generous welfare state in these countries—even at the cost of higher taxes (Figure 7.2).[7]

India's tax collections align with global benchmarks and we only slightly underperform relative to GDP/capita (Figure 7.1). In fact, India has achieved a 17 per cent tax-to-GDP ratio at a lower income than the US or the UK had when they reached this ratio. India's ratio is comparable to Vietnam, which has a similar GDP/capita. Finally, even China had the same tax-to-GDP ratio as India when it had the same level of GDP/capita as India.[8]

There are two key implications for India. First, our revenue collection is in line with global and historical benchmarks. However, we have considerable scope to improve both the quantity and *quality* of revenue collection. In particular, we now have much better technology and data that make it possible to collect higher amounts of tax revenue at lower administrative cost, even at lower levels of GDP/capita.

Second, we need to deliver quality public services and welfare for all Indians, despite having a tax-to-GDP ratio that is only *half* of that in OECD countries. Since spending is constrained by revenue, and tax-to-GDP ratios only grow slowly, we cannot achieve our development goals just by advocating for higher budgets for social sectors. Rather, it is imperative to prioritize value for money in public spending, which is partly why Chapter 6 on boosting quality of public expenditure appears before Chapter 7 on revenue.

Figure 7.1: Cross-Country Comparison of Tax-to-GDP Ratio by GDP/Capita

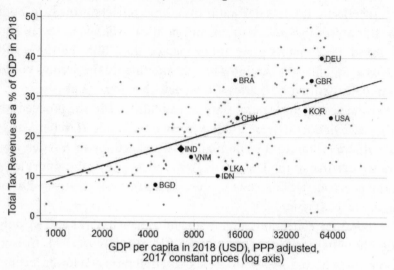

Note(s): Tax revenue data from Our World in Data; GDP per capita from the World Bank; graph created by author.

Figure 7.2: Historical Evolution of Tax-to-GDP Ratio over Time

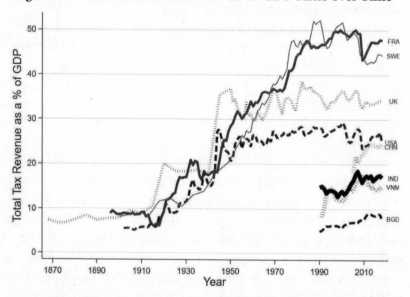

Note(s): Data from Piketty (2014) and Our World in Data, graph created by author.

1.2 Volume and composition of tax collection by level of government

COVID-19-induced disruptions in economic activity starting in March 2020 affected revenue collections in fiscal years 2019–20, 2020–21, and 2021–22, and audited figures for 2022–23 were not available when finalizing this draft. The analysis below therefore uses data from 2018–19, which better represents a steady state.[9]

Figure 7.3 breaks down total tax collection between the Central and state governments in 2018–19. It shows that the Central government collected 63 per cent, with state governments accounting for the remaining 37 per cent. Local governments account for a very small share of revenue and this is discussed in the next chapter.

Figure 7.3: Distribution of Taxes Collected at Central and State Government Levels by Type (2018–19)

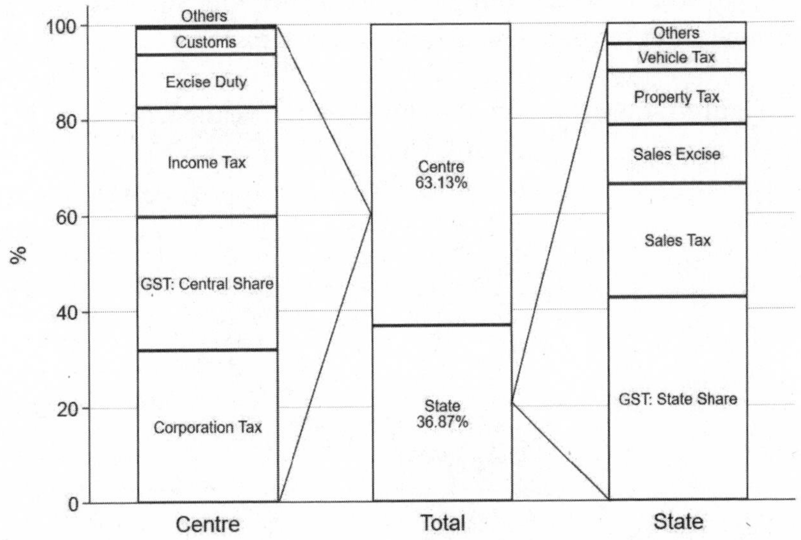

Note(s): Central government data from Bag 5 (Receipts), Ministry of Finance; state government data from the Study of State Finances, Reserve Bank of India (RBI); graph created by author.

The Central government's main revenue sources include income tax, corporate tax and customs taxes. State governments primarily rely on sales tax (mainly on petroleum), excise tax (mainly on alcohol), property and land taxes, and vehicle taxes. The Goods and Services Tax (GST) is jointly administered by the Central and state governments, with revenues shared equally.[10] Tax revenues in 2018–19 were approximately Rs 33 lakh crore. Non-tax revenues (not shown in Figure 7.2) amounted to Rs 4.5 lakh crore yielding a total revenue of Rs 37.5 lakh crore.[11]

While over 60 per cent of India's public revenue is collected by the Central government, around 60 per cent of spending is conducted by states.[12] The difference between state governments' own revenues and spending is accounted for by tied and untied transfers from the Central government (see Chapter 6), and awards of the Finance Commission, which is a constitutional body that recommends a distribution of the 'divisible pool' of national tax revenues between Central and state governments. Finance Commission awards are an important means of supporting equity across India and typically award poorer states larger transfers.[13] Hence, lower-income states rely more on transfers from the Central government, while higher-income states rely more on their own revenues.

Figure 7.4: States' Own Revenue/Total Revenue Expenditure by GDP/Capita

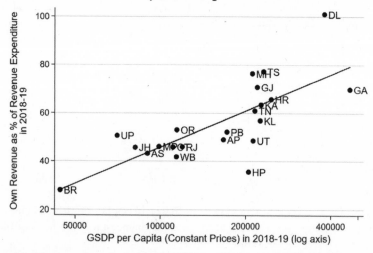

Note(s): Revenue data from 'Study of State Finances', RBI; GSDP data from RBI; Population Data from Ministry of Health and Family Welfare (MoHFW) Projections in 2019.

Figure 7.4 shows the positive correlation between states' GDP/capita and reliance on their own revenues to fund expenditures. The share of states' total spending financed by their own revenues is over 70 per cent for Delhi, Maharashtra, Gujarat, Tamil Nadu, Telangana, and Haryana. In contrast, it is below 30 per cent for Bihar and below 50 per cent for states such as Madhya Pradesh, West Bengal, Jharkhand and Assam. States' own revenue share is also low for special category states with additional developmental challenges, such as Jammu and Kashmir and the north-eastern states.

Figures 7.3 and 7.4 also highlight that states can do a lot on their own to raise revenue. While the introduction of a uniform national GST has removed a key revenue instrument that states used to have control over, they still have numerous levers to raise revenues. These include actions on both tax policy and tax administration.

1.3 Key challenges in the status quo

While India's income-adjusted tax-to-GDP ratio is comparable to other countries (Figure 7.1), we can do much better. There are several weaknesses in both the administration and design of revenue collection in India, which are briefly summarized below.

Staffing

Tax administration in India has a separate structure and staffing at the Central and state government levels, reflecting the different taxes they are supposed to collect. Overall, the Central government has a more robust tax administration. It has two main agencies, the Central Board of Direct Taxes (CBDT) and the Central Board of Indirect Taxes and Customs (CBIC). Both have multiple specialized directorates and field offices, and are staffed by dedicated officers of the Indian Revenue Service (IRS).

However, even these apex central bodies face severe staff shortages. In 2020, 44 per cent of sanctioned posts in CBIC and 40 per cent in CBDT were vacant.[14] This problem has *worsened* over time relative to a staffing shortfall of 29 per cent reported in 2012.[15] While many of these vacancies are in class B and C positions, which may have become redundant with technology, the staffing problem is also acute at senior levels. In July 2021, 400 commissioner-and-above posts, and 73 of the 91 chief commissioner positions, were unfilled in the income tax department, some for over a year.[16] Yet, IRS officer recruitment through the UPSC fell by 74 per cent from 2013 to 2019.[17]

The situation is likely to be similar in states. While systematic state-level staffing data is not easily available, analysis of human resource allocations for GST enforcement in one state found vacancy rates of 15 per cent for GST officers (GSTOs), 24 per cent for GST inspectors (GSTIs) and 54 per cent for assistant commissioners (ACs) in 2021. Further, many staff held additional charges, resulting in a highly uneven workload with the number of taxpayers per GSTO ranging from 3000 to 45,000 across wards.[18]

Data and data analytics

Even the Goods and Services Tax (GST) system, which has the best data by far, faces challenges in adequately analysing this data. The GST taxes value addition at each production stage, with taxpayers reporting total sales and inputs costs, and paying tax on the difference, which is the 'value added'. Since businesses receive input tax credits (ITC) for payments to suppliers, they have incentives to report these purchases truthfully, which makes it difficult for suppliers to under-report their sales. Thus, the GST creates a self-enforcing tax system along the production value chain, with downstream purchasers verifying the sales of upstream suppliers.

The GST was a major tax reform that aimed to promote formalization of the Indian economy, simplify tax administration through digital records, and improve incentives for tax compliance. While it has resulted in substantial improvements in tax administration, and many of its early teething troubles have been addressed, it still faces challenges.

For instance, the GST system has to deal with a burgeoning industry of 'invoice mills' that generate fake invoices and report fake sales to downstream firms that the latter use to claim ITC, leading to considerable tax evasion. A recent government effort in 2023 uncovered fake invoices worth Rs 63,000 crore![19] Further, recovering dues is difficult, time consuming, and slow due to a combination of limited staffing in tax departments, and 'invoice mills' shutting down and re-emerging under new GST registration numbers.

Identifying invoice mills requires sophisticated analysis of GST data. Further, since recovering unpaid taxes is difficult, authorities need to flag suspicious entities early and catch them *before* their invoices are used to evade taxes. This is being done to some extent by the Central government. But states lack similar analytical capacity, and data sharing and validation between Central and state tax authorities is limited, which limits the effectiveness of fraud-detection algorithms, and that of state-level GST staff.[20]

The GST system is, at least, generating data and analysing it. Data quality for collecting other taxes is often worse. For instance, very few municipal corporations in India have a comprehensive list and details of all properties, which is a fundamental requirement for running an effective property tax system.

There is also limited capacity for data analysis in tax administration outside the GST. Tax departments in India gather and even digitize lots of information, but do not use it for regular analysis and insight generation, partly due to a lack of internal capacity to do so. This reflects a legacy of hiring and training staff to conduct field-based assessments as opposed to desk-based data analysis. Further, as noted in Chapter 5, lifetime employment and weak incentives and capacity for retraining make it difficult to pivot staff to a different way of functioning. Thus, data is collected more for administrative compliance, and is not being leveraged to full potential as a powerful tool for tax administration.

Arrears, assessments, and amnesties

One consequence of weaknesses in staffing and technical capacity is that governments in India are often not even able to collect outstanding taxes. For instance, recent CAG audit reports estimate revenue collection arrears of Rs 1,10,000 crore in Maharashtra, Rs 30,000 crore in UP, and Rs 13,000 crore in Rajasthan.[21] Out of these amounts, 27 per cent, 43 per cent and 18 per cent were pending for *over five years*.[22]

Arrears are defined as revenues assessed but not yet collected. But the figures above understate forgone revenue since they ignore irregularities in the assessment itself. For instance, tax officials and taxpayers often collude to lower the amount of tax assessed in return for bribes.[23] Consistent with this, CAG reports routinely note irregularities in tax assessments. For instance, CAG reports estimated irregularities of over Rs 4000 crore in UP and Rs 3500 crore in Bihar based on auditing a *sample* of assessments. Since this is only in the audited sample, the true figure is likely to be considerably larger.[24]

A striking indicator of weak tax administration in India is the use of tax amnesties. These amnesties let tax defaulters pay only a fraction of their dues in return for avoiding prosecution and penalties for past non-payment. Tax amnesties have been used by both Central and state governments, but have had limited success. Such amnesties can *further* reduce tax compliance, as they reward non-payment, and signal the state's limited ability for enforcement.

In addition to the implementation challenges noted above, revenue collection in India also faces many design challenges. These are discussed in the next section.

2. Key Principles and Evidence on Effective Revenue Collection

2.1 Economic principles for revenue collection

Pay attention to the quality of revenue in addition to its quantity

While officials diligently track tax collections and the quantity of revenue raised, they often overlook the *quality* of revenue collected, which is as or even more important.

What do we mean by the quality of revenue collection?

The key point is each rupee raised by the government usually costs more than one rupee. This is because the process of revenue collection creates *additional* economic costs. These include (a) administrative costs of tax collection; (b) time and effort spent in tax compliance, and most importantly; (c) the behavioural changes induced by taxes, including both legal tax avoidance and illegal tax evasion, which can cause large downstream distortions on resource allocation in the economy.

These unmeasured costs, especially from the last category, can be very high. Taxes hurt economic activity by reducing incentives to work and invest. Projects that may be profitable before taxes may not be viable after taxes. Hence, many potentially value-creating projects may not take place once taxes are accounted for. In general, taxation of economic activities raises their costs relative to true cost, and leads to a reduction in that activity below socially optimal levels.[25] These costs result in what economists call the 'deadweight loss' of taxation.

Taxes also generate unseen economic costs as a consequence of people's attempts to evade them. A good example comes from the widespread use of 'black money' in real estate. This increases the cash component of home purchases, which cannot be financed with a bank mortgage loan. This makes it much harder for tens of millions of Indians to buy a home, which is a dream for many of them. The reduced demand, in turn, hurts incentives for construction and expanding housing supply. Thus, India's entire housing sector, which is worth lakhs of crores of rupees and is pivotal for both economic growth and human well-being, has not grown to its full potential, partly due to real estate being a prime sector for tax evasion.[26] These indirect costs are likely to be much higher than the direct cost of forgone tax revenue itself.

So, the quality of revenue can be said to be poor when these additional costs of revenue collection are high. A key concept used by public finance economists to assess the quality of revenue is the marginal cost of public funds (MCPF), which refers to the total social cost of raising an additional rupee of tax revenue.

Based on their extensive work on Indian economic policy, public finance economists Vijay Kelkar and Ajay Shah estimate the MCPF in India to be around 3.[27] This implies that the process of transferring a rupee from taxpayers to the government generates an *additional* two rupees of unseen economic costs in the overall economy. In contrast, the MCPF in a high-income country such as the US is estimated to be between 1.3 and 1.7.

India's higher MCPF relative to richer countries, reflects (a) lower levels of formalization, which makes it harder to collect taxes, (b) a reliance on more inefficient taxes, (c) more human discretion and scope for corruption in tax administration, (d) higher levels of lobbying for differentiated tax rates, which increases both transaction costs and uncertainty, and (e) political constraints on taxation resulting in tax exemptions for large parts of the economy, which contributes to sub-optimally higher taxes on other parts.[28]

Elaborating on the last point, a key result in public finance theory is that the deadweight loss of taxation increases at the rate of the *square* of the tax rate. This implies that the economic cost of a 40 per cent tax rate is *quadruple* that of a 20 per cent tax rate, and that it is more efficient to have lower rates on a broader base of taxpayers than higher rates on fewer payers.[29] So, policies such as zero taxation on agricultural income, and the fact that *only 5 per cent* of Indians pay income tax,[30] result in sub-optimally higher taxes on those who do pay taxes, contributing to a high MCPF in India.

India's high MCPF has three key implications for its public finances. First, it underscores the need to boost the quality of public expenditure, and prioritize high RoI projects. An MCPF of 3 implies that the benefit-to-cost ratio for public spending needs to not only exceed one, but be above three! Much of our public spending does not meet this criterion (see Chapter 6). Second, there is sizeable variation in MCPF across different revenue collection strategies. So, we can improve the average quality of revenue by prioritizing tax instruments with a low MCPF and pruning back those with a high MCPF. Third, improving tax administration and reducing compliance costs can reduce MCPF, which will also improve the average quality of revenue.

Tax public 'bads' to improve quality of revenue

How can we reduce the MCPF and improve the average quality of revenue?

The first point to recognize is that taxing an activity increases its price, and reduces incentives to engage in it. So, increasing income taxes will typically reduce incentives to work, while taxing fossil fuels creates incentives for greater fuel efficiency.

A second key point is that individual decisions can create 'externalities' on others that they may not consider. For instance, when we choose to drive a car instead of taking public transportation, we consider the costs of fuel since we pay for it, but do not usually consider the cost imposed on *others* through increased road congestion or pollution. Similarly, while alcohol use may be a private decision, it can impose costs on others through an increased risk of domestic abuse or drunk-driving accidents.

Taken together, a core principle of public finance is that governments should tax public 'bads' that are detrimental to society. Taxing such activities will increase their price, and better reflect their social costs, inclusive of negative 'externalities' on others. Such taxes can not only raise revenues, but can *increase* social welfare by reducing socially undesirable outcomes like air pollution. Moreover, raising revenue from such sources also allows us to meet revenue targets without increasing taxes on 'good' productive items that we want to encourage, such as working, saving, investing, and innovating.

Tax more 'inelastic' factors of production

While taxing items with negative externalities makes sense, the revenue from these sources alone will not suffice to fund the scope of a modern state. Thus, some taxes on productive economic activity are inevitable. In this case, a core economics principle is that it is better to tax productive activities whose supply will not drop much in response to being taxed. In technical terms, these are referred to as having an 'inelastic' supply.

Items that cannot be moved, such as land, real estate, and natural resources, have a more 'inelastic' supply, making it more efficient to tax these rather than capital, which can be easily moved across borders. Further, while people are less mobile than capital, they can also migrate to other countries if tax rates get too high.[31] Thus, while capital and income taxes are an important component of a country's revenue portfolio, it is more efficient to tax relatively more 'fixed' resources, such as land, real estate, and natural resources.

Even when taxing immobile items such as land, minerals, and spectrum, it is important to design revenue collection instruments to incentivize value addition, and share risks and rewards between governments who own the underlying public asset, and developers who add value to it. So, if the government were to demand large upfront payments for mineral extraction or usage of spectrum, firms may simply not enter the fray. In contrast, revenue-sharing agreements, which share the risk and reward between the government and firms, are more likely to create value and also generate public revenues.

Reduce costs of tax enforcement and compliance, and their
unpredictability

The MCPF can also be reduced by lowering compliance costs. While the government reports its own administrative costs of tax collection, it often overlooks the broader costs of tax compliance borne by citizens and firms. This oversight is evident in frequent tax policy changes, such as GST rate modifications. Each change, including exceptions to rules, creates compliance costs of calculating new tax liabilities and re-optimizing decision-making for tens of thousands of economic actors, which raises the MCPF.

An even greater cost of frequent changes to tax policy is that the resulting policy uncertainty acts as a deterrent to economic activity, and raises the MCPF. Several studies from around the world have shown that policy uncertainty hinders investments and economic activity.[32] Thus, in addition to simplicity, a crucial component of reducing MCPF is to reduce the frequency and unpredictability of changes in tax rates and rules.

2.2 Political principles for revenue collection

People generally dislike taxes, and the political unpopularity of higher taxes is a key safeguard against state overreach into citizens' pockets. Taxation in a democracy should reflect voter consent, and not just 'top-down' decisions of governments. Beyond such philosophical ideals, a key practical consideration is that citizens' willingness to pay taxes is positively correlated with the perceived legitimacy of the taxation system.

What does it take for taxation to be seen as legitimate? Two key components are that citizens should feel that taxes are spent well, and that they have some say in how tax revenues are spent.[33] A recent US study finds that a positive outlook on the government lowers tax evasion.[34] Evidence from China shows that introducing village-level elections and empowering local decision-making *increased* local tax contributions, suggesting that tax payments increase when citizens have more say in how their taxes are spent.[35]

Applying these insights can improve tax compliance in India. India's income-tax paying classes have mostly seceded from public services, and mostly rely on the private sector for core services such as education, health, and even security. Further, government performance in areas they cannot secede from, such as urban roads and air quality, is perceived to be poor. The belief that they receive poor value in return for their taxes leads people to both justify their own tax evasion, and resist tax and fee increases.

In other words, the fiscal compact between taxpayers and the government in India is weak: taxpayers see little connection between the taxes they pay and the services they receive. To some extent, this is inevitable in a modern welfare state. Income-tax payers typically do not benefit from welfare, and welfare recipients do not usually pay income taxes. This is true in higher-income countries as well. However, the key difference is that most taxpayers in high-income countries also use public education and healthcare, and receive retirement social security income from the government, and hence feel a closer connection between taxes paid and services received.

So, we can strengthen the fiscal compact in India by linking revenue streams to specific uses. For instance, revenues from petroleum taxes can be earmarked for investing in public transportation. While funds are, of course, fungible, such earmarking may help build support for taxes and user fees. For instance, a recent survey shows that people's willingness to accept a carbon tax in India increases with education and awareness of the costs of pollution and climate change.[36] While taxes are never popular, conveying that such taxes will reduce pollution and fund environmentally friendly public transport can make them more palatable to the public. Alternatively, increasing local control over tax revenues can strengthen the link between taxation and local public goods that affect the daily quality of life. Specific ideas are discussed in the next section.

2.3 Empirical evidence on effective revenue collection

Beyond these economic and political principles, a growing body of empirical research offers insights on enhancing revenue collection. This is an exciting area of research and often features active collaborations between academics and tax authorities in several countries. Three key insights from this body of work are summarized below.[37]

The first is that high-quality, third-party information significantly helps revenue collection. For instance, income taxes from formal-sector employees can be collected through automatic payroll deductions, with employers serving as third-party reporters of income. This reduces income under-reporting, and boosts efficiency of tax collection.[38] Similarly, studies show that third-party information is a key reason for increased tax compliance under value-added tax (VAT) systems.[39] This is because downstream firms report their suppliers' sales to obtain input tax credits, just like in India's GST system.

A second is the importance of adequate staffing in the tax department. A recent study in Indonesia studied the effect of a reform that tripled staffing in revenue administration by setting up dedicated offices for medium-sized taxpayers. It found that this reform significantly raised collection of a wide variety of taxes, including corporate tax, VAT and payroll tax withholdings. Notably, the investment in personnel was highly cost effective, yielding *sixty-four times* more revenue than the cost of hiring the additional staff![40]

The third is the importance of incentives (or disincentives), for both taxpayers and tax department staff. Multiple studies show that sending deterrence messages to non-compliant taxpayers, with implicit or explicit threats of follow-up action, significantly increases tax payments. Recent studies have also shown that improving incentives of tax department employees, using either performance bonuses or better postings to reward performance, led to significant improvements in tax collections.[41]

At one level, these results are unsurprising since basic economic theory and common sense say that staffing and incentives should matter for revenue collection. But what makes the studies important is that they not only confirm the effectiveness of these interventions, but also find them to be highly cost-effective, generating many times more tax revenue than the cost of implementing them. Further, as discussed in Chapter 5, we *currently do not invest enough* in either staff strength, or in performance management systems in the public sector (including in tax departments). Yet, the evidence suggests that doing so could sharply improve performance and productivity in tax collection.

3. Some Implementable Reform Ideas

Given this book's focus, the discussion below emphasizes ideas that can be taken up at the state level. However, the principles above apply to all taxes, and may be especially relevant to the Central government since it is responsible for over 60 per cent of India's revenue collection, including income, capital gains, customs, and corporate taxes.

3.1 Improve strength, skills, and utilization of staff

The combination of large staff vacancies in tax departments around the country, and the evidence on the large returns to augmenting staffing suggest that this should be a top priority for revenue-collecting departments. At the same time, the problems noted in Chapter 5 also apply to tax department personnel, including lack of relevant technical skills, and weak performance measurement and accountability.

Thus, the ideas of Chapter 5 are especially relevant for tax departments. They should hire more staff, but on five-year renewable contracts. Such an approach will allow them to hire staff with specialized skills for tax collection such as accounting, data analytics and forensics, and law. It will also motivate employees to continually upgrade their skills and perform well since contract renewals will depend on performance. Over time, top-performing staff, who are empanelled for government contractual positions as described in Chapter 5, can be offered full-time positions. Such an approach will improve upon the status quo where candidates are hired into lifetime jobs through a general exam, and may not have the relevant skills, aptitude, or interest in effective tax administration.

This approach can also be used to hire public-spirited chartered accountants and lawyers via lateral entry on five-year contracts. Such professionals with private-sector experience are often best placed to understand loopholes exploited by tax evaders, and can be highly effective in helping the government reduce tax evasion. This process can also be used to identify existing government staff from *any* department who would like to work in the tax department on secondment and have relevant qualifications and aptitude. This would be a form of lateral hiring *within* the government to improve the match quality between the skills and roles of government staff.

It is also essential to upgrade the skills of existing tax department officials. Following the principles in Chapter 5, state governments should both invest in doing so, *and* institutionalize competence and skill-based promotions. The second part is critical to change the culture of tax departments to one that recognizes skills and competence.

Finally, existing staff can be organized and used more effectively. For instance, state GST staff are still organized into geographical wards, which is a legacy of the pre-GST days when tax assessments required a physical interface, and collecting and acting on local knowledge.[42] However, the GST generates massive amounts of data, and the returns to analysing this are now much higher. So, it could be more efficient to organize staff by sectors and value chains, train them to analyse data, identify areas for further scrutiny, and focus on segments with higher unrealized tax potential.

3.2 Strengthen investments in data analytics and forensics

Both research evidence and practical experience suggest that better data analysis can significantly improve tax administration. With thousands of taxpayers per tax officer, data-driven insights are essential for optimal time allocation. Investing in such analysis will not only boost tax collections but can also reduce harassment of honest taxpayers, by enabling precise identification of evaders.

The value of investing in data analysis is magnified by the dramatic increase in data availability after the introduction of the GST.

A data analysis unit can identify sectors, payee types, and specific taxpayer clusters for further scrutiny. It can analyse filing data and send customized deterrence messages to delinquent taxpayers, a strategy proven to be effective by several studies. It can also be used to improve performance measurement and management of officers. Such analysis can also reduce corruption by identifying suspicious assessment patterns, focusing on transactions with high officer discretion, and flag these for audit. Finally, it can improve citizen experiences with tax authorities by using outbound calls to random samples of taxpayers to measure their satisfaction with the tax assessment and payment process (see Chapter 4) and holding tax department officials accountable for these metrics.

Yet, despite these large potential benefits, very few state governments have invested in such analytical capacity. Since existing staff may lack the necessary skills, states should consider hiring external experts, especially those proficient in advanced data analytics and fraud prevention, to help to set up such an analytics unit, and empower them to hire top talent for the unit. These units could also collaborate with national and global academics, research institutions and expert agencies, to boost their capabilities and share learnings. The unit should report to top officials in the commercial taxes department, but should be institutionally stable regardless of transfers of these officials.

3.3 Pay special attention to revenue collection in urban areas

India is transforming into an increasingly urban country. The urban population share grew from 25.7 per cent in 1991 to 35.4 per cent in 2021, and is projected to reach 43.2 per cent (675 million people) in 2035.[43] So, in sheer numbers, 'urban India' will be the third-most populous country in the world after China and 'rural India'. Greater urbanization can catalyse India's development and also improve public service delivery. Cities, with their larger and denser populations, facilitate greater specialization, division of labour, choice for consumers, and competition among producers, all of which boost job creation, productivity, and economic growth (see Chapter 16).[44]

But, our cities cannot fulfil this promise without substantial changes. Indian cities suffer from low revenue, weak public infrastructure, declining air quality, increasing traffic congestion, and severely deficient amenities and services such as clean water and solid waste management.[45] While cities need massive investments to prepare for the urban transition, governments lack the resources to make them, keeping Indian cities stuck in a low-level trap. Fortunately, cities themselves can generate revenue, which can help to both pay for these investments and repay debt taken to finance them. However, urban revenue sources remain mostly untapped and should be a top priority going forward.

Property taxes

The first, and perhaps most important, revenue source we should augment is property taxes, whose current contribution to public revenues is negligible. In 2016, India's ratio of property tax to GDP was 0.07 per cent. In contrast, France and the UK generated nearly *fifty times more*, with ratios of 3.56 and 3.29 per cent respectively. Even among middle-income countries, property tax revenues are around *twenty times higher* in China (1.53 per cent), South Africa (1.33 per cent) and Brazil (1.47 per cent).[46]

Public welfare will be substantially improved if Indian cities can raise more revenue from property taxes. This aligns with several principles from Section 2. First, property is not mobile, making taxes easier to collect. Second, property taxes are controlled by local bodies and fund local public services, such as water, sewage, and transit. This clear link between taxation and services provides property taxes more legitimacy than many other taxes. Third, when tax revenue is used to improve local infrastructure, it can boost property values. This can create a virtuous cycle between taxation, provision of public goods, property value appreciation from the higher quality of life from living in that area, and a further increase in tax revenues to provide even better public goods.[47] Fourth, property taxes are highly progressive, since the poor typically do not own property. So, using the framework of Figure 6.2, raising property taxes would be an R1 reform that would improve both equity and efficiency of revenue collection.

Senior policymakers like Finance Secretary Dr T.V. Somanathan and former CEA Dr Arvind Subramanian have endorsed the importance of property taxes, noting in 2014 that 'few taxes are as compelling'.[48] Yet, a decade later, not much has changed. One reason is that state governments have not invested in building the capacity of urban local bodies to assess and collect property taxes. Areas of underinvestment include satellite mapping; cadastral surveys of land use and property boundaries; updated databases of property, ownership, titles, and liens; and automated systems for generating property tax invoices and following up on non-payment. One reason state governments have not prioritized property taxes is because it accrues to local bodies and not to them.

However, this neglect is short-sighted. Urbanization drives economic growth, and the resulting increase in economic activity will raise state government revenues through higher GST proceeds. So, boosting urbanization is good for states. But, urban growth is constrained by weak urban amenities, which are constrained by low revenues. To break out of this vicious cycle, state governments should invest in the capacity of local bodies to generate more property tax revenue, and make it a top priority. Using the framework of Figure 6.2, increasing property tax revenues would be an R1 idea that would increase both efficiency and equity relative to status quo revenue instruments.

Increase taxes on private transport in urban areas to finance better public transit

A second underused urban revenue source is higher charges for private transport. This can be done through a combination of higher road taxes, registration fees, parking fees, fossil fuel taxes, and congestion charges. These measures not only raise revenue, but also *increase* economic efficiency and population well-being because the current price of private transport overlooks its true social cost. Even excluding climate change costs, private transportation is under-priced due to the health and congestion costs imposed on others. Estimates suggest that urban pollution in India may be responsible for a loss of 650 million years of life.[49] Similarly, a recent NITI Aayog report estimates that traffic congestion in just the four largest Indian cities costs over Rs 1,50,000 crore each year from lower productivity, fuel waste, and accidents.[50]

So, higher carbon taxes and electronic road pricing will not only raise revenues but also improve social welfare by raising prices on activities with negative externalities. Parking fees should be higher and reflect the scarcity and value of urban land. The political costs of these taxes and fees should be managed by earmarking this revenue for investments in urban public transport and communicating the public interest rationale for such policies. This is the approach followed successfully by Singapore where high taxes and fees on private transport (including on cars, roads, and fuel) are combined with investments in and subsidies for socially efficient public transport.

For fossil fuels such as petrol and diesel, states should impose a cyclically adjusted tax that rises predictably over time. This tax would decrease when global oil prices rise and increase when they go down. The average tax rate and target price should rise steadily over time (say 2 per cent annually). Such an approach would (a) provide a steadily growing stream of 'efficient' revenue by taxing a commodity with negative pollution and congestion externalities, (b) cushion consumers from price volatility by aligning taxes inversely with global oil prices, and (c) allow firms and consumers to plan production and purchases of vehicles based on anticipating steady fuel price increases.[51]

Again, earmarking these taxes and fees for visible investments in urban public transport can make them politically palatable and encourage a shift from private transport towards more energy and environmentally efficient high-density public transit.[52] As former mayor of Bogota, Enrique Penalosa, has memorably noted: 'An advanced city is not one where even the poor use cars, but rather one where even the rich use public transport.' India would do well to heed this message. The role model for India's urban future should not be the US with lower population density and higher use of cars, but large European and East Asian cities with similarly high population densities, and high-quality public transit.

User charges for utilities

A third underused revenue source is user charges for urban services such as water and electricity. Studies show that user charges in India are far below the cost of provision. The main reason is the political concern that an increase in charges will be unpopular. But studies have shown that people, including the poor, are willing to pay for services *if they are reliable.*[53] This unwillingness to charge in turn leads to a low-quality trap where quality services cannot be provided because their provision cannot be financed. This perversely results in the poor paying much higher prices for private solutions.[54] So, charging for utilities is essential to provide better quality at lower cost.[55]

How can we balance providing access to basic utilities to the poor, while also charging to finance high-quality provision? One possible solution is to insist on metering and billing for all users, provide a certain number of free units of water or electricity, and have a progressive tariff structure with higher rates for higher use. Even if the number of free units is set at the current usage of a household in the 60th income percentile,[56] and requires government funds to cover the subsidy cost, economic growth will reduce the subsidy burden over time as a fraction of total usage and revenue. By providing reliable revenue streams, such an approach will also make it easier to access private markets to finance the massive infrastructure requirements in the future. This is similar to the approach taken successfully by the Delhi government in recent years.[57]

Bringing it together: Financing urban infrastructure and amenities

India requires an estimated Rs 3.5 lakh crore of investment in urban infrastructure and amenities every year over the next decade. However, we also face a large financing gap, which is limiting our ability to make these welfare-improving urban investments.[58] The principles in this section can help finance such investments.

Consider a project like expanding a bus fleet or building a mass transit system. Based on the principles above, it should be financed using a combination of Central and state government funding, user charges, fossil fuel taxes, parking fees, and property taxes. Such a financing model reflects the distribution of benefits from the investment, and ensures that each contributing party is better off with the project than without.

Specifically, the project will (a) boost economic activity and yield higher GST revenue, justifying government funding; (b) benefit commuters by cutting private transport costs, justifying user charges; (c) facilitate switching from private to public transport, justifying higher fees on private transport to reduce congestion and pollution;[59] and (d) raise property values near transit stops, justifying using some property tax revenues to fund it.

The key takeaway is that consumers, citizens, and property owners will *all* be better off after the project, even with user fees and property taxes, because the benefits will be higher than costs.[60] However, if governments do not collect adequate user charges or property taxes, they may deem the project unaffordable and not undertake it. Thus, designing financing models that better align the benefits and costs of urban amenities can make it politically and economically viable to finance them.

3.4 Use 'sin' taxes to the extent possible and undo the folly of prohibition

As explained in Section 2, levying 'sin' taxes on actions with negative externalities can not only raise revenues, but also improve social welfare. Consider alcohol: Overconsumption imposes indirect costs on others through drunk driving, and domestic violence; and direct costs on consumers by hurting their health.[61] Consequently, some state governments' policy response to alcohol has been to simply ban it, which is also perceived to be a popular policy among women voters.

Yet, alcohol prohibition is almost certainly a mistake. Indian states badly need revenue, and taxing 'bads' is a highly efficient way of collecting it. Prohibition not only deprives the state of revenue, but also drives alcohol-related activity underground, increases crime, and strengthens mafias. This, in turn, diverts scarce law enforcement resources from dealing with more serious crimes. Instead, a better response would be to just tax alcohol more. This would reduce alcohol consumption while raising revenue efficiently.

These points are well illustrated by the case of Bihar. In 2016, the government of Bihar introduced prohibition to combat alcoholism. But this ban has come at a massive cost. The fiscal cost of forgone revenue alone exceeded Rs 4000 crore, or around 16 per cent of Bihar's own tax revenue in 2015–16. For a poor state such as Bihar, with a fifth of the per capita income of Maharashtra, and low tax revenue to begin with (Figure 7.4), this loss of revenue significantly hurt the state's ability to fund essential public services.

Perhaps even worse is the opportunity cost of police and citizen time spent on it. The Bihar police conducted 2,13,000 raids in the first year, and made 1,22,392 arrests in the first two years of the law.[62] Research shows that this diversion of police effort increased other crimes.[63] The ban is also estimated to have cost 35,000 direct jobs from closing 21 alcohol manufacturing plants and 5500 retail outlets, with even higher indirect impacts on jobs and economic activity. It increased bootlegging and smuggling, and contributed to tragic deaths due to the consumption of unsafe, illicitly produced alcohol.[64] It has also created a shadow alcohol economy where revenue accrues to the police and politicians (through bribes) instead of going to the state treasury. Further, when action is taken for violating the law, it disproportionately affects marginalized groups.[65]

Yet, all these facts may not be enough to undo the folly of prohibition if it is seen as politically popular, especially among women. One politically feasible approach may be to repeal prohibition but commit to spending all resulting revenues on women's welfare. For instance, these revenues could be used for monthly unconditional income transfers to women, to hire more female police officers, or provide free public transport to women. While tax revenues are fungible, earmarking revenue from a tax reform to benefit those who would otherwise oppose the change can alleviate political constraints to reforms.[66]

As an example, the Tamil Nadu model of strong public service delivery, with a focus on benefits for women, heavily relies on a similar funding formula. Revenue from alcohol taxes yielded over Rs 36,000 crore in 2021–22, which was around 12 per cent of total budget spending, and 30 per cent of the state's own tax revenues![67] Bihar would do well to follow a similar model, and use the revenue from repealing prohibition to finance programmes to benefit women.

The same logic applies even to higher-income states like Gujarat, which has a similar per capita income as Tamil Nadu, but weaker social development indicators.[68] While the causes of these differences are multidimensional, one simple action that Gujarat can take is to repeal prohibition, tax alcohol, and use those tax revenues to strengthen women-focused public services and programmes. Such a repeal may also help attract more knowledge-based industries, and diversify the economic base of the state.[69]

A similar logic applies to other minor vices like smoking cannabis or marijuana. Despite a long tradition of use in Indian culture, cannabis was banned in India in 1985. Yet, an alternative approach of legalizing, regulating, and taxing its use can yield both revenue and also have several positive spillovers in society as seen recently in the US.

Marijuana was legalized for recreational use by the states of Washington and Colorado in 2012. By 2021, eighteen states had done so, with tax rates ranging from 10 to 25 per cent, generating $2 billion in tax revenue in 2020. In 2021, California alone earned over $1 billion in tax revenue in the first three quarters of the fiscal year.[70] This number is expected to grow six times by 2030, with marijuana tax revenues shortly expected to exceed those from alcohol. Beyond tax revenue, social benefits include the creation of thousands of legal (and hence safer) jobs, curbing illicit trade and money laundering, and improved judicial efficiency from reducing thousands of court cases.

Similar thinking is taking place in India, with some members of Parliament expressing support for legalizing cannabis in recent years. This is an area where states have a legal authority to take the lead, and Himachal Pradesh has recently constituted a committee to examine the trade-offs of doing so. State-level experimentation, as in the case of the US, can help accelerate a similar journey in India.

To summarize, it is much better for society to regulate and tax minor vices like alcohol and cannabis, rather than banning them. Benefits include: (a) increasing public revenue, while also disincentivizing the undesired activity through higher prices, (b) maintaining state control and visibility over the industry, as opposed to losing control to the mafia, (c) reducing crime by curbing diversion of limited police capacity to enforcing prohibition, (d) creating safer legal jobs and economic activity, (e) not criminalizing citizens for engaging in a common recreational activity, (f) reducing the health risks of consuming unsafe, illicit 'banned' products, and (g) treating overconsumption or addiction as public health issues to be addressed with education, counselling, and treatment, rather than as crimes deserving of prosecution and punishment; except in cases of actual threat to the safety of *others* such as drunk driving or domestic violence.

3.5 Tax agricultural incomes above a high threshold

There is also a strong case for taxing agricultural incomes above Rs 50 lakh a year. Such a tax would be highly progressive, and affect only a very small fraction of large landowners. It would also boost efficiency based on the principles in Section 2,[71] and thus be an R1 reform that would improve both equity and efficiency (see Figure 6.2). Several economists and government commissions have endorsed this idea, including the 2014 report of the Tax Administration Reform Commission (TARC), which recommended taxing agricultural income of over Rs 50 lakh a year.[72]

Yet, it has not been implemented due to the political power and resistance of large landowners. Further, the lack of measurement and audit has made agricultural income a lucrative 'conduit to avoid tax and for laundering funds' in the words of the 2014 TARC report itself, which has created additional powerful vested interests against taxing agricultural income.[73] This is similar to how free unmetered power for farmers aids power theft since there is no measurement of actual agricultural power use.

Taxing high agricultural incomes is a reform that is fully within the purview of states, and should especially be considered by pro-poor chief ministers. Pro-poor ideas like land redistribution have been politically unfeasible in most parts of India. Reforms to reduce the pro-rich skew in farm subsidies are difficult because they may also affect poorer farmers. So, the most feasible way to make rural policies more pro-poor may be to tax agricultural incomes over Rs 50 lakh, and use these revenues for pro-poor spending.

3.6 Support a uniform GST rate

The final idea is to highlight the enormous practical benefits of having a uniform single GST rate. While states cannot take this decision on their own, they have an important voice in determining rates in the GST council.

The current GST system has five tax rates: zero on exempt goods, 5, 12, 18, and 28 per cent. This structure aims to be progressive, taxing basic necessities less, and luxuries more.[74] However, it imposes large practical costs. These include the (a) administrative costs of categorizing each good for the right tax rate, (b) complications and increased administrative costs of 'inverted duty structure' when inputs are taxed higher than outputs,[75] (c) time wasted by firms and industry associations in lobbying for lower rates, and by officials in considering these requests, and (d) uncertainty created for industry and consumers due to frequent tinkering of GST rates across thousands of items.

Considering these large costs, India can significantly improve the efficiency of revenue collection with a uniform GST rate (or at least reduce the number of slabs).[76] While this may be regressive, a better way to improve the progressivity of the overall tax system would be through income taxes—including potentially lowering exemption limits so that more people pay them, introducing more progressive taxes on capital income, and taxing high agricultural incomes.[77] Politically, it is essential to communicate to voters that the rich pay much higher income, dividend, and capital gains taxes, and that a uniform GST greatly simplifies tax administration and the ease of doing business.

Further, Scandinavian countries with generous welfare systems also adopt a broad VAT system (similar to India's GST) that is more regressive than their income taxes. Yet, the *overall system is progressive* because the public goods and services funded by these taxes benefit the poor more. Similarly, since the poor in India depend the most on public services, they are likely to be better off if we build a broad and *efficient* tax base through a uniform GST and use the proceeds to fund high-quality public services.

Placed in the framework of Figure 6.2, a uniform GST *on its own* would be an R2 reform that would boost efficiency at the cost of increasing inequity. However, the increased revenue can be used to fund R1 and R4 spending ideas, and the resulting *portfolio* of actions can boost both efficiency and equity. So, to assess the progressivity of public finances, we need to look not only at taxes, but at taxes and spending together.

4. Conclusion

Without revenues, governments cannot perform their core functions. To accelerate India's development, we need to invest in better infrastructure, public goods, and public services. To do this, we need more public revenue, and need to raise it efficiently. While the Central government plays a crucial role in revenue collection, state governments can do a lot more at their level, as this chapter has shown.

Like many government departments in India, those responsible for tax collection also face severe challenges. However, weaknesses in revenue collection can hurt *all* other functions of the government. Further, unlike services such as education, health, or even security and dispute resolution, which can be provided by private parties, only the government can legitimately collect taxes. This makes improving the effectiveness and efficiency of revenue collection a foundational investment in state capacity.

However, given the high additional social cost of raising revenues, it is essential to also improve the quality of expenditure. Indeed, while expenditure and revenue are both essential components of public finance, the expenditure chapter comes first because we need to first improve *how* we spend taxpayer money before seeking to raise more of it.

Governments that try to raise taxes, while wasting lakhs of crores of public money, function with *diminished moral authority to collect taxes*. This, in turn, legitimizes tax evasion in the minds of citizens. Thus, improving the quality of expenditure and public service delivery will also have a positive feedback loop into revenue collection by improving the fiscal compact between taxpayers and the government, and thereby increase citizen willingness to pay their taxes.

One way of transitioning to such a virtuous cycle would be to implement the ideas for raising revenue in this chapter, and earmarking the increased revenues to invest in the ideas for improving the quality of expenditure presented throughout this book. Most of these are R1 ideas (Figure 6.2) that are likely to boost both equity and efficiency, have a high public RoI, and also yield visible benefits to citizens and voters. Thus, earmarking funds from future revenue growth for R1 ideas can accelerate the building of a more effective Indian state, and thereby also accelerate India's development.

Chapter 8

Federalism and Decentralization

India is a federal country with multiple tiers of government. Governments at the national and state levels are primarily responsible for legislation, policymaking, and programme design. These laws, policies, and programmes are then implemented by 'local' governments at the district, block, and local body levels.[1] Thus, the life of Indian citizens is affected by the decisions and actions of government actors at each of these levels.

In theory, federalism is a powerful idea for effective governance. When done well, it can deliver the dual benefits of economies of scale enjoyed by large countries; and better tailoring of policies to local needs, and government responsiveness to citizens as seen in smaller countries. Achieving this federal ideal requires clarity on the optimal delineation of functions across tiers of government, as well as effective coordination between them.

In practice, India's multiple tiers of government often feature overlap and lack of clarity on roles and responsibilities, ineffective coordination, passing the buck for non-delivery, and mismatch between resources available and services to be delivered. It is also common to see turf wars across tiers for both control and credit, which are magnified when different political parties are running different tiers. These structural challenges affect many aspects of governance, and are especially relevant for service delivery.

Thus, understanding and improving how India's federal architecture works is essential for effective governance and public service delivery. This chapter comprises three sections. The first presents the key concepts, benefits, and challenges of federalism. The second discusses the Indian experience with federalism, covering both key facts and rationales for why Indian federalism has evolved the way it has. The final section discusses reform ideas to better align Indian federalism with first principles, and thereby deliver better public services to citizens. Sections 2 and 3 discuss both the Centre-state aspects of federalism, and decentralization from state to local governments.

1. Key Concepts

1.1 How does country size affect the quality of governance?

Imagine you were to be reborn as an average citizen in an unknown country. You are given a single choice: to be born into a large country (by both size and population) or a small one. Where would you expect your quality of life to be higher? The answer is not obvious, because there are both benefits and costs of living in a larger country.

Large countries benefit from economies of scale in several key areas.[2] The first advantage is in national defence. Larger countries have more economic activity and tax revenues, which allows them to support stronger militaries. Historically, this was a key reason for countries seeking to expand their territory. Greater size helped boost economic and military strength, and improve security by deterring aggression. It also allowed rulers to push border conflicts further away from the more productive core of their territories, and better protect citizens and economic activity located there.

Second, investments made for national security can also confer economic advantages. For instance, empires often built transport networks to deploy troops quickly to different regions as and when needed. This also benefited economic activity by integrating markets. Similarly, many critical civilian technologies, such as commercial aviation and the Internet have emerged from publicly funded research and procurement conducted for military purposes.[3] These investments have high fixed costs, and large countries such as the US, and increasingly China, are better positioned to make them.

Thus, large countries obtain economic benefits from military spending even *without* considering the gains from using military strength to directly coerce economic concessions and tributes from other countries, as was the case during colonialism and much of history.

A third advantage is market size. Since internal trade typically faces fewer barriers than international trade, more populous countries benefit from access to a larger domestic market. This scale makes it economically viable to set up high-fixed-cost industries, which require large sales volumes to recover these fixed costs and turn profitable.

A fourth advantage is that larger countries are better able to insure their people against natural disasters such as droughts, floods, and earthquakes. Living in a large country confers two distinct advantages. First, tax revenues from unaffected areas can be used for relief and recovery in affected areas. Second, disaster-affected populations can more easily migrate to unaffected areas within the same country and rebuild their lives.[4]

Finally, larger countries may also find it easier to coordinate policies across jurisdictions. Consider sharing of river waters: upstream regions may overuse water, ignoring claims of downstream regions. However, more equitable sharing would improve both equity and economic efficiency, due to diminishing returns to water. In such cases, it may be easier to negotiate a welfare-improving solution if both regions are part of a larger country, than if they were separate countries (though this is not always true).

Taken together, these advantages may present an overwhelming case for preferring to live in a big country. Yet, there are two important costs of size.

One key cost of size is the need to accommodate more diverse identities and preferences among people as countries expand. National policies must be uniform, but maintaining uniformity is challenging as countries grow larger. Historically, secessionist movements have been more prevalent in the peripheral areas of a country, where people may feel that their interests are not adequately represented by the national government. The difficulty of managing greater diversity of people's identities and preferences with a common set of policies acts as a counterbalance to the benefits of size.

A second critical cost of size is greater distance between citizens and decision-makers. In larger countries, policymakers find it more difficult to stay informed of ground realities and adapt policies accordingly. It is also harder for citizens to access leaders, leading to governance delays and reduced government effectiveness, with adverse consequences for citizen welfare. So, on average, small countries have more agile governments. One measure of the benefits of being small is that *nine out of the ten richest countries* in the world by per capita income are 'small' countries with a population fewer than 10 million, or less than the size of Delhi or Mumbai (see Conclusion for further discussion).

Taken together, the effects of country size on governance and citizens' quality of life depend on how governments are able to balance these costs and benefits. On average, small countries are governed better, but need to worry more about managing external risks, including security and access to markets;[5] whereas larger countries need to worry more about staying united, paying attention to building inclusive governance institutions that can accommodate diversity, and being responsive to local needs.

These factors have affected national boundaries and country size over time. Historically, empires and kingdoms expanded by annexing weaker neighbours, and contracted when rulers overextended, resulting in their being unable to govern large and diverse populations effectively. This dynamic persists even to modern times, as seen in the dissolution of the Soviet Union and Yugoslavia into smaller states in the early 1990s.

This is why a great open question at the time of Indian independence was whether we would stay united as one country given the enormous variation in language, culture, geography, and history across the length and breadth of the country.[6] As we will see below, a key ingredient in India's political success at remaining united has been the institution of federalism and its contribution to accommodating India's diversity.

1.2 The promise of federalism

How can citizens obtain both the benefits of being in a large country and in a small one? The concept of federalism, with multiple tiers of government, offers a promising solution. The key idea is to assign responsibility for functions with greater economies of scale and need for coordination to higher tiers of government, which span larger areas and populations. Conversely, lower tiers of government covering smaller areas and populations are made responsible for functions that need to better accommodate local preferences, gather local information effectively, and act on this promptly.

Functions with economies of scale include national defence, foreign policy, trade agreements, issuing and managing currency, and collecting income and corporate taxes. These roles should and usually do reside with national governments. Similarly, functions requiring coordination across the country, such as national infrastructure projects and river-water sharing, also typically reside with national governments.

Large countries, such as the US, China, Brazil, Indonesia, and India also have state or provincial governments to accommodate regional variations in policy preferences. For instance, people care deeply about preserving local language and culture, which is mainly transmitted through public education systems. So, functions such as education, culture, and tourism often lie in the domain of state governments.

In the Indian case, the formation of states based on language has been a defining feature of our federalism, and may have played a key role in preserving national unity.[7] This approach has enabled states to function not just as administrative units but as governing entities that are able to preserve their distinct languages and cultures. It has allowed citizens to benefit from the economies of scale of being part of India, while better accommodating our enormous linguistic and cultural diversity.[8]

Finally, service delivery tasks, such as street lighting and cleaning, sanitation and waste management, and running schools and clinics are best done by local governments since they need to quickly respond to local information. It is also easier for citizens to hold a proximate local government accountable for service delivery than a more distant one. Local control also makes sense for deciding on local capital expenditures since there may be substantial variation in needs and priorities across communities.

Based on these principles, one key insight is that different functions within the same sector may be optimally located at different tiers of government. Consider the case of education. Functions that benefit from scale, such as funding basic research, are best done at the national level. Functions that need to respect linguistic and cultural diversity, such as setting state board curricula, are best done at the state level. Finally, functions requiring local information and prompt action, such as ensuring teacher attendance, are best done at the local level.[9]

A second key insight is that federalism does *not imply a hierarchy* where national governments are superior to state governments, who are superior to local governments. Instead, the distinction between tiers should be seen in terms of *functions* rather than hierarchy. For citizens' welfare, local governments often matter more than the national one. While changes in foreign policy may affect them over time, lack of streetlights or garbage collection, unpredictable water or electricity supply, and absent teachers and doctors have a much more direct impact on citizens' daily lives.

This discussion underscores the importance of effective local governments to citizens' lives. Based on the first principles of federalism, national or even state governments should have very little role in local service delivery. Yet, as shown in Section 2, governance in India is highly over-centralized, contributing significantly to its low effectiveness. Thus, resetting Indian federalism to better align with the first principles of effective governance will be an essential component of improving the functioning of the Indian state.

1.3 Key tensions in federal governance systems

In theory, federalism offers citizens both the benefits of a large country and a small one. In practice, there are also important tensions in the design of federal governance systems that arise from citizens living under the jurisdiction of multiple governments.

One fundamental tension is the question of whose view prevails when different tiers of government disagree on a law or policy. This is why Constitutions of federal polities try to delineate the topics that are in the domain of different government tiers, often guided by the *subsidiarity* principle of federalism, which recommends that issues be handled at the lowest level of government possible. In India, the Constitution specifies these roles by placing topics in the domain of Central and state governments in the Union and state lists respectively, and placing topics that are in both their domains in the concurrent list.

Despite these constitutional guidelines, disagreements over jurisdiction often arise across tiers of government. These often emerge from new circumstances, technologies, and policy issues that were not envisaged in the Constitution. In other cases, they can result from either overreach by higher-tier governments or a large deviation from national interest by a lower-tier government. When such disagreements cannot be resolved by discussion, they are often escalated to the Supreme Court for resolution. Thus, the question of 'who has the final say' on a given issue is often not a settled matter and is constantly evolving, negotiated, and contested in federal polities.[10]

Second, federal systems also face administrative tensions, especially regarding the extent of local autonomy when there is a clash of values. While greater local autonomy in service delivery is consistent with the subsidiarity principle, there is also a risk of local elite capture to the detriment of the most marginalized sections of society. This is a real concern in the rural Indian setting, where caste- and economic-elites have a long history of aiming to preserve their relative power and status at the cost of marginalized groups.

For instance, devolving control over schools to local governments could improve teacher accountability. However, it could also result in school resources being captured by local elites, who may allocate teacher jobs to their friends and family, or even restrict disadvantaged groups' access to school to maintain their local power.

Similarly, rural landlords who employ labour tried hard to *thwart* the implementation of NREGS, which strengthens the bargaining power of agricultural workers.[11] This is partly why India has often used a centralized administrative structure to implement the laws and programmes of national and state governments that may be resisted at local levels (see Section 2.3).

Third, these tensions can be exacerbated when different parties govern different tiers of government. Beyond differences in ideologies and priorities, conflicts arise in claiming credit for successes and passing blame for failures to other levels of government. For instance, we see increasing cases of tension between Central and state governments over which leader's photo should be on hoardings and scheme materials when programmes are jointly funded by both governments.

1.4 Summary

Successful federal systems balance these tensions and trade-offs effectively, and allow citizens to benefit both from the economies of scale of large countries and from the ability of small countries to better tailor policies to local needs and respond rapidly to citizen needs. However, achieving this federal ideal requires clarity on the roles and responsibilities of different tiers, aligning resources to responsibilities, and effective trust and coordination across tiers. Getting this federal architecture right affects governance and service delivery in *all* sectors and is therefore a core component of state capacity.

2. Federalism: The Indian Experience

2.1 India's federal structure of government

India's federal administrative structure comprises the Union government of India, also referred to as the Central government or just the Centre, twenty-eight state governments, and eight union territories administered by the Centre (some of which also have elected legislatures). States are, in turn, organized into districts, blocks, and urban and rural local bodies.

With an average population of 50 million, Indian states are more populous than most countries! Table 8.1 presents the nearest equivalent countries by population to Indian states, and shows that *each* of India's fifteen most populous states would rank among the forty-two most populous countries in the world, situating them in the 20 per cent of the world's most populous nations. Simply put, governing an Indian state is best thought of as equivalent to running a medium- to large-sized country!

Table 8.1: Indian States Ranked by Population with Nearest Comparable Countries

Rank by Population (2021)	State	Projected Population (2021)	Comparable Countries (2021)	Population rank if the state were a country (2021)
1	Uttar Pradesh	2,30,907,000	Brazil, Pakistan, Nigeria	5
2	Maharashtra	1,24,437,000	Japan, Mexico, Ethiopia	12
3	Bihar	1,23,083,000	Japan, Mexico, Ethiopia	12
4	West Bengal	98,125,000	Vietnam, Egypt, DRC	15
5	Madhya Pradesh	84,516,000	Turkey, Iran	17
6	Rajasthan	79,281,000	Germany	20
7	Tamil Nadu	76,402,000	Germany	20
8	Gujarat	69,788,000	Thailand	21
9	Karnataka	66,845,000	France, UK, Tanzania	22

10	Andhra Pradesh	52,787,000	Kenya, South Korea	28
11	Odisha	44,033,000	Argentina, Spain, Uganda	33
12	Jharkhand	38,471,000	Afghanistan, Poland	38
13	Telangana	37,725,000	Canada, Morocco	40
14	Kerala	35,489,000	Uzbekistan	41
15	Assam	35,043,000	Saudi Arabia	41

Note(s): Population Projections from MoHFW (2020).

Indian districts and sub-districts are also large. India has over 700 districts, averaging around 2 million people per district, and around 7000 sub-districts (blocks), with around 2 lakh people per block. Below the district level, governance structures vary for urban and rural local bodies. As of early 2022, India had around 4750 urban local bodies with an average population of around one lakh, and over 2.5 lakh rural local bodies with an average population of around 3500.[12]

The main point to note is that even districts, sub-districts, and local bodies in India have large populations. An average Indian *district* has more people than eighty-five *countries,* or 36 per cent of the world's countries. Further, India has at least fifteen districts with over 6 million people, which is more than the median population among countries.

2.2 Governance in India is highly centralized

Yet, despite state and local governments representing such large populations, Indian governance is extremely centralized. The centralization spans both political and economic matters, and is seen both between the Central and state governments, and especially between state and local governments.

Political centralization

One striking measure of political centralization in independent India is the history of rampant overuse of Article 356 of the Constitution by Central governments to dismiss *democratically elected* state governments and impose 'President's Rule', whereby the state administration reports directly to the Centre. Intended to be used only under rare, extreme situations,[13] Article 356 was used as a political tool that sharply weakened the authority of state governments. Figure 8.1 shows that, from 1950 to 1990, the Centre dismissed an elected state government *eighty-three times.*

In addition, parties in power at the Centre, historically the Congress and recently the BJP, often replace state chief ministers of their own party to assert central control over state-level governance.[14] Together, these actions severely curb the authority of state-level leaders. There has been a sharp reduction in the use of Article 356 since the 1990s, resulting in chief ministers and state governments having more autonomy.[15] However, for much of the history of independent India, they were quite constrained.

Figure 8.1: Central Government Dismissal of Elected State Governments

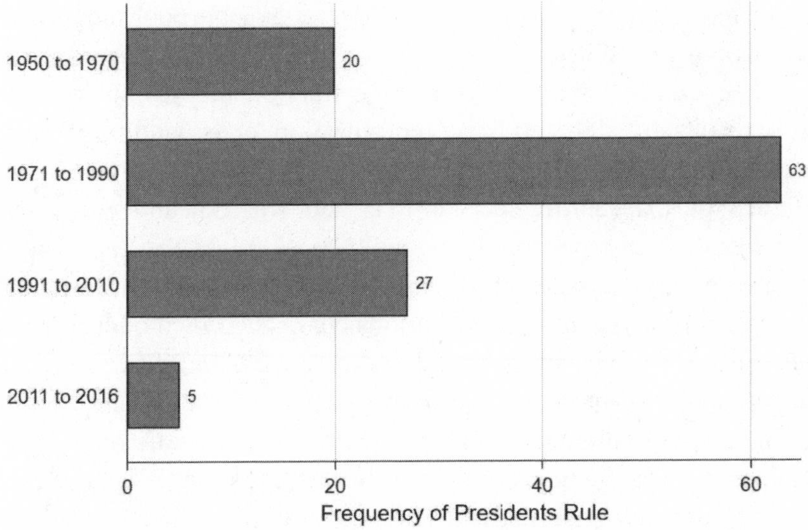

Note(s): Data from Dubbudu (2018); graph recreated by author.

Economic centralization

Key elements of India's economic management are also highly centralized. On the revenue side, the Centre has exclusive authority over major tax categories, including income taxes, corporate taxes, and customs duties, accounting for over 60 per cent of India's tax revenue collections (see Chapter 7). It also collects a majority of the non-tax revenues, including cesses, surcharges, and capital earnings.

The Centre's greater role in revenue collection is in line with the principles of federalism due to economies of scale in administering income, corporate, and customs taxes. Yet, 60 per cent of India's public spending takes place at the state level, which makes sense since states are responsible for most service delivery functions. This gap is bridged by the Finance Commission, a constitutional body that allocates the national divisible pool of tax revenues across the Central and state governments (see Chapter 7).

Historically, the share of the divisible pool allocated to states by Finance Commissions was less than one-third, and the Centre controlled over two-thirds of the national pool of revenues.[16] It is only after the award of the 14th Finance Commission in 2014, that the states' share of the divisible pool went up from 32 per cent to 42 per cent. However, the Centre also raises considerable funds through cesses and surcharges, which are outside the divisible pool and hence, not shared with states.[17]

The Centre's retention of a large fraction of public revenues also results in high levels of centralization of expenditure. This expenditure takes place through Central schemes that are fully funded by the Centre, such as PDS and NREGS; and especially through centrally sponsored schemes (CSS). Under CSSs, the Centre creates programme guidelines and provides funding, but requires states to make matching contributions out of their own budgets and also adhere to the Central guidelines to access Central funds. CSSs are common in many areas, including school education and health (that are primarily in the domain of states), and the ratio of Central and state government funding for different CSSs ranges from 90:10 to 50:50 depending on the state and scheme.[18]

There are good theoretical reasons for CSSs. These include (a) promoting regional equity in spending on basic services, (b) enabling minimum service delivery standards across the country, and (c) economies of scale in creating programme guidelines that reflect high-quality technical inputs and consultations. Some of these benefits are also seen in practice. For example, CSS funds comprise nearly 50 per cent of the school education budget of Bihar, but less than 10 per cent of the same in Maharashtra. This is consistent with Maharashtra's GDP per capita being around five times higher than that of Bihar.[19] Thus, CSS funding plays a crucial role in enabling poorer states to deliver minimum standards of basic services.

However, CSSs have led to excessive centralization of expenditure and impose several costs on effective governance.[20] First is the 'one size fits all' nature of CSS guidelines. Given the wide variation across India, strict guidelines are suboptimal in many parts of the country. For instance, education needs in Kerala and Tamil Nadu are very different from those in Bihar. However, since large amounts of Central funds are tied to CSSs, states often end up following locally suboptimal CSS guidelines to avail this money.[21] The suboptimal standardization imposed by CSSs across a very diverse country is a good example of the governance challenges of larger countries discussed earlier.

A second cost is that they limit state government autonomy on how their *own* sectoral budgets are spent. Since the matching component of the CSS budget contributed by states also has to be spent as per CSS guidelines, the structure of CSSs directs states to spend both their administrative and fiscal resources in line with Central guidelines that may not even be a good fit for the state. In some cases, this mismatch is so strong that states have chosen to completely forgo CSS funds.

A third cost is administrative. Highly granular CSS guidelines impose substantial costs of paperwork. For instance, the National Health Mission (NHM) prescribes over 1500 line items of permitted expenditure and requires state governments to prepare annual project implementation plans (PIP), and submit details of spending under each head. Across twenty-eight states, this results in over 40,000 accounting line items annually for states to create and for the Centre to review.[22] Several senior officials have remarked to me over the years that these onerous requirements serve little substantive purpose and reinforce a 'command and control' culture from the Central government.[23]

A fourth cost is the weakening of state-level policymaking capacity, due to CSSs taking up large shares of states' fiscal and administrative capacity. Even senior state-level officials, responsible for delivering outcomes to country-sized populations, often hesitate to consider policy ideas outside Central government guidelines. The problem is both financial and substantive. Financially, the requirement for states to make matching contributions to avail of CSS funds has reduced budgets available to finance their own initiatives. Substantively, it requires much more work to justify an idea that is not in CSS guidelines. Thus, even a motivated state principal secretary or commissioner will usually find it easier to obtain funding for initiatives if these are within CSS guidelines.[24]

Taken together, though well-intentioned, CSSs have substantially reduced state-level autonomy and initiative in solving their own problems in locally optimal ways.[25] Further, Central government ministries have responded to the increased devolution of funds to states by the 14th Finance Commission by increasing the state's share of contribution to CSSs, which has partly undone the increased financial autonomy given to states by the 14th Finance Commission.[26]

Local-body governments are highly disempowered

The same pattern of over-centralization is seen between state and local governments. While there has been an increase in decentralization to local governments in the political sphere, there has been much less so on economic and administrative matters.

The main marker of political decentralization is that elections are regularly held for rural and urban local bodies, especially after the passing of the 73rd and 74th constitutional amendments in 1993. These elections are conducted by autonomous state election commissions and, for the most part, are free and fair.

However, despite being elected, India's local governments have not been empowered to effectively deliver essential local public services. This is seen in both fiscal and personnel allocations to local governments. A 2015 cross-country study found that India is *one of the least fiscally decentralized countries in the world*, with local government spending accounting for only 3 per cent of total public expenditure. In contrast, China allocates 51 per cent of public spending to local governments, which is *seventeen times higher* than India! Other large countries, such as the US and Brazil, are in the middle, allocating around 27 per cent of total public spending at the local government level, which is still nine times higher than in India (Figure 8.2).[27]

Figure 8.2: Centralization of Government Spending across Countries[28]

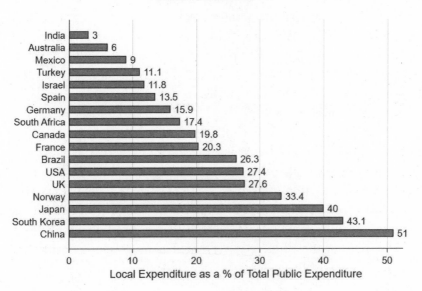

Note(s): Data from Ren (2015), graph recreated by author.

Figure 8.3: Distribution of Personnel across Tiers of Government[29]

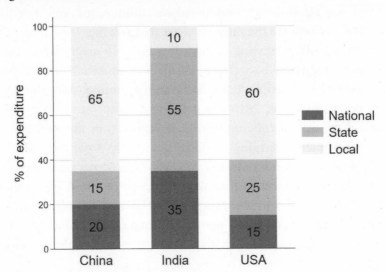

Note(s): Data from Kapur (2020), graph recreated by author.

Similarly, public employment in India is also highly centralized. A study by Devesh Kapur highlights that over 60 per cent of public employees in the US and China work for local governments, compared to only around 10 per cent in India, a six-fold difference! In contrast, the share of national and especially state government employees are much higher in India as seen in Figure 8.3 (reproduced with data from Devesh Kapur).

The comparison with China, the only other country with a similar population as India, is especially instructive. Contrary to common perceptions of China as a strong, centralized state, most government functions that directly affect citizens' daily lives are run by local governments, which account for the majority of both public spending and employment. Thus, the *organization of functions* across tiers of the Chinese government is much closer to the first principles of effective federalism, than in India.

2.3 Why is governance in India so centralized?

The facts above suggest that India is an outlier in terms of how centralized it is and is likely to benefit from greater decentralization.

But, before suggesting reform ideas, it is important to understand *why* governance in India is so centralized.

While drafting the Indian Constitution, members of the Constituent Assembly intensely debated federalism and the optimal division of authority between Central and state governments. Their deliberations spanned many of the same issues covered in Section 1, and concluded that the Central government needed to be stronger than state governments. There were three broad reasons for this view: political, economic, and social.

The political reason was the concern that post-British India would not remain unified, a fear amplified by the Partition of the subcontinent into India and Pakistan.[30] Further, at the time of Independence, *more than 40 per cent* of India's land was ruled by over 500 erstwhile princely states, whose rulers had only recently acceded to the Indian Union, and some had done so quite reluctantly.[31] To understand the enormity of the challenge of uniting the nation, some historical context is useful. In the 2000 years before British rule, even 75 per cent of the Indian Subcontinent was politically unified for less than 200 years: under the peaks of the Mauryan and Mughal Empires (around 300–250 BCE, and around 1600–1700 CE).[32] So, preserving national unity was a top priority for the Constitution's framers. This is why they gave the Central government strong political powers, including the ability to dismiss democratically elected state governments under Article 356.[33]

The economic rationale was the belief that centralized planning and public investments were key for economic growth and development. India's founding leaders also sought to pursue geographically balanced development, which they believed they could achieve through central planning and investment allocation. Since such investments and planning required scale and coordination, economic policy was also highly centralized.

Finally, the social reason was to promote reforms such as eradicating untouchability, and strengthening women's rights.[34] The lack of autonomy to lower tiers of government reflected the concern that local elites would seek to perpetuate patriarchy and caste inequalities, through actions such as denying or limiting education to girls and disadvantaged castes, if they were given power over local service delivery. This lack of trust is perhaps best captured in the famous words of Dr Ambedkar, 'What is the village but a sink of localism, a den of ignorance, narrow-mindedness, and communalism?'[35]

Thus, though the first principles of federalism suggest that local governments should be responsible for service delivery, India's approach to designing a federal governance system has been much more centralized than almost any other country in the world. A key reason for doing this was to have a professional state-level bureaucracy that could implement government policies and programmes to benefit disadvantaged groups, that may have been resisted or even thwarted by local elites.[36]

This tension between traditional society and a modernizing state is still seen today. For instance, in 1993, the government aimed to boost women's empowerment by reserving some village Pradhan (leader) positions for women. Yet, traditional gender norms are often reasserted in the community. As scholars, practitioners, and even the TV series *Panchayat* have highlighted, there may be a female Pradhan on paper, but true power often resides with her husband.[37] Yet, several studies have found that legal provisions to empower women have had positive impacts on outcomes prioritized by women.[38] Thus, despite resistance from local elites, laws and policies of the modernizing state have still managed to help in empowering marginalized groups.[39]

This tension between ethically and normatively informed policy goals of a modern state, and traditional elites who prefer the status quo is not unique to India. For instance, the US Constitution provides more power to state and local governments. But this partly reflects its conservative origins that prioritized individual rights and freedoms and not social reform or justice. When the US later sought to improve racial equality, reforms such as school desegregation and universal voting rights faced stiff resistance from local elites in historical slaveholding regions. Thus, ensuring equal rights for African-Americans required active federal (Central) government interventions, such as passing the Voting Rights Act of 1965 and enforcing it through the federal Justice department. This is an ongoing tension in US law and politics even today.[40] Thus, one way to understand India's high centralization is to note that social goals were integrated into our Constitution at its very inception, rather than added many years later as in the US.

To summarize, India's high centralization reflects our constitutional origins. The political science literature contrasts this with the US, labelling India as a 'top-down' federalism, and the US as a 'coming together' (or 'bottom-up') federalism.[41] This is because, in the US, states were pre-existing units of governance, which came together to delegate a few limited functions with economies of scale, such as defence, to a federal government. Thus, in the US Constitution, any right not explicitly granted to the federal government rests with states by default. In contrast, under the Indian Constitution, the Central government has the final say in any area that is not explicitly in the states' list.[42]

3. Implementable Reform Ideas

The discussion above provides useful historical context to understand why governance in India is so centralized. Yet, in present times, many of these reasons may no longer be valid, and India's over-centralization imposes considerable costs on governance.

Simply put, India is too over-centralized to be governed effectively. With over 1.4 billion people, India's population is similar to that of all the fifty-four countries of Africa put together, and nearly 1.5 times that of North, Central, and South America put together! The only other country of comparable size (China) is *much* more decentralized, with basic service delivery being driven by local governments, as seen in the distribution of public employees and budgets across government tiers.

At the same time, the founders of the Indian Republic had valid reasons for giving more powers to higher tiers of government. Hence, we need a thoughtful, nuanced approach to decentralization that aligns with the principles of federalism, leverages the strengths of different government tiers, and has safeguards against local elite capture. This needs to happen between the Centre and state governments; and perhaps more importantly, between state and local governments. The ideas below cover both these dimensions.

3.1 Consider creating smaller states, districts, sub-districts, and local bodies

One way to address over-centralization is to create smaller administrative units, and there is growing evidence that doing so will be good for governance. At the state level, studies show that the 2001 division of Uttar Pradesh, Bihar, and Madhya Pradesh to create Uttarakhand, Jharkhand and Chhattisgarh improved outcomes in the 'child' states.[43] Smaller states bring capitals closer to citizens, enable more locally tailored policies, and can improve state capacity by increasing public employees per capita. So, the Government of India should consider forming smaller states, especially when there is strong regional sentiment to do so. Such efforts should be pursued in collaboration with state leaders and proceed with mutual consent.

There is also evidence to support smaller administrative units *within* states. A nationally noteworthy reform along these lines was implemented in Andhra Pradesh in 1985 under Chief Minister N.T. Rama Rao, to divide sub-districts (blocks) into three to five *mandals* each. As a result, while blocks in most Indian states have around 2,00,000 to 3,00,000 people; mandals in Andhra Pradesh and Telangana have only 60,000 to 75,000 people. A recent study finds significant improvements in public goods provision in villages whose distance to sub-district headquarters was reduced by the creation of mandals, suggesting that other states may also benefit from similar reforms.[44]

The same pattern holds for local governments. An important recent study in Uttar Pradesh found that villages assigned to smaller Gram Panchayats (GPs) had better infrastructure (roads, schools), house quality (brick houses, toilets, and closed drainage systems), and welfare programme implementation (NREGS, pensions).[45] These villages had greater citizen participation in GPs, were less likely to have candidates and leaders with criminal records, and were more likely to elect a leader from the same village. The study also finds no evidence of increased elite capture. Thus, smaller polities appear to be more effective at both 'selecting' better leaders, and holding them 'accountable', resulting in better implementation of government programmes and development outcomes.

Of course, at some point, the benefits of scale will outweigh those of making administrative units even smaller. However, the consistent findings above suggest that, *at current sizes*, governance and delivery of public goods in India are likely to improve by creating smaller administrative units of governance at all levels. These findings are also consistent with the broader argument that governance in India is too centralized.

3.2 Encourage greater state- and district-level policy experimentation

Thinking more locally can also expedite policy reforms and learning. Most reforms have reasonable arguments for and against them, and also create winners and losers. The combination of plausible public-interest reasons for opposing reforms, the interests of prospective losers in opposing them, a governance system with multiple veto points, and risk-averse politicians and bureaucrats creates a strong status quo bias where reforms are the exception rather than the norm.

So, we are more likely to make progress as a country if we can increase the chances of reform experiments, and reduce the risk of failure. One practical way of doing this is to reduce the size and scope of the geographical jurisdiction where innovations are tried out, by empowering and encouraging lower tiers of government to embark on promising but untested reforms. Such reforms are more likely to be replicated in other locations if they are successful. Over time, such an approach can accelerate the adoption of effective ideas and slow or stop the spread of bad ones.

The central role of competition among political jurisdictions, and the importance of rapid imitation of successful ideas is well illustrated by a historical example.

Comparing China and Europe in the fourteenth century, China was in many ways better positioned to be the world's dominant power. It was technologically more advanced and was also a unified political entity that was not wasting resources on internal wars as opposed to highly fractured Europe, which was plagued by long internal wars. Yet, in practice, European countries became the world's leading powers. Research by economic historian Joel Mokyr suggests that a key reason was policy experimentation across European countries with rapid imitation of successful ideas. Conversely, China's uniformity reduced policy experimentation and made mistakes more costly.[46]

The history of seafaring powerfully illustrates this point. To curb smuggling and piracy, China's Ming dynasty emperor banned maritime trade in 1371. However, this had the unintended negative consequence of limiting China's exposure to the rest of the world and its ideas. In contrast, Columbus's quest for patrons to fund a westward sea journey to the east illustrates the value of political diversity. While he was initially turned down by Portugal, he received support from Spain, leading to the discovery of the New World by Europeans. This success prompted other European powers, including Portugal, to launch their own westward sea voyages. In stark contrast, China remained isolated from global ideas for centuries after its decision to ban maritime trade.

The main lesson here is that the key to success is to try many new things, expand on successes, and correct mistakes quickly! The other key lesson is that some policy mistakes are inevitable, but making them in a big country is more costly. This is not just because the mistake directly affects more people, but also because the lack of self-correcting mechanisms means that it takes much longer to identify and correct the mistake. Fifteenth-century Portuguese leaders made a policy error and so did the Chinese. But the Portuguese mistake was less costly because the Spanish experiment was successful, and it was easy to learn and adapt from a neighbouring country.

The same approach of decentralized innovation, and the rapid adoption of successful ones played a key role in China's remarkable economic growth starting in the 1980s. Allowing and encouraging local governments to experiment with growth-promoting reforms was a critical enabler in transforming the Chinese economy. Reducing the geographic scope of reform experiments helped to manage political risk, and encouraging competition across jurisdictions created the right incentives for effective policies to be replicated.[47]

Similarly, state-led innovation and diffusion of effective reforms can catalyse economic growth and development in India, as elaborated in Chapter 16. A practical way to do so is to modify our approach to the concurrent list of the Indian Constitution. Currently, for items in the concurrent list, Central laws override state laws when the two conflict. However, there is also a Constitutional provision for the President of India to approve state laws that conflict with Central laws on the subject, enabling the state-level law to operate within the state. So, we would do well to consider and allow such exceptions more regularly, to facilitate and encourage state-level policy experimentation.

The same approach can be used by to increase policy experimentation *within* states, including at the district or constituency level. For instance, special economic zones (SEZs) can be used not only to provide contiguous land and facilities for industries, but also to experiment with regulatory reforms (see Chapter 16). Similarly, it may be easier to try out other critical but politically difficult reforms, such as replacing free electricity for farmers with equivalent income transfers, in a few locations to begin with (see Chapters 15 and 16). A key political requirement for reforms is *trust* from citizens, and such trust may be easier to obtain in constituencies of senior leaders or in electoral strongholds of the governing party. Starting reforms on a smaller scale makes it easier for (a) officials to fine-tune implementation, (b) citizens to experience benefits and allay fears, and (c) for leaders to scale up reforms after demonstrating effectiveness.[48]

3.3 Increase both autonomy and accountability in centrally sponsored schemes

Centrally sponsored schemes (CSSs) aim to promote regional equity in basic services. But the challenges faced by the Centre in designing them are similar to those faced by organizations like the World Bank in supporting poor countries. A key concern is that poorer states and countries also have weaker governance. Thus, states that are most in need of extra funds for basic services like health and education often have higher rates of leakage and corruption.[49] Such concerns are partly why the Centre imposes elaborate guidelines on how CSS funds can be spent. However, this approach has been counterproductive for reasons discussed earlier, and creates and perpetuates a culture of accountability based on 'compliance' as opposed to 'outcomes'.

A better approach would be for CSSs to reflect the principle that effective organizations empower frontline staff and managers with autonomy on processes, and combine this with accountability and incentives for delivering outcomes. One way to do this is for the Centre to adopt a 70:20:10 funding formula reflecting the policy goals of equality, equity and effectiveness (as discussed in Chapter 6). Under this formula, 70 per cent of CSS funds could be distributed evenly across states based on population (equality); 20 per cent based on development indicators, with more funds for disadvantaged states (equity); and 10 per cent reserved for a performance-based allocation, distributed annually based on *improvements* in key outcome indicators (effectiveness).

While non-binding central guidelines on CSS spending can be useful for state-level officials, more untied CSS funds will increase their autonomy and initiative to design contextually relevant programmes. Augmenting these funds with performance-based supplemental funds can boost motivation and accountability to focus on improving outcomes, as opposed to having the funds spent ineffectively or captured by local elites. These performance-based funds could, for instance, be partly used for staff bonuses, which could improve the motivation of the entire department.

This approach is consistent with both micro and macro evidence that simply providing resources often fails to improve outcomes. However, resources can be highly effective, when *combined* with incentives to use them well. For instance, in an RCT across 350 schools with over 1,00,000 students in Tanzania, my co-authors and I found that even sizeable school grants had no impact on learning outcomes.

However, these grants were highly effective when combined with outcome-based bonus payments to teachers.[50] Similar results were seen in an influential paper on foreign aid, which finds that such aid had a positive effect on growth in settings where recipient countries had good fiscal, monetary, and trade policies, but had no effect in settings with poor policies.[51]

The number of indicators for performance-based funding should be small to enable prioritization and focus. For health, these could be infant mortality rate below age one and child malnutrition rate at age two. These are critical determinants of long-term human development and also excellent indicators of the quality of health systems (see Chapter 12). For education, these could be foundational literacy and numeracy, which is India's greatest education challenge (see Chapter 11); and girls' secondary education completion rates, which are a critical determinant of female empowerment, age of marriage, total fertility, and child health and nutrition.

The main investment needed to implement outcome-based financing is in independent and credible outcome measurement, as noted in Chapter 4. Ideally, this task should be conducted by an institution like NITI Aayog's Development Monitoring and Evaluation Organization (DMEO). This arrangement facilitates legitimacy, as the measurement would be overseen by a government body, while maintaining independence from states and line departments. Having such data will also allow us to monitor progress towards development goals, facilitate learning about which programmes and initiatives are effective, and accelerate knowledge-sharing of effective practices across states.

Finally, while implementing performance-based financing may take some time due to the need to first build measurement systems, the Centre should immediately implement *performance-based autonomy* for states. India's best-performing states significantly outperform the weakest ones on several human development indicators.[52] Forcing them to comply with norms designed for weaker states constrains high performers and hurts national progress. While these states may still benefit from the technical inputs in CSS guidelines, their track record should earn them more performance-based autonomy. Such autonomy should give them the option to accept only the CSS guidelines that are useful to them, and offer progressively more untied CSS funds with the only condition being that these, and the state's matching funds, be spent on the concerned sector.[53]

3.4 Use principles of federalism to clarify jurisdiction across government tiers

Disputes over jurisdiction between government tiers are common in federal systems. So, greater clarity on the optimal role of different tiers using principles of federalism can improve governance and citizens' quality of life, as shown by the examples below.

Education and Training Credentials

The case of National Eligibility cum Entrance Test (NEET) and National Exit Test (NExT) for medical colleges, mandated by the National Medical Council (NMC), nicely illustrates these issues. The Tamil Nadu government has opposed this mandate, arguing that it infringes on states' Constitutional rights to run their own higher education institutes funded by state governments. It also argues that the NEET hurts disadvantaged candidates, who attend local-language state-board schools, in obtaining admission to medical college. In turn, the Centre contends that since medical education is on the concurrent list, the Constitutional primacy to Central over state laws in cases of conflict allows the Centre to insist on the NEET and NExT to ensure consistent standards across India.

The principles in this chapter can help in finding a practical way forward. The key insight is that we should distinguish between issues that are only relevant within state borders, which should remain in the domain of states; and those with cross-state relevance, where the Centre should have primacy. This reasoning implies that the NEET should *not* be mandatory, since states should have autonomy on filling higher education seats within their borders and funded by them. The same reasoning suggests that the recent attempt by the NMC to cap the number of medical seats in each state is an unwarranted overreach. However, the Centre and the NMC can justify making the

NExT mandatory, because doctors may practice across state borders, which creates a national interest in ensuring minimal credentialing standards for doctors to practice across India.[54]

The case of skilling provides a good example where principles of federalism have been applied well. The National Council for Vocational Education and Training (NCVET), established in 2018, provides considerable autonomy to states and service providers to impart contextually relevant skills training. However, since many workers migrate across the country, the NCVET aims to establish minimum standards for vocational education, and to align these programmes' content and credentials to the National Skills Qualification Framework. The eventual goal is to provide trainees with credible, nationally portable skilling credentials that can be used by employers and employees across India.[55]

Data systems and sharing

While the NEET dispute is better known due to media coverage, similar issues arise in many unseen aspects of governance, such as data systems. For example, the Centre's effort to improve reporting and tracking of child development metrics through the '_Poshan_ tracker' app is commendable. However, the Centre's insistence that states _must_ use it, even when states have their own existing apps to track both national and state-funded programmes, is counterproductive because switching to the national app makes it harder for states to track their own programmes. As a result, some states ask their staff to fill records on both Central and state apps, often in addition to filling paper forms, resulting in substantial staff time and energy wasted on redundant data entry.

A better approach would be for the Centre to allow states to retain their own apps and data systems, but require them to include fields needed for Central tracking and provide an API for the Centre to access the needed data. Many states might opt for the Central system, and it is good for them to have this option. However, while offering a Central app is sensible due to economies of scale in developing, maintaining, and updating the app; mandating it is not. Rather, the API-based approach would facilitate national coordination while respecting states' autonomy to design and track their own programmes.

Reimagining the Concurrent List of the Indian Constitution

India's Constitution reflects the idea that some subjects should be in the domain of both state and Central governments by putting such subjects in the concurrent list. However, the primacy given to Central laws over state ones has led to over-centralization of many concurrent list subjects. It has also contributed to a common but counterproductive view among India's citizens, officials, and leaders that federalism implies government tiers that operate in a *hierarchy*. However, governance and the public interest will be better served if India's government tiers shift away from operating as a hierarchy on the same functions, towards taking primary responsibility for *different functions*, based on the tier at which that function should be optimally done for citizen welfare (see Section 1).

Since disputes over jurisdiction in India's federal structure are often resolved by the Supreme Court, the principles in this chapter may be useful for the Court to consider in such matters. Specifically, the Court should not give the Centre *blanket primacy* over states on all subjects on the concurrent List, as this undermines the very purpose of a concurrent list. Rather, the Centre should have primacy when an issue crosses state boundaries, but mostly not otherwise. Interestingly, the Court has taken exactly this view in a 2021 judgment on the Centre's jurisdiction over cooperative societies.[56] Applying this principle more broadly for Constitutional interpretation on matters of jurisdiction can help accelerate India's development by enabling more state-led policy experimentation on items in the Concurrent list.[57]

Evolving a more sophisticated federal mindset

Finally, since constitutional disputes on jurisdiction can take a long time to be resolved and very few matters reach the Supreme Court, governance in our federal structure will be greatly improved if the *mindset* and daily functioning of leaders, officials, and citizens evolves to better reflect the first principles of federalism. The default mindset is one that focuses on which government tier should have *control* on a subject matter. Rather, we should evolve the mindset to asking which tier is best positioned to perform the specific function needed to best *serve* citizens, and assign roles and resources accordingly.

In many cases, including the NEET and Poshan tracker examples, states *will* benefit from having a central option because of the economies of scale in conducting tests and developing apps. However, it is better to drive usage by making it convenient for states to adopt them rather than mandating their use. Thus, given the scale and diversity of Indian states, the overarching mindset of Central interventions in subjects on the Concurrent list should be to facilitate and help states achieve development goals better while respecting their autonomy, rather than one of command and control.

Note that this mindset shift does *not* mean that the Centre should do less of everything. While India needs much more decentralization on average, the Centre's role will need to *increase* in some areas to serve citizens better. For instance, the greater integration of India's economy through the GST and cross-state worker migration will increase the need for coordination, which the Centre is best positioned to do.[58] Similarly, Central oversight over state debt levels has been an important reason why Indian states have never defaulted on their debt despite being under fiscal stress.[59]

As in all federal polities, disputes over jurisdiction will continue to be contested in both political and judicial arenas. However, the principle of combining central oversight with state autonomy can guide us in many complex issues. For instance, reverting to the old pension scheme for public employees (see Chapter 6) will add great financial stress to states in the future. Yet, state leaders argue for their democratic right to make and fulfil voter commitments using public funds. So, the Centre can balance these considerations by requiring that states provide for the expected future costs of these commitments in their current budget. This approach respects states' rights to make policy commitments, but limits their ability to spend now and transfer the liability to future generations. This is similar to and consistent with the Centre's role in regulating state debt.[60]

3.5 Accelerate decentralization within states

Just as the Central government must decentralize more to states, state governments need to do the same to local bodies. Doing so will both deepen democracy and improve service delivery. This lack of decentralization reflects both constitutional origins and the reluctance of state-level leaders and bureaucrats to relinquish power to governments at lower levels. This phenomenon was well captured in the memorable words of the distinguished public finance economist, Dr Raja Chelliah, who noted that: 'Everyone wants decentralization, but only until his level.'

However, it is simply not tenable for states and chief ministers to demand greater autonomy from the Centre without providing the same to local body governments within states. I discuss specific ways of doing so below.

Improve autonomy and accountability of district-level officials

The same approach outlined for reforming CSS, integrating ideas from Chapters 4 to 6 can also be used *within* states. Specifically, states can use annual district-level data on key development outcomes from a KPI survey (Chapter 4) to allocate funds across districts using the 70:20:10 formula (Chapter 6), with some of the 10 per cent performance-based funds being usable for district-level bonus payments to staff (Chapter 5), as well as for funding discretionary programmes identified at the local level.

It is considerably easier to implement this reform within states than from the Centre to states because the scope of measurement will be more manageable. Further, both budgets and personnel for service delivery sectors are primarily controlled by state governments. Such an approach can be transformative for service delivery in India. It would move the focus of governance from inputs to outcomes, and empower and motivate frontline staff and managers to proactively take initiative to improve outcomes, rather than just passively following orders and focusing on compliance and paperwork.

Decentralize service delivery to local bodies with checks and balances

In addition to better 'top-down' accountability by linking funding to improved outcomes, states can also improve 'bottom-up' accountability for service delivery. First principles of federalism suggest that service delivery should primarily be a local government function. Further, *states are more responsible* for over-centralization in India than the Centre (see Figure 8.3). Finally, studies show that bringing government closer to the people, and reducing polity size improves governance and development outcomes.

Thus, one of the *most important governance reforms* we need is to shift responsibility for service delivery from states to local bodies. This will improve both the accountability of public employees to locally elected leaders, and of elected representatives to voters. Unlike Parliament and assembly elections, where multiple issues are salient, local body elections are primarily contested on issues of service delivery. Thus, empowering local bodies with greater authority on funds and personnel will improve both service delivery and the functioning of Indian democracy itself. It is perhaps no accident that the Indian chief minister who has most notably focused on improved service delivery (Arvind Kejriwal) is better thought of as India's most empowered mayor of a large city (Delhi).

One way to balance the trade-offs between local accountability and the risk of local elite capture is by decentralizing with checks and balances, whereby higher government tiers set standards and lower tiers ensure accountability. For instance, for teachers, the state government can stipulate that they will only pay salaries for qualified teachers, from an empanelled roster of eligible teachers. Empanelment can be based on a combination of credentials, scores on the Teacher Eligibility Test, and years of teaching experience.

Crucially, simply being empanelled would not guarantee a job. Teaching positions would be filled and renewed by local governments, and government school teacher posts would essentially become local posts, subject to quality control by the empanelment process. This approach limits local elite capture (because the empanelment process is determined and implemented at higher levels of government) but increases the accountability of teachers to the communities they serve. It would also increase their connection to communities, with a reduced rate of transfers between schools.

An even stronger form of local control would be to transfer budgets to local bodies, and allow them to set salaries of service providers. Currently, 85–95 per cent of a village school's operating costs (of around Rs 10–15 lakh/year) goes to teacher salaries, leaving very little for other education needs.[61] Further, these salaries are *much* higher than market norms, and are not linked to performance (see Chapters 5 and 9). So, having control of the budget would give local bodies the flexibility to hire more teachers at lower salaries if they wish, and to pay effective teachers more to retain and motivate them.[62] Administrative oversight can be maintained by requiring local bodies to hire empanelled teachers and maintain school accounts that would be subject to audit. A similar approach can be used for primary health centres and anganwadi centres.[63]

Decentralization will not eliminate corruption. For instance, local contract teacher hiring is often influenced by bribes or connections.[64] Yet, evidence suggests that they are still at least as effective as regular teachers, *despite* much lower pay and qualifications, and potential irregularities in their hiring.[65] This finding highlights how the combination of greater accountability and connection to the community can compensate for other weaknesses. Further, it is not uncommon even for regular qualified teachers to have paid bribes for their jobs or postings. So, avoiding decentralization due to the *potential* for local corruption would be misguided. Instead, policies should build checks and balances that leverage the power of local accountability for service delivery, while exercising some oversight from higher government tiers, such as via empanelment.[66]

Structural reforms like those proposed above will probably face resistance from vested interests, such as teacher unions in the case of education. Chief ministers will therefore need to advocate for such reforms and marshal public support by highlighting how these reforms will empower citizens. One way of reducing the political risk of attempting such reforms is to first conduct them in the chief minister's own constituency, or another party stronghold, and demonstrate effectiveness before scaling up.

Empowering local bodies enables citizens to use their vote in local elections to reward improved service delivery. It can also help to bridge the trust deficit between citizens and the government by giving citizens more voice in service delivery, and enabling local governments to deliver better services. Doing so can also improve the fiscal compact between citizens and the state and make citizens more willing to pay their taxes, which itself would be a marker of increased trust in the government (see Chapter 7).

Invest in revenue generation capabilities of local bodies

A key reason for the low empowerment of local bodies is that they have few revenue sources, and depend largely on transfers from the state and the Centre. They also do not have the resources to cover the fixed costs of investing in their own revenue generation capacity. So, states should prioritize implementing the ideas in Chapter 7 to help local bodies develop such capacity. Such an investment will not only boost overall government revenues, but it will also raise the *quality* of revenue by increasing receipts from property taxes, and urban user charges (see Chapter 7). Beyond the benefits of generating revenues to finance investments in urban amenities, the greater long-term benefit may be that it also helps accelerate decentralization in India, by increasing the share of total public revenues and expenditure at the local government level.

Greater decentralization is also good for politicians and quality of political leadership

A final point to consider is the incentives of politicians themselves. In many cases, chief ministers, MLAs, and MPs resist decentralization because they do not want to create alternative centres of power. However, empowering local governments is also good for politicians because it will create many more jobs for political leaders that come with *real* authority.

In theory, MLAs and MPs are elected to draft and enact laws. Yet, in practice, voters mainly expect them to deliver local services. Thus, elected leaders spend time trying to influence the local administration to meet voter demands, but without direct control on either personnel or budgets. This is frustrating for MLAs and inefficient for citizens.[67] In contrast, if local bodies are empowered, many MLAs may find it more satisfying to serve as mayors of medium and large cities. As empowered mayors, their roles and responsibilities will better align with what their voters actually want them to do! Such local empowerment can also improve coordination across departments, which is key to improving service delivery, because many governance problems result from departments working in silos and passing responsibility to others.[68]

Shifting political accountability to the level where services are delivered can also create a performance-based pathway for ascending to senior government positions. It is worth recalling that stalwarts of India's independence movement, such as Jawaharlal Nehru, Sardar Vallabhbhai Patel, C. Rajagopalachari, Chittaranjan Das, and Rajendra Prasad started their public careers as mayors or chairpersons of municipal boards of Allahabad, Ahmedabad, Salem, Kolkata, and Patna, respectively. Thus, a chief minister who embarks upon an agenda of greater decentralization of authority to local bodies is likely to not only improve service delivery but strengthen Indian democracy itself.

3.6 The delimitation challenge and opportunity

The year 2026 will mark an important challenge for Indian federalism, since that is when the next electoral delimitation exercise is due. The current allocation of parliamentary seats to states is based on 1971 population figures, as a result of the 42nd Constitutional amendment in 1976 to freeze parliamentary representation based on the 1971 census for twenty-five years. This amendment, passed during Prime Minister Indira Gandhi's tenure, aimed to not penalize states that were effective at controlling population growth. This freeze was extended for another twenty-five years in 2002 through the 84th Constitutional amendment during Prime Minister Vajpayee's tenure with broad-based political support.

A key challenge posed by these freezes is that the current representation in Parliament has deviated significantly from the 'one person, one vote' principle. At present, MPs from UP and Bihar represent over 50 per cent more people than those from Kerala or Tamil Nadu. So, it would be natural to reallocate seats based on current populations to return to a democratic ideal. However, doing so will lead to a dramatic shift in the relative influence of different states in Parliament and, by extension, in the Central government.[69] This would hurt better-performing states, with higher human development and GDP per capita, both politically and economically, and is likely to be resisted by them.[70]

This tension poses a fundamental challenge for India because there are two valid principles that are in conflict. As per the 'equality of all citizens' principle, delimitation is long overdue and should be done in full. However, as per the 'federal' principle, which treats states as meaningful entities in the national polity in their own right, delimitation would not only be unfair, but also break a promise designed to incentivize states to control their populations, which the better-performing states have done—especially by investing heavily in women's health and education.

In practice, large federal systems aim to balance the 'equality of citizens' principle with an 'equality of states' principle to protect the interests of less populous states from being overwhelmed by those of larger ones. For instance, in the US Congress, the House of Representatives follows the 'equality of citizens' principle, with regular population-based delimitation. However, the US Senate follows the 'equality of states' principle, and has two senators from each state regardless of population. Since laws and budgets have to pass both chambers of Congress, this structure balances the two principles.[71]

So, we will need to explore a wide range of solutions and compromises that can adequately balance these and other considerations that are unique to India. In addition to the options of full delimitation or extending the freeze, some intermediate options include: (a) implementing delimitation in the Lok Sabha, but modifying the rules of the Rajya Sabha so that it functions more like the US Senate where each state has an equal vote, (b) continuing to freeze political representation based on the 1971 census, but using current census figures for economic transfers, and (c) reforming the Seventh Schedule of the Constitution to substantially increase state-level fiscal and policy autonomy so that a relative reduction in Parliamentary representation has less impact on citizens' lives in states that experience such a reduction.[72]

This last point is why the challenge of delimitation can also be an *opportunity* to revisit and reoptimize India's federal compact. As shown in this chapter, India is the most over-centralized large country in the world, which reflects unique concerns that the founding framers of our Constitution had. As we enter our seventy-fifth year as a sovereign Republic, much has changed. The political unity of India is far more robust now than in 1950; central planning is much less important for our economic well-being than state-led dynamism; and sharp increases in education and access to information make it easier for local communities to resist elite capture.[73] These changes make it both feasible and optimal to decentralize much more, while maintaining essential checks and balances.

The delimitation challenge is both complex and sensitive, and addressing it will require extended deliberations and trust across the polity. Further, the details of how we resolve it will fundamentally shape India's future for decades to come—far more than any single election. So, it would make sense for all parties to come together and appoint a credible non-partisan Commission to assess and deliberate on a wide variety of options, and present recommendations for leaders and citizens to consider. This process also offers an opportunity to revise India's federal compact to better align with the first principles of federalism and thereby improve governance, service delivery, and citizens' lives.

4. Conclusion

While living in a large country has many benefits, global evidence suggests that smaller countries on average deliver better governance and development outcomes. Nine of the world's ten richest countries by per capita income have populations under 10 million.[74] Further, out of the world's top twenty countries by GDP per capita, sixteen are 'small' by population (below 20 million), two are 'medium' (20 to 50 million), and only two are 'big' (over 50 million).[75] Thus, the key to being a successful large country lies in effectively applying the principles of federalism and decentralization as noted in this chapter.

However, both theory and evidence suggest that India is highly over-centralized, especially compared to other large countries such as China, the US and Brazil. This has contributed to (a) weak democratic accountability for service delivery, (b) governments that are slow to respond to citizen needs by being too far away from the people, (c) ineffective public expenditure that is not a good fit for local conditions, and (d) limited development of local capacity and leadership for governance and service delivery.

The greatest cost of over-centralization may be the weakening of Indian society and democracy by reducing citizens' agency, engagement, and initiative in solving their own problems at a local level, and instead looking to a distant '*sarkar*' (government) to do so. Greater decentralization will increase the number of people engaged in governance, and reduce the time taken to respond to local problems. This point has been succinctly captured by decentralization advocate Ashwin Mahesh, who has noted that: 'The best way to solve our numerous problems is to increase the number of problem-solvers'.[76]

India would do well to heed this message. We need much more decentralization of funds, functions, and functionaries, both from Central to state governments, and especially from state to local governments. Higher government tiers remain important, but their focus should shift from micromanaging programme designs to encouraging much more decentralized innovation, providing technical support, setting standards and providing light-touch checks and balances, and designing systems to reward performance. This is an aspect of India's development journey that chief ministers have considerable influence over, because they can lead in increasing decentralization of powers to local bodies. As with most of the ideas in this book, it only takes a few to lead the way.

Chapter 9

The State and the Market

Central and state governments in India spent over Rs 13 lakh crore in 2022–23,[1] or over 15 per cent of the total budget, on education and health, with most of these funds being used to directly provide services. These services are provided either free of charge or at highly subsidized prices. Yet, a remarkable 30–70 per cent of Indians choose to forgo *free* public options for education and health in favour of fee-charging private providers.

This mass exit to the private sector is a striking critique of the quality of public services in India. Journalist Shankkar Aiyar has recently written an entire book on the topic of public failures and private solutions in India, and notes that 'millions of Indians are disinvesting from hope in the government's promises and adopting alternatives in the wake of such glaring public policy failures.'[2]

The large-scale prevalence and use of private services has both benefits and costs. On the positive side, competition for paying customers makes private providers more accountable, innovative, cost-effective, and responsive to user needs (on average). Further, better-off citizens are more likely to use private services. This can help free up scarce public resources for the poor, who most need public options.

Yet, the large market share of private providers also has notable downsides. First, it creates glaring disparities in access to essential services based on economic status. Since education, health, clean water, and security are key enablers of opportunity for future generations, inequality in these sectors is socially and ethically more problematic than in other areas. Second, when affluent and influential sections of society—including most income taxpayers, policymakers, opinion leaders, and government employees—opt out of public services, there is much less impetus to improve them. Finally, private providers of essential services often exploit their power over consumers and behave unethically, with citizens having limited means of recourse against such behaviour.

As a result, debates on the appropriate role of private providers in delivering services like education and health are often ideologically contentious. On one side, economists like Amartya Sen and Jean Drèze have argued that the de facto privatization of essential services is undesirable, and that we should focus on strengthening public systems for service delivery.[3] Conversely, economists like Jagdish Bhagwati and Arvind Panagariya argue that the problem of improving public sector efficiency in service delivery is almost insurmountable. They suggest that public-private partnership models could be a more effective approach, by combining public financing for universal access with private provision for greater operational efficiency and accountability.[4]

Both these views have merit. However, the traditional state *versus* market debate may be less useful in the Indian setting, where both public and private providers play a large role in service delivery. Instead, this chapter argues that policymakers should focus on how we can use both the state *and* the market for effective service delivery. The goal of policy should be to improve outcomes for *all* citizens— regardless of service provider. So, this chapter argues that we should design systems to leverage strengths and mitigate weaknesses of both public *and* private providers, rather than exclusively relying on either. Thus, governments should view the state and the market as complements that can strengthen overall service delivery, rather than as substitutes for each other.

Yet, even if policymakers leverage private providers for service delivery, it is essential to strengthen public-sector capacity. Improving public service delivery offers dual benefits. First, it directly benefits users of public services. Second, it also indirectly benefits non-users by putting pressure on private providers to improve quality. Thus, improving public service delivery will provide citizens with a strong public option, force private providers to improve, and thereby raise the average quality of services for *all* citizens. Further, even with greater private provision, the government needs to build effective regulatory capacity to ensure that private providers function in the public interest.

A key conceptual point highlighted in this chapter is that the government plays three distinct roles in service delivery: policymaker, regulator, and service provider. Crucially, the way the government should view the private sector varies across these roles. Much of the confusion and unpredictability in how the government interacts with the private sector reflects a lack of clarity regarding these roles. Thus, creating an effective service delivery architecture that leverages both public and private providers for citizen welfare will require the government to separate these roles and perform each of them well.

The discussion in this chapter focuses on primary education and health for three reasons: (a) these sectors have the most extensive research and evidence, (b) they feature a large private sector market share of 30–70 per cent, (c) they are crucial for development, and (d) they comprise large shares of both public and private spending. Yet, many of the concepts in this chapter are also likely to be relevant for other sectors with both public and private providers, such as water, electricity, municipal services, and public sector enterprises, and may also be useful for policymakers in these areas.[5]

This chapter comprises four sections. The first one presents key facts and summarizes high-quality evidence on public and private service delivery in India. The second offers a conceptual framework for the roles of the state and the market in service delivery. The third discusses how the government can make markets work better for all citizens, and the last one discusses policy ideas to leverage markets to better serve the poor.

1. Key Facts and Insights on State and Market Provision of Services in India

1.1 Private options are increasingly popular even when the public option is free

Private schools account for over 50 per cent of school enrolment in urban India and around 30 per cent in rural India.[6] Most of these are not 'elite' private schools but rather 'budget' or 'affordable' private schools. These budget private schools deliver education at a much lower cost per child than government schools. However, since they charge fees, their users on average are better off than those using government schools.[7]

Similarly, in healthcare, nationwide data show that nearly 70 per cent of Indian households report seeking care from private providers.[8] Further, the market share of private health providers is high even when villages have public clinics with qualified staff.[9] Thus, the high market share of private providers is not simply because the public sector is absent but is also a reflection of the quality and reliability of public provision.

Water is another essential service where the private sector plays a large role. While municipal corporations supply piped water in major Indian cities, most cities also have an active private market for water tankers that provide water to locations unconnected to piped water and act as a backup water source to connected locations.[10]

The private sector also plays a growing role in providing security. In 2015, around 7 million people were employed in private security, a figure expected to grow to 12 million by 2022. In contrast, the sanctioned police strength in 2018 was around 2.6 million, with only 2.1 million posts filled.[11] Thus, measured by employee headcount, the private sector is over three times larger than the public sector.

1.2 Private providers (in health and education) have fewer credentials but are better managed and work harder

On average, private providers are less qualified than their public counterparts. For instance, private school teachers typically have fewer years of education, less teacher training, and less teaching experience. They are also paid much lower salaries than government school teachers, often *one-fifth to one-tenth* as much.[12] Thus, on paper, private school teachers appear to be of lower quality than those in government schools.

However, private school teachers are managed much better,[13] and work harder than government school teachers. In a study in unified Andhra Pradesh, we found that private schools had longer school days (by around forty-five minutes), longer school years (by two weeks), much lower teacher absence rates (9 per cent versus 24 per cent), and higher engagement in active teaching during unannounced school visits (51 per cent versus 34 per cent). Similar patterns are seen in older all-India data.[14] Further, lower teacher salaries allow private schools to hire many more teachers. As a result, private schools typically have lower pupil-teacher ratios, and much lower rates of multi-grade teaching, where the same teacher teaches students across multiple grades simultaneously.

These patterns are mirrored in the health sector. The majority of private health providers in India lack formal medical qualifications. For instance, in a study in Madhya Pradesh, my colleagues and I found that 77 per cent of household medical visits were to private providers with no recognized medical qualifications. A nationwide 2010 survey revealed that 79 per cent of households had sought care from unqualified private providers in the past month.[15] Even using more conservative estimates, at least half the patient interactions in India are with unqualified healthcare providers.[16]

Here, too, there is evidence that private health providers, though less qualified, exert more effort than their government counterparts. Using nationwide data from surprise visits to a representative sample of over 1500 public healthcare clinics across nineteen Indian states, my colleagues and I found that around 40 per cent of doctors were absent during working hours.[17] Another study not only confirmed high doctor absence rates in public health centres, but also found it to be unpredictable.[18] This unpredictability is especially costly for the poor, since they cannot afford the time and travel cost of going to a government clinic and not finding a doctor there.

Even when public providers see patients, they expend limited effort. Using detailed observations in public clinics, a study in Delhi found that the average doctor-patient interaction lasts only 3.8 minutes, with the doctor asking only 3.2 questions on average. The short interactions were *not* driven by long patient queues, suggesting low effort in the public sector rather than high patient loads. Remarkably, these patterns persist even when doctors knew they were being observed, suggesting that low effort is typical.

In contrast, in the private sector, absence is much less of a problem because doctors do not get paid if they do not see patients. Multiple studies also find that private providers spend more time with patients, and ask more questions in the diagnostic process.[19]

1.3 Private providers deliver comparable quality—at a significantly lower cost

Both public and private sectors offer unique advantages in service delivery. The public sector benefits from: (a) lacking a profit motive, allowing more resources for service delivery, (b) larger scale and lower costs of capital, (c) lower marketing costs, and (d) more qualified staff. Private-sector strengths include: (a) greater accountability to parents, (b) a focus on cost effectiveness, and market-linked salaries and procurement, and (c) better management and accountability of staff. So, a key question for both citizens and policymakers is to compare the overall quality of public versus private providers. However, doing so is difficult due to other confounding factors.

For instance, in education, private school students have better learning outcomes, but this could merely reflect the fact that they come from higher socio-economic status (SES) households, with greater income, wealth, and more educated parents. Similarly, in health, more complicated cases may be referred to higher quality hospitals, making indicators like 'patient survival rates' an inaccurate and misleading measure of quality.

So, isolating the effects of attending a private school or clinic requires a study design where the *only* difference across participants is the type of institution they use. Economist Venkatesh Sundararaman and I conducted one such study using a large-scale randomized controlled trial (RCT) across five districts in unified Andhra Pradesh.[20] Around 2000 low-income students, who would normally have attended a government school, were selected by lottery to receive a voucher that covered all costs of attending a private primary school, and their outcomes were tracked over four years. Since these vouchers were randomly assigned, comparing outcomes between lottery winners and losers allowed us to isolate the impact of attending a private school.

The findings from the study highlight the complexity of the public versus private debate and the need for a nuanced assessment. On the one hand, after four years, there was no test score difference between lottery winners and losers in maths and Telugu. This suggests that the perceived superiority of private schools, often based on higher *levels* of test scores, mainly reflects selective enrolment of students from higher SES families rather than private schools being more effective at *improving* learning.[21]

On the other hand, private schools allocated much less instructional time to these main subjects (40 per cent less on Telugu; 32 per cent less on maths), and more time to English, science and social studies (EVS), and Hindi. Reflecting this time allocation, voucher winners had modest gains in English and large gains in Hindi.[22] Further, private schools operated at less than one-third the per-child spending in government schools.

Taken together, these results suggest that private schools more than compensated for lower teacher qualifications and pay with higher teacher effort. They delivered learning gains that were either comparable (in math, Telugu and EVS) or better (in Hindi and English) than government schools, and did so at one-third the per-child cost. However, despite being more cost-effective, their absolute effectiveness was not much higher.

In another study, my co-authors and I measured the differences in healthcare quality across public and private providers in rural Madhya Pradesh using highly trained actors. These actors presented symptoms of three standardized medical cases to different providers and carefully recorded all actions taken, including case-appropriate diagnostic checklist completion rates, time spent, all treatments provided (later coded as correct, unnecessary, and incorrect), and prices charged.[23] Since outcomes are compared on how different providers treat the *same* case, the study is able to compare public and private providers without the confounding factor of case complexity.

As in education, this study also found that private providers were less qualified but exerted greater effort, spending 50 per cent longer with patients and completing 50 per cent more items on a diagnostic checklist. Further, the quality of care was comparable across public and private providers—at least for common ailments such as coughs, fevers, aches, and diarrhoea, for which people seek primary care. However, the cost per patient interaction was over five times higher in the public sector, due to higher salaries and lower utilization (see Chapter 12 for more details).

One limitation of our current policies is that they often assume that qualifications are synonymous with quality. However, quality depends on both provider knowledge *and effort*. A key finding from high-quality research over the past decade, in both health and education, is that private providers compensate for lower qualifications with greater effort and deliver comparable or slightly better quality of services, at a significantly lower unit cost than the public sector.

However, while private providers deliver slightly better services more cost-effectively, it is crucial to note that their *absolute* quality of service delivery is still low. For instance, nationwide data from ASER surveys show that only 38.5 per cent of Class 5 students in government schools in rural India can read a Class 2 level paragraph. While the private school figure is higher at 56.8 per cent, it is worth noting that even in private schools across rural India, over 40 per cent of Class 5 students cannot read at a Class 2 level.[24]

The situation is well illustrated by a story of two men in a forest being chased by a bear. The first says: 'We better outrun the bear', to which the second responds: 'I only need to outrun you!' Similarly, as a country, we are being chased by the bear of illiteracy and poor health. The private sector is like the second man in the story. It is slightly better than the public sector, and hence attracts customers, but is also no match for the bear.

This is why I believe that the public *versus* private debate can be a distraction. Rather, we need to focus on designing systems that will improve the quality of *both* public and private options, and thereby improve service quality for *all* users.

1.4 Quality of public and private providers within a market are highly correlated

A key insight from recent research is that the quality of public and private providers is positively correlated within markets. In our study of healthcare in rural India, we found that villages with better public primary healthcare options *also* had better private options.[25] This is also true at the state level. While Kerala and Tamil Nadu have better functioning public health systems than Bihar or UP, these have not displaced the private sector. Rather, the private sector in these states is *also* better than in UP and Bihar. Similarly, a recent high-quality study in Pakistan found that improving public schools led to a significant improvement in *private* schools in the same market. Finally, in my research on NREGS in Andhra Pradesh, we found that improving its implementation led to higher private market wages as private employers had to compete with NREGS.

Thus, studies across education, health, and labour markets show that public and private options compete in a market and do not operate in isolation. This is a critical insight for policy because many Indian elites who use private services think of these providers as operating independently of the public system. However, the findings highlight that this is not true, and that private providers respond to changes in the quality of the public option. This is why improving the quality of public options matters *even* for those who never use public services, because it is a foundation for improving the *overall* system through a cascade effect along the quality distribution of private providers.

So, just like the second man in the story above was motivated to outrun the first one to stay ahead of the bear, helping the first one (public sector) run faster forces the second one (private sector) to also run faster. This increases the chances that *both* of them can outrun the bear, which represents the danger of poor education and health.

2. Conceptualizing State and Market

As noted above, private providers play a large and growing role in delivering essential services in India. However, governments and civil society often hold mixed or even negative views towards them. This ambivalence often contributes to unpredictable and arbitrary government actions towards private providers, which creates an uncertain policy and regulatory environment for both providers and consumers.

To optimize the government's interface with the private sector, it is essential to have conceptual clarity on its three distinct roles in shaping the service delivery ecosystem: policymaking, regulation, and direct provision. As policymakers, governments enact laws regarding private participation in a sector, make commitments on public service delivery, and allocate budgets to meet them. As regulators, they set and enforce rules for providers covering parameters such as safety, quality standards, transparency, and pricing. Lastly, as providers, they directly run public systems to deliver services.

Distinguishing between these three roles is crucial because the government's approach towards the private sector should vary in each role. As policymakers, governments should view the private sector as an *ally*, because they contribute to service delivery, and policymakers should aim to ensure that citizens obtain high-quality services *regardless* of whether they use public or private providers. As regulators, governments should treat the private sector as an *equal*, applying regulations uniformly to all providers, regardless of public or private status. Finally, as providers, governments may see the private sector as a *competitor* since they compete for users.

In practice, the majority of government personnel and budgets are allocated to its role as a provider. So, the default pattern of thinking within government often focuses on its direct provision role. As a result, the policymaking function ends up focusing more on the interests of the department as a 'provider' rather than the interests of citizens.

For instance, in education, district education officers (DEOs) oversee both the operation of government schools, *and* the inspection and regulation of private schools in their district. Consequently, numerous private schools across India were shut down for not meeting provisions of the 2009 Right to Education Act, even though many government-run schools were also in violation of these same provisions. Since DEOs in their 'provider' role see private schools as undesirable, it is not surprising that they try to use their 'regulator' role to disproportionately target private schools. Ultimately, citizens who were deprived of access to options they preferred are the ones who paid the price.[26]

The social cost of such role ambiguity is seen in other sectors as well. For instance, for many years, the civil aviation ministry (the policymaker) implemented policies to favour Air India, which was a government-run airline till recently. Rather than focusing on improving aviation options at lower prices for *all* Indians, such as through an open skies policy welcoming all airlines, India's aviation policy focused on protecting the interests of Air India through negotiating bilateral landing rights with other countries. This priority contributed to lower overall aviation capacity, and flights to and from India. Since foreign carriers were more competitive, expanding capacity would hurt Air India, whereas restricting capacity helped preserve some market share for Air India.

The government's inability to effectively separate its duty as a policymaker (which was to maximize national welfare) from its concerns as a provider (which was to protect Air India) could partly explain why India, despite its millennia-old civilization and culture, remained a relatively less sought-after tourist destination. In contrast, a tiny country like Singapore for many years had more tourists than India in part because of its open skies policy that allowed any airline to fly passengers in and out of Singapore. In the end, it is the Indian economy and citizens who suffered from the lost opportunity of fewer tourists.

Distinguishing between these roles and having staff serve in only one role at a time will increase role clarity and reduce conflicts of interest within the government. As policymakers, governments should implement policies that maximize the *overall* quality of services offered to all citizens. As regulators, they should ensure a level playing field across providers, address market failures, and make it easier for users to hold *both* public and private providers accountable. Finally, as providers, governments must improve the quality of services they offer, per rupee spent, to ensure the existence of high-quality public options that can guarantee universal access to essential services.

Since most of this book focuses on ideas for improving government performance as a provider of services, the ideas in this chapter focus on how the government can improve its performance as a regulator and policymaker. Doing so can help markets work better and also leverage non-government providers, both for-profit and non-profit, to improve public welfare. This is a critical area that needs more clarity and attention since policy and regulatory decisions shape the entire ecosystem of supply and demand, which affects all Indians. Yet, governments in India do not pay enough attention to their policy and regulatory functions because they focus on their role as a provider.

3. Making Markets Work Better for Overall Welfare

A core principle in economics is that increasing choices for consumers and competition among providers promotes welfare by offering more options, and inducing productive efficiency. India's own liberalization experience illustrates this point well. Growing up in the 1980s, it was normal to experience shortages and waiting lists for a wide variety of products. This changed after the transformative economic reforms of the 1990s. A key component of these reforms was reducing entry barriers for new firms and products, both domestic and foreign. In turn, this led to increased supply, higher quality, and lower costs across sectors, which improved the welfare of hundreds of millions of Indians.

It is perhaps no accident that the greatest challenges for the Indian economy are in sectors such as education and health that have not seen similar reforms. Quality service delivery in India is constrained in large part by the *low supply* of high-quality options. This shortage, in turn, leads to queues and waiting lists for access and increases the pricing power of the few high-quality providers.[27] Thus, Indian policy should place a very high priority on expanding the supply of high-quality service providers, regardless of whether they are in the public or private sector.

However, improving education and health by increasing choice and competition is much more difficult than in sectors like cars or computers. In part, this is because the relation between observable short-term provider actions and long-term outcomes is less clear, which makes it difficult for consumers to assess provider quality. Health and education are also labour-intensive sectors that require personalized provision, which makes it difficult to scale up uniformly high-quality production, unlike in the case of manufactured goods, where economies of scale can both increase supply and reduce cost per unit of quality more easily. Yet, despite this caveat, governments can still do more to increase choice and competition in service-delivery sectors, and make markets work better.

3.1 Regulate with a light touch, based on disclosures rather than mandates

The simplest way to increase choice and competition is to reduce regulatory barriers to the entry of private service providers. Yet, there are also several good reasons for service-delivery sectors to be subject to regulation. First, service provision often takes place in quasi-public spaces such as schools and hospitals, which warrant minimum standards of physical safety. Second, there is considerable information asymmetry between providers and consumers: for instance, patients often do not know what they need and are hence vulnerable to doctors and hospitals recommending unnecessary medications and procedures to increase their fees and profits. Third, power asymmetry between providers and consumers can make it more difficult for consumers to enforce accountability: for instance, an accident victim who desperately needs hospitalization is unlikely to be able to compare prices across hospitals and negotiate fees in advance.

These challenges do warrant regulation. Yet, though they may be well-intentioned, regulations in India are often heavy-handed and arbitrarily enforced. Regulatory norms are often imposed without considering whether their social benefits exceed the costs of compliance. Private service providers are constantly wary of violating some regulation or the other. In some cases, they find it impossible to not be in violation because different rules and regulations may be in contradiction with each other. This, in turn, gives wide discretionary power to officials, who can shut down facilities for a variety of reasons and extort bribes from providers in return for overlooking regulatory violations.

Many of these problems are seen in education. The Right to Education (RTE) Act imposed strict input-based norms on private schools, which forced many low-cost schools that were valued in their communities to shut down.[28] Other norms reduced schools' ability to optimally allocate resources to improve education. For instance, the RTE requires *all* teachers to be qualified. While well-intentioned, such a mandate is counterproductive because there is no evidence that teaching credentials in India improve teacher effectiveness.[29] Some states also prescribe minimum teacher salaries in private schools that are well above the market rate. This stipulation negates a key source of private school efficiency, which is that lower teacher salaries allow them to hire more teachers at any given budget, and deliver comparable or slightly better education quality than the government system, but at a much lower cost.

These rules leave many private schools with only two options: to either shut down, or falsely report compliance with regulatory norms, especially on teacher qualifications and pay, while deviating from them in practice.[30] In the second case, it is not uncommon to bribe school inspectors to turn a blind eye to this deviation. The current unrealistically high input-based norms, which cannot be met by many schools, make it difficult for honest operators to enter this space. They also cede market share to less honest providers who claim compliance on paper, while not being compliant in practice.

An alternative approach to regulation would be as follows: Rather than input *mandates*, regulators should require a public *disclosure* of key school inputs. This approach would acknowledge the wide variation across India and allow diverse models of schooling to emerge at different levels of cost and affordability, while still using regulation to mitigate market failures. Thus, schools could be sanctioned, or even shut down, for *lying* about their teachers' qualifications but would not be forced to hire *only* credentialled teachers. This approach to regulation recognizes that *every mandate costs money*, which has to be recovered through higher fees, and allows the market to determine if a qualification is worth paying a premium for. It may also have the downstream benefit of rewarding teacher training programmes that actually prepare their graduates to become more effective teachers as opposed to simply providing a certificate.[31]

More generally, regulation based on disclosure would improve market functioning, and allow for variation in approaches across locations, providers, and price points. It will also make the environment less 'corrosive' by moving from a low-level equilibrium of unrealistic norms that are not enforced uniformly and associated with bribes and corruption, to a more transparent policy regime based on disclosure of the truth and letting citizens decide on the inputs that they want providers to focus on.

3.2 Invest in providing information to allow for informed decision-making

Regulation based on disclosure can also help citizens make informed choices. Markets flourish when providers compete, when consumers are well informed about price and quality differences across providers, and providers are rewarded for improving quality or lowering cost with greater market share and profits. For instance, a key success driver of e-commerce websites is that they help markets work better by enabling consumers to read reviews and compare prices, and thereby make more informed choices.

But in service delivery sectors, citizens often cannot make such informed decisions, in part because product quality is difficult to measure. For example, parents may know differences in fees across schools but often know less about the quality of classroom instruction, or how they vary across schools. Similarly, patients often find it difficult to assess the quality of medical care they receive.

At present, one way the market tries to address this problem is that providers invest in branding and reputation, and users seek recommendations and referrals from friends and family. However, the highly fragmented landscape of health and education providers limits the effectiveness of these solutions. Hence, governments may be able to significantly improve public welfare by investing in independent measurement of provider quality and providing easily accessible public reports of quality.

This conjecture is supported by recent studies. For example, an important study in Punjab (Pakistan) found that providing parents with credible information on school quality, for both public and private schools, through 'school report cards' led to a significant improvement in average learning outcomes as well as a *reduction* in fees charged by private schools. This was driven by increased competitive pressure created by the availability of better information on school prices and quality. In India, a similar study in Rajasthan found that school report cards improved private school quality, though there was no improvement in public schools in this case.[32]

These results suggest that regulators can help markets work better by creating and maintaining a public database where all recognized schools are listed, along with information on key parameters such as facilities, teacher details, learning outcomes, and fees. This can be seamlessly combined with the previous idea of regulation by disclosure. Schools would update their information online annually, and that information would automatically be reflected in a publicly searchable database. Certain fields in the database such as results from independent assessments of learning, as well as audits of disclosure can be filled over time. It may also be possible to add information on (verified) parent ratings and feedback.

A similar approach could also be considered for health clinics and providers. One natural starting point for this database could be the list of empanelled providers under publicly funded health insurance schemes. While assessing quality is difficult, simply providing information on qualifications, experience, number of patients seen, fees charged for different services and potentially including patient ratings could significantly improve the information available to patients while choosing a provider. Such an initiative could be considered under the National Digital Health Mission. This is also an area where states can create their own initiatives, including inviting neutral third parties, such as patients' rights organizations, to design and maintain such a database.

Of course, the private sector could also create such information portals, but their effectiveness is limited by their need to find sustainable revenue models. For instance, private rating agencies often charge the entities that are being rated for the costs of assessment, which can create a conflict of interest. Other revenue models are based on subscription fees, but the poor typically cannot afford to pay for high-quality information.

Good information provides public benefits beyond what can be monetized by a private provider. This is why public investments in information to make markets work better can be a highly cost-effective intervention to improve overall service delivery quality. This is also an area where philanthropic funds supporting high-quality non-profit organizations can sharply improve public welfare at a low cost (see Chapter 18). These efforts could also draw on private sector expertise to replicate practices of successful e-commerce platforms who invest heavily in fraud analytics to identify and delete fake reviews, and in building a reputation for integrity by not allowing firms to delete negative reviews.

These ideas are not rocket science and can be implemented within a few years, at least in a few cities with a dedicated team with the requisite skills. However, governments often do not think about acting along these lines because they focus most of their attention on their role as a provider as opposed to functioning as an enabler of an *ecosystem* of high-quality, accountable public *and* private providers. For example, most health ministers and secretaries think of their job as running the public health system, though this only accounts for 30 per cent of primary healthcare sought in India.

This is an area where reimagining the government's role, guided by the principles and evidence in this chapter, can yield enormous benefits to public welfare. An approach to regulating *all* providers based on disclosure, transparency, and quality ratings with user inputs, will allow governments to enhance accountability for providers, and enable more informed choices for consumers. This can be a highly cost-effective way of improving citizens' access to better quality services through both private and public providers.

4. Leveraging Markets to Better Serve the Poor

The ideas above can help the government be a more effective regulator to increase the supply and quality of private providers. I now discuss how the government, in its role as a policymaker, can leverage markets, choice, and competition to better serve the poor.

Markets have many great strengths, including providing incentives for innovation and efficiency. Combined with choice and competition, markets have contributed immensely to human welfare in India and around the world. Yet, the market also has a fundamental limitation, which is that it values people and allocates resources to them based on their purchasing power. In short, competitive markets are wonderful in the aggregate but do not care for people without purchasing power.

While the democratic ideal is 'one *person*, one vote,' markets allocate resources to people on the basis of 'one *rupee*, one vote'. Thus, while both democracy and markets have many virtues, including valuing individual freedom, there is also constant tension between them that democratic market-based societies need to navigate. This is a key reason why governments try to ensure access to essential services such as education and healthcare for all through providing free or subsidized public services. However, as noted above, these publicly provided services are often of poor quality, while markets may offer services of comparable or better quality at a much lower unit cost.

4.1 Vouchers and public-private partnerships (PPP)

How can we combine the strengths of markets such as accountability, efficiency, and responsiveness to users while mitigating the proclivity of markets to exclude the poor?

One simple but powerful idea is to provide the poor with purchasing power equivalent to government spending on public services, enabling them to access market solutions. For instance, the government could issue the per capita expenditure that it incurs in service provision directly to citizens as a voucher, which is redeemable across a choice of public and private providers. Citizens, including the poorest, would be able to choose their provider, pay by voucher, and the government would reimburse providers directly.

As a concrete example, governments in India spend over Rs 30,000 annually per child on school education but obtain poor value for money, due to a combination of very high teacher salaries relative to market norms and low accountability (see Chapter 5). Distributing even 80 per cent of these funds directly to parents as a voucher would empower them to choose private schools costing up to Rs 2000 per month, which will cover the fees of most private schools in the country.[33]

Another approach is to use public-private partnerships (PPPs) to contract private providers to deliver services. An example would be charter schools in education. Charter schools are operated by private providers, often non-profit organizations, but retain 'public' characteristics by not engaging in selective admission, not charging fees beyond those permissible in public schools, and following a recognized curriculum. They are reimbursed a per-student amount by the government for every student they enrol. However, they maintain autonomy on teacher hiring, management, and compensation. While they have not yet been evaluated in India, global evidence suggests that charter schools have often been able to deliver significantly better learning outcomes than default public schools at equal or lower cost per student.[34]

4.2 Exit and voice

Approaches such as vouchers and PPPs can not only improve efficiency and value for money, but also boost empowerment of marginalized groups. In his classic book *Exit, Voice, and Loyalty*, Albert Hirschman noted that people can improve how they are treated in a relationship through 'voice' and 'exit'.[35] The voice mechanism works by providing feedback and hoping that it is heard and acted upon. In contrast, the exit mechanism works by forcing improvement through the threat of exit to a competitor.

Accountability in markets is mainly influenced by exit, while accountability in policy is driven more by voice. If consumers are unhappy with a product, they usually switch ('exit') to a competing offering. However, if citizens are unhappy with a policy, it is more common to vote, organize, and lobby to change the policy using their 'voice' as citizens than to 'exit' the country! However, both voice and exit mechanisms matter across contexts. Companies respond to customer feedback (voice) as well as the loss of customers (exit). Similarly, political leaders respond to voter opinion (voice) and also to voters opting for other candidates (exit).

A critical point to note is that voice is typically more effective when there is a credible threat of exit. Companies and organizations are more likely to respond to customer or employee feedback if they have an option to switch to someone else. This principle also applies to personal relationships. For instance, many women in India and globally remain in abusive domestic relationships due to limited exit options, driven by a lack of economic means to provide for themselves. Thus, greater economic empowerment of women not only increases their ability to exit abusive relationships, it also empowers them to assert their rights within existing relationships by strengthening their voice.[36]

This framework highlights why the poor are doubly disadvantaged in the status quo. First, they have limited voice to improve service delivery, partly because of the power asymmetry between poor beneficiaries and service providers such as teachers and PDS dealers, and partly because of their lower levels of education and awareness. Second, their lower ability to pay for market solutions means that they become 'captive customers' of public providers without a credible exit option. This further limits their voice, and reduces pressure on public providers to deliver better services.

Thus, providing vouchers to the poor and marginalized directly strengthens their ability to exit to private providers, and *also* boosts their voice, as they would no longer be captive customers for an inefficient public sector. Importantly, this choice can improve the quality of public provision even without users actually exiting to private providers, because the mere *option* of doing so will put pressure on the public system to improve.

Note that vouchers and charter schools *do not privilege private options* over public ones. Rather, what they do is to empower the poor with more options using the *same* amount of taxpayer funds that are already being spent in their name, but which they can currently avail only through the public system. Thus, for the government as a policymaker, vouchers and charters offer the double advantage of empowering the poor *and* increasing the accountability of the government as a provider.

The idea of combining public financing for universal access to services for the poor with choice across both public and private providers for better accountability is an old one. For instance, Nobel Prize-winning economist Milton Friedman proposed vouchers for education in 1963. However, one reason for limited take-up of this idea, in addition to strong political opposition from public-sector unions, is that there are also several challenges in effectively designing and implementing voucher and PPP-based models.

Some of these challenges and potential solutions are discussed below.

4.3 Designing vouchers and PPPs for equity

Ensuring that vouchers or PPPs deliver equitable access requires careful design. This is because the cost of providing services often varies substantially across people. For instance, even if the value of a voucher equals the *average* cost per student in a government school, private schools may refuse to accept students with special needs or disabilities, because the costs of serving them are higher. Similarly, private schools and clinics are unlikely to move to remote rural areas with low population density.

This is why government provision is often considered the only way to provide universal access. However, it is often ignored that the government *also* incurs much higher costs per user to provide access in remote areas. This is because the fixed costs of setting up and running a facility are distributed over a much smaller user base. For example, India has over one lakh small schools with fewer than twenty students across grades 1–5, primarily located in low-density, rural areas.[37] The combination of low enrolment and minimum staffing norms of at least two teachers per school, results in much higher per-student costs in these sub-scale schools. For instance, the average cost per student exceeds Rs 75,000 per year in schools with less than twenty students, compared to around Rs 30,000 per year in schools with over sixty students.

Thus, a crucial point to appreciate is that government provision conceals the enormous variation in costs of service provision across locations and users. While private schools may be unwilling to operate in remote rural areas at an average voucher value of Rs 30,0000, they may be happy to do so if the voucher value matched the true cost of public service provision in that area; say Rs 75,000, as in the example above. At a higher voucher value, private schools may also develop more cost-effective models, like organizing transportation for students from remote areas to a centrally located school, and investing the savings in improving school quality. Of course, the government can do the same thing and run buses to provide access while also obtaining the quality benefits of larger-scale facilities (see

Chapter 11). The problem is that governments are *much* slower to consider and implement such innovations.

The same logic of adjusting voucher values for equity applies to children with special educational needs or disabilities. Again, it is believed that only governments can fulfil the social responsibility of providing equitable educational access for such children. Yet, we forget that the government also incurs higher costs in doing so. Accounting for the full cost of providing special educational services, and augmenting voucher values for such children, can make it economically viable for private or non-profit schools to cater to their needs.[38] In many cases, motivated non-profit and civil-society organizations may do a better job of educating students with special needs than the government, because staff in public facilities can often be callous to the needs of the disadvantaged.

Overall, achieving equity goals as a society requires constant attention, *regardless* of whether providers are public or private. A key insight from this section is that it is *not* true that the only option for achieving equity goals is public provision. If there is accurate accounting of the full cost of public service provision to disadvantaged or remote populations, setting voucher values equal to these costs may make it attractive for civil-society or private providers to serve more of them. This approach, along with robust regulations, can help governments augment national capacity for meeting equity goals.

So, to promote equity, the government as a policymaker should empower the poorest and most disadvantaged with *options* for accessing both public and private providers. As a regulator, the government should require disclosure on equity arrangements by providers, and monitor compliance with equity commitments made to receive voucher or charter funding. Finally, as a provider, the government should offer high-quality services that the poor choose willingly, rather than out of necessity from not having other options.

4.4 Procurement and contracting

Another key challenge is procurement. This is a complex topic on which much has been written, especially in the case of large infrastructure projects.[39] Two central issues are incomplete information on provider quality at the time of procurement, and inability to write complete contracts that specify the obligations of the public and the private parties under all future states of the world.

Both points are well-illustrated by an important recent study on PPPs in education in Liberia.[40] Using a high-quality randomized evaluation, the study found that students who attend PPP schools have significantly higher test scores on *average*. However, there was a large variation in quality across private school operators, with some being no better than the public schools and others being much better. The problem, however, is that there was no way of knowing these quality differences at the time of procurement.

The second problem is also illustrated by the same study. Standard concerns of PPPs in education, such as selective admission of students and charging extra fees, were *not* seen because the contractual terms prohibited them. However, one large PPP operator chose to unenroll students to control class size. While this may have helped those who were retained, it imposed substantial hardship on those who were forced to switch schools. This was clearly socially undesirable, but the operator acted fully within the terms of the contract because there was no stipulation preventing such an action. This example highlights the problem of incomplete contracts, as it is often not feasible to write a contract with private parties that anticipates and addresses all eventualities.

These are complex issues that have posed challenges for PPPs in many sectors, including infrastructure. In practice, the optimal way of addressing them will depend on the context and sector-specific details. But the good news is that, unlike procurement decisions for large infrastructure projects that lock in the government for a long time, users can switch providers more easily in the case of health and education.

So, a practical way forward would be for governments to create a list of empanelled providers based on a few basic metrics of quality, where vouchers may be redeemed. Over time, providing voucher users a choice across both public and private providers is likely to be an effective way to (a) weed out low-quality private providers, (b) create incentives for high-quality private providers to expand capacity to respond to higher demand, and (c) put pressure on public systems to improve their quality to match the more effective private providers.[41] Paying providers dynamically on a per-user basis, verified by electronically matching user and provider IDs, can also help reduce fraud.[42]

4.5 Targeting and fiscal implications

Implementing voucher and charter-based models can also pose a fiscal challenge for the government by attracting people who are currently availing of market solutions on their own. For instance, if the government were to implement a universal school voucher system by providing *all* children with a voucher equal to the per-child cost in the public system, many families who are currently paying for private schools on their own would also obtain the voucher. This could sharply increase the fiscal costs of the voucher programme by directing public funds to households who would have otherwise covered the costs of private schools by themselves.

Thus, reforms that aim to empower the poor to access market-based solutions will need to pay careful attention to targeting to manage fiscal costs. In practice, identifying households to target for voucher eligibility will require using other databases such as the Below Poverty Line (BPL) database, Socio-Economic and Caste Census (SECC), or the systems used to determine eligibility under the Economically Weaker Sections (EWS) clause of the Right to Education Act. Over time, as targeting databases get stronger, it may make sense to offer a sliding scale of voucher values with larger amounts of public funding for poorer and more disadvantaged households. Such a sliding scale of vouchers can increase the overall progressivity of India's tax and transfer systems.[43]

4.6 Importance of investing in a robust public option

While governments should consider ways of leveraging private providers to better serve the poor, the most important thing they can do to make the private sector work better that is directly in their control is to improve the quality of *public* service delivery using several of the ideas suggested in the previous five chapters and also in the sectors chapters. Going back to the analogy of the chasing bear, if the government can get the first man (public sector) to run faster, the second one (private) will also run faster!

A high-quality public option is also critical because it provides citizens with a strong 'default' option. This matters because, even though it is important for consumers to have choices, a recent body of evidence has highlighted the possibility of 'choice overload'. While standard economic models assume that more choice is always good, it does not account for the cognitive cost of making decisions across many choices. After accounting for this cost, research has shown that expanding the number of choices beyond a point can actually *reduce* consumer welfare.[44]

This risk is magnified for the uneducated and the poor. Several studies have shown how companies exploit unsophisticated consumers by hiding consumer-unfriendly terms and conditions in the fine print.[45] Further, recent evidence has shown that poverty-induced stresses can impair decision-making.[46] In settings where the consequences of decisions manifest only far in the future, expanding choices need not improve consumer welfare. For instance, a study by Nobel Prize-winning economist Richard Thaler showed that expanding investment options in retirement savings plans could worsen portfolio returns via an increase in 'naive' diversification.[47] There is also evidence from India that less-experienced investors may do worse when their investment options are expanded.[48]

These results highlight an important challenge for policy. On the one hand, democracy is premised on respecting the choices of every citizen, regardless of education or income. Thus, expanding choices for the poor should be desirable because it enhances their agency. As Amartya Sen has noted: 'Development consists of the removal of various types of unfreedoms that leave people with little choice and little opportunity of exercising their reasoned agency'.[49] On the other hand, there is also evidence showing that, when given too much agency, people make bad decisions, which they *regret* in hindsight. Studies also show that interventions that limit citizens' ability to make suboptimal choices can improve their welfare.[50] How should we balance this trade-off?

One way to address this complex issue is the idea of 'benign paternalism' suggested by Richard Thaler and Cass Sunstein. Several studies find that default options have a strong influence on decision-making. So, one way to protect people from poor decision-making *without* constraining their choices is to have a publicly vetted default option. This default would not restrict choice but would provide a convenient automatic option for those who do not want to expend effort in making a choice. This approach is also used for helping employees make investment choices for retirement savings plans, where the hundreds of available options can quickly become overwhelming. So, retirement plans often offer a default option based on employees' expected retirement age, which many employees choose to use. But they are free to change the investments if they want to.

Similarly, a high-quality public option for basic service delivery can serve as a default option that citizens can use even without thinking too much. However, giving citizens a choice of availing private options with comparable levels of per-unit funding will empower them and increase accountability of public providers.

4.7 Some practical examples

The two examples below integrate and illustrate the ideas in this section.

Example 1: Choice-based DBT in the PDS

One application of these ideas could be in India's Public Distribution System (PDS). The PDS delivers highly subsidized food grains to the poor, and is India's largest welfare programme. Yet, it also has problems of leakage and quality (see Chapter 6). Many experts have recommended replacing subsidized food with an income transfer equal to the subsidy value. This could (a) reduce corruption and leakage by eliminating the dual-price system and bypassing intermediaries, (b) reduce administrative costs of storage and transportation, and (c) increase beneficiary flexibility over what foods to consume and facilitate dietary diversity away from the rice and wheat provided under the PDS.

At the same time, replacing in-kind entitlements of the PDS with income transfers made as a direct benefit transfer (DBT) also poses considerable risks. These include (a) poor implementation, which may make beneficiaries worse off, (b) the value of transfers may be inadequate, especially if not indexed for inflation, (c) access to banks, ATMs, and markets may vary across locations, and (d) the possibility of worsening women's positions within households, since studies show that women are more likely to control use of food grains, whereas men are more likely to control the use of cash. Given compelling arguments on both sides of this debate, how should policymakers decide?

A simple but powerful solution would be to offer beneficiaries a choice. Rather than policymakers deciding between PDS and DBT and imposing this decision on the entire population, beneficiaries could choose what they would prefer: the subsidized food or the cash transfer. Crucially, under a choice-based system, the default option would continue to be in-kind benefits through the PDS shop. However, households could also choose to avail of a pre-specified income transfer (DBT) instead of their in-kind PDS benefits, with funds transferred into the account of the female household head.

This approach is now feasible since the PDS has been digitized with e-PoS machines and Aadhaar-based authentication. Thus, beneficiaries can record their choice on the e-PoS machine, and avail the option that best suits them. Choice-based DBT preserves the PDS as the default, but weakens the monopoly of PDS dealers by providing citizens with an exit option. Further, even if they continue using the PDS, the mere presence of the DBT option will put pressure on the PDS system to reduce leakage and deliver better quality service. To make it economically viable for PDS dealers to operate even with a reduced market share, they can be encouraged to function like general *kirana* stores that sell multiple items, with the PDS grains just being one of their product lines.

The choice-based approach also reduces the political and ethical risk of reforms. Since the PDS will remain the default option, beneficiaries who are happy with the PDS can continue as before. However, those who would prefer DBT can avail of the option. This approach recognizes the enormous variation across time and space in beneficiary conditions and preferences, and enables food security policy to move from a 'one-size-fits-all' approach towards one that is better customized to local needs and preferences. Such an approach can be piloted in a few urban areas to begin with, and expanded based on evaluation of its impacts and citizen feedback.

Such a choice-based architecture is an example of how we can design systems so that the poor have access to multiple providers and are not captive customers of a public monopoly. It is likely to improve service delivery by empowering the poor with an 'exit' option, which will also strengthen their 'voice' within the public system. It would also give citizens a direct voice in determining how budgetary allocations made in their name are actually spent. Thus, a choice-based system would also represent a strengthening of democracy by giving citizens a regular say in how they avail their benefits.

Example 2: Charter Schools

These principles can also be applied to the case of education. A specific idea for state governments to consider is to pilot a charter school model, whereby the government engages high-quality non-governmental education providers and signs a management contract with them to operate government schools.

While details vary, charter schools typically have the following broad characteristics.

First, they are 'public' in the sense that they cannot selectively admit students, or charge fees other than those permissible in public schools. Second, they are reimbursed a fixed amount per student, pegged at a fraction of the per-student spending in the government system, with the fraction depending on the extent to which the government provides its own facilities to the charter operator. Third, while their curricula need not be identical to that of public schools, they must follow the curriculum of a recognized board. Fourth, they have considerably more managerial autonomy, especially with regard to the hiring, retention, compensation, and performance management of teachers and staff.

A natural starting point for such pilots is in urban areas where government schools often occupy prime land, and have decent infrastructure and facilities. However, they have very low enrolment due to weak demand. One way to address this challenge is to offer high-quality private school operators management contracts to run underutilized government schools, with a fixed per-child reimbursement. This will incentivize them to improve quality and attract students to the 'public' charter schools, and away from lower-quality public and private schools. Further, high population density in urban areas ensures that parents will continue to have a choice across public, private, and charter school options. This is consistent with the principle of ensuring adequate choice and competition.

Charter school pilots should be framed as 'grand challenges', inviting motivated, high-quality school operators to undertake the challenge of delivering quality education at scale for low-SES students. Ensuring quality education to tens of millions of first-generation learners is a formidable challenge that India has not yet solved. Hence, a charter school 'grand challenge' should be seen as expanding the portfolio of options that we develop as a country to address this pressing challenge.

5. Conclusion

The core challenge of service delivery in India has been succinctly summarized by Manish Sabharwal, who has noted that: 'The government has an execution deficit, the private sector has a trust deficit, and civil society has a scale deficit.' In other words, the government has scale and legitimacy but has weak implementation; the private sector can implement well and at scale, but is not trusted due to its profit motive and exclusion of those who cannot pay; and civil society organizations are trusted and can implement well, but are limited in scale due to constraints in staff and funding.

So, we need innovative collaborations across all three sets of actors to provide high quality services at scale, while ensuring access to *all* Indians, regardless of their ability to pay. Several commentators, including researchers and former senior officials, have urged the government to harness the dynamism of the private sector and the public-spirited motivation of civil-society organizations for better service delivery.[51] Yet, these calls often get entangled in ideological debates about the role of the state and the market in society and service delivery. This chapter has aimed to demonstrate that this debate may be a distraction. We would do well to think less in terms of state *versus* market, which is how the government may think in its 'provider' role; and more in terms of state *and* market, which is how the government should think in its 'policymaker' role.

State governments should therefore aim to expand the supply of cost-effective, high-quality private providers, improve the quality and accountability of public providers, and empower all citizens— including the poor—to choose from a broader set of options. To do this effectively, they must separate the roles of government as a policymaker (where the private sector is an ally), provider (where the private sector is a competitor), and regulator (for whom the public and private sectors should be equal).

As regulators, governments can greatly improve market functioning by focusing on transparent disclosure rather than imposing uniform input mandates, and by investing in providing credible information on the quality of all providers in a market. Doing so will boost entry and competition, informed consumer choice, and overall quality of services. As policymakers, governments should explore models of public financing and private provision to empower the poor with better exit options, which will also strengthen their voice within the public system that otherwise treats them poorly as captive customers.

Designing systems to do all this will require careful attention to sector-specific details. It will also require investing in *other* areas of state capacity such as regulation, procurement, and independent quality audits that have been neglected due to the government's focus on its provider role. But this is an area where state governments have considerable autonomy, and states that take the initiative to experiment with such models (and evaluate them carefully) may be able to sharply improve the quality of services available to their citizens and emerge as national role models.

Section III

Accelerating India's Development

Chapter 10

Shifting the Preston Curve for Development

India faces enormous development challenges, as outlined in Chapter 1. At the same time, we also have much to be proud of. Despite the governance challenges described in Chapters 2–9, we have done reasonably well when considered in a global perspective. As we will see in this chapter, India's development outcomes closely track per capita GDP, and have improved along with GDP growth, especially since the 1980s. Overall, India's development performance can be graded as a solid B+, reflecting our above-average performance on some metrics and average performance on others.

Yet, we have the potential to excel at an A or even A+ level. The problem is not that we are doing badly. It is just that we can do *much* better if we improve the effectiveness of the Indian state. Chapters 4–9 provide a roadmap for doing so by strengthening key systemic components of governance. Chapters 11–16 apply these principles to outline evidence-based reform roadmaps to improve outcomes in the key sectors that are crucial to India's development.

This chapter serves as a key conceptual bridge between the governance themes in Chapters 4–9, and the sectors in Chapters 11–16. It lays out a vision for how we can accelerate improvements in human development at any level of income, and thereby shift the Preston curve for development (an idea explained further in this chapter). Accelerating human development can, in turn, accelerate economic growth, and thereby jumpstart a virtuous cycle of faster development and growth. It also aims to highlight that investing in improving state effectiveness should be a top priority for development discourse, by noting that weak state capacity is a *critical* binding constraint to achieving national and global development goals.

It comprises three sections. The first presents India's development performance in a global comparative context. The second discusses the 'growth' versus 'development' debate, and its implications for India. The third presents scenarios for India in 2047, and shows that we will have unacceptably poor development outcomes if we continue along our existing trajectory. It then shows how improving public systems, state capacity, and public expenditure quality can spark a virtuous cycle that can accelerate both human development and economic growth. Doing so will also reduce inequity and allow many more Indians to both participate in and contribute to accelerated economic growth.

1. Benchmarking India's Performance

The absolute levels of human development outcomes in India leave much to be desired. However, we need to assess India's performance in the context of our much lower per capita income because there is a strong and consistent positive correlation between per capita income and key human development outcomes, as seen in the graphs below.

Figure 10.1: Health—Life Expectancy by GDP/Capita[1]

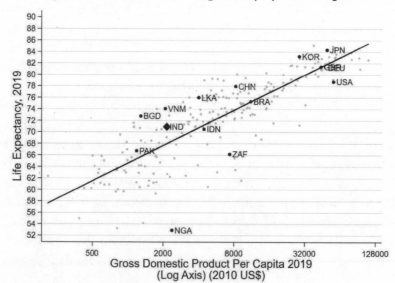

Note(s): Data from the World Bank, graph created by author.

Figure 10.2:   Health—Infant Mortality by GDP/Capita

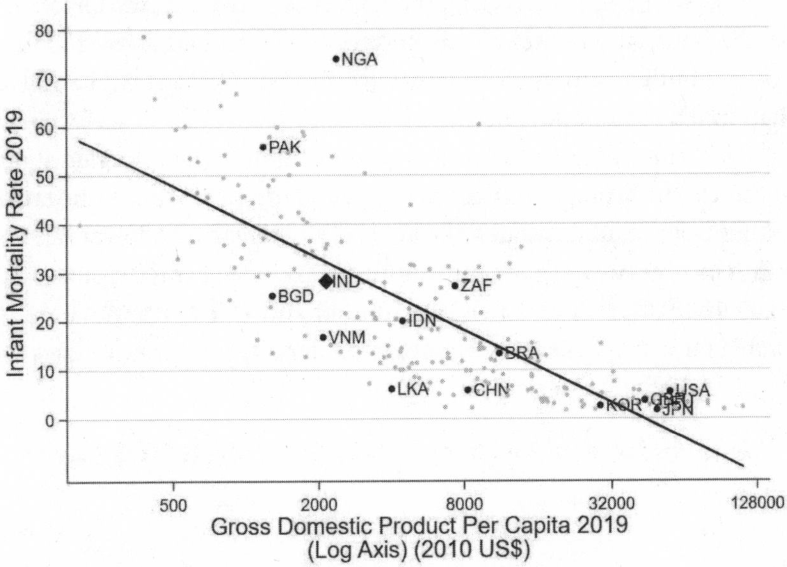

Note(s): Data from the World Bank, graph created by author.

There are three key messages in these figures. First, GDP per capita really matters for development outcomes. Richer countries have better human development outcomes across health (shown above), education, and public safety.[2] This reflects a combination of households in richer countries having more resources (including parental education, which strongly benefits child health and education), as well as governments having higher tax revenues as a fraction of GDP per capita to invest more in these areas.

Second, India's performance aligns closely with our GDP per capita. In fact, the figures above suggest that we do slightly better than expected on infant mortality and life expectancy after adjusting for GDP per capita. The same is true for crime—though this could also reflect poor crime reporting (see Chapter 13). Finally, while India does not participate in the internationally comparable PISA tests, other cross-country studies have estimated that (a) there is a strong correlation between education quality and GDP per capita, and (b) India's quality of education is in line with its GDP per capita.[3]

Third, at any given income level, there are notable outliers. On an income-adjusted basis, countries like Nigeria (NGA) underperform on infant mortality and life expectancy, while those like Bangladesh (BGD), Sri Lanka (LKA), Vietnam (VNM), and China (CHN) do better. Thus, in seeking role models to learn from, we should look at positive outliers among countries with similar GDP per capita rather than much richer countries.[4]

The same patterns are seen across Indian states. Richer states do better on average, but there are also large positive and negative outliers. For instance, states like Kerala (KL) have much lower rates of infant mortality even after controlling for GDP per capita. Conversely, states like Uttar Pradesh (UP), Uttarakhand (UK), Haryana (HR), Delhi (DL), and Gujarat (GJ) have considerably poorer outcomes for their level of GDP per capita.

Figure 10.3: Infant Mortality by State by Net State GDP/Capita

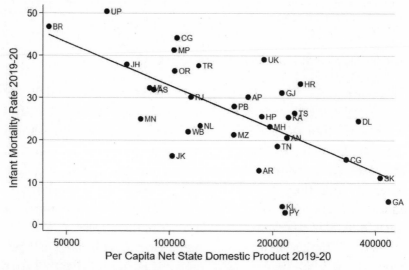

Note(s): NSDP per capita from the Statistical Appendix of the Economic Survey 2023–24; Infant Mortality from NFHS-5.

2. The Growth versus Development Debate

The graphs above provide the backdrop for one of the key debates in the discourse on development. While economists often focus on GDP per capita as the key measure of economic development, income is only an instrument for improving well-being and is not an end in itself. For example, countries with a high GDP per capita may have very high inequality, limited freedom for women, or high levels of pollution. In these cases, GDP per capita may be high, but the well-being of large groups of citizens may be low.

Amartya Sen has therefore famously argued that development should be measured less in terms of GDP per capita, and more in terms of enhancing human 'capabilities' to enable people to live a meaningful life of their own choosing. In this view, the ultimate goal of development is to improve human freedom and agency.[5] Thus, improving education, health, and safety can be seen as essential components of enhancing human freedom and capability.

The capabilities framework has significantly shaped global development discourse. The United Nations' Human Development Index (HDI)—which evaluates countries on education, health, and GDP per capita—embodies this concept. Similarly, all eight of the United Nations' Millennium Development Goals (MDGs), and the majority of the seventeen Sustainable Development Goals (SDGs) prioritize human development outcomes such as health, nutrition, education, and women's empowerment, rather than just income.

However, while the conceptual distinction between HDI and GDP per capita as metrics of development is important, country rankings on both metrics are very similar. This reflects the fact that richer countries also have more resources, both private and public, to invest in health and education, and is consistent with the patterns in Figures 10.1 to 10.3.[6] This raises the question: How much does the distinction between HDI and GDP matter in practice? Primarily, it has mattered in debates on the *direction* of causation between income and human development, which shapes thinking on how governments should prioritize resource allocation between 'growth' and 'development' sectors.

The 'growth' view, championed among others by Jagdish Bhagwati and Arvind Panagariya, posits that economic growth is the primary driver of development, including human development.[7] They contend that even if we accept the intrinsic importance of health and education, the best way to improve them is to boost economic growth. For instance, India and China had a similar GDP per capita in 1980, but China's roughly 2 per cent higher average annual growth rate over forty years not only increased GDP per capita, but also significantly improved human development outcomes.

The practical implication of this view is that governments should prioritize infrastructure, law and order, and policies that promote private productive investments, which are the key to economic growth. In this view, human development is driven more by demand than supply. Thus, increasing growth will boost health and education because people will demand more of these as they grow richer. Economic growth also increases the value of education, motivating people to invest more in education. So, as per this view, India's gains in school enrolment since the late 1990s may owe less to higher public education spending, and more to increasing economic opportunity due to faster growth, which has increased household *demand* for education.[8]

In contrast, the 'development' view, championed notably by Amartya Sen and Jean Drèze, emphasizes that countries *do not need to wait to get rich* to deliver high levels of human development to their citizens. They point to positive outliers in Figures 10.1–10.3 like Vietnam, Sri Lanka, and Kerala to show that it is possible to deliver impressive human development even at modest levels of per capita income, by prioritizing public social sector spending and greater equity in health and education systems.[9] A striking illustration of such possibilities is that Sri Lanka and Kerala have a life expectancy that is similar to the US despite the US having over fifteen times higher GDP per capita![10]

Further, Drèze and Sen argue that prioritizing human development will also boost economic growth, as more educated and healthy citizens will also be more productive. They point to high-performing East Asian economies, such as South Korea, Taiwan, Singapore, Hong Kong, and later China and Vietnam, as examples. They argue that these nations' high investment in primary education and health early on was the key to their faster economic growth over time. So, the 'development' view is that focusing on human development is not only good ethics but also good economics.

Both perspectives have substantial merits, and are backed by empirical evidence. Several studies confirm that income growth results in higher household spending on education and health.[11] Conversely, studies also show that investing in health and education in early years leads to higher long-term wages and income.[12] So, both logic and evidence suggest that there is a *virtuous cycle* between higher growth and improved human development, highlighting the need for both.

In practice, the relative priority governments place on 'growth' versus 'development' spending often reflects ideology. Centre-left governments in India, and globally, tend to prioritize equity and social spending, whereas centre-right governments focus more on infrastructure. These ideological differences often make the growth versus development debate more polarized than it needs to be. We clearly need both, and governments on average spend considerable amounts on both physical infrastructure and social sectors.

Rather, as shown in Chapter 6, our bigger problem is that we spend public money badly *regardless* of whether we spend on infrastructure or social sectors! So, zero-sum ideological debates on how budgets should be allocated across infrastructure and social sectors may be distracting us from the much more important task of improving the effectiveness of public expenditure. One of the *most important messages of this book* is that shifting our focus from how budgets are allocated to how effectively they are spent will allow us to sharply accelerate both development and growth as illustrated below.

3. Accelerating Development *and* Growth

Clearly, we care about both growth and development. Yet, we are a lower middle-income country, with tight budgets and high levels of debt (Chapter 6). Thus, a critical question to focus on is: 'How can we deliver better development outcomes at *any* given income level?' The good news is that we have evidence that this is possible.

3.1 The case for optimism: shifting of the Preston curve for life expectancy

The case for optimism comes from asking: 'What do low- and middle-income countries have that today's high-income countries lacked when they were at a comparable per capita income?' This question highlights a key advantage that countries like India have: access to much better knowledge and technologies than today's rich countries had in the past. For example, we now have the knowledge and technological capacity to mass-produce low-cost life-saving interventions such as vaccines for previously lethal diseases and antibiotics for otherwise fatal bacterial infections. As recently as 100 years ago, even the son of the US President could not survive a simple bacterial infection.[13] Today, even a poor wage labourer can do so, due to the easy availability of antibiotics.

The power of better technology to dramatically improve human possibilities at any given level of income was beautifully illustrated in a famous 1975 paper by demographer Samuel Preston, who plotted the average life expectancy in countries against GDP per capita and noted that this curve was shifting upwards over time.[14]

Figure 10.4a plots the 'Preston curves' at different points in time, and shows that in 1960, countries had considerably higher life-expectancy than those with the *same* level of GDP per capita in 1930. The increase is higher for poorer countries, which were further behind the technological frontier. This reflects the fact that it is easier to copy effective technologies than to innovate from scratch. More recent and updated analysis by Harvard health economist David Bloom and colleagues shows that the Preston curve has continued to shift upwards from 1960 to 2015 (Figure 10.4b).

Figure 10.4a: Scatter Diagram of Relations between Life Expectancy at Birth and National Income per Head for Nations in the 1900s, 1930s and 1960s

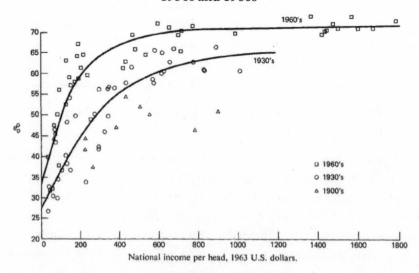

Notes: Graph directly taken from Preston (1975).

Figure 10.4b: Preston Curves for 1960 and 2015

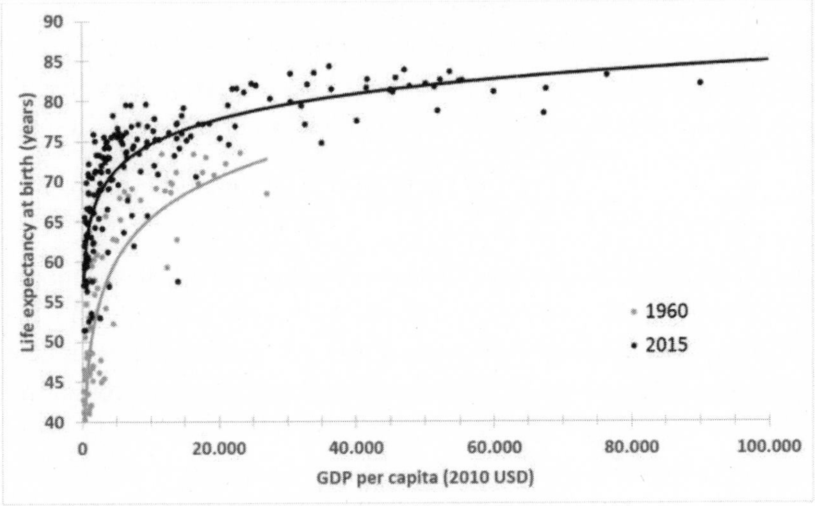

Note(s): Graph directly taken from Bloom et al. (2018).

3.2 Shifting the Preston curve for *all* development sectors

The lessons from how societies managed to shift the Preston curve for life expectancy apply to *all* development goals. As in the case of health, we now have access to better knowledge and more advanced technologies, which allow us to pursue all development goals more effectively. In particular, we now have *much better data and evidence* to guide cost-effective public spending. This knowledge creation has accelerated in the last few decades due to the rapid increases in computing power and data availability, and advances in research methods. However, we are not yet using these possibilities effectively. Doing so will allow us to sharply improve the effectiveness of public spending, and shift the Preston curve upwards in other development areas as well.

Consider education: India has significantly increased education spending in the last three decades, and also sharply increased enrolment. Yet, the translation of higher spending and enrolment into better learning outcomes has been very poor. High-quality research evidence from the last two decades shows that there is striking variation in the effectiveness of education spending items. We spend lots of money in ineffective ways, leaving us short of funds to invest in highly effective and cost-effective programmes (see Chapter 11). Therefore, moving public spending from less to more cost-effective programmes and policies will allow us to deliver substantially improved education outcomes *at any given level* of public expenditure. Doing so will allow us to achieve a lot more with our limited resources and shift up the Preston curve for education.

3.3 Shifting India's Preston curve for development between now and 2047

What will India's development indicators look like in 2047 if we proceed at the current rate, and how can we do better and accelerate national progress? To make these projections, Table 10.1 uses data across Indian states over time to quantify the relationship between income and development outcomes. It presents estimates of income elasticity (e) of key development outcomes, which measure the extent to which these outcomes improve when GDP per capita goes up by 1 per cent.

Table 10.1: Income Elasticity of Key Human Development Indicators

Human Development Indicator	Cross-section elasticity	Time-series elasticity
Health—IMR (deaths per 1000)	-0.553	-0.434
Health—Life Exp. at Birth (LEB)	0.046	0.053
Health—Stunting (per cent under 5)	-0.167	-0.224
Violent Crime (rate per 1,00,000)	-0.136	-0.196
Education—ASER Reading	0.409	0.438
Education—ASER Mathematics	0.369	-0.032

Note(s): Data on Net GSDP per capita at constant prices from the National Statistical Office; data source for infant mortality (2004–18 annually) and life expectancy at birth (2004–17 annually) from Sample Registration System, Government of India; data source for stunting is NFHS collated by Global Data Lab (years 2006, 2016, and 2019 by survey waves); data source for violent crime rate is NCRB (years 2015–19 annually); data on education indicators are from ASER (years 2006–18 annually, excluding 2015 for reading and 2013–18 for mathematics).

These estimates are calculated in two ways. The cross-section elasticity shows this relationship across states at the same point in time, using the latest year in which comparable data across states are available. This estimate is informative of the extent to which richer states do better on average. The time-series elasticity estimates this relationship over time—typically, the most recent ten to fifteen years (see table notes). The two estimates are similar in most cases, except mathematics. However, the time-series elasticities show how income growth has translated into better outcomes *over time* and may hence be a better estimate for projecting outcomes into the future.[15]

Table 10.1 shows that every 1 per cent income increase over time has been correlated with a 0.434 per cent reduction in infant mortality, a 0.224 per cent reduction in stunting, a 0.196 per cent reduction in violent crime, a 0.053 per cent increase in life expectancy, and a 0.44 per cent increase in the fraction of fifth-grade students in rural India who can read at the second-grade level on ASER reading assessments. These estimates allow us to project how India will do on key development outcomes in 2047 when the modern Indian state turns 100, under various scenarios as shown in Figure 10.5.[16]

An achievable base case scenario would be an annual GDP per capita growth rate of 6 per cent, in line with our growth rate between 2009 and 2019 before the COVID-19 pandemic. A highly optimistic scenario would be one of 8 per cent growth, in line with India's peak growth years since 1991. Both scenarios are somewhat optimistic because they assume (a) that these growth rates can be *sustained* for over twenty years, and (b) that these are *per capita* growth rates. At a 1 per cent annual population growth, these cases assume GDP growth rates of 7 and 9 per cent respectively.[17]

Even with a strong GDP per capita growth rate of 6 per cent, projections for 2047 paint a sobering picture if we maintain our current course (Figure 10.5—Scenario 1). While India's infant mortality is projected to halve from 27 per 1000 births to 13 in 2047 (Figure 10.5a), it will still be well above China's *current* rate of 8. Child stunting will only decrease from 35.5 to 25 per cent (Figure 10.5b), which is only a 10.5 percentage point or 30 per cent reduction in nearly 25 years. In rural India, 16 per cent of children in Class 5 will still not be able to read at a Class 2 level, and 55 per cent of them will still not be able to do division at the Class 3 level (Figures 10.5c and d). Finally, the rate of violent crime is projected to fall by less than 30 per cent from its current rate (Figure 10.5e).

Figure 10.5a: Projections of Infant Mortality Rate till 2047

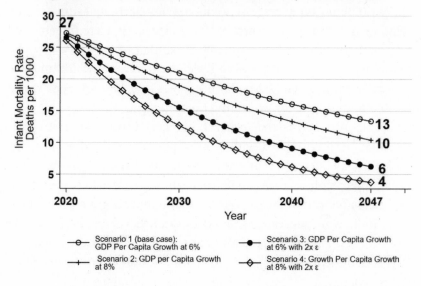

Figure 10.5b: Projections of Child Stunting Rate till 2047

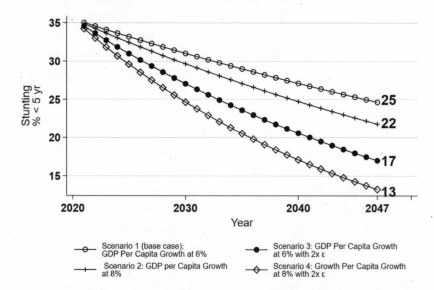

Figure 10.5c: Projections of Reading Competencies till 2047

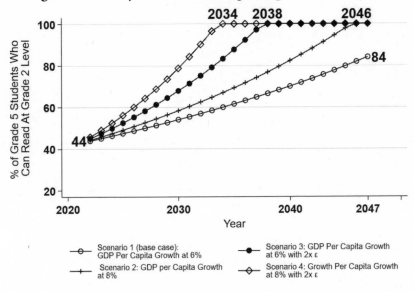

Figure 10.5d: Projections of Mathematics Competencies till 2047[1]

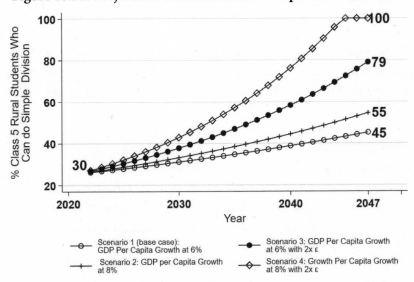

---

[1] Note that unlike the other projections, which are based on the time-series elasticities in Table 10.1, these projections are based on the cross-section elasticities

Figure 10.5e: Projections of Violent Crime Rate till 2047

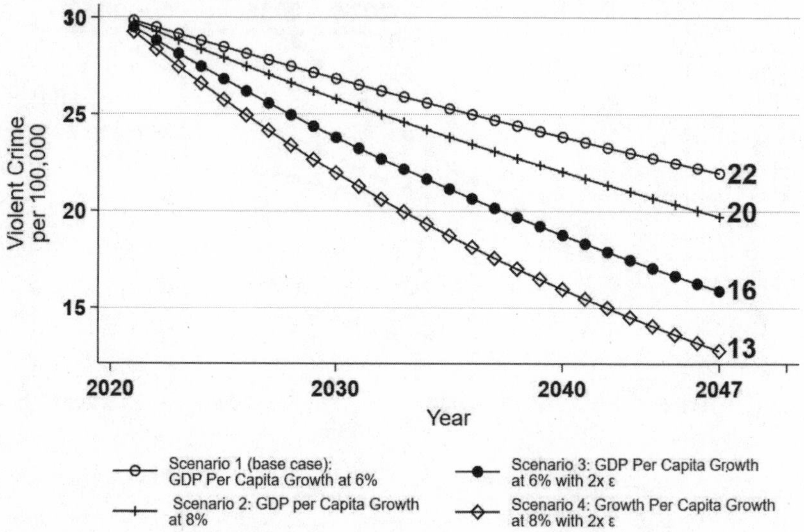

Note(s): Figures 10.5a-e show projections of key development indicators in India till 2047, under different scenarios of economic growth, and efficiency of translation of income into outcomes using estimates of time-series income elasticities of outcomes from Table 10.1.

Faster economic growth will help, of course. But, even under a highly optimistic scenario of sustaining annual GDP per capita growth rates of 8 per cent till 2047, progress on key human development indicators will be unsatisfactory (Figure 10.5a-e—Scenario 2). For instance, 45 per cent of rural Indian children will still complete primary education without being able to do simple division. The stunting rate will remain at 22 per cent, and the multiplier of improvement relative to the base case is only 1.2–1.5 across indicators.[18]

Sectoral advocates should also note that the projected outcomes at 8 per cent growth are likely to be an upper limit on what is achievable by increasing 'government as usual' sectoral budget allocations under 6 per cent annual growth. For instance, starting from an education budget share of 3.5 per cent, if the budget share grows by 2 per cent annually for twenty-five years, it will hit 5.75 per cent of GDP, which is close to the 6 per cent target sought by education advocates. Yet, even such a large budget increase under 6 per cent growth will *at most* yield a similar impact to keeping the current budget share at an 8 per cent growth rate.

This is true for at least two reasons. First, raising education budgets by 2 per cent annually with 6 per cent GDP growth will yield the same absolute increase in public spending as an 8 per cent GDP growth without budget changes. However, the projections at 8 per cent growth include increases in *household* income and spending and not just higher public spending. So, the gains from just increasing public education spending at 6 per cent growth will be lower. Second, increasing the education budget share requires *cutting* the budget elsewhere. If cuts affect other social sectors like health or poverty alleviation, it could offset benefits from increased education spending. If cuts come from infrastructure, it could slow the growth of household incomes, which would also offset the benefits from increasing public spending on education.

This is why neither a 'growth' focus (even one that increases GDP per capita growth rates to an impressive 8 per cent a year) nor a 'development' focus (that increases budget allocations to social sectors) is likely to get us to satisfactory development outcomes if we stay on our current trajectory of converting spending into outcomes.

How can we do better? Scenarios 3 and 4 in Figure 10.5 show what we can achieve if we can double the income elasticity of development outcomes going forward. This is an ambitious goal, because these elasticities depend on both private and public spending, whereas policymakers can only directly affect the effectiveness of public spending. Yet, it is feasible because (a) many of the ideas in this book are likely to be over *ten times* more cost-effective than the status quo, (b) the doubling is only assumed to apply to *future* spending, reflecting the political reality that cutting existing spending is difficult even if it is inefficient, (c) development challenges are concentrated among the poor who depend more on public services, implying a high translation from improving public spending to better development outcomes, and (d) well-designed public spending can also improve the effectiveness of household spending.[19]

Figure 10.5 shows that even at 6 per cent growth, a doubling of the income elasticity of development outcomes will achieve better results than 8 per cent growth without efficiency improvements. If we can combine 8 per cent growth with a doubling of the income elasticity, we can achieve three to four times greater improvements than the base case. The graphs for Scenarios 3 and 4 illustrate this shifting of the Preston curve for several development outcomes. Doing so can accelerate Indian development relative to our current trajectory at *any* given level of income.

Such an acceleration can dramatically improve human welfare. At our current rate of progress, we will not reach universal functional literacy even in 2047. Even with an 8 per cent growth rate (Scenario 2), we will only get there in 2046. Yet, if we can double the income elasticity of education outcomes by improving the impact of every rupee spent, we could reach this goal by 2038 at 6 per cent growth (Scenario 3), and 2034 at 8 per cent (Scenario 4). If we stay on our current trajectory, another *200 million* children are likely to complete primary school by 2047 without basic literacy.[20] Scenario 3 would lower this number to 108 million, and Scenario 4 to 80 million, potentially ensuring foundational literacy for an additional 90 to 120 million children (see Figure 10.6).

Figure 10.6: Estimated Cumulative Number of Children Who Will Complete Class 5 without Being Able to Read at a Class 2 Level between 2022 and 2047

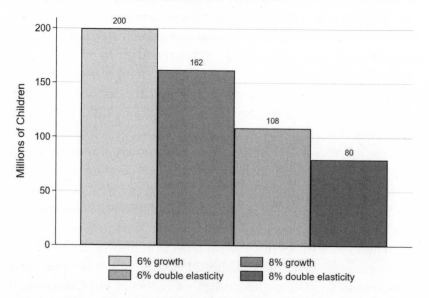

Note(s): Figures calculated by adding annual projections in Figure 10.5c.

Pursuing this agenda will also accelerate equity. Many of our development challenges are rooted not just in poverty, but also reflect deep-rooted inequalities—especially of caste and gender. Underprivileged groups have poorer average development outcomes in nearly every area, including nutrition, education, and vulnerability to physical and economic risks. They also disproportionately rely on the state for basic services, and suffer the most from weak state capacity. Hence, improving the Indian state's effectiveness at delivering basic services will also help improve equity at scale.

This discussion is also consistent with the macro development economics literature that explores the drivers of income variation across countries. A well-known paper estimates that 20 per cent of variation in per capita incomes across countries can be accounted for by variation in physical capital, 10–30 per cent by variation in human capital, and 50–70 per cent by differences in productivity, also known as total factor productivity (TFP).[21]

Placed in this context, the 'growth' view of public spending priorities can be considered as analogous to prioritizing physical capital (like infrastructure), the 'development' view to focusing on human capital (education and health), and the 'state capacity' and quality of expenditure view as analogous to focusing on improving productivity. These estimates from the macro development literature are consistent with my argument that while both physical and human capital matter for development, the greatest gains are likely to come from improving productivity—in this case, the TFP of public sector spending—which we have mostly ignored in India's development discourse.[22]

3.4 Bringing 'state capacity' to the centre of the development discourse

Intellectually, my focus on shifting the Preston curve for development by increasing the TFP of public spending integrates and builds on the contributions of three sets of Nobel laureates in development economics: Amartya Sen (1998), Angus Deaton (2015), and Abhijit Banerjee, Esther Duflo, and Michael Kremer (2019). Sen underscored that the goal of development should not just be to increase incomes, but to enhance human capabilities.[23] Deaton highlighted the critical role of better knowledge on the causes and cures of diseases, and of public actions based on this knowledge in shifting the Preston curve for life expectancy over time.[24] Finally, the push to generate better evidence on the impact of development interventions using RCTs championed by Banerjee, Duflo, and Kremer has helped to highlight the large variation in the effectiveness and cost-effectiveness of policies and programmes that aim to improve development outcomes.[25]

This book reflects these influences by focusing primarily on human development (Sen); by emphasizing that new knowledge, and acting on it, can shift the Preston curve for development outcomes beyond health (Deaton); and by synthesizing evidence from a large number of empirical studies, often using RCTs, to highlight the new knowledge created in recent years that can be used to significantly improve development outcomes (Banerjee, Duflo, and Kremer). Yet, it goes beyond them by recognizing the central role of building effective states to the development process itself. This is critical because even if we have better knowledge and technical answers to the question of *what* low- and middle-income (LMIC) governments should do, effectively translating these ideas into reality requires a capable state.

Traditional approaches to development often assume a capable state, and focus more on *what* the state should do rather than *how* it will do it, or *whether* it even can. This frequently results in 'well-designed' policies that fail due to weak implementation.[26] Another approach is to treat weak state capacity as given and try to work around it by creating project management units or using external consultants. However, this limits the scale and sustainability of interventions.[27] This book argues for a third approach: acknowledge that weak state capacity is a *critical binding constraint* to achieving global and national development goals, and make it a top priority to invest in strengthening it.

In doing so, it aims to move the development discourse beyond the traditional questions of 'What sectors and policies should governments prioritize?', and the more recent ones of 'What evidence-based programmes should governments scale up?', to focus more on the question of 'How can we make the state itself more capable?'[28] It contributes to this goal by identifying systemic components of state effectiveness and using evidence to understand them better (social science); and combining this understanding with a recognition of political, bureaucratic, judicial, and social incentives and constraints to propose practical ideas for strengthening these systems (systems engineering).[29]

To make the case for prioritizing state capacity in development thinking and practice, this book synthesizes insights from several studies to highlight a key pattern: investing in state capacity and governance is often far more cost effective at improving outcomes than more 'government as usual' spending. This micro-founded view is also consistent with macroeconomic evidence that differences in TFP are the most important driver of cross-country outcome differences. So, building a more effective Indian state can accelerate national progress by improving the TFP of public spending at any level of GDP per capita, and thereby shift the Preston curve for all development outcomes.[30]

3.5 Jumpstarting a virtuous cycle of faster development and growth

While Chapters 4–9 discuss how to build a more effective state, Chapters 11–16 focus on the sectors where we should prioritize deploying these enhanced capabilities. The discussion above on growth and development informs the choice of sectors: education and skills; health and nutrition; police and public safety; courts and justice; social protection and welfare; and jobs and productivity. In focusing on these sectors, we do not have to choose between 'development' and 'growth' because they matter for *both*.

Improving education, skills, health, nutrition, safety, and justice is *intrinsically* valuable to citizens' quality of life. But it is also *instrumentally* valuable because it will improve individual and aggregate productivity, and thereby contribute to economic growth.

This argument also applies to well-designed welfare programmes, which can improve both equity *and* productivity (see Chapter 15). Further, a credible social safety net can make it politically more feasible to implement reforms that may be disruptive to individual workers who are displaced from low-productivity jobs, but will significantly increase aggregate productivity and creation of higher-quality jobs (see Chapter 16).

Thus, improving the quality of public expenditure in these sectors can not only shift the Preston curve upwards for development outcomes, but also create a positive feedback loop to accelerate economic growth. So, starting at our current average per capita growth rate of 6 per cent and implementing the reforms outlined in this book can move us from Scenario 1 to 3 in Figure 10.5, and the corresponding increase in productivity makes it more likely that we achieve an 8 per cent per capita growth rate and attain Scenario 4.

As we try to accelerate growth, development, and equity, it is worth reiterating the foundational importance of implementing the measurement ideas in Chapter 4. Such data is critical not only for improving government effectiveness but also for tracking state and national progress towards development goals. Better data will help us to celebrate if progress is accelerating, and to course correct if it is not. In the context of this chapter, such data will be essential to verify whether we are shifting the Preston curve for key development outcomes, and accelerating progress in the coming years.

3.6 The importance of jobs, productivity, and economic growth

The most important long-term asset of a country is its people. So, improving human development is a foundational investment that will enable many more Indians to participate in, and contribute to the growth process. However, it is also critical to create the enabling conditions for boosting jobs, productivity, and economic growth, which are the *engines* that will pull our economy forward and help accelerate India's development.

The examples of Cuba and Kerala illustrate both the strengths and limitations of a human development focus. On the one hand, they represent impressive success stories of societies that have delivered universal, high-quality health and education at a relatively low level of per capita income. They illustrate that we do not need to wait to get rich to deliver better universal basic services, and have high levels of human development.

However, while some policy choices (such as investing in health and education) made by governments in Cuba and Kerala have contributed to strong human development performance, others (such as discouragement of private capital) may have inhibited investments, productivity, and job creation. Thus, despite creating highly educated populations, these societies have struggled to create adequate jobs; contributing to high levels of outmigration, and local economies that depend heavily on remittances.[31]

Note that there is nothing wrong with this approach. In many ways, it makes more sense to focus on developing *people* rather than *places*. Productivity and wages are higher in urban areas, and wages are even higher overseas. So, the best way for states to boost their citizens' life prospects may be to invest in their human capital, and enable them to seek the highest return to these skills by migrating to any location in India or the world. Remittances from these migrants can then be considered as part of the return on investment to the societies that invested in their human capital.[32]

Yet, leaders and citizens also value *local* development, especially because many would prefer to thrive in their home states close to their families and cultural roots, without needing to uproot themselves and migrate to earn a better living. Chapter 16 addresses this crucial issue, and discusses how states can boost jobs, productivity, and economic growth. Acting on these ideas can be a force multiplier that allows states to reap the economic benefits of making the investments in Chapters 11–15. India also needs state-level leadership on the jobs and economic growth agenda because many of the key policy levers in this area are in the domain of state governments.

A good model for Indian states is Vietnam, which delivered high-quality education and health to its citizens and is a consistent positive outlier on human development indices. This base of strong human capital has helped Vietnam to benefit from its investment-friendly policies because companies and investors care about human capital as well as policies to attract investors. This synergy has contributed to a boom in investments and job creation in Vietnam as global firms diversify production out of China.[33]

Economic growth is key for both individual and societal development. Higher incomes boost individual freedom and capabilities to exercise choices in the market. Harvard economist Benjamin Friedman has also noted that economic growth and higher tax revenues enhance the *moral capacity* of societies, by enabling them to better support their most vulnerable citizens.[34] On average, richer countries have better health insurance systems, better support for children with special needs, and more robust disability insurance. Thus, even for those committed to Mahatma Gandhi's vision of caring for the most disadvantaged in society, it is critical to support economic growth.

4. Conclusion

Placed in historical and global contexts, India has done reasonably well at delivering both growth and development. However, we have the potential to do *much* better, and a key enabler for reaching this potential is to build a more effective Indian state. Doing so will allow us to improve the translation of public spending into outcomes, and thereby accelerate development, growth, *and* equity.

The state capacity agenda should therefore unite both the economic left and the right. Beyond charting out a roadmap for national progress, a key goal of this book is to build a broad consensus on the importance of this agenda by taking a non-ideological, non-partisan, evidence-based, centrist approach that aims to combine the strengths of both centre-left and centre-right views, while mitigating their limitations.

This centrist approach can be characterized as being to the centre-left in terms of goals, and centre-right in terms of means. The goal of better human development, and the choice of sectors in the coming chapters reflect the centre-left 'capabilities' framework that emphasizes equity and justice. Further, the focus on improving the capacity of public systems echoes the centre-left view that the state has a pivotal role in ensuring the delivery of essential services. Yet, many of the practical ideas in this book recognize that delivering better development outcomes at scale will require us to deploy centre-right principles including: (a) sharply improving management quality, accountability, efficiency, and cost-effectiveness within government; (b) designing systems that align incentives of all stakeholders to deliver improved outcomes; (c) not assuming that well-intentioned laws and higher budgets will yield better outcomes by themselves; and (d) treating markets and the private sector as an ally in achieving development goals.[35]

Chapters 11 to 16 apply these principles to key sectors that matter for India's development. These topics are complex enough to each warrant a separate book. To keep the scope of the chapters manageable, they focus on highlighting the most important issues in the concerned sector, discuss relevant evidence, and present actionable reform ideas that: (a) reflect the ideas in Chapters 4–9, (b) can accelerate both development and growth, and (c) have the potential to yield meaningful and visible improvements within the five-year term of state leaders, which will allow them to take a track record of genuine accomplishments back to their voters.

Chapter 11

Education and Skills

Education exemplifies a sector that is both intrinsically and instrumentally important. Instrumentally, it increases 'human capital' and productivity, which are key drivers of economic growth. It also helps inclusion, by enabling citizens to participate in the growth process by obtaining better paying jobs. Education is also intrinsically valuable because it enhances citizens' capabilities and empowerment in several spheres of life, beyond jobs and income.[1] Thus, education contributes to both 'growth' and 'development', and building an effective education system is a foundational investment in India's future.

In the early decades after Independence, India paid more attention to tertiary education than primary education, and focused on setting up high-quality technical institutes like the IITs and IIMs. This decision reflected the importance placed on creating a technically trained workforce to support India's modernization. However, this came at the cost of underinvestment in universal primary education. This choice was in contrast to countries in East Asia that prioritized universal school education, and basic literacy and numeracy.

These early education policy choices have shaped the Indian economy even today. We are globally competitive in skill-intensive sectors such as IT, pharmaceuticals, and high-skill manufacturing. But we lag in low-skilled labour-intensive manufacturing sectors such as textiles and shoes, which require large numbers of workers with basic skills.[2] Success in these sectors was key to moving

325

tens of millions of people out of poverty in East Asia. Thus, delivering broad-based inclusive growth in India depends critically on providing *all* children and youth with adequate education and skills.

Starting in the 1980s, the Government of India started prioritizing primary education, increased education spending, and launched several schemes for school education.[3] These efforts have contributed to near universal school enrolment: in 2022, 98.4 per cent of children aged six to fourteen were enrolled in schools even in rural India.[4]

Yet, despite enrolment gains, learning levels remain very low. Nationally representative surveys show that around 50 per cent of Class 5 children in rural India *could not read* a Class 2 level paragraph in 2018. This figure had worsened to over 57 per cent in 2022 after the pandemic and school closures.[5] This learning crisis, whereby schooling is not translating into learning, is clearly visible in the labour market. On the one hand, we have millions of unemployed 'educated' youth, and on the other, employers report that the majority of 'qualified' candidates do not possess the skills to be employable.

This learning crisis is one of the greatest challenges we face as a country today. While we have challenges at all levels of education from preschool to university, it is critical to prioritize the quality of primary school education, since these foundational years shape *all* future learning and skill acquisition.

Fortunately, this is an area where the last two decades have yielded many new insights from high-quality research. We now have a much better understanding of the impacts and cost-effectiveness of a wide range of education interventions. Acting on this knowledge, and implementing the principles in the chapters in the previous section, will allow us to substantially improve learning outcomes at any given level of resources, and accelerate national progress on education goals, as noted in Chapter 10.

This chapter has two main sections. The first presents key facts and evidence to better understand school education in India. The second presents administratively and politically feasible, evidence-based reform ideas that can be carried out by any state.

1. Understanding the Indian School Education System

1.1 Key facts and trends

Total budgeted education spending across Central and state governments in 2022–23 exceeded Rs 7,50,000 crore, or around 3 per cent of the GDP.[6] These funds are mainly spent on teacher and staff salaries, school construction and maintenance, and student inputs like midday meals and textbooks.

The good news on education in India is that there has been steady growth in enrolment and average years of schooling. In addition to near universal school enrolment, average years of schooling among people aged twenty-five or older increased from 3 in 1990 to 6.5 in 2018.[7] This increase is seen in almost every population subgroup, and has contributed to increasing convergence in average years of schooling between rural and urban populations, boys and girls, and SC/ST and the general population.[8]

However, the bad news is that enrolment gains have not translated into better learning. Nationally representative data from rural India suggest that learning outcomes have been mostly flat or even declining during the period from 2005 to 2022.[9] More detailed data from studies in several states including Delhi, Rajasthan, MP, AP, and Telangana confirm that average learning levels, especially in government schools, are substantially below grade-appropriate standards.

Poor learning outcomes are the single biggest challenge for Indian education. Research evidence shows that what matters for translating education into higher productivity and wages (at the individual level), and economic growth (at the aggregate level) is not just the quantity of education measured by years of schooling, but the *quality* of education, as measured by learning outcomes.[10] Thus, the low average level of skills in the Indian workforce severely limits the ability of millions of young Indians to contribute to and participate in India's growth and development.

1.2 Our default approach is not working

Sectoral advocates routinely argue that we should increase public education spending from 3 to 6 per cent of GDP. However, there are two problems with this argument. First, the 6 per cent benchmark comes from high-income countries with a tax-to-GDP ratio of around 35 per cent, whereas India's tax-to-GDP ratio is around half of this (Chapter 7). So, as a fraction of the budget, India's education spending is in line with other countries.

Second, the evidence suggests that additional spending is not likely to be very effective if we simply spend more along existing patterns. We can partly infer this from the fact that increases in education spending over the last two decades have not led to meaningful gains in learning outcomes. Since this pattern may be confounded with other variables, the discussion below summarizes high-quality micro evidence to explain why this may be the case. It is organized along India's three main components of education spending: infrastructure, teacher salaries, and student inputs.

Infrastructure

While building schools in areas without access to a school improves enrolment and learning outcomes, upgrading school infrastructure has typically been found to have no effect on learning.[11] Why may this be the case?

First, better facilities may make school attendance more pleasant, but may not affect learning much if instruction quality is weak. For instance, a study on the quality of scientific research in German universities after World War II found that universities that lost their buildings due to bombings had fully recovered within a decade of the war. However, those that lost a large number of top scientists (which happened in universities with more Jewish faculty) had not recovered even many decades later.[12] Similarly, constructing school buildings may not be enough if the teaching and learning processes are ineffective, as we will see below.

Second, even when schools get facilities, they might not be used. For instance, my data and field experience show that school toilets are built but often not used due to a lack of running water or staff to clean them.[13] Similarly, computer labs and libraries are built but often kept locked and unused because teachers were more concerned about resources not being damaged or stolen than about them not being used (see Chapter 3).

Finally, it is possible that improving infrastructure has modest positive annual impacts on learning that may be meaningful if aggregated over the (say) twenty-year depreciation period of capital projects. However, the annual effect may be too small to be statistically significant in studies of the impact of improving infrastructure on student learning.

Overall, while improving school infrastructure may create an enabling environment for better learning, the evidence suggests that it may not be enough on its own, unless *accompanied* by other enabling conditions.

Teachers

Several studies suggest that teacher quality is a key determinant of education quality. However, the problem for policy is that variation in teacher quality is poorly predicted by characteristics such as age, experience, qualifications, training, and salary.[14] In other words, while good teachers are incredibly important, the standard measures we use as proxies for teacher quality are not effective at identifying who the good teachers are. As a result, we spend a lot of money on things we *think* are effective, but are actually not.

In particular, two commonly suggested ways of improving teacher quality are to pay them more, and to hire only 'qualified' teachers. Yet, studies find very little impact of increasing pay or having teaching credentials on teacher effectiveness at improving learning outcomes.[15] Further, several studies find that locally-hired volunteers, who have completed only the tenth or twelfth class, have no training credentials, and are paid much lower salaries, can be highly effective at improving basic literacy and numeracy.[16] Thus, higher teacher salaries, which absorb most of the education budget, are neither necessary nor sufficient for effective teaching, at least for primary school. Similarly, teaching credentials are also neither necessary nor sufficient for teaching effectiveness.

As a professional educator who believes in the value of teaching and training, I find this to be a disappointing and puzzling result. As noted in Chapter 5, these findings likely reflect a combination of three factors. First, teaching credentials may not matter because many of them are fake. Second, even genuine teacher training programmes devote little time to practical training in effective pedagogy, and mostly focus on the history, philosophy, sociology, and theory of education, and test these by rote memorization on an exam.[17] Finally, even if teacher training has useful content, it may not be used in practice due to a lack of either rewards for effective teaching, or penalties for poor performance.[18]

Increasing the number of teachers does not seem to help much either. One of the most expensive components of the 2009 Right to Education Act was to reduce pupil-teacher ratio (PTR) norms from 40:1 to 30:1. However, evidence suggests a weak relationship between PTR reduction and learning gains. For instance, a study by Abhijit Banerjee and colleagues found no effect of smaller class sizes on student learning.[19] In my own work, we found that reducing PTR by hiring regular government teachers led to modest learning gains, but would yield a low rate of return on public spending.[20]

Several reasons could explain this finding. First, smaller class sizes matter most for younger children, who need more attention.[21] However, since PTR norms are set at the school level, senior teachers often teach a small class in grade 5, leaving larger groups of younger children to newer teachers. Second, multiple studies find that hiring extra teachers leads to *increased* absence rates among existing teachers.[22] Third, many teachers are posted to small or tiny schools with fewer than fifty or twenty students, respectively.[23] Thus, despite low PTRs, teachers teach multiple grades at the same time. The widespread prevalence of multi-grade teaching in government schools may also limit the effectiveness of PTR reductions. Finally, as discussed below, a key binding constraint to effective teaching in India is that students are several grade levels below curricular standards. In such a setting, hiring more teachers may not be effective if the teacher is simply teaching from the textbook to complete the curriculum.

To summarize, translating increases in teacher hiring, pay, and training into improved learning outcomes requires a lot more work than simply spending on these line items. It also requires careful attention to the deployment of teachers across and within schools, to governance and monitoring, and the specifics of pedagogy.

Student inputs

The final major category of public education spending is on student inputs such as midday meals, books, computers, uniforms, and other materials. However, several studies suggest that budgets sanctioned for these inputs have, at best, modest effects on learning outcomes. There are several possible reasons for this.

First, money may not reach schools on time, or may not reach at all (see Chapter 6). Second, even if funds and resources reach schools, they are often not used, or used improperly. As discussed above, books and computers are often kept locked up to reduce the risk of theft. In another well-known study in Romania, providing free computers to high school students led to a *reduction* in test scores because computers were used to play games rather than to study.[24] Third, households may reduce their own spending on inputs in response to public provision.[25] Finally, the inputs may not alleviate binding constraints to learning. For instance, free textbooks may not be very useful if children are not able to read.[26] Similarly, expensive programmes such as 'One Laptop Per Child' had no impact on learning outcomes, in part because there was limited integration of the technology with pedagogy.[27]

Yet, input-based programmes *can* be highly effective in some cases. In a study with Nishith Prakash, we found that the Bihar government's 2006 programme of providing free bicycles to girls enrolled in secondary school was highly effective and cost-effective at improving three key goals of education policy: access, equity, and quality. The programme led to a remarkable 32 per cent increase in girls' age-appropriate secondary school enrolment, a 40 per cent reduction in the gender gaps in such enrolment, an 18 per cent rise in the number of girls taking the tenth-standard board exam, and a 12 per cent increase in the number who passed the exam.[28]

The programme's success can be attributed to several factors. First, it was a top priority for the chief minister and was implemented well, on time, and with minimal corruption. Second, it alleviated a clear binding constraint to girls' school attendance: the time and safety cost of going to school outside the village. Third, the girls did not have a bicycle to begin with, and household substitution was therefore not a concern. Also, the public distribution of bicycles in school ceremonies made it socially costly for parents to resell bicycles. Fourth, non-use was not a concern since the cycle was used every single day to go to school. Finally, the collective provision of the cycle to all secondary school girls, which enabled them to cycle to school in *groups*, may have contributed to a relaxing of patriarchal social norms that prevent adolescent girls from leaving the village.

Thus, the implication of this discussion should not be that inputs do not matter. Rather, it is that simply providing inputs may not be enough to ensure learning *unless we also address other binding constraints to converting inputs into outcomes.*

1.3 Does anything work?

The summary above makes for depressing reading because it shows that most of our education spending does not seem to be effective at improving learning outcomes. On a more optimistic note, there is strong evidence that two classes of interventions—governance and pedagogy—are both effective and cost-effective.

Governance

A key reason for the poor translation of spending into learning is weak governance and personnel management in the public education system, including a lack of accountability for non-performance, and inadequate rewards and recognition for good performance. Poor accountability is exemplified by high rates of teacher absence, which was around 26 per cent in rural government schools in 2003, and 24 per cent in 2010, and continues to be high in more recent data.[29] The fiscal cost of this absence, based on 2010 salaries, is around Rs 10,000 crore per year. A key reason for teacher absence is poor monitoring and supervision, driven in part by vacancies in supervisory positions. As noted in Chapters 1 and 5, allocating funds to filling these vacancies and thereby reducing teacher absence would be ten times more cost-effective at reducing *effective* pupil-teacher ratio than hiring more teachers.[30]

The importance of accountability is also seen in several studies which find that locally hired contract teachers, who are less educated and less trained, are at least as effective at improving primary school learning outcomes as regular civil-service teachers, even though the latter are paid at least five times more. Contract teachers also have significantly lower rates of absence, driven by a combination of being from the local community and being on renewable contracts without lifetime job security.[31]

Further, the value of recognizing and rewarding good performance is seen in multiple studies showing that even modest amounts of performance-based pay can significantly improve teacher effort and student learning outcomes. In contrast, multiple studies find zero correlation between salary *levels* and productivity in public schools.[32] In a large nationwide study in Indonesia, my co-authors and I found that even *doubling* teacher salaries had no impact on student learning.[33] Put together, a large body of evidence suggests that improving governance and management, with a focus on improving teacher effort and accountability, will be much more effective and cost-effective than simply spending more along existing patterns.

Pedagogy

Despite absence rates of around 25 per cent, many government teachers are sincere, and do their best under adverse conditions.[34] However, even motivated, sincere teachers are often quite ineffective at improving learning for the *average* student in an Indian classroom. This is because they spend most of their time completing the textbook and curriculum to prepare students for exams, whereas a large fraction of students, especially in government schools, are far behind curricular standards. Thus, grade-level instruction may be quite ineffective for these students.

Figure 11.1 illustrates the magnitude of this problem, and provides several key insights into the Indian education system. Using data from a large sample of over 5000 students across four districts in Rajasthan, it plots the mathematics learning levels of students by grade. The x-axis shows the grade students are enrolled in, the y-axis shows the grade of their actual learning level, and each dot represents ten students. The 45-degree dotted line is where students would be if they were at a grade-appropriate standard, and the solid line is where the true average learning level is at.

Figure 11.1: Learning Levels in Government Schools in Rajasthan[35]

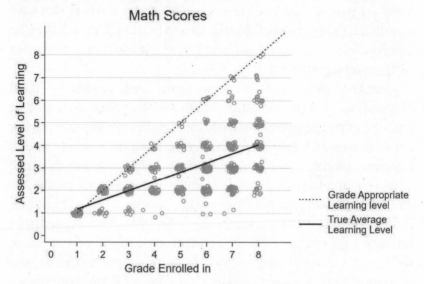

Note(s): Muralidharan (2019); graph recreated by author.

I consider this to be perhaps the *most important figure* for understanding the Indian education system. There are three key insights in this figure. First, the average rate of learning progress is only *half* the rate envisaged by the syllabus and textbooks. Second, as a result, the gap between average learning levels and the curriculum standards in the textbook grows over time. Third, there is enormous dispersion in within-grade learning levels: for instance, students enrolled in Class 8 range from Class 2 to Class 8 in their learning levels. Similar patterns are seen in data from other studies of mine in Delhi, Madhya Pradesh, Tamil Nadu, and Telangana.

The figure highlights both how far behind grade-level curricular standards students are, and also the striking *variation* in student learning levels within a class. This variation, in turn, illustrates how difficult it can be to teach and learn when teachers have to cater to students of such varying preparation. Even if a teacher is highly qualified and motivated, students will struggle if the level of instruction is not matched to their level.

நான் தமிழில் எழுதத் தொடங்கினால், நான் என்ன சொல்கிறேன் என்று உங்களுக்கு ஒரு வார்த்தை கூட புரியாது. நான் மிகவும் தகுதிவாய்ந்த மற்றும் ஊக்கமுள்ள ஆசிரியராக இருக்கலாம், மேலும் சிறப்பாக கற்ப்பிப்பதில் அக்கறை காட்டலாம். ஆனால் நான் உள்ளடக்கிய பொருள் உங்கள் புரிதலின் அளவை விட அதிகமாக இருந்தால், அது வேறு மொழியில் பேசுவது போல் இருக்கும்.

The shift to Tamil above may be confusing, but it shows how teaching at the level of the textbook is akin to teaching in a foreign language, when students are many grade levels behind. The sense of helplessness that non-Tamil readers may feel in trying to decipher one paragraph provides a glimpse into the lived daily experience of tens of millions of children in our schools. In fact, it is a miracle that more do not drop out given how demoralizing it must be to attend school without following much of what is going on.

Figure 11.1 and the Tamil paragraph may also help explain why our default policies are not working. We could increase the education budget by an additional Rs 1,00,000 crore but improvements in infrastructure, teacher credentials, teacher pay, or student inputs will have very little impact on learning if the instruction is above students' level of comprehension. Consistent with this view, my co-authors and I found in a study in Delhi, that students in the lowest third of baseline test scores within Classes VI to IX make *no progress* in learning during the entire school year despite being enrolled in school.[36]

They also highlight the value of 'Teaching at the Right Level' (TaRL), where instruction is tailored to students' current learning level, rather than their expected grade level. The TaRL approach has been tested and validated in multiple studies across India, led by Abhijit Banerjee and Esther Duflo, and this work was prominently mentioned in their Nobel Prize citation. They have shown that supplemental instruction delivered even by modestly paid volunteers with limited training and only a secondary or high-school education, can be highly effective at improving basic literacy and numeracy when they focus not on completing the textbook but on teaching at the child's learning level.

One reason that well-intentioned policies fail is that they are often designed by elites who do not face the same constraints as the policies' target populations. For instance, a policymaker might provide free textbooks with good intentions, without considering the possibility that most students are so far behind grade-level standards that they may not even be able to read the textbook. Similarly, adding a teacher to reduce class sizes may be of limited use if the teacher focuses on completing the textbook and syllabus while student learning levels are far behind. These examples illustrate how acting on high-quality research evidence can sharply improve the effectiveness of public spending.

1.4 Putting it together

How and why have we designed such an inefficient education system? To answer this question, it is useful to step back and examine the role of education in society itself. Historically, education systems have served three distinct roles in society. The first is to *teach* knowledge and skills to make students more productive. The second is to use tests and exams to *identify* students of high academic ability, and channel them towards more technically demanding higher education, and thereby to occupations that require greater skills and knowledge. The third is to provide all citizens with a common set of facts and values that create a shared sense of identity.[37] These three functions can be referred to as the 'human development', 'sorting', and 'socialization' roles of education.

While all three functions have mattered historically, in India, our education system has primarily been driven by 'sorting' rather than 'human development'. Indeed, the Indian education system in its current form is perhaps best understood as a 'filtration' system that focuses on *identifying the few* academically talented students rather than an 'education' system that effectively *teaches all* students.

This framework helps to make sense of several deep structural challenges of the Indian education system.

First, there are massive inequalities in the education system. At one level, the Indian education system can appear highly effective based on the impressive success of the Indian diaspora around the world, as exemplified by Indians becoming CEOs of several iconic global companies including Microsoft, Google, IBM, Pepsi, Mastercard, Federal Express, and Starbucks.[38] On the other hand, India also produces millions of students *annually* who complete primary school without being able to read a simple paragraph at the second-grade level. How do we make sense of this paradox?

This contrast is no longer a puzzle once we recognize that the Indian education system mainly functions as a 'filtration' system that is very effective at *identifying* highly talented individuals who are then likely to do great things. However, since the 'system' only cares about students at the top of the distribution, students who fall behind early—who are disproportionately first-generation learners from disadvantaged backgrounds—are left behind in perpetuity.

Second, even students who have 'passed' exams and possess paper qualifications have limited practical skills or conceptual understanding, as memorably depicted in the movie *3 Idiots*. This is a natural consequence of a 'filtration'-based education system where students primarily use rote learning to pass exams as opposed to aiming to obtain conceptual understanding that can be applied and used in practical situations. Rote learning is also prevalent because the only viable strategy for students who fall behind is to cram and hope to pass exams by memorizing past exam questions. Conceptual understanding is not prioritized as it is not rewarded by the exam system.

Third, many students lag so far behind curricular standards that they resort to cheating, necessitating stringent security for board exams. The scale of the exam-cheating crisis is seen by noting that the pass rate in Class 10 and 12 board exams fell sharply when UP introduced a strict 'anti-copying' law in the 1990s. As noted by journalist Shankkar Aiyar, 'The phenomenon of mass copying symbolizes everything that is not right and everything that has gone wrong (with our) broken education system.'[39]

Note that exams and 'sorting' are not inherently problematic. Globally, societies aim to identify talented individuals for leadership roles and occupations that benefit society as a whole.[40] Higher-education institutions and employers also need credible signals of student preparation, and it makes sense for students to try to provide them.[41] So, the main problem with our 'filtration' based education system is not exams per se, but its failure to offer 'teaching at the right level' for children who are behind grade-level standards. This leads to a massive waste of both time and money. Money is spent on building schools and hiring teachers, and efforts are taken to keep children in school to prevent dropouts; but very little actual learning is taking place.

Thus, the central design challenge for the Indian education system is to move from a 'sorting' system to a 'human development' system that equips and empowers *all* citizens with the skills and knowledge needed to contribute to and participate in the economic growth process. We now turn to ideas for achieving this goal.

2. Evidence-Based Reform Ideas

Despite the formidable challenges documented above, the evidence that improving governance and pedagogy can yield sharp gains in learning outcomes should offer hope. This section discusses actionable, evidence-based ideas that state governments can implement to significantly improve education quality in a cost-effective manner. These ideas include elements of all the thematic ideas in Chapters 4–9.

2.1 Foundational literacy and numeracy mission

The most important goal for education policy in India should be to deliver *universal* foundational literacy and numeracy (FLN) by the end of primary school. Foundational skills are critical because you need to 'learn to read' to be able to 'read to learn'. Every child who is not able to read functionally by Class 3, and fluently by Class 5, is a child whose future learning prospects are likely to be permanently compromised.

This is an achievable goal with focused efforts. The key components of an FLN mission include the following:

1. **System alignment on goals:** The first step is to establish universal FLN as the top priority across *every* level of the education system: from political leadership; to officials at state, district, and block levels; to teachers, parents, and students.

2. **Clarity on standards:** The focus of assessment in primary school should move away from marks and ranking, towards assessing *absolute* proficiency standards, that include both competence and fluency.[42]

3. **Aligning pedagogy to FLN goals:** Teachers should be encouraged to prioritize universal FLN over textbook completion. Since they will still need to complete the syllabus, one practical way to balance these two goals would be to use sixty to ninety minutes every school day for small group instruction focused on FLN, where children are grouped by their current learning levels.

4. **Accountability for outcomes:** An FLN mission is unlikely to succeed without continuous tracking of levels and improvements in student learning, and holding the 'system' of teachers and administrators accountable for progress.

   a. A critical component of such accountability is the integrity of administrative data. Without this, the system will naturally inflate data on learning levels (see Figure 4.1). Implementing 'nested supervision' where teachers record learning data digitally, and supervisors re-test a random student sample on a sample of the same questions, will allow the creation of truth scores to improve administrative data integrity (see details in Chapter 4).

b. A second key component is an annual district-level KPI survey including learning outcomes (see Chapter 4), which will allow policymakers to independently verify learning levels in government schools, and also help monitor learning in private schools. The latter is essential for tracking state and national progress, given their large enrolment share (see Chapter 9).

5. **Staffing:** The reforms above should improve FLN, even at current staffing levels. However, widespread multigrade teaching is a key constraint to delivering FLN. Thus, augmenting and rationalizing staffing to reduce multigrade teaching, and enable supplemental small-group instruction, can accelerate universal FLN. Sections 2.2, 2.3, and 2.5 discuss practical, cost-effective ideas for doing so.

6. **Flexible resources:** A final component is to allocate some flexible financial and human resources for district- and block-level initiatives to improve FLN. This will boost the autonomy of frontline administrators to deploy resources as they see fit to best deliver the goal of achieving universal FLN. Over time, parts of the budget for annual staff salary increases can go to a performance-based pool, from which modest salary supplements (of 5–10 per cent) can be paid based on independently validated performance. This can help boost 'autonomy on process, and accountability for outcomes'.

The National Education Policy of 2020 recognizes the centrality of FLN, and the Union Ministry of Education (MoE) has launched the *Nipun Bharat Mission* with the stated goal of achieving universal FLN by 2026–27. This is a laudable initiative. Yet, as is well-known, the real challenge is in translating this intent into improved outcomes. The mission has focused on points 1–3 above, which is a good start. But, we will need to pay attention to points 4–6 if we are to deliver on this goal.[43] These in turn reflect the three key themes of data, personnel, and budgets discussed in Chapters 4–6.

The importance of independent measurement of learning is seen from the cautionary tale of the Shaala Siddhi programme. This was an ambitious attempt to improve school governance in India using structured assessments and school improvement plans. The programme reflected several global best practices and high-quality technical inputs. Yet, in an independent evaluation conducted from 2014 to 2018, Abhijeet Singh and I found that the programme had *no impact* on any outcome that we care about, including teacher and student attendance, teaching activity, or student learning.[44]

Yet, the programme was scaled up to over 6,00,000 schools across India despite a lack of any impact. Further, qualitative investigation revealed that the programme was perceived to be successful because all paperwork and forms were immaculately filled out, and uploaded on dashboards. However, neither teaching nor learning changed in practice! This example highlights how bureaucratic incentives at all levels often reward the *appearance* of activity rather than the consequences of that activity.

Interventions that succeed at scale have often had visibility on outcomes that enabled senior officials to monitor *outcomes*. So, while the Nipun Bharat FLN mission is doing many things well, it is crucial to not assume that FLN is being delivered just because there is a mission for it. We need to continuously measure outcomes independently, celebrate progress based on genuine improvements, and course-correct if we are not seeing them. This underscores the centrality of investing in independent outcome measurement as described in Chapter 4 for accelerating India's development.

As noted in Chapter 10, if we continue on our current trajectory, then by 2047, India will have added another *200 million* children who complete primary school but who cannot read a simple paragraph. On an optimistic note, this *future is yet to be written*, and it is completely in our hands to change this dismal projection. Building an education system that can deliver universal FLN over the next five to ten years will allow us to reduce this number by over 100 million children. Every education minister and secretary in India should structure their priorities and their departments around delivering this goal.

2.2 Implement a practicum-based teacher training and selection programme

We can accelerate universal FLN by augmenting teaching staff in schools to reduce or eliminate multigrade teaching and provide small-group instruction to first generation learners. As discussed in Chapter 5, a practicum-based training and apprenticeship model of staffing can be a powerful way to cost-effectively augment state capacity and improve education outcomes in both the short and long run.

The key idea is to create a two- to four-year-long practicum-based elementary school teacher training programme (two years for a diploma, four years for a degree). It would blend three months of theoretical modules per year, with eight months of practice-based components. The highest-scoring Class 12 board exam candidates from each panchayat would be eligible, with priority given to locations with the greatest staffing needs. This training would be free, provided through District Institutes of Education and Training (DIETs) or other high-quality accredited institutions, and can be funded jointly from the education and skilling department budgets. Apprentices would receive modest stipends during their practicum, making it attractive for candidates who have passed Class 12.

During the practical training, candidates would actively teach under the supervision of a senior teacher. Specifically, they could focus on small-group instruction for young children to support the goal of universal FLN. During the practicum, they would also have access to digital training content and resources, and peer support groups through smartphones. Upon completion, participants would receive either a diploma or degree in education, recognized for both public and private employment. Finally, the government teacher recruitment process should be modified to provide extra points for each year of practical experience, including those obtained during the practicum-based training.

This approach improves upon the status quo in several ways, as noted in Chapter 5. These include (a) improving training quality by integrating theory and practice, (b) enabling a fiscally-feasible expansion of front-line teaching staff at a lower stipendiary pay scale than regular government salaries, (c) reducing the geographic mismatch between teachers and schools by assigning local candidates to practical training in their home locations, and (d) improving long-term quality of government school teachers selected by providing weightage for actual experience on the job in regular hiring and not just exam performance, which is often not correlated with teaching quality.

This approach also offers several benefits to teacher trainees: (a) the government will cover the training fee, sparing them the cost, (b) they will earn a stipend during their practical training, (c) the training quality will be higher, (d) they will receive a credential valued in both the public and private sector, and (e) those genuinely committed to teaching, demonstrated by undergoing the practicum-based training, will have improved their prospects of securing a job as a government teacher, by gaining an edge over candidates who mainly apply for teaching jobs to attempt the government job lottery.[45]

Based on over twenty years of work on education, this is perhaps the single-most important idea that I would recommend to a state education minister. It would enable additional staffing to provide the small group instruction needed to deliver universal FLN, in a fiscally feasible way. It would improve teacher training and skills, long-term recruitment quality, and also boost female empowerment and labour force participation.

2.3 School size optimization

While the policy push in the last two decades to create schools in every habitation may have helped to improve school enrolment, it has also led to a proliferation of subscale schools. Economist Geeta Gandhi Kingdon has shown that in 2016 over 4,00,000 (40 per cent) of India's government schools were 'small' with fewer than fifty students, and over 1,00,000 (10 per cent) were 'tiny' with fewer than twenty students.[46]

Such small schools hurt education quality on several dimensions, including pedagogy, governance, social integration, and value for money. Pedagogy is hurt by the need for multigrade teaching in small schools. Governance is hurt by the difficulty of monitoring distant schools. Social integration is hurt by caste- and community-based segregation of schools, reflecting segregation of rural habitations on these lines. Thus, a critical social cost of a school in each habitation is high socioeconomic segregation across schools.[47] Finally, value for money is poor because the norm requiring at least two teachers per school combined with low enrolment leads to much higher per-child costs. Specifically, schools with under twenty students spend over Rs 75,000 per child annually in teacher salary costs, versus around Rs 25,000 per year in schools with over 150 students.[48]

Thus, we can improve pedagogy, governance, social integration, and value for money by consolidating schools to a fewer number of larger schools serving 120–250 students each, or roughly one or two schools per GP. With over 120 students, schools can have at least five teachers based on the minimum PTR norm of 30:1. This will eliminate multigrade teaching, by providing a teacher for each primary grade. Larger schools also benefit from economies of scale, enabling the appointment of a dedicated principal for better management, and provision of better facilities such as computer labs, libraries, and play areas. Having fewer, larger schools will also promote social integration by reducing the transmission of residential segregation to segregation in schools.[49]

The main argument against school consolidation is the belief that a school in every habitation is essential for universal enrolment and attendance. While this is a valid concern, the vast cost savings from school consolidation could easily fund a bus or auto service to pick up every child at or near their homes. The success of the Bihar girls' bicycle programme shows that providing transport can be an effective and cost-effective way of ensuring school access while also obtaining the educational advantages of larger schools. While this approach may not have been feasible a few decades ago, it has become viable due to extensive rural road construction in the past two decades.

It is also important to consider political factors in adopting such a policy. Many Indian communities obtained schools after years of demand and pressure, and may feel pride and attachment to their local school. Thus, a top-down decree to close these schools could be politically unpopular. A better way to approach school consolidation would be to offer GPs the option to adopt a consolidated model, with resources for upgrading the nodal school, and for running a bus service. This approach would allow GPs to choose consolidation, lending democratic legitimacy to the policy and ensuring it only occurs in places where it has community support. The approach can be expanded over time based on its success and popularity.

Such a policy would also improve teachers' quality of life and working conditions. They would benefit from a larger community of peers, better school facilities, and elimination of multigrade teaching. It would be easier to attend training workshops, as there will be other teachers to cover for them, unlike in small schools with just one or two teachers. Moreover, since most teachers commute to school from nearby towns, larger, centrally located schools would be more accessible. Finally, while school consolidation may reduce the number of teacher posts over time, it would not affect incumbents. Thus, the combination of improved working conditions for teachers and community validation before implementation can make the idea politically feasible.

This approach was implemented in Rajasthan under the Adarsh (model) school scheme. A recent study finds that the reform created better-resourced schools with improved governance and reduced multigrade teaching. It finds suggestive evidence of lower dropout rates after Class 8, and improved learning outcomes.[50] However, the same study also finds that there was a slight decrease in enrolment of marginalized student groups, suggesting that concerns of exclusion are real. Thus, it is important to combine school consolidation with a bus or auto service to ensure universal access, which was not done in Rajasthan at the outset of the reforms.

2.4 Invest in strengthening public preschool education

Global evidence consistently shows that early-age interactions of children with parents and caregivers profoundly shape their cognitive and socioemotional development. Further, a key reason that students fall behind curricular standards even in early grades, is the large number of first-generation learners in the Indian schooling system. These learners often lack the educational home support that higher SES children have, and are also less likely to attend private kindergartens. Thus, there is a strong case for investing in universal preschool education to support school readiness, improve equity, and help achieve the goal of universal FLN.

Indian policymakers have recognized the importance of early-childhood education, including in the 86th Constitutional Amendment of 2002, which notes that: 'The State shall endeavour to provide early childhood care and education for all children until they complete the age of six years.' Similar commitments have been made in the Right to Education Act of 2009 and the National Education Policy of 2020, which declared that universal preschool education is a national policy goal. However, as in many sectors, India's main challenge is not so much the lack of intention to deliver development goals, as much as the lack of capacity to do so.

This challenge is clearly seen in the Integrated Child Development Services (ICDS). The ICDS is India's main vehicle for delivering public early childhood interventions, and provides services through over 1.35 million anganwadi centres (AWCs). However, it has limited funding and staffing. Typically, a single anganwadi worker (AWW) is responsible for both nutrition and pre-school education services. The AWW has to cater to the very different needs of children aged zero to three by visiting homes; and aged three to six, through AWC-based activities.[51] She is also responsible for copious paperwork and record-keeping.[52] Thus, it is not surprising that very little early childhood education is provided in AWCs. In a recent study, my co-authors and I found that even in a high-capacity state like Tamil Nadu, the average AWC spent only thirty-eight minutes a day on pre-school education.

A simple, scalable way to improve early childhood education is to add a second worker to AWCs to focus on preschool education. There is strong evidence that doing so would be both highly effective and cost-effective. In a recent study, my co-authors and I found that adding an extra locally hired early-childhood care and education (ECCE) facilitator to anganwadis in Tamil Nadu doubled daily preschool instructional time. After eighteen months of the intervention, we found large gains in students' maths, language, and executive function skills. We also found a significant reduction in child stunting and malnutrition, with the existing worker increasing time spent on nutrition-related activities.

We estimate that the social return on this investment was around thirteen times the cost, or a remarkably high 1200 per cent! This estimate is conservative because it does not account for the improvements in nutrition. Further, we estimate that the social rate of return on public funds invested in such a programme would be *infinite*. This is because the increase in future tax revenues from higher long-term productivity would exceed the upfront cost. However, we found no impact of raising salaries of existing workers. This is a key result because in practice, budget increases are mainly absorbed by pay raises for existing staff, who are politically more powerful, leaving little funds to hire new staff.

This study reinforces several key points in this book. First, it shows that augmenting frontline staffing for service delivery can yield high returns. Second, hiring local staff on renewable contracts promotes both cost-effectiveness and accountability.[53] Third, the ECCE facilitators typically had only a Class 10 or Class 12 qualification and received only one week of training, and were still highly effective. While this does not imply that training *cannot* be useful, it reinforces the point that formal qualifications may not be essential for basic service delivery, and that it may not make sense to insist on such credentials for hiring local service delivery staff.

Adding a second worker to the anganwadi system is an easily scalable way to augment state capacity for child development in a cost-effective way. Doing so will also boost female empowerment and labour force participation—both directly through the additional jobs created, and indirectly by providing better childcare for working mothers. Further, the hiring of the extra anganwadi workers will also be politically popular and is something I would strongly recommend to any chief minister as one of the lowest hanging fruits we have for accelerating human development in India.

2.5 Consider implementing volunteer-led after-school programmes

A noteworthy recent innovation in public education is the Illam Thedi Kalvi (ITK) programme in Tamil Nadu, which means 'education at doorstep'. ITK was designed to remediate learning losses from COVID-19-induced school closures, and employed over 2 lakh volunteers for sixty to ninety minutes a day at a modest stipend of Rs 1000 per month to conduct after school remedial classes.[54] The sessions typically ran in the school premises in the afternoon and were open to all students free of cost. Conceived in late 2021, ITK was scaled up to reach over 30 lakh students by early 2022.

In an independent evaluation, my co-authors and I found that ITK was highly effective at bridging learning losses. It also improved equity because participants were primarily drawn from government as opposed to private schools. ITK was also remarkably cost-effective: it used only 2 per cent of the state's school education budget, but improved learning by over 30 per cent, suggesting that it was over ten times more cost-effective than the typical school education spending in the state.[55] Further, ITK contributed to boosting female labour force participation and empowerment by providing flexible work, that was valued and respected in the community.[56] One measure of the popularity of ITK among the volunteers is that the Tamil Nadu government received nearly four applications for every open position despite only paying a stipend of Rs 1000 per month.

The combination of effectiveness, cost-effectiveness, reduction in learning inequality, and positive effects on female labour force participation makes ITK worthy of replication as an after-school programme, even beyond its short-term use for mitigating COVID-19 learning loss. As an after-school programme, ITK complements rather than replaces existing teachers, and also engages the community to deliver education.[57]

Since private-school students are more likely to attend private tuition, programmes like ITK that are mainly used by government school students can help bridge socioeconomic gaps in learning, and promote universal FLN. So, it can be considered as equivalent to a government-supported, community-led, after-school tuition programme that is primarily meant to provide learning support for children attending government schools. Further, since ITK has *already* been deployed at scale across Tamil Nadu, it may be possible for other state governments to implement similar programmes at scale.

2.6 Leveraging technology for improving pedagogy and governance

Historically, newer technologies have been the key to increasing productivity, and many experts believe that using technology in education can similarly facilitate sharp gains in learning outcomes. Reasons include the possibility of using technology to, (a) deliver uniform, high-quality content from top teachers to overcome limitations in teacher knowledge and quality, (b) deliver interactive content for greater student engagement, (c) increase student motivation through gamification and rewards, (d) provide rapid feedback to students to clarify misconceptions in real time, based on analysis of mistakes made, and perhaps, most importantly, (e) personalize the type and difficulty of content based on each student's learning levels. This is a compelling list, and has led some evangelists to proclaim that technology will 'disrupt' and 'transform' education.

Yet, despite this promise, the evidence on the effectiveness of technology in improving learning is mixed. For instance, an evaluation of the highly hyped 'one laptop per child' (OLPC) programme found that it had no impact on student learning.[58] Several other studies around the world have also found limited impact of hardware provision. In fact, one well-known study of the impact of providing computers to secondary school students found a *negative* effect on learning outcomes, since students may have used it to play computer games, as opposed to studying.[59]

On a more optimistic note, other studies have found positive effects when technology is effectively integrated with pedagogy. In particular, multiple studies in India have found very large positive effects on learning outcomes when technology is used to *customize* instruction to each students' learning level.[60] In one study, my co-authors and I evaluated the impact of Mindspark, a personalized education software developed by an Indian company, on students in Classes VI–IX in Delhi. After just five months of exposure to Mindspark, we found dramatic increases in learning outcomes, with a rate of progress more than double that of the control group. The learning gains achieved per unit of time were greater than in *any* other middle school intervention evaluated to date.

A key reason for these large effects was the software's ability to accommodate the large variation in within-class student learning levels (seen in Figure 11.1) by customizing instruction to the level of each student. Figure 11.2 shows how the dynamic adjustment of content on the Mindspark platform allows different students *sitting in the same class* at the same time to be *learning completely different content* based on their current learning level as opposed to the grade they are enrolled in.

Figure 11.2: Customization of Educational Content by the Mindspark Software

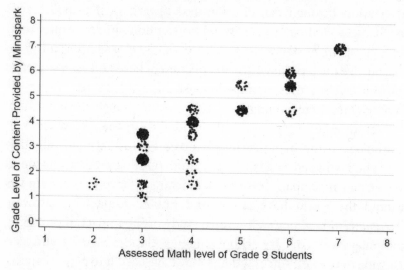

Note(s): Data is from Muralidharan, Singh, and Ganimian (2019); graph recreated by author; the X-axis shows the true mathematics learning level of each student in Class 9 in our Delhi study. The Y-axis shows the grade level of the content provided to each student by the Mindspark software during one session. The graph shows that the content for each student is centred on their assessed grade level, with some questions that are slightly below or above this level.

Our findings suggest that the personalized instruction on Mindspark benefited all students equally, regardless of their initial learning level. Further, while the *absolute* effect of Mindspark was similar for all students, the *relative* effects compared to the progress in the control group were highest for the *lowest* achieving students. These students were so far behind grade-level standards that they learnt almost nothing during the school year. So, the value of 'teaching at the right level' enabled by Mindspark was especially high for these students. While equity advocates correctly worry that increasing the use of technology in education may increase inequality because of the digital divide, these results show that a well-designed personalized instruction programme may be able to reduce inequality by reducing the extent to which weaker students fall behind.

Taken together, the evidence highlights the promise of technology-enabled education to deliver improved learning outcomes at scale. However, it also cautions that simply providing hardware is unlikely to be effective. In this sense, the results are consistent with the broader pattern reported in Section 1, which is that simply providing inputs (in this case, computers) is unlikely to improve learning, without addressing binding constraints such as pedagogy and governance.

Technology can also be used to improve education governance, especially exam and data integrity. As shown in Chapter 4, official learning data is often inflated. In a study in Andhra Pradesh, Abhijeet Singh showed that using tablet-based assessments reduced cheating by 90 per cent compared to paper-based testing (see Figure 11.3).[61] Reasons included (a) randomizing test questions from a large digital question bank, which makes it difficult for students to copy or for teachers to share solutions, and (b) immediate grading and data transmission, which makes it difficult to manipulate grading.

More generally, using technology to provide every student with a personalized ID to log in and work on content and modules at their own pace can also provide visibility to teachers and administrators on the rate of learning progress that students are making and provide early remediation when needed. Used this way, technology can improve both pedagogy—by allowing customization of instruction with high-quality content; and governance—by improving data integrity and visibility into student learning.

Figure 11.3: Fraction of Schools Flagged for Cheating in Paper vs Tablet-Based Tests

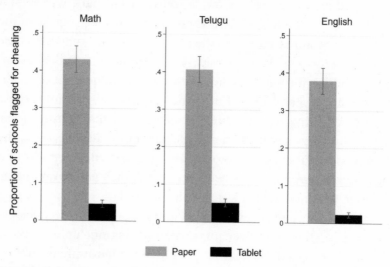

Note(s): Data is from Singh (2023); graph recreated by author.

Unfortunately, education technology policy focuses more on inputs and procurement of computers and less on how they are actually *used* to improve instruction or governance. The evidence suggests that this approach is highly unlikely to improve learning. Rather, what state governments need to do is to leverage the resources for hardware provided by the Central government and invest in systems to effectively *use* the technology to improve pedagogy and governance, and monitor progress on learning outcomes.

The Government of Andhra Pradesh has taken some steps in its procurement of education technology to reflect these insights, and NITI Aayog has recently piloted a 'results-based financing' framework for education technology vendors. While these have not been evaluated yet, they are promising steps that other states should replicate.

2.7 Exam reform

A key challenge for the Indian education system is to move from a 'sorting' or 'selection' paradigm towards a 'human development' one. Achieving this shift will require reforming our exam system, which is mainly oriented towards the sorting function. This requires changing the exam system to capture not only the marks and 'relative' ranking of students, but also the 'absolute' level of skills and knowledge. A system that focuses on 'ranks' is zero-sum by construction because only one person can be first, whereas one that focuses on knowledge and skills is positive-sum because *everyone* can get better.

Exam reform is crucial because the content and structure of the exam system is a critical determinant of what teachers, parents, and students work towards. Indeed, the exam system is the proverbial tail that wags the dog of the entire education system. Thus, focusing on supply-side reforms in how we deliver education may have only a limited impact if we do not also change what parents and students *demand*—which in turn is driven by what the exam system focuses on.

Thus, a key reform is to have a national or state testing agency to set standards for 'absolute' levels of proficiency, broken down granularly by grade, subject, and topic. This is similar to how education software platforms like Khan Academy and Mindspark are structured. The availability of modular assessments organized in ascending order of skills will provide a critical source of feedback to parents, teachers, and students about the absolute competence that a student has attained, and about the progress made at regular intervals such as a week, month, quarter, and year.

While some exams will still serve a 'sorting' function, focusing student report cards on measures of absolute learning will allow teachers, students, and parents to focus on each student's *improvement* over time, rather than their class rank. So, assessments should evolve from saying 'Student X scored Y per cent in the Class 5 exam' to being able to say that, 'Student X has demonstrated the following levels of competence in various topics and domains'. The levels can range from 'not demonstrated' to 'mastered' and would aim to provide feedback to parents, students, and eventually employers, about functional competencies as opposed to arbitrary marks.

Over time, technology-based platforms can administer such assessments at scale, to enable dynamic adaptive testing and ensure test integrity through large question banks. In the short term, preprinted worksheets for various topics can be used for such assessments. This is a critical reform to ensure that the millions of children who are behind grade level and at risk of being left behind permanently are encouraged to make 'absolute' progress regardless of their level. It is also a crucial enabler of skilling and vocational education for students who may not take an academic track.

Prioritizing absolute competence over ranks can also help India's education system balance reservations and high standards. Given our long history of social stratification and discrimination, using only ranks for admission to higher education will result in substantial under-representation of disadvantaged groups. This is why nearly all Indian institutions have reservations. Yet, though reservations facilitate access to higher education, real-world job opportunities prioritize skills more than degrees. So, it is imperative for both individual and social welfare that students from reserved categories have opportunities to both improve and demonstrate their absolute skill levels.

The example of NEET and NExT in Chapter 8 illustrates how such a balance can be achieved. The NEET aims to *rank* students on an admissions merit list. So, reservations may be needed for equitable access to medical education for disadvantaged groups.[62] However, the NExT should test *absolute* levels of medical knowledge to ensure that candidates meet the minimum competence threshold needed to practice medicine. So, a strategy that combines affirmative action for admissions, targeted tutoring, and coaching as needed, and high absolute standards to practice, can help integrate equity in access to medical education with high professional standards.

2.8 Take skilling and vocational education seriously

The jobs crisis in India is, in large part, a skills crisis. On the one hand, we have millions of 'educated' unemployed youth. On the other, employers routinely complain that they cannot find adequately skilled manpower. An important reason for this skills crisis is the focus of the education system on passing exams, usually by cramming, resulting in millions of students having neither an understanding of academic subject matter, nor any practical skills that are valued by employers.

Indian youth, and the country, will be better served if we pay more attention to improving skilling and vocational education. There are four essential things that we need to do.

First, we must deliver universal FLN in schools. Students entering skilling or job-training programmes often lack basic literacy and numeracy skills, leaving them ill-prepared for even skilling curricula. The problem is that students are directed to vocational tracks only when they have fallen far behind the curriculum. At this point, they also have weak basic skills. So, as Manish Sabharwal has noted: 'The best skilling programme is a better-quality school education.' This reinforces the centrality of the FLN mission and exam reforms to emphasize *absolute* skills so that all students make progress in school.

Second, we need to better integrate vocational education into school curricula. While research in India is limited, evidence from the US highlights the importance of such integration. For instance, a recent study shows that high-school curricula in the US used to have substantial vocational content up to the 1950s but that this changed in the 1960s to focus almost exclusively on college preparation. While this made sense for students who did go on to college, it may have *worsened* labour market outcomes for those who did not. This is because their high-school education no longer prepared them for the labour market compared to previous curricula with more vocational content.[63]

India should not repeat this mistake. Many world-leading education systems, including those in Singapore, Germany, and Switzerland, track students into vocational streams after grades 6 or 8. This tracking allows students to obtain *more* human capital than they would on a traditional academic track, through a mix of vocational classroom training and practical training or apprenticeships. In turn, this allows skilled workers to earn middle-class incomes even without completing more than a high-school education.

Such an approach will benefit millions of Indian students who 'pass' exams but lack employable skills. Effective vocational programmes require collaboration between employers, curriculum developers, teacher trainers, and administrators. Given limited state capacity, partnering with non-profits and industry associations can help state governments to innovate, test, and scale effective models. For instance, organizations like 'Lend A Hand India' have developed scalable models to integrate vocational skills into high-school curricula, and states should consider partnering with such entities to do so. Effective integration should also enable students who choose a vocational track in high school to attend college later if they wish to do so. The key is to ensure that high school is not *solely* viewed as preparation for college, but also as a pathway to vocational skills and employment.

Third, a key market failure that governments can mitigate, in partnership with industry, is the lack of a *credible signal* of quality of vocational qualifications. The skilling sector in India is stuck in a low-level equilibrium, because (a) many skilling providers are of low quality, and so employers often do not pay higher wages to 'skilled' candidates due to not knowing their true skill levels, (b) since the market will not pay more for skills, the youth do not value skills and prefer to focus on the government-job lottery; see Chapter 5, and (c) as a result, the skilling ecosystem is sustained by subsidies from the National Skills Development Corporation (NSDC). But since these subsidies are usually not linked to placements, wages, or credible signals of candidates having obtained skills, there is limited incentive for skilling providers to improve their own quality.

Thus, as noted in Chapter 9, governments can improve market functioning by investing in credible, independent skill certification. The National Skills Qualification Framework maps the skills needed at different proficiency levels for several professions, and the National Council for Vocational Education and Training aims to align skilling programmes' content with these proficiencies. However, what is missing is credible, third-party verification of these skills. Investing in such certification can create a virtuous cycle: employers would offer higher pay to candidates with such certification, and high-quality skilling providers would be able to build a reputation based on students' performance.

India's information technology (IT) revolution illustrates the importance of skills and their certification. A key role in preparing lakhs of youth for well-paying IT jobs was played by high-quality technical institutes like NIIT and Aptech, and not just engineering colleges. These institutes focused on imparting skills, offered certificates and not degrees, trained candidates from diverse backgrounds, and combined effective training with *credible certifications* in a sector with booming market demand. India will do well to learn from this success, and try to replicate it in other skill-intensive sectors with growing demand.

Fourth, we need to change social attitudes. Vocational education is often seen as a less desirable option, only chosen by academically weaker students. This perception can make students worse off by leading them to pursue 'degrees' that provide few skills. This is why it is essential to build an ecosystem where investing in skills and taking up vocational tracks can provide decently paying jobs, professional identity, and dignity. If we can do this, social attitudes towards vocational education will also change.

Implementing practicum-based training and credentialing programmes in key sectors, as discussed in Chapters 5, 11, 12, and 13, can also increase the value placed on practical skills in Indian society. This is because a major factor driving the demand for 'degrees' is the pursuit of government jobs, which offer lucrative terms based on exam results and paper qualifications, and not on either skills or performance. This public-sector labour market structure contributes to the high demand for 'degrees' over 'skills'. Reforming public-sector hiring to prioritize practical skills and sector-specific experience can also help to shift what is valued in society. If the economic return to a 'degree' without skills falls, it will also reduce the demand for such degrees and raise the demand for skills.

2.9 Leverage private schools for the public good

This chapter has focused on improving the public education system, which is under direct government control. However, from a policy perspective, we should care about improving outcomes for *all* children, whether they attend government or private schools. This is especially important for India because private schools account for around 30 per cent of enrolment in rural areas and 50 per cent in urban India.

As noted in Chapter 9, the government affects the service delivery ecosystem in three roles: as a policymaker, regulator, and provider. To avoid repetition, this section provides brief summaries of how governments can improve private-school quality, leverage private schools for the public good in their regulatory and policymaking roles, and refer readers back to Chapter 9 for details.

In their regulatory role, governments can make markets work better by (a) regulating private schools based on truthful disclosure of key inputs as opposed to input-based mandates, and (b) creating platforms that provide credible independent information and ratings on schools. The former will allow multiple differentiated models of instruction to flourish and will better cater to the varied needs of parents and students in different parts of the country. The latter will improve school accountability, empower parents, and make markets work better for all citizens (see Chapter 9 for details).

In their policymaking role, state governments can consider pilots of a charter-school model, whereby the government engages high-quality non-profit education providers and signs a management contract with them to operate underutilized urban government schools. The schools would remain 'public' in terms of not charging fees or practising selective admissions, but the charter-school operator would have autonomy on teacher hiring, pay, and management. Providing such operators with a per-child reimbursement will incentivize them to improve quality and attract students back to the 'public' charter school, and away from lower-quality private schools (see Chapter 9 for details).

Charter-school pilots should be framed as 'grand challenges,' and encourage high-quality non-government school providers to deliver quality education at scale for low-SES students. Providing quality education to tens of millions of first-generation learners is a daunting task that we have not yet solved as a country. The reform ideas for the public schooling system in this chapter are based on high-quality evidence, and I am optimistic that they will help. However, there is no guarantee that they will be effective or enough. Thus, a charter school 'grand challenge' should be seen as expanding the portfolio of options that we develop as a country to address this pressing challenge.

3. Conclusion

India's public education system exemplifies our weak state capacity and poor quality of public expenditure. This view is confirmed by several experts, including former school education secretary Anil Swarup, who has presented a scathing indictment, noting that, 'Except getting most of the children to school, everything that could go wrong has gone wrong with school education in India.'[64]

To fix the problem, we first need to acknowledge it. Indian elites have mostly ignored the crisis in public education, because they have exited to private solutions. Officials mostly focus on input-based policies, often ignoring the fact that higher spending has not led to better learning. For over fifteen years, the official reaction to inconvenient data on poor learning outcomes reported by Pratham, and confirmed by independent studies, was largely one of denial. As shown in Chapter 4, this denial is supported by inflated official learning data, as per which there is no learning crisis at all! Therefore, the first step is for all stakeholders—students, parents, teachers, officials, politicians, and civil society—to face the reality of our dysfunctional education system. In other words: *'System ko asliyat se lagav hona chahiye'* (the system has to care about reality).

A succinct summary of this reality is as follows: Millions of Indian students complete primary school *every year* without even being able to read. Yet, they are promoted to higher grades to comply with the 'no detention' provision of the RTE. Many of them drop out after Class 8 without even basic literacy and numeracy skills.[65] Finally, even many of the students who continue to further schooling and who have 'passed' exams have done so through rote learning without understanding at *best*, and copying and cheating at worst. This in turn explains India's crisis of an 'educated' but unemployable workforce that threatens to squander our much-vaunted demographic dividend.

The National Education Policy of 2020 acknowledges many issues highlighted in this chapter, and offers a strong foundation for reforming India's education system.[66] Yet, India frequently sees well-drafted policy documents that are barely implemented. For instance, the Twelfth Five-Year Plan of 2012 declared that it would be a top priority to ensure that all children completing five years of primary school would have achieved at least a Class 3 level of literacy and numeracy.

However, a decade later, there has been little progress in meeting this goal. In the ten years since the Twelfth Plan, India has added *over 130 million children* who have completed primary school without being able to read.[67] These are children whose future learning has likely been permanently compromised because you need to 'learn to read' to be able to 'read to learn'. We simply cannot allow this crisis to continue year after year, especially when we know so much about how to fix the problem.

This chapter outlines a set of practical, evidence-based steps that can significantly, and cost-effectively, improve our education system. Each new cohort of children gives us a fresh chance to make a real difference. Hence, acting urgently can deliver visible gains within just five years. A chief minister who starts implementing this roadmap at the start of a five-year term should be able to deliver *universal* foundational literacy and numeracy within five years. This would be a signature achievement that they can not only back take to voters for re-election, but also secure their legacy with.

Chapter 12

Health and Nutrition

Securing and improving population health is a fundamental development goal with both intrinsic and instrumental value for societal well-being. On the instrumental side, health is a key component of 'human capital' since it directly affects productivity. Poor health and nutrition can also create a 'poverty trap' by limiting people's ability to work and earn a living, which can perpetuate poverty and impede investments in improved health. So, public investments in health and nutrition can jumpstart a virtuous cycle of better health and productivity, especially among those who are poor and malnourished to begin with.[1]

However, health also matters intrinsically because people value good health for its own sake over and above its contribution to their productivity. Good health is also a critical enabler of individual agency and dignity that allows people to live on their own terms. Correspondingly, both national and global development goals—such as the UN's Millennium Development Goals and Sustainable Development Goals—aim to improve key indicators of population health.

Healthcare is also subject to many market failures, including asymmetric information between providers and patients, the inability of patients to negotiate prices during health emergencies, and under-provision of public goods such as infectious disease control. Large, unexpected healthcare expenses are also a leading cause of families sliding into poverty. As a result, most public policy experts believe that a combination of effective regulation and targeted government interventions can enhance the functioning of healthcare markets in the public interest. This perspective is eloquently expressed by Nobel Prize-winning economist Kenneth Arrow, who asserted that 'it is the general social consensus, clearly, that the *laissez-faire* solution for medicine is intolerable'.[2]

Reflecting this view, governments in India, and globally, play an active role in the healthcare ecosystem spanning policymaking, regulation, and direct provision. Yet, playing this role well requires an effective state. So, the broader weaknesses in the functioning of the Indian state are also reflected in the condition of healthcare in India.

Health, healthcare, and health policy are incredibly complex subjects that are difficult to address comprehensively even in a book-length treatment. Therefore, this chapter aims to offer a focused discussion on key facts and principles needed to understand these topics in the Indian context (next section). It then presents specific ideas to improve population health, with a focus on ideas that reflect the themes of this book, and can be implemented at the state level (section 2).

1. Key Facts

1.1 India's performance on health outcomes

Two widely used indicators of population health are life expectancy at birth and infant mortality. Life expectancy reflects the cumulative effect of health quality experienced at all ages, from infancy to old age, making it a good composite measure of a nation's health status. Correspondingly, it is the only health indicator used in the United Nations' Human Development Index (HDI). Reducing infant mortality is one of the most effective ways of increasing average life expectancy.[3] Further, we already *know* a lot about how to reduce infant mortality, and so the extent to which societies manage to achieve this in practice is a good indicator of the quality of their health *systems*.

India has improved considerably on both indicators over the last fifty years. Infant mortality declined from 142.6 per thousand live births in 1970 to 28.3 in 2019, and life expectancy at birth has increased from 41.4 in 1960 to 69.4 in 2018. These are impressive achievements and reflect a combination of economic growth, availability of newer and more effective health technologies, as well as policy and programmatic interventions to deploy newer knowledge and technologies where needed.

However, India's performance lags when we compare it to China (which is of comparable size), Vietnam (comparable GDP per capita) and Bangladesh (comparable initial conditions). As of 2019, infant mortality in India was more than four times higher than that in China (28.3 vs 6.3), 78 per cent higher than that in Vietnam (28.3 vs 15.9), and 10 per cent higher than Bangladesh even though Bangladesh had a higher infant mortality rate than India in 1970 (just before it was formed). We see similar under-performance relative to these three countries on life expectancy, which is 7.3 years higher in China, 5.9 years higher in Vietnam, and 2.9 years higher even in Bangladesh.

While life expectancy is a key indicator of population health, it does not capture the overall quality of life. The World Health Organization (WHO) adjusts for this using a metric called 'Healthy Life Expectancy' (HALE), which accounts for the reduction in effective years of life due to morbidities and illnesses. In 2016, India's HALE was 59.3, which was 10.1 years less than the life expectancy of 69.4 in 2018. The adjustment for HALE affects other countries as well, but the gap between life expectancy and HALE is lower in China (8 years), Vietnam (7.8 years), and Bangladesh (9 years). Taken together, we see that not only is average life expectancy in India lower, but the additional years of effective life lost due to poor health is also higher.

Another key indicator of long-term health is early childhood nutrition, measured by child height for age. Children falling more than two standard deviations below the global child growth

Table 12.1: Key Health Outcomes over Time for India and Comparison Countries

Country	Infant Mortality			Life Expectancy at Birth				Healthy Life Expectancy at Birth			Stunting	
	1970	1990	2019	1960	1990	2018		2000	2016		1987–90	2013–18
India	142.6	88.6	28.3	41.4	57.9	69.4		53.5	59.3		62.7	34.7
China	79.5	42.1	6.8	43.7	69.1	76.7		64.8	68.7		38.3	8.1
Vietnam	54.4	36.9	15.9	59	70.6	75.3		64.3	67.5		61.3	23.8
Bangladesh	148.7	99.7	25.6	45.4	58.2	72.3		56.5	63.3		63.4	30.8

Note(s): Data for infant mortality, life expectancy, stunting from World Bank, HALE from the World Health Organization (WHO); stunting measured for India in 1989 and 2017, for China in 1987 and 2013, for Vietnam in 1988 and 2017, and for Bangladesh in 1990 and 2018.

benchmark are classified as stunted. Several studies show that child stunting is correlated with a higher lifetime probability of illness, and lower lifetime education and earnings.[4] India has reduced the fraction of children under five who are stunted from 62.7 per cent in 1989 to 34.7 per cent in 2017. This is solid progress, but not nearly enough. India's stunting rate is 4.3 times higher than in China (34.7 vs 8.1), 46 per cent higher than in Vietnam, and even 13 per cent greater than in Bangladesh.

Overall, the data present a mixed picture. On a positive note, India's health indicators have improved substantially over the years. At the same time, we could do much better. China's outperformance reflects a combination of much faster economic growth as well as better public service delivery. The comparison with Vietnam is especially instructive because Vietnam has delivered significantly better health and nutrition outcomes despite having a comparable GDP per capita. Finally, there may also be useful lessons to learn from Bangladesh, which had poorer health indicators than India in 1970, but has improved them more rapidly in the last fifty years.

Beyond global comparisons, there is also much to learn from the large variation in these metrics across Indian states. For instance, as per the fifth round of the National Family Health Survey (NFHS-V), infant mortality rates in states like UP (50.4), Bihar (46.8), Chhattisgarh (44.3), and Madhya Pradesh (41.3) were *eight to ten times* higher than in states like Goa (5.6) and Kerala (4.4), and around 2–2.5 times greater than in Tamil Nadu (18.6). As noted in Chapter 10, and seen in Figure 10.3, this variation partly reflects differences in state-level GDP per capita. But, there are also notable positive and negative outliers, even after adjusting for income, which likely reflect differences in state-level conditions and policies.

1.2 Health expenditure: public and private

This section highlights five key facts about healthcare expenditure in India. In the discussion below, the term 'government health spending' refers to *all* spending by the government on health, whereas the term 'public health spending' refers to spending on *public* health that focuses on *preventive* measures at the *population* level, such as infectious disease control, as opposed to spending on *curative* private health at the *individual* level, such as clinics, hospitals, procedures, and medicines.

First, India's total health spending per capita is comparable to peer countries in South Asia, but lower than in other regions. As per World Bank figures, India's total health expenditure in 2017 was estimated at 3.5 per cent of the GDP, compared to 3.5 per cent for South Asia, 6.6 per cent for East Asia, and 5.1 per cent even for Sub-Saharan Africa.[5]

Second, in 2017, government health spending in India was 1.2 per cent of the GDP, and comprised 32 per cent of total health spending in India.[6] Government health expenditure in India has increased after the pandemic to around 2 per cent of the GDP, but it is still low by global standards.[7] It is less than half that in East Asia (4.4 per cent), and similar to Sub-Saharan Africa, which averages 1.9 per cent.

Third, higher state government health expenditure per capita is correlated with better health outcomes including lower infant mortality and prevalence of infectious disease, and higher life expectancy and rates of immunization.[8] These relationships hold even after controlling for state GDP per capita, and are especially strong for public health outcomes such as infectious disease control. Thus, variation in the level and quality of state-level government health spending likely contributes to explaining the positive and negative outliers in the state-level income-outcome trend lines in Figure 10.3.

Fourth, within government spending, the Central government share is 20 per cent, and states account for 80 per cent (see Chapter 5). While this 80 per cent includes Central transfers and state matching contributions for centrally sponsored schemes (CSS), these figures highlight that there is considerable room for states to shape their health expenditure and improve its effectiveness.

Finally, the majority of health spending in India is allocated to curative as opposed to preventive healthcare spending. In 2016–17, preventive care constituted only 6.8 per cent of total health expenditure, compared to 85.8 per cent for curative care, covering costs of outpatient and inpatient care, medications, and tests.[9]

A direct consequence of low government health expenditure in India is the high share of out-of-pocket healthcare spending. Household survey data show that people frequently fall sick and seek curative care. For instance, studies in rural Rajasthan and Madhya Pradesh, and urban Delhi found that the average household had sought care .51, .83, and 2.1 times in the month before the day of the survey.[10] Importantly, a large fraction of these visits were to fee-charging private healthcare providers (see more below).

The high dependence on private healthcare imposes a significant burden on household budgets. Data from the 2012 NSS shows that healthcare spending accounts for 7.7 and 5.7 per cent of total household spending in rural and urban areas. Further, nearly 19 per cent of rural and 16 per cent of urban households reported that out-of-pocket healthcare spending comprised over 10 per cent of their expenditure. Overall, both qualitative and quantitative studies have highlighted that unexpected illnesses and healthcare spending are a major source of economic vulnerability across India.[11]

1.3 Access to healthcare in India

The Government Healthcare System

India's government-run healthcare system aims to provide universal access to healthcare delivered by qualified health workers. The system is structured as per WHO guidelines and comprises five tiers: district and sub-divisional hospitals, community health centres (CHCs), primary health centres (PHCs), and sub-health centres (SHCs).[12] This tiered structure aims to offer increasing levels of speciality care at higher-level health centres serving larger populations.

Table 12.2: Structure of India's Public Health System

Tier	Staff	Facilities	Population served
Sub-Health Centre	ANM (Auxiliary Nurse Midwife) + MPHW (Multi-Purpose Health Worker)	Outpatient only	5000
Primary Health Centre	MBBS doctor + ANM + pharmacist	Inpatient capacity for admitting 4–6 patients	25,000
Community Health Centre	~5 doctors (including ob-gyn, paediatrics, anaesthesia and general surgery)	Inpatient capacity for admitting ~30 patients	1,00,000
Sub-divisional Hospitals	~20 doctors covering all major specialties	First referral unit for specialized care; inpatient capacity for admitting 31–100 patients	5,00,000
District Hospitals	~30 doctors covering all major specialties	Apex referral hospital in the district; inpatient capacity for admitting 101–500 patients	2–3 million

Medical staff at the level of the PHC and sub-centre are supported by ASHA (Accredited Social Health Activist) workers. The ASHA workers are all female, required to have at least completed Class 8, and undergo a month of training. They serve as the primary point of community health outreach and focus on pre- and post-natal care of mothers and infants, promoting institutional childbirth, and child vaccinations.

In theory, the public health system described above is meant to provide universal free or nominally priced care, delivered by appropriately qualified staff. In practice, access is constrained by both staff vacancies and high levels of healthcare worker absence.

Even as per official government statistics, as of 2018, 23.5 per cent of sanctioned doctor posts and 8.8 per cent of ANM positions were vacant. However, these average figures understate the problem of lack of staff in many parts of the country. In particular, there are often *more* doctors than sanctioned posts in accessible urban PHCs while positions in remote rural PHCs remain vacant.[13] There is also enormous variation across states, with high doctor vacancy rates in states like Chhattisgarh (59 per cent), MP (48 per cent), and Jharkhand (50 per cent), and much lower vacancy rates in states like Kerala (0 per cent), Karnataka (1 per cent), and Andhra Pradesh (8 per cent).[14]

Even when vacancies are filled, there are severe accountability problems in the public health system, exemplified by high rates of staff absence. In an all-India study in 2003, featuring surprise visits to over 1500 health clinics across 19 Indian states, my co-authors and I found that 43 per cent of MBBS doctors in CHCs and PHCs were absent, and 40 per cent of nurses were absent during working hours.[15]

These findings were replicated in a more detailed study in Udaipur district of Rajasthan by Abhijit Banerjee, Angus Deaton, and Esther Duflo during the same period.[16] They found 45 per cent of health personnel absent in sub-centres, and 36 per cent absent in PHCs and CHCs. Sub-centres *were closed 56 per cent of the time* during scheduled hours, due to absence of the single assigned nurse.[17] Further, doctor absence was not only high, it was also *unpredictable*. Even with a 40 per cent absence rate, users can adapt if they know which three days of the week the doctor will be available. However, the unpredictability of absence can sharply deter usage because patients have to pay transport and time costs (including lost wages) to visit a clinic. Unfortunately, doctor absence continues to be a problem, with a more recent study in Karnataka finding that doctors were present in the PHC only 36 per cent of the time.[18]

Private Healthcare Providers

The combination of vacancies, and high and unpredictable staff absence in public clinics may partly explain the high market share of private healthcare providers in India, as seen in data from several household surveys. This is a well-known fact to those working on healthcare in India. Yet, there is remarkably little systematic understanding of the landscape of private healthcare providers because of a lack of data. Since many private healthcare providers are unqualified and practice illegally, they are not included in official government data and are almost 'invisible' to policymakers.

To fill this gap, my co-authors and I conducted a nationwide study in 2010 to collect data on the prevalence, qualifications, and competence of both public and private healthcare providers in rural India. The study collected data from a representative sample of over 1500 villages across twenty major Indian states and conducted a *census* of all healthcare providers in these villages, and reports several striking findings.[19]

First, the average village had 3.2 healthcare providers, with 88 per cent of them being private providers (2.8 out of 3.2), and only 12 per cent being public.

Second, most private providers had no formal qualifications: only 2.8 per cent had an MBBS degree, 16.8 per cent had an alternate (AYUSH) medical degree, 62.8 per cent reported having no formal qualification in healthcare, and another 17.6 per cent gave no response. If we assume that those who were interviewed but chose to not respond were not qualified, *over 80 per cent* of private providers had no formal medical qualifications!

Third, while there is variation across states in the fraction of private providers, their presence is nearly ubiquitous. The share of private providers was over 75 per cent in every state except Kerala, where it was 47.4 per cent. The share of private providers was over 95 per cent in states like West Bengal, Bihar, and Jharkhand.

Private healthcare providers are also widespread in urban areas. While there is no analogous nationwide census in urban areas, a detailed study in Delhi estimated that the average household has access to seventy healthcare providers within a fifteen-minute walking distance, and that 78 per cent of them were in the private sector.[20] While there are more qualified private providers in urban areas, a large fraction of them also have no formal medical qualifications! How, then, do they learn what to do?

Field interviews suggest that private providers in both rural and urban areas typically obtain medical knowledge informally. A common pathway for many of them is to have spent time, ranging from months to years, as a compounder or ward boy assisting a senior provider. Many private providers report having learnt their trade during these stints by close observation, and then setting up practices in their own community. They also report ongoing learning from pharmaceutical representatives who provide samples of medicines along with information on how to use different medications to treat specific symptoms. While these representatives likely have incentives to exaggerate the effectiveness of their products, they also maintain long-term relationships with informal providers, and hence also have an incentive to build some credibility and reputation.

Thus, informal providers do have some medical knowledge despite lacking formal qualifications. Of course, there is likely to be considerable variation in the quality of the senior providers who were shadowed—who themselves may not be qualified, and in the quality of the pharmaceutical representatives providing information. It is therefore not surprising that there is also enormous variation in the quality of informal providers.

The discussion above covers healthcare availability inside a village. However, people often travel further to access healthcare. So, the effective market is often larger than the village. In a more detailed study across 100 randomly sampled villages in five districts of Madhya Pradesh (MP), described further below, my co-authors and I listed *all* the healthcare providers used by residents both in their village and beyond.

A key finding was that healthcare *markets* extend well beyond a village, and include clusters of private providers in small towns and in 'market' areas along main roads. On average, villages had four providers within the village, and another 7.7 in nearby market areas, implying that the total number of accessible providers was nearly three times greater than those in the village. Around 34 per cent of healthcare consultations in the month before the survey were sought outside the village. Finally, patients who travelled further to access healthcare visited a higher-quality provider (as defined below).[21]

Putting it together (access)

Put together, the facts above highlight the central role played by private providers in Indian healthcare. They comprise *over 80 per cent* of providers in an average Indian village. Even considering the larger 'market' we studied in MP, which typically includes a public PHC, we found that 66 per cent of all providers were private, and that a striking 89 per cent of all patient visits in MP were to private providers.

This pattern is also seen in nationwide data. As per NSS data from 2017–18 nearly 70 per cent of Indian households report that their ailments were treated outside the public health system, with high private-sector market shares in both urban (74 per cent) and rural (67 per cent) areas. The 2019–21 National Family Health Survey (NFHS-V) finds that 50 per cent of surveyed households report that they generally do not use government health facilities. The top three reasons they gave were poor quality (48 per cent), long and unpredictable waiting times (46 per cent), and low and unreliable access (40 per cent). Many respondents reported more than one of these reasons.

However, while users may choose private providers because they are more present and available when needed, the quality of healthcare they receive may be poor since these providers are mostly unqualified. We turn next to understanding the quality of care.

1.4 Quality of healthcare across public and private providers

Measuring healthcare provider quality is not easy. Challenges include (a) defining the relevant outcomes, (b) measuring them consistently and accurately, (c) accounting for both undertreatment and overtreatment, and (d) adjusting for case complexity. For instance, patients with complex cases often seek care from higher quality providers. So, assessing doctor quality by an outcome such as fatality rates can be highly misleading. Conversely, doctors who appear to be good by providing symptomatic relief, may also prescribe lots of unnecessary medications with negative long-term effects. Accounting for these different dimensions of quality is very difficult, and health researchers have spent considerable effort to improve our ability to measure healthcare provider quality.

One approach is to use clinical vignettes, a standard tool used in medical school assessments. Students are presented a hypothetical case with a set of symptoms, and asked to describe how they would proceed. Their responses (such as questions asked, tests recommended, diagnosis made, and treatments prescribed) are assessed against a checklist of recommended actions for that case, and a summary score of their medical competence is calculated based on these responses. This same approach has been used by researchers to assess the competence of practising healthcare providers.[22]

Multiple vignette studies show that the quality of healthcare provided in India is poor. In our all-India rural healthcare study, providers were presented with cases of tuberculosis, diarrhoea, dysentery, or preeclampsia (a pregnancy-related complication that requires immediate care, and is responsible for a large fraction of maternal deaths). These are conditions that every doctor in India is likely to come across.[23] Overall, we found that less than half the providers were able to correctly diagnose and manage all four cases. We also found many interesting patterns in provider knowledge.

First, nationally, among MBBS providers, 71 per cent demonstrated the requisite knowledge to manage all cases correctly, compared to 40 per cent of Ayush providers and 44 per cent of unqualified providers who manage all cases correctly. Thus, having an MBBS degree is clearly correlated with better doctor knowledge, but at the same time, it appears to be neither necessary nor sufficient to ensure quality.[24]

Figure 12.1: Provider Knowledge by Degree and State

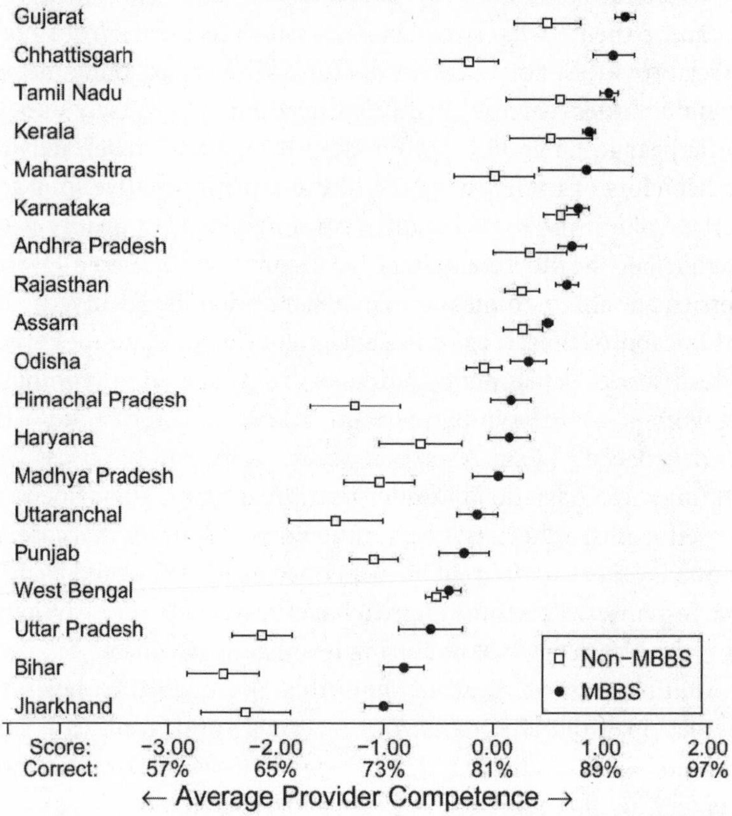

Note(s): Figure reproduced from Das et al (2022); this figure reports the competence score of the full sample of providers who participated in the vignettes testing; it includes a sample of 1738 providers who reported having an MBBS degree, and 2091 who did not.

Second, there is considerable variation in knowledge levels even among similarly qualified providers across states. The average MBBS doctor in Jharkhand and Bihar is around one standard deviation below the national average, while the average MBBS provider in states like Gujarat, Tamil Nadu, and Kerala is one standard deviation above the national average (see Figure 12.1). This translates to a

20–30 percentage point increase in the likelihood of knowing how to correctly manage a case.

Third, the medical knowledge of non-MBBS providers is highly correlated with that of MBBS providers in the same state, and even the same district (Figure 12.1).

This could reflect a combination of variation in the quality of medical education across states, and competitive pressures within markets. Specifically, higher-quality free public services may force low-quality private providers in those states to shut down, and put pressure on the remaining ones to boost quality to remain competitive. This may also explain the striking finding that unqualified informal providers in high-performing states such as Gujarat, Tamil Nadu, and Kerala exhibit greater medical knowledge than even MBBS providers in low-performing states such as Bihar, Jharkhand, and UP. Thus, equal qualifications do *not* imply equal quality across states.

While vignettes measure healthcare providers' *knowledge*, they may not provide a full picture of quality since providers may not always apply their knowledge in *practice*. For instance, a study in Bihar evaluated providers' ability to correctly diagnose and treat a case of diarrhoea. In the study, 72.4 per cent of them *said* they would offer ORS (Oral Rehydration Supplements) to the patient, which is the correct treatment as per WHO guidelines. However, only 17.4 per cent did so in practice.[25] This disparity between doctors' knowledge and their actual practice, referred to as the 'know-do' gap, has been documented in many studies across India. This makes it important to measure not only what doctors know, but also what they do in practice when they see patients.

One novel approach to doing so is to deploy trained actors to portray standardized ('fake') patients (SPs), who present themselves to providers with simulated symptoms. Quality of care is then assessed based on the providers' actions. Quality measures may include time spent with the patient, completion of items from a checklist of essential diagnostic questions and measurements, and treatment quality accounting for both correct and incorrect or unnecessary treatments. The use of SPs to evaluate quality of care is a well-established method, and is used in medical schools to test students.[26]

Using this method, my co-authors and I conducted a study to compare the quality of care across private and public providers in rural MP.[27] We sent highly trained SPs to a random representative sample of public and private healthcare providers in sixty villages across three districts in MP.[28] This 'representative sample' allows us to compare the typical experience of a patient visiting a public and a private clinic. This captures both the differences in composition of providers as well as differences in effort.

We found that, on average, public providers spent *only 2.4 minutes* with the SP per interaction and completed only 16 per cent of checklist items for the cases presented. Private providers were not much better in *absolute* terms, but were significantly better in *relative* terms, spending over 50 per cent more time with the SP (3.7 vs 2.4 minutes) and completing 40 per cent more checklist items (22.3 per cent vs 16 per cent). Turning to treatment, private providers on average were slightly *more* likely to provide a correct treatment, though this difference was not statistically significant. Also, in many cases, when the SP visited a public clinic, the care was provided by an unqualified ward boy or assistant because the qualified provider was absent or unavailable.

We also collected data in a 'dual-practice' sample where we identified public MBBS doctors who also had an (illegal) private practice. Over a period of three to six months, different SPs presented the *same case* to the *same doctor* in both their public and private practices.[29] The comparison across this 'dual sample' allows us to isolate the effects of the differential incentives for the *same* provider across their public and private practices.

We find that *every* metric of quality of care was higher in the doctor's private practice. Compared to their own public practice, doctors in private practice spent 86 per cent more time engaging with patients (3 vs 1.6 minutes), completed 60 per cent more checklist items (28.3 vs 17.7 per cent), and were 52 per cent more likely to provide the correct treatment (56.6 vs 37.3 per cent). They were also 20 per cent less likely to provide a palliative treatment (that eased symptoms but did not address the underlying condition), 29 per cent less likely to prescribe an antibiotic (which was not indicated for the condition), and dispensed or prescribed the same number of total medications.

These results highlight the nuanced ways in which market incentives can play out. On the one hand, we do find that there are market incentives for excessive treatment: prices charged are higher when more medications are provided. On the other, the *overall* level of medication provided is comparable to that of the public sector.

This apparent contradiction can be explained by two opposing factors. On the one hand, private doctors have incentives to over-treat. On the other, they also have incentives to exert higher diagnostic effort. A key result we find is that prices charged are positively correlated with both diagnostic effort and the number of medications provided. These are both proxies for quality that *patients can observe*. Thus, the greater diagnostic effort may increase the accuracy of doctors' diagnosis, potentially reducing the need for over-treatment. These opposing factors may also explain another surprising finding: public providers *also* dispense a large amount of unnecessary medication, even though they have no financial incentives for doing so. One possible explanation suggested by the study is that public providers may be using over-treatment to compensate for low diagnostic effort, especially because the medicines are free.

Taken together, these findings offer valuable insights about healthcare in India. The most important point is that quality of healthcare is a combination of providers' medical knowledge, which increases with but is not guaranteed by better qualifications, *and* their effort. On average, the public sector has more qualified providers. Yet, the evidence suggests that private providers can compensate for their lower qualifications with greater effort, ultimately resulting in quality of care that is comparable to that delivered by better qualified public providers. Interestingly, this pattern mirrors what we see in the case of primary education (see Chapters 9 and 11).

1.5 Cost-effectiveness

In addition to access and quality, we need to consider cost-effectiveness to maximize quality for every rupee spent. The studies above also provide insights on cost-effectiveness both within the public sector, and between the public and private sector.

Our nationwide study finds that there is enormous variation in the cost per patient even within the public sector across Indian states. Since staff salaries are the largest cost component, and are also fixed costs, the variation in cost per patient is largely driven by variation in the utilization rate of public facilities. For instance, doctor salaries in Tamil Nadu and Uttar Pradesh were quite similar. However, the number of patients per month per public MBBS provider was six times higher in Tamil Nadu (1848 vs 293). Hence, the cost per patient in Tamil Nadu was six times *lower* than in UP despite the quality being *higher*. These results are striking and show that states like Tamil Nadu (and also Kerala, Karnataka, and Andhra Pradesh) deliver higher quality at a lower cost!

One key likely factor behind these states' ability to deliver higher-quality healthcare at a lower cost is their much greater investments in medical education, including permitting and promoting the creation of private medical colleges.[30] This increase in the supply of doctors and other medical staff may have enabled the public system to hire more staff without salaries increasing too much (as seen by the comparable salaries of public doctors in UP and Tamil Nadu), and also improved provider quality in the private sector.

A second noteworthy point is that though fee-charging private providers cost users more than free public care, the true taxpayer-funded cost per patient in the public sector, is much higher. For instance, in our MP study, we estimated that the cost per patient in public clinics was over *four times greater* than the average fee charged in the private clinics. This is conservative because it only counts the salary cost of staff in the public clinics and excludes costs of infrastructure and facilities, whereas private providers' fees have to cover *all* their costs. As noted above, a key driver of high cost per patient in MP's public health clinics is their low utilization. On average, clinics saw 1000 patients per month and employed 13.5 staff. Assuming twenty-five working days per month, this translates to only three patients per day per employee.

1.6 Putting it together: access, quality, and cost

To summarize, there are six key facts about healthcare in India, three each on private and public provision. First, the fee-charging private sector accounts for 70–80 per cent of market share for primary care. Second, most of India's healthcare providers are in the private sector and unqualified. Third, despite limited qualifications, private providers on average seem to provide comparable quality of care to that in the public sector, at least for primary care. This appears to be driven by a combination of higher effort and a reasonable amount of informally obtained practical medical knowledge.

Fourth, there is substantial variation across states in the quality and cost-effectiveness of public healthcare, underscoring the potential for public healthcare systems to function much better. Fifth, the strong correlation between public and private providers within a given market highlights the dual benefit of improving public provision: (a) it directly helps those who use public services, and (b) it also benefits those who use private services by exerting competitive pressure on private providers to improve their quality. Sixth, the combination of people being willing to travel to access higher-quality providers, higher unit cost of providing quality care in low-density areas, and greater difficulty of ensuring provider attendance in remote areas suggests that we can improve access to quality care by improving connectivity and not just by adding facilities in low-density areas.

Taken together, the main policy implications of these facts are that the government should both focus on strengthening the quality and cost-effectiveness of public healthcare, and also make it easier for markets for private healthcare to function better.

1.7 The nutrition challenge

Beyond healthcare, India faces a significant challenge of child stunting. Stunting reflects several factors, including poverty and low incomes, food expenditure, nutritional quality of diet, women's empowerment within households,[31] population disease burden, and poor sanitation. Together, these factors contribute to inadequate net nutrient intake for children to grow, resulting in slower child growth. However, while this physiological adaptation enables children to survive in adverse conditions (smaller bodies require fewer minimum calories to survive), it severely limits their ability to lead healthy lives.

Several global and Indian studies have shown that stunting during childhood imposes large long-term costs on health and well-being. These costs include slower cognitive development, higher likelihood of illness, lower educational attainment, reduced lifetime earnings, and shorter life expectancy. Crucially, for policy and public welfare, targeted interventions to reduce stunting at young ages can deliver lifelong benefits that far exceed the costs.[32] Thus, reducing child stunting is a critical investment in the long-term health of India's population.

The Central government has recognized the importance of child nutrition by establishing a National Nutrition Mission. Yet, success will mainly be determined by state-level actions, which can be made more effective as discussed in Section 2.6.

1.8 The pollution challenge

Finally, it is critical to recognize the cost of environmental degradation on population health. India has the unfortunate distinction of having thirteen of the fifteen cities with the *worst air pollution in the world* in 2020.[33] The WHO recommends a maximum safe concentration level of PM2.5 (particulate matter of size less than 2.5 microns) in the air at 10 micrograms/m^3. However, India's average PM2.5 level in 2019 was nearly six times higher, at 58 microgram/m^3. This is also 1.5 times higher than the national benchmark of 40 microgram/m^3. The situation is meaningfully worse in the winters when many Indian cities are classified as unhealthy or very unhealthy by WHO standards. Economist Rohini Pande and co-authors have estimated that 99.9 per cent of India's population is breathing air that is more polluted than the WHO benchmark.[34]

The Energy Policy Institute of Chicago (EPIC) estimates that reducing India's air pollution to WHO benchmarks could boost average life expectancy by around four years, which would halve our life expectancy gap with China. Even if we reduce pollution to comply with our own national standards, average life expectancy would increase by 1.3 years. EPIC Director Professor Michael Greenstone has noted that: 'Particulate air pollution is the greatest external threat to human health on the planet. When you focus on developing countries, the effect is even larger.'

Further, a growing body of research finds direct links between reducing air pollution and increased productivity.[35] This is especially true in urban areas, where both economic activity and the burden of air pollution are higher. So, we should see not see spending and regulations to improving air quality as a drag on economic activity, but as an investment that will improve both health *and* productivity.

2. Principles and Policy Ideas

Section 1 shows that public spending on health in India is below global norms. However, it also shows that the effectiveness of existing spending is low due to (a) prioritizing curative over preventive care, and (b) low productivity in government-funded curative care. The latter point is exemplified by high and unpredictable public health worker absence rates, leading to low utilization, and high costs per patient.

So, while there is a strong case for higher public spending on health, simply expanding 'government as usual' health spending may not meaningfully improve population health outcomes. Rather, we should use the framework of Figure 6.2 to identify R1 ideas that can improve both equity and efficiency, and prioritize scarce public funds on such ideas. The discussion below outlines key principles for identifying R1 ideas, and then presents specific ones for improving population health.

2.1 Prioritize preventive *public* health over curative *private* health

For health policy, it is crucial to understand the distinction between public and private goods. One common misconception is to think that a public good is something that is provided by the government. But this is not true because the government often provides goods for private consumption, such as subsidized food grains or healthcare. These are not public goods, but publicly provided private goods.

Rather, the technical definition of a public good is something that is: (a) non-excludable—i.e. it cannot be denied to someone who does not pay for it; and (b) non-rival—i.e. one person's consumption of the good does not impede someone else's consumption of the same good. Classic examples of public goods include national defence and streetlights. Another good reason for governments to provide certain goods is when they generate social benefits to *others*. Such items are also, reasonably, referred to as public goods.

In health, examples of public goods include infectious disease control and reducing air pollution, which meet the conditions above. In contrast, curative care is a private good since the benefits mostly accrue to individuals and their families. Programmes like vaccination and sanitation campaigns (that include toilet construction for the poor) provide direct benefits to recipients, but are closer to public goods since they provide large *indirect* benefits to non-recipients by reducing the spread of infectious diseases.

Public goods have two other key traits. First, their social benefits usually greatly exceed those of private goods because they benefit many more people. Second, they will typically be *underprovided* if left to individual actions alone, since individuals weigh *personal* costs and benefits in their decision-making, but usually neglect the broader social impacts of their actions. For instance, it may be individually optimal for farmers to burn stubble, but this decision ignores the additional social costs of pollution. So, a core policy principle to guide the allocation of scarce public resources should be to prioritize spending on public goods that will be underprovided otherwise.

This is why health policy should prioritize preventive public health over curative private health. For instance, the public RoI on reducing infectious disease transmission is much higher than spending on curative care after an infection. Further, individuals can and do spend on curative care, but are less able and likely to spend on preventive public health measures, which magnifies the importance of public expenditure in this area.

However, India's public spending on health is heavily skewed towards curative care (see Section 1.2). This pattern is consistent with several studies showing that people underinvest time, effort, and money in simple preventive healthcare behaviours relative to how much they spend *after* falling sick.[36] It is also consistent with the fact that it is often politically more rewarding to give fewer people large, visible benefits (like hospital reimbursements), than to give many more people smaller, less visible benefits (like prevention) that they are less likely to give politicians credit for (see Chapter 2).

Thus, the patterns of public spending on health may simply reflect citizen and voter demand, and politicians catering to it. However, given our tight fiscal constraints, policymakers should aim to use public funds judiciously and maximize the public RoI of health spending. So, they should prioritize additional public spending on preventive public health and also explain the importance of doing so to voters and citizens.

A recent co-authored study in Jharkhand shows the value of public health investments. We studied the impact of two years of cash transfers worth Rs 500 per month to mothers of zero-to-two-year-old children, on child development outcomes.[37] We found that the transfers improved food consumption, dietary diversity, and nutritious food intake among mothers and children. However, we found no improvement in child growth on average, but only in areas with low open defecation rates. Thus, the sanitation environment, which is mostly determined by the actions of *others* in the neighbourhood, played a critical mediating role in converting food intake into better child growth. These results illustrate that initiatives to eliminate open defecation, like the Swachh Bharat Mission (SBM), are a good example of public health interventions that offer spillover benefits to communities, over and above benefits to individual households.

2.2 Consider health impacts of actions *outside* the health ministry

Health ministers and secretaries often view their main role as running the public health system, and to some extent regulating private providers and medical education. Yet, it is critical to recognize that the most effective health-promoting investments for India may lie *outside* the health ministry, as shown in the examples below.

Air and water quality

As discussed earlier, a growing body of evidence points to the long-lasting negative effects of air and water pollution on health. Improving environmental quality is also a classic example of an underprovided public good. While the details of environmental policy, regulation, and enforcement are beyond the scope of this book,[38] recognizing the centrality of the environment for health may help to reinforce its importance for policy.

Public discourse on environmental regulation often frames it as a trade-off between economic activity and livelihoods, and environmental protection. This can contribute to a view that environmental regulations are obstacles to development and job creation. Further, issuing environmental certificates is often a source of corruption, which reduces the credibility and standing of environmental regulation in the business community.

However, our current approach to environmental protection significantly underestimates, or even ignores, the health costs of pollution. Proper accounting of these costs would reveal the large social welfare benefits of higher investments in upfront pollution mitigation. So, a practical recommendation for Central and state health ministries is to quantify the cost of different kinds of pollution, and ensure that these costs are factored into the design and enforcement of environmental regulations.

Such calculations can also help to build support for politically difficult policy actions. For instance, raising taxes on petroleum products is politically unpopular. Yet, as explained in Chapter 7, it is better for society to raise public revenue by taxing items like pollution, that we want to reduce; than by taxing earnings and consumption, that we want to encourage. Presenting clear charts and figures showing the health benefits of petroleum taxes and urban congestion charges could make such policies politically more viable. Labelling these as 'green taxes' and earmarking the proceeds for investments in public transportation could further clarify the policy rationale to the voters.

Roads, broadband, and market access

Delivering quality healthcare in rural areas faces two major challenges. First, qualified providers do not want to live there, and commuting from further away is a key driver of absence. Second, low population density and facility utilization sharply increases per patient costs. Combined with evidence that patients are willing to travel to access higher quality care, a simple insight that may be missed by health policymakers is that public investments in roads may also be an effective way of promoting healthcare access. A recent study on India's rural roads programme, Pradhan Mantri Gram Sadak Yojana (PMGSY), confirms this, and finds that PMGSY led to a significant increase in institutional prenatal care and deliveries, and vaccination rates.[39]

Similarly, high-quality broadband Internet access in rural areas can enable rural residents to easily consult with specialists in higher density urban areas. Several promising models of telemedicine have been developed and deployed in recent years. Such models can sharply bring down the quality adjusted cost of healthcare per patient, and will be easier to scale with public investment in broadband access.

A twenty-first-century health ministry should imagine its role as extending beyond just running public healthcare systems, to becoming the primary advocate within the government for actions that promote population health. While decisions on issues like environmental mitigation, road construction, and rolling out fibre-Internet connections will lie outside their domain, health ministries should calculate the health benefits to these investments and share them with the finance department and concerned line departments to ensure that they are accounted for in deciding how to allocate scarce public resources.

This is an obvious insight to economists and public policy experts.[40] Yet, government functioning is so fragmented across ministries that implementing this idea would be a profound departure from 'government as usual'. It would be bold and unconventional for a health ministry to seek additional resources not for itself, but for policies to improve air quality or child nutrition. However, doing so may have a much greater positive impact on population health and well-being than additional funding for clinics and hospitals.

2.3 Invest strategically in medical education

A key constraint to delivering quality healthcare in India is the scarcity of adequately trained professionals. As noted earlier, there are large vacancies in doctor and nurse positions, especially in poorer states and in rural and remote areas. These vacancies are driven by: (a) fewer medical training institutions in poorer states, and (b) qualified medical providers being less willing to work in rural and remote locations.

There is striking variation in medical college seats per capita across Indian states (see Figure 12.2). Telangana and Karnataka, for instance, have four to five times more seats per capita than Bihar and Jharkhand. This disparity drives variation in doctors per capita across states because (a) 85 per cent of seats are reserved for students from the same state as the college is, and (b) doctors are much more likely to practise in their home states, or where they obtained their medical education. Hence, investing in medical education generates public benefits by expanding the supply of well-qualified healthcare staff for *both* public and private clinics in the state.

Figure 12.2: Medical College Seats per 1000 Population across States

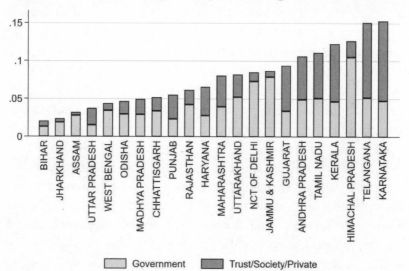

Note(s): Population from 2011 Census; number of seats from the National Medical Council website; states with population >50 lakh included.

However, the cost of setting up medical colleges is high. So, the variation in medical seats per capita across states is mainly driven by private medical colleges. These are more economically viable in higher-income states where more students can afford their high fees. So, it is essential to develop lower cost models for training healthcare workers to facilitate large-scale, cost-effective expansion of healthcare. Further, it is not enough to just train more people; they also need to be willing to work in underserved areas. The idea below aims to address both of these challenges.

Set up practicum-based nurse training programmes

The core idea has been discussed in Chapter 5, and applies well to all three critical labour-intensive service sectors: education, health, and public safety.

States can increase the supply of qualified healthcare workers by introducing practicum-based nursing courses lasting three to four years, after Class 12. These courses would blend three to four months of theoretical modules and exams, with eight to nine months of practical training in a PHC or a sub-centre, under the supervision of an ANM. The government would cover course fees and offer a modest stipend (say Rs 3000–6000 per month) during the practicum. These features would make the course highly attractive to young women, and it would admit candidates based on Class 12 marks. To augment healthcare staff in underserved areas, candidates from areas with the most need for medical staff would be prioritized. For instance, the top scoring applicant from each GP in a district would be considered for selection, with slots filled in descending order of staffing needs.

Ideally, every district would have one such training institute, with curricula and course content developed by top state and national training institutes. The district institute would have (or contract with) a hostel where female candidates would be able to stay during their theoretical training phase. While doing their practical training in their home areas, trainee nurses would receive smartphones, enabling them to (a) log their efforts and update patient medical records, (b) consult experienced providers for advice, (c) create virtual communities of practice with their training cohort, through

WhatsApp groups for instance, and (d) continue to receive modular training content digitally.[41]

Creating such a programme would offer several benefits. First, it is more cost-effective to expand the supply of medical workers through nursing programmes than to establish MBBS colleges, making it scalable in poorer states with acute health worker shortages. Second, interspersing theory and practice will improve training quality.[42] Third, admitting candidates from GPs with the greatest staff shortages and situating the practicum in the home GPs helps to address the vexing problem of spatial mismatch, where qualified staff do not want to work in underserved areas. Fourth, it promotes female employment, especially in patriarchal communities, by locating the practicum in the home GP.

This idea shares important similarities with the nationally successful ASHA worker programme, which was scaled up after successful pilots by Dr Abhay and Rani Bang in Gadchiroli district of Maharashtra. The key insight of the ASHA model is that rather than expecting highly qualified candidates, who prefer living in urban areas, to serve in rural areas, it may be more effective to identify talented and motivated young women from local communities, and upgrade their skills to equip them to provide basic health services in their own communities. However, the ASHA model has not been leveraged to full potential because of under-investment in training and capacity building. The practicum-based nurse training programme could be used to upgrade ASHA workers' skills, and offer them a career ladder based on competency and performance.[43]

Upon completing the practicum, candidates would earn an ANM qualification, reflecting their total theoretical training being similar to that received by ANMs. However, this course's extensive practical training will produce more skilled candidates than traditional ANM courses, which offer less practical training. Also, most ANM training courses are run by private institutions charging fees of around Rs 25,000 to Rs 50,000, which is a barrier for qualified, but economically disadvantaged, candidates.

In the proposed practicum model, the training would be free, with the cost to taxpayers being paid back by providing healthcare services during the practicum. This approach sends a powerful message to youth, saying that the government would invest in them to enable them to serve their communities. At the time of regular recruitment of ANMs, graduates of the practicum-based course would receive extra points for each year of practical experience (as explained in Chapter 5). So, these candidates could either be employed as public sector ANMs, or in the private sector where nearly 80 per cent of ANMs work. Such public investment in medical education would benefit all citizens by increasing the supply of qualified health workers to both the public and private sectors.

Set up practicum-based training programmes for other health workers as well

The same approach can be used to develop other types of health workers. While ANMs focus on obstetrics, gynaecology, and maternal and childcare, the health system also includes male and female multipurpose health workers (MPHW). MPHWs are trained to provide public health services, and assist doctors in various functions. A similar practicum-based course can be used to increase both the numbers and skills of MPHWs, and thereby enhance the overall quality of community health services.

This approach could also be used for training mid-level health providers (MLHPs) and regular nurses, who are more qualified than MPHWs and ANMs, but less so than MBBS doctors. The new approach would improve upon the status quo by helping to reduce spatial mismatch. Under the status quo, candidates self-fund their training and prefer to be posted in urban areas. In the new model, the government would pay for training candidates from underserved areas, and improve service delivery in these areas via the practicum component, during which candidates would serve in their home areas.

2.4 Strengthen public health systems for both curative and preventive care

Despite the large market share of private providers in India, the foundation of universal healthcare is the government-run system. So, improving its functioning should be a top priority. The discussion below suggests some practical ideas for doing so.

Augment staffing—especially with locally hired personnel

A key staffing challenge for healthcare provision in India is spatial mismatch: qualified staff prefer to live in urban areas, whereas the most severe staff shortages are in rural and remote areas. Further, it is not socially efficient to put highly qualified staff in rural areas since low caseloads result in underutilization of scarce qualified staff and a much higher cost per patient.

Therefore, a better way to augment staffing in rural areas is to identify motivated, local, personnel and augment their skills to (a) provide better quality *primary* care in rural areas, (b) teach them when to refer complex cases to more qualified providers, and (c) leverage technology to consult more qualified providers in urban areas. One way to do this is to implement the modular practicum-based training programmes described in the previous section. After these candidates graduate from the programme, they could be given preference for being hired as regular ANMs and MPHWs in their own GPs.

Improve incentives

A critical reform to strengthen public health systems is to improve staff motivation and recognize effective performance. Under the status quo, doctors and healthcare workers often have *negative* incentives to work hard. While they may work diligently up to a point due to intrinsic motivation, their only reward for providing good care is that they will get *more* patients, without *any* increase in either resources or pay. This makes it rational for even motivated healthcare workers to limit their effort in the public system. It also makes it logical for doctors to have a private practice on the side, offer basic care to the poor who come to public clinics, and direct those who can afford to pay to their private practice, where they provide better quality of care and get compensated for doing so.

It is tempting to paint doctors as villains in this situation, since private practices are often illegal. However, it will be more productive to recognize that the root cause of the problem is poorly designed incentives in the public healthcare system. Under the current system, providing better care results in more patients and work with no extra pay. Furthermore, punitive top-down actions against health workers are unlikely to be very effective. They may ensure attendance, but cannot inspire greater effort or quality of care. Such actions can even backfire by reducing healthcare workers' intrinsic motivation.

A more promising approach may be to reward providers for effort and quality of care. One idea is to provide additional revenue to public clinics for every verified patient visit. These extra funds can go into a discretionary clinic account and be used to either hire extra staff, or pay bonuses to existing staff. This approach has been successfully used in the mohalla clinics in Delhi. Of course, there is a risk of fraud and registering fake patient visits, necessitating robust verification systems. The National Health Authority is already building such systems under the National Digital Health Mission. States can use this as a base to implement better incentive systems for public clinics to attract patients.

Over time, with the growth of digital health records and unique health IDs, governments could design systems to empower poorer patients to seek care in either public or private facilities, and directly pay them based on verified patient use (see Section 2.5). While designing such systems is challenging, the current system is clearly not working. So, the benefits from implementing systemic reforms that improve incentives and accountability in the public health system are likely to be substantial.

Build second district hospitals

The reforms suggested above can greatly improve the public health system. However, bureaucracies usually find it easier to do more of what they know how to do, than to reform existing systems. So, it is inevitable that governments will build more facilities and hire more staff in the coming years. In this case, it will be much better to invest these resources in building a second high-quality district hospital in every district rather than spreading these resources out thinly with several smaller facilities.

This is because the problems of provider absence, low utilization, and higher per-patient costs are all more acute in remote and rural areas. Unlike schooling, where proximity is crucial due to daily travel by children, people are more willing to travel for better quality healthcare because (a) usage is more episodic, (b) better quality providers are available in densely populated areas, and (c) larger facilities have less staff absence, even in the public sector. Given significant improvements in road construction and connectivity over the last two decades, investing in fewer, larger-scale hospitals at the district level will be more effective than spreading out the same capacity in sub-scale, remote facilities. This approach has also been endorsed by Abhijit Banerjee.[44]

Create a dedicated public health cadre

A key recommendation for state governments is to create a dedicated public health cadre to focus on tasks like disease surveillance, vector control, health communications and messaging, and monitoring *other* departments responsible for functions that matter for population health—such as waste management, water, and sanitation. As explained earlier, investing in preventive public health is likely to yield much higher social returns than spending more on curative private health. However, most states, except Tamil Nadu and Maharashtra, rely on medical doctors to provide public health services. This approach is less effective because medical doctors are primarily trained to provide care to individual patients, and not for managing population-level health outcomes.[45]

Hence, state health systems will greatly benefit from having a dedicated team of public health specialists. Expert committees and policy documents have long made this recommendation. For instance, the Twelfth Five-Year Plan in 2012 noted the: 'urgent, real need for a dedicated public health cadre backed by appropriate regulation at the state level'. The National Health Policy of 2017 reiterated this need, highlighting that this cadre should be multidisciplinary and professionally qualified. It declared that a public health cadre was a prerequisite to effectively address social determinants of health and enforce regulatory provisions. However, not much progress has been made in practice.

Setting up a dedicated public health cadre is likely to be one of the most efficient ways to improve population health. A cross-state report showed that Kerala and Himachal Pradesh had the best health indicators, but also had the highest health expenditures.[46] However, it reported that Tamil Nadu had similarly good indicators, but below-average health spending, and notes that 'its consistently good indicators despite low expenditure have been attributed to the long-standing presence of a Public Health Cadre and Act in the state.' Echoing this view, a *Lancet* review paper on 'Good Health at Low Cost' notes Tamil Nadu's success and says: 'In Tamil Nadu, we doubt whether many innovations would have been successful without the state's unique public health management cadre at district level, with power to plan and manage services.'[47] So, while a national public health mission can expedite the creation of such cadres across India with funds and technical support, states can also learn from Tamil Nadu and do so on their own.

2.5 Improve the functioning of healthcare markets

Beyond its role as a provider, governments also shape the healthcare ecosystem as a policymaker and regulator. However, since government budgets and staff are mostly allocated to healthcare provision, most health ministers and secretaries tend to focus on managing the public healthcare system. However, this is a limited view, since over 70 per cent of healthcare in India is provided by the private sector. So, the government should aim to improve the *overall* healthcare system and not just the public one. The discussion below builds on Chapter 9, with specific ideas in the healthcare context.

Understand and mitigate market failures

In most markets, consumers identify their needs, and seek the best value for money. However, healthcare is different, and suffers from many market failures, including information asymmetry, conflict of interests, and inability to comparison-shop when ill.

For instance, patients may know they are unwell, but usually lack knowledge about their illness or the required treatment, relying on doctors to tell them. This information asymmetry hinders patients' ability to evaluate the quality of care. They can observe a doctors' behaviour, and tell if their symptoms get better, but usually cannot assess the long-term effects of treatments or procedures, or if they were even necessary.

This information asymmetry can also lead to a divergence between doctor and patient interests, if doctors are compensated for prescribing more medicines or doing more procedures. Global evidence shows that the likelihood of unnecessary procedures increases when doctors' are rewarded for them.[48]

Market-based accountability in healthcare is further weakened by patients being price insensitive when ill. An accident victim will want to be taken to the nearest hospital, and does not have the luxury of bargaining to obtain the best possible price. Conversely, hospitals have considerable pricing power when patients are in acute need.

These reasons explain why standard market-based accountability may be inadequate for healthcare. This is also partly why healthcare training and provision is regulated, globally. The medical profession tries to mitigate the power and knowledge imbalance between doctors and patients by promoting ethical behaviour, exemplified by the Hippocratic oath, as part of medical training. Training and practice guides also aim to establish standardized care protocols to provide a benchmark for doctor actions. Partly as a result, the vast majority of doctors are intrinsically motivated, altruistic, and act in patients' best interests. However, they are also human, and respond to incentives to recommend treatments and procedures that are not always necessary.

Yet, the existence of market failures does *not* imply that the government should always intervene, because such intervention can make matters worse. For instance, imposing price caps can benefit a few, but hurt many more by restricting supply. In other cases, regulation can become an excuse for extracting bribes. Further, while the government can stipulate rules and regulations, it also has limited capacity to enforce them.

Given limited state capacity, the best way to improve the functioning of healthcare markets may be to promote greater transparency and disclosure among healthcare providers. For instance, the government should not try to fix prices for hospital procedures, but it can require transparency in pricing, and for similar prices to be charged for regular and emergency patients. Such an approach enables patients to make more informed choices without heavy-handed interventions.

Governments could set up, or contract the creation of, a portal listing healthcare providers by area. Providers would be encouraged to register on this portal with practice details such as their qualifications, experience, number of patients seen, and fee ranges for various services. The portal could also indicate if the provider is recognized by publicly funded programmes such as Ayushman Bharat, or state equivalents such as Aarogyashree in AP and Telangana. Over time, it could include feedback from *verified* users, akin to platforms like Amazon or Flipkart. Generating and sharing credible information on healthcare provider quality is a public good, creating a strong case for governments, or philanthropy, to fund the creation and distribution of such information.

If done well, such a system can foster a virtuous cycle in private health markets. It would improve consumer awareness and choice, and encourage providers to improve their quality and cost-effectiveness. Over time, it would increase the market share of high-quality providers and encourage them to expand, while reducing market share of lower quality providers, potentially leading to their closure. This approach could also inspire the establishment of organizations, both for-profit and non-profit, that operate chains of high-quality, low-cost primary care clinics that leverage scale to keep costs low, and have reputational incentives to maintain quality standards.

This disclosure-based regulatory approach is a departure from the status quo where governments often try to shut down unqualified providers but are unsuccessful because they often resume practice after being 'shut down'. In contrast, under the disclosure-based approach, unqualified providers will typically not register, and patients can use this information to gradually shift away from them towards higher-quality providers.

Training and credentialing of informal providers

A critical area where thoughtful interventions can improve market-level healthcare quality is training and skilling of the lakhs of informal healthcare providers across India. These providers are usually ignored in policy discussions due to very limited data, and because their practices are illegal since they are mostly unqualified. So, policymakers often prefer to ignore their existence because they are not supposed to be practising. However, these providers *account for the majority of healthcare provision in India!*

Ignoring this vast segment of informal providers is a massive blind spot in our current approach to health policy. Research shows that despite lacking formal qualifications, they are often as effective as those in the formal public system, at least for primary care. They are also available when needed, unlike frequently absent public staff, and have long-standing relationships in their communities. They make up for lower knowledge with higher effort, and have incentives to deliver at least symptomatic relief, to build and maintain their local reputation. Further, while their over-prescription of medication is a real problem, this is often driven less by unscrupulous providers and more by *patient demand* for symptomatic relief.[49] This demand reflects the fact that getting back to work soon is the overriding goal for the poor who depend on daily-wage work for a livelihood.

The best long-term solution to the problem of untrained informal providers is to increase the supply of trained providers, who will be *willing to practise in the communities* served by the informal providers. A natural place to start is by training the informal providers themselves since they are already providing healthcare services in their communities. An important study by Abhijit Banerjee, Jishnu Das, and others found that training informal providers in West Bengal significantly improved the quality of care they provided.[50] However, this was a one-off experiment, and has not been institutionalized.

A practical strategy to improve the skills of unqualified, informal providers at scale is to offer them preferential access to the modular, practicum-based, ANM, MPHW, nurse, or mid-level health provider training programmes described in Section 2.3, based on their formal education level. The government would fund the theoretical training modules, but not offer a stipend since they would not be doing a practicum in a public clinic. Rather, these providers would continue practising in their communities (which would be their practicum equivalent), and gradually increase their knowledge, get better connected to peer networks, and access modular training through smartphones. Importantly, such training can better equip informal providers to detect complex cases early and refer these to qualified doctors, and thereby improve healthcare quality by reducing harm.

A crucial mindset shift we need in thinking about informal providers is to stop viewing them as malevolent actors, operating illegally. Their widespread prevalence and use is a response to the gaps in state-provided healthcare, and their ability to offer more predictable access to healthcare than the public system. Thus, improving their training and skills can significantly improve healthcare quality for hundreds of millions of Indians, and also reduce their likelihood of doing harm.

Improving healthcare access in India depends critically on: (a) increasing the number of well-trained healthcare providers, and (b) doing so cost-effectively. The latter is as or *more* important if we want to scale up equitable access. India's policies on medical education and health investments are heavily influenced by elites, including top doctors who are super-specialists. However, creating more AIIMS or super-speciality hospitals will not solve the problem of *cost-effective*, equitable access to basic care for all Indians.

In contrast, large numbers of informal providers already exist. They are trusted and embedded in their communities, and practise medicine anyway. Thus, upgrading their skills through training and credentialing at the level of a nurse or mid-level health provider (*not* an MBBS doctor) may be one of the most effective and cost-effective policy options for improving access, quality, and equity in healthcare at scale.

A longer-term architecture for healthcare

Designing effective healthcare systems is an incredibly complex problem. There is also considerable path dependence in countries' choices, which makes it important to get the health system architecture right at the outset. As India embarks upon building a twenty-first-century healthcare system, we have the opportunity to get the first principles right.

One key principle is that health systems should provide incentives for quality care but avoid incentives for over-treatment. One approach is a system where people register with a primary care physician or practice annually, and the government provides a fixed annual payment per registered patient to the chosen provider or practice. This payment would apply to *both* public and private clinics, and be linked to Aadhaar or the ABHA number,[51] to ensure each citizen selects only one primary practice. Thus, the government would essentially provide an 'annual voucher' for universal health access, redeemable with the patient's preferred healthcare provider each year. Initially, voucher eligibility can be limited to the very poor, as done with Ayushman Bharat. Over time, it could be offered to more people with the voucher value decreasing with income.

Such a system architecture, where the 'money follows the patient' offers several benefits. It motivates providers to build a reputation for quality care, so that people register with their practice. Yet, the fixed annual payment limits incentives for over-treatment. It will also increase the market share of qualified providers, since the voucher will only be redeemable with accredited or empanelled providers. It will also sharply improve incentives for effort in *public* clinics, because they will now receive an extra payment for every patient registered with them.

Most importantly, this approach empowers the poor with purchasing power, via a voucher, and can encourage private and non-profit entities to create scalable, low-cost, healthcare models that can better serve millions of Indians. For instance, companies may invest in high-quality remote telemedicine services, where rural primary clinics are staffed by qualified nurses who examine patients, record their medical histories, and transmit this data to a central hub staffed with qualified doctors. Nurses can provide primary care for routine ailments, and easily consult doctors for more complex cases. Advances in communication technology may also enable qualified doctors to remotely examine patients, assisted by onsite nurses.

These healthcare concepts are not new, and many organizations (both for-profit and non-profit) are already exploring them. However, these models primarily cater to paying customers, excluding those who cannot afford to pay. The key innovation in the proposed approach is empowering the poor with a healthcare voucher, which will sharply increase the scale and speed of innovation targeted at serving low-income populations, and thereby improve equity and inclusivity in our healthcare system.

India is already embarking on this approach to healthcare under the Ayushman Bharat scheme, which is a large-scale insurance programme. However, it is only being applied for tertiary care.[52] Extending this model to primary care could substantially improve long-term cost-adjusted quality of care in India. While implementing this approach nationally may be financially challenging, states can test it with their own budgets. This approach could also appeal to international development finance organizations, and attract subsidized loans, technical assistance, and even grants to states willing to pilot it.

The reforms in this subsection can be implemented individually, but combining them could yield synergies, and deliver higher overall benefits. In particular, pairing voucher-based financing for the poor and better provision of information on provider quality can significantly improve the functioning of healthcare markets, and improve both equity and efficiency, making it an R1 reform (see Figure 6.2).

This approach does not privilege the private sector, as the public clinic will be the default option. Users not registered with any provider would be automatically enrolled with their local public clinic. A significant fraction of public clinics' costs, say 70 per cent of staff salaries, could be pre-paid by the government. The voucher value for patients choosing public clinics could be split, with 70 per cent returning to the government to cover the pre-paid amount, and 30 per cent retained by the clinic for variable staff compensation. This way, public clinics will remain the foundation of the healthcare system, but will face greater accountability and incentives, since they will lose funds and variable pay if patients are unsatisfied with the public clinic, and shift to other providers.

Implementing such a system will require many practical details to be worked out, such as reimbursement rates for different procedures, fraud prevention, and adjusting voucher values for patients with pre-existing conditions. However, the core conceptual point is that this architecture improves incentives for both public and private providers, and empowers the poor with more choice. It exemplifies the 'exit and voice' framework discussed in Chapter 9, and illustrates how offering the poor an option to 'exit' out of the public system will also improve their 'voice' in improving it.

2.6 Improve child nutrition in mission mode

The single-most important investment we can make in India's future is to improve early childhood health, nutrition, and education. We can address this challenge at scale by making a few key investments to strengthen the ICDS. As noted in Chapter 11, the ICDS is the world's largest provider of early childhood health and education services, but is both understaffed and under-resourced relative to its importance for India's future. In particular, a single anganwadi worker (AWW) is tasked with delivering a wide range of early-childhood health, nutrition, and pre-school education services in addition to large amounts of paperwork and record-keeping.

One simple, scalable, evidence-backed idea that state governments can immediately act on is to add an extra worker to AWCs, so that one can focus on health and nutrition, and the other on pre-school education. In a recent study in Tamil Nadu, my co-authors and I found that doing so led to a significant reduction in child malnutrition and stunting, in addition to boosting early childhood learning outcomes. We estimate that the benefits of an extra worker were thirteen to twenty-one times the cost, yielding an RoI of 1200–2000 per cent! Further, the public RoI would be *infinite* since the discounted present value of higher future tax revenues would more than pay for programme costs.[53]

These results suggest that adding an extra worker to AWCs can be a highly effective and cost-effective strategy for improving early childhood health, nutrition, and education. Similar to the success of the ASHA worker model, this study provides another example of the substantial benefits of augmenting staffing in public facilities with locally hired employees.[54] Further, since the AWC system already exists, this is an idea that can be implemented quickly and at scale. Finally, this idea should also be politically attractive since it will create more jobs for women in their communities, and be financially feasible since the costs are modest. Put together, this is an exemplar of an R1 policy that can sharply improve both equity and efficiency, and should be a top scaling-up priority.

The results in our Tamil Nadu study may be an underestimate of the long-term benefits of strengthening the anganwadi system because it did not include governance reforms over and above the extra worker. Global evidence suggests that combining additional inputs with improved staff motivation and accountability can be especially effective at improving outcomes, and be much more effective than adding inputs on their own.[55]

So, we can significantly and rapidly reduce child malnutrition and stunting by implementing a data-driven nutrition mission, incorporating ideas from Chapters 4–6. Such a mission would feature: (a) a second worker in each AWC as outlined above, (b) technology-enabled measurement and real-time reporting of child-level growth data, covering *all* children in an AWC's catchment area, and not just those who attend it, (c) a strong focus on data integrity, (d) supplemental resources and coaching to AWWs, via software on smartphones to target interventions for malnourished children and their families, and (e) competence- and performance-based rewards to AWWs and supervisors based on independently verified improvements in key indicators.

The mission should also use technology to simplify workflows and reduce paperwork, allowing AWWs to spend more time on actual service delivery, and focus on outcomes as opposed to compliance and paperwork. It should coordinate and 'converge' at the last mile of delivery with other related departments including health, water and sanitation, and Panchayati Raj, since many of the most important actions for improving child nutrition—like improving sanitation— lie *outside* the ICDS programme. Finally, it is critical to engage with the community and women's self-help groups to ensure that supply-sided initiatives from the government are coordinated with local knowledge and initiative to identify and support the most vulnerable households and children.[56]

Many of the pieces above are being put in place, but they can be much more effective if integrated together with additional resources in the most critical area (the extra worker), better convergence across departments as well as the Centre and states, and a greater focus on outcomes.[57] The annual district-level KPI survey outlined in Chapter 4 is especially critical to ensure that we hold ourselves accountable for accelerating progress and shifting the Preston curve for stunting every year (Chapter 10).

At our current rate of progress, we will add *150 million* more stunted children by 2047, with the stunting rate projected to still be 25 per cent (see Chapter 10).[58] This slow projected progress underscores the need for a more integrated, mission-mode strategy to accelerate national progress.[59] The good news is that most of the 150 million projected stunted children in the next twenty-five years are not yet born. Changing their destiny is therefore in our hands. We just need to do it!

3. Conclusion

Good health is both intrinsically valuable for a high quality of life, and instrumentally important for individual and aggregate productivity. It is also an area prone to several market failures, and under provision of valuable public goods. Research and evidence over the past two decades have revealed several insights that can guide more effective policymaking to improve the quality of health spending, and thereby deliver much better health outcomes at any given level of expenditure.

Investing more in health and nutrition, using evidence on cost-effectiveness, is likely to yield a large social RoI. Priority areas include, investing in underprovided *public* goods for health, including in areas outside the health ministry's purview, rather than just spending more on curative care; augmenting locally hired staff in the public health and anganwadi systems; and improving health worker education and training, especially through practicum-based courses. Further, the large market share of private providers makes the principles in Chapter 9 especially relevant for health. Clarifying the government's distinct roles as policymaker, regulator, and provider; and implementing the ideas in this chapter to improve performance in each of these roles, can improve population health far more than focusing only on the public healthcare system.

The COVID-19 crisis highlighted the deficiencies of India's healthcare system, and made it visible to all Indians. This experience provides a policy window where leaders, officials, and citizens appreciate the importance of building a stronger health system for India. Yet, given the large inefficiencies in our existing public healthcare system, simply spending more in a 'government as usual' way will not be very effective. This chapter lays out both key principles and practical evidence-based ideas for state governments to invest in with increasing budgetary allocations. Doing so can improve efficiency, equity, citizens' daily quality of life, individual productivity, and economic growth.

Chapter 13

Police and Public Safety

Policing and public safety are essential duties of a state. A 'state' itself is often defined as an entity with a monopoly on the legitimate use of force within its borders. In other words, only governments have the legal authority to limit citizens' freedoms, using actions such as fines, imprisonment, and other punishments. These coercive powers, in turn, are meant to help ensure maintenance of law and order, and public safety.

The state's coercive powers are primarily exercised through a combination of the police, the courts and the legal system. The police are granted considerable powers to maintain law and order, and ensure public safety. However, these powers are circumscribed by laws and due process to safeguard individuals and organizations from oppression by the state. Thus, while the police are authorized to enforce laws, it is also essential that they follow the law themselves. Overall, a well-functioning police system will deter crime and promote public safety while following the law and due process to minimize disruption to, and harassment of, citizens.

Like health and education, public safety is both intrinsically and instrumentally important for human welfare. Intrinsically, physical safety and freedom from fear directly enhance citizens' welfare. Instrumentally, these factors are key contributors to economic activity and labour force participation (especially for women) that drive economic growth. So, the quality of policing matters for both individual and aggregate welfare, and is a key component of state capacity. Indeed, a 'failed state' is often defined as one that is unable to enforce law and order within its borders.

Overall, India's performance in policing has been a mixed bag. On the positive side, law and order have mostly been upheld, with a police system that is capable of maintaining it and swiftly responding to major threats to public safety. Yet, as shown in this chapter, day-to-day police functioning leaves much to be desired. This weakness reflects both chronic under-investment in police capacity, and political incentives to deploy the police to serve narrow political interests rather than the broader public interest.

Like in education and health, Indian elites and middle classes have responded to state weaknesses by seeking private solutions. One striking indicator is that India's private security industry employs over 7 million people, which is 3.5 times the total headcount of around 2 million police personnel across the states and the Centre.[1] Additionally, as with health and education, the costs of weaknesses in policing are disproportionately borne by the poor and disadvantaged. They are both more likely to need protection, and less able to access the police or private security solutions.

This chapter comprises two sections. The first presents key facts and evidence on police functioning in India. The second presents reform ideas that draw on the themes discussed in Chapters 4–9, and are likely to be both effective and cost-effective.

1. Key Facts on Policing in India

1.1 The big picture

The positive side of policing in India is that the police system has enough capacity to maintain law and order. While India has seen incidents of extreme threat to law and order, such as communal rioting, the evidence suggests that these riots and loss of property and life have usually taken place when they have been *politically* condoned. Conversely, the police have shown that they are capable of maintaining and rapidly restoring order, when there is clear political direction to do so.[2]

India's performance in public safety has steadily improved over time, especially since the late 1990s. Research by political scientists

Devesh Kapur and Amit Ahuja reveals a steady decline in various forms of violence, including homicides, terrorism, riots, and insurgencies.[3] While this decline likely has many causes (including faster economic growth), they attribute it, at least in part, to improved state capacity for policing and internal security—with increased investments in people, equipment, and technology.[4]

Figure 13.1: Correlation between Crime and GDP Per Capita

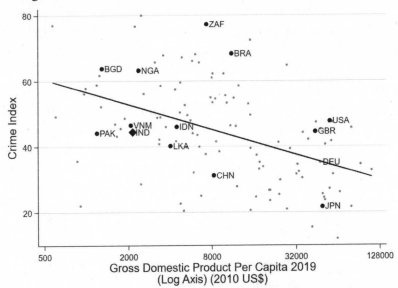

Note(s): GDP data from World Bank; crime index from World Population Review on Crime Index; graph created by the author.

India's crime index, adjusted for GDP per capita, also aligns with global comparisons. Figure 13.1 plots the crime index of various countries against their GDP per capita, and shows that richer countries have less crime. Further, Figure 13.1 suggests that India does *better* than expected relative to its per capita income. Thus, while there are many ways in which policing in India can be improved, India's performance in controlling crime is not below global standards after adjusting for GDP per capita.

However, there are two key limitations in interpreting these data in a positive light. First, the crime index reflects *reported* crimes and not actual crimes. As shown later, there is severe under-reporting of crime in India. While crime could also be under-reported in other countries, if under-reporting is more severe in India, the picture above may present a rosier picture than warranted by reality.

Second, even if the data were reliable, India's strong performance in controlling crime may be coming at the cost of excessive violations of individual rights and due process. The central tension in policing is the need to balance deterring crime and maintaining law and order on the one hand, and minimizing police excesses against citizens on the other. This creates a perennial trade-off between policing that is too strict versus too lenient. The former approach may deter crime effectively, but increases the risk of human rights abuse and harassment of innocent citizens. More lenient approaches protect individual rights better, but may fail to adequately deter crime and criminals.[6]

In most modern democracies, laws prioritize protecting the innocent, even if this raises the risk of not punishing genuine offenders. In contrast, 'security states', which typically prioritize the interests of the ruling classes over citizens, tend to have the opposite priority. They place greater emphasis on punitive action against offenders and deterring crime, even at a higher risk of punishing innocents and disregarding individual rights.

India is an interesting hybrid case where the letter of the law includes some protections for individual rights, consistent with a modern democracy; whereas the *practice* of policing often violates individual rights and protections, consistent with a security state.

One indicator of police abuse is data from India's National Human Rights Commission (NHRC), which estimates a total of 17,146 custodial deaths between 2010 to 2020, averaging five deaths every day in police custody and jails.[7] Not all these deaths are due to police abuse, as they include prisoners who die of natural causes in custody. But, the number is still an indictment of our police and legal system (see Chapter 14). A second indicator comes from detailed reports by human rights organizations, investigative journalists, documentary makers, and book authors.[8] A third telling indicator is the frequent depiction in movies and television shows of prison abuse, torture for information or confessions, and 'encounter' killings of suspects as commonly used police practices.[9]

Overall, policing in India has been reasonably effective at crime control and prevention, but weaker in safeguarding individual rights. As noted by several experts and scholars on Indian policing, this record reflects the greater political priority placed on maintaining law and order, than on safeguarding human rights.[10] This approach also primarily serves the interests of elites and ruling classes. Distinguished retired IPS officer Prakash Singh encapsulates this point succinctly, stating that: 'The police in India serve those in power and not citizens. That has been its history.'[11]

1.2 Colonial origins

This feature of Indian policing is best understood by noting that it is built on the same structure as the British colonial police system, which was not designed to serve people, but to *rule* over them. The colonial police's main role was to ensure law and order, which would facilitate economic activity that could be taxed to finance the Imperial treasury. Their goal was to keep the population docile and fearful, focused on working for survival, and with minimal rights. Essentially, the colonial police primarily functioned as the 'muscle arm' of an extractive state, with little regard for public welfare.

Consistent with this goal, colonial British law in India provided sweeping powers to the police that prioritized law and order over individual rights. The long shadow of colonial law on current policing practices in India is seen in the fact that many of our legal frameworks for policing are unchanged from the 1861 Police Act of India. These include powers to pre-emptively arrest citizens without cause, and keep them detained for extended periods under broad and vague justifications of being threats to public safety.

On the positive side, the Indian Constitution aims to secure at least some individual rights against state overreach. For instance, Article 32 guarantees citizens recourse against unlawful detention through the right of *habeas corpus*, under which police need to obtain judicial sanction to continue detaining the petitioner.[12] However, in practice, the daily functioning of the police often ignores legal due process in their interactions with potential informants or suspects. S.R. Darapuri, a former inspector general of police, has described this process as: 'Investigation typically is the form of coaxing statements pleading guilt from "suspects" via torture.'[13]

Why do the police in democratic India continue to function in ways that resemble a colonial police force? In addition to its colonial institutional and cultural legacy, a key reason is the chronic underinvestment in police capacity. This has led to an understaffed, under-equipped, under-trained, and poorly motivated police force, as shown below. Thus, while many of the laws of democratic India reflect the aspirations of a modern citizen-centred polity, the police simply *do not have the capacity to implement these ideals* in practice. In the face of severe capacity and resource constraints, the police often resort to more heavy-handed approaches to law enforcement than what a modern rules-based democracy should find acceptable.

1.3 Police in India are underfunded, understaffed, and overworked

Low budgets

On average, police expenditure is under 3 per cent of state budgets. A 2019 report showed average spending on the police to be 2.96 per cent of state budgets in 2014–15, and 2.85 per cent in 2017–18.[14] For comparison, Indian states spend 0.3 per cent of GDP on the police, whereas the US spends double (0.6 per cent of GDP), and European Union (EU) countries spend triple (0.9 per cent of GDP).

Understaffing

The low budget allocations directly translate into staff shortages. India has an average sanctioned police strength of 195 police personnel per 1,00,000 people, around 12 per cent lower than the UN's recommended 222 per 1,00,000 people. Further, this figure includes a substantial number of district and state armed reserve police forces and the Indian Reserve Battalion, who are typically not used for community policing. Data from the Bureau of Police

Research and Development (BPRD) shows that, excluding the armed police, the ratio falls to 124 police personnel per 1,00,000 people.[15]

In addition to low staffing norms to begin with, actual staffing is even lower due to vacancies at all levels of the police force. Recent estimates reveal an average vacancy rate of 24 per cent among state police staff. After accounting for vacancies, the average police strength per capita in the state forces falls to 99 per 1,00,000.[16]

The limited availability of police for general public safety is exacerbated by significant disparities in police staff allocation across areas and people. For instance, police per capita is much higher in more affluent areas.[17] One example of skewed police allocation is the case of VIP security. A report by Lokniti and CSDS estimates that an average VIP has a security detail of 3.39 police staff. In other words, the police to citizen ratio is over *1700 times higher for a VIP* than for an average citizen.[18]

Overwork and mental health challenges

A natural consequence of being understaffed is that existing police personnel are severely overworked and stretched beyond their capacity. A key source of stress is the need to be available 'on call' practically on a 24x7 basis. Since the incidence of crime is higher in the dark, constables are regularly expected to work in the evenings and even at night in addition to regular daytime office hours.

The combination of overwork, unpredictable hours, frequent time away from family, and poor working conditions leads to severe mental health challenges among the police. The extreme stress under which the police function directly contributes to their abusive behaviour towards suspects. A large body of psychological research shows that people under high stress vent their frustrations on those less powerful than themselves. Thus, while citizens often perceive police constables as bullies who exercise power arbitrarily, as a society we should view our police forces through a more sympathetic lens.

1.4 Police are also poorly trained and underequipped

In addition to being understaffed and overworked, police in India are also poorly trained.

Multiple official committees including the Padmanabhaiah Committee on Police Reforms (2000) and the Second Administrative Reforms Commission (2005) have noted that low education levels (Class 10) and lack of soft skills training have hindered the constabulary in ensuring adequate public safety. These and other committees have all highlighted the importance of soft skills training in building a more citizen-friendly police force.

Yet, in practice, nothing has been done to implement these recommendations. The scale of the problem is noted by the India Justice Report, 2019, which reports that only 6.4 per cent of the police force has received *any* in-service training. This lack of training reflects both low budgets, with a training budget of just Rs 8000 per employee during their *entire* career; and severe understaffing, which makes it difficult to release police personnel from active duty to attend training programmes.[19]

Weakness in training extends beyond the constabulary. Training in forensics and investigative techniques is supposed to be provided to cadres at and above the sub-inspector level, but the quality of training is low, and it is rarely used in the field.[20] The practical use of modern investigative techniques is also severely hampered by understaffing above the constabulary level. Constables comprise 86 per cent of the police personnel, but do not receive training in forensics and investigative techniques.

Consequently, police investigations often rely on extracting confessions through torture, leading to both human rights abuses and ineffective results, as such cases often get dismissed in courts for want of concrete evidence.[21] The knowledge that criminals are likely to be acquitted by courts for lack of evidence, in turn, contributes to police feeling justified in the use of violence on suspected criminals. This process makes a mockery of 'the rule of law', and the principle of being 'innocent until proven guilty' as suspects face severe punishment in police custody long before courts pronounce an actual verdict.

The frustrations of the police are exacerbated by not even having budgets for basic equipment like vehicles or fuel, let alone computers or other modern technologies. In some cases, police stations even operate from temporary structures like tents, due to lack of funding for proper buildings. As highlighted in the TV show *Satyamev Jayate*, there are cases where police stations are unable to even pay their electricity bills. Beyond these anecdotes, the impact of staff and equipment shortages is reflected in a study by Common Cause and CSDS, which found that in Rajasthan, police reached the crime scene on time in only 4 per cent of cases over a two-month period.[22] Police personnel are *not even able to reach* a crime scene, let alone solve it.

1.5 Police are not representative, and have limited connection to communities

The police also have serious challenges with representation. As the 2019 India Justice Report highlights, women constitute only 7 per cent of the police. The report notes the sluggish progress in boosting female representation and estimates that at the current recruitment rate, it may take over 100 years to reach the recommended 33 per cent. It also notes that Muslim representation in police forces is disproportionately low at 4 per cent compared to their population share of 14.2 per cent. Finally, it notes that vacancies among underrepresented categories (SC/ST/OBC/Women) exceed average vacancy rates, despite the existence of reservations to improve representation.

Inadequate representation can adversely affect policing quality. Effective policing relies on strong community connections, which are difficult to establish if large sections of the population are not represented in the police force. Police-community connections are also weakened by limited staffing, especially in rural areas. As per 2019 data on police presence and 2011 census data on populations, there are sixty-five revenue villages and twenty-five gram panchayats per police station.[23] The situation is particularly severe in UP and Bihar, which have among the lowest police to population ratios in the country. In many districts, there is only one police station for over 1,00,000 people in rural areas and almost no direct police presence in most villages.

1.6 Poor public perception and low public trust in the police

The factors above collectively contribute to negative public perception and low trust in the police. This sentiment is echoed in media portrayals, where police are often depicted as subservient to the powerful and oppressive towards the weak.[24] A study on the Indian police summarizes this point and notes that: 'News and entertainment media, as well as other modes of public culture, broadly portray police either as incompetent fools with inadequate tools, as little more than "yes men" to more powerful figures, or as brutal and corrupt "little tyrants".'[25]

These qualitative points are also validated in surveys using larger samples. The 2018 State of Policing in India Report (SPIR) conducted extensive surveys across twenty-two states to study various aspects of citizens' trust and perception of the police, and reported that 55 per cent of respondents feel that the police is corrupt and does not do its job well. Only 29 per cent mentioned having 'a lot of trust' in senior police officers, with the figure falling to 23 per cent for local police officers, and 16 per cent for traffic police. For comparison, 54 per cent of respondents reported a lot of trust in the army.

The survey also reported that 44 per cent of respondents were either highly (14 per cent) or somewhat (30 per cent) fearful of the police. Specific fears included being beaten up (44 per cent), being arrested (38 per cent), being falsely implicated in a case (38 per cent), and being approached at home (38 per cent). Fear of the police is more pronounced among religious minorities, especially Muslims, and marginalized groups like Scheduled Castes. Unsurprisingly, such fear is highest when respondents perceive the police as discriminatory. Finally, illiterate and poorer households are more likely to have a negative perception of the police.

Taken together, the data validates the view that the police are not well regarded by citizens on average, and also that the police engender greater fear and distrust among more vulnerable groups. One clear testament to the fact that the police primarily serves to 'rule' the people rather than 'serve' them is the fact that such a large fraction of the population *fears* the police rather than being reassured by them.

1.7 Chronic under-reporting of crime

One consequence of low trust in police is that many crimes are simply not reported. Thus, reported crime data severely understate the true level of crime.

A 2017 report by the IDFC Institute, based on surveys in Chennai, Bangalore, Mumbai, and Delhi, found that over 90 per cent of thefts were unreported among surveyed victims.[26] A 2018 investigative article in *Mint* compared sexual assault rates reported in the National Family Health Survey (NFHS) 2015–16 with National Crime Records Bureau (NCRB) data, and showed that only 15 per cent of crimes get reported to the police, even for a serious crime like sexual assault.[27] Finally, even when crimes are reported to the police, the fraction of complaints that are converted into First Information Reports (FIR), a crucial first step in formal police investigations, is low. For instance, the complaint to FIR conversion rate was 25 per cent in 2019.[28]

Under-reporting of crime occurs for several reasons. On the victim's side, these include not wanting to be stuck in police and court proceedings, fear of victim-shaming by the police (especially in sexual assault cases), and doubts about the police taking the complaint seriously.[29] On the police side, they are often judged by crime statistics at the police-station level, incentivizing under-reporting. Further, given their limited resources, the police may rationally only file FIRs for more serious crimes, as recording any crime requires them to allocate resources to solving the case.

Similar to education and health, our understanding of police and public safety in India is severely constrained by poor data quality. In health and education, we at least have representative household surveys like the NFHS and Pratham ASER. In the case of public safety, we have no such household data and have to rely solely on official data that likely under-report crime. Recognizing this data lacuna, the Ministry of Home Affairs initiated the All India Citizens Survey of Police Services in 2019. However, results are not available as of the time of writing, with the effort likely delayed due to COVID-19.

1.8 Limited professional autonomy and institutionalized corruption

Finally, police effectiveness in India has been deeply compromised by their use as a political tool. Regardless of which party is in power, it is common for political parties in power to use the police as a tool to (a) collect revenue through petty corruption, like bribes and protection money, (b) selectively pursue cases and investigations against political and business rivals and their supporters, and (c) ignore violations of laws by political and business allies, including those who simply pay for this benefit.

Politicians use frequent transfers of IPS officers as a means to 'control' the police and reduce their autonomy to enforce the law. Stable tenures are vital for effective policing, as they allow officers to learn about the context, and implement effective management practices. However, as with IAS officers, IPS officers are also frequently transferred: analysis of BPRD reports from 2016 to 2020 show that around 25 per cent of IPS officers were transferred within a year of their posting. In some states like UP, the *average* tenure of IPS officers was less than a year.[30] Conversely, transfers among constabulary staff are less frequent, with typically longer durations at their postings.

The regular turnover of senior officers, coupled with a more stable frontline police force, hinders the ability of even motivated IPS officers to systematically improve policing. However, it facilitates the persistence of institutionalized corruption. Anecdotal evidence and portrayals in movies (*Gangaajal* is a good example) and TV shows suggest widespread corruption in the police system. Former IAS officer N.C. Saxena has noted that IPS officers are transferred even more frequently than IAS officers leading to a quip that 'if we are posted for weeks, then all we can do is to collect our weekly bribes.'[31]

The fact of institutionalized corruption within the police came to the fore in March 2021, when Param Bir Singh, the former commissioner of the Mumbai Police, openly accused the Maharashtra home minister of corruption and interference in police work. In an open letter to the chief minister, he alleged that the minister instructed officers to 'collect money' from restaurants, pubs, bars, and hookah parlours, setting a monthly target of Rs 100 crore. This is consistent with research papers by retired IPS officers who have noted that police routinely charge weekly protection money (*hafta*) from a variety of vendors. They report that these funds are distributed 'up the chain', with the majority going to politicians, who use the funds for themselves and their parties.[32]

Taken together, control of the police is a 'golden goose' for politicians, which largely explains the low political priority placed on improving the autonomy and capacity of police forces in India. This view is supported by Justice Thomas, a retired Supreme Court judge and head of the monitoring committee overseeing the implementation of Supreme Court directives in Prakash Singh vs Union of India (2006). He has noted widespread disregard by states of the directive to have an independent committee for postings, transfers, and promotion of police staff.[33]

2. Implementable Reform Ideas

The issues above are well-known to scholars and observers of the Indian police. Multiple committees have been set up over the years, to suggest reforms to improve police functioning in India.[34] These bodies, comprising distinguished retired police officials, judges, and senior home ministry officials with a deep understanding of the relevant issues, have produced detailed, well-researched reports. For instance, the Padmanabhaiah Committee on Police Reforms proposed 208 reform ideas. However, these recommendations have mostly been ignored, despite the Supreme Court urging Central and state governments to implement them.[35]

The main challenge in implementing police reforms is political. A core recommendation of the commissions above is to increase police autonomy, and give the police independence from day-to-day political control. Such autonomy is a key trait of effective and credible police forces globally, as well as bureaucracies in general, as noted in Chapter 3. However, politicians view control over the police and its functioning as crucial to their ability to exercise power. Thus, no political party or state government has been willing to act on these committees' reform recommendations.

The political apathy towards police reforms has been well captured in the opening epigraph of the Malimath Committee Report on Criminal Justice Reforms. It starts by quoting a French thinker who observed that:

'Everything has been said already, but as no one listens, we must always begin again!'

Such political apathy makes significant police reforms unlikely without concerted efforts from citizens and civil society (see Chapter 18) and electoral reforms (see Chapter 17). Since these changes may take time, the key to improving police functioning in the short and medium run is to find ideas that are both effective and politically feasible. While political leaders may be unwilling to increase the autonomy and independence of the police in the short run, even politicians may benefit from improving the *capacity* of the police to improve public safety. This may be especially true if these capacity improvements lead to visible benefits to voters and communities. The following section discusses three practical, politically feasible ideas that extend *beyond* those in police reform commission reports, which are based on the themes in Chapters 4–6.

2.1 Improve measurement of public safety

As discussed earlier, we have very little reliable data on the key metrics of public safety. Large gaps in crime reporting can make official statistics almost useless for monitoring police effectiveness. In fact, the status quo creates perverse incentives where improving police performance may result in an *increase* in reported crimes if people have more confidence that action will be taken when they file a complaint. So, the police leadership may look bad if they do well, and look good if their true performance is poor!

Thus, a foundational investment in improving public safety in India will be to generate reliable data on crime and public perceptions of safety *directly* from citizens so that it is not confounded by the large gaps in crime reporting. This is one area that past police commissions have not paid much attention to, perhaps because it may have seemed unrealistic and prohibitively expensive to conduct such an exercise.

However, as outlined in Chapter 4, advances in measurement technology now enable annual household surveys in representative district-level samples at a cost of less than 0.02 per cent of state budgets. These multisector household surveys can include a module on public safety that captures key variables such as: (a) frequency of various kinds of crime in the past year, (b) citizens' safety perceptions for engaging in various activities, (c) how citizens access the law and justice systems (both formal and informal), (d) time and financial cost of accessing law and justice, and (e) confidence in police and institutions for crime prevention, and dispute resolution.

Having such data can transform policing and public safety in India. At present, while there is data on actual cases of violent crime, there is no systematic data on citizens' exposure to violence, their experiences of fear, their perceptions of safety, or on how these are changing over time. This matters because fear of violence shapes people's lives and decisions regarding education and employment. For example, an important recent study in Delhi shows that women often choose lower-quality colleges than they are eligible for, to reduce the safety risks of travelling further to a better college.[36]

Consistently measuring crime incidence and safety perceptions using representative household surveys will ensure that policymakers' understanding of crime is not biased by the large gaps between actual crime incidents and those that are formally reported. It will provide policymakers with direct visibility into citizens' *perceptions* of safety, and increase the policy salience of the central but neglected topic of public safety.

Access to regular, representative citizen-level data will help policymakers and senior police officials to evaluate whether their interventions are effective. For instance, many police departments are launching initiatives like citizen helplines, women-only police stations, desks for women and children, and installing CCTV cameras.

However, there is no systematic way to gauge: (a) citizen awareness of these initiatives, (b) the extent of citizen engagement with them, or (c) their impact on boosting citizen confidence. Currently, effective interventions may lead to an *increase* in crime reporting, and it is impossible to know if this is because crime has gone up or because reporting has gone up. Thus, having direct citizen-level data on the *true* rate of crime is a foundational investment in understanding whether policing interventions are truly effective.

This data will also enable police leadership to focus on impactful long-term initiatives and track their effectiveness over time. This approach contrasts sharply with the status quo, where policymakers only focus on public safety issues following heinous violent incidents that draw disproportionate media and public attention. Responses to such incidents are often ad hoc and driven by the need to *appear* to be taking action, as opposed to doing things that are most likely to be effective. So, police leadership should greatly welcome such a measurement effort because it will: (a) provide regular salience to policing and public safety in the policy discourse, (b) help obtain resources for investing in this critical area, and (c) allow them to focus on things that truly matter as measured by systematic improvements in real and perceived public safety over time.

Such measurement can also help shed light on the differences in police perception by socioeconomic categories. While the poor and less educated are more likely to fear the police globally, having regular data on citizens' perception of the police may help spur efforts to reduce these inequalities. As mentioned in Chapter 4, a key hurdle to greater equity in India is the *invisibility* to elites of the living conditions and daily experiences of the poor and marginalized. Thus, collecting such data should be especially championed by politicians representing marginalized communities, and by civil-society organizations focused on improving the welfare of these groups.

As discussed in Chapter 4, better measurement has been the foundation of human progress in almost every area of life. Thus, improving the quality, reliability, frequency, and spatial disaggregation of measurement of crime and public safety will be a foundational investment in improving this neglected area of governance and service delivery in India. Conducting such measurement in conjunction with a multisector household survey will be highly cost-effective and state governments can easily do it.

The fact that the Union Home Ministry commissioned such a survey in 2019 suggests that senior policymakers are aware of the value of such an exercise. Implementing the approach suggested in this section will allow states to make this a regular annual exercise that can drive goal setting, progress-monitoring, and course correction. It will allow states to institutionalize data-driven decision-making in this key area, and will be much more useful than just conducting a one-off survey.

2.2 Competency-based career management for existing staff

Several police reform commissions have highlighted the importance of: (a) improving the training of existing police personnel, and (b) instituting performance-based career progression for police personnel. Both ideas are fundamental to well-functioning organizations, and I fully endorse them, as seen in Chapter 5.

However, figuring out the practical *details* of performance measurement and management of the police is a very difficult problem. Tracking and rewarding metrics like notifications issued, complaints registered, or arrests made can easily lead to overzealous police behaviour that *worsens* citizen welfare. This is an example of the well-known multitasking problem whereby tracking some metrics and not others can lead to suboptimal outcomes. This has been shown, for instance, in a classic paper by Nobel prize-winning economists Bengt Holmstrom and Paul Milgrom.[37]

Since implementing performance-based career management may be difficult in the case of the police, it is more realistic to implement *competency-based* career management, which will still yield a meaningful improvement over the status quo. This requires serious investments in training and alleviating the barriers to improving the quality of in-service training. These barriers include: (a) understaffed police forces are unable to spare staff time for training, (b) limited budgets for in-person training, and (c) lack of adequate skilled trainers to ensure consistent quality of training.

All three constraints can be addressed by creating modular training content on digital platforms. Such content should be created by high-quality master trainers, and combine lectures, case studies, and practical demonstrations of effective policing techniques using short videos. Content can be organized into modules, and modules into courses, with all content being available digitally to all serving police staff. All constables should be required to complete a certain number of hours of in-service training every year, and be guided to the modules and courses that are most relevant to them, given their seniority, current role, prior courses completed, and identified competence gaps.

Most of this training can be completed flexibly, whenever staff have downtime on duty. This flexibility is critical for the police because the unpredictable and time-sensitive nature of policing work requires them to constantly be 'available', while also including periods of downtime when they are simply waiting in their police stations. This need to have police staff constantly 'available' makes it difficult for senior officers to sanction full-time absences for training, especially given large staff vacancies. However, having short digital modules that can be absorbed on a smartphone allows police personnel to get trained while continuing to be available in the police station if needed.

Completion of digital training modules and courses can be followed up by workshops and peer-group discussions, to reflect on the training content and its practical application in daily policing tasks. These workshops can be conducted digitally through videoconferencing, to sharply reduce time and travel costs. This approach also enables master trainers to moderate and facilitate many more workshops than they could if they had to travel in person. The widespread adoption of videoconferencing and digital meetings in response to COVID-19 induced restrictions has shown that virtual meetings can deliver most of the value of an in-person meeting, but at a much lower cost.

Each training module should have an assessment at the end that tests candidates' understanding and mastery of the module's content. Candidates should also have the option of taking formal invigilated exams at the end of a digital course, and obtaining certificates of course completion, as well as grades such as Pass, Merit, or Distinction, as appropriate. The importance of in-service training and upgrading of skills can be institutionalized into the culture of police departments by implementing a system of competency-based promotions and career planning.

For instance, completing a minimum number of annual hours of training can be made a requirement for obtaining annual increments. Completion of entire courses and scoring well on them can be given weight in promotion decisions as opposed to simply following seniority. This approach can be used for constables, sub-inspectors, inspectors, and potentially even IPS officers. Just like doctors and medical professionals are required to recertify their competence every ten years through medical board exams, a similar approach of requiring a continued demonstration of relevant knowledge (especially for promotions), will be a significant improvement over the status quo.

Over time, this competency-based approach can be used not just for promotions but also for job postings, aligning candidate skills with position requirements. In a competency-based career progression framework, candidates can build their skill profiles in various areas of policing, such as law and order, forensics, investigation, preparing evidence and paperwork for prosecution, crimes against women and children, cyber security, financial and white-collar crimes, and data analysis for crime detection and prevention. Records of module and course completion, and grades would become part of personnel files, which can be used to improve the job posting process.

Such a system will significantly boost staff motivation by providing a tangible link between their efforts in upgrading their competencies and capabilities, and the postings that they receive. Over time, it would even make sense to allow candidates to apply for specific posts and signal their interest as well as preparedness for the role.

Overall, given the difficulty of performance measurement at the level of individual police personnel, a competency-based framework for career trajectory management is much more likely to be implementable, and will be a substantial improvement over the status quo. Importantly, it is also likely to be supported by police unions because it is objective, and would invest in improving their skills, which is sorely lacking in the status quo.

At senior levels, it may be possible to also institute some performance-based career management. For instance, data from annual district-level household KPI surveys can be used as an input in the performance evaluation of district superintendents of police (SP). The performance metric can include weightage on both levels and improvements in key outcomes as appropriate. Holding district-level leadership accountable for actual performance will also improve their incentives to invest in the capacity of their police forces to deliver better overall performance in their districts.

2.3 Create a practicum-based diploma and degree in public safety

Indian police forces are understaffed and over-stretched, undertrained and underequipped, and not adequately embedded in the communities they serve. At the same time, budgets are tight, which has made it difficult to find funds to augment police staffing. We therefore need cost-effective solutions to augment both the quantity and capacity of police forces in India. How do we address this challenge?

A practicum-based training course, as detailed in Chapter 5, can be designed for policing as well. State police academies can create a two- to four-year long practicum-based training course that leads to a diploma or degree in public safety. The course would admit candidates after Class 12, with a view to preparing them for a constabulary track through a two-year diploma course or a sub-inspector track for top candidates via the four-year degree course. The course would modularly intersperse three months of theory and exams, with nine months of practical training where trainees will be assigned to a police station, and an actual beat. The course itself would be free, and apprentices would be paid a modest stipend during their practical training. Such a programme will be appealing and aspirational, and have no problem attracting strong candidates.

The course can start with the basics of law and principles of effective community policing, which will allow candidates to become useful in the field even after the first three to four months training module. Later modules can cover topics such as citizen-friendly policing, gender-sensitive policing, community engagement and confidence building, information and intelligence gathering, data analysis and reporting, mediation and de-escalation of disputes (including domestic ones), and crime prevention. The course will likely not include firearms training, which is expensive to provide and regulate.

The apprentices will *not* have formal police powers of arrest and coercion during their practicum-based training. However, their primary function will be to act as the eyes and ears of the police in the community during their beat, and to act as a trusted liaison between communities and the police. They could also help with administrative tasks that currently absorb a lot of police time.[38] They could be given distinct uniforms with one, two, or three stripes indicating the number of years completed in their course. This would both give them community standing, and enhance their own identity and dignity.

Even without having formal police powers, such trainees can augment the capacity of our overburdened police system by improving its ability to gather information from local communities, build trust and credibility in the formal police system by enhancing its presence in communities, and by pre-emptively resolving minor disputes before they escalate. The trainees can also be equipped with smartphones to allow them to participate both in groups of peer trainees, as well as the larger group of police officials in their assigned police station. This will allow them to rapidly bring important matters to the attention of the formal police system, as appropriate.

While the model will have to be piloted and evaluated in an Indian setting, there is suggestive evidence on the potential efficacy of such a model.[39] The key insight is that even without formal police powers, informal community-based police can be highly effective because of their enhanced ability to draw the attention of formal law enforcement to matters that would otherwise go unnoticed. Their role as a bridge between communities and the formal police system can provide them with legitimacy to often be able to resolve situations at their own level. Over time, their presence in the community can help to deter crime and enhance public safety.

This approach can also be used to increase the share of female public safety staff from the current low rate of 7 per cent, by reserving 33 per cent of positions for women. A recent large-scale RCT in Madhya Pradesh found that having women's help desks in police stations led to a significant increase in the number of cases of gender-based violence registered, and that this was especially high when the help desk was staffed with a female police officer.[40] Similarly, having female public safety personnel available in communities could make it easier for women to register cases when needed.

The *lack* of formal police powers for trainees might be beneficial, as it can make people more comfortable in interacting with the police system. Many Indians, especially less educated citizens, say that they do not trust the police. A system where citizens' first contact with the police system is with personnel who do not have punitive powers, and whose main role is to facilitate public safety, could bridge the social and psychological gap between the police and the public. Thus, the practicum-based training model could both enhance police effectiveness, and boost public confidence in them.

In contrast to practicum-based training for teachers and nurses, where it makes sense to locate the practicum in the candidate's own community, the ideal location for policing practicums is less clear. The advantages of local placements include: (a) familiarity and integration with the community, (b) greater community acceptance, and (c) lower costs for the candidate by living at home. The disadvantages are greater risk of: (a) being dominated by local authority figures, and (b) biased reporting reflecting the candidates' connections to local power structures and prejudices. In the absence of evidence, the details of candidates' selection and posting should be tailored by state and local authorities, based on contextual factors, such as potentially posting female trainees in their home GPs and male trainees outside. These pilots should be evaluated, and the findings should be used to iteratively improve programme design.

Upon completing this training course, candidates will have acquired both conceptual and practical skills to become effective public safety professionals. This level of training would exceed what is currently provided to police constables, and align with many of the recommendations from police reform commissions. Crucially, this training would occur *before* regular government employment, which would increase the incentives of trainees to absorb the training content. In the status quo, candidates' interest in training is often limited because: (a) they already have been confirmed with formal employment, and (b) their career prospects do not depend on demonstrated competence.

As noted in Chapter 5, this practicum-based course would be not an employment programme, but a *training* programme that will boost the quality of public safety professionals in *both* the public and private sector. The public police stations should be seen as practicum sites, where candidates *learn* the practical aspects of working in public safety. However, the recruitment process for regular constables and sub-inspectors should provide extra points or marks for years of practicum experience, and also provide extra credit for performance in the practicum-based course. The course can also include assessments of various personality and psycho-social traits that are shown by research and evidence to be good predictors of effective police personnel. These scores can also be given some weight in the regular recruitment process.

Such a structure will also enhance the quality of candidates hired into permanent police positions, improving both their training and experience, and ensuring a better fit for the job. Currently, hundreds of thousands of youth take exams to become police constables and get selected based solely on exam and physical test scores, without an assessment of their actual aptitude for the job. In the revised system, candidates who do not enjoy the job during their practicum-based course, may opt for alternative careers, and those who get selected are more likely to be those who are a good fit for the job.

The practicum-based courses should also coordinate with the private security industry to enhance job prospects of graduates who do not obtain government positions. Private security firms in India employ lakhs of staff, and spend heavily on training them. For instance, Shankkar Aiyar notes that in 2019, the firm Security and Intelligence Services (SIS) had over 2,00,000 employees, and trained over 20,000 security staff annually in its own academies.[41] While Aiyar views the rise of private security firms as indicative of state failure (which is true), their prevalence and scale also present an opportunity for governments to develop a high-quality skilling programme for security personnel, incorporating expertise from both the private sector and police training academies.

Just like medical education, this is another example where investing in high-quality training and skilling will benefit not only the public sector but society as a whole. For instance, even if they are employed by private companies, graduates of the practicum course will have active networks of peers who are in the public police system, and will be much more likely to share information that can be useful in preventing crime and promoting public safety. One of the most important inputs into effective policing is credible real-time information. Given the extreme paucity of public police personnel, the public interest will be well served by leveraging the private security industry as well.

Private security guards primarily protect their clients' property, but since they observe their communities closely, they can also contribute to public safety by acting as sources of information for the police when needed. While such information transmission cannot be mandated, it is more likely when private security staff are public spirited and can easily share information with the formal police system. This sense of public duty is likely to be stronger among graduates of the practicum-based training course since the government would have paid for their training, and they would have received practical training in public police stations. Also, since their course peers will be in the police, it becomes easier to share information. Finally, their experience in community policing during training equips them to contribute to public safety in their communities as well.

If I were advising a state government on cost-effective ways of improving public safety, piloting, testing, refining, and scaling, this idea would be my top recommendation. This investment can enable us to move from a vicious cycle of staff scarcity, ineffectiveness, and lack of public confidence in the police to a virtuous cycle of enhanced capacity, effectiveness, and public trust in the police. Further, an approach focused on building skills and providing meaningful employment that offers dignity, purpose, and a modest stipend, will be politically attractive given the widespread crisis of unemployed youth. Beyond police department funds, this initiative could also be partly financed by leveraging resources provided under national skilling and gender programmes.

A useful case study to examine is Tamil Nadu's Special Police Youth Brigade (SPYB) programme in 2013, which aimed to cost-effectively augment police capacity, while also providing youth employment. It featured some of the ideas discussed here, including basic training for four weeks, using candidates for support functions to free up scarce police officer time, and a modest stipend.[42] However, the programme just saved on one year of salary costs, and had limited long-term impact as most SPYB candidates were regularized after a year. In contrast, implementing the practicum-based training approach will deliver substantially greater benefits over both the short and the long run.

A key lesson from the SPYB experience is that it is critical to set the right expectations for candidates at the outset so that they understand that the practicum is a part of their training, and *not* a guaranteed pathway to a government job. While doing well on the course would increase the probability of obtaining a government position, it would not guarantee it. Since private security firms employ over three times as many staff as the public police system, the most likely jobs will be there. But the training programme should still be attractive to the youth given the free training, stipends, and increased likelihood of meaningful employment in either the government or private sector.[43]

While policing is a state subject, the Union Home Ministry and national institutes such as the National Police Training Academy and the Bureau of Police Research and Development can contribute to accelerating the deployment of such a model by: (a) designing the modular training programme in consultation with states and top private security agencies, (b) creating templates that states can modify as per their requirements, and (c) providing funds and personnel, especially master trainers, to cover the fixed costs of designing state-level programmes.

States can also pilot such an approach on their own. Designing such a course should not be very expensive, and motivated leaders in state police training academies could do so with support from department, administrative, and political leadership and inputs from experts and the private sector. States may also be able to obtain concessional funding from entities like the World Bank or other agencies to design such a course. As with most of the ideas in this book, it only takes one state to lead the way!

3. Conclusion

On the positive side, the police in India are effective at maintaining law and order, and India's reported crime statistics align with income-adjusted global norms. Research by Devesh Kapur and Amit Ahuja also finds a steady decline in crime and violence in India over time. However, Indian policing also has notable weaknesses including excessive use of force against suspects, harassment of citizens for bribes, and not having enough capacity to instil public confidence. These weaknesses have been documented in both official reports and popular media, and underscored by the fact that 44 per cent of citizens report *fearing* rather than being reassured by the police.[44] Overall, policing in India exemplifies the Indian state's incomplete transition from a colonial state meant to *rule* people, to a modern democratic state designed to *serve* them.

Numerous police reform committees have proposed excellent recommendations for improving policing in India. However, their reports have typically not considered *cost-effectiveness* or sought to prioritize among the long list of recommendations. Given limited budgets and policymaker attention, we need to prioritize interventions based on cost-effectiveness to maximize public return on investment. Reforms also need to be politically attractive. So, this chapter focuses on just three ideas that are likely to be effective, cost-effective, and politically feasible.

Even implementing these three ideas can meaningfully improve police capacity and effectiveness. However, given the limited empirical evidence on police reforms in India, it is important to first pilot such initiatives, and continuously fine-tune programme details based on practical feedback, and high-quality process and impact evaluations. Such initiatives are primarily in the domain of states, and provide another opportunity for state-led innovations to accelerate India's development.

Chapter 14

Courts and Justice

Resolving disputes and delivering justice are fundamental roles of a state. These are typically performed by courts and the judicial system. The judiciary, comprising all levels of courts, is an equal and independent branch of the state along with the legislature and the executive, and has the final word in interpreting the law and resolving disputes. Thus, the quality of the judicial system is a central component of state capacity.

As with the other core functions of the state, our courts and justice system also perform poorly. The Indian court system is understaffed, under-resourced, and bursting at its seams. Across Indian courts, over *34 million* cases are pending for over a year, with the backlog growing rapidly every year.[1] This is both a moral and an economic failure.

A high-quality justice system is both intrinsically and instrumentally important for human welfare. Intrinsically, a slow and costly system denies many citizens access to justice. It also leads to large numbers of citizens being held as undertrials in police custody for extended periods even without having been convicted. Thus, the justice process itself becomes the punishment, undermining the principle of 'innocent until proven guilty'. Instrumentally, effective contract enforcement and dispute resolution directly contribute to boosting economic activity and growth. As we will see in this chapter, investing in our justice system is likely to pay for itself many times over by increasing economic activity.

However, unlike other sectors, where the executive can lead reforms, judicial reforms are more difficult. Even well-intentioned attempts by elected leaders to improve judicial efficiency can be perceived as intruding on judicial independence, and face resistance from the judiciary. Thus, judicial reform initiatives should clarify that the judiciary retains exclusive control over the *content* of justice. However, all three branches of the state—the legislature, the executive, and the judiciary—need to collaborate to improve the *process* of justice, including reducing time and costs of case resolution.

The legislature can ease the judiciary's burden by simplifying laws, repealing outdated and conflicting statutes, and paying attention to the transaction costs of enforcing and adjudicating laws. The executive can contribute by working with the judiciary to jointly determine *process* performance targets, say for reducing backlogs, and funding the staff, training, and technology needed to do so efficiently. Finally, the judiciary can streamline processes, and hold itself accountable for improving case disposal efficiency.

As with the other sectors covered in this book, improving judicial functioning in India also largely requires state-level actions, as over 80 per cent of cases are resolved at or below district courts. Thus the highest return on effort will come from focusing on the lower judiciary. As discussed in the chapter, there is a lot that can be done by chief ministers, state governments, and state legislatures working in coordination with high court chief justices, to strengthen the lower judiciary.

This chapter comprises two main sections. The first offers a brief overview of key facts on the Indian justice system, including relevant evidence from empirical studies. The second presents reform ideas for state-level implementation.

1. Key Facts on Courts in India

1.1 Structure of the Indian justice system

The Indian judiciary has a unitary structure, with the Supreme Court of India at the apex, followed by 24 state-level High Courts,

672 district-level courts, and 6591 subordinate courts.[2] The original jurisdiction of most disputes rests with the district judiciary, which includes the District and Sessions Court as the top court for the district, and various sub-district courts divided into civil and criminal courts. The determination of where disputes are initially filed depends on both the territorial jurisdiction of the matter and its monetary value, with higher value cases usually filed directly at the district level.

In practice, the vast majority of cases in India (about 87 per cent) are filed in district or lower courts. Among these, 26 per cent are civil, and 74 per cent are criminal.[3] The most common civil cases involve land or property (66 per cent) and financial disputes (18 per cent), together accounting for over 80 per cent of the total civil caseload.[4]

Constitutionally, the judiciary is an equal and independent branch of the state whose judgments are final and only subject to appeal to the higher levels of the judiciary itself. By law, the police and other arms of the executive are expected to help enforce the judgments of the judicial system. However, the Constitution does not provide for a prescribed minimum level of funding for the judiciary.

Thus, the executive directly affects judicial capacity through its control over budget allocations. It supplies the judiciary with land, courtrooms, and funding for staff, infrastructure, and technology. The responsibility for framing policies and securing budgets for the judiciary lies with the Ministry of Law and Justice at the Central government level, and with analogous departments at the state level.

1.2 Delays and backlog in courts

One striking metric of the weakness of India's judicial system is the large number of pending cases in our courts. As of 26 April 2022, there were nearly 30 million cases pending for over one year in the district judiciary, and nearly 5 million such cases in the High Courts.[5] Among cases pending for over a year in district courts, 29 per cent have been so for over five years, and 11 per cent have been pending for over ten years.[6] In sum, over 3.5 million cases have been pending in our district courts for over ten years.

The problem of case backlog worsens every year. On average, district and subordinate courts in India receive around 1350 new case filings per year, but they only resolve around 1000 cases per year.[7] So, each district court accumulates a backlog of around 350 cases every year. Not only are they not making adequate progress on reducing the case backlog, they are not even able to keep pace with the annual flow of new cases.

1.3 Understaffed and under-resourced courts

One key reason for the large and growing backlog of cases is the severe understaffing and under-resourcing of our judiciary. The number of sanctioned judge positions in India is twenty judges per million people, which is very low to begin with. In comparison, it is 51 in the UK, and 107 in the US.[8] Thus, per capita judicial capacity in the UK is two and a half times higher than in India, and five times higher in the US.

The situation is worsened by vacancies against even these low numbers of sanctioned positions. As of 2022, judicial vacancies were estimated at 21 per cent in the Supreme Court, 30 per cent in High Courts, and 22 per cent in district courts. In addition, 26 per cent of non-judicial court staff positions were also vacant.[9] Courtroom infrastructure is also inadequate with a 15 per cent shortfall in courtrooms relative to sanctioned judge posts. Many courtrooms also lack essential productivity tools such as computers and internet access.

The judicial system's limited capacity, in terms of both infrastructure and personnel, is largely a result of low budgetary allocations. On average, states spent only 0.54 per cent of their budgets on the judiciary, which is a minuscule 0.07 per cent of India's GDP. By comparison, the US spends around 0.7 per cent of its GDP on its courts and justice system, which is ten times more as a fraction of GDP than India. Even accounting for India's tax-to-GDP ratio being around half of that of the U.S., we spend only one-fifth as much of the government budget on the judicial system.

1.4 High procedural inefficiencies

Judicial efficiency in India is also hampered by procedural complexities, exacerbated by the numerous steps in a typical case, and the need to coordinate across various parties. A standard case process involves fifteen steps, including: (i) filing, (ii) registration and case categorization, (iii) document verification/*vakalatnama*, (iv) preparation of order sheet summarizing case details for the principal judge, (v) case assignment by principal judge to a courtroom, (vi) date of first hearing, (vii) summons to defendant, (viii) return notice/*vakalatnama* by defendant, (ix) written statement and counter-statements by litigating parties, (x) framing of issues under appropriate law and section, (xi) presenting of evidence, (xii) cross-examination of witnesses, (xiii) oral arguments, (xiv) pronouncing of judgement, and (xv) issue of final decree on a stamp paper.

Even under optimal conditions, the time to resolve a case from filing to verdict can take a full year. However, several procedural inefficiencies can extend this timeline. A critical source of inefficiency is the high frequency of lawyers asking for and being granted adjournments, often to gather more evidence or find witnesses. Legally, adjournments make sense to grant if parties need more time to adequately prepare their case. So, the problem is not adjournments per se, but the *uncertainty* around whether an adjournment is going to be sought on the scheduled court day.

The uncertainty regarding adjournment requests on hearing dates creates enormous inefficiencies. A case where an adjournment is sought and given can be disposed of in five to ten minutes. In contrast, a case where both sides are ready to present evidence or oral arguments will take more time. However, because nobody knows at the start of the court day as to how many adjournments will be granted, it is common for as many as 100 cases to be listed on a daily court calendar.[10] Lawyers on both sides often simply wait in the court just in case their matter ends up being heard that day.

Further, busy senior lawyers, who often depute others to wait in court and summon them if their case is called, may not be available when required, leading to more adjournments. The cost of these adjournments, including lawyer fees and delayed justice, is passed on to litigants, which increases the cost of accessing the legal system. The frustration faced by common citizens in accessing the formal justice system was vividly portrayed by Sunny Deol's famous '*Taareekh-par-taareekh*' (date after date) dialogue in the movie *Damini*, where he expresses despair that the justice system only gives him dates after dates (for hearings) but no justice.

The culture of adjournments has directly contributed to the delays in our court system. A study analysing inefficiencies and judicial delays in the Delhi High Court revealed that 91 per cent of all delayed cases had at least one adjournment and 70 per cent had three. Lawyers sought 80 per cent of adjournments, and the other 20 per cent were due to court-related constraints, such as absent judges or insufficient hearing time.[11]

1.5 Costs of weak judicial processes, and returns to augmenting judicial capacity

India's weak judicial system imposes both intrinsic and instrumental costs on our citizens. At an intrinsic level, it hurts human rights and individual welfare. At an instrumental level, it hurts economic activity and growth.

One striking measure of these intrinsic costs is the large number of defendants held in custody pending trial and judgment. Recent data show that 76 per cent of all prisoners in India are 'undertrial', which means that they are being detained despite *not* yet having been found guilty.[12] Further, members of scheduled castes and tribes are much more likely to be detained without being convicted than their population share.[13] Thus, the most vulnerable Indians are also most likely to bear the cost of our weak justice system.

In addition to being denied their freedom, undertrials are often held in the same jails as convicted criminals. Since conviction rates in India are very low, convicted inmates are more likely to have committed heinous crimes.[14] For instance, 50 per cent of convicted criminals in jail have been convicted for murder.[15] So, even if undertrials are being tried for minor crimes, they are exposed to much more dangerous and hardened criminals while in custody pending trial and judgment. This not only exposes them to greater physical danger and abuse while not yet convicted, it raises the likelihood that they also become hardened criminals, as jails can inadvertently serve as 'crime schools'.[16]

The 1894 Prisons Act mandates separate quarters for undertrials and convicted criminals, but the limited capacity of our jails makes it difficult to implement this policy.[17] While discussing jail reform is beyond the scope of this chapter, the sorry condition of our jails underscores the humanitarian costs of a weak justice system, which routinely incarcerates suspects awaiting trial.[18] For many, this period spent in jail even *without* being convicted of a crime is the most feared aspect of interacting with India's police and justice system, as captured vividly in multiple television programmes and films.[19]

Educated elites and middle classes might not worry too much about these risks, since the connected and powerful often secure bail easily if they are at risk of being put in custody while under trial. However, beyond the moral cost of condoning and ignoring these systemic issues, we *all* pay for the weak justice system through the instrumental costs imposed on the economy. These include both the direct time and opportunity costs of going through the legal process, and the indirect costs to the economy of unutilized factors of production, especially land and capital, that are stuck in litigation.

The 2016 Access to Justice Survey conducted by Daksh, a non-profit legal think-tank, estimates that the annual *direct* cost for individual litigants of engaging with the court system is 0.48 per cent of India's GDP. This is nearly seven times the total spending on the judiciary, which is 0.07 per cent of the GDP. So, it is unsurprising that research studies find large positive social returns from investments that strengthen the judiciary.

For instance, a cross-country study shows that judicial reforms to boost trial efficiency significantly increased firms' perception of judicial efficiency, and increased productivity in contract-intensive industries. A study in India found that the creation of debt-recovery tribunals in the late 1990s reduced loan delinquency by 28 per cent and contributed to lower interest rates, with likely downstream benefits for the entire economy.[20]

An important recent study finds that adding a judge to district courts in India resolved 200 pending cases and reduced backlogs by 10 per cent. It also led to a significant increase in bank credit circulation within the district, and increased the total wage bill and profits.[21] Further, since these gains were in the formal sector, the study estimates that the government could recover six times the cost of hiring extra judges through increased tax revenue, with the total economic benefits to society being over *thirty times* higher. This study illustrates the critical role of well-functioning judicial institutions to debt recovery, credit circulation, and economic activity, and the large social returns from investing in core components of state capacity like the judiciary.

These humanitarian and economic costs do not include the broader costs of weak trust in core state institutions. In particular, the statistics above are only based on cases that are actually filed. However, the well-known financial and time costs of accessing formal justice systems often drive citizens towards informal dispute resolution mechanisms including *khap* panchayats, religious figures, or even local mafia. These 'alternative dispute resolution' mechanisms draw their authority from different sources, including community recognition, moral or spiritual authority, and the threat of force or violence.

Thus, the near absence of the state on the ground limits our ability to implement the law of the land. For instance, khap panchayats often issue rulings that violate individual freedoms or anti-discrimination laws. Similarly, in the absence of meaningful presence of police and courts, local mafias and strongmen often run a parallel 'law enforcement' system that undermines the authority and efficacy of state laws and regulations.

While policy debates pay a lot of attention to crafting and refining laws, the effectiveness of these laws is substantially constrained by weak state capacity for enforcement. However, this issue gets much less systematic attention, and reinvesting in core police and judicial state capacity needs to be a top priority for India.

2. Implementable Reform Ideas

In line with the book's focus, my emphasis below is on ideas that can be implemented at the state level to increase the chance that at least some states will consider some of them, and thereby help move the country forward in this important area. Crucially, these ideas uphold the autonomy and independence of the judiciary regarding the *content* of justice, and focus on boosting judicial capacity and improving judicial *processes*. State governments can initiate these ideas by offering to finance them, but they will have to be implemented in close collaboration with the state's judicial leadership.

2.1 Fill district court vacancies and sanction more posts

As documented earlier, we now have credible empirical evidence on the large social returns from augmenting judicial capacity. Importantly, the evidence suggests that governments will *more* than recover the annual salary cost of hiring more district judges through increased tax revenue. After including the gains to economic activity and job creation, the economic returns are likely to be over thirty times the cost.[22]

Thus, one simple and impactful action that state governments can take is to provide budgets to fill judicial vacancies in district courts and below. This will significantly reduce case backlogs and shorten average case resolution times. It will directly improve the lives of citizens whose cases get resolved more promptly. More importantly, it will indirectly benefit *all* citizens because speeding up case resolution will boost overall economic activity, job creation, and wages by freeing up capital and land to be put to productive use as opposed to being underutilized when stuck in a litigation process.

Similarly, the social RoI of increasing the sanctioned strength of the lower judiciary is also likely to be high. The 1987 Law Commission Report recommended a target strength of fifty judges per million people at that time. However, the strength remains around twenty judges per million even now, and the number of judicial posts has not kept pace with population growth.

The cost of understaffing is seen in the growing backlog of cases. District courts have an average of five judges and resolve around 1000 cases a year, implying an average productivity of 200 cases per year per judge. The average number of new cases per year is around 1350, which adds around 350 cases a year to the backlog. This implies that we will need to hire at least two extra judges per district court to keep pace with the current flow of new cases, and start clearing the backlog of accumulated cases.

So, it should be an immediate priority for every state government in India to increase the number of operational judicial posts by an average of two judges per district court. However, a practical constraint to implementing this idea is the limited pipeline of candidates qualified to be judges.[23] Thus, while governments should provide the budget to hire more judges, additional strategies may also be needed to boost judicial capacity.

2.2 Create a judicial clerkship programme to boost productivity of district judges

One idea for augmenting judicial capacity quickly and cost-effectively is to create a judicial clerkship programme that provides all district judges with two recent law school graduates as judicial clerks. The position would be a two-year contractual appointment, open to all final-year LLB candidates or recent LLB graduates through a competitive exam. Clerks would receive a monthly stipend of Rs 20,000 to Rs 30,000, and work in the chambers of district court judges for two years after graduation.

The judicial clerks can significantly boost a judge's efficiency by providing analytical support, and expediting decision-making and drafting judgments. Areas of support could include (a) fact-finding, (b) assessing the quality of evidence submitted by contesting parties, (c) researching legal precedents, and (d) creating first drafts of judgments for judges to review, edit, and finalize. Investing in two clerks per judge could significantly augment judicial capacity even with a fixed number of judges.[24] It could improve the quality and the speed of judgments by providing judges with capacity for research and writing, and free up judge time to focus on assessing evidence and making judgments.

Younger clerks are also likely to be more adept with technology and can help speed up the adoption of digital case management practices in lower courts. While current court digitization initiatives provide hardware, the pace of change is often constrained by the inability of existing judicial staff to use technology. Clerks could help by serving as point persons for accelerating the digitization of lower courts. Crucially, they would not just be technology operators, but be trained and credentialled lawyers who are fully integrated in the judge's chambers. They would therefore have the judges' authority to accelerate the use of technology in case management.

Such a judicial clerkship programme would also significantly improve the quality of legal training of young law graduates. It would augment their classroom and exam-based knowledge of the law with direct exposure to the application of the law in practice and make them much better lawyers at the end of their two-year clerkship. Thus, young lawyers who have successfully completed a clerkship are likely to have better employment prospects and market value both with law firms and in private practice. In turn, this would make the clerkship a highly prestigious and career-boosting step that will be attractive and even aspirational to young law-school graduates.

Setting benchmark standards of legal knowledge and training for the clerkship programme can also help improve the quality of law school education in India. As with all areas of higher and technical education in India, the landscape of legal training institutions is also characterized by a few top-quality national institutions and hundreds of others with low and variable quality. The quality problem is so severe in many state-level law colleges that the Madras High Court recommended closing 85 per cent of law colleges due to their low quality of education and sale of fake law degrees.[25]

Thus, the entrance exam for the judicial clerkships can itself play an important role in shaping the standards of law-school education. It can also provide students with a metric for assessing the quality of law schools based on the success of their graduates in obtaining these clerkships. This is another example where a thoughtful policy intervention can improve quality not just in the public system, but can also induce private law colleges to improve, and thereby benefit the overall economy.

The actions to set up such a programme include: (a) creating and running an annual judicial clerkship exam, which can be run by state public service commissions with input from bar associations, (b) developing a three-to-four week clerkship training programme, which can be run by premier law schools with input from judges, (c) determining the selection and posting procedures, which can be done by law ministries, and (d) sanctioning the required budgets, a task for the finance ministry.

Conservatively, the total annual cost of a clerk would be Rs 5 lakh.[26] With about twenty judges per district, a full-scale programme would need forty clerks per district, and cost around Rs 2 crore annually per district, or Rs 60 crore annually for an average-sized state with about thirty districts. However, this modest investment would: (a) deliver a cost-effective and feasible augmentation of judicial capacity by boosting judge productivity,[27] (b) facilitate the acceleration of digitization of court records, processes, and case management, (c) force law colleges to improve their quality, and (d) improve the training and long-term quality of lawyers in the country by increasing their practical exposure to the law while serving as clerks.

The practice of using law clerks to support judges is well-established globally, especially in the US.[28] India would do well to adopt a similar system, and reap its multiple benefits.

This is a variant of a unified idea across Chapters 11–13, which is to use practicum-based training courses to cost-effectively augment staffing for service delivery, while also improving skilling for the sector, which will benefit trainees in their future careers *regardless* of whether they are employed in the public or private sector. It may actually be easiest to implement the idea of judicial clerks because (a) the numbers are smaller, (b) it does not require setting up a new type of training course, and will simply add a practicum-based job that law graduates can apply to, and (c) the benefits will be immediately visible. As in the other sectors, this should be a top recommendation for state governments and high courts to consider.

2.3 Improve operational efficiency of courts

Technology and digitization can significantly enhance court efficiency.[29] A critical area of improvement is reducing inefficiencies caused by frequent and unpredictable requests for adjournment. The problem is not just the delays due to adjournments themselves, but the time wasted by lawyers, witnesses, and other relevant parties due to the *uncertainty* about whether their case will be heard on a scheduled court day.

A simple reform to the adjournment process can be as follows: adjournments would have to be requested electronically five to ten working days before the hearing date, along with written justifications and documentation as needed. Judges, aided by clerks, could review these requests outside court hours, and grant or deny the request three to five days before the hearing. All parties would have electronic access to adjournment requests and decisions, and lawyers would be notified of any change in case status. Since judge time in court is extremely limited, resolving adjournments electronically, with support from clerks, can sharply improve the use of scarce judge time.

This reform would preserve the judicial need for adjournment for valid reasons, like gathering evidence or finding witnesses, while reducing the inefficiency of the process. With adjournments granted or denied three to five days in advance, the daily court docket can be shorter with a much higher probability that a case will be heard on the day it is listed for. This would greatly reduce the time wasted by lawyers, witnesses, and disputing parties who currently need to be available just in case their matter comes up for hearing.[30] The adjournment process is perhaps the greater source of frustration and inefficiency in the status quo, and using technology as outlined above can significantly improve efficiency.

The idea is quite similar to the electronic ticketing system used to manage the pilgrim flow for *darshan* at the Tirupati temple, which reduced the average time spent waiting in line by pilgrims from twelve hours to one or two hours.[31] If the Lord of Seven Hills can use an electronic ticketing system to reduce the waiting time for devotees by a factor of ten, surely the lords of our courts can do the same for supplicants seeking justice!

2.4 Executive actions to reduce the need for litigation

An even more effective way of reducing case backlogs, and the burden on the judiciary, is to reduce the number of cases in the first place. The executive can directly contribute to this goal by undertaking actions that are fully in its domain.

In particular, land and property disputes account for nearly *two-thirds* of civil cases in Indian district courts, largely due to the absence of a unified land titling system.[32] Land ownership is frequently disputed because there are multiple ways to establish claims, and relevant documentation can be issued by different government departments as well as by courts. In addition, both custom and law provide tenants and sharecroppers use-rights to land, without the rights to sell or mortgage the land. Further, these claims may be accepted in the community but not documented legally.[33] Family land disputes are also common, due to the frequent lack of a formal will by a deceased family head.

Land disputes not only contribute to court backlogs, they also hurt land productivity due to unclear use rights, and disincentives for land improvement amid uncertain property rights. So, state governments should prioritize establishing a comprehensive electronic land records and titling programme. This would feature a master database of all land parcels in the state, with clear ownership and title details, linked to Aadhaar for unique identification. It would also track zoning status, changes in land-use classification, current land use, and any encumbrances or liens for collateral. An accessible, comprehensive, integrated system across various departments and court records will sharply reduce land disputes, and the burden on courts. This will have the direct benefit of unlocking land value and encouraging investments, and the indirect benefit of reducing judicial backlog by freeing up time for other cases.

Of course, implementing this seemingly simple reform is incredibly challenging and there are many special cases that will require customized political, administrative, and legal solutions.[34] However, even starting with establishing and providing a clean title to less complicated cases will alleviate the burden on the judiciary and have a substantial positive impact on the ease of conducting economic activity.

Many states have launched initiatives to conduct a comprehensive digitization of land records. There is also a Central programme, which aims to issue a Unique Land Parcel Identification Number (ULPIN), also called Bhu-Aadhaar, to do so. However, this initiative has been ongoing since 2008, and it is important to accelerate progress, and track impacts on the ultimate outcomes of interest, including sharply reducing the number of land disputes that are pending in courts.

2.5 Legislative actions to improve judicial capacity

Legislatures can also take actions to improve the effective capacity of our court system. Clearly written laws make it easier to adjudicate disputes around interpretation. Thus, one important way in which legislatures can contribute is to repeal obsolete laws, simplify existing ones, and clarify laws that have frequently resulted in court cases.

A practical way to get started would be to analyse data on cases under various sections of the law, and measure both the number and duration of cases brought under different statutes. This process can help identify the specific laws that create the largest burden on the courts, and flag these for scrutiny to see if reforming or clarifying the concerned law may help to reduce the adjudication burden on the courts.

One good example is the case of bounced cheques. As per the current law, any bounced cheque is considered a criminal offence on the basis that cheques should be considered as legal tender, and that a bounced cheque indicates an intention to defraud on the part of the cheque writer.[35] In practice, given the possibility of payment delays by vendors, many bounced cheques simply reflect the timing of when the cheque was presented. In other words, a routine cash flow, or working capital, problem for a small business can often result in a serious criminal charge. Since a criminal charge is punishable by jail, the accused party will have to appeal for bail, which substantially increases the time and transaction cost of processing the case.

As of 10 March 2021, about *30 per cent of criminal trials* in district courts across India are 'Negotiable Instruments Sec 138' cases, concerning bounced cheques.[36] This high number reflects the fact that all such cases are treated as criminal offences, regardless of the cheque's value. A legislative amendment to categorize bounced cheques under a certain amount (say, Rs 1,00,000) as civil offences could significantly reduce the time and cost of adjudication. Bounced cheques above this threshold could remain a criminal offence to deter non-payment of substantial debts. However, the benefits of this change, in terms of reduced case transaction costs, must be balanced against the potential for greater default due to reduced penalties. So, it would make sense to evaluate the impact of the reform, and consider adjustments based on the findings.

More generally, the discussion above highlights the crying need for more empirical analysis of the consequences of various laws in India. In many cases, our laws represent ideals and aspirations borrowed from societies with much greater per capita income, and police and judicial capacity for enforcing the laws. However, in settings of weak enforcement such as India, well-intentioned laws can often lead to perverse unintended consequences. For instance, multiple studies have shown that the costs of prohibition of alcohol in states like Bihar likely far exceed the benefits (see Chapter 7).

A study by economist Prashant Bharadwaj and co-authors presents a striking example. It finds that laws banning child labour in India may have inadvertently *increased* its presence.[37] The underlying logic is that households resort to child labour not because they do not want their children in school but because they need a minimum income for survival, and rely on child labour income. In practice, laws against child labour could move work from better-paid formal jobs, where the law could be enforced, to less well-paid informal tasks, where enforcement was more difficult. Such moves would on average reduce household income, which can lead to households compensating by *increasing* the extent of child labour. This is exactly what the study finds.

This is a morally difficult example to grapple with. The purpose of highlighting this study is *not* to argue against progressive laws. Such laws serve an intrinsically useful purpose as a statement of social values and public signalling that some actions, like child labour, are inherently undesirable.[38] However, it is crucial to recognize that our laws' aspirations often surpass our capacity to implement them. Empirical studies show that even well-intentioned laws such as banning alcohol, dowry, and prostitution, can *worsen* outcomes in the desired domain itself.[39] Generally, in settings of weak enforcement, banning undesired behaviours can worsen outcomes by pushing the concerned activity underground, reducing safeguards, and increasing incentives to bribe law enforcers.

This increases the importance of carefully evaluating not just the intentions of laws and regulations, but also their *consequences*— after accounting for enforcement costs and the changes in incentives to both citizens and the law enforcement machinery of the state. Among Indian thinkers and policymakers, Bibek Debroy has notably led efforts to repeal obsolete laws. However, there is still much to be done in this area, and building a body of empirical evidence on the costs and benefits of various laws can help inform potentially high-return legislative reforms, that can also reduce the burden on the courts.

State legislatures can also support the rule of law and the quality of our justice system by passing laws to guarantee minimum capacity of the judicial system. As shown in this chapter, the public welfare gains from augmenting judicial capacity far exceed the cost. Yet, governments often prioritize short-term, visible projects over long-term investments in core state capacity. In this context, individual or groups of MLAs can make a meaningful impact by proposing laws to mandate a certain minimum number of judges per population and to ensure a minimum budgetary allocation to the justice system. Such a legislative foundation to building a more effective judiciary can help to ensure a minimum functional standard in our courts system.

2.6 Making it happen

The inefficiencies of our judicial system and the problem of large and increasing case backlogs are well known to everyone in the legal system, and most policymakers and business leaders as well. Further, the backlog *increases every single year*, and everyone can see this happening. Why then are we not doing anything about it?

The main challenge is that *no one* in the system is responsible for the problem. Judges mainly focus on delivering judgments, and not on improving the functioning of the judicial system. Further, judicial appointments have been bureaucratized, and follow a mechanical seniority system. This results in very short tenures for chief justices of under two years and often even less. Thus, while High Court chief justices have the authority to initiate reforms to improve district court functioning, even those who are motivated to make systemic changes are hampered by not having enough time to do so.

Another problem is that High Court chief justices are appointed from *outside* the state. While the rationale is to curb corruption, a key cost is that High Court chief justices may not have either the institutional knowledge or relationships in the state to build the consensus needed to pursue reforms. Between short tenures and being outsiders, it is almost impossible for a High Court chief justice to design and implement even the most basic procedural reforms. Further, judicial accountability to the public is almost non-existent under the status quo, which makes it possible for the 'system' to continue in its dysfunctional state. Everyone knows it is broken, but no one seems to be able to fix it!

Political and bureaucratic leaders are aware of the problem but have hesitated to act due to several factors. These include: (a) judicial pushback against perceived executive encroachment on their domain, (b) concerns about public perception of political interference in the judiciary, (c) prioritizing other areas, believed to yield quicker, visible results. My personal experience confirms this. For instance, when I raised this issue with a state chief secretary, he told me that 'this is an important issue, but the return on time invested will be low because coordinating with the judiciary is too difficult'.

However, this is too important an issue to ignore. Chief ministers are responsible for delivering economic growth and development, and are accountable to citizens through elections. This gives them the democratic legitimacy to initiate reforms to improve judicial processes, speed up dispute resolution, reduce the backlog of cases, and reduce the costs of accessing the justice system. While the *content* of justice should be determined solely by judges, improving the *process* of justice is well within the scope of what the executive branch of government should be concerned about.

A practical way forward would be for chief ministers to set up a state Judicial *Process* Reforms Commission headed by a recently retired Supreme Court judge or High Court chief justice. The commission could have five members, and include another judge, a senior advocate, a senior retired IAS officer like a former home or finance secretary, and a senior retired IPS officer to reflect the perspective of the police who play a critical role in pre-trial actions. Recently retired judges and officers are ideal for such a role because they have (a) the seniority and understanding needed to do a good job, and will also have credibility and respect within the system, and (b) the *time* to focus exclusively on this critical problem. Serving judges and officers simply do not have the time to both do their jobs, and redesign the system at the same time.

Commission members should have five-year terms, and can include both full-time and part-time members. The commission should be given a time-bound target of getting the system to a point where the annual number of cases disposed of is *greater* than the new cases filed, which is the only way to *reduce* the case backlog. Commissioners should be appointed in a bipartisan manner in consultation with the Opposition, and the chairman of the commission should provide an annual progress report to the legislative assembly to ensure accountability and public salience for their work.

Having the commission led by a former High Court chief justice, or Supreme Court justice from the state will provide it with legitimacy and credibility, and make it clear that reforms are being driven by members of the judiciary themselves. Having a former home or finance secretary on the commission can help ensure an effective interface with the government, especially for sanctioning funds. The commission should be provided with the resources and mandate to engage in wide consultations and design, implement, and monitor a five- to ten-year reform agenda that delivers the goals above.

Over time, such a commission could also take up matters such as improving equity in access to justice, and advising the government on data and evidence-based reforms to improve the process of justice, reduce its costs, and improve citizen satisfaction with the justice system. It can also obtain technical assistance from legal think tanks and non-profit organizations like the Vidhi Centre for Legal Policy, Daksh, and Agami, as well as from academic experts.[40] Given the importance of such an effort not just for India, but for other low-income countries as well, it may also be possible for states to obtain financial and technical assistance from international development agencies.

3. Conclusion

Our very viability as a society governed by the 'rule of law' depends on having a law enforcement and justice system that inspires confidence in the people. The discussions in the previous and current chapters highlight both the scale of the challenges in these areas, and the large public returns that can be obtained from even modest investments in strengthening these core functions of the state.

The judiciary in India is a constitutionally equal and independent branch of the state, but is hampered by its dependence on the executive for funding. A poignant symbol of the crisis in the judiciary was the former chief justice of India (T.S. Thakur) breaking down in tears at a conference of chief ministers and chief justices in 2016, noting that the judiciary was unable to function adequately given its limited resources.[41] At the same time, institutional features of the judiciary are also partly responsible for its sorry state of affairs. These include (a) a lack of initiative to act on its own abysmal functioning at a systemic level, (b) resistance to accountability of any sort, and

(c) designing systems primarily for the benefit of senior lawyers and 'insiders' rather than the public.[42]

Further, given tight budgets and compelling spending needs in several critical sectors, it is essential to prioritize improving judicial efficiency. Implemented ideas like electronic adjournments, and introducing a judicial clerkship programme to boost the productivity of district judges and improve the quality of legal education are practical ways of doing so, quickly. It is also essential to focus not just on programmes and schemes, but on the ultimate outcomes of interest such as speed of case resolution, reduction of backlogs, improved efficiency of time use, and greater citizen confidence in the justice system.

Chief ministers who can improve judicial efficiency in their states will not only improve citizens' lives, but also have a signature achievement to present to investors. Investors feel the pain of our weak justice system on an ongoing basis, and over time, states that address these issues are likely to see rapid rewards in terms of increased investments, economic growth, and job creation. Such an approach, focused on alleviating frictions to economic activity, could be a much more effective long-term strategy for attracting investors than the current one of offering tax cuts and other concessions (see Chapter 16).

As we enter our seventy-fifth year as a sovereign Republic, the weakness of our courts and justice system is a core failing that we need to urgently rectify. It is also an area where states and chief ministers can do a lot to lead the way forward for their state and for India as a whole.

Chapter 15

Social Protection and Welfare

India's universal franchise democracy provides incentives for both voters and politicians to prioritize public spending on welfare and subsidy programmes. This priority is reflected in our budgets, with 30–50 per cent of discretionary Central and state government budgets (excluding salaries, pensions, and interest) being allocated to such spending items.

Public discourse on welfare programmes in India is often polarized. On the one hand, many income-tax paying elites and middle classes often deride them as 'freebies' and view them as politicians buying votes with their taxes. On the other hand, advocates for a more equitable and just society see them as a lifeline for the poor and marginalized, and believe that the government should expand social protection and welfare programmes. How can we reconcile these divergent views? Is it even possible?

One way to find common ground is to move beyond thinking about welfare spending in aggregate terms, and pay more attention to the *details* of the design and implementation of specific subsidies and welfare programmes. As shown in the conceptual framework of Figure 6.2, and expanded in this chapter, poorly designed subsidies can hurt *both* equity and efficiency, while well-designed welfare programmes can promote both goals. So, shifting public funds from the former to the latter, and improving their delivery will allow us to support the poor better, and also increase economic productivity and growth. This is an agenda that should be appealing to both the economic right and left.

As with the other sectors discussed in this book, a robust social protection and welfare system is both intrinsically and instrumentally important for society. Intrinsically, it can protect individuals from the vagaries of life, and mitigate extreme poverty and adversity resulting from the morally arbitrary circumstances of one's birth. Instrumentally, it can help people escape poverty traps and give them the support needed to become more productive. This can help transform poor citizens from passive 'beneficiaries' of government support to productive contributors to their own and national progress.

A well-functioning social protection system can also boost state capacity for economic reforms that enhance productivity and job creation. While such reforms can improve overall well-being, they can adversely impact some groups who may try to block the reforms. An effective social protection system can make it easier to compensate these groups or at least mitigate their losses, and reduce political barriers to reforms that increase aggregate welfare. Thus, systems that 'protect' citizens from the vagaries of life and the market, can also facilitate policies that 'promote' average well-being by fostering economic dynamism and job creation (see Chapter 16).

This chapter comprises three sections. The first briefly overviews key facts on welfare spending in India; the second discusses principles and evidence regarding the effective design and delivery of welfare programmes; the final one discusses implementable reform ideas to build a better welfare and social protection architecture for India.

1. Key Facts on Welfare Programmes in India

Both Central and state governments allocate substantial portions of their budget to subsidies and welfare programmes. Welfare programmes are broadly defined as those transferring public resources to private citizens, either through income support or by providing free or subsidized in-kind benefits. This definition excludes costs of direct provision of services such as education or health (these are primarily salary costs), but includes in-kind benefits in these sectors, such as midday meals in schools.

At the national level, key welfare programmes include the Public Distribution System (PDS) for subsidized food; National Rural Employment Guarantee Scheme (NREGS) offering public employment to the rural poor; PM Awas Yojana (PMAY) for subsidized housing for the poor; and the National Social Assistance Programme (NSAP), providing pensions to the elderly poor. In addition, the budget for the school midday meal scheme for children is comparable to NSAP's allocation for the elderly.

The agriculture budget also includes large spending items aimed at supporting farmer welfare. These include fertilizer subsidies, interest subsidies on farm loans, farm loan waivers, free or subsidized crop insurance, and the PM-KISAN programme, which offers income support to farmers. While these policies can partly be justified as helping to improve agricultural yields and ensure national food security, they are largely driven by the political need to support farmer welfare.

Table 15.1 presents the spending on these schemes, and shows that they totalled nearly Rs 4,21,000 crore in 2019–20. This constituted 15.7 per cent of total Central government spending, and 32.7 per cent of its discretionary spending (excluding salaries, pensions, and interest). Beyond these 'broad' welfare schemes, there are also numerous smaller welfare schemes targeted at 'narrow' groups of beneficiaries, typically under various disadvantaged categories. The figures do not include costs for reimbursing private schools under the Right to Education Act or private hospitals under the Ayushman Bharat scheme, which are included in the education and health budgets.

While there is variation across states, most states also spend 25 to 50 per cent of their discretionary budget on subsidies and welfare programmes. Some large expenditure items include free electricity to farmers, state-specific farmer welfare schemes (such as Rythu Bandhu in Telangana and KALIA in Odisha), state-level pension schemes, affordable housing schemes, and loan waivers.[1]

Overall, both Central and state governments in India spend large portions of their discretionary budgets on subsidies and welfare schemes. This spending reflects voter demand and politician supply of welfare, and is a natural consequence of India's universal franchise

Table 15.1: Major Central Government Welfare and Subsidy Spending

Scheme	2019–2020		
	Expenditure in Rs crores	Per cent of total expenditure	Per cent of discretionary expenditure
Food Subsidies and PDS	1,08,688	4.0%	8.5%
Fuel Subsidies	38,529	1.4%	3.0%
Fertilizer Subsidies	81,124	3.0%	6.3%
PM KISAN	48,714	1.8%	3.8%
Interest Subvention	16,219	0.6%	1.3%
Crop Insurance	12,639	0.5%	1.0%
MGNREGS	71,687	2.7%	5.6%
NSAP	8,692	0.3%	0.7%
PMAY	24,964	0.9%	1.9%
Mid-day Meals	9,699	0.4%	0.8%
Total	**4,20,955**	**15.7%**	**32.7%**

Notes: Data from Bag 6 (Expenditure), Ministry of Finance.

democracy (Chapter 2). India's primary challenge is to improve the *quality* of our welfare spending. Doing so requires us to understand key principles for designing and implementing an effective social protection architecture.

2. Principles for Effective Social Protection and Welfare Programmes

2.1 Analyse welfare programmes through the lens of equity and efficiency

The stated policy goal of most welfare and subsidy spending is to help the poor. Yet, there are many cases where such spending is disproportionately availed by the better-off. Thus, even if spending items are publicly justified as intended to improve equity, we cannot assume that they do so in practice.

Similarly, welfare programmes can both hurt or help economic efficiency. Sources of spending inefficiency include administrative costs and leakage, and distortion of resource allocation in the economy due to subsidies (see Chapter 6). Further, the need to raise taxes to finance higher welfare spending will also typically increase economic inefficiency (Chapter 7). As noted by Vijay Kelkar and Ajay Shah, every rupee raised by the government costs the economy between two and three rupees.

So, when the government spends Rs 100 on subsidies and welfare, the amount that reaches beneficiaries is well below Rs 100, and the cost to taxpayers is well over Rs 100. This reflects inefficiencies and transaction costs in both taxation and redistribution. Thus, it can cost the Indian economy say Rs 200–300 for every Rs 70 delivered to beneficiaries through subsidies and welfare programmes. This is why the default view in economics is that there is an inevitable trade-off between equity and efficiency.[2]

However, this default view reflects the intellectual tradition of 'public finance' economics, which has mostly been developed in higher-income country contexts. In contrast, a key conceptual result in 'development' economics is that people who are extremely poor can be stuck in 'poverty traps'. In such situations, well-designed welfare programmes can not only reduce human suffering, which is intrinsically and ethically desirable, but *also* make people more productive. Thus, they can improve *both* equity and efficiency.

For instance, malnourished children face lifelong disadvantages in health and cognitive development. In such cases, inexpensive early life interventions can not only improve the lives of these children, which is intrinsically desirable; but *also* pay for themselves by increasing lifetime human capital, productivity, incomes, and future taxes. Similarly, farmers might hesitate to invest in new, potentially more profitable crop varieties due to the risks of adopting new technologies; it is in fact typical to first make losses on a new crop before making profits after going through a learning process. In such a setting, having a backup income source like a rural public employment programme, can not only protect the poor from adverse economic shocks, but also facilitate the risk-taking needed to grow farm productivity and incomes.[3]

The concept of a 'poverty trap' is relevant not just for individuals, but for economies as well. Countries can get stuck in a low-productivity, low-income trap due to limited demand in high-poverty contexts. Low demand makes it difficult for firms to invest in productivity-enhancing capital because they cannot recover the fixed costs of their investments.[4] This is why exports have usually been critical for poorer countries to grow faster, as demand from high-income foreign markets allows producers in low-income countries to make fixed-cost investments to increase productivity, which then increases wages and domestic demand over time (see Chapter 16). A key implication for India is that, though we have a large domestic population, high poverty and inequality limit the *effective* market size for domestic industry. In such a situation, well-designed welfare programmes can also boost productivity and growth by increasing demand.

Thus, one of the most important messages of this chapter is that it is essential to consider the *details* of specific welfare and subsidy programmes before assessing whether they are a good use of scarce public funds. In some cases, the total benefits can be much greater than the cost, and in others they can be much less than the costs.

A powerful way of analysing the quality of welfare spending is to consider its impacts on both equity and efficiency, as defined in Chapter 6, using the framework in Figure 6.2. Figure 15.1 does this and situates specific welfare spending items in this 2x2 framework. The main insight here is that there is enormous variation in the equity and efficiency impacts of spending items. Some items worsen *both* equity and efficiency and fall in Region 3 (R3); others improve both and are in Region 1 (R1). There are also items in Regions 2 and 4 that are positive on one dimension but negative on the other. Figure 15.1 classifies major spending items, based on a combination of calculations, research evidence, and judgement.

An example of a highly inefficient 'welfare' programme in R3 is free electricity for farmers (item 10), which is arguably one of India's *worst* economic policies. As Chapter 6 shows, it is terrible for equity: the top 5 per cent of landholders receive nearly 50 per cent of farm electricity subsidy spending; however, the poorest,

Figure 15.1: Characterizing India's Welfare and Subsidy Spending by Equity and Efficiency Impacts

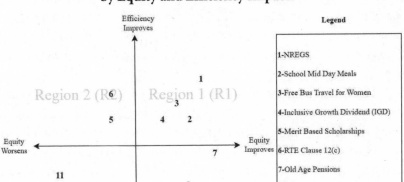

Legend
1-NREGS
2-School Mid Day Meals
3-Free Bus Travel for Women
4-Inclusive Growth Dividend (IGD)
5-Merit Based Scholarships
6-RTE Clause 12(c)
7-Old Age Pensions
8-PDS
9-NYAY
10-Free electricity to Farmers
11-Fertilizer Subsidies
12-Farm Loan Waivers

like landless labourers, barely benefit. It also hurts efficiency by encouraging the cultivation of water-intensive crops in arid areas. This practice, driven by free electricity, significantly contributes to India's groundwater crisis and ecological stress, and also exacerbates north India's pollution crisis through paddy stubble burning by farmers in Punjab and Haryana.

It also hurts the broader economy since state power distribution companies (DISCOMs) try to cover the losses from free electricity to farmers by charging industrial users more. This hurts the competitiveness of Indian industry, leading to reduced investments, and fewer jobs (see Chapter 16). It also allows DISCOMs to hide their inefficiencies. Since agricultural power use is often unmetered, other inefficiencies and theft are hidden in this category.[5] Beyond the direct fiscal costs to state treasuries, the financial stress of DISCOMs also hurts power generation because DISCOMs struggle to pay power producers on time. Overall, the insolvency of DISCOMs is a major economic policy challenge for many states, and free agricultural power is a large contributor to this crisis.

Fertilizer subsidies (item 11) are also in R3 since they mainly benefit large landowners. They also create inefficiencies by encouraging the overuse of urea. However, they are not as inefficient as free electricity, because they do play a key role in allowing multiple crops from land within a calendar year, which contributes to national food security.[6]

Farm loan waivers (item 12) are another example of R3 spending that are justified as promoting farmer 'welfare'. They are highly inequitable as larger landowners, who tend to borrow more, benefit more; whereas small and marginal farmers, often reliant on informal lenders, miss out on formal bank loan forgiveness. Loan waivers also create perverse incentives by rewarding those who do not pay back loans, and penalizing those who did. So, loan waivers can raise default risk, and make banks wary of lending, which hurts credit availability, economic activity, and job creation. However, they are less inefficient than free electricity because they are sporadic and not annual, and less inequitable because the waiver amounts are often capped.

The point of these examples is not to criticize farmer welfare spending, but to highlight how the *specific* ways in which we do so hurt both equity and efficiency. As shown in Section 3.4, we can deliver farmer support in *much* more efficient ways. Also, when we criticize farm loan waivers for being in R3, it is important to acknowledge that corporate loan waivers through writing off non-performing assets (NPAs) of public sector banks are even worse. These are even more inequitable, as big business owners are usually wealthier than large landowners, and hurt efficiency for similar reasons.[7]

In contrast, the NREGS is one of India's most effective welfare programmes. It improves equity by providing work to poor rural households. The work requirement improves targeting, and reduces inclusion errors whereby ineligible beneficiaries receive funds. Further, NREGS indirectly boosts wages for *all* rural workers, by offering them a better 'outside option' and reducing desperation for low-wage work. These wage increases primarily benefit landless labourers, who are typically poorer, and appear to persist year-round, even beyond the lean season when NREGS is primarily active.[8]

While boosting wages of the rural poor is good for equity, it may hurt efficiency if higher wages reduce employment. However, multiple studies (including my own) have shown that NREGS *increased* employment and economic activity. Potential reasons include: (a) improved rural assets from NREGS projects, (b) counteracting collusion among employers to keep wages and employment down ('monopsony' power), (c) improved credit access from higher wages, (d) greater willingness to undertake risky investments due to wage insurance, (e) increased mechanization of agriculture due to higher wages, which could boost productivity, and (f) increased demand for local enterprises from higher rural incomes, creating a positive local multiplier effect.[9] So, NREGS improves both equity and efficiency, and is an excellent R1 programme (item 1).

Another example of an R1 programme is school midday meals (item 2). They improve equity since they mainly cater to lower SES children who attend government schools. Studies also show that they have positive long-term effects on school attendance, nutrition, and learning outcomes, though the magnitude of the effects are modest.[10]

Free bus travel for women (item 3) is another example of an R1 policy. It improves equity by promoting mobility and empowerment of women in our still patriarchal society, and can also improve efficiency by making it easier for women to work or study. Further, since the well-off do not use public transport, it is well targeted by design. As shown in Chapter 11, the provision of free bicycles to girls in Bihar led to a significant increase in girls' secondary school participation. This suggests that schemes that reduce the daily cost of commuting to school or work for women can be highly effective.

Pensions for the elderly poor (item 7) effectively improve equity, as beneficiaries are mostly poor and vulnerable. They are also implemented well with limited leakage since targeting is easier, and payments are regular and predictable.[11] While they do not boost productive efficiency, they improve equity without much inefficiency, other than the cost of raising taxes to finance them.

The Nyuntam Aay Yojana (NYAY), proposed by the Congress party before the 2019 elections, aimed to boost equity by giving the poorest 20 per cent of households a minimum income of Rs 72,000 per year. While this would have likely improved equity, it risked considerable inefficiency for multiple reasons.

First, because benefits were so generous, non-poor households would be incentivized to exploit connections to get included in beneficiary lists, excluding the neediest. This risk is real, as marginalized groups often struggle with paperwork to prove programme eligibility. Second, the design of NYAY would disincentivize work. Since households would lose all benefits if they climbed from the twentieth to the twenty-first percentile of the income distribution, NYAY could sharply reduce incentives for work near this threshold and reinforce a poverty trap, whereas the goal of welfare programmes should be to help the poor escape a poverty trap instead of incentivizing them to stay poor.[12]

The Public Distribution System (PDS) also promotes equity but at the cost of economic inefficiency (item 8). It improves equity by providing food security to the poor, and may even help efficiency by boosting their caloric intake and productivity. On the other hand, its dual-price system is prone to leakage through diversion of subsidized commodities to the open market. Further, the PDS is made possible by government actions to procure rice and wheat from farmers at or above minimum support prices. While some buffer stocks are needed for national food security, India's food grain policies generate large inefficiencies. These policies violate basic economics in both production, by purchasing grains *above* market prices, and in distribution, by selling grains *below* market prices.[13] Thus, while the PDS helps both equity and food security, there may be more efficient ways to deliver similar levels of support to the poor.

Merit-based scholarships (item 5) likely improve efficiency by incentivizing student effort, and aiding meritorious students obtain a higher quality of education. However, they are more likely to go to better-off students, with the support and resources needed for academic success. Similarly, under Clause 12(c) of the Right to Education Act, the government reimburses students from Economically Weaker Sections (EWS) who attend private schools (item 6). While this may improve efficiency by helping them attend higher-quality schools, recent evidence suggests that it is not very effective at promoting equity: beneficiaries are mostly those who would have gone to a private school anyway, and the most disadvantaged students did not have the documents or the know-how to access programme benefits. Thus, though the programme was meant to promote equity, in practice the benefits are mainly availed by better-off households.[14]

This discussion and Figure 15.1 convey several crucial insights. First, there is usually a trade-off between equity and efficiency, but this is not always true. Second, rather than assessing welfare spending in the aggregate, we need to pay careful attention to the *details* of specific proposals, since they can have widely varying impacts on equity and efficiency. Third, it highlights the value of research and evidence on the efficiency and equity impacts of specific programmes, to inform public discourse on their social value.

For instance, when NREGS was launched in 2005, many economists, including myself, were sceptical about its impacts due to concerns of corruption, and worrying that increasing rural wages without corresponding productivity growth may hurt employment and economic activity. However, evidence from multiple studies, including my own, has helped to shift this view.[15] The depiction of spending items in Figure 15.1 and most of this book relies on research and evidence.[16] When designing new programmes where we do not have such evidence, we should analyse likely impacts on both equity and efficiency as part of the budgeting process, as suggested in Chapter 6. Such analysis can promote a more informed policy discourse on how best to use scarce public funds.

Reasonable people may disagree on whether to prioritize spending in R4 or R2, based on their relative emphasis on equity or efficiency. However, we should build a national consensus to phase out R3 spending, or limit its growth, and reallocate these funds to R1 ideas. More broadly, in designing and reforming public spending programmes, we should aim to continuously improve either equity or efficiency, and ideally both.

2.2 Help the poor through income support rather than price subsidies

A fundamental economics principle for policymakers and the public to understand is the crucial role of competitive market prices in promoting efficiency. Prices allocate scarce resources like land, labour, and capital to their most valuable uses, as determined by what people are willing to pay. High prices are a signal to producers to increase supply, as they can now afford to pay more for the inputs needed to increase production. This increase in supply enables broader access to goods or services, and eventually lowers prices. In contrast, policy interventions aiming to help the poor by controlling prices of 'essential' goods, often result in shortages and poorer long-term outcomes.

For example, rent control policies benefit the *few* who are currently in rental housing, but often deter new housing investments, exacerbating the challenge of affordable housing for *many more* people. Similarly, allowing electricity prices to rise in summer when demand is high encourages more supply by producers, and greater conservation by consumers. This allows more people to consume electricity. In contrast, trying to control prices usually results in shortages. Akshay Jaitly and Ajay Shah explain this point by noting that we do not have ice cream shortages in summer, despite higher demand then, because we allow market prices to rise to reflect changes in supply and demand. In contrast, we constantly have power shortages in the summer because we try to control prices in ways that make it unattractive for producers to increase supply.[17]

Of course, as noted in Chapter 9, a key limitation of the market is that it does not value those who cannot pay. This creates tension between market logic and democratic principles and pressure. While the democratic ideal is 'one person, one vote', the market functions on a 'one rupee, one vote' principle. This is why democratic societies, globally, try to soften the rough edge of markets and aim to support the poor to access essential goods and services. India is no exception, and so governments may be fine with ice cream prices rising in summer, since ice cream is not considered essential. But, they try to control electricity prices to provide access to the poor.

This is a worthy goal. However, trying to improve access to the poor by controlling electricity prices incurs high efficiency costs, weakens price signals, and results in shortages for *all*. A better approach is to provide users with a *fixed* amount of free or subsidized units of consumption, after which they have to pay market prices. The price schedule can rise with usage, making those who use more pay proportionately more, effectively eliminating subsidies above a consumption threshold. Such an approach, used by Delhi, can improve equity at a much lower cost to efficiency.

2.3 Make social protection programmes systematic and reliable

Social protection programmes are more effective if they are predictable and reliable. This enables citizens to plan their lives with the confidence that welfare support is available if needed. For instance, a reliable NREGS as a backup option, can give a small farmer the confidence to try a riskier, but potentially more profitable, new crop. So, a welfare system that can credibly 'protect' individuals from risk can also help 'promote' investments that increase both individual productivity and aggregate economic growth.

However, in practice, India's welfare spending is often sporadic and unreliable. This is partly due to politicians seeking electoral gains from announcing schemes like loan waivers or income transfers before elections, and partly because of weaknesses in delivery systems. It is often easier to announce new programmes than to ensure that they effectively reach intended recipients.

A 2022 report by Dvara Research on the 'state of exclusion' in India's welfare schemes highlights several challenges beneficiaries face in accessing benefits.[18] These issues arise at every stage of the process: (a) proving eligibility and applying, (b) application processing and inclusion in beneficiary lists, (c) timely payment disbursal, and (d) collecting payments smoothly. These barriers stem from: (a) gaps in beneficiary literacy and awareness in filing paperwork, (b) bureaucratic approval processes that reject applications for even minor paperwork issues, (c) non-release of funds due to budget constraints, and (d) difficulties in accessing cash points, especially in rural areas.

These challenges affect every major welfare programme. Even flagship schemes like NREGS are hampered by delayed and unpredictable payments.[19] This is both a moral and practical failure. Morally, it is egregious when workers do hard labour on NREGS and then do not get paid for weeks or even months. Practically, such unpredictability greatly diminishes NREGS's effectiveness for social protection in the lean season.

Similarly, one-off farm loan waivers before elections may offer temporary relief but do not typically lead to 'productive' investments that lift people out of poverty. In contrast, an income transfer scheme giving farmers equivalent funds *before* the planting season can enable investments in higher-yielding seeds or crops, that farmers may not try with borrowed money. If such transfers become reliable, they could help farmers potentially break free of the cycle of debt in the first place.

The key point to note is that the *same* amount of public resources spent on welfare can yield greater social benefits if implemented predictably and reliably, because it allows recipients to better plan the rest of their actions. Such reliability will also help improve trust in the state, which is a key enabler of more far-reaching reforms (see Section 3.4).

2.4 Build social safety *trampolines* rather than social safety *nets*

The term social safety 'net' reflects the idea that life is unpredictable, and people are vulnerable, and so society should build a safety net to catch them when they fall. However, the 'net' metaphor implies a state of absorption where people are protected from falls but stay stuck in the net. Rather, our approach to social safety should be to provide support in ways that help people bounce back from adversity or climb out of poverty, but not in ways that they prefer to remain in the net or are unable to leave it.

So, to use a phrase coined by Tharman Shanmugaratnam, the current President of Singapore, our approach to social safety should be to build 'trampolines' rather than 'nets'.[20] In the Indian context, even a thinker who prioritizes social justice, like Yogendra Yadav, has noted that our welfare discourse should stop thinking of recipients as '*labharthis*' (beneficiaries), implying that they are passive recipients of government largesse, and move to thinking of them as '*purusharthis*' (hard workers), who are empowered by government support to contribute to personal and national progress.[21]

3. Implementable Reform Ideas

The reform ideas below reflect the principles discussed above and will help us improve the quality of subsidy and welfare spending by moving it towards R1 in Figure 15.1. These include four broad ideas to boost the effectiveness of existing welfare spending, followed by two proposals for new welfare programmes that can improve the overall quality of social protection in India.

3.1 Harmonize and simplify welfare schemes

Several reports note that people are frequently unaware of welfare schemes they could benefit from. Even if they are, they often do not know how to complete the paperwork and apply for specific programmes. One reason is the proliferation of small schemes under both Central and state governments. For instance, the 2022 Central government budget listed 740 central-sector schemes, and over 65 Centrally sponsored schemes.

The political rationale for numerous small schemes is to allow politicians to demonstrate their efforts for various population subgroups. Small schemes also reflect a politics of clientelism, whereby state resources are directed to narrow as opposed to broad groups (Chapter 2). However, this proliferation of schemes makes it difficult for citizens to track them, and increases the risk that public welfare funds do not reach the vulnerable and needy. It also leads to several schemes with small budgets, which are susceptible to changes in political priorities. Finally, all schemes have fixed costs of administration. So, the fraction of the budget that reaches citizens is lower in smaller schemes. All these factors combine to severely limit the reach, impact, and value of small schemes.

So, we can significantly improve the effectiveness of India's welfare spending by phasing out many small schemes, and reallocating funds to key flagship programmes like food security, employment guarantees (for those who can work), and pensions (for those who cannot work). The funds saved could also be used to finance a modest universal supplemental income transfer (see Section 3.5). Such rationalization will also help focus limited administrative capacity on better implementation of flagship schemes, ensuring that they reach the most vulnerable. In contrast, several small schemes make it more likely that their benefits reach the advantaged who know how to access them.

Consistent with the principles of federalism discussed in Chapter 8, the Centre should lead on welfare programmes that are near-universal, nationally portable, and benefit from scale economies. However, states are better positioned to lead on schemes that benefit from local information on design and targeting. So, the Centre should focus on funding a few key flagship national welfare schemes well, phase out smaller ones, and let states lead on more narrowly targeted schemes while focusing on broad ones. Better clarity on Central and state schemes will also reduce political tussles over credit, and help citizens know which benefits are portable across states and which are not.

3.2 Create a dedicated implementation quality cell for all welfare programmes

An effective social protection system requires attention to both design and *delivery*. As noted in Chapter 1, several studies have documented weaknesses in last-mile delivery of welfare programmes as well as the large return on investment (RoI) from investing in better delivery of welfare programmes.[22] These results suggest that there are likely to be large returns to public welfare if state governments were to systematically invest in creating a dedicated implementation quality cell for welfare programmes.

The key to the effectiveness of such a cell is having reliable, actionable data. The ideas in Chapter 4 offer ways of collecting such data: outbound phone calls, field truthing of administrative data, and district-level surveys. Key metrics to monitor could include receipt, exclusion, leakage, timeliness, and reliability of welfare programmes.

The cell should report directly to the chief minister's office, to drive follow-up actions, and close the loop from performance measurement to personnel management.

In addition to the above methods of measuring system-level quality of welfare delivery, we also need effective grievance redressal mechanisms for *specific* complaints. Many states have inbound call centres to receive complaints, but few have formalized follow-up processes with legal service level commitments. Such a commitment can be quite effective as shown by recent research, which has found that Bihar's grievance redressal act, which enabled citizens and their local representatives to file formal complaints for non-delivery of services, was highly effective at improving service delivery.[23]

Together, the data from outbound call centres and inbound complaints will provide the basis for improving both performance measurement and management of government staff (as noted in Chapters 4 and 5). A senior IAS officer once memorably mentioned to me that getting government employees to work well required a combination of *bhayam* (fear) and *bhakti* (devotion). Thus, well-designed and managed public systems will improve both employee motivation (*bhakti*) and accountability (*bhayam*).

These ideas of effective management are well-known to senior officials, but we have not built systems to institutionalize and implement these ideas at scale. An implementation quality cell, as described above, can improve both staff motivation and accountability. It makes it possible to both recognize good performance, and to identify and address poor performance using objective real-time data. It can also help departments make the case for additional staffing and resources when their current levels of resourcing are not enough to meet service quality expectations. Investing in such a cell can yield visible improvements in citizen-centred governance, and would also be politically rewarding.

3.3 Empower citizens with choices regarding accessing welfare programmes

A key mindset shift that we need to make in designing welfare programmes is to move from thinking of citizens as passive beneficiaries, and think of ways of empowering them to make their own decisions regarding how they access the benefits that they are legally entitled to. In particular, we would do well to use the ideas laid out in Chapter 9 and give citizens more choices in how they access welfare benefits.

For instance, as noted in Chapter 9, one powerful way of both empowering citizens and curbing leakage in the PDS is to give beneficiaries the *choice* of opting for an equivalent income transfer sent to their bank accounts as a Direct Benefit Transfer (DBT). The in-kind benefits of the PDS would still be the default option. However, the choice of DBT weakens PDS dealers' monopoly, by providing beneficiaries with additional options.

Over the past decade, my colleagues and I have piloted this choice-based approach in the PDS in multiple states and have found strong support for the idea.[24] In our first pilot in Bihar in 2012–13, *over 80 per cent* of beneficiaries chose a cash option equal to the subsidy's fiscal value. In fact, leakage and non-availability of grains in the PDS were so severe that over half the beneficiaries chose the cash option even when its value was only 60 per cent of the subsidy's fiscal value. Thus, the PDS in Bihar in 2012–13 was clearly delivering much less value to beneficiaries than the fiscal cost of providing it.

In more recent pilots in Maharashtra, around 25 per cent of PDS beneficiaries opted for DBT, likely reflecting better governance in the state, and nationwide improvements in PDS implementation in the past decade. Yet, 96 per cent of beneficiaries in our Maharashtra study strongly valued the *option* of availing DBT if they were to choose to do so. These results reinforce a key point in Chapter 9: providing citizens with an option to exit the public system can empower them, and offer an important disciplining device for improving service quality in the public system.

The Central government has already introduced some choice in the PDS by enabling portability of benefits across PDS shops anywhere in India under the 'one nation, one ration' scheme. This excellent initiative enables workers to seek jobs across the country, without losing PDS benefits. It also exemplifies how investing in Aadhaar has enhanced state capacity to serve citizens. Implementing portability requires a dynamic PDS inventory management system, which is feasible using Aadhaar-authenticated transaction records, but was not possible with paper-based record-keeping. With this technological infrastructure in place, it is now feasible to further empower beneficiaries by offering the choice of income transfer by DBT in lieu of in-kind PDS benefits.[25]

This example illustrates the power of incorporating citizen choice into welfare programme design. The fiscal cost per beneficiary will be unchanged, but the value derived by citizens can be significantly enhanced by moving from a 'one-size-fits-all' system to one that better accommodates variation in citizens' needs and preferences.

3.4 Replace agriculture subsidies with income-based support

State governments spend tens of thousands of crores annually on free electricity for farmers. However, these subsidies hurt equity and efficiency, and are also a leading contributor to India's groundwater crisis. Simply put, they are just not sustainable.

So, a transformative reform for chief ministers to consider is phasing out free electricity for farmers and replacing it with an equivalent income transfer. The basic idea is to calculate the average cost of electricity needed to irrigate an acre of land and to transfer this per-acre amount to farmers at the start of the agricultural season. However, farmers would need to install meters and pay for their electricity usage. This reform would have been infeasible even a decade ago. But with programmes like PM-KISAN successfully transferring funds to bank accounts of tens of millions of rural households, India now has the state capacity and systems to reform the design of farmer support programmes.

This reform is politically feasible since farmers will receive the *same* subsidy amount as they currently do. If their electricity usage does not change, they will not be worse off. The crucial difference is that they will now have an incentive to conserve electricity, and thereby groundwater, as any unused electricity translates into money that they would get to keep. Further, farmers themselves know that current farming practices are ecologically unsustainable with ever-depleting groundwater tables. Therefore, this reform could be framed as a '*paani bachao, paisa kamao*' (save water, earn money) initiative, mirroring the name of a recent pilot along these lines in Punjab.[26]

Initially, this reform will *not* reduce government spending, as the same subsidy amount will be paid to farmers as a lump sum. However, it will generate considerable taxpayer savings over time because the value of the income transfer will be set based on the *current* electricity usage. While the per-unit subsidy value should be adjusted for inflation in the cost of electricity, the number of units will be fixed. In contrast, persisting with free electricity for farmers will require increasing subsidies over time since *more* electricity will be needed to extract the *same* amount of groundwater as levels deplete.

This reform represents a win-win-win deal for taxpayers, farmers, and the environment. The government and taxpayers will save money over time, and will also benefit from improved financial viability and accountability of electricity DISCOMs. Farmers will make extra money by being more judicious in their water use and making more contextually appropriate crop choices that reflect the true cost of water. The reform may also help increase farmers' long-term income by promoting crop diversification. The environment (and citizens) will benefit from slowing down groundwater depletion, and improved air quality in north India due to reduced cultivation of water-intensive paddy in Punjab and Haryana, and the resulting reduction in stubble burning.

One concern is the possibility that farmers may collect the income transfer, but refuse to install meters or pay electricity bills. If this happens, it may be politically difficult to cut electricity to defaulting farmers. However, advances in digital metering make it easier to remotely monitor electricity usage, and remotely disable connections if bills are unpaid. To mitigate non-payment risk, a virtual account could be established for each farmer with the DISCOM. The subsidy value could be transferred into this virtual account at the start of a year, with deductions based on actual electricity usage. The balance in this virtual account would be visible to farmers in real-time to motivate conservation. Net balances can be transferred to farmers' bank accounts every quarter.

The specifics of implementation will have to be piloted and refined based on the context. Since free electricity for farmers is primarily a state-level policy, states are well positioned to spearhead serious pilots in consultation with farmers' associations. It may also make sense to de-risk the reform and start in areas where the chief minister or senior leaders of the party in power have strong political support and trust.

This reform is so crucial to our collective welfare, that political parties should collectively grasp the severity of the fiscal and ecological crisis from free electricity for farmers, and agree to support piloting and evaluating reforms along these lines. Broad consensus can also help alleviate farmers' concerns that the government may renege on promises of transferring the subsidy value as a DBT, after abolishing free electricity. One way to build trust and confidence on this issue is legislative backing for a scaled-up reform that legally commits to the per-acre compensation to farmers in lieu of free electricity, and makes an annual budgetary provision for at least ten years, and potentially longer. While pilots and evaluations can be done based on government orders, legal backing for scaled-up reforms will help to both institutionalize key commitments and build trust.

This example illustrates three key principles for policy reforms in a democracy like India. The first is the power of incentives. Where do the benefits of this reform magically come from? After all, subsidies paid to farmers will be the same both before and after the reform. The key difference is that in the modified structure, farmers have an incentive to conserve water because they face the true social costs of using additional water, and are compensated when they save water. The better alignment of private incentives with the public good is the magic ingredient that generates positive outcomes for everyone.

The second is the importance of political economy considerations. Even reforms that boost overall welfare are difficult to implement if sizable groups of people lose from it. They will try to make the reforms politically difficult, as seen in protests against farm law reforms. Successful reforms often involve adequately compensating the losers. In this example, governments might be tempted to focus on fiscal savings as the motivation for reducing farm electricity subsidies. However, this would make the reforms politically unfeasible. In contrast, committing to provide the same fiscal support, but as a flat transfer, makes everyone better off while also improving the alignment of incentives as noted above. The fiscal savings will come over time due to improved efficiency.

The third principle is the critical role of public communication and trust in facilitating complex reforms. People worldwide are nervous about change, and often block reforms simply due to a status quo bias. This is why the successful implementation of programmes like Rythu Bandhu, KALIA, and PM-KISAN is a key enabler of the proposed reform. It has shown farmers that income transfers can be made reliably, and this demonstration can build the trust needed for complex reforms. It is also vital to implement reforms gradually, identify and address implementation challenges, communicate with the public about reform goals and how it will benefit everyone, and work to make farmers *want* to adopt the reform and not force it on them. Once established, such a system can pave the way for further reforms to improve agricultural productivity (see Chapter 16).

3.5 Consider implementing an inclusive growth dividend

Many leading economists, including Pranab Bardhan, Vijay Joshi, Sudipto Mundle, Debraj Ray, and former CEA Arvind Subramanian, have recommended that India should adopt variants of a universal basic income (UBI), noting that doing so could nearly eliminate poverty.[27] A UBI would lower targeting and administrative costs, minimize exclusion errors, and offer flexible benefits. Further, global and Indian studies have shown that income transfers are highly beneficial to the poor greatly, and that they spend the money productively and not on alcohol or other 'sin' goods.[28]

Yet, the UBI concept has not gained momentum in India, partly due to the high cost projections, ranging from 3.5 to 10 per cent of GDP. To make a poverty-eliminating UBI fiscally feasible, some proponents have suggested replacing existing welfare schemes, including NREGS and PDS, with a UBI. However, this is politically difficult and may not even be desirable given these programmes' benefits. A more practical approach to deliver the benefits of income transfers may be to decrease the transfer value and introduce it as a *supplement* rather than a substitute to existing programmes.

One specific idea that I have proposed in an essay with Paul Niehaus and Sandip Sukhtankar, and in a detailed paper with Maitreesh Ghatak, is an 'Inclusive Growth Dividend (IGD)', pegged at 1 per cent of GDP (Rs 140/month per person at present). This sum would be transferred monthly to every Indian, with children's allowances paid into their mother's accounts. The investments in Aadhaar and Jan Dhan accounts make it feasible to implement an IGD at scale at a modest administrative cost.[29]

Though the IGD is a universal income transfer, it differs from UBI in key aspects, reflected in the term 'Inclusive Growth Dividend'. First, 'dividend' implies it is one part of a *portfolio* of people's income, unlike 'basic income' which suggests an amount that is enough to live on. Second, 'inclusive' denotes the universality of a programme that reaches every citizen without any exclusion error. As the amount is the same for all citizens, it is proportionately higher for the poor, which makes the IGD inherently progressive and equity-enhancing. Finally, 'growth' signifies that the benefit will expand with the economy, giving every citizen a stake in national growth.

An IGD could be transformative for India. Even at a modest value of Rs 140/month (or around Rs 600/month for a typical household) it would notably reduce poverty, boosting consumption for the poorest 50 per cent of the population by over 10 per cent, and for the poorest 10 per cent by 20 per cent. By allocating children's allowances to their mothers, it would enhance female empowerment and agency. It would boost financial inclusion by activating dormant Jan Dhan accounts, and enable the poor to build savings. It would also facilitate access to lower-interest rate credit, as predictable cash flows improve creditworthiness, and empower the poor to make productivity-enhancing but risky investments, like planting a new crop, by providing some consumption insurance.[30]

An IGD also offers several benefits over alternative ideas like NYAY (explained above), which proposes larger transfers to a smaller, poorer, group. First, it eliminates targeting costs and minimizes exclusion errors. Second, the IGD's modest amount can mitigate poverty, without reducing work incentives, unlike in larger transfer programmes. Third, targeted benefits need to be phased out as incomes grow, which creates disincentives to work because of the potential loss of benefits. Finally, sociological evidence suggests that people care about not just their absolute income, but also their relative position in a community. As a result, non-beneficiaries often resent and try to undermine targeted welfare programmes that reverse community prosperity rankings. An IGD elegantly avoids this challenge by being universal and lifting all boats equally.

Successfully implementing an IGD would boost both the capacity and credibility of the Indian state. Consistently delivering an IGD would mark the first instance of the Indian state reliably providing a benefit to *every* citizen every month. On its own, this would be a signature achievement. Beyond the money, the IGD would foster greater trust in the government among citizens, which can further strengthen state capacity and expand the range of viable policy options. For instance, replacing farmer electricity subsidies with income transfers will be more feasible once the government has proven its ability to reliably deliver regular income transfers to hundreds of millions of Indians.

An IGD can also contribute to economic growth by stimulating demand. Analysts of the Indian economy like Haresh Chawla and Rathin Roy have noted that India's post-1990s economic growth has largely been a top-down growth story. The highest-earning 5–10 per cent of the population drives consumption, indirectly supporting the next 30–40 per cent in smaller enterprises and service jobs catering to this affluent group. However, the bottom 50 per cent has largely been left out of India's growth story.

By putting more money in the hands of the poor, an IGD could provide a bottom-up demand stimulus to the economy. It would not only raise income, but its *predictability*, a crucial factor for demand.

An important recent study of unconditional income transfers in Kenya finds an economic multiplier of 2.4, meaning every dollar given to the poor increased total local income by 2.4 dollars.[31] While boosting demand in settings of full employment usually increases inflation, this study found no increase in inflation, suggesting there was considerable unused capacity. This is a familiar situation in India, with high levels of disguised unemployment and slack capacity (see Chapter 16).

These findings in the Kenya study are also consistent with my own findings that improving NREGS implementation led to a substantial increase in the number of non-agricultural firms and employment in the local economy. More generally, both theory and evidence suggest that a broader consumption base promotes development by allowing firms to recover the fixed costs of investing in more productive capital and technology. Thus, an IGD is likely to have a substantial multiplier effect on the economy by boosting domestic demand, and thereby enhancing both equity and efficiency.

Stronger social protection can also help growth by supporting migration. Globally, cities are growth engines, and migration to cities is a key pathway out of poverty.[32] Research shows that even modest support to the rural poor can increase their productivity and income by covering the cost of *searching* for better opportunities.[33] Thus, a portable IGD can boost both incomes and aggregate productivity by helping workers to seek the best possible livelihood anywhere in India. Conversely, an IGD can also help protect migrants in urban areas from adversity. For instance, the tragic episode of lakhs of migrants walking back to their villages during the COVID-19 lockdown might have been avoidable with an IGD. Having such a system in place could have enabled governments to increase transfers to registered migrant workers, providing them with the means to sustain themselves in cities amidst job losses caused by the lockdown.

Having the IGD infrastructure will also enable integrating beneficiary choice into welfare spending. For instance, people may prefer to delay receipt of IGD funds to receive a lump sum later, to be used for durable goods or other investments.[34] It also facilitates offering citizens a choice between in-kind public benefits such as PDS, schooling, or healthcare, or an income equivalent DBT, allowing them to choose what works best for them. Such a choice-based system can improve the quality and accountability of public services because the government provider will no longer have the poor as captive customers with no other option (see Chapter 9). While choice-based architectures will have to be designed separately by sector, the IGD infrastructure makes it easier to implement such a system at scale, thereby boosting state capacity.

An IGD is also likely to be politically rewarding. Prime Minister Narendra Modi's stated goal of 'Sabka Saath, Sabka Vikaas, Sabka Vishwaas' is laudable, but credibly delivering it is not easy. An IGD provides a promising way of doing so through its combination of universality (sabka saath), promoting broad-based development (sabka vikaas), and building public confidence in the state by credibly delivering a benefit to every Indian every month (sabka vishwaas).

Finally, an IGD can serve as a powerful symbol of social solidarity that all Indians experience together, regardless of their station. The government could consider an option for the wealthy to 'give it up' for some fiscal savings, and thereby build shared solidarity, but the IGD is universal by design with the goal of creating something that is shared equally by every Indian. The idea that such a programme can help create shared citizenship and solidarity has also been highlighted by political scientist Sunil Khilnani, who has made a case for a similar programme.[35]

A well-designed social protection system should ideally promote both equity and long-term growth and development. An IGD would do exactly this, and is hence placed in R1 of Figure 15.1 (item 4). It will support the poor, give them the means and confidence to migrate to better job opportunities, boost demand and productivity, build social solidarity and state capacity, and lay the foundations for broad-based long-term prosperity.

While it may be too early for the Centre to make a fiscal commitment to an IGD for the full country, state governments should consider implementing and evaluating IGD pilots. They could begin in the poorest blocks within the state and implement a universal IGD in these areas. The simplicity of the idea allows any state to implement it on its own.

In recent years, political parties across the ideological spectrum, including the DMK in Tamil Nadu, TMC in West Bengal, Congress in Karnataka, and BJP in Madhya Pradesh have announced or launched income transfer schemes providing Rs 1000 to Rs 2000 per month to female heads of households meeting minimal eligibility criteria, like having a ration card. While not an IGD, they are similar in spirit, as the IGD also proposes larger transfers to women by sending children's entitlements to them. These trends suggest that policymakers are moving in a direction akin to the IGD. Given their large fiscal implications, it is advisable to evaluate these initiatives, and generate insights that could inform state and national discussions on scaling up similar programmes.

Another option is for mining rich states like Odisha, Jharkhand, and Chhattisgarh to use their District Mineral Funds (DMF) for IGD pilot projects and evaluations. DMFs were established to return a portion of natural resource royalties to the residents of mining districts. In practice, DMFs have substantial unspent funds, due to onerous project design and approval rules for utilizing these funds. An IGD using DMF funds would be especially fitting for a pilot and evaluation, as it would pay citizens a 'dividend' based on the mining resources that they have a natural claim over.

Many of India's flagship welfare programmes were scaled up after successful pilots and implementation at the state level. Examples include NREGS (Maharashtra), school midday meals (Tamil Nadu), and PM-KISAN (Telangana). The idea of an IGD is similarly ripe for state-level leadership in both design and evaluation.

3.6 Consider piloting and evaluating an urban employment guarantee programme

While average earnings are higher in urban areas, the migration of lakhs of workers back to their villages during the COVID-19 lockdown revealed that vulnerability may also be higher in urban areas.[36]

This reflects a combination of (a) weaker integration into social and community networks of social insurance in urban areas, and (b) a greater policy priority on providing social protection in rural areas, exemplified by the existence of NREGS in rural areas without a corresponding equivalent in urban areas.

As discussed earlier, research finds that areas that better implemented NREGS had higher wages, employment, and incomes, which far exceed the direct income provided by NREGS. These promising results combined with India's growing urban population suggest that it may make sense to also consider an urban employment guarantee scheme for India. Such a programme could provide modest amounts of training, and create a roster of semi-skilled workers who could be usefully employed in a wide variety of urban public service roles, given the staff shortages in local governments. As with NREGS, the greatest value of such a programme may lie less in the public employment per se, and more in putting upward pressure on the quality of urban private sector jobs.

While details will need to be worked out, there are enough inputs available for states to pilot and test different kinds of models. For instance, Jean Drèze, who played a crucial role in the design of NREGS, has proposed a template for states to consider called DUET (Decentralised Urban Employment and Training), and researchers from the Azim Premji University who produce the annual 'State of Working India' report have also made several suggestions that could be considered for such pilots.[37] Crucially, these pilots should be carefully evaluated to study both processes and impacts, and the results of these studies can inform if and how such programmes should be expanded.

4. Conclusion

A well-functioning social protection and welfare system can promote equity and justice, and also support people in making investments to improve their productivity and thereby contribute to personal and national progress. It is therefore a crucial area that contributes to both growth and development.

Most welfare programmes redistribute resources from taxpayers to those who are less well-off. However, such redistribution typically comes at the cost of reduced efficiency, as shown in this chapter. Modern democracies are willing to make this trade-off because of the intrinsic and instrumental reasons noted above, and also because the democratic process and voter demand provide legitimacy for redistribution and welfare. But, given the very real trade-off between equity and efficiency, it is in the broad social interest to identify policies and programmes where the trade-off is limited, and ideally to focus on R1 ideas that can improve both equity and efficiency.

A central insight of this chapter is that our public discourse on welfare initiatives should move beyond simplistic discussions of whether they are 'freebies', and examine the *details* of design and delivery of specific programmes. As seen in this chapter, we have large categories of 'welfare' and subsidy spending that hurt both equity and efficiency, others that help both, and some that are good on one dimension and weak on the other. Having this conceptual clarity can then help guide reform efforts towards reducing spending on R3 ideas that hurt both equity and efficiency, and increasing fiscal allocations to R1 ideas that help both.

Implementing the ideas in this chapter can help to improve both the design and delivery of welfare programmes in India, and thereby accelerate our progress towards growth, development, and equity goals. While the Centre has a key role to play in designing the architecture of nationwide welfare programmes, there is much to be done at the state level. As with most ideas in this book, state-level leadership on these reforms will not only deliver meaningful improvements in the lives of state residents, but also contribute to shaping the national discourse.

Chapter 16

Jobs, Productivity, and Economic Growth

Economic growth is essential for the quality of life of a nation's citizens. It is a key driver of poverty reduction, and enhances well-being through improved access to food, housing, health, education, and security. Increased tax revenues from growth enable better public goods, service delivery, and programmes to support inclusion. This creates a virtuous cycle, and makes faster economic growth critical for India's development.

Economic growth has two main drivers. The first is mobilizing factors of production such as land, labour, and capital for productive use. The second is increasing productivity to produce *more* output with the *same* amount of inputs. While both channels matter for India, the most important long-term driver of economic growth is higher productivity.

Boosting productivity is also crucial for raising wages and job quality. India's main jobs challenge is not job quantity but job *quality*—defined by wage levels, stability and reliability of wage income, and benefits such as pensions and paid medical leave. However, offering better wages and benefits costs money, and employers can only do so sustainably when the value of employees' output exceeds their cost to the employer. Thus, boosting productivity is the key to steadily improving the quality of jobs in India.

Productivity growth is driven by both firms and governments. While firms are the primary actors in adopting practices and techniques that increase productivity, governments play an essential role in creating the enabling environment for higher productivity.

Government actions profoundly affect productivity in the economy through laws and regulations governing the use of land, labour, and capital; by policies on taxation, bankruptcy, environmental regulation, and promoting competition; and by investing in police and courts to facilitate safety, contract enforcement, and dispute resolution. They can also help improve productivity by building infrastructure such as roads, railways, and ports; providing reliable, competitively priced utilities such as electricity, water, and communications; and improving the quality of education and skilling.

So, improving government effectiveness in providing these enabling conditions can catalyse productivity and economic growth. However, India's public discourse on growth mainly focuses on Central government actions to promote it, though many of the key issues above are in the domain of state governments. So, it is critical to analyse and improve the effectiveness of state-level actions for boosting productivity and job quality. State-led initiative and innovations, followed by rapid replication of successful ones can play a key role in accelerating both growth and development in India.

Boosting productivity and job quality is both intrinsically and instrumentally important for national well-being. Intrinsically, a job is not just a source of income. It also provides identity, dignity, and social engagement. With over 95 per cent of India's population relying primarily on labour income for sustenance, improving job quality will directly improve the welfare of hundreds of millions of Indians.[1] While China's sustained high growth rate has delivered the instrumental benefits of making China an economic and military superpower, it has also transformed the quality of lives of hundreds of millions of Chinese citizens. Increasing productivity has been the key to this transformation.

Increasing economic productivity is much more complex than improving service delivery in a single sector, because it involves improving the functioning of the *entire* economy. Further, most drivers of job creation and economic growth are in the private sector and not in the government. Therefore, achieving this goal will require policymakers to have a nuanced understanding of (a) how high-quality jobs are created, (b) how policies in one sector affect others, creating what economists call 'general equilibrium' effects, and (c) the necessity of transcending individual government department silos for a coordinated policy framework on jobs, productivity, and economic growth.

The chapter comprises three sections. The first outlines key facts on jobs in India. The second presents a conceptual overview of the basic economic determinants of jobs, productivity, and wages; and highlights key challenges faced by the Indian economy. The third presents state-level ideas to improve jobs, productivity, and economic growth. It also discusses how we can balance social goals of worker welfare and environmental protection, alongside policies to promote economic dynamism and growth.

1. Key Facts on Employment and Wages in India

Table 16.1 provides a snapshot of India's employment landscape using data from the 2022–23 Periodic Labour Force Survey (PLFS) for the working age population, defined as those aged fifteen to sixty-four. It presents both overall estimates, and the breakdown by gender and rural versus urban areas.

Key insights from these figures include: only 56 per cent of India's working-age population is in the labour force, with 15 per cent in education or training, and 29 per cent neither looking for work nor studying. Among those in the labour force, 50 per cent are self-employed, 45 per cent work for wages, and 5 per cent are unemployed. Labour force participation is significantly lower for women (34 per cent) than men (79 per cent), and higher in rural (61 per cent) compared to urban areas (53 per cent). However, urban areas have a higher rate of wage employment than rural areas (53 vs 35 per cent), while rural areas have much higher self-employment (61 vs 40 per cent).

Table 16.2 presents key facts on job quality. Self-employed individuals earn an average of Rs 10,331 per month. Among wage

Table 16.1: Snapshot of Employment (15–64 Age Group) by Percentage of the Population

Metric	Total	Male	Female	Rural	Urban
Neither looking for work nor in education	29	5	52	25	31
In education or training	15	16	14	14	16
Labour Force Participation Rate (LFPR)	56	79	34	61	53
Unemployed	*5*	*5*	*6*	*4*	*7*
Self-employed	*50*	*47*	*56*	*61*	*40*
Wage-employed	*45*	*48*	*38*	*35*	*53*

Notes: Data from the Periodic Labour Force Survey (PLFS) 2022–23, in % for the 15–64 age group; numbers are rounded to the nearest integer. The calculations use the 'current working status' (CWS) variable.

workers, those on monthly salaries earn Rs 20,071 per month, over double the earnings of casual labourers, who earned only Rs 9,109 per month.[2] Salaried employees with a written contract earn 1.8 times more than those without one (Rs 28,800 vs Rs 15,946). In every category, men earn more than women, reflecting both more days worked and higher wage rates.[3] Finally, urban earnings were also higher in every category.

These figures highlight that India's primary jobs challenge is job *quality*. While the unemployment rate is only 5 per cent, 70 per cent of those who do work are either self-employed (50 per cent) or in casual wage employment (20 per cent). Both are characterized by low productivity, and low earnings averaging around Rs 10,000 per month. Other key indicators of job quality include having a written contract, which correlated with higher job stability and earnings; and social security benefits such as gratuity, provident fund, health, or maternity benefits. Panels B and C show that only 21 per cent of those in wage jobs have a written employment contract, and only 22 per cent have any social security. These shares represent only

Table 16.2: Quality of Employment (15–64 Age Group)

Metric	Total	Male	Female	Rural	Urban
Panel A: By Earnings					
Self-employed Gross Earnings (past 30 days)	50 per cent of Working Population				
Average Monthly Earnings (Rs)	10,331	13,838	3,533	7,585	14,175
Salaried Wage (calendar month)	30 per cent of Working Population				
Average Monthly Earnings (Rs)	20,071	21,593	16,031	16,817	21,129
Average Monthly Earnings with Written Contract (Rs)	28,800	30,769	23,657	23,879	31,242
Average Monthly Earnings with No Contract (Rs)	15,946	17,285	12,361	11,407	17,113
Casual Wage (weekly earnings in past 7 days scaled to month)	20 per cent of Working Population				
Average Monthly Earnings (Rs)	9,109	10,076	5,736	8,628	9,990
Panel B: By Contract—among wage employed; [per cent of all those who are employed]					
Written Contract	21 [10]	21 [10]	23 [9]	19 [7]	23 [13]
No Contract	79 [90]	79 [90]	77 [91]	81 [93]	77 [87]
Panel C: By Benefits—among wage employed; [per cent of all those who are employed]					
No Social Security	78 [90]	78 [89]	78 [91]	82 [93]	75 [86]
Any Social Security	22 [10]	22 [11]	22 [9]	18 [7]	25 [14]

Notes: Data from the Periodic Labour Force Survey (PLFS) 2022–23, in % for the 15–64 age group.

10 per cent of the labour force, and under 6 per cent of the working age population.

Beyond low wages, the poor also face considerable uncertainty in *whether* a job will be available on any given day. These costs are captured well in a recent feature story on unemployment in India, which notes that:

> On a wintry morning, even as the smog remains, hundreds of men and women gather on the sidewalk on the outskirts of Uttar Pradesh's capital city, Lucknow. A truck approaches the gathering, and a man sticks out his head from the truck and yells out the number of people he's hiring that day—ranging from a couple dozen to the hundreds. Immediately, he's ambushed by people with raised hands, hoping to get paid a daily wage so they can feed their families.[4]

This story reflects the struggles of millions of Indians reliant on casual wage labour for sustenance. These human costs are magnified, as the average income-earner supports 2.7 dependants.[5] This is why improving living standards in India depends critically on improving worker productivity and creating more high-quality jobs to generate higher, more reliable incomes. Creating better jobs may also raise labour-force participation, as people are more likely to work if better jobs are available. This will further boost GDP, GDP per capita, and economic well-being.

However, while there is broad agreement on the need for higher-quality jobs and faster growth, there is less clarity or consensus among policymakers on the most effective, and cost-effective, policies to promote this goal. This is partly because job creation mainly happens in the private sector, and the ways in which public interventions affect private sector actions are often indirect and not easily visible. In fact, many of India's policies that aim to support jobs actually *hurt* job creation. This is why we need to first understand key economic concepts that drive productivity, jobs, and wages.

2. Key Concepts

2.1 Some basic economics of growth, productivity, jobs, and wages

The output of an economy depends on two key factors. First is the quantity of inputs like land, capital, and labour—known as 'factors of production'—mobilized for production. Second is the productivity of these inputs, known as 'total factor productivity' (TFP). So, countries can increase production by (i) mobilizing more factors of production, and (ii) increasing TFP. Investing in education and health is usually considered as increasing an input ('human capital') into production, but it can also be considered as boosting the productivity of labour, since it increases output per worker.[6]

Lower-income countries can grow through both channels, because they have more room to increase factor mobilization. So, countries like India can increase per capita income by boosting labour force participation (especially for women), channelling savings from unproductive assets like gold into productive investments, and improving the quality of education and health. However, over time, once the gains from increasing input mobilization are realized, the main source of growth is increasing TFP, which can come from adopting new technologies, better management, and economies of scale.

Most production in an economy takes place within firms of various sizes. Firms create jobs when hiring someone brings in more revenue than the cost. The quality of jobs, reflected in wages and benefits, depends on employee productivity and the demand for their skills. In competitive labour markets, with many potential employers, wages will typically reflect worker productivity. This pattern is confirmed in Indian data, where there is a strong positive correlation between workers' productivity, and their earnings.[7] Thus, the best long-term way to improve job quality is to increase worker productivity.

There are three main ways of increasing worker productivity. First, increasing physical capital per worker: for instance, a farmer can plough more land per hour with a tractor than with a bullock. Second, increasing human capital (education, skills, and health), as healthier, more educated workers are typically more productive. Third, by using better management techniques and deploying newer technologies. Note that the last two channels are connected, since better education is often a prerequisite for workers to be able to use more advanced technologies.

Increasing worker productivity usually leads to higher wages and incomes. But, this need not be true if the productivity growth is in a sector with slow-growing demand. Here, higher output can lower prices, and offset productivity gains.[8] This issue is commonly seen in agricultural staple crops. For instance, despite rising rice productivity per acre in India, farmers' incomes have not matched productivity growth since demand for rice has grown slower than growth in output, putting downward pressure on prices.[9]

Thus, while productivity growth is very important for economic growth, it is *not enough* by itself to generate wage and economic growth. Converting productivity growth into economic growth also requires *dynamism* in the economy whereby the resources (especially labour) that are freed up by increasing productivity in sectors with slow-growing demand are absorbed in other sectors with greater demand and value addition.

This point highlights the potential conflict between boosting productivity and jobs. Often, increasing productivity may *reduce* jobs, as fewer workers can do the same work. This tension has historically made workers, social thinkers, and even Mahatma Gandhi wary of labour-saving technologies, favouring higher employment even at the cost of lower productivity.[10] However, this view is misguided because it assumes that the economy is static. However, dynamic economies create new products and services that deliver value to consumers. So, even if a firm hires fewer workers due to a new technology, the higher wages and profits that result will create demand and jobs in *other* sectors. This raises the question: Where do the new jobs in other sectors come from?

Entrepreneurs and business leaders play a key role in this process. They identify new opportunities for creating value; mobilize factors of production to create goods and services (and thereby create jobs); and manage production, distribution, sales, and revenue generation. They also innovate to improve productivity and reduce costs, and create new products that generate value for consumers. Of course, firms themselves can get complacent over time. This is why it is essential for policymakers to promote competition and entry of new firms to facilitate a dynamic economy.

Over time, the combination of *new* products, competition among producers, and choice for consumers has been one of the most important sources of improving human welfare.[11] One way of seeing this is that nine out of the ten most valuable US firms in 2017 *did not even exist* fifty years earlier in 1967! Further, forty-one out of the fifty most valuable US firms in 2017 were not on this list in 1967.[12] This process of firms getting created and shut down, and growing and shrinking, in response to changing technology and tastes, is an essential part of the dynamism of an economy and is what was famously referred to as the process of 'creative destruction' by economist Joseph Schumpeter.

To summarize, accelerating the creation of high-quality jobs requires (a) boosting productivity in all sectors of the economy, and (b) increasing the dynamism of the economy to allow factors of production like land, capital, and labour to be easily reallocated to the firms and sectors of the economy that generate the most value.

2.2 Structural transformation and Indian exceptionalism

Over time, countries have improved productivity, created higher-quality jobs, and got rich through a process of structural transformation, in which the share of workers in primary sectors (agriculture, forestry, mining, and fishing) decreases and the share in the secondary (manufacturing) and tertiary (services) sectors increases.[13] Historically, the greatest gains in output per worker have come from moving workers from agriculture to manufacturing. There are three reasons for this.

First, and most important, moving workers out of agriculture into assembly-line manufacturing enabled specialization, division of labour, more capital per worker, better management, and economies of scale. This combination enabled a dramatic increase in worker productivity.[14] Second, the exportability of manufactured goods allowed countries to access much larger markets, which in turn, enabled further economies of scale and productivity gains.[15] Third, it enabled the creation of large numbers of higher-paying and more reliable jobs (compared to agriculture) which were accessible even to those with only basic education. This contributed to *broadly distributed prosperity*, which boosted demand in all sectors and made it viable for firms to invest in capital and technologies in other sectors, as well as new research and knowledge. Over time, this allowed countries to develop a diverse set of technologically sophisticated industries.[16]

Unfortunately, India's growth trajectory has been hampered by policies that made it difficult to develop low-skill intensive manufacturing in India (discussed briefly in the next section). However, despite its relatively poor performance in building low-skill intensive manufacturing, India managed to accelerate growth in the 1990s and especially in the 2000s based on exporting knowledge-intensive services.

India's unique journey, diverging from historical norms, was facilitated by several factors. Crucially, the arrival of the Internet in the 1990s significantly reduced global communications costs, transforming many non-tradable services into IT-enabled *tradable* ones. Second, India's focus on tertiary education (see Chapter 11), and legacy of English-medium instruction provided a large pool of English-speaking graduates who could provide IT-enabled services globally at much lower costs. Third, the setting up of backend offices by world-leading companies trained Indian managers and employees to meet global standards of quality and reliability. These managers later moved to other firms or set up their own IT-service firms, and accelerated the rapid diffusion of IT-enabled service firms in India who could serve global markets.[17] Today, more than 1400 multinational corporations (MNCs) have set up global capability centres in India that employ 1.4 million highly skilled Indians and generate revenues over $35 billion.[18]

India's service sector has served us well. However, while it has succeeded at building scale and exporting to global markets, it has been less successful at creating large numbers of good-quality jobs for *low-skilled* workers.[19] On the positive side, well-paid professionals producing tradable output for the global 'dollar economy' create demand and jobs for construction workers, drivers, cooks, security guards, and other non-traded service providers in the local 'rupee economy'.[20] This helps India, because non-traded service sector workers earn *more* than they would in agriculture. However, the limitation is that these non-traded service sectors, employing large numbers of Indians, are likely to have slower productivity growth than what is possible in low-skilled manufacturing.

This discussion has three main implications for India's jobs strategy. First, we need to accelerate structural transformation by sharply reducing the fraction of our workforce in the primary sector. Second, expansion of low-skilled manufacturing, for both domestic and global markets, is crucial for creating millions of productive salaried jobs for workers without a college degree. Third, we need to continuously improve service sector worker productivity through better education and skills, management, and technology; and use technology to make more services tradable to benefit from both global scale, and the higher ability to pay in richer countries, which in turn will sustain higher wages in India.

However, we have a long way to go in our journey of structural transformation. A striking indicator is that over 45 per cent of India's labour force is still employed in agriculture.[21] This is over *60 times greater* than the 0.7 per cent in a high-income country like the US, and also much higher than that in middle-income countries like Brazil (9.4 per cent), Mexico (13.4 per cent), and China (27.7 per cent). The large share of India's workforce in agriculture is one of the key drivers of low productivity in the Indian economy, and is a specific example of the more general problem of factor misallocation.

2.3 Factor misallocation

A key driver of productivity in an economy is whether factors of production are allocated to their most valuable use. In other words, they should be deployed to the sectors that create the most value, and to the most productive firms within each sector. Economists use the term 'misallocation' to describe inefficient factor allocation. Intuitively, societies with high barriers to reallocating factors of production from less to more productive uses have higher misallocation. Unfortunately, the Indian economy suffers from high factor misallocation, which contributes to low productivity as seen in the examples below.[22]

Labour

A leading indicator and driver of low productivity in India is the large share of the workforce in agriculture and in rural areas. Agricultural productivity in India is low due to small and fragmented land holdings, limited mechanization, and subsidies that encourage small farmers to continue in agriculture despite low productivity.[23] Further, agricultural work is seasonal, with many days requiring minimal labour. Thus, averaged over the year, rural workers often face high 'disguised' employment, which refers to the idea of being 'employed' but working below full potential.[24]

In contrast, urbanization boosts productivity for several reasons. First, it provides larger market sizes, which facilitates greater specialization, division of labour, and scale.[25] Second, it increases the varieties of products and services available, making it attractive to live in urban areas. Third, the greater ease of interaction with large numbers of people is vital in creative and knowledge sectors that rely on frequent exchange of ideas. This is why urban areas attract highly educated and productive workers, whose presence generates an employment multiplier with each skilled job creating additional unskilled jobs.[26] Fourth, higher population density and lower search costs improve productivity by increasing choice for consumers and competition among providers, compelling them to improve the quality and cost-effectiveness of services provided.

Overall, urbanization is a key driver of productivity growth, higher incomes and higher quality of life through the availability of a larger number of differentiated products and services.[27] A simple way to see this is that GDP per capita is more than three times higher in urban versus rural India, and a primary channel for reduction in rural poverty is the migration of a working-age member to urban areas.[28] Indeed, Harvard economist Edward Glaeser has described the *city as mankind's greatest invention*, and a critical driver of the increase in living standards since the Industrial Revolution.[29]

It is critical to understand the close link between urbanization and higher productivity, given India's history of policies that encourage people to stay in rural areas. For instance, the NREGS is only available in rural areas, and the PDS was historically not portable, and only accessible in one's home area ration shop. Thus, migrants have to give up access to the two most important social welfare benefits. Further, agricultural subsidies are only available in rural areas, which also induces people to not migrate. On the other side of the equation, we also deter migration through under-investment in urban rental housing and other urban amenities. Yet, the fact that people still *choose* to migrate from rural areas highlights how much worse their prospects in the villages are.[30]

Put together, the combination of low productivity and disguised unemployment in rural areas, and much higher productivity in urban areas, suggests that increasing rural to urban migration, and reducing the fraction of workers in agriculture, will raise output per worker in *both* rural and urban areas.[31] While considerable migration is happening, it is likely too little, reflecting policy choices that inhibit rather than promote migration.

There is also significant misallocation of labour across firms *within* the manufacturing sector. Given productivity differences across firms in a sector, overall productivity can be increased by reallocating workers from less to more productive firms. This would imply growing productive firms, which would further improve economies of scale and efficiency, and shutting down less productive firms. In practice, several policies in India have constrained and continue to limit such reallocation.

These include: (a) the history of reserving low-skill labour-intensive products for small-scale industries, which restricted the growth of productive firms,[32] (b) stricter labour laws for firms with more employees, which deterred firms from growing, (c) restrictions on closing non-viable firms, which kept workers in low productivity jobs, and (d) regulatory red tape for setting up new firms.[33] While these constraints are being eased, their cumulative legacy still lingers. One indicator is the smaller scale of Indian manufacturing firms. For instance, even garment-exporting plants in India rarely employ more than 2000 workers, whereas in Bangladesh, many such plants have over 10,000 workers.[34] This disparity in scale directly affects productivity, leading to higher unit costs in India.[35]

India's emphasis on tertiary education over primary education and skills, combined with regulatory hurdles for larger-scale plants, has led to better performance in high-skill intensive manufacturing industries (requiring fewer workers), than in low-skill intensive ones like apparel, shoes, and toys which could employ millions. As economist Rathin Roy has noted, India is good at making high-quality shirts priced at Rs 2000, but average-quality Rs 300 shirts are more likely to be imported from Bangladesh, or Vietnam. This represents a significant missed opportunity, given the larger market size and job-creating potential in this low-cost segment.

In summary, reducing labour misallocation is crucial for improving productivity, wages, and living standards. As Manish Sabharwal has noted, this requires accelerating multiple transitions: farm to non-farm, rural to urban, subsistence self-employment to wage employment, and from informal to formal firms (also a proxy for firm size).[36] Achieving this will require both a reduction in reasons for workers to remain in low-productivity roles, and an increase in the capacity of industry and services to absorb more workers. It will also require reducing misallocation of *other* factors of production.

Credit and Capital

Credit and capital are key inputs into production. A well-functioning financial system plays a critical role in economic growth by directing funds from savers looking for high rates of returns to the most promising businesses and entrepreneurs who can generate those high returns.[37] Conversely, if the financial system is weak, productive and innovative firms find it difficult to obtain capital and grow.

Several studies show that Indian firms are credit-constrained, and often have rates of return to capital that are much higher than the going interest rate.[38] This implies that expanding credit to these firms would allow them to grow. However, this growth is not happening because firms are unable to obtain credit.

Why would banks not make loans to such firms, even if the loans would be profitable? The problem is that businesses are risky, and while they may be profitable on *average*, individual businesses will often fail. Thus, a key determinant of banks' economic viability is their ability to minimize losses and recover loans made to unsuccessful businesses. This requires a speedy and transparent bankruptcy and debt-recovery process.

However, India's slow and opaque bankruptcy process impedes banks' ability to recover bad loans, also known as non-performing assets (NPAs). This has two costs. First, funds tied up in NPAs are unavailable to lend to productive high-growth firms, limiting their access to credit. Second, it makes bank officials risk-averse in lending since they are more likely to be penalized for unrecovered loans than rewarded for successful ones. One measure of this risk aversion is the large proportion of banks' assets held in low-yielding but safe government securities, far in excess of their regulatory requirement for maintaining a minimum statutory liquidity ratio (SLR).[39] Consequently, a large fraction of Indians' savings funds government expenditure (which is often very inefficient as seen in Chapter 5) rather than productive investments in the private sector.

Overall, weaknesses in India's debt recovery institutions have led to considerable misallocation of savings and credit. Large amounts of national savings are tied up in unproductive 'bad loans', making these funds unavailable to productive firms to start or expand. On the positive side, studies show that better debt recovery institutions, and reducing judicial vacancies (see Chapter 14), can alleviate credit constraints and boost economic activity. These results highlight the importance of investing in state capacity for contract enforcement and dispute resolution for accelerating economic growth.

Land

A third key factor of production is land. Similar to capital and labour, land is misallocated when used for low productivity purposes as opposed to higher productivity ones. Thus, enabling smooth transfer of land across uses and users is key to reducing land misallocation and increasing overall productivity. Unfortunately, the Indian state has underinvested in public goods for efficient land markets, and overinvested in rules and regulations that inhibit efficient land use.

One example of underinvestment is the absence of a unified land titling system, which inhibits the use of land as collateral for credit, as well as leasing and selling land to those who can make more productive use of it. One measure of the cost of unclear land titles is the large volume of land-related litigation, with nearly two-thirds of all civil litigation in trial courts stemming from land disputes (see Chapter 14).

Governments in India also place several, often unnecessary, obstacles in converting agricultural lands to more efficient uses. A recent article by an entrepreneur trying to start a business on *his own* agricultural land noted how painful the process was even in a state like Maharashtra, which leads on ease of doing business indicators.[40] While governments have tried to simplify some steps and improve their 'ease of doing business' score, this score only captures rules on paper and not how they are enforced in reality. In practice, local officials have significant discretion in approving land conversion requests, and delay projects extensively, often to extort bribes.

India's land regulations, aimed at protecting small and marginal landholders from exploitation and displacement, inadvertently limit economies of scale, which are critical for productivity in both agriculture and industry.[41] While safeguarding such landholders is essential, measures like the Land Acquisition Act of 2013 may have excessively hindered efficient land use and productivity growth. Thus, a key policy design challenge is to develop strategies to optimize the productive potential and value of land on one hand, and ensure that the poor can obtain a share of this value on the other.

Misallocation of other factors

India also suffers from misallocation of intermediate production inputs such as electricity and transport. While the fiscal and environmental costs of free electricity to farmers have been discussed in Chapters 6 and 15, this policy also adversely affects industry. In theory, subsidies for agricultural power should be financed in state budgets, but in reality, states often cannot afford to meet DISCOMs' losses. This results in higher tariffs for industrial users to cross-subsidize agricultural users, increasing the costs faced by Indian industry relative to global competitors, and reducing its competitiveness. Similarly, using higher freight tariffs in railways to cross-subsidize passenger traffic increases the logistics costs of Indian manufacturing relative to competitor nations.

Charging higher prices for water, electricity, or transport to high-income *end users* to subsidize low-income users can be justified, akin to a progressive consumption tax. However, charging higher prices to *intermediate* industrial users who use these inputs for final production hurts economic activity, output, and employment. This is exactly analogous to the costs of high import tariffs prior to the 1991 reforms. Although intended to raise revenue from duties on luxury goods and to protect domestic industries, these tariffs impeded the import of essential intermediate capital goods for potential exporters. Just like eliminating tariffs on intermediate goods helped boost productivity, exports, and economic activity in India,[42] removing the intermediate input cross-subsidy burdens on industrial users will reduce misallocation and increase economic efficiency and activity.

Summary of misallocation

There are five key messages from the discussion above: (1) India suffers from significant misallocation of key factors of production, and reducing misallocation will directly improve productivity, (2) there are many *unseen* intersectoral linkages created by policies like cross-subsidies and rural-biased welfare programmes that contribute to misallocation, (3) taxes and subsidies usually increase misallocation by altering competitive market prices, implying that policies to support the poor should use income transfers more than price subsidies (as noted in Chapter 15), (4) regulatory frictions to closing non-viable firms on one hand, and to the creation and expansion of new firms on the other, contribute to misallocation and low productivity, and (5) policies that inhibit productive firms from scaling contribute to misallocation since larger firms are typically more productive, and reallocating factors of production from inefficient smaller firms to larger firms will usually increase average productivity.

2.4 Multiple binding constraints

The issues discussed above are well known to economic policy commentators in India. Several reports, including government-commissioned ones, have stressed the need to reform labour laws, simplify land acquisition for industrialization, reduce logistics costs, and speed up debt recovery. However, each reform has political costs, and generating political support for reforms requires demonstrating their positive impact to voters.

The problem in practice is that investment decisions by private companies may not respond much to individual reforms, if there are still *other* binding constraints to scale. So, for instance, labour law reforms by themselves may not suffice to expand scale and productivity if firms still face higher costs of capital, land, and logistics compared to global competitors. Thus, while individual reforms are likely to help on the margin, they may not generate enough 'visible' impact to be worth the political cost.

This is why successful reforms that have generated a major impact on productivity and economic growth (such as in the early 1990s) have often taken place during times of stress and external pressure that made it possible to alleviate *multiple* binding constraints at the same time. The key lesson for chief ministers who seek to jump-start jobs, productivity, and economic growth in their states is to identify politically feasible ways of simultaneously alleviating multiple constraints to productivity and scale.[43]

3. An Action Agenda for State Governments

3.1 Assign responsibility for jobs, productivity, and economic growth

Despite the centrality of jobs and economic growth to citizens' welfare, *no one* in a state government is primarily responsible for delivering this goal, due to the excessive siloing of ministries and departments and limited coordination across them. The Central government has entities like the Department of Economic Affairs in the Ministry of Finance, and NITI Aayog that aim to take an integrated view of the economy, and help with policy coordination. However, such entities are generally lacking at the state level.

Finance departments allocate budgets, but focus on the *affordability* of departmental requests rather than the implications of spending for growth. Commercial Tax departments focus on GST *collections* but not on promoting economic growth. State Planning departments typically focus on collating data and reports, and play limited roles in policy formulation or coordination. Departments of Labour monitor compliance with labour laws but do not focus on creating *new* jobs. Rural Development departments have programmes for rural livelihood generation, but often overlook that aiding rural-to-urban migration may create better jobs for the rural poor. Municipal and Urban Administration departments struggle to meet existing urban needs, and rarely encourage more migration to urban areas. Housing departments aim to build subsidized housing on government-owned land for some beneficiaries, but seldom consider facilitating markets for affordable *rental* housing in urban areas.

Even among ministries promoting economic activity, there is excessive siloing, typically into departments such as industries, MSME (micro, small, and medium enterprises), textiles, and cooperatives. Further, these ministries mainly focus on securing budgets for subsidies and incentives and on how to allocate them, as opposed to promoting overall economic activity. For instance, even in a highly industrialized state like Maharashtra, the first policy listed on the Ministry of Textiles' homepage is the provision of power subsidies![44] However, subsidies by themselves rarely improve productivity.

So, a top priority for state governments should be to constitute an empowered task force, reporting to the chief minister, focused on improving job quality, *productivity*, and economic growth (JPEG). Led by the chief secretary, or equivalently senior officer,[45] the JPEG task force should include key secretaries and department heads. Its main role would be to take an *integrated view of the economy*, paying attention to the many ways policies and actions in one department affect others, and identifying the most effective combination of top-down and bottom-up actions to boost productivity, and job quality. Specific actions for such a task force are discussed below.

3.2 Focus less on concessions to specific investors and more on providing high-quality public goods, which benefits *all* actors in the economy

An encouraging development for India is that several states have started getting serious about crafting and executing economic transformation strategies, with states like UP, Maharashtra, Tamil Nadu, Gujarat, and Karnataka setting targets to rapidly become trillion-dollar economies. However, in practice, the main strategy to achieve this goal has centred on identifying priority sectors for the state, and attracting investors by providing concessions or incentives.

However, a key limitation of an incentive or concession-driven approach is that it can lead to a competitive race to the bottom among states, draining them of resources needed for investing in public goods that improve *overall* productivity. A second concern is that it favours large industrialists who can negotiate across states and obtain favourable terms, disadvantaging thousands of smaller enterprises who generate far more jobs. Finally, a system of 'customized' incentive packages is a fertile setting for corruption and crony capitalism, whereby industrialists pay off politicians and decision-makers, receiving taxpayer funds as 'incentives' in return.

States should indeed compete for investment, but the competition should be based on improving fundamentals of doing business, that benefit *all* firms and not just a select few. This highlights the importance of strengthening the areas covered in Chapters 11–15. As those chapters note, these topics are both intrinsically important for better quality of life, and also *instrumentally* important for improving productivity and growth.

Improving education and skills will directly boost productivity and wages over time. Better health and lower pollution will also boost productivity. Improving policing and public safety will boost labour force participation, especially among women, and directly boost economic output. Investing in judicial capacity and improving contract enforcement will unlock land and capital for productive use, and encourage additional investments. Finally, reliable, portable social protection systems will give workers the confidence to pursue productivity-enhancing activities like migration. Importantly, each of these points can also be used to market a state and attract private investments.

This is not a utopian ideal. For instance, Gujarat attracts investors with fewer subsidies because it reformed electricity distribution so that industrial users are not overcharged to cross-subsidize power for agriculture. Similarly, states that invest in district courts and bring down case pendency rates can use this data to attract investors. Actual data on such metrics may be more credible to investors than 'ease of doing business' rankings that are based on paper metrics, as opposed to ease of doing business in practice.

In many ways, the 'incentive-based' approach to attract investments reflects the need to *compensate for state failures* in providing the core public goods and services needed to build a better India. The problem is that this risks a negative cycle of public funds being deployed for incentives to *individual* investors rather than being used to invest in public goods that will benefit all citizens. Rather, states should aim to create a 'virtuous cycle' whereby they invest in better public goods and policies to attract investments, which will generate higher tax revenues, which can be reinvested in even better public goods.

In my conversations with senior officials, many have agreed with these concerns and privately express doubts about the incentive-based approach to attracting investments. However, they often face a 'race to the bottom', with firms shopping across states for the best deal they can get and threatening to invest elsewhere if a state does not match other offers. So, it may not be practical to avoid incentives altogether. Further, attracting large investors can have genuine economic benefits, including forward and backward linkages with distributors and suppliers. So, how should state governments proceed? The principles and ideas below may offer some guidance.

First, aim to attract investments by alleviating multiple binding constraints such as land, utilities, transport connectivity, and single-window clearances for setting up operations and annual renewals. One way to do this is to use special economic zones (SEZs) more effectively to focus on scale. While SEZs have been set up in many Indian states, they have underperformed relative to SEZs in China and even Bangladesh. One reason is that we have too many sub-scale SEZs as opposed to a few truly large ones that can achieve globally competitive scales.[46]

Second, utilize SEZs for more than just single-window clearances; use them to pilot deeper reforms to reduce factor misallocation. States could rationalize labour laws, simplify regulatory burdens, and lower compliance costs within SEZs. While these reforms could be done state-wide, political challenges may make SEZs more practical for initial experimentation, mirroring China's approach. If successful, these reforms can be expanded across the state. This approach ensures that *all* firms within the SEZ benefit from regulatory reforms and not just those with favourable deals.[47] Further, SEZs should be jointly owned by the government and a private-sector partner, with the latter managing operations.[48] This will allow the SEZ to be run with private-sector management standards, and with well-aligned incentives for making it a success.

Third, to the extent that large investors expect additional concessions, it would be better to offer wage subsidies, based on the number of people employed rather than a capital subsidy based on the volume of investment. Indian industry is already capital-intensive, and what we need to encourage is more labour-intensive rather than capital-intensive industries. It may even make sense to offer an increasing schedule of wage subsidies as a function of people employed to encourage truly large-scale manufacturing units that employ tens of thousands of workers in sectors like apparel and shoes.

Fourth, aim to subsidize training and skilling. Since employers often best understand their skill needs, state governments should incentivize large employers to establish dedicated training institutes, offering to fund the training of workers employed by the investor. This could be a more effective use of skilling budgets than spending it on skilling 'degree mills' who lack strong industry connections. It would be a win-win subsidy that benefits both investors and workers. In exchange for paying for the training, governments could negotiate with employers to certify the acquired skills and provide a credential to workers. This will improve worker mobility and bargaining power, enabling them to obtain higher wages corresponding to their improved skills and productivity.

The last two recommendations contrast with India's production-linked incentive (PLI) scheme, which provides incentives to manufacturers in fourteen selected sectors based on production volume. The PLI scheme incentivizes scale, which is sensible. However, one key limitation is that it mainly targets knowledge and capital-intensive sectors rather than low-skill labour-intensive ones. So, while it *may* serve national security purposes, like reducing import dependence in critical sectors, the PLI scheme in its current form is unlikely to create the millions of low-skilled jobs we need.[49] Further, investing for strategic security reasons is best done at the national government level. So, it makes even more sense for states to attract investment by subsidizing wages and training to encourage large-scale investments in low-skilled labour-intensive manufacturing.

In summary, my advice for state governments on attracting investments centres on four key principles. First, strengthen the provision of essential public goods and use outcome data from such investments to attract investors. Second, alleviate multiple constraints together to see a meaningful increase in investments, and use SEZs for this purpose. Third, while it is fine to motivate reform actions by wanting to attract a few key investors such as anchor investors in an SEZ, governments should focus on actions that benefit *all* firms in *all* sectors and not just a favoured few. While some sectoral emphasis is fine, particularly in low-skill labour-intensive sectors, the focus should be on policy actions to boost productivity and job quality in the *overall* economy. Finally, if firms still expect incentives and subsidies, they should be directed towards labour and not capital.

3.3 Launch a structural transformation mission

One way for the JPEG task force to focus on the fundamental drivers of productivity is to launch a structural transformation mission. Such a mission would recognize that growth will not come simply from setting aspirational targets, or even from attracting investments, but that it will be the organic result of accelerating deeper structural shifts in the economy: from agriculture to manufacturing or services; from rural to urban; from informal to formal; and from self-employment to wage employment.

This acceleration will require both reducing frictions that sub-optimally keep people in agriculture and rural areas, and those that hinder migration into urban areas. For example, India's agriculture policies contribute to slowing structural transformation. While these subsidies are often critiqued for their fiscal burden, their deeper cost may be that they impede structural transformation by keeping small and marginal land under cultivation, even when these are not economically viable without subsidies.

Fertilizer and electricity subsidies artificially lower the cost of agricultural inputs, while procurement subsidies inflate the selling price. Profitability analysis suggests that many small and marginal farms in India *destroy* value, as the true unsubsidized cost of inputs deployed, including family labour, far exceeds the output's economic value.[50] Economically unsustainable agriculture is also extended by episodic loan waivers.

This plethora of subsidies is justified by the need to (a) support farmers, and (b) ensure food security for the country. Both are worthy goals. But it is possible to achieve both goals much more efficiently. Food security can be achieved with greater productive efficiency by making it easier to consolidate land and farm at larger scales. Farmers can be supported more efficiently by making unconditional income payments rather than through subsidies. Overall, India needs an economic strategy that reduces the number of workers in agriculture and increases productivity and incomes of those who remain.

The good news is that Indian policymakers in recent years have started switching to income-based support for farmers such as Telangana's Rythu Bandhu scheme, Odisha's KALIA scheme, and the nationwide PM-KISAN scheme. However, while it is politically much easier to *add* benefits, no state has yet combined the expansion of income-based support with a corresponding *reduction* in distortionary subsidies.

A far-reaching reform for states would be to craft a 'structural transformation' strategy, whereby they phase out major subsidies such as free electricity for farmers, and replace them with an equivalent unconditional annual income transfer to farmers proportional to land holding, capped at 5 or 10 acres. Such a strategy would compensate farmers for the subsidy loss, while incentivizing water conservation, and selection of crops suitable for their agro-climatic zones. A similar approach could apply to fertilizer subsidies (especially urea), though this comes under the purview of the Centre.[51]

A former state finance secretary once sagely told me: 'It will be much better for the country, if we simply take the total cost of our agricultural subsidies and provide it as a lump-sum annual payment to farmers. This will reduce ecologically unsustainable agriculture, and also free up land and labour for more productive uses.' This is exactly right, and states that are able to embark on reforms along these lines will be able to accelerate their structural transformation and development trajectories.

An even bolder reform would guarantee these payments to farmers for five to ten years, even if they *do not cultivate* anything, and even if they *sell* their land. While paying farmers for not cultivating might seem counter-intuitive, the fiscal cost would be equivalent to current subsidy expenditures. The aim of the income transfer is to maintain the social protection provided by current subsidies, while freeing farmers to deploy their land to its most productive use, which need not be farming. Such an approach will both unlock the value of small and marginal land holdings, and also increase average agricultural productivity. As many experts have noted, the best way to double farmers' income may be to reduce the number of people in farming, and increase the productivity of the remaining ones.

This shift out of agriculture need not involve people changing their occupations after decades of farming, which is difficult and disruptive. Rather, we should aim to accelerate the transition of the better-educated *children* of farmers and farm labourers out of agriculture. This is consistent with evidence that nearly half the global decline in agricultural employment over time was driven by new cohorts entering the labour market.[52]

Public discourse on reforming agricultural subsidies often focuses on the fiscal burden. However, the problem with this approach is that it loses the trust of farmers who see the reforms as trying to cut their benefits, and protest in response. Rather, the more critical reason to reform the subsidies is to reduce misallocation of land, labour, and water, and increase overall productivity in the economy. Farmers themselves understand that our current model of agriculture is both economically and ecologically unsustainable. So, shifting the public discourse on subsidy reform by highlighting its importance for water conservation, and boosting growth and productivity while preserving the *same fiscal value of support for farmers*, may help make these reforms more politically feasible.

One concern with stopping cultivation on unviable farms is that it may hurt food security. However, there are many untapped ways of boosting agricultural productivity, especially by increasing the scale and mechanization of farms. One promising approach may be to encourage more large-scale contract farming, whereby large buyers can help improve farm productivity by enabling scale and simultaneously alleviating several constraints, including seeds, extension services, credit, price guarantees, and marketing. Of course, in practice, private companies may exploit farmers due to their asymmetry in power, which has made policymakers wary of allowing contract farming. However, rather than discouraging contract farming, a better approach to protect farmers would be to encourage competition among contract farming companies, including by creating *public* and cooperative options; consistent with the principles outlined in Chapter 9.[53]

To accelerate structural transformation, we need to both decrease employment in rural areas and increase migration to urban areas. This will be facilitated by building a robust, portable welfare system using ideas such as making PDS benefits portable, providing a portable income supplement like the Inclusive Growth Dividend (IGD), and having an urban jobs guarantee programme (all discussed in Chapter 15). Such measures will enable those stuck in low-productivity rural jobs to more confidently look for higher-productivity urban options. This discussion highlights that a well-designed social protection architecture should be viewed not merely as welfare, but as an investment for improving individual and aggregate productivity in the Indian economy.

More generally, the JPEG task force should recognize that an *urbanization strategy* is vital for boosting productivity and earnings. So, state governments should proactively invest in urban infrastructure to make rural-urban migration more attractive. Currently, most urban policymaking in India is reactive, playing 'catch-up' to cope with past migration. However, we need to invest in urban public goods to encourage *more* migration, not only in state capitals, but also in tier-2 and tier-3 cities. Proactive planning for urban expansions can also help minimize environmental damage caused by ad-hoc settlements in environmentally-sensitive locations that get regularized over time.

A specific idea is to increase the supply of low-cost rental housing, including dormitories for single workers or those migrating without their families. While home ownership is an aspirational goal for many, more *rental* housing is crucial for dynamic labour markets by enabling worker mobility. A related idea is to progressively raise the floor-space index (FSI), to enable many more high-rise buildings to expand housing supply. Given India's large population density, we need cities to grow vertically, with commensurate increases in urban infrastructure, amenities, and public transportation. More generally, research by urban planners shows that building regulations in urban areas impose substantial costs that impede affordable housing in India.[54] Understanding and alleviating these regulatory constraints should be a top priority for the JPEG task force.

The larger point is that urban policy and governance should not be seen only in terms of catering to current urban residents.

Rather, they should be seen as key enablers of *future* urban growth, and thereby playing an integral role in accelerating India's structural transformation. Reforms to strengthen the capacity of local governments to raise property taxes and revenue (Chapter 7) should also be seen in this light—they are not just about boosting revenue, but about accelerating India's structural transformation.

3.4 Reform public-sector hiring to create more jobs both directly and indirectly

A critical, but underappreciated, driver of educated youth unemployment in India is the structure of public-sector jobs. As Chapter 5 notes, government jobs typically offer much more generous terms than market norms, attracting hundreds of applicants per opening. This not only leads to inefficient use of public funds for service delivery (we should pay less, and hire more), but also drives high unemployment among educated youth. Many of them spend years trying to win the government-job lottery: a recent study estimates that *80 per cent of unemployment* in this group is due to preparing for government job exams.[55] Since less than 1 per cent of aspirants will win this lottery, the structure of public-sector jobs and recruitment imposes heavy time and financial costs on the other 99 per cent, who gain few real skills in the process beyond cramming for exams.

So, reforming public-sector hiring is crucial not only to improve state capacity, but also for *overall* economic efficiency. This is why the practicum-based training and hiring model detailed in Chapter 5, and expanded upon in Chapters 11–13, is among the most important reform ideas in this book. Implementing this model offers three key benefits for job quality and productivity in India. First, sectors like education, health, and public safety, which are labour-intensive, less prone to automation, and employ millions in the *private* sector, will see higher productivity and wages, through improved skilling via this model. Second, it cost-effectively boosts state capacity by using apprentices to support public service delivery, enhancing education and health services, which will boost human capital and productivity over time. Third, by linking public-sector hiring to *sector-specific* interest, competence, and experience rather than just passing an exam, this model will also reduce labour misallocation in the broader economy.

Similarly, hiring for many government roles on renewable three-to-five year contracts instead of lifetime ones, as described in Chapter 5, offers several benefits for jobs and skilling: (a) it enables governments to hire more people, directly creating jobs, (b) it boosts demand for in-service training and skilling due to the renewable nature of the contracts, and (c), it boosts demand for skills in the broader economy. Since the government is the largest and most lucrative employer in the economy, its hiring processes significantly shape education, training, and job-seeker behaviour by affecting what is rewarded. Currently, India's education system produces degree-holders and exam takers without real skills because the largest and most lucrative employer hires based on degrees and exam-taking ability, and not based on skills! Thus, reforming government hiring to place more emphasis on skills and performance will have positive spillovers on the entire economy.

A final action on government hiring that can be done immediately is to take a policy decision to shift to a two-worker anganwadi model in the ICDS. The benefits of doing so for early childhood education and nutrition, its long-term benefits, and cost-effectiveness have been discussed in Chapters 11 and 12. But, it will also have large positive effects on jobs by: (a) directly creating an extra 1.3 million jobs for women, and (b) making it easier for *other* women to work by providing better childcare in the ICDS, and thereby reducing a critical barrier to female labour force participation. Again, the spillovers of government hiring actions to the private market can be quite substantial.

A good example of the importance of such spillovers comes from the NREGS. Multiple studies find that NREGS significantly raised market wages, despite its small share in rural employment. My own research finds that over 85 per cent of income gains to the poor from improving NREGS implementation, came not from NREGS itself, but from increases in *market* earnings.[56] This example powerfully illustrates how government hiring can shape the entire labour market. I similarly believe that the spillovers of reforming public-sector hiring on job-creation and skilling in the Indian economy are likely to be massive. This is another example of inter-sectoral linkages in the economy that are typically ignored in our siloed approach to policy, and highlights the importance of 'systems' thinking in economic policymaking.

3.5 Measure and monitor key indicators of productivity and misallocation

The JPEG task force should also identify a few metrics of overall economic productivity and factor misallocation to both set goals and track progress.

One key indicator that we should monitor better is the *quality* of jobs. Existing surveys, including the PLFS, measure wages, benefits, and whether jobs are in the formal sector. This is useful, but not enough. For instance, we also have very little understanding of the dynamics of income volatility, uncertainty in finding jobs, or the job search process, in part because most surveys in India do not track the same respondents over time.

A simple way to address this gap is to include a module on jobs and livelihoods in the KPI survey discussed in Chapter 4. Doing so will provide policymakers with *annual district-level* data on key labour market indicators, offering systematic insights into their state's structural transformation. It will also help to better identify labour market frictions, craft solutions to mitigate these, and design outreach and training for firms and workers on how to use these systems. This is important as many governments, companies, and NGOs are launching technological solutions to reduce labour market frictions such as job portals, and referral and screening services. But we have no visibility on whether citizens are aware of and using these solutions.

Collecting and publishing such data can also motivate NGOs and firms to develop solutions to reduce labour market frictions. For instance, a recent study in South Africa found that giving job seekers assessments of their skills that they could *credibly share* with employers improved their job search efficiency, leading to increased employment and earnings.[57] More generally, while policymakers often focus on designing schemes and programmes, they may have a much greater positive impact on the economy by deploying low-cost interventions to *make markets work better* (as noted in Chapter 9).

The task force should also track metrics of locked-up factors of production, such as the value of land and credit tied up in courts, arbitration, and bankruptcy proceedings. Publishing this data, alongside information on pending cases, can highlight the social importance of better contract enforcement and dispute resolution. It can also increase the public salience and urgency of improving court functioning (see Chapter 14).

The task force should also track outstanding payments to MSMEs, who often face delayed payments. A recent study estimated delayed payments of around Rs 10.7 lakh crore or 5.9 per cent of gross value added.[58] The resulting increases in working capital costs are substantial, and even lead to business closures. Government departments and enterprises are themselves often guilty of delayed payments. Thus, a simple but highly effective way for governments to support the MSME sector is to pay their own dues on time. Reducing these payment delays could offer more value at much lower cost than all the credit-access schemes run by state governments to support MSMEs.

Finally, the adoption of GST provides an excellent metric to track the economy. This is already being done at an aggregate level, but the data can be used to generate many more insights on economic activity at granular levels, aiding in improved planning and aligning incentives and accountability (see below). State governments can also leverage this data within the new account aggregator framework, and support lenders in making lower-cost working capital loans to firms based on their GST-transaction data.

A key message of this chapter is that state governments should focus less on identifying sectors to support and high-profile investors to attract, and much more on *reducing frictions* that hamper the optimal utilization of factors of production like land, labour, and capital in the entire economy. Designing a monitoring framework that identifies key metrics of frictions and misallocation, and aims to reduce these steadily, can play a critical role in sustainably accelerating productivity, job quality, and economic growth.

3.6 Improve alignment of incentives within the government

The final structural challenge to address is the weak alignment of incentives down the chain of government. Even when political leaders and senior officials recognize the need to improve business climate and boost investment, lower-level officials often lack incentives to facilitate this goal. Indian businesses, especially MSMEs, frequently face harassment over obtaining necessary forms and certificates at the local level. Local officials' discretion to delay or deny approvals enables them to extract bribes and side payments from businesses. So, we can accelerate investments and job creation if we can better align local officials' incentives with these goals.

This is the key challenge that China successfully identified and addressed in the 1980s. The story of Deng Xiaoping's market-friendly reforms is well known, but the crucial role of China's *bureaucratic reforms* in catalysing growth is often underappreciated. These reforms involved regular performance assessment of local and provincial officials, with significant emphasis on growth in investments, jobs, and local tax revenue. Officials received substantial bonuses based on these performance metrics, and promotion prospects were linked to these performance evaluations.[59]

This approach was critical in making local officials and leaders proactive champions of local industries, and of minimizing business hurdles to attract new investments. Several accounts by business representatives, including from India, recall visits to China in the 1990s where they were actively courted by mayors and local party officials to invest in their areas. Local leaders also enjoyed significant autonomy to mobilize resources, and to streamline permits and approvals needed to attract investments. Thus, the Chinese approach to development in the 1990s exemplifies the effectiveness of granting local leaders 'autonomy on process' while maintaining 'accountability for outcomes'.

The significance of these reforms is underscored by a Chinese scholar's observation that China's economic reforms were first and foremost *governance reforms*.[60] A crucial lesson from China's experience is that linking the compensation and career prospects of officials with the economic growth of their jurisdictions aligned local, provincial, and national interests, and unleashed local initiatives to attract businesses and investments. This led to officials acting as *minority shareholders* in the economic performance of their jurisdictions, whose personal growth was effectively linked to the larger public good.[61]

In contrast, while major investors may receive expedited clearances and obtain red-carpet treatment in India, the majority of MSMEs often face harassment from local officials for bribes to issue permits and certificates. This situation arises because the pay and career prospects of local Indian officials are completely unrelated to either their performance or that of the local economy. Thus, their incentives are often to extract bribes from businesses rather than facilitate their growth. In short, *they have no skin in the game*. Under such an incentive structure, even directives from the prime minister and chief ministers to improve the 'ease of doing business' may have little bearing on the ground realities faced by Indian businesses.

So, a transformative reform Indian chief ministers can initiate is to combine GST data and job-quality data from the KPI survey (or, initially, just GST data) to create a district-level index of economic performance. With credible measurement in place, there are several ways to motivate local officials, such as collectors and district industries' centre heads, to improve these metrics. These include: (a) annual competitions and rankings for the fastest-growing district, (b) incorporating economic growth metrics as a key component of the annual performance appraisal of district officials, and (c) directly rewarding faster growth through performance-linked bonuses, or postings.

This approach can be extended to measuring GST and job growth at the parliamentary and assembly constituency levels. Party leaders could use metrics of local growth as an input in deciding whether to retain sitting MLAs, and to identify promising local leaders for promotion. Doing so can help improve political incentives to deliver not just visible schemes but on the more important goal of better-quality jobs and economic growth.

While India cannot and should not fully replicate the Chinese model given our unique political and institutional setting, the discussion here underscores the critical importance of better aligning incentives of local officials and leaders with the broader public interest. Even modest steps towards this alignment can significantly shift governance culture in India. It also highlights the far-ranging governance benefits of investing in better measurement systems as outlined in Chapter 4.

3.7 Balancing economic dynamism with worker protection

Many reform ideas in this chapter have been suggested by other economists, but have been politically difficult to implement due to their perceived adverse impact on working classes, who are predominantly poor. Inefficient agricultural policies persist because they are seen as essential to support poor farmers. Counter-productive labour laws are sustained by the belief that they protect worker interests. Decisions like reserving entire sectors of the economy for small-scale industries, which hindered India's potential as a global hub for low-skill intensive manufacturing, were driven by a desire to protect artisans from mechanization and global competition.

Protecting workers is a vital social and policy goal. The problem is that many of our misguided policies try to protect *jobs* instead of protecting workers. However, this approach is unsustainable in the long run because *many jobs become obsolete over time* due to technological advances in production, and shifting consumer preferences. This is why achieving India's JPEG goals requires us to build a dynamic economy that can reallocate labour from lower to higher value-added tasks. At the same time, it is undeniable that job losses are disruptive, and it is natural for incumbent workers to seek support in maintaining their jobs and minimizing disruption to their lives.

The way we should aim to balance the twin goals of worker protection and economic dynamism is to aim to *protect workers and not jobs.* In other words, as a society, we should aim to accelerate the creation of new jobs that add more value and not try to preserve jobs that are not economically viable. However, we should invest in better systems to support workers during the disruptive period of job transitions.

Some of the ideas for doing so, including a portable safety net, an inclusive growth dividend, and an urban employment guarantee programme, have been discussed in Chapter 15. An idea in this chapter is to reform farm subsidies *without* cutting subsidy budgets in the short run, and preserving the social protection of farmers provided by the status quo while reforming their structure. Finally, improving our education and skilling system, and supporting citizens with vouchers for lifelong learning that can be augmented at times of job loss, will make it easier for them to handle the disruptions of job losses and get retrained to find jobs in growing segments of the economy.

More broadly, this is why a robust social protection infrastructure should not be thought of as charity, but as providing a foundation for a dynamic economy that is ethically just, economically efficient, and politically sustainable.

3.8 Balancing economic growth with environmental protection

India must also balance economic growth with environmental protection. With thirteen of the world's fifteen-most polluted cities, we simply cannot afford to grow first and clean up later. Growth must be clean, and mitigating environmental damage must accompany faster economic growth. There is also growing evidence that pollution hurts productivity, and that higher temperatures also hurt productivity, further reducing the conflict between abating pollution and boosting productivity.[62] While suggesting detailed environmental protection strategies are beyond the scope of this book, I offer four ideas aligned with the themes of the book: two for better measurement, and two for better aligning private and public incentives.

The first idea is to institutionalize environmental quality in our development discourse by reporting 'Green GDP'. The idea, endorsed by several prominent economists, is to adjust standard

GDP figures for the costs of environmental deterioration, and the use of non-renewable natural resources. While such calculations require many assumptions, even attempting and reporting them annually can improve public discourse and policy by quantifying the cost of environmental degradation and making environmental quality a priority for policymakers. We would not stop tracking GDP growth, but reporting 'Green GDP' growth alongside will help the public understand and track the *quality* of GDP growth as it relates to the quality of lives. Green GDP growth can even be *higher* than GDP growth if environmental quality improves in the relevant time period.

The second idea is to invest in advanced real-time measurement systems to monitor pollution from key sources like factories and power plants. Modern sensor technologies now enable easy and cost-effective tracking of emissions. Currently, regulation relies on periodic physical inspections, which can be easily manipulated,[63] and are a ripe avenue for bribes to inspectors in return for turning a blind eye to violations. Mandating firms with high pollution potential to install modern sensor-based emission tracking systems, and always keep them on, will sharply reduce monitoring and compliance costs. It also allows surprise physical inspections to verify the *truth* of the *reported data* and penalize firms for false reporting. This approach echoes the 'truth score' idea in Chapter 4, and illustrates the broad applicability of those principles.

Improving pollution measurement at the macro and micro levels leads to the third idea: leveraging market-based incentives for changing firm behaviour. A practical model is for states to adopt a 'cap and trade' emission control system. This system sets a cap on total permitted emissions, allocates initial emission rights to firms, and allows them to trade these rights with each other. The system's efficiency comes from enabling firms that can reduce emissions easily and cheaply to sell their entitlements to those for whom reducing emissions is costlier. It maintains a fixed emission level, while lowering mitigation costs by maximizing reductions among the firms who have the lowest cost of mitigation. This approach also incentivizes investments in newer, lower-emissions technologies, aligning firms' private incentives with public goals of lower emissions.

The effectiveness of a 'cap and trade' system for pollution emission isn't just theoretical. A recent study on a pilot programme in Gujarat found a 20 to 30 per cent reduction in emissions compared to the traditional command and control system, where firms have fixed pollution quotas. The study also estimated that the abatement cost under the trading system was 12 per cent lower than the status quo.[64] Other states could benefit from studying and replicating such market-based models for emission reduction, thereby reducing both quantity of emissions, and the cost to firms of lower emissions.

Finally, investing in better pollution measurement could also facilitate India's access to global sources of 'green finance'. Several key sectors, including manufacturing and transport, can boost both productivity and energy efficiency by upgrading capital stock. Credible quantification and certification of the emission reductions resulting from such capital upgrades is the crucial step needed to access global financing for carbon offsets and credits. Helping Indian firms to access such financing for capital upgradation presents an opportunity for state governments to enable a win-win arrangement that improves productivity, energy efficiency, and environmental quality.

4. Conclusion

Promoting the creation of high-quality jobs, improving productivity, and accelerating economic growth is perhaps the most important thing that state governments can do to drive improved prosperity and well-being for their citizens. While the engine of economic growth will be driven by the private sector, the government plays a critical role in the JPEG agenda by creating the enabling conditions for factors of production to be used and redeployed efficiently. Playing this role well will allow private enterprises to flourish and create the jobs needed for broadly shared economic prosperity.

Much has been written about the reforms that India needs to accelerate progress on these dimensions. Yet, economic policy commentators have focused disproportionately on actions that the Central government needs to take. However, many of the most important policy levers, including regulations on the use of land and labour; investments in enabling conditions for property rights, dispute resolution, and skilling; and aligning incentives of local officials are in the control of state governments.

Many chief ministers are increasingly concentrating on growing their states' economies. However, state-level growth strategies have mainly focused on attracting investments. While this is a good start, it does not address the deeper question of *how* exactly to boost productivity, job quality, and economic growth. This chapter has aimed to provide some conceptual clarity on these points, along with practical ideas on how to achieve these goals, and thereby accelerate both growth and development.

Section IV

Making it Happen

Chapter 17

Reimagining Institutions

Why do policies, programmes, public spending priorities, and (cumulatively) the trajectory of countries evolve the way they do? A useful framework for understanding these is the '3i framework' of ideas, interests, and institutions.[1]

Ideas and ideologies (which are more rigid manifestations of ideas) are a fundamental determinant of policy choices. They do so by driving both the public discourse on what problems to focus on and how to solve them, and by shaping the world view of leaders who make the decisions that determine the trajectory of countries. The impact of both local and global ideas on Indian policy choices is seen in critical decisions like the adoption of universal franchise democracy and a government-led development strategy after Independence, as well as in the economic liberalization of 1991.

However, even good ideas will struggle to get adopted if they are not aligned with the interests of decision-makers, or those who have the most influence on decision-making. Conversely, ideas that hurt the public interest may get adopted if they benefit those in positions of power. Indeed, the term 'interest-group politics' captures the fact that policymaking usually reflects a political process whereby groups lobby for their interests. Thus, policies, programmes, and reforms are more likely to happen when there is a larger coalition of interests that lobbies for them, and less likely when there isn't.

A third key determinant of how societies function is the nature and quality of their institutions. Institutions matter because they set the 'rules of the game' within which individuals and organizations act on their ideas and interests, and interact with each other. Institutions matter both at the macro level—by formulating and implementing the rules that determine who has decision-making power in the polity and how they interact with and constrain each other, and at the micro level—by shaping the routines by which agents of the state go about their daily work.[2]

Thus, accelerating India's development will require us to not only have better and more effective *ideas*, but also to improve the alignment of *interests* between decision-makers and the public good to increase the chances that these ideas are adopted. Effective *institutions* are a key mechanism for promoting this alignment.

This is why the technocratic core of this book that lays out reform ideas (Chapters 4–16) is bookended by a discussion of the incentives and constraints of the key actors in the polity—politicians, public officials, institutions, citizens, and civil society. Chapters 2 and 3 describe the *current* incentives and constraints of politicians and bureaucrats, and aim to make the case for why the reforms in Chapters 4–16 would make sense for them to adopt even under the status quo. Chapters 17 and 18 discuss ways in which we can *modify* these incentives and constraints to increase the chances that those in positions of power will take the actions that will promote the broader public interest. This chapter focuses on institutions, and the next one on citizens and civil society.

Institutions can be both formal (e.g., parliaments, courts, election commissions, and central banks) and informal (e.g., culture, values, and norms). Formal public institutions are set up by the state and their rules are enforced under law by the state, whereas informal institutions are created by society, and their rules are enforced by social recognition and sanctions. Together, formal and informal institutions shape the roles of different actors in society, help ensure cooperation, restrain their actions, and provide checks and balances across them. Since this book focuses on effective governance, the discussion below focuses on strengthening formal public institutions.[3]

A large body of research has shown that countries with better public institutions have higher rates of economic growth, and superior development outcomes.[4] An influential summary of this work is presented by Daron Acemoglu and James Robinson in their book *Why Nations Fail*, where they argue that societies with 'inclusive institutions' that allow for broad participation in economic and political activity, constraints on rulers, and orderly transitions of power do much better than those with 'extractive institutions' that favour a narrow elite and help them stay entrenched in power, and garner most of the resources in society at the expense of the common good.[5]

However, designing, building, and sustaining inclusive public institutions is not an easy task. This is because a key role of institutions is to put *constraints* on elite behaviour and limit their ability to act in their private interest, when such actions are detrimental to the public good. However, elites do not like constraints on their own power, and it is the same elites who need to invest in institutions that can do so. This is why it usually takes a combination of public-spirited and sagacious elites, and effort and vigilance from citizens and civil society to build and maintain effective public institutions.

As with many of the topics in this book, the Indian experience with institutions is a mixed bag. On the positive side, the Indian Constitution has provided a world-leading example of establishing a set of 'inclusive institutions' of governance, and India's institutions set up in the 1950s were among the very best in the world for low-income countries. On the negative side, there has been a steady decline in the autonomy and effectiveness of India's institutions over time. I briefly discuss both sides of the story in the next section.

The gradual weakening of Indian institutions is a direct contributor to India's weak state capacity. Many commentators on India have noted that we need to renew and reinvest in building the capacities of India's key public institutions.[6] However, most of this discourse has focused on national-level institutions. A key point of departure in this chapter is to highlight the importance of state-level institutions, and the considerable opportunities that states have to design, build, and invigorate their institutions.

This chapter calls on state-level leaders, citizens, and civil society to embark on a process of reimagining both economic and political institutions at the state level, and to make a set of institutional investments that will position their states to thrive in the years to come, and provides a roadmap for doing so. To keep its scope manageable, the chapter focuses on ideas for institutional reforms that will strengthen state capacity and make it easier to 'institutionalize' the implementation of key ideas in earlier chapters.

As with many of the ideas in this book, state-led actions may be the most promising way of taking India forward. With nearly four times the population compared to what we had at Independence, building nationwide consensus on key institutional reforms can be much more difficult now than during the Constituent Assembly. Therefore, states and chief ministers who initiate a process to design and build institutions for their next phase of development can not only lay the foundations for long-term success of their own state, but also contribute to institutional renewal across India by their examples.

This chapter comprises three sections. The first provides a brief overview of India's institutions and their performance, and highlights the opportunity that states have to contribute to India's institutional renewal. The second discusses ideas for state-level institutions to strengthen the key themes of state capacity covered in Section II. The last section discusses ideas for reforming electoral rules to improve the alignment between the private incentives of people's representatives and the public interest, and thereby improve the functioning of Indian democracy itself.

1. India's Institutions: A Brief Overview

India's Constitution is a masterpiece of institutional design that lays the foundation of the modern Indian Republic. The Constituent Assembly comprised leading minds of the time as well as stalwart leaders of the Independence movement, representing a broad diversity of views, perspectives, global exposure, and personal experiences. Further, the process of framing the Constitution was both deliberative and inclusive, and the resulting framework of the Indian Republic is an exemplar of 'inclusive' institutions.[7]

The most striking illustration of India's inclusive institutions was the audacious decision to adopt democracy based on *universal* franchise at Independence. This made India a global outlier, since there was no precedent of a country doing so at such low levels of literacy and per capita income (see Chapter 2). The Constitution also established several autonomous institutions with responsibility for crucial public functions, to diffuse power and ensure checks and balances.

At the apex, are institutions representing the legislature (Parliament), the executive (Prime Minister and the Cabinet), and the judiciary (Supreme Court), which have the final say in making, implementing, and interpreting the laws of the land. However, the framers of the Constitution recognized that the effectiveness and credibility of even these apex institutions in turn depends on the quality of *other* public institutions.

For instance, the Election Commission is meant to ensure public credibility of the elected leadership; Public Service Commissions are meant to ensure the integrity of recruitment into public service and thereby contribute to both the quality and credibility of the executive; the Controller and Auditor General (CAG) is meant to ensure probity in public expenditure; and the Reserve Bank of India (RBI) is supposed to maintain the credibility of currency and resist urges to expand the money supply for meeting short-term spending needs at the cost of higher inflation.

Of course, it is not enough to just have institutions. They also need to be effective. Key features of effective public institutions include: (1) being *specialized*—with well-defined roles and responsibilities, (2) being *capable* of performing their designated roles, with adequate numbers of suitably qualified and motivated staff, (3) following well-defined professional rules of action, and thereby building *public trust* in their functioning, and (4) being accountable to elected authorities for outcomes, but having professional *autonomy* in how they function, and being insulated from pressure to make decisions that are expedient in the short run, but may be costly for public welfare in the long run.

Effective institutions accumulate competence and organizational capacity over time. Combined with public trust and autonomy, this allows them to build positive institutional identity, culture, and norms of functioning. These traits in turn help them maintain strong performance regardless of changes in personnel or political leadership. A reputation for competence and integrity also generates public recognition for effective institutions and their employees, and helps to establish the institution as a pillar of the country's governance architecture. Such public recognition helps to sustain norms of institutional autonomy, and institutionalize the idea of checks and balances over time.

India is fortunate to have several high-quality national institutions. These include a professional civil service that attracts some of the most talented individuals in the country, an election commission that is a world leader in conducting free and fair elections, and a central bank that has successfully managed monetary and exchange rate policy and ensured (together with the finance ministry) that India has rarely suffered from a macroeconomic shock in increasingly globalized financial markets.

At the same time, experts and scholars of Indian institutions also agree that the effectiveness of India's institutions has been steadily declining over time. An excellent scholarly treatment of India's public institutions is provided in the 2005 book *Public Institutions in India: Performance and Design*, edited by Devesh Kapur and Pratap Bhanu Mehta, and in a follow-up volume in 2017 that was also edited by Milan Vaishnav.[8] The narrative of declining institutional effectiveness is seen in several of the essays in these volumes and applies to a wide range of India's key institutions. This decline has been driven by a combination of factors, and I summarize three of the most important ones.

The first reason is chronic understaffing, especially in key technical roles. Many of India's leading institutions have significant vacancies even against sanctioned posts, let alone adding staff to keep pace with the growing population and complexity of tasks that these institutions are meant to take on. Over time, this lack of institutional capacity has led to an eroding of both the functioning and credibility of several key institutions. These challenges are similar to those faced by the bureaucracy (Chapters 3 and 5).

The second is political interference in the functioning of institutions and the gradual erosion of their autonomy. In some cases, the interference has been direct. In other cases, it has been done indirectly through the appointment of favoured officials to key institutional roles after retirement. Political interference has been especially severe in the case of institutions of law enforcement, which has compromised both their effectiveness and their public image.

The third channel is through the weakening of institutions that impact the effectiveness of *other* institutions. For instance, the independent CAG routinely documents violations of public expenditure norms. However, the mechanism by which CAG reports are meant to enforce accountability on the executive is through the legislature. Since Central and state legislatures have increasingly become subservient to the executive, CAG reports have mostly become toothless because legislatures rarely act on them.[9] Similarly, an independent judiciary is not enough to ensure justice when the quality of investigation and presentation of evidence is constrained by a weak police system.

The last point underscores the need to think about institutions in a systemic framework. In a system of interconnected institutions, weaknesses in one can hurt the effectiveness of others. This also means that improving just one institution may not be very effective without also strengthening other related institutions. This point applies to state capacity more generally where the different themes discussed in Section II are similarly connected, where investments in one area (like better data) allow improvements in other areas (like personnel management and quality of expenditure).

To summarize: India was fortunate to have an inclusive and deliberative constitutional process that yielded a well-designed institutional architecture to govern India. Many of India's institutions have served us well and continue to do so. However, like other parts of the Indian state, they have suffered from under-investment, political interference, and lack of systemic efforts to improve their functioning. Thus, a key mechanism by which we can build a more effective Indian state is to reimagine our institutional needs seventy-five years after Independence and to make the investments needed to both renew existing institutions and design and build new ones.

1.1 The state-level opportunity

Discussions of India's institutions, including in the books referred to above, have typically focused on national-level institutions. This focus mirrors India's broader approach to institutional design, which has relied on the national government to design institutional frameworks that are then copied and replicated at the state level. This approach is also consistent with the first principles of federalism described in Chapter 8, because there are economies of scale and scope in institutional design.

National institutions have typically performed better than their state-level counterparts on both competence and integrity. As an example of the former, the erstwhile Planning Commission attracted national and global leaders in statistics, and played a formative role in shaping state planning departments. Correspondingly, the abolishing of the Planning Commission has also led to a weakening of state-level planning departments. A good example of the latter is the fact that the Union Public Service Commission has largely been scandal-free in hiring civil servants. In contrast, several state-level public service commissions have been embroiled in recruitment scams.

National-level institutions usually outperform state-level counterparts for several reasons. First, they can draw from a broader national (and even global) talent pool, and the greater scope and potential impact of national roles helps to attract top-tier candidates. Second, they have more interaction with global counterpart institutions, enabling access to global knowledge and best practices. Third, they are typically better resourced and have greater access to government and international donor-funded programmes for institutional strengthening. Finally, they are more likely to be under the scrutiny of the national media, which makes integrity violations more costly.

However, while national-level institutions outperform their state-level counterparts on *average*, the *best* state-level institutions often perform better. For instance, Kerala has done far more on police reforms than the government of India; Gujarat has taken the lead in market-based regulation of pollution, which is more efficient than the command-and-control approach used by national environmental regulators (Chapter 16); and Telangana has launched its own annual multisector district-level KPI survey (as suggested in Chapter 4), whereas there are no such equivalents at the national level.

This is not surprising because statistically, it makes sense that the *best* out of twenty-eight states in any given domain of policy may often be better than the national equivalent. Further, evolving a national consensus on institutional reforms may be more difficult now than at the time of the Constituent Assembly. Thus, there is considerable potential for state-level leadership in designing and building institutions that will help us govern India better.

However, our public discourse and states' own imaginations have not recognized these possibilities. While we do discuss state-level leadership in sector-specific reforms, we have paid less attention to the possibility of state-level leadership in the design of *institutions of governance* themselves. This is a missed opportunity. The fifteen largest Indian states would each be in the world's top 20 per cent of countries by population. So there is no good reason why states should not think for themselves and put in place an institutional architecture that can accelerate their and India's collective progress. State-level leadership will then enable replication of successful innovations. I now present specific examples of such institutional reforms that states could consider.

2. Institutional Reforms to Strengthen State Capacity

There are many areas where states can take the lead in setting up institutions for better governance. For brevity, I focus on ideas for institutions to improve three core areas of state capacity—data, personnel, and public finance. Specifically, I recommend that states set up three sets of state-level institutions (a) a Statistics Commission, (b) a Public Human Resources Commission, and (c) a Public Finance Commission to strengthen these critical functions that underpin state effectiveness.

While many of the reform ideas in Chapters 4–7 should be implemented within concerned government departments themselves (planning, personnel, and finance/revenue), there are at least four reasons to set up dedicated institutions for these functions: (1) to draw in relevant expertise from outside the government, (2) to provide *institutional continuity to the reform agenda* when there is a turnover of department leadership (which happens very often), (3) to provide some insulation for these key functions from short-term political pressures by building these institutions outside the direct control of the executive, and (4) to have a long-term horizon focused on system strengthening, whereas officers are usually busy running their departments.

Using the car analogy from Chapter 1, current political and bureaucratic leaders are focused on driving the car that is the state, whereas the commissions would focus on redesigning and building a better car. An alternative framing is that current leaders would focus on the *substance* of governance, whereas the commissions would focus on strengthening the *systems*.

Some features should be common across these institutions. They should be created after passing enabling legislation with wide consultations and bipartisan support. The legislation should specify roles and responsibilities of the commissions, ensure adequate funding, and mandate expedited functioning—with time-bound targets and annual progress reporting to the legislature. Imposing time-bound targets and ensuring public accountability for the commission's work is essential to prevent them from becoming post-retirement sinecures for favoured officers, as seen in some cases.

Members of the commissions should be seasoned *experts* from government, the private sector, academia, law, and civil society. They should be tasked with outlining a five-to-ten-year strategic vision depicting the 'steady state' of a high-functioning system. Members should be appointed on five-year terms and the commissions should be given the resources and support to implement the reform roadmap, including dedicated staff to build expertise and preserve institutional memory. The commissions would identify the concerned line departments responsible for implementing specific reforms, providing both guidance and oversight. I now outline specific roles for these three institutions.

2.1 State Statistics Commission

As emphasized in Chapter 4, reliable, real-time, granular data on process and outcomes is a crucial input into effective policymaking and management. Yet, many decisions within government are still taken based on anecdotes as opposed to data and evidence. Changing this *culture* of how the government functions is a long-term project and will require a correspondingly long-term institutional investment.

States should therefore establish a state-level Statistics Commission, to provide a framework and technical guidance not only for data collection and reporting, but to support a process whereby all government departments can access, analyse, and *use* data for better decision-making. While much of the work will happen within planning and line departments, the commission should be accountable for driving the process. It should create a framework to improve data collection, analysis, and use in all departments; ensure that they have adequate resources to implement these reforms; establish implementation timelines; and conduct regular follow-ups.

On data collection, Chapter 4 provides three practicable ideas that the commission can help planning departments to set up and institutionalize. These include (a) an annual district-level survey for tracking key development outcomes, and thereby shifting the focus of government departments from schemes and inputs to ultimate outcomes, (b) a high-capacity call centre to make *outbound* calls to gather real-time data on citizen access to government programmes and benefits, and (c) a systematic effort to improve administrative data quality in all departments.

On data analysis, the commission should help to create a 'data analytics unit' in the planning department. This unit, using various public and private data sets, would generate real-time data on economic activity and development indicators. Over time, the analysis produced by this unit should become an integral part of government decision-making, target setting, monitoring and evaluation, and course correction. The unit could be staffed with a combination of full-time employees, and contractual staff.

Finally, on data use, the commission should anchor a process whereby departments develop and implement a data use strategy at all levels. This will involve creating a culture where junior and middle-level officials not only *transmit* the data to higher level officials, but actively engage with and *use* the data for their own roles. An effective data use strategy should (a) think about how better data can help improve functioning at all levels, including frontline workers, supervisors, block and district level administrators, and senior policymakers, (b) ensure that the most relevant data is available at each level, (c) systematically build capacity for data use, and (d) promote a culture where key decisions are driven by data more than anecdotes and opinions.

The commission can also help departments to simplify workflows, reduce redundancies in data collection, and explain statistical concepts. For example, many politicians and officials often do not grasp the subtle point that the precision of sample-based estimates mostly depends only on stratification and sample size and *not* on the ratio of sample to the total population. In extreme cases, this lack of understanding can lead to their insisting on censuses and not accepting sample surveys, which can *reduce* data quality and increase cost (as seen in the example of agriculture yield estimation in Chapter 5).

The commission should also be responsible for the following tasks: (1) setting high technical standards for data collection, analysis, and reporting, (2) designing protocols for protecting the anonymity of unit-level data while improving transparency of aggregate-level data, (3) staying abreast of technological improvements that enable faster data collection and analysis, and aim to accelerate the adoption of these techniques in the government, and (4) creating regular timeframes and processes for releasing key reports to the public to disconnect these from electoral cycles.

Taken together, the role of the Statistical Commission would be to professionalize, institutionalize, and depoliticize data collection and use within the government, and to do the same for the public communication of data.

Revamping our statistical infrastructure and building a culture of data use within government should ideally happen across India. However, this is a daunting task—especially given the wide variation in capacity across states. Moreover, investing in data for governance and service delivery (as opposed to just tracking progress) is much more important at the state level, since constitutionally, most service delivery functions are the responsibility of state governments. So, the goal of encouraging state-level innovation is to see if at least a few can take the lead in building a twenty-first century statistical infrastructure and provide templates that other states can rapidly adopt.

2.2 State Public Human Resources Commission

As noted in Chapter 5, research shows that the quality of personnel management is one of the most critical determinants of organizational effectiveness. Unfortunately, it is also an area where Central and state governments in India are especially weak. While we do have institutions focused on public sector personnel, they are too fragmented. There are different institutions responsible for recruitment (Public Service Commissions), training (various training centres), and pay (Pay Commissions), but there is no entity that is responsible for strategic human resource management across the entire government.

States should therefore set up a public Human Resources Commission (HRC) tasked with overseeing the design and implementation of a strategy to strengthen all aspects of public personnel management, including recruitment, training and capacity building, posting, pay and promotions, and performance measurement and management.

To start with, the commission could convene relevant departments to create an implementation plan and timeline for the ideas in Chapter 5, and assign primary responsibility to appropriate departments. Some of the agenda items would include: (a) building an integrated HRMIS, using this data to analyse managerial vacancies and tenure, and striving to minimize vacancies and increase stability of tenure in these roles, (b) mapping competencies required for all government functions against those possessed by existing staff, using this data for better assignment of talent to roles and building a competence-based career progression system, and (c) designing and implementing practicum-based training programmes that would both augment service delivery staff strength with apprentices and improve the long-term quality of talent in both the public and private sectors for key service delivery functions.

Over time, the work of Pay Commissions should be subsumed into the HRC. Several Pay Commissions have recommended that at least some elements of pay should be tied to performance. But Pay Commissions are set up episodically and wound up after submitting their recommendations. In practice, their recommendations on pay increases are accepted, but those on performance management get ignored, in part, because there is no entity with the mandate to focus on it. Since pay is crucial for employee motivation and management, it should be integrated into the HRC's work, so that pay and promotions are better linked to performance over time.

The commission should also undertake a systematic study of the use of consultants and contractual employees in the government and develop standardized guidelines to optimize their use. As noted in Chapter 5, it may make sense to reduce the use of external consulting firms, and instead hire employees on fixed-term, renewable contracts of three to five years to get the benefits of greater flexibility, accountability, and ability to cater to the changing skills needed in the government. The commission could oversee policies for recruiting contractual employees, and empanelment of top non-selected candidates from the UPSC exam for contractual positions (as suggested in Chapter 5).

It may also make sense to bring an administrative tribunal under the HRC's jurisdiction to handle all public personnel-related disputes. As Chapters 3 and 5 note, excessive litigation on personnel matters and bottlenecks in the judiciary cause severe challenges to governments. Transferring these disputes from courts to a dedicated administrative tribunal could both declutter the courts and boost the executive's capacity by rapidly resolving public personnel-related disputes that often drag on for years in the courts.

Unfortunately, administrative tribunals alone will not solve the backlog of personnel-related litigation, because courts often permit litigants to appeal tribunal decisions. Hence, tribunals may have made matters *worse* by adding an extra layer to the process.[10] Nonetheless, the most efficient way to speed up personnel litigation is to use tribunals and for courts to refuse to consider appeals of tribunal decisions except under extreme circumstances. So, the commission will need to analyse data from personnel litigation, tribunal decisions, and court reviews to persuade courts to refrain from admitting review petitions of tribunal decisions. Having the case made by a statutory body like a Human Resources Commission that is outside the executive may make courts more willing to look at the data and modify their actions accordingly.

None of these ideas for improving personnel management are 'rocket science'. At the same time, none of them are being done in a systematic way, resulting in unacceptably low quality of public personnel management in India. The Central government has launched Mission Karmayogi to take some much-needed steps to improve capacity-building. While this is a good start, it is still not a unified strategic human resource framework. States have the advantage of being able to work on a smaller scale, and setting up a Public Human Resources Commission along the lines proposed here will have long-lasting positive effects on state capacity and government effectiveness.

2.3 State Public Finance Commission

The final pillar of governance that would benefit from a dedicated institution is public finance—spanning both expenditure and revenue. While finance and commercial taxes/revenue departments carefully monitor the *quantity* of expenditure and revenue, they pay much less attention to their *quality*. This may partly explain the inefficiencies in public expenditure (Chapter 6), and the poor quality of revenue, whereby the economic cost of every rupee of revenue collected may be as high as three rupees (Chapter 7).

As with human resources, we do have institutions dedicated to state finances. However, they are fragmented and do not provide a unified strategic framework to boost the *quality* of revenue and expenditure. State Finance Commissions are episodic and focus primarily on devolution of funds to local bodies. They often suggest measures to boost revenues of local bodies but are unable to follow up because they get disbanded after making recommendations. State-level offices of the CAG probe public accounts for irregularities and corruption but have been ineffective in improving expenditure quality.

States should therefore create a Public Finance Commission (PFC) to take a long-term institutional approach to improving the quality of expenditure, and quantity and quality of revenue. The PFC could initiate its work based on the ideas in Chapters 6 and 7.

Key expenditure-side ideas include: (a) conducting better analysis of public expenditure on effectiveness, cost-effectiveness, distributional impacts, and downstream effects on the economy, (b) institutionalizing a focus on evidence and cost-effectiveness in approving departmental budgets and spending programmes, (c) analysing procurement data to improve value for money and post-award performance by vendors, and (d) monitoring fund flows and reducing delays in disbursement. Revenue-side ideas include: (a) improving data analytics for tax compliance, (b) strengthening the capacity of urban local bodies for property tax collections, (c) implementing user fees for cost recovery and sustainable service delivery, (d) improving quality of revenue by taxing items with negative externalities, including congestion, fossil fuels, and alcohol and tobacco, and (e) using outbound call centres to measure taxpayer satisfaction to act as a safeguard against harassment of citizens by tax department officials.

While these functions could be done within finance and revenue/commercial taxes departments, locating them in an institution like a state PFC will enable analysis to be conducted independently without political pressure. Ideally, all significant spending proposals (say, over Rs 500 crore) should be subject to independent analysis that is shared publicly for debate and deliberation. Over time, the PFC can perform functions similar to that of the Congressional Budget Office

(CBO) in the USA, which 'scores' laws with major fiscal impact and presents projected fiscal implications to the legislature.

Further, state governments largely operate on an annual 'cash accounting' basis, with spending in any year directly linked to revenue. Thus, there are limited mechanisms for smoothing spending amidst revenue volatility. The PFC can help states create and implement a medium-term expenditure framework that uses a combination of borrowing and building reserves to smooth expenditure. It can also analyse the sustainability of state borrowing and help boost the credibility of states with bond markets by making such sustainability analyses publicly available.[11]

Finally, just like the work of (episodic) Pay Commissions can be subsumed into that of a permanent Human Resource Commission, the work of (episodic) State Finance Commissions (SFC) can be folded into that of a permanent Public Finance Commission (PFC). This would improve upon the status quo because setting up and disbanding SFCs every five years leads to a loss of institutional memory and makes it more difficult to follow up on SFC recommendations.[12]

2.4 Summary and common themes

None of these ideas are particularly difficult or controversial. Yet, we are not making these basic institutional investments because officials are so overburdened with running the car that is the Indian state that they do not have the time or mental bandwidth to think about redesigning the car, and upgrading its systems. Building just the above three institutions and giving them the mandate and resources to perform the functions outlined above can be a transformative investment in building a more effective state.[13]

While the Government of India can do more to rejuvenate India's institutions, it only has direct authority over its own personnel and budgets. Since states collectively account for 60 per cent of public expenditure and 79 per cent of public employment in India,[14] it is essential for national progress that states take the lead in making the next wave of institutional investments that India needs—especially in critical areas like management of public finances and public human resources.

However, as noted earlier, building effective institutions is not easy because it requires leaders to be willing to accept *constraints* on their own behaviour. An effective statistical commission will make it more difficult for leaders to hide inconvenient data. An effective human resources commission will make it more difficult for public personnel actions to be taken at the behest of individual politicians if they violate transparent and objective standards. Finally, an effective public finance commission will make it more difficult to undertake politically expedient but economically unwise expenditure.

However, just like human productivity and welfare can be increased by *constraining* access to choices that provide short-term pleasure at the cost of longer-term welfare,[15] the long-term productivity and effectiveness of the government can also be increased by well-designed institutional *constraints*. Such institutions do not infringe on political leaders' ability to design policies or programmes, but they will improve the ability of the state they lead to actually deliver against their goals. Over time, this is likely to deliver *political* benefits through higher voter satisfaction and the likelihood of re-election.

Effective chief ministers already understand these points. Better-governed states typically have longer tenures for senior officials, provide more autonomy to effective officials, make better use of data and technology for governance, and appoint external experts as advisers. However, these practices can be fragile and easy to undo under a different government. Thus, the main value of building newer state-level institutions focused on better data availability and use, public personnel management, and public finance management is to *institutionalize* these good practices and locate them in entities who have a dedicated mandate to improve these systems within government.

To summarize, none of the governance reforms outlined in this book can happen without political interest and support. However, converting the desire of leaders who want to improve government functioning into *sustained* results will require these leaders to also invest in systems to institutionalize key reforms. Investing in state-level institutions will be a critical enabler of such sustainability and longer-term impact. Finally, while it will be ideal if such an institutional renewal agenda is led by political leaders themselves, citizens and civil society can increase the chances that such a renewal happens through greater engagement with these issues (see Chapter 18).

3. Institutional Reforms to Make Indian Democracy Work Better

The ideas in this book, and the institutional reforms above will help politicians who actually want to serve citizens better. However, as noted in Chapter 2, many of our challenges reflect misalignment between politicians' private incentives and the broader public interest. Even the best policy advice is unlikely to be acted upon, if the incentives of key decision-makers are not better aligned with the broader public interest.

So, a key question for the institutional design of Indian democracy is: How do we get more politicians in office who are mainly focused on improving public welfare? Seventy-five years after Independence is a good time to take stock of our political institutions and consider tweaks to the 'rules of the game' of Indian democracy to improve the alignment of private interests of the political class, and the broader public interest.

The question of how to improve democratic functioning is a complex topic worthy of extended deliberation. This section presents two specific ideas that could significantly strengthen the functioning of Indian democracy. Consistent with the book's emphasis on state-level reform ideas, both ideas can be piloted and tested at the state level.

3.1 Replace 'first past the post' with 'ranked choice voting'

As explained in Chapter 2, many of the perverse political incentives in Indian democracy can be attributed to our first-past-the-post election system. One simple but far-reaching reform is to adopt a ranked-choice voting (RCV) mechanism. The properties of an RCV system have been studied extensively, and several scholars—

including multiple Nobel Prize-winners—recommend it over the status quo of first-past-the-post elections.[16] I first describe the RCV process, and then discuss its many advantages over the status quo.

The key idea of RCV is that voters not only pick their top choice, but rank as many candidates as they want in descending preference order. The election winner is determined sequentially. Candidates are initially ranked by first choice votes. If a candidate gets over 50 per cent of first-choice votes, they win. If not, the lowest-ranked candidate is dropped and the votes of those who ranked them first are transferred to their second-choice candidates. This process continues until a candidate receives over 50 per cent of votes. If no winner emerges at an early stage, there will eventually be only two candidates left, at which point, the one with the majority of votes is elected.

The example below shows how an RCV system would work. Consider an election with five candidates (A to E) and ten voters (1 to 10). Column (1) in Table 17.1 shows voters' preference ranking over candidates, which reflects their vote under an RCV system. Column (2) shows their vote if limited to their top choice, as they do under the status quo (assuming no strategic voting, a point discussed further below).

Under the status quo, candidate A would win with three out of ten votes, with only a 30 per cent vote share. This reflects the current reality of many Indian elections (see Chapter 2). However, Column (1) shows that 70 per cent of the voters (all except 1, 2, and 7) prefer candidate C to A. Thus, the majority of voters would have preferred a different candidate to the one who was elected: a perverse outcome for a democracy.

In contrast, under RCV, candidate E, with the fewest first-choice votes (one out of ten) would drop out after the first round. Voter 10's vote would then be transferred from their first choice E (who is no longer in contention) to their second choice (candidate C). After this, candidates A and C are tied for first place with three out of ten votes each, while B and D have two out of ten votes. So, in the next round, candidates B and D drop out and the votes of those who ranked B and D first (voters 3, 5, 8, and 9) would be transferred to their next choice. Since all four of them prefer C to A, C would win with 70 per cent of the vote.

Table 17.1: Ranked-Choice Voting versus First-Past-the-Post Election Outcomes

	Actual Preference Ranking of Candidates (also expressed in Ranked-Choice Voting)	Status quo (First Past the Post)—assuming no strategic voting
	(1)	(2)
Voter 1	A > B > C > D > E	A
Voter 2	A > C > D > B > E	A
Voter 3	B > C > D > A > E	B
Voter 4	C > D > B > A > E	C
Voter 5	D > C > B > A > E	D
Voter 6	C > B > D > A > E	C
Voter 7	A > D > C > B > E	A
Voter 8	B > C > D > A > E	B
Voter 9	D > C > A > B > E	D
Voter 10	E > C > D > A > B	E
Election result	C wins with 70 per cent of the votes. (C is preferred to A, B, and D by 70 per cent of voters, and to E by 90 per cent of voters).	A wins with 3/10 votes. (B, C, and D each have 2/10; E has 1/10)

As a simpler example, consider three candidates (A, B, and C) who receive thirty-six, thirty-four, and thirty votes respectively out of a hundred. However, twenty out of the thirty supporters of C prefer B to A, and rank B as their second-choice vote. Under the status quo, A would win with just thirty-six votes. But under an RCV system, C would drop out after the first round, and twenty of their thirty votes would be awarded to B and the remaining ten to A. Thus, in the second round, B would win with fifty-four votes against forty-six for A.

An RCV system can strengthen Indian democracy in several ways. First, it ensures that election winners are preferred over other candidates by a majority of voters, as seen in the examples above. This is good intrinsically because the election winner will better reflect voter preferences, and instrumentally because it would improve the incentives of politicians to better represent the interests of a *broad* set of voters. As shown in Chapter 2, the arithmetic of a politics of patronage and polarization works if you can win an election with around 20–25 per cent of registered voters, but does not work if you need over 50 per cent to win, as would be the case under an RCV. Thus, an RCV would shift political incentives away from narrow vote-bank politics that benefit smaller groups of voters, towards a broader and more inclusive politics.

Second, RCV will reduce the role of 'nuisance' and 'spoiler' candidates. In our current system, major parties often support spoiler candidates, who have no chance of winning, but may cut into the votes of viable opponents. This is highly undesirable, both because of the socially useless effort and cost spent on propping up spoiler candidates, and more importantly, because spoilers can distort electoral outcomes from the preference of the majority.[17] Under an RCV system, spoiler candidates will matter a lot less, since many of their votes will get transferred to more viable candidates.

Third, RCV removes incentives for strategic voting. In our current system, voters often worry that their vote may be wasted if their most-preferred candidate is unlikely to win. So, they spend time and effort to guess which *other* candidate might be most likely to win, and try to vote strategically to prevent their least-preferred candidate from winning. The need for strategic voting weakens democracy by discouraging voting according to citizens' true preferences. With RCV, strategic voting becomes unnecessary since votes are transferred to the next most preferred candidate if higher-ranked choices do not win.

Fourth, RCV can reinvigorate our democracy by reducing barriers to political entry. We need new leaders and parties who are focused on issues like decentralization, urban governance, environmental quality, police reform, education, health, and jobs. However, our current system makes it difficult for new parties to gain traction because voters may hesitate to waste their vote on parties who are unlikely to win. However, with RCV, there is no wasted vote because votes transfer to the next choice if the top choice does not win. Consequently, even if new issue-based parties do not win, they can still influence politics because larger parties will be incentivized to address these issues to receive these parties' second-choice votes. Thus, RCV can empower voters to better express their priorities and facilitate the entry of new leaders and issues in the political arena.

Fifth, RCV makes it easier for parties to form coalitions without complex seat-sharing negotiations. Currently, parties resist giving up seats to coalition partners because their own support base may erode if they are not contesting. Under an RCV, parties can be in a coalition and also nurture their support base, since they can all contest and instruct their voters to list their coalition partner as the second-choice vote. This enables political coalitions while also preserving the identity and relevance of smaller coalition partners in every seat, and not just the ones that they are allocated in seat-sharing negotiations.

RCV systems have been successfully used in settings ranging from Australia to US state-level elections. While more research is needed on their impacts, existing evidence based on these experiences suggests that they have promoted the election of a more diverse set of candidates, and that they are more likely to lead to the election of moderate as opposed to extreme candidates.[18] Interestingly, we *already* use the RCV system in India for the election of the Indian President, and for elections to the legislative council in several states. Hence, there is no constitutional or legal barrier to adopting the system, given that the precedent already exists within our democratic framework. So why not extend the RCV to other elections as well?

546 Accelerating India's Development

The main concern about RCV is that it may be too complex for voters, especially for the illiterate. However, both voter literacy and technology have improved dramatically over the past seventy-five years. India's use of electronic voting machines (EVMs) makes it easy to implement a voice-guided system for voters to rank candidates. Importantly, voters need not need rank *all* candidates: they would have the option of ranking as many candidates as they like. Even allowing voters to rank up to three candidates would be a major improvement, and would be easy to communicate to voters.[19] EVMs can easily tabulate the votes, and election commissions can transparently show the counting process by which winners are decided.

Switching to an RCV system can transform Indian democracy. It could accelerate a transition from a politics that rewards polarization, vote banks and patronage to one that rewards better governance for all citizens. It would better align the incentives of politicians with the broad public interest, allow voters to express their true preferences without needing to vote strategically, reduce the role of spoiler candidates, facilitate coalitions, and energize public life by easing the entry of new issue-based parties.

3.2 Pilot 'citizen assemblies' with randomly chosen citizens as members

While RCV can improve the *mechanics* of democracy by reducing spoiler candidates and strategic voting, and rewarding parties who can target broader coalitions of citizens, several deeper challenges remain. Three of the most critical ones are the growing role of money in politics, under-representation of marginalized groups, and low citizen engagement. These concerns are relevant for democracies globally, including India.

The growing role of money in politics presents a fundamental challenge. Parties are estimated to have spent ~Rs 35,000 crore and ~Rs 55,000 crore in the 2014 and 2019 general elections, respectively, with the costs of state and municipal elections adding to this total.[20] The need to raise large sums of money to contest elections is the *root cause* of many of the pathologies of Indian democracy. It fuels both petty corruption and harassment of citizens and firms by officials (with money often flowing up the chain to political leaders), and grand corruption where policies, contracts, and procurement are influenced by industrial houses, lobbies, and contractors in return for campaign contributions. It also validates corruption in the minds of the political class as an unavoidable 'democracy tax' that even personally honest politicians have to pay to even be able to participate in Indian democracy through elections.

Moreover, the high cost of campaigns acts as a barrier to the entry of public-spirited, honest Indians who may wish to contest elections and serve their fellow citizens. Even worse, the advantage enjoyed by those who can self-finance election campaigns has contributed to the entry and success of criminals in politics. Thus, the increasing role of money in politics contributes to a vicious cycle whereby there are both negative *selection* effects in *who* becomes a politician (criminals are more likely to contest and win elections), and negative *incentive* effects in what politicians *do* after getting elected (their actions are at least partly motivated by the need to make money to recover their investments in contesting elections, and to be able to finance future elections).

Money in politics is a vexing challenge for democracies worldwide, and poses both practical and philosophical problems. Practically, even if election commissions stipulate spending limits, they are difficult to enforce, and such limits are routinely violated. Philosophically, one can argue that citizens in free societies should have the freedom to spend their money as they wish, including lobbying for preferred policies. Indeed, the US Supreme Court ruled in 2010 that the right to make campaign contributions is akin to the right to free speech, and made it more difficult to enforce election spending limits.[21]

A second challenge is the under-representation of many disadvantaged demographic groups. While the Constitution provides for reservations for scheduled castes and tribes, other disadvantaged groups are significantly under-represented in positions of power. For instance, Muslims comprise 15 per cent of India's population, and have much poorer development outcomes, but make up only 5 per cent of our MPs. Women comprise 50 per cent of the population but only 9 per cent of all MLAs. As noted in Chapter 1, this under-representation of women may have directly contributed to our collective underinvestment in state capacity and service delivery.

A third challenge is the lack of ongoing mechanisms for citizen engagement in decisions that affect their well-being, such as identifying priorities for public spending. India's democracy uses elections to provide legitimacy to people's representatives, but does not provide a way to incorporate citizen voices or feedback in governance. Over time, this structure has contributed to creating a ruling class of political and bureaucratic elites who are separated from the people in how they live and function. This sentiment is reflected in the popular refrain about many politicians that 'they come to citizens to seek votes every five years, and are not seen after that till the next election'.

These problems seem almost insurmountable and democracy advocates have struggled to find good ways of addressing them. Is there a practical way to proceed?

Helene Landemore, a political scientist at Yale, has suggested an innovative approach in a 2020 book called *Open Democracy*.[22] The idea is to create citizen assemblies by *randomly* selecting citizens to serve from among those registered to vote. Such assemblies could deliberate budget trade-offs and oversee the use of public funds, offer citizen inputs into policies, and even have a say in the drafting and passing of laws.

Serving on the assembly would be similar to *jury duty*. Members would serve only one term; bring their knowledge and perspectives to their public role; aim to represent the public interest while serving; and revert back to being regular citizens at the end of their term. Thus, they would primarily be *citizens* as opposed to career politicians. A similar idea put forth in 2014 by philosopher Alexander Guerrero advocated for random selection of citizens into political decision-making roles instead of elections.[23]

The ideas of Guerrero and Landemore have been praised by scholars as an intriguing possibility for addressing some of the deep challenges faced by modern democracies. While the idea may be too radical and risky to implement as a *replacement* for existing political structures, it has several attractive features that make it worth experimenting with and testing. In particular, it could make sense to pilot the idea as a *supplement* over and above existing structures for *local* governance.

To pilot this approach, we could create a citizen assembly of ten to twenty members, randomly selected from voter lists, for a few municipal governments. Assemblies would provide inputs on spending priorities and approve municipal budgets and contracts. Serving would be a part-time role requiring ten to fifteen hours per week, and be modestly compensated (say at the semi-skilled labour wage rate) to ensure that loss of earnings would not be a barrier for the poor to participate. While those selected could choose to opt out, the expectation would be that selection is a rare privilege that should not be turned down. Members would go through a basic training course to understand their roles, and serve for two-year terms, with half the cohort refreshed annually. Members would be assisted by officials (just like elected political leaders are assisted by bureaucrats) but would be entrusted with taking decisions on behalf of the people.

There are many attractive features of such an idea of political representation.

First, it would elegantly break the link between campaign spending and the probability of being a people's representative, and thereby address one of the root causes of political corruption. Since money would no longer matter for getting elected, representatives will not have to worry about fundraising and have both the opportunity to be honest and to spend more time on effective governance. While other elected offices would still need campaign funding, a representative citizen assembly for local government with budget oversight, could curb corruption and improve the provision of local public goods.[24]

Second, it would ensure equal representation of all groups *even without any quotas*. The framers of India's Constitution extensively debated the question of how to ensure adequate representation of underprivileged groups. In the end, reservations were instituted for some disadvantaged groups (scheduled castes and tribes) but not for others (Muslims or women). This was a politically acceptable compromise, but an ethically arbitrary outcome. In practice, reservations have helped the groups who have received them,[25] but have not solved the problem of under-representation of *other* marginalized groups. Quotas along some dimensions may have also made it harder to acknowledge the multidimensional nature of identity and deprivation. Even if these other dimensions are acknowledged, it would be practically very difficult to implement quotas to adequately represent *all* under-represented dimensions of human identity.[26]

Under this proposal, every registered voter would get an equal opportunity to represent the public and have a voice in decision-making. Thus, by the law of averages, *every* under-represented group will be proportionately represented, *including intersectional categories of deprivation*.[27] Members will bring perspectives representing the full diversity of Indian society. However, they will serve primarily as *citizens* and not as representatives of a quota-defined group. This is an intrinsically valuable model of representation, and also adds instrumental value by incorporating a wider variety of voices and inputs into governance, thereby making our democracy more inclusive.

Third, it would empower marginalized groups who will now be represented by *average* citizens, and not by privileged members within disadvantaged groups, as often happens with reservations. It will improve citizen empowerment by making officials accountable to a group of average citizens. Unlike the status quo, the assembly would be likely to include extremely disadvantaged citizens who usually only enter government offices as supplicants for benefits, but would now have actual authority over officials.

Fourth, it would create a new civic space where all citizens are truly equal regardless of their status outside the assembly. It could increase intergroup contact, engagement, and empathy in our highly stratified and unequal society. While India has a vibrant civil society, there is almost no public space where citizens are completely equal and have to engage with each other on an equal footing. An institution like a citizen assembly could help bridge social and economic divides by creating such a public space. Working together to deliberate and decide on local public goods is an ideal practical setting in which to build more connective tissue across *all* Indians.[28]

Fifth, it would deepen our democracy by increasing civic engagement in governance. Citizens would not only be engaged in governance while serving on the assembly, they would gain knowledge about governance during their term, and are more likely to stay engaged civic participants even after their term ends. Over time, the citizen assembly would create several cohorts of alumni who engage more actively in shaping their communities. Some of them may even choose to run for elected office, and thereby diversify and broaden the pool of candidates for elected office over time.

Sixth, it can accelerate our ability to decentralize governance. As noted in Chapter 8, India is highly overcentralized, and local governments are better suited to ensure quality service delivery. However, sceptics of decentralization worry that local elites will capture public funds and deny services to marginalized groups, and that local communities do not have the capacity to administer public funds well. A representative citizen assembly can solve both problems by making elite capture more difficult, and creating a diverse pool of citizens who would have built greater capacity for local governance.

The notion that 'locals cannot govern themselves' is the same excuse used by the British to delay Indian independence. However, the experience of governing cities and then states over time allowed Indian leaders to learn how to manage public affairs, and to also prove their ability to do so. Similarly, creating citizen assemblies with limited but meaningful authority over local budgets can be both a training ground and proving ground for a new generation of inclusive and broad-based leadership for India.

While the idea may seem radical, it is consistent with existing efforts to boost citizen participation in local government. Ideas such as 'Gram Sabhas' open to all citizens are already in the 73rd Constitutional Amendment as a building block of local government, and the 'Mohalla Sabha' proposed by the Aam Aadmi Party has similar goals. However, in practice, it becomes unwieldy for *all* citizens to participate, and actual participation is skewed towards the elite.[29]

So, the proposed idea can be considered as analogous to a modified Gram Sabha or Mohalla Sabha, that aims to increase average citizens' participation in local governance by (a) only expecting selected members to engage, but ensuring equal representation to all (b) making it easier to participate by compensating them for their time, and providing training and administrative support, and (c) framing participation as a civic duty (akin to jury duty) and a rare opportunity to have a voice in public decision-making.

Overall, representative citizen assemblies with random selection is a deeply democratic idea that entrusts citizens with decisions impacting their collective good. While it may seem radical, it is no more so than India's original democratic experiment of providing voting rights to all citizens—regardless of education or wealth—at Independence. Further, *every* household knows how to manage a budget, and seek value for money, with average citizens often *more* conscious of these issues than elites. Since the main role of these assemblies will be to allocate and oversee the use of taxpayer funds for local public goods—and not to make policy or laws—there is reason for cautious optimism that an assembly of average citizens will discharge this responsibility well.

Finally, a more modest way of piloting this idea could be to restrict the lottery-based selection to citizens who agree to serve on the assembly by filling a simple candidacy form. While this may skew participation away from the most vulnerable, who may opt to not be considered, it will still be a much more inclusive process than the status quo. It has the added advantage that everyone who is chosen will *want* to perform the role.

Abraham Lincoln described democracy as a government 'of the people, by the people, and for the people'. Our democracy is good at being 'by' the people (through elections), but weak on being 'of' the people (elites are much more likely to contest), and 'for' the people (private interests of politicians often diverge from the public interest). A citizens' assembly would be better at being 'of' the people (through equal selection chances for all), and potentially stronger 'for' the people (for the reasons described above). It would be weaker at being 'by' the people because representatives are not elected, and accountability may be poorer because of a lack of elections. However, holding a referendum to validate the creation of such a representative body could address this concern. If approved, the entire system would have been endorsed 'by' the people.

Finally, why would incumbent parties and candidates support this approach when it would diminish their own power? The answer is that incumbents may not, but Opposition parties looking for fresh ideas to revitalize Indian democracy may find it worthwhile to develop the idea further and include it in their manifesto. If these parties win elections by promising more 'power to the people', it could serve as the referendum suggested above to allow a pilot in a few places. Alternatively, an incumbent party aiming to leave a legacy of deep governance reforms may want to pilot the idea.

It is also an idea that civil society and democracy-promoting organizations may want to develop further, and build broader support for. Scholars of decentralization have noted that elites rarely give up power on their own and in that sense, the *struggle for decentralization is similar to the struggle for democracy itself.*[30] The proposed approach could be one concrete way of channelizing a push for better representation, inclusion, and decentralization in decision-making for local governance.

3.3 Some practical considerations

Even within democracies, the rules of how representatives are chosen can significantly shape political incentives. While democracy should be considered sacrosanct as India's system of government, it is worth reassessing our electoral rules to see if we can mitigate some of the weaknesses of the status quo. Both the ideas above have the potential to significantly improve the functioning of Indian democracy.

However, my recommendations are based on the conceptual merits of these ideas, and we do not yet have empirical evidence on their effectiveness in India. Thus, a central challenge for reform is our understandable risk aversion to sudden nationwide changes in electoral rules. But a fear of change can also trap us in a never-improving status quo. This is why state-level experimentation may be the key to electoral reforms. It can help us to pilot and test electoral reforms at a smaller scale, and thereby de-risk the process of testing ways of improving our democracy.

While the National Representation of Peoples Act governs parliamentary and assembly elections, states have more autonomy over sub-state elections, subject to approval by the State Election Commission (SEC). Reforms like rank-choice voting (RCV) preserve and *enhance* our democratic ideals and are within India's constitutional framework. Similarly, adding a local governance layer such as a citizen's assembly with lottery-based selection of members aligns with ideas like the Gram Sabha, which are already in the Constitution. Thus, a proactive chief minister, in consultation with Opposition parties, the SEC, and legal experts, could pilot these ideas in a local body election.

These political reforms are not essential for implementing the other ideas in this book. However, we cannot deny the reality that many of our governance challenges are a result of the divergence of interests between the political class and citizens at large. So, it is worth considering 'meta' reforms to tweak our electoral rules to make Indian democracy work better. The two ideas above are offered for consideration in this spirit, and because state-led experimentation may be especially useful for trying such reforms.

4. Conclusion

While India was fortunate to have been endowed with an impressive set of 'inclusive institutions' at Independence, their functioning has deteriorated over time. Further, India has evolved considerably since the time of the Constituent Assembly's deliberations. In particular, voter literacy, access to information, awareness of local and national issues, and technological possibilities have dramatically improved over this period.

Thus, seventy-five years after Independence is a good time to critically examine the performance of our economic and political institutions, and to make a renewed commitment to reimagining, redesigning, and reinvesting in our institutions. Moreover, while it will be wonderful if we can reach nationwide consensus on these issues, states can play a key role in accelerating this process, by taking their own initiatives and leading the country by experimenting with new institutional possibilities.

Most of this book has focused on specific practical ideas to improve governance. However, to have lasting effects, we need to institutionalize these new ways of functioning. Implementing the ideas in Section 2 of this chapter will allow chief ministers to go beyond announcing new programmes and schemes, and institutionalize better governance for the long run. Reforming electoral rules with the ideas in Section 3 will allow them to have an even more fundamental impact on long-term governance by improving the functioning of Indian democracy itself.

Chapter 18

State, Citizen, and Society

The main goal of this book is to help accelerate India's development and thereby improve the lives of over 1.4 billion people in the coming years. To achieve this goal, it has focused on providing a roadmap for improving governance and state capacity, which will enable the state to deliver essential services better for *all* Indians.

The focus on the state reflects the fact that it is by far the largest actor in providing essential services, and improving its effectiveness is the best way of delivering better outcomes for all Indians at scale. Further, improving the quality of public services will put pressure on private service providers to improve, and thereby *also* benefit those who do not use public services (Chapter 9). Finally, the state is critical for promoting equity. In our democracy, the main instrument for the disadvantaged to seek greater equality is the state, which is the one entity that they have an equal claim on along with every Indian citizen. Thus, the Indian state's weakness in delivering basic services limits our ability to translate the political equality of our democracy into greater equality in access to essential services like education, health, safety, and justice.

This is why the agenda of building a more effective Indian state is *the great unfinished task of Indian democracy.* This is because 'democracy before development' has given all Indian citizens the ability to make a claim on the state, but has not by itself provided either the resources or political incentives to build the capacity of the state to satisfy these aspirations.[1] Correspondingly, this is a task that *we all* have a stake in.

The good news is that trends in voter behaviour suggest reasons for cautious optimism that it will be in the interest of political leaders to act on this agenda. However, we can accelerate this process by constructing a broad coalition of citizens and civil society to demand, encourage, support, and reward state actions that can improve governance, and thereby boost both growth and development. This final chapter discusses ways in which each of us can contribute to this goal and has three key messages.

First, our public discourse often suffers from a zero-sum mindset where various interest groups lobby for a fixed pie of public benefits. While such 'big fights' make for good media theatrics, they distract us from focusing on the large set of feasible positive-sum actions that can both expand the size of the pie *and* also promote equity. We would therefore be much better off as a society if we could focus our energies on identifying such positive-sum ideas, and implementing them well.

Second, we cannot sit back and expect the government to do better without actively engaging with it, nudging it to do better, and supporting it where possible. It is common for the tax-paying elites and middle classes to respond to a problem in the public sphere by saying that 'it is the government's job' or 'what do we pay taxes for?' While this view may work in high-income countries with better state capacity, it hinders progress in a low-capacity setting like India. Effective democracy requires active citizenship, and the quality of governance will also reflect the extent and quality of citizen engagement.

Third, achieving the two goals above can improve trust among citizens, and between citizens and the state. This is because there is a virtuous cycle between improving state effectiveness in public good provision, citizen engagement, and increasing trust in the government. An increase in trust will in turn make it easier for us to tackle much more difficult problems and implement complex reforms that require some upfront costs but can generate large longer-term gains for *all* Indians.

This chapter comprises three sections. The first lays out a framework for constructive civic engagement whereby citizens, civil society, and the state can work together to accelerate India's development. The second outlines ways in which each of us can contribute to this goal in our own way. The last one discusses how acting on the ideas in this book will not only strengthen India, but also help us lead the world. India matters both intrinsically and instrumentally for global welfare, and accelerating India's development will also speed up global development.

1. A Framework for Constructive Civic Engagement

1.1 Understanding how class structure has shaped the status quo

A key reason for India's weak performance in universal service delivery is our elite bias in both policies and public spending. The facts highlighted in this book are consistent with economist Pranab Bardhan's argument that three groups of elites—government employees (Chapter 5), large landowners (Chapters 6 and 15), and big businesses (Chapters 2 and 16)—have captured the lion's share of public resources.[2]

More generally, we see a pattern of elite bias in *every* sector discussed in this book. A common truism about India is that 'everything that is true about India, the opposite is also true.'[3] For instance, the Indian education system produces some of the world's greatest talents, but also has the largest number of children who complete primary school without being able to read. We have some of the world's best healthcare for those who can afford to pay, but also have the largest number of stunted children. These extremes partly reflect India's vast population, with outliers on both ends of the outcome distribution. But they also reflect the elite skew in our policy priorities.[4]

For instance, our focus on higher education over primary education mainly benefited students who attended private schools or public schools like the *Kendriya Vidyalayas* that served children of government employees.[5] While elite universities and institutions had 'meritocratic' admissions, the under-investment in universal high-quality school education meant that the stepping stones to compete in meritocratic entrance exams were never built for most Indians. Consistent with this elite bias, cross-country analysis shows that the Indian education system is one of the most unequal in the world.[6]

Similarly, many of our travails in health reflect policies that cater to elite interests. For instance, doctor lobbies and private medical college operators have contributed to the low investment in medical education—where limiting supply benefits incumbents, but at great cost to the public.[7] Similarly, the under-investment in preventive public health relative to curative private health partly reflects the fact that top doctors in India enjoy great influence in health policy by being personal physicians to the elite.[8,9]

Policing is also an area where the system is mainly set up to serve elites, at the cost of the poor and vulnerable, as discussed in Chapter 13. The elite bias of the police is best captured by former DGP Prakash Singh, who has noted that 'police in India are primarily used to serve the ruling class, and not the citizens'.

Our slow justice system also favours the rich and connected. Delays increase the cost of justice and benefit those who can hire legal teams for longer. They hurt the weaker party in a dispute who has less 'staying power' and may therefore give up even when wronged. Delays also benefit lawyers who get paid more when cases drag on for longer.[10] Finally, the composition of both the bar (lawyers) and the bench (judges) is stacked towards elites and those with a family history in the legal profession.[11]

Even our welfare and subsidy spending is often skewed towards the better-off. Electricity and fertilizer subsidies, and farm loan waivers are promoted as farmer welfare programmes but are mostly captured by large landowners. Further, the poorest are often unable to even access welfare schemes because of not being aware of them or not being able to complete the necessary paperwork (Chapter 15).

Finally, as noted in Chapter 16, job creation in India has favoured the highly educated who have benefited disproportionately from globalization and trade. Further, state strategies to attract investments and even the PLI scheme have prioritized incentives for capital over labour, and for sectors intensive in high-skilled labour.

Thus, we subsidize the elites and the middle classes both at the time of education *and* at the time of job creation.

The challenge of elites having a disproportionate voice in policy and obtaining more than their fair share of public resources is not unique to India and is seen in many societies around the world. But it is important to recognize that the patterns of public expenditure documented throughout this book are not just a set of technocratic facts, *but also reflect the distribution of power and access in our society.*[12]

One reason for cautious optimism is that these patterns do not necessarily imply a malevolent elite. Rather, they more likely reflect a standard political process where different social and economic groups lobby for their interests. Since elites have greater access to power, policy decisions often reflect their preferences. This is why the agenda of improving governance and service delivery will be furthered by showing that it will be in *everyone's* interest to do so— including the elite—as further elaborated below.

1.2 From class conflict to collective action

This skewed distribution of economic and political power partly explains why civil society movements that advocate for the poor and marginalized have strong elements of class conflict. For activists focused on the vulnerable, witnessing deprivation and injustice, alongside elite capture of public resources—both through grand corruption at the policy level and petty corruption at the local level— almost inevitably fuels a sense of class struggle. Further, since they perceive (often correctly) that the state is captured by the rich and powerful, their activism is often directed against the state itself.

Partly drawing from Mahatma Gandhi's approach against the British, India's civil-society organizations (CSOs) and activists have used a combination of methods including petitions, marches, sit-ins, protests, hunger strikes, voter mobilization, and court cases, to both get the state to cease some actions, and to start others.[13] For instance, they have challenged the eviction of tribal populations from their lands for mining and dam construction without adequate compensation, and advocated for better rehabilitation of displaced people.[14] Other examples include lobbying the government to pass the Right to Information (RTI) Act to improve government transparency and the National Rural Employment Guarantee Act (NREGA) to provide employment to the rural poor.

These examples illustrate the value of a vigilant civil society in holding the government accountable, especially when state actions are arbitrary or harm the vulnerable. India is a democracy, which implies governance by 'majority rule'. However, we are also a Constitutional *Republic*, which means that the majority cannot run roughshod over the legal rights of individuals. While these rights are in theory protected by the law, in practice, civil-society activism is a key instrument in helping the vulnerable secure their legal rights against state overreach.[15] The examples also highlight the value of CSOs in promoting progressive legislation that elected governments may not enact on their own.

At the same time, despite these efforts, the facts on elite skew of public spending and weak public service delivery suggest that we may need different social strategies to alleviate these structural problems. This section argues that, while civil society vigilance against state overreach is important, progressive civil society movements will be more effective in helping the disadvantaged at scale by working in *partnership* with the state and forming coalitions with elites (or at least subsets of them) to build more effective public systems rather than predominantly functioning in an adversarial mode.

My reason for this view is that we are not dealing with an oppressive colonial state, that needs to be constantly opposed. Rather, we are mainly dealing with a democratic but *overwhelmed* state. Thus, while lobbying for more rights and legislative protections and entitlements for the poor is useful, the key binding constraint to delivering on democratic aspirations for all Indians at scale is not intention as much as weak state capacity.[16]

However, building a more effective Indian state is a much more complex and long-term endeavour than getting governments to launch a pro-poor programme or policy. While pro-poor advocacy may accomplish the latter, the former needs a broad and sustained social coalition, including elites who recognize that *even they* are hurt by an ineffective state. Elites exert disproportionate influence in every society, including India.[17] Thus, activists and CSOs might achieve more for the disadvantaged by shifting from an approach of class conflict to one based on collective action around positive-sum ideas.

Specifically, the Indian state's ability to serve the poor is constrained by (a) limited resources, (b) skewed spending towards elites, and (c) poor translation of spending into outcomes. The best way to relax the first constraint is faster economic growth.[18] The second constraint can be eased by prioritizing ideas with elite and middle-class support, and by mobilizing voters to provide *political support* to reform inequitable and inefficient subsidies. Finally, alleviating the third constraint is what this book has focused on, by presenting data and evidence-based ideas to facilitate this goal. This is also the area where more focus will yield the *highest* social returns, as shown in Chapter 10.

1.3 Economists, activists, and finding common ground

Civil-society groups often criticize finance department officials (and economists who advise them) for not allocating more funds to social sectors. However, such criticism does not appreciate the enormous pressure these officials face. As one exasperated finance secretary said to me: 'Everyone wants more spending on their pet area, but no one talks about what to cut or recognizes the precarious fiscal situation.'

As a result, the engagement between activists and CSOs on one side, and economists and officials in the finance department, can often be adversarial.[19] However, as economist *and* activist Jean Drèze has noted, both groups will benefit from understanding each other since they often have similar goals, but approach development problems with different perspectives and priorities.[20]

The differences are both philosophical and epistemic. Philosophically, economists prioritize efficiency and economic growth, whereas activists prioritize equity and state action to mitigate injustices of accidents of birth. Economists focus more on improving *average* outcomes over time, whereas activists take more of a human rights perspective and focus on outcomes of the most vulnerable. Epistemically, economists privilege quantitative evidence based on representative samples of data, and credible causal estimates of the impacts of policies and programmes, consistent with their focus on averages. In contrast, activists make greater use of qualitative data, field notes, and case studies, consistent with their focus on understanding and telling the stories of the vulnerable, and highlighting human experiences and not just statistics.

Economists, including myself, put great emphasis on efficiency, markets, and evidence. This is because well-functioning markets with competition among producers and choice for consumers are a powerful tool for boosting efficiency and productivity. These in turn are key to economic growth, which is the most important driver of long-term welfare. They also see evidence on the impact and cost-effectiveness of public spending as a key tool for boosting efficiency due to the lack of market discipline in the public sector.[21]

However, pro-poor activists and intellectuals are often wary of economists, seeing these arguments as supporting the existing power distribution. While free-market capitalism may promote efficiency and growth, it often widens inequality by mainly benefiting elites with financial, physical, and human capital. Market-led growth processes can also make the vulnerable worse off, unless the state acts to widely distribute the benefits of growth. However, growing inequality increases the risk that elites capture political processes, entrench their power and advantage, undermine state support for the poor, and make institutions more extractive than inclusive. These are not just theoretical concerns. Global evidence has documented elite capture of institutions to perpetuate their advantages in many settings, with signs of similar dynamics in India as well.[22]

On evidence, the pushback is more tactical. While not against quantitative evidence in principle, activists worry that waiting for evidence before acting can delay pro-poor initiatives, and can even become a stalling tactic for those who resist pro-poor spending.

Thus, in this view, demanding evidence before acting can create a conservative bias in favour of the status quo—especially if one insists on expensive large-scale and long-term impact studies before scaling pro-poor policies and programmes.

Put together, a common view among pro-poor activists is that (a) the state favours elites by default, necessitating continuous pressure for pro-poor policies, and (b) because of this pro-elite bias, they should be opportunistic in getting pro-poor programmes and laws passed when there is a political window of opportunity—without waiting for data or evidence on effectiveness. Yet, despite these philosophical and epistemic differences between economists and activists, there is much common ground to be found.

Economists will do well to recognize the blind spots of the economics discipline regarding power, and how power differences shape both the state and the market. Further, as the discussion in Chapter 15 shows, local elites often resist even well-designed welfare programmes like NREGS, because they threaten their authority over the poor. Given such resistance, even *efficiency-enhancing* welfare programmes like the NREGS would have never come into being without the sustained advocacy of CSOs and activists over decades, which illustrates the value of such pro-poor advocacy.

At the same time, activists should recognize that passing laws and raising budgets are *not enough* to improve outcomes for the poor. As shown throughout this book, the translation of laws and budgets into outcomes is often weak, and the impact of laws, policies, and programmes vary enormously. Paying more attention to evidence and cost-effectiveness to inform the *specifics* of what CSOs lobby for will yield much better outcomes for the poor at any given level of spending. For instance, while NREGS was a highly effective programme, several well-intentioned elements of the Right to Education (RTE) Act have been ineffective, or even harmful for education.[23]

This is why activists and economists can be more effective by working together. To build a better India for *all*, we need to (a) reduce the elite bias in our public spending, and (b) sharply improve the effectiveness of public money spent on pro-poor causes.

Activists and CSOs are better positioned to lead on the first goal by directly engaging with citizens and building movements to create political support for pro-poor initiatives, *and* for reducing inequitable, inefficient subsidies to free up funds for pro-poor spending.

Economists and economic reasoning can help with the second goal by using theory, data, and evidence to improve the effectiveness of pro-poor public spending. Economic analysis of subsidy spending can also help CSOs mobilize support for policies that reduce subsidies to the rich. Given our tight fiscal situation, improving effectiveness of public spending should not just be a technical task for economists. Rather, it is a *moral imperative* for *all of us* because doing so will allow us to deliver much more for the poor.

Turning from data and evidence to markets, activists and CSOs should recognize that well-regulated competitive free markets are the most powerful poverty alleviation tool we have ever known! This is best seen in the transformative growth in China and India after adopting market-based reforms in the 1980s and 1990s, resulting in more people escaping poverty than any period in human history. The power of free markets comes from two main elements: (a) using market prices as a signal for resource allocation, and (b) using these prices to create incentives for both efficiency and innovation.[24] Overall, societies that rely more on free markets than state control to allocate scarce resources have on average delivered higher economic growth *and* more human development.

Beyond efficiency, free markets also have moral virtues. The main moral attraction of a free-market transaction is its basis in voluntary exchange. No party can coerce the other to buy or sell unless they *both* benefit from the transaction. This is an exemplar of a win-win exchange, and illustrates how markets promote freedom. Consistent with this view, there is evidence that market-led growth in India has accelerated the empowerment of scheduled castes. Studies show that reforms and growth helped them upend rigid social hierarchies by expanding their economic opportunities, freedom, and mobility.[25]

However, despite these virtues, a key weakness of markets is that they only care for those with purchasing power. So, while a market transaction makes both sides better off, the market does not question the justice (or lack thereof) of the initial position at the start of that transaction.[26] Economists should acknowledge this fact more often, and recognize the tension between markets and democracy: while the democratic ideal is 'one person, one vote', markets treat people on a 'one rupee, one vote' principle.

This tension lies at the core of several policy dilemmas we face in India: efficiency will typically be higher if we follow market principles, whereas politicians are under pressure to provide more equal access to basic goods and services regardless of people's ability to pay. Navigating this tension is the primary challenge for Indian political economy. Intervening too much in free markets, and doing so inefficiently, will reduce efficiency and growth, and hurt *everyone*, including the poor, over time. However, doing nothing to mitigate injustices due to accidents of birth is ethically undesirable, politically not viable in a democracy, and *also* economically inefficient by limiting the potential of hundreds of millions of Indians to escape the low-capability traps that they are born into.

Global evidence and India's own experience suggest that the most effective way to balance these goals is to allow well-regulated competitive markets to function freely to maximize efficiency, while the state focuses on providing essential public services and well-designed welfare programmes to promote equity. Doing so will boost growth, and empower many more Indians to participate in the growth process, and create a positive feedback loop to faster growth by making people more productive. A central goal of this book is to present ideas that will allow us to improve both equity *and* efficiency and to accelerate both development *and* growth. This is a goal that activists and economists spanning the economic left and right should be able to find common ground on.

1.4 Building trust between the state and civil society

Just as civil society's efficacy increases when it partners with the state, governments become more effective when they can build trust with citizens. Trust is critical for a society's ability to undertake 'positive-sum' actions, which require forgoing immediate benefits for higher long-term returns. However, if citizens distrust the government, they will be less willing to make short-term sacrifices for longer-term gains, and it can be difficult to implement even welfare-improving reforms, as seen in the examples below.

For example, Aadhaar-linked benefit transfer programmes were launched to improve the delivery of welfare schemes for the poor. The government highlighted the gains from reduced leakage and corruption, and improving beneficiary empowerment through portability of benefits. Yet, civil society opponents were suspicious on grounds ranging from increased exclusion, loss of privacy, and data leaks to corporate interests. While the project did proceed, it was acrimoniously litigated all the way to the Supreme Court. Some of this conflict may have been avoided by having better and more timely data, and improving government transparency to boost trust (as explained in Chapter 4).

Low trust is also partly why advocates for the poor prefer legislative guarantees to *in-kind* benefits (like subsidized food) as opposed to income equivalents, despite the latter being more efficient. This is because income-based benefits can be devalued by inflation, and the government has a poor track record of indexing benefits for the poor. For example, the National Old Age Pension was set at Rs 200 per month in 2006 and was unchanged for over a decade, implying substantial value erosion due to inflation.[27] Such actions not only privilege powerful insiders over vulnerable outsiders (pensions of officials are inflation indexed, but those for poor widows were not), they also undermine citizen trust, which hurts our collective capacity to undertake positive-sum actions.

This is also why agriculture subsidy reforms are so difficult. First, they must be well designed to be technically feasible and align incentives. Second, for political feasibility, they should ideally not make anyone worse off. Third, even if such designs are created (like in Chapters 6, 15, and 16), they cannot be implemented without extensive trust-building between the government and farmers because farmers will have to agree to give up a 'bird in the hand' today in return for promises of continued future payments.[28]

Effective political leaders understand the centrality of public trust for their governments' effectiveness. Prime Minister Narendra Modi demonstrated this by modifying his original 2014 slogan promising a governing philosophy of *sabka saath, sabka vikaas* (with everyone, for the development of everyone) to include *sabka vishwaas* (with everyone's *trust*).[29] Interestingly, he later added *sabka prayaas* (with everyone's effort) to this slogan, which is consistent with the goals of *this* chapter, reflecting the view that building a better India will take a collective effort that we all can and need to contribute to.

How can the government make this slogan a reality and build more public trust? One way is to invest in state capacity to deliver better public services and improve citizens' experiences with receiving them. A second is to further decentralize governance, which can boost both performance and trust by reducing the gap between citizens and the government (Chapter 8). A third is to not over-promise relative to state capacity to deliver, since this will inevitably lead to broken promises and erosion of trust. This can be very difficult for politicians facing electoral pressures, which is why the institutional investments discussed in Chapter 17 that *constrain* the ability of politicians to act in their short-term interest can help to build citizen trust in the state. A fourth is better and more transparent data, and to *explain* the rationale behind policy and budget choices to the public to clarify the thinking that has informed policy choices (Chapters 4 and 6).

Such public reasoning can make our democracy more mature by helping citizens and civil society understand and debate trade-offs, as opposed to only making demands of the state.[30] Understanding resource constraints can also help to build public support for cost-effectiveness and value for money in public spending. It can also help build public support for reforms that may hurt a few concentrated elite interests, but generate large gains in public welfare. Such a process will also build mutual trust over time and make it easier for the state, citizens, and civil society to work together to build a better India.

1.5 Building a broad social coalition to improve public service delivery

The discussion above highlights the value of collaboration and building trust across state and civil society. Yet, the track record of Indian elites in supporting pro-poor policies is not very inspiring. So, a natural question to address is why should elites and middle classes support the reform agenda in this book even though they currently enjoy a disproportionate share of public resources, and have mostly seceded from receiving public services? There are at least three reasons—altruism, patriotism, and self-interest.

Many Indians exhibit altruistic behaviour in their private lives. However, the best way to help the less fortunate at *scale* is to improve state effectiveness to serve them better. For the patriotically motivated, the best way to improve India's global standing is to boost economic growth. However, growth is hampered by low individual and aggregate productivity due to weak education, health, safety, and justice. Finally, beyond altruism and patriotism, a key reason to support this reform agenda is that weaknesses in governance and service delivery *also* hurt elites and middle classes.

Elites, like firm owners and industrialists, are hurt by low productivity of poorly educated and skilled workers. They are hurt by lower worker attendance and productivity due to the increased risks of falling sick (from pollution and higher disease burden) and low quality of curative care. They are directly hurt by pollution and an inability to enjoy outdoor spaces. The lower willingness of women to travel to work due to poor public safety deprives their firms of a large pool of productive employees. Finally, while they can afford lawyers to fight their own cases, the painfully slow justice system locks up key factors of production including credit and land, and thereby increases their costs.

Salaried middle-classes have also turned to private solutions and exited from public services.[31] But they are also hurt by weak public service delivery (which gives private operators more power over them) and by misguided policy and regulatory actions that constrain the creation of more high-quality private options (Chapter 9). Further, their ability to 'buy their way out' of state failures is less than that of elites. Thus, while it is rational for individual middle-class families to exit to private options, it will benefit them as a collective if we improve public services. This is why it makes sense for all strata of Indians to form a broad coalition to advocate for improving state capacity, quality of expenditure, and public services, and it also makes sense for political leaders to aim to craft such a winning coalition around improved service delivery.[32]

1.6 Section summary

Beyond limited resources and inefficiency, weak public service delivery in India also reflects elite capture and elite apathy. To accelerate India's development, it is essential for Indian elites and middle classes to understand that weak governance and service delivery hurts *all* of us, contributing to poor development outcomes for most Indians and limiting economic growth. This is why this book has aimed to present ideas that will benefit all sections of society and thereby generate broad coalitions of support.

Acting on these ideas will allow us to improve efficiency and equity, and also empower the most vulnerable. It will allow us to expand the economic pie to benefit all, while also bending the arc of India's progress towards justice, and help realize Dr Ambedkar's hope that democratic equality should also contribute to greater social and economic equality and justice.[33] Critically, this pathway for greater social justice does not rely on redistributing a fixed pie, or stifling entrepreneurs and businesses like our failed socialist policies of the past. Rather, it aims to do so by enlarging the pie by making high-return public investments that will make *all* members of society more productive.

While the language in this book may focus more on technocratic notions of efficiency than on ethical notions of justice, the goal is very much to promote the latter. The book's approach reflects the idea that effective leaders 'campaign in poetry, but govern in prose'.[34] Similarly, poetic advocacy for equality and social justice may stir idealism and build mass movements more effectively than prosaic discussions of data, evidence, and cost-effectiveness. Yet, given our limited resources, improving the quality of public spending and service delivery using these tools is the most *practical* way to improve equity and better *deliver* on the promise of democracy for all Indians. It is also the approach that is most likely to garner broad support across all sections of society.

2. How Can We All Contribute to Accelerating India's Development?

We are more likely to build a better India if we work together. Yet, the way we can best contribute varies by our position in society. Specifically, the poor can contribute by being more *empowered*, middle classes by being more *engaged* in civic life and shaping the public sphere, and elites by being more *ethical*—lobbying not just for themselves, but for the collective goods and governance reforms that will make all Indians better off. Some of this is already happening, but we will achieve more by accelerating these trends. This section *briefly* discusses ways in which various social actors can use the ideas in this book to undertake actions that will help to accelerate India's development.

2.1 Government

Political leaders

In our democracy, elected political leaders have the legitimacy and authority to create policies, allocate public funds, and initiate reforms to improve public welfare. India's politicians face increasing pressure to meet voter demands, but a key challenge they face is in identifying the best way to do so with limited resources. They may know *what* they want the state to deliver, but may not know *how* best to make it deliver efficiently.

This book aims to offer a menu of *implementable*, evidence-based, and cost-effective ideas that are likely to deliver at least some visible results in a five-year time frame. So, political leaders in search of practical ideas that will appeal to voters can engage with this menu, and include ideas they like in their party's election manifesto. Further, while they can implement these better if they are elected, engaging with the menu can also give political leaders constructive ideas to advocate for when they are in opposition.

Ideally, these ideas will resonate with both governing and Opposition parties, fostering a broad political consensus on the centrality of improving state capacity for public welfare. Simply put, regardless of the direction a party may want to drive the car that is the Indian state, *every* party will benefit from being able to drive a better-functioning car.[35]

Beyond adopting specific ideas, the most important step that political leaders can take to accelerate India's development is to prioritize a new politics of governance and service delivery over the old politics of identity, polarization, and patronage. Doing so can jumpstart a virtuous cycle because when parties do better on governance, they will have less need for polarization. In addition to top leaders focusing on governance, it is crucial for party leaders to create pathways for rising up their party hierarchy that reward effective governance rather than polarization.

This is another key reason why more decentralization is good for Indian democracy. At present, lower-level leaders do not have many ways of either developing their skills in administration and governance or of demonstrating these to senior party leaders. As a result, they often resort to making provocative, polarizing statements to draw attention from the media and party leaders. In contrast, having more local government positions with meaningful authority will benefit junior politicians, parties, and citizens by creating opportunities and incentives for many more politicians to deliver better governance.

Senior bureaucrats

While political leaders set government priorities, senior bureaucrats are key players in both policymaking and implementation. Most of the issues identified in this book are well known to them due to their extensive experience in government. However, they are often unable to fix them for the reasons noted in Chapters 3 and 5. A key goal of this book is to make these issues that are well known within the bureaucracy into *common knowledge* across Indian society so that there can be a greater impetus for change.[36] Senior officials can drive reforms to boost state effectiveness in at least three ways.

First, as many officials know, reforms happen when preparation meets opportunity. Political leaders are so busy that their attention windows for specific policy areas can be unpredictable. However, when they do focus on an issue, they expect quick options from senior officials. Inspired by the 1991 example, when senior officials had a well-prepared blueprint ready when political leaders sought ideas for economic reforms, this book offers a menu of options for governance reforms that senior officials can have on hand to present whenever there is political demand for ideas to improve governance or outcomes in specific sectors. Further, since most of these are state-level reform ideas, *many more* officials will have the opportunity to engage with and consider them for their states and sectors than if we were to rely only on reformers in the Central government.

Second, even without waiting for political leaders, senior officials can prepare reform roadmaps based on these ideas that are customized to their sector and state. They can champion reforms, promote cross-departmental coordination and collaboration, and proactively build coalitions of reformers. They can present these reform roadmaps and their potential to accelerate India's development to political leaders. In practice, policymaking reflects both political and bureaucratic leadership. As trusted advisers on policy matters, senior officials can proactively shape the thinking of political leaders.

Third, even when there is political support for specific reform ideas, senior bureaucratic leadership is essential for converting ideas into policy roadmaps, driving high-quality implementation, iterating ideas based on practical feedback, and institutionalizing them.

Frontline workers and managers

Many of the costs of weak public systems documented in Chapters 3 and 5 are borne by frontline government staff. Over time, the 'system' has converted them into order-takers, reducing their autonomy and agency to do their jobs better. Several reform ideas in this book aim to boost the capacity and agency of frontline staff and managers, which in turn will increase both their effectiveness and job satisfaction. Correspondingly, government staff should themselves champion these ideas.

Ideally, causes such as reducing paperwork, improving time use and staff management, and continuous capacity-building should be taken up by public employee associations. In practice, these associations have focused more on bargaining for better pay and service conditions for insiders rather than spearheading cost-effective reforms that improve service to the general public. But even if associations do not take up these causes, proactive public-spirited employees and managers can still systematically document their challenges and suggest solutions based on the ideas in this book.

Government employees are much more educated than the average population, and comprise the top 5 to 10 per cent of Indian society by socioeconomic status. They also have the deepest understanding of the practical challenges of service delivery. Their leadership in internalizing the need for reforms, proposing cost-effective solutions, and championing their implementation will significantly contribute to building a better India.

2.2 Civil society

India has a vibrant civil society, with active civil-society organizations (CSOs) that span every arena of our public life. These CSOs are integral to our democracy, and have also played an important role in advocating for public programmes that help the poor. However, CSOs can be much more effective by using data and evidence on cost-effectiveness to inform *what* exactly they lobby for, as seen in the examples below.

Education and human development

Education CSOs in India often advocate for increasing education spending to 6 per cent of GDP. However, it is not clear that higher spending will improve learning outcomes if we spend more in a 'government as usual' way (see Chapter 11). The 6 per cent target is also unrealistic since it reflects the norms of OECD countries who have *double* India's tax to GDP ratio (35 per cent versus 17–18 per cent in India). If we consider the budget share spent on education (and not share of GDP), India aligns with other nations.

Rather than looking at OECD norms, India's education system would have done better by learning from China and Vietnam. A key, but not well-known, fact is that relative to GDP per capita, average government teacher salaries in India are *three times* higher than in China and Vietnam.[37] Since teacher salaries account for most of education spending, China and Vietnam have achieved much better education outcomes than India despite allocating a *lower* share of their budget to school education.

This comparison highlights how ignoring cost-effectiveness has set India back and hurt the poor and vulnerable the most. Education advocacy in India aimed to scale up a high-cost model with many small schools, high teacher salaries, and low accountability and blamed the finance ministry for not allocating more funds. However, these demands were unrealistic at India's tax to GDP ratio. Thus, we would have been better off if we had learnt from China and Vietnam and prioritized *cost-effective* solutions for delivering primary education at scale. In practice, India's approach prioritized the interests of upper middle-class government teachers over those of the poor and marginalized.[38]

This is why CSOs can help by not just lobbying for more spending, but also paying attention to data and evidence to advocate for initiatives that are effective, cost-effective, and benefit disadvantaged children the most. The ideas in Chapter 11 aim to meet all these criteria, and are more likely to be adopted if championed by CSOs.

Similarly, ICDS budget increases over the years have mostly been used to raise the pay of existing anganwadi workers rather than hiring more of them. Yet, a large-scale RCT in Tamil Nadu found that adding staff at current salaries significantly improved child development outcomes, while raising pay for incumbents did not.

Thus, child rights advocates will deliver much more for children (and for women's empowerment) by lobbying for hiring additional workers rather than raising the pay of incumbents.[39]

The ICDS example highlights how researchers and CSOs can complement each other. Child-rights advocates have long urged the addition of a second worker to anganwadi centres, but governments have not acted—citing fiscal constraints.[40] Yet, robust RCT evidence, showing that staff augmentation in the ICDS was highly effective with estimated benefits of thirteen to twenty-one times the cost, has helped to reinforce the case. Bibek Debroy, chairman of the Economic Advisory Council to the Prime Minister, cited the study in a recent column recommending nationwide adoption, and multiple states have shown interest in testing the model.[41] Thus, good evidence can help CSOs with advocacy, and CSOs can help accelerate the translation of evidence to policy.[42]

Healthcare

Similarly, health advocates lobby for higher budgets for the health sector. Yet, more government spending along existing patterns (mainly on curative care) will not be nearly as effective as investing more on preventive public health. Similarly, increasing the supply of high-quality medical education institutes, and creating competence-based pathways to credentialing the large numbers of informal providers will do much more for long-term population health by bringing down costs of healthcare provision.

We must not forget that we are *not* a rich country. Thus, improving healthcare delivery at scale requires a focus on reducing the cost of quality-adjusted provision rather than expanding inefficient, high-cost models. While we *do* need to increase government health spending, CSOs will be much more effective if they focus on lobbying for cost-effective and high-return investments, including the ideas in Chapter 12.

Agriculture subsidy reforms

As noted in Chapters 6, 15, and 16, India's farm subsidies are costly, inefficient, and highly skewed towards large landowners. Despite economists' emphasis on reforming these subsidies, the political influence of large landowners makes such reforms very difficult. However, this diversion of public funds towards the elites mainly hurts the poor who bear the costs of lack of public funds to invest in better basic service delivery.

This is why CSOs can do more to increase pro-poor spending if they also identify and lobby against subsidies that hurt both equity and efficiency, and are in R3 of Figure 6.2. Generating such mass support will be easier if the fiscal savings from cutting bad spending are earmarked for a policy or programme that will benefit many more people. This is what the ideas in Chapter 15 and 16 aim to do. But they are more likely to happen with mass public support, which economists and technocrats cannot provide, but CSOs can be more effective at.

Other reform ideas

Nearly every idea in this book should appeal to pro-poor CSOs. For instance, ideas such as building better systems for collecting data on outcomes and citizen receipts of welfare programmes; conducting spatial and economic incidence of public expenditure; using this data to allocate public funds based on principles of equality, equity, and effectiveness; improving the functioning of markets through better disclosure; and apprenticeship-based training and hiring for service delivery jobs should be strongly supported by progressive CSOs because they aim to systematically reduce the pro-elite bias in our public spending, and deliver more for the poor at any given level of spending.

Paying attention to the political economy of reform

While it is good to build broader awareness of the elite-skew in public spending, and for CSOs to support attempts to reduce this skew, it is important to recognize the power of entrenched elites to block reforms. This is why most reform ideas in this book are designed in ways that existing beneficiaries of the status quo are *not* made worse off, but that we can improve the quality of public expenditure *going forward*.

Thus, despite high public-sector salaries and poor accountability, this book does not recommend salary reductions or removal of non-performers as these are political non-starters. Instead, the focus is on apprenticeship-based pathways for *future* hiring, which can deliver many improvements over the status quo, as seen in Chapters 5 and 11–14. Crucially, this reform will not threaten current employees, and will in fact make their life easier by boosting staffing. Similarly, the approach to agriculture subsidy reform in Chapters 6, 15, and 16 does not target immediate fiscal savings. Instead, it aims to reduce economic distortions and inefficiency while keeping subsidy value unchanged. The fiscal savings will come over time from increased efficiency as shown in Chapter 6.

The history of policy analysis in India is full of economically sound reform ideas that are not undertaken because of political constraints. This is why this book focuses on ideas that should be politically popular, and that should be able to build a broad coalition of support across stakeholders and ideologies. India's vibrant civil society will have a crucial role to play in supporting the adoption of these ideas to build a better India.

2.3 Entrepreneurs and business leaders

As noted in Chapter 16, these groups have a critical role in accelerating development by boosting innovation, productivity, and job creation. Yet, they can do much more.

Business leaders

Business leaders can contribute by using their collective voice— especially through industry associations—to push the government for better delivery of essential public services. Weak public service delivery raises costs for businesses and makes them less competitive. Thus, fixing these issues will have a much greater long-term impact on economic growth than short-term fixes like capital subsidies and tariff protections.

This is why citizens should be wary when firms lobby for protection from imports. The higher cost of doing business imposed by weak public service delivery may not matter much for firms in domestic markets because local competitors *also* face these costs. But they matter in global markets because higher production costs make Indian industry less competitive. Protection allows industry to make up for these cost disadvantages in the domestic market, but the costs are paid by Indian citizens in the form of higher prices.

The greater long-term social cost may be reduced incentives for businesses to advocate for better public service delivery because 'band-aid' solutions like tariffs and subsidies can delay system-level actions to address the deep wounds of weak public services. Recall that a self-interested reason for business elites to support better public services is that *they* also pay the costs of weak public services in the form of lower productivity and higher input costs. However, if these costs are mitigated by 'deals' they negotiate with politicians, citizens lose a vital voice in lobbying for better public service delivery. It also becomes easier to get stuck in a low-level political economy cycle where business elites and politicians exchange electoral financing in return for tariffs or investment subsidies where *they* are both better off, but at a large cost to average citizens.

This is why it is essential for business leaders and industry associations who care about India's long-term development to champion the agenda of building a more effective Indian state that can better deliver essential public services. Beyond advocacy, they can also contribute by using their personal wealth and corporate social responsibility (CSR) funds to make strategic philanthropic investments, as expanded on in Section 2.6.

Entrepreneurs

One of India's great strengths is its vibrant ecosystem of innovators and entrepreneurs. However, many start-ups have found themselves chasing a relatively small addressable market. As noted by investors like Haresh Chawla and Sajith Pai, the perception of a 1.4 billion-strong Indian market is mostly a myth since only 10–15 per cent of this population has purchasing power after meeting basic needs.[43]

Instead of importing ideas and business models from high-income countries to cater to a limited segment of India's population, entrepreneurs can contribute more to India's development by focusing on frugal innovation—developing cost-effective solutions for India's domestic needs. The good news is that many successful entrepreneurs are already doing this, and there is funding available for such efforts from both standard investors and 'impact investors' who seek a 'double bottom line' of both commercial and social returns. The ideas in this book can hopefully provide some fuel for Indian entrepreneurs by identifying key missing markets and products to direct innovation at.[44]

2.4 Academia and think tanks

Academics and intellectuals can play a crucial role in accelerating India's development. They have the ability and the time to deeply study complex issues, and share their understanding with decision-makers and the public. They also shape the world views and actions of future generations through their teaching. Yet, they can do much more.

Academics and researchers

Officials often need research-based inputs to solve practical problems, but might not know which researcher has the relevant expertise or interest. Conversely, academics often have valuable insights for policy, but do not know how to connect with decision-makers, or whether their inputs will be appreciated. Therefore, we will all benefit from creating structures that enable researchers and officials to interact more.

One idea is to create a state-level policy forum that brings together policymakers and leading researchers for an annual discussion of the state's policy priorities. These fora could be sector specific for more focused discussions. The agenda should focus on two key points: 'What decisions do policymakers expect to make that will benefit from having better research?', and 'What knowledge do researchers already have that they feel is not being adequately reflected in policy?'[45] Policymakers should present, and academics should reflect on the first question, with roles being reversed for the second. Even if such a forum results in a few good engagements, it would be worthwhile.

A second idea is for states to create part-time advisory roles for leading researchers, enabling engagement with government departments in their area of expertise.[46] While many academics would prioritize research and writing, having even a few policy-motivated scholars in these roles could help bridge gaps between officials and relevant academic expertise. Importantly, the adviser's role is not to *have* all the answers, but to connect officials with the right expert or organization when specific questions arise.

Third, this book could serve as a resource for public-spirited academics to gain insights into governance issues, and propose projects that could improve welfare at the state or local level. While the first two ideas require government initiative, acting at the local level makes it easier for academics themselves to initiate public-interest engagement.

Fourth, since officials may be busy and not have time to engage even with well-meaning academics, another entry point for working on public-interest issues is by reaching out to relevant CSOs. Many CSOs have deep sectoral knowledge, as well as programme data that can provide insights, but often lack dedicated staff for analysing such data. Collaborations between academics and CSOs can be a win-win arrangement where the CSOs get analytical support, and academics can contribute to the public interest.[47]

Finally, academics should aim to include their students in these projects.[48] Such projects will equip students with skills, experience, a deeper understanding of complex issues, and a chance to contribute to the public good. Even without a formal partner engagement, faculty can encourage students to analyse public-interest issues for their assignments, come up with potential solutions, and facilitate sharing of the best of these analyses and ideas with stakeholders in and outside the government.[49]

Think tanks

Think tanks occupy an important place in effective policymaking. Unlike academics, who mainly focus on teaching and publishing research papers, think-tank staff are primarily motivated by translating research insights into tangible policy solutions. India has many good think tanks, working on a range of policy issues. However, India's think-tank ecosystem is predominantly Delhi-based, and focused on national-level issues.

My main suggestion to think tanks is to increase their focus on state-level issues, and to create policy templates and roadmaps usable at the state level. Many of India's most pressing issues—including education, skills, health, environment, safety, and jobs—require urgent action at the state level. Yet, state and local governments are relatively underserved by India's think-tank ecosystem. Hence, the practical impact of think tanks can be much higher at these levels. Some think tanks are already doing this, but the collective impact of India's think tank ecosystem will be higher if they institutionalize thinking about state-level actions and prioritize them as much as national ones.[50]

2.5 Media

The media is a key contributor to our public sphere. It shapes both public discourse and opinion, and is often referred to as the fourth branch of government. Yet, in part due to commercial pressures, the media in India and globally has seen a deterioration in the quality of discourse.[51] Even when public life is covered in a factual and non-partisan way, the coverage treats politics more as a spectator sport and focuses on who is winning and losing power, rather than the substance of policies and governance.

The media can help to build a better India by increasing coverage of the fundamental issues discussed in this book. Despite the belief that audiences have a short attention span, and want to be entertained more than educated, the popularity of TV shows like Aamir Khan's *Satyamev Jayate*, and long-form podcasts like Amit Varma's *The Seen and the Unseen* suggests that there is a demand for deep, well-researched content on substantive issues. The challenge is to make this kind of programming more commercially viable.

One idea is to design TV shows that make governance exciting. Imagine a gameshow with elements of *Kaun Banega Crorepati* and *Satyamev Jayate* featuring governance heroes and highlighting their work. It could invite nominations from across India, showcase citizen or official initiatives to improve governance, and have audience members and live viewers vote on winners. It can be commercially viable by attracting corporate sponsors who value the positive brand association with a public cause, as seen in the environmental sustainability-themed show, *Godrej Green Champion*.[52]

The other key media trend is the rise of individual content creators on platforms like YouTube, who have developed direct relationships with viewers. Such creators are increasingly influential since young audiences obtain more information from them than from traditional media. They can play an important role in India's future by helping to educate citizens about substantive issues that affect their well-being, *including in regional languages*. There are several facts in this book that may not be widely known, which in turn can provide new ideas for content creators to take to their audiences.

Addressing the deeper structural challenges of the media is beyond the scope of this book. However, given the importance of the media in shaping our public discourse, the two ideas offered above are modest attempts to suggest ways whereby public-spirited traditional and new media content creators can use the ideas in this book to educate citizens on these essential issues, and on potential ways of addressing them.

2.6 Philanthropy

India has a long tradition of philanthropy, which has been growing in recent years—spurred by economic growth and rising individual fortunes. It has also been accelerated by the legal mandate for companies to set aside funds for CSR. Such philanthropy has the potential to bring about transformative changes in India. However, just like public funds can be spent more effectively, so can philanthropic funds.

Traditional versus strategic philanthropy

Traditional philanthropy often aims to fill gaps in the delivery of social welfare that are left by the government. Historically, before the advent of the welfare state, support to the vulnerable and afflicted was led by society through a combination of religious and community organizations, rather than by the state.

Indian philanthropy mostly reflects this view, and has created and funded organizations focused on activities such as: (a) alleviating human suffering through providing food and medical assistance to the needy, (b) serving local communities by running or supporting schools, clinics, and community centres, (c) supporting disadvantaged populations who are underserved by the state, (d) creating centres of excellence—such as high-quality schools or hospitals that also cater to the poor, (e) offering merit scholarships to talented individuals of limited means, and (f) supporting programmes to empower marginalized communities.

In contrast, strategic philanthropy—a more recent concept—aims to identify the areas with the highest social return on philanthropic investment. Examples of causes funded include: (a) fundamental research and innovation, with transformative potential for human welfare, (b) scaling up evidence-based, cost-effective programmes, and (c) improving the effectiveness of the state itself, which is still in its infancy.

The strategic philanthropy opportunity

Traditional philanthropy serves crucial social functions. However, with the increase in philanthropic funds in India, we can expand strategic philanthropy without reducing funds for traditional philanthropy. The numerical example below illustrates how strategic philanthropy focused on improving state effectiveness can be transformative.

Indian governments spend over Rs 7,50,000 crore on education annually. A gift of Rs 1000 crore to build schools raises the budget to Rs 7,51,000 crore. In contrast, a strategic philanthropic investment of the same funds that improves the effectiveness of public spending by even 1 per cent would yield efficiency gains of Rs 7500 crore. If the gain comes from improving public _systems_, they would occur annually in _perpetuity_. Using a 10 per cent discount rate, this implies a net present value of Rs 75,000 crore or *75 times higher* than the return to traditional philanthropy! Rohini Nilekani has echoed this sentiment by noting that: 'If more CSOs could focus on better governance, I think we could all become more effective more quickly.'[53]

Another way of thinking about this difference is that traditional philanthropy is *additive* to the public budget, whereas strategic philanthropy that even modestly improves state effectiveness can generate *multiplicative* benefits because of the vastly greater *scale* of government spending. This is not a pipe dream given how much low-hanging fruit there is in improving government effectiveness as shown throughout this book. To borrow from venture capital parlance: there are many 20–100x social RoI opportunities in this space. Even at a success rate of 20 per cent, a *portfolio* of such investments would likely yield a 10x return on philanthropic funds invested.

Proceeding with both ambition and humility

Strategic philanthropy shares key principles with effective public spending. Both will maximize welfare by (a) identifying and correcting market failures, (b) investing in high expected RoI activities, and (c) considering how their actions will affect other actors and the overall ecosystem. However, despite these similarities, there are notable differences in the opportunities and the constraints faced by philanthropy and government.

The main advantage of philanthropy is its ability to move fast, and make data-driven investments to maximize public good with fewer procedural constraints than a reformer within the government would face. This freedom allows it to be bold, take risks, and aim for 'moon shots' with transformative potential, albeit with lower success rates. Its main constraint is the lack of a democratic mandate, which can limit its legitimacy to influence government functioning. This could be why philanthropy in India has focused on low-risk non-controversial, *additive* activities, such as building schools and hospitals, rather than higher-return *multiplicative* activities that can amplify government effectiveness but require both a stronger appetite for failure and navigation of political sensitivities.

However, given the sheer scale of the state, Indian philanthropy can turbo-charge India's development by helping to improve government effectiveness. One way to do this while remaining apolitical is to support activities that improve delivery in the government's *own stated tasks*. This way, the regular political process determines *what* the government does, while philanthropy can help to improve execution.

Actions to improve state effectiveness should ideally originate within the government. However, even when government leaders wish to do so, they may lack the capacity to do so due to the 'chicken and egg' problem: you often need capacity to build capacity! Strategic philanthropy can help by supporting government leaders who wish to improve state functioning by funding staff and organizations to help accelerate this process.

Some of this is already happening. For example, field staff provided by the Tata Trusts helped in implementing the Swachh Bharat Mission, providing not just an additive, but a multiplicative contribution by supporting better utilization of public funds.[54] Other examples include organizations like Pratham, EkStep, Madhi, and Central Square Foundation in education; Janaagraha in urban governance; and eGov Foundation in e-governance. They are all funded by philanthropy, and work with national, state, and local governments to boost their efficacy. The key value of philanthropic funding is that it allows mission-driven social entrepreneurs and organizations to hire mission-oriented *professional* talent to build both the internal capacity to deliver, and to build trust with governments by not seeking contracts and payments as commercial vendors would do.

While the examples above are a good start, a lot more can be done. Given the scale of India's problems, we need to improve government effectiveness across the board, and not just at a project level. But building a more effective Indian state is a colossal task! It requires ambitious organizations and similarly ambitious funders. Beyond individual philanthropy, CSR funding can do a lot more to support strategic initiatives to boost government effectiveness. Since individual companies might lack the scale to identify such opportunities, this is an area where industry associations can take the lead.

At the same time, it is essential to be humble and recognize the extra constraints that governments operate under compared to the private sector (Chapter 3). Philanthropists should guard against the potential hubris that their financial success in one industry gives them the knowledge to take on complex problems of public policy and designing effective public organizations. They should therefore combine ambition to tackle our most challenging problems with the humility to recognize the associated complexities.[55] Further, while strategic philanthropists can have a transformative impact on public welfare, they need to be patient and take a long-term view of success, while being thoughtful about setting intermediate targets for the organizations they fund.

2.7 Individual citizens

Finally, how can citizens contribute to building a more effective Indian state? It is easy to think that individuals have no say over the massive and distant state, and for citizens to therefore not try to engage with it. However, this is a mistake. Active citizenship is the bedrock of democracy, and we can all do more to make the Indian state function better.

The crucial starting point is a mindset shift. We need to stop thinking of politicians and officials as rulers, and citizens as subjects—a misconception that gets entrenched in our collective consciousness when the media refers to governing political parties as 'ruling' parties. Such terminology is an outdated relic of our colonial and feudal history, and of security states where subjects followed rulers' orders in return for protection and basic sustenance. In a democracy, politicians in office derive their authority from the people, and are meant to function in the public interest. Simply put, in a modern democracy, the state exists to serve the citizens and not the other way around.

This mindset shift should clarify that our 'ruling classes' are actually 'employed' on behalf of the public, and paid with taxpayer funds. Just like employers cannot assume that employees are doing their duties, citizens cannot assume that agents of the state are functioning in the public interest. At the same time, just as employers cannot expect staff to deliver unrealistic quantity and quality of output with limited time and resources, citizens cannot expect the state to deliver beyond its fiscal and administrative capacity. So, just like effective managers and supervisors support and monitor their employees, and *prioritize* their tasks; citizens need to do the same with the state.

There are many examples of how citizen engagement with the state can have a positive impact. An illustrative example comes from economist M.R. Sharan's recent book on citizen actions to improve NREGS in Bihar.[56] The story's key protagonist is an individual citizen (Sanjay Sahni) who downloads NREGS data from a government website and uses it to verify if people had been paid for the work reported against their names. While this effort led to a larger civil-society movement, the *spark was a single individual* who decided to understand the system, engage with it, and convert informed engagement into empowerment by asking questions of the concerned authorities.

This example highlights three key steps to active citizenship. The first is to *educate* oneself about public issues. The second is to *engage* with the state, community, and other stakeholders to help improve the situation one is concerned about. The third is when educated engagement creates *empowerment*, which can then be deployed in the public interest. Across households, community organizations, and workplaces, those who care the most and actively engage usually wield disproportionate influence, as well-captured in the adage that '80 per cent of success is just showing up.'[57]

Many citizens are frustrated by poor public-service delivery, but find it easier to exit to private solutions than to try and improve the functioning of the state.[58] But it is *our* taxpayer money that is spent badly and *our* public employees who are managed poorly, and citizens are the ultimate stakeholders in improving the status quo. This book seeks to help with the first step of citizen empowerment by *educating* them about the underperforming Indian state, and the deep structural reasons for this.[59]

The second step is more citizen engagement. In addition to engaging with public issues through participating in CSOs and associations, a specific idea for citizens to contribute to the public sphere is to get more engaged in the functioning of their *local* government. While state and national governments are quite distant, the local government is both accessible and meant to deal with issues of basic service delivery.

Greater engagement of citizens with local government can be a force multiplier for building a better India. It can help (a) prioritize what the government does, (b) improve the efficiency of use of existing resources, and (c) augment state capacity through citizen contributions of time, money, and other in-kind resources. CSOs like *Janaagraha* have developed actionable templates for how citizens can better engage with and support the functioning of their local government, and these provide a natural starting point. Such engagement has also become much easier due to technology. Many cities now have apps that allow citizens to report issues, and citizens in turn can help create a virtuous cycle of better local governance by engaging with these platforms.

Of course, this suggestion faces a collective action problem: everyone benefits if *other* citizens engage to improve local government, and so people may not do so themselves. However, voting is not a rational activity either—an individual vote rarely decides an election. Yet, hundreds of millions of Indians vote—in part because of the intrinsic value of participating in the democratic process. However, if citizen engagement is limited to voting, we should not be surprised if politicians do the same thing—asking for votes every five years and doing little between elections. So, just like voting, engaging with local government can be an intrinsically meaningful form of civic participation; but it can also yield the instrumental benefits of making leaders more responsive to citizens.[60]

Finally, increasing engagement will increase citizen empowerment, a long-term bedrock of a better India. Empowered citizens can both push the state to better do what it should be doing, and push back against the state when it does what it should not. Over time, increased engagement by empowered citizens may be the most effective way of getting the institutional reforms India needs, including greater decentralization of governance, police reforms, electoral reforms, and setting up institutions to increase and safeguard the quality of data, public finances, and public human resource management.

As noted in Chapter 17, we need to create and strengthen institutions to make the Indian state better serve the public interest. However, such changes are resisted by those in power because it requires them to accept constraints on their own behaviour. So, we cannot just wait for benevolent leaders to implement these reforms. We can accelerate them by increasing citizen demand for them. As activists and scholars have noted: 'Power is not given, it has to be taken.'[61]

India did not achieve Independence by just waiting for the British to leave on their own. It was expedited by years of citizen effort through a freedom struggle. Similarly, if we are suffering from the consequences of a state that is primarily serving elite interests, and has underinvested in its own capacity to serve citizens, it is partly because citizens have chosen to passively accept the weak performance of the state. To improve state functioning, citizens must internalize the dictum that *engagement creates empowerment*. Educated engagement with issues of governance, starting at the local level, will over time empower citizens to push for the investments in state capacity and the institutional reforms needed to make the Indian state work better for all Indians.

Students and youth

India's youth are critical stakeholders in this reform agenda because their lives will be the most affected by it. Historically, student and youth movements and protests, fuelled by their idealism and energy, have helped bring about social change in many parts of the world. However, while protestors are often clear on what they are opposing, they are typically less clear on *how* they will achieve the goals they are protesting for. This often leads to disillusionment among idealistic youth as they get older.

This book aims to educate students and youth about India's deep systemic constraints to delivering better development outcomes. Just like changing the driver does not fix a dysfunctional car, merely replacing leaders or parties is unlikely to alleviate our systemic constraints. Doing so will take sustained engagement, regardless of the party in office. This book hopes to empower motivated, idealistic youth with the understanding needed to augment the poetry of protest with the prose of policy, and thereby help to create more effective change agents for a better India. Given that India has the world's largest youth population, their actions will not only shape India, but the entire world.

Section summary

Accelerating India's development will need a combination of top-down actions from enlightened and sagacious leaders, and bottom-up actions by engaged and empowered citizens. While I believe that it makes political sense for elected leaders to act on the roadmap in this book, we can increase the likelihood that these actions are taken if educated and empowered citizens *demand* better governance as well.

3. Strengthening India, and Leading the World

As the world's most populous nation, accounting for over a sixth of humanity, India is increasingly important for global welfare. In line with this importance, Indians should remember that we are also global citizens. Correspondingly, this final section of the book discusses the possible global impacts of acting on its reform roadmap in India.

3.1 Finding solutions that are 'made for India'

India's unique combination of large population, unparalleled diversity, and early democracy makes us a global outlier. This uniqueness often presents a challenge for policy innovators. Foreign ideas risk rejection on the basis that the Indian context is too different, whereas homegrown ideas can face scepticism for lack of a global precedent!

This book aims to address these concerns by primarily drawing on research and evidence from India. While it incorporates universal *principles* like incentives, efficiency, and equity, it tailors the diagnosis of our challenges and proposed solutions to account for India's political, administrative, judicial, and social realities. This approach reduces the risk of 'isomorphic mimicry', whereby we simply copy ideas and best practices from other settings that may not work as well in India.[62]

However, focusing on new homegrown ideas means that there are no global templates to follow. Several specific ideas in this book, like those for a new data and measurement architecture (Chapter 4); using apprenticeship-based training programmes to boost public sector staffing and improve hiring quality (Chapter 5); nuanced decentralization to balance local control with some checks from higher levels of government (Chapter 8); or for building an architecture for service delivery that effectively leverages both public and private options (Chapter 9) have not been tried at scale anywhere else. This raises the valid concern that the ideas may not work, or potentially even backfire.

This book addresses these concerns by emphasizing ways to minimize the risk of policy innovation and experimentation. A key reason for focusing on state-level reform ideas is to encourage states to experiment with different subsets of these ideas, and generate data, evidence, and stakeholder feedback on how they are working in practice. While these ideas reflect my considered judgement that they are likely to be effective in the Indian context, there is no guarantee that they will work. Thus, while they provide a starting point for reforms to improve governance and state capacity, it is important to take an iterative approach and refine implementation roadmaps based on ground-level feedback and evidence from state-level (and even sub-state level) experimentation.[63]

The Aadhaar example

Aadhaar, and the wide range of citizen services enabled by digital public infrastructure (DPI) built on top of it, also known as the India Stack, is an excellent case of a home-grown solution to India's development needs.[64] The project is an exemplar of clear thinking; high-quality execution; and government leadership in understanding the idea's transformative potential, bringing its visionary (Nandan Nilekani) into government, and supporting him in realizing this vision. It also reflects bipartisan political support for good ideas, with the UPA2 government launching *Aadhaar* and the NDA2 government integrating it into numerous welfare schemes.[65]

The challenge for homegrown innovators was seen in the response of early critics who pointed out that such an ambitious biometric ID programme had not been implemented anywhere globally, even in wealthier countries with much smaller populations. However, Aadhaar proponents argued that the value of biometric technology was especially high in India's setting of low adult literacy. They also argued that biometric technologies had advanced dramatically since the time other countries designed their ID systems, which, combined with the rapid spread of mobile phones in India, made us ready for such technology-based leapfrogging.

Despite some challenges, including increased exclusion of genuine beneficiaries during the transition to Aadhaar-authenticated welfare delivery,[66] large-scale surveys in 2018 and 2019 indicated widespread citizen satisfaction with Aadhaar.[67] This was even without considering the wide range of public and private services that have been built on it since then, including the transformative Universal Payments Interface (or UPI), which has significantly increased the ease of making digital payments, and doing business. The Aadhaar example illustrates the value of keeping the strength of our convictions to design and scale homegrown innovations for India's problems.

3.2 Strengthening India's position in the world

Homegrown innovations in governance can also boost India's standing in the world. This matters because our future depends both on actions we take to strengthen ourselves internally, as well as actions we take to create and promote a global environment that is conducive to India's development.

Scholars and analysts of international relations use the ideas of 'hard' and 'soft' power to characterize countries' ability to shape the global environment to advance their own interests.[68] A country's 'hard power' reflects its ability to *coerce* others to promote its interests.[69] Hard power is influenced by factors like total GDP, per capita GDP, tax to GDP ratio, and military strength, which determine countries' ability to wage economic or military warfare and bear the costs of doing so. In contrast, a country's 'soft power' reflects its ability to *co-opt* other countries to be favourable to its interests by aligning values and culture. Soft power is boosted by building goodwill among other countries that can be tapped in times of need, and used to further mutual national interests.

Historically, post-Independence India has had more soft power than hard power in the international arena. This reflected (a) the broad global appeal of India's democracy, respect for diversity, and history of not waging wars of aggression, (b) the global popularity of Indian culture spanning movies, food, and music, and (c) our relatively weaker military and lower GDP per capita, which limited our hard power.[70]

In recent years, India's standing in the world has been steadily rising. The combination of India's democracy, steady economic growth, large domestic market, favourable demographics, vibrant innovation ecosystem, and highly successful diaspora are both indicators of success as well as enablers of a bright future. Together, these factors have contributed to India's growing international stature as a key pole of a multipolar global order that can both drive global economic growth, and contribute to the provision of global public goods like security, vaccines, and mitigating climate change.[71]

However, we also face several internal challenges—especially in basic service delivery to *all* citizens. This challenge is so severe that scholars like Anirudh Krishna have argued that the majority of Indians outside a narrow elite face a *broken ladder* whereby they simply 'cope' but are not able to 'advance' to prosperity.[72] This broken ladder not only limits the potential of the affected individuals, but also limits India's overall potential by not leveraging the talents of over a billion people. This is why acting on the reform roadmap in this book will help India boost both its soft and hard power.

Boosting India's soft power

While India's conditions are unique, our problems are not. Most low- and middle-income countries (LMICs) in the world face similar challenges, spanning education, health, public safety, access to justice, building effective social safety nets, and creating jobs. They also struggle with weak governance and state capacity. Hence, the roadmap in this book is not just relevant for India but also for global development more broadly. So, testing these ideas and developing new solutions to India's governance challenges can also help other countries, and thereby boost India's global goodwill and soft power.

Again, the case of Aadhaar, UPI, and the India Stack exemplifies a set of innovations that have strengthened India internally and also boosted India's soft power by providing a global roadmap for building digital public infrastructure. For instance, the World Bank has an ID4D (Identity for Development) group to help countries build out digital ID and public infrastructure, and their templates draw heavily from India's Aadhaar experience. In keeping with India's global leadership in this area, the World Bank ID4D group has organized learning missions for officials from several LMICs to India in recent years.

This mirrors how India's leadership in measurement of living standards using sample-based household surveys in the 1950s set the standard for global measurement of poverty. Similar to the initial scepticism around Aadhaar, many experts thought that the household surveys India was trying to conduct would not work at the proposed scale. But India proved the sceptics wrong, and the World Bank's Living Standards Measurement Survey (LSMS), which has formed the basis for globally comparable measurement of living standards, drew heavily from the Indian template.

Another recent example of global leadership from an Indian *state* is the government of Tamil Nadu's *Illam Thedi Kalvi* (ITK) programme to remediate learning losses due to COVID-19 induced school closures. Employing over 2 lakh volunteers and reaching over 30 lakh children, ITK was the world's largest programme of this kind. As detailed in Chapter 11, ITK was effective, highly cost-effective, and also improved equity.[73] Notably, we presented these results in a session at the UN General Assembly meetings in New York in 2022.[74] This led to global appreciation for ITK, and several countries expressed interest in learning from Tamil Nadu.

The key takeaway is that Tamil Nadu did not wait for global or national guidelines on how to respond to an urgent crisis.

They devised their own solutions and implemented them at scale. Similarly, many ideas in this book are tailored to India's needs and address critical challenges. These ideas are ripe for state-level experimentation, and successes can be replicated not just in other states but in other LMICS as well.

India's bold democratic experiment made us a global moral example in the post-colonial period, and gave us considerable soft power. However, our struggle to deliver economic growth and address our own development challenges diminished the appeal of the Indian model over time. In contrast, China's rapid economic growth and its ability to finance infrastructure investments in LMICs gradually increased China's global influence relative to India's. However, China's move towards greater authoritarianism under Xi Jinping, its strategic use of debt to obtain concessions from LMICs, and growing aggression towards its neighbours has made the world increasingly wary of China.

These conditions create room for India to positively shape the world order to benefit both India and the world.[75] However, the appeal of the Indian model will be considerably strengthened if we implement governance reforms to build a more effective state that can accelerate development for *all* Indians and not just a narrow elite. Showing that we can deliver both high economic growth *and* rapid human development while maintaining democracy and respect for diversity will increase India's soft power, and make it a global exemplar for other LMICs to follow and learn from.

Boosting India's hard power

While soft power is very helpful, it may be insufficient when facing a hostile neighbour with greater hard power. Thus, given geopolitical challenges in our neighbourhood, we also need adequate hard power. While India does not seek hard power to impose its will on the world, we need enough hard power to make aggression against us unacceptably costly to potential adversaries.[76] Hard power also allows us to contribute to essential global public goods such as freedom of navigation.

The main practical constraint to building India's hard power is our much lower GDP per capita compared to other powers.[77] Thus, as strategic experts have noted, the best way to build India's hard power is to have faster economic growth. Further, even if India grows faster than China for a few years, China's total GDP will grow much more in this period because their starting level is four times higher.[78] So, the military gap between China and India is likely to grow in the near future even if India grows faster than China for a few years.[79] Bridging this gap requires us to *sustain* annual growth rates over 8 per cent for a couple of decades.

However, this is unlikely if the productivity of over half our population is constrained by poor education, skills, health, and safety, and if key productive inputs like land, credit, and labour are allocated inefficiently. Simply put, we are not firing on all cylinders and are therefore functioning significantly below our potential. This is why acting on the roadmap in this book is needed to improve both human development *and* economic growth, and thereby boost both India's soft and hard power in the world. In other words, even for those who care primarily about India's standing in the world, acting on this domestic agenda may be the most important action item to focus on.

Summary

Many believe that this could be 'India's moment' to rise in the global order. Yet, despite favourable external circumstances, we still face enormous domestic challenges. The good news is that we are largely in control of our own destiny. Moreover, large parts of the world *want* India to succeed. India matters intrinsically for human welfare by being over a sixth of humanity; and instrumentally as a provider of global public goods, and as a source of product and policy innovation that can also benefit other countries. This global goodwill should be leveraged to accelerate development in India and the world.[80]

4. Conclusion

As we reflect on seventy-five years of independent India, we have much to celebrate. But we also face many challenges, especially in improving human development outcomes. These poor outcomes reflect weak public service delivery, which reflects years of under-investment in the capacity of the Indian state and its public systems to deliver against democratic expectations. This is why building a more effective Indian state is the great unfinished task of Indian democracy itself, and is a task that we all have a stake in.

Based on two decades of research, this book has argued that making data and evidence-based investments in governance and state capacity will have a much greater impact on improving citizens' lives for every rupee spent than simply spending more in a 'government as usual' way. Doing so will help us accelerate *both* human development and economic growth by jumpstarting a virtuous cycle between them (Chapter 10). It is therefore an agenda that will benefit *all* Indians. Finally, growing voter demand for better governance and service delivery makes this an opportune moment for India's political leadership to invest in building the state's capability to deliver better for voters. Simply put, acting on this roadmap can be both good policy and good politics.

A key innovation of this book is to move away from our Delhi-centred public discourse, and focus on actions that can and should be taken by states. Most service delivery functions are constitutionally in the domain of states, and states collectively spend 50 per cent more than the Central government. So, we cannot build a better India without more effective state governments. The focus on states also makes it more likely that at least some states try out some of these ideas in some of these sectors! Given the complexity of reforms and the potential for mistakes, it is essential that we both increase the chances of reforms and mitigate their risks. A strategy of state-led experimentation, rapid replication of successes, and course correction in the case of failures, sharply increases our collective ability to experiment while reducing the risk of failure.

Seventy-five years after Independence, it is good to see political leaders announcing ambitious goals for the size of the national and state economies. However, while useful for focus, setting goals is easier than achieving them. As the projections in Chapter 10 show, if we continue on the same 'government as usual' path as the status quo, we are likely to fall well short of our development goals, which will also act as a drag on growth.

If we want to achieve lofty goals, we will need to build better *systems* of governance that will enable us to reach these goals. This book's focus on improving public systems is consistent with author James Clear's observation in his bestselling book *Atomic Habits* that the key to successful individuals and organizations is not only to set ambitious goals, but to develop and *consistently implement better systems*. As he has memorably noted: 'You do not rise to the level of your goals. You fall to the level of your systems.'[81]

Building effective states and public systems is a long and arduous process that has taken high-income countries several generations to achieve. Fortunately, we have the knowledge and the technology to expedite the building of an effective Indian state, and thereby accelerate both development and growth. Doing so over the next twenty-five years is perhaps *the most important task* we need to complete to get to our full potential. However, while we may be able to compress the timeframe of building an effective state to one generation, it is still a long journey. Getting to this destination over the next twenty-five years will require both *Tejas* (conceptual clarity), and *Tapasya* (sustained hard work), and this book hopes to contribute to that journey.

Notes

Chapter 1: India@75: The Imperative of State Capacity

1 See Guha (2007) for an extensive discussion of the concerns that India would not remain united and/or that it would not be able to maintain a democracy for a sustained period after Independence.

2 While autonomous institutions that are critical for democracy (including the courts and the election commission) have been subject to various forms and extents of political pressure over the years, electoral democracy itself has endured except for the brief period of the Emergency from 1975 to 1977. See Varshney (2013) for an illustrative discussion of India's improbable democracy. Further, even the Constitutions of most countries have been quite unstable: the average written Constitution after 1789 only survived for seventeen years, and only 19 per cent of them survived for fifty years (Elkin, Ginsburg, and Melton 2009). Thus, India is a meaningful outlier on this dimension of political stability as well.

3 See Lamba and Subramanian (2020). They note that countries that have grown faster than India—Singapore, South Korea, Taiwan, Malta, Hong Kong (SAR), China, and Thailand—have been less democratic. Indeed, the only country that has remained fully democratic and grown faster than India since World War II is Botswana, with a population of 2.5 million, which is less than 2 per cent that of India!

4 The most recent estimates of poverty that are comparable over time are based on the 2011–12 round of the National Sample Survey. The 21.9 per cent figure is from the World Bank (2020).

5   See Kapur (2020) for an excellent discussion of this issue. Also, see Chapter 3.

6   Data sources and calculations for the points in the next six paragraphs are in Chapters 11–16.

7   The demographic transition is the process by which countries move from having high fertility and high mortality, to low fertility and mortality. The demographic dividend is associated with the period when countries have a high ratio of working-age population to dependents (children and elderly), which happens only once during the demographic transition.

8   As estimated in 2020. See data sources in Chapter 12.

9   Quote from Lant Pritchett in the article 'Battling the Babu-raj' in the *Economist* (2008).

10 See Mohan (2018), p. 39. Mohan (2019) calls for serious thinking around third-generation reforms to improve the functioning of the Indian state, and Lall (2023) makes a similar point. This book aims to contribute to this process.

11 This framing is adapted from Mankiw (2006), who notes how economists can function as both 'scientists' (focused on deep understanding of the world) and 'engineers' (focused on problem-solving).

12 See Chapter 6.

13 See Fukuyama (2005) for a more detailed discussion of the idea of 'scope' and 'strength' of states.

14 Prominent scholars who have focused on the capacity of a state to defend its borders and enforce law and order within its boundaries include Max Weber, Samuel Huntington and Charles Tilly. See Weber (1968), Huntington (1968) and Tilly (1975) for classic references. Besley and Persson (2009) focus on state capacity for collecting revenue and supporting markets (which in turn support growth).

15 Another way of seeing this point is to note that the British colonial state was weaker than the modern Indian state in *absolute* terms of what it could accomplish, but it was stronger in *relative* terms because it had only two main goals—maintaining

law and order and collecting revenue—and it did those tasks well. Conversely, the modern Indian state is more capable than the colonial state in absolute terms but is weaker in relative terms, because the democratic aspirations of Indian citizens are now much higher. For instance, a colonial state could maintain law and order by imprisoning innocent civilians and creating fear in the population. However, a modern democratic state needs to maintain law and order, while also respecting individual rights and freedoms and minimizing the use of force against (potentially) innocent citizens. It is relative to this *higher* standard that the Indian state often falls short (see Chapter 13).

16 This distinction has notably been made by Devesh Kapur (see, for example, Kapur 2020). He urges social scientists to not just study how the state as an institution affects downstream development, but to spend more effort on studying the state as an organization, and to better understand its inner workings so that its effectiveness as an institution may be enhanced. This book aims to contribute to this goal.

17 One metric of this atrophy is the extent to which government departments in both state and Central governments increasingly depend on external consultants to staff key projects.

18 See Bandiera et al. (2009). The study is set in Italy, but the lessons apply broadly.

19 See Jensen (2022).

20 Of course, the founding generation of leaders made several mistakes, including in their choice of a state-led economic model, and neglecting to invest in universal primary education and preventive public health (see Chapters 11 and 12, as well as Mody 2023). However, the main point to note is that the founding generation functioned more in a 'nation-building' mode than in an 'election-winning' mode.

21 Kothari (1964) and (1970) are classic references on the Congress 'system' and how it accommodated a wide variety of factions and interest groups within a 'broad tent' for two decades after Independence.

22 See Andrews, Pritchett, and Woolcock (2017).

23 A similar point is made by Kelkar and Shah (2019), and by Chhibber and Soz (2022). The same point applies to time management, where task prioritization is essential for completing the most important ones.

24 See the discussion between Ajay Shah and Amit Varma on this point in Episode 211 of the podcast series *The Seen and the Unseen*. Also, see the discussion in Chapter 18.

25 I have personally known of cases of small enterprises going out of business because payments due to them from the government had been repeatedly delayed. See Rajshekhar (2021) for examples of state governments not paying their employees for months.

26 See Shultz (2020).

27 See Basu (2018), p. 40.

28 See Aiyar (2020) for a detailed treatment of elite and middle class exit from public services in India.

29 For instance, Ahuja and Mehta (2023) show that economic growth has led to greater improvement in public services used by elites and middle classes (such as passport services), than in those where elites have exited to the private sector (such as education and health). Similar patterns are seen in data from my own all-India studies, where we found that teacher absence rates in government schools were lower when more elected Gram Panchayat (GP) members sent their own children to that school.

30 See Ambedkar (1936). A strong social norm of intra-caste marriage is a key factor in the transmission of caste identities over generations. More recent scholarship on caste such as Jodhka (2015) notes that though the ideological basis for caste in India has weakened over time, caste identities are still associated with economic and social inequalities, and still create and reproduce discrimination. See Deshpande (2011) for an economists' perspective on caste-based discrimination in India.

31 See *Democracy without Associations*, Chhibber (2001) for an illustrative discussion of this point.

32 See Ahuja (2019) for an insightful discussion of this point.

33 The best example of such thwarting may be the case of landlords (who are disproportionately from advantaged castes) resisting the implementation of the NREGS. See Khera (2011b), Anderson et al. (2015), Jenkins and Manor (2017), and Sharan (2021) for illustrative examples. Similar concerns have been widely documented historically with respect to providing education to disadvantaged caste groups.

34 In many cases, these power structures are replicated within the state itself since upper castes and privileged demographic groups are more likely to be employees of the state. At best, this can contribute to apathy by actors of the state for the marginalized; at worst, it can cause these actors to undermine the implementation of programmes and policies intended to serve the marginalized.

35 This legacy is seen in several metrics including sex ratios at birth, measures of empowerment, and representation in various public decision-making bodies.

36 See Chattopadhyay and Duflo (2004). On representation more generally, only 5 per cent of MPs in the first Lok Sabha were women, growing to just 14 per cent even in the 2019 Lok Sabha.

37 See Kapur and Mehta (2005) and Kapur, Mehta and Vaishnav (2017).

38 I thank Mukhmeet Bhatia for suggesting replacing my original term of 'business as usual' spending with the more precise term 'government as usual'.

39 See Muralidharan, Niehaus, Sukhtankar and Weaver (2021).

40 See Muralidharan, Niehaus and Sukhtankar (2016).

41 See Muralidharan, Das, Holla and Mohpal (2017). Fiscal costs are calculated by multiplying the total teacher salary bill by the estimated rates of unauthorized absence. The estimated cost of Rs 10,000 crore per year is based on 2010 salaries. These costs are likely to be considerably higher now.

42 For instance, the Right to Education (RTE) Act stipulated that lakhs of new teachers should be hired to reduce pupil–teacher ratios from 40:1 to 30:1, at an estimated cost of over Rs 25,000 crore per year. The calculations suggest that filling supervisory

positions could have been ten times more cost effective at reducing the *effective* pupil–teacher ratio by curtailing absence rates of existing teachers.

43 See Muralidharan and Sundararaman (2011), Muralidharan (2012), and de Ree et al. (2018).

44 See Ganimian, Muralidharan and Walters (2023).

45 See Rao (2022).

46 This assessment is similar to that of former Chief Economic Adviser Ashok Lahiri, who notes in his recent book that India's performance has been 'good, but not great' (Lahiri 2022).

47 For instance, China has a highly capable state that has delivered rapid economic growth and better development outcomes than India. But, the Chinese state also uses its capabilities to curb individual freedoms at will, with little public accountability. This trade-off may be unacceptable to most Indians who value their democratic freedoms, as demonstrated by the repudiation of the Emergency at the ballot box.

48 Of course, money and influence can help even in dire times, but everyone will be better off if the plane does not crash. In that sense, the sinking of the *Titanic* is also an apt transportation metaphor for the experience of April–May 2021. The rich and middle classes were more likely to obtain a lifeboat but also perished in large numbers, and would have clearly been better off if the ship were not sinking.

49 See, for instance, the accounts by Baru (2016), Sitapati (2018), Mohan (2018), and Ahluwalia (2020). One example of an internal government document that reflected this new thinking is the M-document authored by Montek Ahluwalia that had been circulated internally in the finance ministry in the late 1980s. These policy notes in turn reflected a body of deeper academic research including Jagdish Bhagwati and Padma Desai's classic analysis and critique of state-led planning (see Bhagwati and Desai 1970). See 'The 1991 Project' for an excellent documentation of the research, and people who contributed to the landmark 1991 economic reforms that transformed India's economy (https://the1991project.com/).

50 See Muralidharan and Singh (2021) and (2023) for illustrations of this point.

51 In their book on bridging technology and human needs titled *Bridgital Nation*, Chandrasekaran and Purushothaman (2019) have also highlighted the centrality of putting people's needs ahead of technology per se in using technology to solve India's development problems.

52 Specifically, agriculture is discussed in Chapters 6, 15, and 16; urbanization in Chapters 7, 8, 15, and 16; and environment in Chapters 7, 12, and 16.

53 Understanding variation in development outcomes across Indian states is a major scholarly endeavour by itself. Some notable works in the last decade that have examined this question using case studies of a few states include Vivek (2014), Singh (2016), and Ahuja (2019). For a recent summary of the stark differences across northern and southern states, see Nilakantan (2022).

54 One noteworthy recent work that pays attention to state-level governance challenges in India is the book *Despite the State* (Rajshekhar 2021), which provides a sobering narrative of governance failures in six different states of India based on extensive on-the-ground reporting.

55 In their recent book, *State Capability in India*, senior IAS officers, T.V. Somanathan and Gulzar Natarajan use a similar analogy where they describe state capability as 'analogous to a hose used to deliver water' with the quality of the hose being measured by how much water is transferred from the point of input to the point of delivery (Somanathan and Natarajan 2022).

56 This balance is also reflected in the tone throughout this book, avoiding both the excessive optimism of those who believe that the twenty-first century is *destined* to be India's century (as proclaimed by many corporate CEOs), and the excessive pessimism of those who argue that India is 'broken' (such as Mody 2023). The tone of this book is perhaps closest to that of Joshi (2016), who acknowledges India's key challenges and offers a measured evidence-based discussion of policy options to improve outcomes.

57 Landes (1999), p. 543.

Chapter 2: The Politicians' Predicament

1 As we will see in Chapter 7, tax-to-GDP ratios increase with per capita income. So, the diversion of public resources towards elite interests has greater social costs in low-income countries because the social opportunity cost of these diverted funds is higher. This is consistent with the evidence of very high public rates of return from investing in state capacity in India (summarized in Chapter 1).

2 This section presents my short synthesis of a vast academic literature on historical political economy.

3 See Pincus and Robinson (2016) for a detailed discussion and references to individual studies estimating the share of military expenditure across France, Russia, Austria, and Holland in the seventeenth century (all of which ranged from 75–90 per cent). While historical data is more limited, studies cited by Pincus and Robinson (2016) have estimated that states in ancient Rome and Egypt also spent around 80 per cent of their revenue on the military.

4 As noted on p. 112 in Giddens (1985), 'It was war and preparation for war that provided the most potent energizing stimulus for the concentration of administrative resources and fiscal reorganization' (of early modern states). This view has been reinforced in several later works, including Besley and Persson (2009), who note: 'War placed a premium on sources of taxation and created incentives for governments to invest in revenue raising institutions.'

5 Tilly (1975), p. 42.

6 Key features of the Industrial Revolution included mechanization, division of labour, and specialization, which greatly increased economies of scale in production. Thus, it became much more cost-effective to produce at large scales in a few locations and transport these goods to others, which greatly raised the economic returns to building better transportation infrastructure.

7 As noted by Pincus and Robinson (2016): 'The eighteenth-century British state was the first European state to begin to shift

the balance away from fiscal-military expenditures and towards other budget items that promoted colonial development, education, (and) the development of infrastructure.' They also note that the productivity gains and economic growth enabled by these investments allowed Britain to 'transform its military into the world's foremost fighting machine and simultaneously spend a relatively *smaller* percentage of the budget on exclusively fiscal-military matters'.

8   Note that the quality of life of kings and ruling classes did grow in this period because an expanding population increased tax revenue to finance more opulent lifestyles for them. This was true globally as well as in India. However, the quality of life of the average citizen or peasant improved much less in the pre-Industrial period (Clark 2007).

9   In the language of economists, these correspond to physical, financial, and human capital.

10 Thus, in the terminology of Fukuyama (2005), they expanded the *scope* of the state to cover welfare only after achieving the *strength* to do so.

11 It is easy to measure a state's fiscal capacity using the tax-to-GDP ratio, and document that it increased during World War II. However, it is likely that administrative capacity also increased during this period as governments commandeered many parts of the economy for the war effort, and drafted many of their best thinkers and managers into improving government functioning as part of the war effort.

12 The decision to do so reflected a combination of voter and elite preferences. Of course, there was still considerable variation in the extent of the welfare state across countries—especially the US and those in Western Europe. See Alesina and Glaeser (2004) for a discussion of these differences.

13 Rulers and elites also routinely violated individual rights in the name of providing 'security'. While distasteful, the philosopher Thomas Hobbes provided a moral justification for the 'security state' by noting that it was still an improvement over the

alternative 'state of nature'. As he famously described it, the life of humans in the state of nature would be 'nasty, brutish, and short' (Hobbes 1651). Thus, he argued that people would be better off by entering into a 'social contract' where they gave up individual rights to the sovereign, to enable the king and his forces to better protect life and basic liberty by providing security.

14 See, for instance, Keyssar (2000) on the struggle to expand the right to vote in the US.

15 Husted and Kenny (1997) analyse the relationship between welfare spending and voting rights with US data and find support for a 'redistributive' model whereby shifting the median voter to one with lower income (which is what franchise expansions have typically done) increases welfare spending. Haggard and Kaufman (2008) assess the link between expansion of voting rights and welfare spending across Latin America, East Asia, and Eastern Europe and confirm that these are positively correlated. Fujiwara (2015) uses a natural experiment in Brazil to show that the expansion of *effective* voting rights of less-educated voters (due to the introduction of a new voting technology) led to an expansion of healthcare spending, which is particularly beneficial to the poor.

16 See Gupta (2013) for a discussion of how elites have led the creation of progressive policies both in Western countries and in India. However, it can also be counterproductive to adopt Western policy norms in India given our much lower fiscal and state capacity. See Rajagopalan and Tabarrok (2019) for an illustrative discussion of the costs of premature adoption of Western policies in India.

17 Even after the abolition of slavery, black Americans were effectively denied voting rights for much of the twentieth century through state-level laws that made it much more difficult for black voters to register to vote. Instruments of disenfranchisement included poll taxes (a per head tax that was a much bigger burden for the poor, who were disproportionately black) and literacy tests (which again discriminated against former slaves with no formal education) as requirements to vote.

18 GDP Data from the Maddison Project (2020), which reports figures in comparable 'International Dollars' at 2011 prices.

19 Note that some of these schemes were introduced by elites on moral grounds (like the midday meal scheme in Tamil Nadu) and not created by mass movements or democratic pressure (consistent with Gupta 2013). However, the fact that they would be popular and win votes was also an important reason for their implementation. Thus, policy choices reflect both ideas and interests (also see Chapter 17).

20 Many scholars have noted that the adoption and persistence of democracy in India is a deep puzzle, and have tried to understand this 'exceptional' phenomenon (see Varshney [2013] for an illustrative discussion of India's 'improbable democracy'). While this body of work aims to understand the *causes* of Indian democracy, my focus here is on its *consequences*.

21 In the terminology of economics, the very existence of high marginal returns to investing in state capacity that are *not* being acted upon suggest an optimization failure.

22 For instance, the last two national elections (2014 and 2019) saw an average of fifteen contestants per seat across the country. Average voter turnout in the 2019 national election was 67 per cent.

23 All election data reported in this chapter was obtained from the Trivedi Centre for Political Data.

24 The point that politicians can often find it more electorally advantageous to concentrate public benefits on a narrower group of voters is well-documented in the academic literature. See Lizzeri and Persico (2001) and Besley and Persson (2009) for illustrative examples.

25 See Thakur (2000), and Mathew and Moore (2011).

26 See Mathew and Moore (2011). Specifically, the Yadav community benefited disproportionately from government spending and hiring, and the main benefit provided to the Muslim community was physical safety, with the police being instructed to prioritize prevention of communal violence.

27 He also legitimized this approach among his base voters by arguing that he was acting in their interests. For instance, he

would tell them that he did not invest in roads because doing so would only benefit contractors and the wealthy, who had cars.

28 His base voters also supported Lalu Prasad Yadav intensely, because just the fact of his being chief minister delivered respect and empowerment to socially disadvantaged groups, who had been left out of the post-Independence power structures of Bihar.

29 See Alesina and La Ferrara (2005) for a discussion of the conceptual issues relating to ethnic diversity and economic performance and a review of empirical evidence. Pranab Bardhan discusses these issues in the Indian context in Bardhan (1984), and makes a more general argument in Bardhan (2004).

30 Political scientists broadly refer to these three kinds of actions as clientelism, patronage, and corruption. While all these actions benefit favoured groups, the *distribution* of benefits *within* the group will often vary by the form of action. Targeted government policies are more likely to benefit the poor, favouritism in hiring is more likely to benefit the middle class, and corruption usually benefits elites within the group in power. Note that such behaviour is seen around the world. See Nichter (2018) for an excellent scholarly analysis of clientelism in Latin America. The evocatively named book, *It's Our Turn to Eat,* provides a more journalistic account of the same patterns in Kenya (Wrong, 2010).

31 See Pratap Bhanu Mehta's classic essay, 'The Burden of Democracy', for a discussion of how the nature of social cleavages and hierarchies in India has contributed to the zero-sum nature of our politics and made it difficult to build broad coalitions for public goods (Mehta 2003). Chhibber (2001) is a classic reference on how political parties have exacerbated social cleavages because this helps them electorally. These discussions also highlight the value of the legacy of India's freedom struggle that helped make common cause across a very wide variety of Indians. Further, the founding leaders of India reflected this legacy in an inclusive Constitution, and a post-Independence focus on national integration.

32 As explained in Mancur Olson's classic book *The Logic of Collective Action* (1965).

33 This numerical example is consistent with basic economic theory, which highlights the 'deadweight loss' from tariffs and show how the benefits accrue to producers, while costs are borne by consumers. More advanced dynamic trade theory models provide a potential justification for tariffs based on the possibility of learning by doing, knowledge spillovers, and reducing costs over time. However, even under these models, there is only a justification for *temporary* tariffs. In practice, once tariffs are introduced, they can be difficult to reverse because of the lobbying considerations explained in this paragraph.

34 Several studies of grassroots participation by citizens in social groups discuss how the social capital formed by such interactions is an important mechanism by which citizens access the state. Examples include Krishna (2002) and Kruks-Wisner (2018). For those without direct social capital, accessing the limited resources of the state typically requires the use of an intermediary or broker, who provides access in return for a payment (Krishna 2013a).

35 Data from the Association of Democratic Reforms.

36 See Vaishnav (2017) for several examples of politicians with a long list of criminal charges against them, including extortion, kidnapping, and even murder, but who were still popular with their base voters. This is a well-known feature of 'tribal' politics, where voters are willing to condone faults and even criminal behaviour of leaders as long as they represent *their* interests.

37 See Krishna (2013a). This idea has also been captured in movies. For instance, in the 2018 Telugu movie, *Bharat Ane Nenu,* the attempt of an honest chief minister to empower citizens by transferring funds directly to villages is resisted by traditional political leaders who argue that this will reduce their own value and importance in society.

38 See Mani and Mukand (2007) and Vaishnav (2015).

39 A large literature in psychology has documented what is known as 'Weber's Law' of just-noticeable differences, whereby small

differences are typically not noticed and where the threshold of noticeability grows in proportion to the size of the original stimulus. See Namboodiri et al. (2014) for a review.

40 Kapur and Vaishnav (2018) note that the total expenditure on general elections in India grew from an estimated $2 billion in 2009 to around $5 billion (~Rs 35,000 crore) in 2014. See the collection of essays in Kapur and Vaishnav (2018) for an excellent review of electoral financing in India.

41 See Usmani (2019).

42 In the tariff example of Section 2.2, implementing a tariff would generate Rs 1000 crore for politicians, and Rs 2000 crore for steel producers but at a cost of Rs 7000 crore to consumers. Thus, political and business elites will both be better off under this arrangement, but at a large aggregate cost to national welfare. For a candid and disturbing account of the 'business' of politics in India, see Joseph (2016).

43 See Vaishnav (2019) for a discussion of electoral bonds. Also see Bussell (2018) who interviews several Indian politicians, and notes that many of them acknowledge the importance of illicit, untraceable funds in elections because of the need to spend far in excess of official Election Commission limits.

44 The challenge of money in politics is a universal issue, and not limited to India. For instance, the influence of lobbies in the US is so strong that laws often reflect the interest of well-funded special interest groups rather than the general public. However, the US and other democracies at least mandate the disclosure of most forms of political financing, enabling citizens to track and scrutinize it.

45 A nationwide survey in 2018 by CSDS-Lokniti and Azim Premji University found that political parties had the lowest level of trust among sixteen different institutions in India. A 2019 Pew Survey found that 64 per cent of respondents agreed that the statement 'most politicians are corrupt' described India well.

46 See Bardhan (1984).

47 For instance, large landowners often had considerable influence on the voting behaviour of agricultural labourers who depended on them for their livelihood, and government teachers had a similar influence on illiterate votes by virtue of often being the most educated members in the community. .

48 Beyond their ability to protest, government employees like teachers were also politically very powerful due to their role in conducting elections and staffing election booths. See Kingdon and Muzammil (2009) for an illuminating case study of the channels through which teachers command political power in UP.

49 See Khan (2010), Levy et al. (2014), and Kelsall et al. (2022) for references on political settlement analysis and their implications for both conflict and development. In the language of game theory, political settlements are sustained when the 'continuation payoff' to maintaining the status quo and partaking of one's share of the economic pie is higher than the 'expected payoff' from disrupting the status quo and reducing the size of the pie, but with the possibility of obtaining a larger share of a smaller pie.

50 See Poonam (2018) for a collection of vignettes that captures the frustration of youth who have been left out of India's progress. The case of Brexit provides a good recent example of popular disruption of an elite-biased political settlement. Brexit clearly reduced average welfare in the UK, but large numbers of voters who had been left out of the benefits of greater integration with the EU felt that their positions had worsened substantially under integration, and therefore preferred to vote to 'leave' and thereby shake up the political settlement that had skewed too far towards benefiting elites possessing physical, financial, and human capital at the cost of those who did not.

51 See Vaishnav and Swanson (2015). Arvind Subramanian, the former chief economic adviser of India, has made the same point, writing, 'Since independence, many Indian voters have reflexively ejected politicians from office even when they had

compiled decent records in power [. . .] Recently, though, Indian voters have started to reward good performance, especially in state-level politics' (Subramanian 2009).

52 See Gupta and Panagariya (2014).

53 See Bussell (2018).

54 The study was conducted using a large-scale randomized controlled trial (RCT). See Muralidharan, Niehaus, and Sukhtankar (2016).

55 Consistent with this view, our study found that over 90 per cent of beneficiaries preferred smartcards to the old system because they received more money, with fewer delays. Interestingly, intermediaries who tried to get the smartcard programme scrapped tried to argue that it was inconveniencing beneficiaries due to difficulties in authentication. In other words, they tried to protect *their* 'interests' (of *not* reducing corruption) by claiming that they were worried about beneficiaries. Our data was directly used by senior officials in the government to assure the political leadership that beneficiaries highly valued the reform.

56 Dr Santhosh Mathew was then a joint secretary in the Ministry of Rural Development (responsible for NREGS). This comment was made in a public workshop on the findings of the study, as is available for viewing at https://www.youtube.com/watch?v=3Cnxghjk6tQ&t=2877s.

57 This is also an example where the constraint of concentrated costs of the reform (to the intermediaries who lost their ability to siphon funds) versus diffuse benefits (to a much greater number of poor beneficiaries) was overcome because the chief minister chose a strategy of delivering better services.

58 See Jha (2017) and Mehta (2022) for insightful discussions of the combinations of factors that contribute to the BJP's electoral strength.

59 See Vaishnav (2015) for a data-based discussion on understanding the Indian voter.

60 Examples include schemes such as Ujjwala for providing cooking gas to poor households, PM Awas Yojana for constructing homes

for the rural poor and Swachh Bharat Abhiyaan for constructing tens of millions of rural toilets. Many of these schemes also existed under prior governments, but the quality of delivery noticeably improved under Prime Minister Narendra Modi. See Gupta (2019) for an illustrative discussion on the importance of better delivery of schemes in explaining the BJP's re-election in 2019.

61 See Verma and Barthwal (2022) for an illustrative discussion.

62 In the words of veteran journalist and political commentator Shekhar Gupta, the number one lesson from the 2023 Karnataka state election is: 'If you run a really bad state government, nothing can redeem you. Voters will then toss aside the charm of your national leaders, nationalism, polarization, religion and a partisan news media.' (Gupta 2023).

63 See Deshmukh and Guru (2023) for further validation of this argument.

64 See Muralidharan, Niehaus, Sukhtankar, and Weaver (2021).

65 See Kapur and Vaishnav (2018) for a comprehensive discussion of political finance in India, with several examples on this point.

66 See Chauchard (2018) for an elaboration of this point.

67 See Deshmukh and Guru (2023) for a more extended discussion of this point.

68 See Chapter 2 in Rukmini (2021) for detailed data on this point.

69 Consistent with this view that 'elections are a waste of time', 58 per cent of the respondents in a 2019 Pew Survey agreed with the statement that 'no matter who wins an election, things do not change very much' compared to only 29 per cent who disagreed with the statement.

70 Doucouliagos and Ulubasoglu (2008) conduct a meta-analysis of relevant studies and conclude that democracy appears to have no direct effect on growth but has an indirect positive effect through improved human capital and lower political instability and inflation. More recently, Acemoglu et al. (2019) conclude that democracy does have a positive effect on economic growth.

71 For instance, see Mobarak (2005), Yang (2008), and Cuberes and Jerzmanowsky (2009).

72 See the article by Cai et al. (2023) in the *New York Times* for a
    detailed analysis of 'How Xi Returned China to One-Man Rule'.
    More generally, scholars of Chinese politics note that though
    it may seem like there is not much political change in China
    because of single-party rule, in practice, the *details* of how the
    Chinese state functions have changed significantly over time.
    See Ang (2019) for a primer.

73 See Padmanabhan (2018). For reference, during the period
    1969–2019, the average growth rate under single-party national
    governments was 4.7 per cent, whereas it was 5.7 per cent under
    coalition national governments. Of course, there are also other
    differences across time and so this analysis should only be
    considered suggestive and not as definitive causal evidence. The
    same caveat applies to the analysis of Chinese performance over
    time in the previous paragraph.

74 See Nooruddin (2011) for both theory and evidence on this point
    using both cross-country quantitative analysis and multiple case
    studies. Chapter 5 of Nooruddin (2011) expands on this point in
    the Indian context.

75 Remarks made by Dr Ambedkar to the Constituent Assembly on
    25 November 1949.

76 This dynamic applies to many other low-income democracies
    as well. The agenda for investing in state capacity outlined in
    this book is therefore likely to be relevant to many other country
    settings as well.

Chapter 3: The Bureaucracy's Burden

1   In other words, we have expanded the scope of the state without
    investing in its strength to deliver against this expanded scope.
    See Kapur (2020) for further discussion on this point.

2   The story is from the opening lines of the Woody Allen movie
    Annie Hall.

3   Data is from the Economic Survey of India (2017–18), which
    reports that there were around 7.2 million state and 2.5

million Central government employees as of 2012 (excluding the ministry of defence and paramilitary forces of the home ministry). This figure does not include quasi-government staff or local government staff. See Economic Survey (2017–18) for details. Recent estimates suggest that state governments account for 79 per cent of all public employees in India: https://forumforstatestudies.in/.

4   See the UNESCO 2021 report titled, 'No Teacher, No Class', p. 30. School-level vacancies are often higher than average vacancies in the system because of inefficiencies in how teachers are allocated across schools. So, schools in desirable urban locations will often have a 'surplus' of teachers, while schools in less desirable rural locations are more likely to be understaffed.

5   See Muralidharan et al. (2017).

6   13th Joint Review Mission Monitoring Report of Sarva Shiksha Abhiyan (2011).

7   See Dasgupta and Kapur (2020).

8   The data is from Saxena (2019).

9   See Kremer et al. (2005) and Chaudhury et al. (2006).

10 See Muralidharan et al. (2017). Note that the 2003 round of surveys included rural and urban areas (with the rural teacher absence rate being 26.2 per cent). The 2010 round only resurveyed rural areas.

11 See Muralidharan and Singh (2023).

12 Specifically, in our 2003 study (Kremer et al. 2005), we found that only one head teacher out of over 3000 government schools we surveyed had ever managed to suspend a teacher for absence. In contrast, 35 out of around 600 private school principals reported having taken action against absent teachers. Thus, private schools were 175 times more likely to take action against absent teachers.

13 Lemos, Muralidharan, and Scur (2023). We found that the personnel-management score in private schools was *four standard deviations higher* than in public schools, which is an enormous difference.

14 Civil Services Survey—A Report (2010).

15 *Panchayat*, Season 1, Episode 5: 'Computer Nahin Monitor'.

16 See Mangla (2015) for a case study of education across states. He argues that education outcomes are better in Himachal Pradesh relative to neighbouring Uttarakhand (despite their being neighbouring states with similar geographic conditions) because officials in Himachal operate under a more 'deliberative' model, whereby officials and community members work collectively to design solutions that are appropriate to the local context (which is a measure of greater autonomy). In contrast, he categorizes Uttarakhand as operating under a more 'legalistic' model that prioritizes strict adherence to rules, procedures, and hierarchies (with reduced autonomy). In a different sector (environmental regulation), Duflo et al. (2018) show how officials closer to the ground have more information on how best to do their job, and how providing them the autonomy to act on this information can be in the public interest. Finally, Kala (2022) shows that increasing autonomy of public-sector enterprises boosted their profitability.

17 See Bandiera et al. (2021). In a different context, Rasul and Rogger (2018) study the effectiveness of Nigerian Civil Service officers and find that increasing bureaucratic autonomy is associated with higher project completion rates.

18 Civil Services Survey—A Report (2010).

19 See Muralidharan and Sundararaman (2013).

20 In a written response to a parliamentary question in early 2021, the Government of India responded that over 42,000 positions reserved for Scheduled Castes (SCs), Scheduled Tribes (STs), and Other Backward Castes (OBCs) were vacant (Dasgupta 2021).

21 See Muralidharan and Sheth (2016) for evidence on how being taught by a female teacher can help bridge the gender gap between girls and boys in learning.

22 As discussed in Chapter 1, multiple studies show that the quality of public services is higher when they are also used by elites and middle classes.

23 See Weber (1968) for a classic reference. This view is reinforced by more modern discussions of building effective human resource systems for the public sector (Daly 2010 and Berman et al. 2016).

24 See Ganimian, Muralidharan, and Walters (2023). Similar estimates are reported in Kondepati (2013).

25 See Mathur (2015).

26 See Muralidharan and Singh (2023).

27 See Gupta (2012).

28 The divergence between administrative records and reality in India has been documented in multiple studies. See Tarlo (2000) and Singh (2020) for illustrative examples.

29 See Romero and Singh (2023).

30 See Aiyar and Bhattacharya (2016).

31 See the *Mint* story by the 'How India Lives' team (22 April 2019).

32 See evidence from interviews of education department officials in Muralidharan and Singh (2023). See Iyer and Mani (2012) for a systematic analysis of the costs of frequent transfers of officials.

33 Note that the Mughal state—which preceded the colonial state, as well as many princely states (that were contemporary to the colonial state) *also* focused primarily on extraction of surplus from peasants to finance the military and opulent lives of the rulers. I highlight the extractive colonial state because the structures of the modern Indian state are built on it.

34 This scenario was memorably depicted in the Hindi film *Lagaan*, where Captain Russel epitomizes the detached colonial administrator, focused on tax collection and leisure activities like hunting and cricket. In contrast, his sister Elizabeth mingles and interacts with the local population, develops empathy with their struggles, and ends up supporting them against her brother— effectively 'going native'!

35 In the words of a former IAS officer recounting an experience as a district collector: 'I was once trying to find out who was at fault for a particularly shoddy roadwork for which huge sums had been spent multiple times in my district, but it was *impossible* to pinpoint anyone.' This idea was also captured memorably in the TV show *Yes*

Minister, where Humphrey Appleby notes that: 'Arnold reminded me (as if I didn't already know) that we already move our officials around every two or three years, to stop this personal responsibility nonsense'! (*Yes Minister*, Season 3, Episode 2: The Challenge).

36 It also contributes to reduced levels of connection and trust between public employees and the communities they are meant to serve, lower accountability for performance, and longer durations of both staff and managerial positions being vacant, which directly hurt service delivery.

37 Recruitment scams that have come into public attention recently include the Vyapam scam in MP (Mitra and Tomar 2018), the teacher recruitment scam in Haryana (for which a former chief minister was convicted; see IANS 2019), and the resignation of a railway minister in response to allegations that he was selling positions on the apex Railway Board (Vij-Aurora and Jolly 2013). Corruption in public-sector recruitment has long been widespread in India. See Wade (1985) for a classic reference and Sukhtankar and Vaishnav (2015) for a fuller set of references.

38 See Saxena (2019) for several detailed examples.

39 Das (2021). Also, see Donthi (2011) for an extensive investigative report on how politically motivated decision-making over the years contributed to the decline of Air India.

40 This is why employees of the Telangana Road Transport Corporation (RTC) went on strike in 2019 demanding that the RTC be taken over by the government. This way, the losses of the RTC (driven by a combination of poor management and high employee salaries) would get hidden in the government budget and employees would face less risk of being laid off.

41 The issue of integrating seniority lists can be such a bottleneck to governance that the chairperson of the Prime Minister's Economic Advisory Council, Dr Bibek Debroy, wrote an entire column on it as a key factor delaying the implementation of railway reforms. See Debroy (2020).

42 See Somanathan and Natarajan (2022), pp. 108–09 (emphasis added). They also note that: '. . . the huge administrative burden that falls on senior managers is an important reason why they

are reluctant to recruit more people or fill posts—more staff means more administrative work and more litigation.'

43 See Sneha et al. (2021).

44 Union Finance Secretary Dr T.V. Somanathan, who has also written about these issues in Somanathan and Natarajan (2022), released new procurement guidelines in 2021 to make it easier to include quality parameters in tender evaluation (see PIB release 1767545). However, there is still a long way to go in converting these enabling provisions into changes in actual procurement—especially at the state level.

45 I recall hearing this quote from England goalkeeper Peter Shilton in an interview in the 1980s.

46 See Banerjee (1997).

47 See Andrews, Pritchett, and Woolcock (2017).

48 This characterization also sheds light on a subtle distinction between the judiciary and the executive. The judiciary often focuses on addressing *individual* cases of injustice that appear before the court, whereas the role of the executive is to improve *average* outcomes to the extent possible. Thus, while judicial interventions in cases against the government might benefit the individual petitioner, they may have the unseen cost of diverting executive time and attention from tasks that affect many others. Of course, this need not always be true—if, for example, the case serves as a precedent for future executive action. But, in practice, the greater constraint to executive effectiveness is often not intention but capacity. Hence, a focus on addressing individual grievances may sometimes compromise broader outcomes.

49 See Jesudasan (2018). The ostensible reason given for the rotations was to improve governance but there is no good reason to think why this may be the case.

50 As quoted in Krishna (2020).

51 See, for instance, Mahadevan-Dasgupta (2020).

52 See Saxena (2019), p. 204.

53 Another example of such behaviour is the resistance of insiders to lateral entry. Many key players in India's transformative economic reforms of the 1990s—such as Montek Ahluwalia,

Rakesh Mohan, Shankar Acharya, and Arvind Virmani—were professional economists with global exposure who made mid-career entries into the government as 'economic advisers'. This allowed them to learn the nuances of how government works while bringing their more conceptual and research-based inputs into policymaking. However, Indian Economic Service (IES) officers felt that such lateral entry hurt their career prospects and lobbied to reserve the post of Economic Adviser for the IES. This may have benefited the careers of IES officers but has arguably weakened economic expertise within the government by depriving it of top mid-career economists with global exposure (see Ahluwalia and Rajagopalan 2023).

54 See Saxena (2019) for several anecdotes and case studies of insiders confirming this view.

55 These 'notes' need not be provided directly. They could also be provided indirectly through means such as preferential awarding of contracts or offering government jobs to effective political mobilizers.

56 Of course, officials should be prudent and not be reckless in their actions. But, political leaders need to encourage initiative and protect officials from good faith errors, which are almost inevitable when attempting complex projects.

57 Recent research shows that providing public sector undertakings with greater autonomy led to improved performance on several metrics, including profitability (Kala 2022).

58 See Ang (2016) for a summary and references to further primary sources.

59 See Dercon (2022) for an anecdote where a leading Chinese scholar tells the author that the key to Chinese economic development was not economic reforms, but *governance* reforms.

60 See Jha (2017) and Singh (2019) for illustrative discussions.

61 See Muralidharan and Sundararaman (2011). Specifically, over 75 per cent of government teachers who had participated in a pilot programme of performance-linked pay in (undivided) Andhra Pradesh were in favour of having at least 10 per cent of their pay linked to their performance in improving student learning.

Chapter 4: Data and Outcome Measurement

1   According to the Oxford English Dictionary, the German *statistisch* comes from the Latin *statisticus*, meaning 'of or relating to the state, statists, or statecraft' (OED.com, accessed 7 October 2020).

2   See Menon (2022) for a detailed discussion of how these systems were set up, and the central role of P.C. Mahalanobis and the Indian Statistical Institute in doing so.

3   See the *Mint* essay by data journalist Pramit Bhattacharya, 'How India's Statistical System Was Crippled', for a detailed narrative of the technical and political reasons behind the progressive weakening of India's statistical system (Bhattacharya 2019), and his more recent working paper for suggestions on national level reforms (Bhattacharya 2023). Also, see Chapter 6 of Rukmini (2021). My focus in this chapter is less on the technical and political challenges with the NSS data, and more on how our data systems are inadequate for governance even if NSS data are released in a timely manner.

4   As per the 2023 ASER Report (based on surveys conducted in 2022), only 1.6 per cent of children aged 6–14 in rural India are not in school (ASER 2023). Assuming similar rates in urban areas, over 98 per cent are enrolled in school.

5   Data on enrolment and learning outcomes are both from ASER (2018).

6   See Muralidharan, Niehaus, and Sukhtankar (2017).

7   In any case, data from grievance redressal calls would only reflect the inputs of proactive citizens who know how to call and complain, and would not be a good data source for representative population-level estimates of the quality of service delivery.

8   See Figure 2 in Singh (2020). Interestingly, the ranking of students was unchanged between the administrative data and the independent tests, suggesting that teachers are conscious of the importance of the rank in student outcomes. But they inflated the *levels* of reported learning across the board.

9   See Singh (2020). Note that the problem of over-reporting student learning was found in both private and government

schools in AP, suggesting that the government has to worry
about the problem of over-reporting outcomes both in its role as
a provider, and in its role as a regulator (see Chapter 9).

10 We have wasted over fifteen years because the first ASER report
showing very low levels of learning in rural India came out in
2005. However, governments have mostly preferred to deny this
data and rely on official data—which severely overstates learning
levels and understates the learning crisis.

11 These results were obtained as part of the fieldwork conducted
for Ganimian, Muralidharan, and Walters (2023).

12 See Bansal (2021) for a recent investigative journalistic account
of how inflation of education learning outcome data in Rajasthan
led to a 'fictional education revolution'.

13 One teacher in Madhya Pradesh actually told a colleague of mine
that if he marked a child as achieving a D or F grade then he
would have to conduct extra remedial classes, which he did not
have time for!

14 These technical design challenges underscore the importance of
close collaborations between academic experts and the government,
as was the case in the 1950s, where faculty members of the Indian
Statistical Institute worked closely with officials of the Planning
Commission to design India's statistical infrastructure (see Menon
2022). One example of the need for statistical sophistication in
interpreting data is the common mistake of policymakers over-
reacting to changes in rankings, which can often reflect sampling
variation and measurement error, as opposed to actual changes.

15 Some of these limitations include: NAS excludes those who are
out of school, in unrecognized private schools, or absent on the
day of testing. It only asks grade-appropriate questions, which
means it cannot capture how far below grade level students might
be. And it may suffer from the same data integrity problems that
have been documented by independent researchers, because
it is perceived as a high-stakes accountability exercise for the
public-school system (see Bansal 2021 for an illustration of these
pressures on the ground in Rajasthan). These limitations are so
severe that a recent study (Johnson and Parrado 2021) concluded

that 'NAS state averages are likely artificially high and contain little information about states' relative performance'. It noted that 'the presence of severe bias in the NAS data suggests that this data should be used carefully or *not at all* for comparisons between states' (emphasis added).

16 The ASER data also has challenges and limitations, though not as severe as those with the NAS. See Johnson and Parrado (2021) as well as Rukmini (2014) for illustrative discussions.

17 This is common in all high-quality survey operations and is referred to as a 'backcheck'.

18 A key technical issue in ensuring that such surveys are representative of the population is to have a sampling frame of the entire universe of households. One practical and cost-effective option is to use voter registration lists, which are public information, as the sampling frame for such an exercise. The Election Commission updates this list faster than even the census, and the voter rolls are therefore likely to be the most current sampling frame. See Joshi et al. (2022) for results from a field-based validation to assess whether voter rolls provide a suitable sampling frame for household surveys in India.

19 For instance, if a respondent says 'Yes' to a question, there will usually be follow-up questions. If they say 'No', then the surveyor will have to jump to the next section. In a paper-based survey, this would often entail turning pages manually to reach the right sections, which increases error rates and chances of incorrectly skipping pages. This problem is eliminated by digital data collection. Similarly, software can be pre-coded to flag entries that look incorrect to prompt real-time checking by enumerators and reduce common errors in field data entry, such as adding or forgetting a digit while recording data.

20 In fact, one of the main goals of the ADP is to develop governance templates at the district level that can then be scaled up through states. The Consumer Pyramids survey of the Centre for Monitoring the Indian Economy (CMIE) is another large-scale household survey covering around 1,70,000 households

three times a year, further confirming that such large-scale high-frequency surveys are feasible.

21 The cost estimates are based on inputs from organizations who conduct large field surveys.

22 While generating precise district-level estimates requires a sample size of around 2000 households per district, precise state-level estimates require much smaller samples. So, adding ten different modules in ten different subsamples (of 200 households per district), will allow governments to obtain state-level estimates of the evolution of the quality of life of the average citizen every year. Examples of topics for deeper exploration in these '10 per cent samples' include health-seeking behaviour and healthcare usage, employment and job search behaviour, agricultural production, time use, credit and savings, etc.

23 This is exactly what happened under the 'Results Framework Document' exercise conducted by the Performance Management Division (PMD) set up in the Cabinet Secretariat in 2009. Departments were asked to identify their key performance indicators, and the school education department mostly came up with input-based indicators with a minuscule weight on learning outcomes.

24 Assessing access from the household's perspective and not just that of school construction can also encourage innovative solutions to improving school access such as providing transport, which will often improve learning by enabling governments to build larger, higher-quality schools (see Chapter 11).

25 I have served as a technical adviser to this project, with operational support provided by a team from the Centre for Effective Governance of Indian States (CEGIS), a non-profit organization that I have co-founded to help state governments in India improve governance, including by helping to create practical roadmaps to implement the ideas in this book that state governments may be interested in adopting.

26 See Muralidharan, Niehaus, Sukhtankar, and Weaver (2021).

27 Of course, even planning departments may need to engage technical partners for some of this work since they may not have the capabilities internally but planning and/or IT departments are the logical nodal departments for such an effort.

28 This was driven by a combination of ABBA being launched in Jharkhand at a time when 23 per cent of beneficiaries had still not seeded their ration cards, and by the way grain stocks were replenished after the reform. See Muralidharan, Niehaus, and Sukhtankar (2022) and (2023b) for details.

29 See the discussion in Muralidharan (2020b) for more details.

30 I thank Dr Santhosh Mathew for coining the term 'truth score' in our conversations on this topic.

31 The value of sample-based field surveys to validate administrative data has also been noted by Dr P.C. Mohanan, former acting chairman of India's National Statistical Commission (see Mohanan 2019).

32 I thank Rajendra Kondepati for coining the term 'nested supervision' to describe this approach during our discussions on this topic.

33 The structure of nested supervision makes it difficult for a DEO to argue that a case of data fudging found in a school audit is an isolated exception. This is because CRCs are supposed to visit *every* school multiple times in a year, and so there should be no fudging if CRCs are doing their job properly. Further, since BEOs are supposed to audit every CRC, they should be able to identify cases where CRCs are not doing their job properly. Finally, DEOs should be able to do the same for every BEO.

34 Such protocols are standard in both commercial market research and in academic research and should be straightforward to transfer to this setting as well.

35 Public disclosure of data need not prevent government departments from pressure testing it before it is finalized. A good balance will be for preliminary reports to first be shared internally within the government for review, followed by a public release of summary statistics at the district or block level.

36 This analogy is inspired by Amit Varma's podcast titled *The Seen and the Unseen.*

37 See Landes (1998) on the impact of clocks on productivity and Baker and Hubbard (2004) on how on-board GPS devices helped change contractual structure and productivity in the long-distance trucking industry.

38 The exact number of economists and data scientists employed by Amazon is not public information, but a 2019 CNN report noted that Amazon had hired more than 150 PhD economists in just the past few years (see DePillis 2019). Current and former Amazon employees I have spoken to estimate that there are 1000–2000 PhD holders working there, mostly focused on data analytics. Pat Bajari, Amazon's chief economist, has noted that better data, analysis, and experimental testing of new ideas have helped to sharply reduce guesswork and waste, and have thereby greatly improved efficiency.

Chapter 5: Personnel Management

1 See Bloom and Van Reenan (2007, 2009, and 2010), Bloom et al. (2013), and Bloom et al. (2015). They decompose management quality into operations, strategy, and personnel management. While all of these matter for overall management quality, they find that personnel management is by far the most important. My colleagues and I find similar results in the Indian context (see Lemos, Muralidharan, and Scur 2023).

2 The wage compression ratio is defined as the ratio of pay and benefits of the highest-paid employees in an organization to that of the lowest. In India, this ratio is typically under 15 in the government, whereas it can easily exceed 100 in private firms. As a result, the most senior government employees are often paid much less than their private-sector counterparts, whereas public employees at lower levels (who make up larger numbers) are paid much more.

3 See Table 1 and Figure 1 in Finan, Olken, and Pande (2017). The 'public-sector pay premium' is defined as the *extra* pay in

the public sector after controlling for observable individual and job characteristics. It finds that lower-income countries typically have a higher public sector pay premium, with India ranking among the world's top three (consistent with the 2003 World Bank report cited later in the paragraph).

4   See Drèze and Sen (2013).

5   As cited and reported in Saxena (2019), p. 92.

6   See a review of several studies in Kingdon (2020).

7   Note that this is in a sample of low-cost 'affordable' private schools, which comprise the vast majority of private schools in India and not the 'elite' private schools that cater to affluent populations.

8   See more details on the new and old pension schemes in Chapter 6.

9   CSDS-Lokniti-KAS Survey of 'Attitudes, Anxieties and Aspirations of India's Youth: Changing Patterns' conducted in 2016 (Kumar and Gupta 2018). 19 per cent said they preferred to set up their own business.

10 See Mangal (2023).

11 See Verma (2015).

12 Examples include the Vyapam scam in MP (Mitra and Tomar 2018), and the teacher recruitment scam in Haryana (see IANS 2019). These are only a selection of cases that have been exposed and led to some follow-up action. However, corruption in public sector recruitment has long been known to be widespread in India. See Wade (1985) for a classic reference and Sukhtankar and Vaishnav (2015) for a fuller set of references.

13 More generally, this is another example of how fertile ground for corruption is created whenever a government tries to set prices (in this case wages) that are disconnected from market prices. The same problem is seen in other cases of governments trying to run 'dual-price' systems in areas ranging from PDS grains to electricity for farmers (see Chapter 6 for further details).

14 See Hanna and Wang (2017). While this need not be driven by corruption in hiring (it could simply reflect opportunities for corruption while having a government job), it does suggest

that the status quo may be attracting less honest candidates for government jobs.

15 There are also political advantages to episodic 'bulk' recruiting. If timed before elections, politicians can take credit for 'providing' jobs and use their influence in recruiting to reward supporters with lucrative jobs. This is consistent with political incentives to view public sector employment more through the lens of providing jobs to a few rather than providing better services to many (see Chapter 2).

16 See Hemrajani (2018).

17 Note that I have also seen many committed and passionate teachers and so the field notes above do not suggest that *all* government teachers lack passion and interest in their job. But it is also true that for many of them, the primary attraction is the government job, and not teaching *per se*.

18 The full title of the book is *Timepass: Youth, Class and the Politics of Waiting in India* (Jeffrey 2010).

19 See Mangal (2023). Consistent with this point, all-India NSS data also shows much higher unemployment rates for educated males under the age limit for entry into many government jobs.

20 See, for instance, the reports by Accenture-NSDC (2013) and EY-FICCI (2013). Interviews with placement managers (conducted by Abhijit Banerjee and Gaurav Chiplunkar) confirm this with quotes along the lines of: 'Attrition post-placement is one of our larger concerns. While most candidates complete two-to-three-month-long training sessions, very few of them eventually stick on in the labour market.'

21 In practice, many of these applicants do combine their exam preparation with various formal and informal jobs and so not all their time is wasted. Nevertheless, obtaining a public-sector job and studying for the selection exams is typically the main focus of these youth, as opposed to obtaining skills that are rewarded in the broader economy.

22 This was part of the Andhra Pradesh Randomized Evaluation Studies (AP-REST), conducted in partnership with the Azim

Premji Foundation, which collected data on learning outcomes in 500 schools across five districts of AP, between 2005 and 2009.

23 Measuring employee productivity in the public sector is challenging because it is difficult to attribute outcomes to specific employees. However, in primary education, we can measure a teacher's 'value addition' (or effectiveness) by tracking student learning progress and attributing it to their teachers in that subject and year. This measure of effectiveness can then be correlated with employee characteristics such as education, training, experience, pay, and contractual structure to study the extent to which these factors predict teacher effectiveness. While estimating teacher value-added requires addressing several technical issues, high-quality long-term studies find that students with a 'high-value-added' teacher in school have better long-term economic outcomes (Chetty et al. 2014a and 2014b). See Bassiri (2015) for a discussion of the technical issues in estimating and interpreting measures of teacher value addition.

24 See Muralidharan and Sundararaman (2011), and Muralidharan (2012). Both studies find a negative (but statistically insignificant) correlation between teacher pay and effectiveness in government schools.

25 See Kremer et al. (2005) for evidence on levels and correlates of teacher absence in India.

26 See Das, Holla, Mohpal, and Muralidharan (2016).

27 See Lemos, Muralidharan, and Scur (2023) for evidence from India and Bau and Das (2020) for very similar findings in Pakistan.

28 See Ganimian, Muralidharan, and Walters (2023).

29 See De Ree, Muralidharan, Pradhan, and Rogers (2018).

30 See Ganimian, Muralidharan, and Walters (2023), and Muralidharan and Sundararaman (2013).

31 Unfortunately, actions like reverting to the more expensive old pension scheme go in the opposite direction—further raising compensation for privileged insiders at the cost of funds for hiring more staff.

32 See Muralidharan (2013) for a review of the evidence.

33 The problem is so severe that former School Education Secretary Anil Swarup has referred to these low-quality teacher training institutes as a mafia. See Swarup (2019).

34 In mathematical terms: If Quality (Q) = Knowledge (K) * Effort (E), then $dQ/dK = E$. Thus, the marginal impact of improving K on Q is higher when E is higher.

35 See Muralidharan and Sundararaman (2011) and Muralidharan (2012), which show there is no correlation between possessing a teacher training credential and teacher value-added in a typical government school. On the other hand, in schools randomly selected for a performance pay experiment, trained teachers were significantly more effective.

36 For detailed descriptions of the status quo of Indian classrooms as well as the regulations and norms surrounding teacher recruitment, training, deployment, transfers, and pay, see Ramachandran et al. (2016) and Ramachandran (2016).

37 Ganimian, A.J., Mbiti, I.M., and Mishra, A. (2022).

38 See Bloom, Genakos, Sadun, and Van Reenen (2012) for a review.

39 We studied the quality of management practices across public and private schools in (unified) Andhra Pradesh, and found that private schools scored 1.4 standard deviations higher on overall management scores, but scored 4.8 standard deviations higher on personnel management. This is an enormous difference, and the weaknesses in public personnel management accounted for the majority of the overall differences in management quality (see Lemos, Muralidharan, and Scur 2023).

40 There is very little systematic data on managerial vacancies, but I have personally seen vacancies in the 40–60 per cent range in block-level supervisory positions in multiple states and sectors.

41 These private sector management practices include actions such as (a) termination of employment for non-performance, (b) provision of large bonuses or equity compensation for strong performance, and (c) performance-based promotions. These are all much more difficult ideas to implement in the public sector.

42 For instance, government payrolls include large numbers of excess clerks and stenographers, whose roles have shrunk in importance since technology allows us to easily digitize government records.

43 This also applies to courts, who face limited competition and have perhaps, as a result, not felt the pressure to modernize their processes (see Chapter 14).

44 For instance, one of my studies showed that, on average, contract teachers lived 1 km away from the school, whereas regular teachers lived over 12 km away (Muralidharan and Sundararaman 2013).

45 See Béteille (2009) for an illustrative discussion.

46 For instance, the placement algorithm would know employees' priority ordering for postings (based on currently used criteria such as seniority, performance, family considerations, etc.); employees can indicate their ranked preferences over available postings; and the algorithm can implement the assignments based on the official policy. Thus, the main thing that the HRMIS would enable is a smoother, faster, more transparent, and less corrupt implementation of the official policy. While they have not developed a full HRMIS, several state governments, including Karnataka and Haryana, have implemented such an online transfer system for teachers, and qualitative reports suggest that such systems have been highly effective at both reducing corruption and improving teacher morale.

47 To keep the information in the system current, it should be required that all personnel actions taken in the government (including postings and transfers) be recorded digitally in the HRMIS.

48 As an example, government norms say that teachers should receive twenty days a year of in-service training, but multiple reports point out that this norm is rarely implemented in practice. As noted by Ramachandran et al. (2016): 'None of the (nine) states in this study have an effective policy for in-service training of teachers; training is carried out in an ad hoc manner . . .'

49 See Banerjee et al. (2021). Examples of soft skills taught included training on how to communicate with victims and record complaints in a more sensitive way.

50 To my knowledge, the term 'competency passbook' was coined by Dr Santhosh Matthew. The term is now being used more widely in the government in the context of Mission Karmayogi.

51 The first draft of this chapter was written in late 2019, before the Government of India announced Mission Karmayogi in September 2020, and many ideas in this sub-section have since been reflected in Mission Karmayogi. This validates the point that many of the ideas in this book are implementable, and also shows that they are being thought of independently by senior government officials.

52 Networking and mentoring matter a lot for promotions, and women and under-represented groups may be disadvantaged by their limited access to, or opportunity to participate in, social spaces outside the office. Organizations like WomenLift Health aim to bridge gender gaps in leadership positions in the health sector by facilitating such mentoring and networking for mid-career women. The proposed approach can help institutionalize the building of a diverse pipeline of leaders within public systems.

53 The main difficulty in implementing performance-based career progression in the government is the challenge of measurement of performance and attribution of individual contributions in team-based settings. In contrast, it is easier to observe if candidates have continued to accumulate relevant skills and competences over their career, and this is also something that is in the control of individuals.

54 This approach allows for provisions for reservations and quotas to be met at a district level.

55 These programmes should ideally be designed by apex government training institutions, but they can also be supported by high-quality private and non-profit organizations.

56 Much of this research has been conducted in the healthcare context, and the extensive use of practical training in medical

education through internships, residencies, and fellowships partly reflects the evidence on the effectiveness of such forms of training. See Zendejas et al. (2013) and Chang et al. (2017) for illustrative examples. There is similar suggestive evidence in education, though the number of high-quality studies is smaller than in medicine. See Muralidharan (2016) for references. A similar philosophy informs the design of 'co-op' based university programmes in practical fields such as engineering.

57 Bang et al. (1999) and Haines et al. (2007) show that community health workers, who receive limited training and are paid much more modest stipends than regular government health workers, were able to improve health outcomes in underserved rural areas in India. Note that the training in more theoretical course components will have to happen in person in a district headquarters, for which hostel accommodation may be needed. However, candidates can be based at home during their practicum.

58 Of course, this ratio will be lower for the graduates of the practicum-based skilling programme, but if such programmes are scaled up to every district, it is likely that the number of graduates from the programmes will exceed the number of government job openings.

59 For instance, many high-income countries face both ageing populations and shrinking working-age populations. This could lead to growing need for personalized care-giving services, potentially opening doors for foreign workers on short-term work visas. Graduates of high-quality practicum-based training programmes may be well-positioned for these jobs, which will likely pay well.

60 See Muralidharan and Sheth (2016).

61 See Jensen (2012).

62 See Singh, Romero, and Muralidharan (2022) for a more detailed description of the programme and its impact. Assuming 75–90 minutes of work per day for 20–24 days a month, the effective hourly wage rate would be Rs 50 per hour, or a daily wage rate of Rs 400, which is above the state minimum wage.

63 This concern was typically raised by organizations such as the National Council of Educational Research and Training (NCERT), and the National Institute of Educational Planning and Administration (NIEPA). See Kumar (2001), and Govinda and Josephine (2005) for an illustration of these objections.

64 See Dayaram (2002) for an overall review of the para-teacher model and related concerns including the frequency of litigation on compensation-related issues (p. 7).

65 Also, in many cases, the political pressure for regularization also reflects the *replacement* of regular hiring with contract workers as substitutes. In contrast, the proposal above aims to *supplement* existing staff with apprentices, without stopping regular recruitment.

66 Some elements of this idea are seen in the Agniveer scheme of the armed forces, including four-year tenures, and absorption of the top 25 per cent of candidates into regular positions. The Agniveer model more closely resembles recommendations I had made in an earlier policy paper (Muralidharan 2016). However, I believe that the modified approach in this chapter— anchoring apprenticeships *within training programmes*, with the practicum-based training being performed in a public facility— is much better, especially for frontline service delivery jobs with ample private sector demand. On Agniveer itself, the model may be better suited for support functions (such as cooks, cleaners, and drivers) than for combat troops. Reasons include: (a) the high training cost of a combat soldier implies a longer payback period, making short tenures less attractive, (b) combat roles demand unit solidarity and a willingness to risk life, which may be compromised by the Agniveer model, and (c) there are fewer private sector jobs that require a trained combat soldier. None of these concerns apply to support staff.

67 See Mazzucato and Collington (2023) on the costs of governments becoming overly dependent on consultants, including the key cost of weakening their own internal capacity.

68 To manage the logistics of offering such a course to five or ten times as many candidates as in the status quo, it can be delivered

in a blended manner with a combination of online content and assessments so that candidates can build their competency passbooks, and in-person training sessions.

69 See Chapter 11 of Iyer (2021). These young professionals were called *Zilla Swasth Bharat Preraks*.

70 In commenting on a draft of this chapter, a mid-career IAS officer noted: 'I think this is one of the most critical requirements at the cutting edge of service delivery. We need a dynamic, data-driven, young team at the disposal of Collectors and District Magistrates.'

71 See Somanathan and Natarajan (2022) for an extensive discussion of these issues.

72 While I have often observed this myself, this point was reinforced by Mahima Vashisht in her interview with Amit Varma on episode 293 of *The Seen and the Unseen* podcast.

73 Such a structure would be analogous to the 'Short Service Commission' in the armed forces.

74 TV shows like *The Aspirants* and the recent movie *12th Fail* provide a vivid sense of the effort, commitment, and dreams of UPSC aspirants, that are mostly dashed by the cruel reality of the very low odds of getting selected. Implementing the proposal in the text would be a substantial improvement over the status quo both for the government and for the aspirants.

75 In the words of a senior IAS officer (in a personal note to me): 'Much of the time is consumed in generating multiple reports for superior officers on a daily basis. Based on personal experience, I would say that this activity of preparing and sending reports must be consuming anywhere between 15 and 20 per cent of officers' time on a daily basis.'

76 This is based on fieldwork in one state. The discrepancy in *total area* sown was much less than 25 per cent because officials extrapolated from other data sources for the totals. The 'making up' of data was seen more at the individual plot level, reflecting officials making a 'guesstimate' without visiting the plot.

77 As observed in *High Output Management* (Grove 1983).

78 This calculation assumes that the additional work that can be done with the 5 per cent time of existing staff will reduce hiring needs by the same amount and thereby save these funds. In practice, the social value of the employee time saved could be greater or less than the salary cost of that time, depending on how the saved time is deployed to other tasks or to improve the quality of work done on existing tasks.

79 See Muralidharan and Sundararaman (2011), Duflo, Hanna and Ryan (2012), Muralidharan (2012), and Mbiti et al. (2019) for examples from education; Mohanan et al. (2021) for one from health; and Khan, Khwaja, and Olken (2016), and Khan, Khwaja, and Olken (2019) for examples from tax collection.

80 See Bansal (2021) for one such cautionary tale.

81 The focus on these three key sets of indicators for performance management is also why Chapter 4 discusses how to measure them in some detail. Finally, the last goal will also require and motivate departments to coordinate better across departments, and to think about their role not just as a 'provider' of services but also as a regulator and policymaker whose actions affect quality and availability of services through private providers, and non-governmental organizations as well (see Chapter 9).

82 Performance evaluations can also explicitly include equity goals, such as improvements in outcomes for women and marginalized groups.

83 Issuing a notice to the agitators to rejoin work, the Principal Secretary noted that: 'Regularization of service of any contract employee cannot be for all but will be subject to the assessment and evaluation of their performance by a committee appointed by the government. Those whose performance is found to be satisfactory can only be regularized.' See the story by The Hindu news bureau dated 8 May 2023.

84 See Bhargava (2022) for more details on this unique pilot. Like the KPI survey described in Chapter 4, this project also had programme management support from the Centre for Effective Governance of Indian States (CEGIS) and technical inputs from academic researchers, including myself. The importance of

changing employee culture from the outset was highlighted to me by the commissioner who initiated the project. He valued the new performance measurement system so much that he requested CEGIS's assistance to help him implement it in his subsequent department as well. However, he noted later that it was more difficult to do so when existing staff were used to the old ways of functioning, compared to a setting where fresh recruits were hired with the expectation that their performance will be measured.

85 See:https://static.pib.gov.in/WriteReadData/specificdocs/ documents/2023/apr/doc2023417181801.pdf.

Chapter 6: Public Finance—Expenditure

1 Such goods often exhibit some or all of the following features: (a) high fixed costs, beyond what firms can take on, (b) non-rivalry in consumption, which means that one person's usage does not limit others' ability to benefit from the good (as in infectious disease control or defence), (c) non-excludability, which means it is difficult to exclude those who do not pay from receiving benefits (as with national defence and disease control), and (d) they generate externalities, whereby one person's consumption also affects others, such as with pollution or congestion. All these features can result in individuals and markets not adequately providing these goods relative to socially optimal levels.

2 A good example is ISRO, whose Chandrayaan-3 was the world's most inexpensive moon mission.

3 For instance, one well-known study estimates that only around 17 per cent of waste in government is due to 'active' waste or corruption and the remaining 83 per cent is due to 'passive' waste or inefficiency (Bandiera et al. 2009). While the study is set in Italy, this insight is likely to be widely applicable.

4 For instance, Central government spending on food subsidies increased nearly five times from Rs 1,09,000 crore in 2019–20 to Rs 5,41,000 crore in 2020–21, and remained atypically elevated at 2,89,000 crore in 2021–22. Further, tax revenues were significantly depressed by lockdowns and reduction in economic

activity in these two fiscal years, implying higher borrowing than usual. While the economy and public finances started returning to normal in 2022–23, audited accounts for this year were not available across the Central and state governments at the time of finalizing the manuscript. Hence discussions of public spending in this book use the audited 2019–20 figures.

5   Source for Central government spending: https://www.indiabudget. gov.in/doc/Budget_at_Glance/bag6.pdf; source for data on state government spending: RBI, Study of State Finances. While many states augment food subsidies provided by the Central government through the PDS, this line item is not reported separately in a standardized way across states and is hence set to zero above, and included in the 'others' category.

6   These include forces such as the Central Reserve Police Force (CRPF), Border Security Force (BSF) and the Central Industrial Security Force (CISF), which together have over 7,00,000 active staff.

7   In 2019–20, Central government spending was Rs 26.87 lakh crore, while states spent Rs 34.96 lakh crore, implying a combined expenditure of Rs 61.83 lakh crore. Yet, the Rs 26.87 lakh crore figure includes Rs 6.3 lakh crore the Central government transferred to states, which are already included in state spending figures, causing double counting. Adjusting for this, the actual total spending is Rs 55.5 lakh crore.

8   Of the Rs 6.3 lakh crore of transfers, Rs 3.1 lakh crore (or around half the total) were 'tied' transfers under centrally sponsored schemes. These are assigned to a sector based on the scheme, and then split equally across the Central and state governments. The remaining transfers of Rs 3.2 lakh crore, which are mostly untied, are assigned to states. These include Rs 1.2 lakh crore under Finance Commission transfers; and Rs 2 lakh crore under other transfers to states, which includes compensation for revenue loss under GST, transfers for disaster relief, etc. The Forum for State Studies, comprising eminent Indian public finance economists, has also independently estimated the total

share of state spending in India to be 60 per cent. See: https://
forumforstatestudies.in/.

9   Data sources: Government of India Budget Documents for
    Central government figures; RBI, Study of State Finances for
    state government figures. Funds transferred to states by the
    Central government are apportioned the same way as in Table 6.1
    and reflected in the 'other spending' category.

10 The old pension system (OPS) is a 'defined benefits' system that
    promised a perpetual pension based on the final salary, for the
    retiree and surviving spouse. In contrast, the new pension scheme
    (NPS) is a 'defined contribution' scheme where employees
    save for retirement with matching contributions from the
    government. The NPS is more cost-effective and fiscally prudent
    as the pension costs of employment are fully accounted for in
    the same year, rather than deferred to the future. A key reform
    in 2002 transitioned new public employees from the OPS to
    NPS from 2004. The recent pressure to revert to the OPS, partly
    influenced by strong public-sector unions, will not only limit
    future funds for public investments but is also inequitable, given
    government employees' substantial pay relative to market and
    global benchmarks (see Chapter 5). For a detailed discussion of
    pensions, refer to Episode 347 of Amit Varma's *The Seen and the
    Unseen* podcast with Ajay Shah and Renuka Sane.

11 This is what happened under the UDAY scheme where
    state governments assumed 75 per cent of the liabilities of
    electricity distribution companies, and issued new debt to
    finance this. This process was supposed to be accompanied
    by reforms to the electricity sector, but the reforms have
    mostly not happened yet. See Tanwar (2019) for a discussion.
    Similarly, public-sector banks have also periodically needed
    infusions of public taxpayer money to get recapitalized after
    accumulated losses.

12 These investment figures themselves are higher than historical
    norms and reflect an increase in the budget share allocated to
    capital expenditure in recent years.

13 In economics terminology, governments should focus on activities where they have a 'comparative advantage' relative to other social actors such as individuals, firms, and social organizations.

14 Chapter 2 discussed this trade-off with examples from railways and utilities such as water and electricity. Other examples are discussed in Chapters 15 and 16.

15 Spending on interest subsidies on farm loans was Rs 16,219 crore and on PM-KISAN (that made income transfers to farmers) was Rs 48,714 crore.

16 Source: Budget at a Glance, Government of Punjab. https://www.cbgaindia.org/wp-content/uploads/2020/03/Budget-at-a-Glance-2020-21-Punjab.pdf.

17 See Desai et Al. (2010).

18 See Drèze, Gupta, Khera, and Pimenta (2019).

19 Note that the SECC does not include homesteads and small homestead farms in landholding, and therefore shows a higher rate of landless rural residents than the NSS.

20 Of course, the landless would also benefit indirectly from the creation of jobs in agriculture. However, as we will see further in Chapters 15 and 16, these are low-productivity jobs and are only sustained by subsidies. This actually *hurts* workers over time by delaying their transition to more productive jobs.

21 In all cases, the top category of households are those with more than 10 acres of land. The average landholding in this group is 19 acres in Punjab, 17 acres in Maharashtra and 15.7 acres in (unified) Andhra Pradesh, including both present-day AP and Telangana. All data is from the 2011 SECC.

22 See Romero and Singh (2023).

23 See Alexander and Padmanabhan (2019a).

24 See Rukmini S. (2019) for this analysis.

25 Leakage can be calculated by comparing average disbursals at the district level and average receipts reported in household surveys like the NSS. This is the methodology used, for instance, by Himanshu and Sen (2011) as well as Khera (2011a) to estimate leakage in the PDS.

26 See Muralidharan, Niehaus, and Sukhtankar (2016, 2023b).

27 See Niehaus and Sukhtankar (2013).

28 See George and Subramanian (2015). See Chapter 15 for additional examples of this point.

29 The calculation of fiscal cost is based on an estimate of unauthorized absences. See Muralidharan, Das, Holla, and Mohpal (2017) for details.

30 For instance, rent control laws aim to subsidize housing for the poor. However, several US studies show that rent control hurts social welfare by reducing the supply of housing over time and misallocating scarce housing stock. See Diamond et al. (2019) and Glaeser and Luttmer (2003) for examples.

31 Historically, India's welfare spending largely took the form of price subsidies, due to the absence of a system for direct income transfers to citizens. With the widespread adoption of Aadhaar and bank accounts, it is now feasible to transition many welfare programmes from price subsidies to income transfers, as has been done successfully for LPG (liquefied petroleum gas) subsidies. See Barnwal (2023) for evidence that this reform significantly reduced corruption and leakage in LPG subsidies.

32 Alexander and Padmanabhan (2019b) detail how perverse farmer incentives caused by free electricity are a key driver of India's groundwater crisis.

33 For instance, the Kaleshwaram lift irrigation project, started in 2016, was one of the most important political priorities for the government of the newly formed state of Telangana.

34 See Chokkakula, Kapur, and Singh (2021) for key facts on water resource management in India.

35 The Accelerated Irrigation Benefits Programme (AIBP) was launched in 1996–97 to provide Central assistance for major irrigation projects. This has since been subsumed under the Pradhan Mantri Krishi Sinchai Yojana (PMKSY), but most of its funds are still allocated to major irrigation projects.

36 See Chokkakula, Kapur, and Singh (2021). They note that irrigation investments in Maharashtra have been characterized by 'highly uneven development and inequalities across geographic regions'.

37 See CAG AIBP Report, 2018.

38 See Iyer (2019) for an illustrative account of corruption scandals in irrigation projects.

39 See CAG AIBP Report, 2018.

40 Ibid.

41 Ibid.

42 The PAISA report was produced for several years by the Accountability Initiative at the Centre for Policy Research. See Accountability Initiative (2012) for an illustration.

43 See Choudhury and Mohanty (2018).

44 On a more optimistic note, the study also highlights how process reforms in Odisha reduced the number of steps needed to access funds.

45 This is a global problem and there is high-quality evidence even from the US showing that there is a sharp increase in public spending in the last week of the fiscal year, and that the quality of this expenditure is significantly lower (Liebman and Mahoney 2017).

46 See Mathew, Purohit, and Sharma (2024) for a detailed discussion of the problems with the PFMS and how these weaknesses in the PFMS contribute to poor value for money in public spending in India.

47 This would be analogous to companies borrowing for high RoI projects. Debt is a valuable tool in such a setting, because it enables high RoI projects to be undertaken that may not otherwise be possible.

48 Another cost of free agricultural power is increased theft of power, which is easier to hide under 'agricultural use' because agricultural power use is often not even metered. This power theft also contributes to the financial stress and insolvency of power distribution companies.

49 See Choudhury and Dubey (2020)

50 In Western philosophy, a similar idea that policies and programmes should be assessed by their impact on the most disadvantaged members of society has notably been made by US

philosopher John Rawls in his famous book *A Theory of Justice* (Rawls 1971).

51 There is a large academic literature on measuring poverty and inequality that has devised several ways to measure them. So, the impact of policies on reducing inequality will vary by the kind of measure used.

52 If printed in colour, R1 would be in green, R3 in red, and R2 and R4 in yellow to reflect that we should be moving spending from R3 to R1, and that items in R2 and R4 may need further discussion and debate.

53 In the words of a senior IAS officer who commented on a draft of this chapter: 'In the current system, there is absolutely no incentive for being cost effective, while there are good number of reasons for the opposite.' As with many insights about government, this point has also been eloquently articulated in the *Yes, Minister* series, where Sir Humphrey Appleby memorably says: '. . . the Civil Service does not make profits or losses. *Ergo*, we measure success by the size of our staff and our budget.'

54 This would imply that disadvantaged areas would get more staff, which is the opposite of what often happens under the status quo.

55 Note that given statistical concerns of measurement error making changes in rankings quite noisy, these district-level pools for performance-based funding should ideally be given on a continuous sliding scale of measured improvements as opposed to being fully awarded to a few winning districts.

56 See Mbiti et al. (2019).

57 I was not able to find an official figure for the total value of public procurement from private vendors. However, since the total capital expenditure is over Rs 8 lakh crore/year, this will be true if even two-thirds of all such expenditure is undertaken by contractors (which is likely an underestimate).

58 The problem of poorly rated companies shutting down and re-emerging under a new name can be mitigated by requiring companies to list their directors and their unique Director

Identification Number (DIN), which is issued by the Ministry of Corporate Affairs. Thus, analysis of company reputation can include both the institutional reputation of the entity and the individual reputation of its directors.

59 Further ideas for improving the process of fund flows and PFM systems are presented in an excellent recent book dedicated to the subject (see Mathew, Purohit, and Sharma 2024).

60 See 'Charting a Course for the Indian Economy' by Muralidharan and Subramanian (2015).

61 For instance, the former Indonesian finance minister said to me in 2015: 'How I wish we had your study [showing no impact of doubling teacher pay] in 2005 when we were debating the policy in the government. We had our doubts, but had no evidence to inform the decision that cost billions of dollars, but delivered little benefit.' Similarly, in my work with Indian state finance departments, I have heard similar requests for high-quality economic analysis.

62 The Government of Andhra Pradesh issued a notification dated 2 January 2023 announcing the creation of a Centre for Strategic Planning and Governance (CSPG) that lays out similar roles and responsibilities to the ones mentioned in this chapter.

63 We also need more well-trained economists who can conduct such analysis. However, with the growing popularity of economics and public policy as subjects, I am optimistic that there will be a strong pipeline of motivated high-quality candidates for such roles in the coming years. What is missing is an institutional structure that can create meaningful career trajectories for policy economists to do good work and have this work reflected in policy. Institutions such as the NIPFP and the RBI are natural places to house such economists so that they can benefit from the scale of these institutions for exposure to new ideas and technically strong peers, while also working on deep state-level fiscal analysis.

64 For instance, one state education commissioner told me that department initiatives to reduce fake enrolment saved hundreds of crores of rupees, but the finance department took this money

back and refused to fund other department priorities for improving student learning. Such actions strongly discourage line departments from taking initiatives to save money.

65 While employee pay should be linked to state revenue growth, the multiplier from revenue growth to pay growth should be less than 1. This will ensure that revenue growth also creates increases in fiscal space to hire more employees or make other R1 investments.

66 This is what happened during the COVID-19 pandemic.

67 Thus, the variable pay pool will be the same as set aside at the time of Pay Commission raises. It will start by being linked only to state revenue growth, but over time, it can include weights for measures of performance as well as demonstrated competence (as outlined in Chapter 5).

68 The main cost of implementing performance-based pay systems is not the pay itself (as discussed above) but rather the cost of measuring performance. However, as discussed in Chapter 4, this cost is likely to be very small (~0.025 per cent of a typical state's budget or ~0.1 per cent of the salary cost).

69 See Muralidharan and Singh (2023) for an example.

70 See Levine (2017) for a discussion of the moral case for evidence in policymaking.

Chapter 7: Public Finance—Revenue

1   As James C. Scott argues in his book *Against the Grain: A Deep History of the Earliest States*, the advent of crop production which was 'visible, divisible, assessable, storable, transportable, and rationable' made it easy to collect taxes. Recent research has confirmed that the ability of rulers to easily collect a share of cereal production as taxes was even more important than land productivity per se in explaining the origins of the modern state (see Mayshar, Moav, and Pascali 2022).

2   The *Arthashastra* memorably captures this sentiment by noting sagely that 'the king should collect taxes from his subjects exactly the same way a honey bee collects nectar from flowers'. In other

Notes: Chapter 7

words, revenue should be collected with minimum disruption to the underlying production and producers.

3   RBI Study of State Finances for the state figure and Budget at a glance (Bag 5) for the Central figure.

4   Greater formalization is associated with increasing division of labour and economies of scale, which in turn drive greater productivity and economic growth. It is also associated with moving home production, which does not enter the national income accounts, to market production, which does. These factors increase GDP per capita, and also make economic activity easier to track and therefore to tax.

5   This is also consistent with the historical pattern that increases in state fiscal capacity were driven by the need to finance war efforts as noted in Chapter 2.

6   This choice reflected a combination of expanded voting rights (see Chapter 2), and greater national solidarity engendered by the war effort, which in turn created broad public support for a welfare state.

7   See Alesina and Glaeser (2004) for a comparative discussion of welfare states in the US and in Continental Europe.

8   India had a tax-to-GDP ratio of ~17 per cent in 2018–19 at PPP-adjusted GDP/capita of $6800. In comparison, the UK and the US only reached a 17 per cent tax-to-GDP ratio at a PPP-adjusted GDP/capita of $8200 and $10,500 respectively. China had a PPP-adjusted GDP/capita of $6600 in 2005 and a tax-to-GDP ratio of 18.3 per cent at that point, which is comparable to where India was in 2018–19. All these numbers are based on the underlying figures used in Figures 7.1 and 7.2.

9   For instance, the tax-to-GDP ratio fell to 16.1 per cent in 2019–20, likely reflecting the lockdown in March 2020 and the slowing of economic activity before that. However, Chapter 6 uses figures from 2019–20 as the lockdown in March 2020 did not significantly affect government expenditure in the last two weeks of the fiscal year, and only did so in 2020–21.

10   The division of revenue sources reflects constitutional guidelines earmarking different taxes as being in the jurisdiction of Union

and state governments respectively. Sales taxes on goods were in the domain of states whereas those on services were with the Union government. However, the GST Constitutional Amendment of 2017 unified these two sets of taxes to create a national GST. This change reflects the greater national integration of the economy over time and the importance of having a unified tax regime to realize the benefits of the economies of scale from integrating India's national market.

11 Non-tax revenues include cesses, surcharges, mining royalties, and capital earnings such as proceeds of asset sales, and dividends paid to the government from publicly owned companies and the RBI.

12 This difference is consistent with the principles of fiscal federalism whereby it is usually more efficient to collect many kinds of taxes at the national level (to leverage economies of scale and to minimize tax competition and a race to the bottom across states) and more efficient to spend at a local level (to better reflect variation in needs and preferences across locations).

13 The divisible pool includes all direct (income tax, corporation tax, tax on transaction of securities and other commodities) and indirect (CGST, central excise, customs) central taxes net of collection costs. It excludes all non-tax revenues of the Centre, cesses and surcharges. The Finance Commission determines two key parameters: (a) the division of funds between the Union and state governments (vertical devolution), and (b) the division of the state pool across states (horizontal devolution). The horizontal devolution component includes a weight on underdevelopment, which results in additional fund allocations to underdeveloped states to promote more equitable development across the country.

14 See Ganjapure (2020) in the *Times of India*.

15 As reported in an *Economic Times* news story dated 07 December 2012.

16 See Seth (2021) in *Business Standard*.

17 See Dhingra (2019).

18 Estimates are based on work done by the Centre for Effective Governance of Indian States (CEGIS).

19 See Sinha (2023) in the *Hindu BusinessLine*.

20 Specifically, the Business Intelligence and Fraud Analytics (BIFA) division of the GSTN and the Directorate General of GST Intelligence (DGGI) of the CBIC conduct fraud analytics on GST data at the national level. However, this analytical work is not fully integrated with state-level field operations. For instance, BIFA sends states a list of suspicious accounts for field verification, but at the time of writing, there was no institutionalized way for the results of this field verification to be fed back into the BIFA fraud detection algorithm, which is needed to refine its predictions and thereby make better use of limited staff capacity for field verifications. This limited coordination reflects the legacy of GST implementation, with responsibility for taxpayers being divided between the Central and state governments, resulting in two parallel systems of field enforcement rather than a unified and harmonized one.

21 Estimates rounded to nearest Rs 1000 crore. These are the states with the most recent CAG audits. Source: 'Report of the Comptroller and Auditor General of India on Revenue Sector'; Uttar Pradesh (2020), Bihar (2021), Rajasthan (2020), and Maharashtra (2019); https://cag.gov.in/en/audit-report.

22 These numbers reflect both weak tax enforcement capacity, and court-related delays, since some cases of uncollected arrears are due to litigation stuck in courts.

23 In practice, the opposite is also known to happen where tax officials make high assessments and then demand bribes to reduce the assessment. This reflects the conflicting pressures faced by officials. On the one hand, they are given revenue targets to meet, which are helped by high assessments on those who will pay high taxes. On the other, they benefit from receiving bribes to lower assessments. While some officials are scrupulously honest, others aim to balance these two conflicting goals by delivering 'enough' revenue to not attract suspicion, while also collecting bribes where possible.

24 Source: 'Report of the Comptroller and Auditor General of India on Revenue Sector'; Uttar Pradesh (2020), Bihar (2021); https://cag.gov.in/en/audit-report. These CAG audit reports could be even more useful if they were conducted using a stratified random sample, because the data can then be reweighted to produce population-level estimates of irregularities, which are currently not available as far as I know.

25 This is analogous to the distortionary costs of subsidies discussed in Chapter 6, where we noted that free electricity to farmers has not just a direct fiscal cost but also large indirect costs by making the price of water zero and thereby not reflecting the true social cost of water use. In general, both taxes and subsidies impose unseen costs on the economy by introducing a wedge between the true economic cost of an activity and the price actually faced on it by economic actors.

26 Of course, the demand for cash payments in the housing sector also reflects the corruption in issuing and obtaining the necessary permits for construction, which also often need cash. But, the supply of cash to real estate reflects the demand from tax evaders for investments where they can park black money. See Kapur and Vaishnav (2018) for an extended discussion of the close links between builders and politicians, with the latter providing permits and the former providing election finance.

27 Kelkar and Shah (2019).

28 See Shah (2016) for a more detailed discussion on MCPF and why it is high in India.

29 Consider a government that can meet a revenue target in three ways: (a) impose a 10 per cent tax on all citizens, (b) impose 20 per cent on one half and none on the other half, and (c) impose 40 per cent on one quarter of the citizens, and none on the other three quarters. In this case, public finance theory tells us that option (c) is twice as socially inefficient as option (b) and four times as inefficient as option (a). Of course, in practice, we have progressive taxation with higher tax rates for higher earners

because we also care about equity. The discussion in this section of the text focuses on efficiency.

30 See Daniyal (2022).

31 A recent analysis of data from the UN Department of Economic Affairs estimated that 17 million Indians were living abroad in 2017, making India the largest source country for international migrants (Sanghera 2018). In 2020, 5000 high-net-worth individuals (2 per cent of all such individuals in India) emigrated from India (Mohan 2022). This point is corroborated by analysis on the destination side where the great success of the Indian diaspora in the US is mainly explained by 'selection' whereby the most talented Indians are disproportionately likely to migrate to the US (Chakravorty, Kapur, and Singh 2017).

32 Basic economic theory shows that firms and consumers invest less under uncertainty (Dixit and Pindyck 1994). See Bloom (2009) and Basu and Bundick (2017) for examples of empirical studies. An illustrative Indian example is the 2012 retrospective taxation case, where the Government of India introduced legislation to undo the Indian Supreme Court ruling in favour of Vodafone on taxing capital gains. This action is widely believed to have hurt business confidence and investment in India, with some commentators even referring to it as 'tax terrorism' (see Venkataramakrishnan 2021 for an example).

33 Studying the extent to which citizens are willing to pay taxes is an active area of research in public finance. See Luttmer and Singhal (2014) for a synthesis of the literature on tax morale and tax payments.

34 See Cullen, Turner, and Washington (2021).

35 See Martinez-Bravo, Padro i Miquel, and Qian (2012).

36 See Gupta (2016).

37 See Pomeranz and Vila-Belda (2019) for an excellent review of this body of work. The summary in this section draws heavily on this paper.

38 See Jensen (2022) for micro evidence that transition from self-employment to jobs as paid employees is correlated with increasing tax capacity of societies over time.

39 See Pomeranz (2015).

40 See Basri et al. (2021).

41 See Pomeranz and Vila-Belda (2019) for references to various taxpayer communication studies and Khan, Khwaja, and Olken (2016 and 2019) for evidence on impacts of incentives to tax officials.

42 This is not too different from a policeman on a 'beat' who knows local information and sources well.

43 Projected estimates are from the United Nations *World Cities Report* (2022).

44 Despite having only a third of India's population, Indian cities contribute 59 to 70 per cent of India's GDP (Mitra and Mehta 2011). See Glaeser (2011) for an excellent review of the ways in which urbanization promotes economic growth and development.

45 See Hingorani et al. (2019).

46 See UNU-Wilder Government Revenue Dataset.

47 For instance, Cellini, Ferreira, and Rothstein (2010) found that successfully issuing bonds for school construction and improvement in the US led to an increase in property prices that was greater than the interest cost of paying back the bonds, suggesting that the investment created net positive social value.

48 See Kapur, Somanathan, and Subramanian (2014).

49 The estimates indicate that 200 million people who live in 180 cities would lose an average of 3.3 years of life due particulate matter concentrations over India's standards, implying over 650 million years of life lost. See Greenstone and Pande (2014) and Gupta and Spears (2017).

50 See Juyal et al. (2018).

51 High-quality global evidence shows that fuel prices are an important determinant of the extent to which consumers demand and firms prioritize innovation in energy efficiency. See Newell, Jaffe, and Stavins (1999) for an illustrative example.

52 These revenues can also be used to finance politically popular initiatives like free bus travel for women, which may have social benefits such as increased female labour force participation (see Chapter 16).

53 See Venkatachalam (2015) for an example.

54 As an illustration, see Subramanian (2017) for an excellent discussion of the economics of the private water tanker business in Bangalore. Also see the discussion in Aiyar (2020).

55 A good illustration of the 'low-level equilibrium' of not charging (or being able to charge, due to theft) for electricity, and low quality of provision is illustrated by the documentary *Katiyabaaz*. Private solutions such as water tankers or electricity generators have much higher unit costs due to the smaller scale.

56 Just as in Figure 6.1, the total electricity and water usage of the lowest 60 per cent of users will be considerably less than 60 per cent.

57 The discussion in the text focuses on the policy question of how to balance access and user charges. There is a different *operational* question of how to improve the efficiency of utilities, which includes questions of privatization and competition. This question is beyond the scope of this book, though some relevant principles are discussed in Chapter 9.

58 World Bank report on *Financing India's Urban Infrastructure Needs* (Athar, White, and Goyal, 2022).

59 Note that such fees on private transport make economic sense even without earmarking them for public transport. However, to the extent that transit is almost a necessity for modern urban life, investing in public transport makes such fees economically and politically more practical.

60 Commuters are sure to be better off because they will only avail the new option if the price is less than the value they obtain. Similarly, any increase in property taxes will only be a small fraction of the increase in their property values, and so they will also be better off.

61 To the extent that this results in seeking care from the public health system, it also imposes costs on others by using taxpayer funded services.

62 The points in this paragraph draw from Srivastava (2017), Manur (2018), and Parth (2020).

63 See Dar and Sahay (2018).

64 See Jha (2022), and Malhotra (2022) for examples. Editorials in the *Times of India* (2022) and *The Hindu* (2021) have also noted that prohibition in Bihar is not working.

65 See Parth (2020).

66 Long-term earmarking of such revenues can be suboptimal due to unforeseen future changes. So, it can make sense to have a sunset clause where revenue earmarking lasts for a fixed period, say five or ten years, and then needs to be reauthorized. This approach can balance the benefits of obtaining political support for reforms against the costs of making potentially inefficient long-term commitments.

67 Total Tamil Nadu government spending was Rs 2,95,000 crore in 2021–22, while own tax revenues were Rs 1,23,000 crore. The gap between own tax revenues and spending was bridged by central transfers, non-tax revenues, and borrowing. Source: Parliamentary Research Service (PRS) state budget analysis.

68 See Kalaiyarasan (2014).

69 Despite prohibition, alcohol is widely available in Gujarat (see Jadeja 2023). However, its illegal status confines consumption indoors and in known company. In my discussions with executives in knowledge industries, prohibition is often mentioned as a deterrent to attracting young professionals to Gujarat, since such talent values public opportunities for socialization and networking, which is limited by prohibition.

70 See Braun (2021).

71 The principles are that (a) land is immovable, (b) the deadweight loss of taxation increases with the square of the tax rate, and so the economic cost of increasing a tax from 0 to 20 per cent is much lower than that of increasing one from 20 to 40 per cent. Thus, holding revenue targets constant, the MCPF from raising agricultural taxes from zero will most likely be lower than further increasing existing taxes.

72 See Alagh (1961) for an illustrative early example, and the 2002 Kelkar committee report and the 2014 TARC report for more recent ones. See Mohanty (2020) for a summary of the relevant issues.

73 Technical concerns such as the difficulty of measuring agricultural profits can be addressed using data on average acreage, yields, and costs of cultivation—which are calculated by the government anyway. So, tax assessments on large landholdings can be based on these averages as opposed to estimating profits on each plot of land.

74 Progressive tax systems are those that tax a higher proportion of the income of richer citizens. Changes that reduce the progressivity of a tax system are referred to as regressive.

75 In these cases, firms selling the product in a lower tax category have paid a higher tax on their inputs and are eligible for a refund under some conditions. This creates additional administrative work for both the taxpayers and government and increases working capital costs for firms who have to wait for the government to refund extra taxes collected.

76 The chairman of the Prime Minister's Economic Advisory Council, Bibek Debroy, has made a similar argument and called for a uniform GST. See Debroy (2022).

77 Since less than 5 per cent of Indians pay income tax (see Daniyal 2022), we will do well to not raise the minimum threshold for income taxes further so that more earners come into the income tax fold over time.

Chapter 8: Federalism and Decentralization

1 Some smaller states do not have block panchayats and have a two-tier Panchayati Raj system.

2 The discussion of the benefits and costs of country size is based on Alesina and Spolaore (1997) and (2003). These, in turn, build on classic papers on federalism such as Tiebout (1956) and Oates (1972).

3 Specifically, military procurement from Boeing to develop and produce planes for the air force during World War II spilled over into dramatic improvements in commercial aviation. Similarly, the modern commercial Internet originated in technologies developed for rapid military communications.

4   See Hornbeck (2012) for an illustration of how migration within the US was key to reducing the long-term costs of being exposed to severe erosion of the US's plains in the 1930s, which sharply reduced agricultural productivity (an episode known as the Dust Bowl). In principle, these benefits can be provided through foreign aid and international migration. In practice, political support for helping areas and people in another country is often much lower than within the same country.

5   A key factor that has enabled smaller countries to thrive in recent years is that the post-World War II international order saw both a reduction in wars of territorial annexation and an increase in market access and free trade. Both these factors reduced the benefits of country size and made it possible for smaller countries to be prosperous and maintain their own identity (see Alesina and Spolaore 1997 and 2003).

6   See Guha (2007) for an extended discussion of these concerns.

7   The founding leaders of India disagreed considerably on this question with Gandhi advocating the linguistic division of states since as early as 1918, and both Nehru and Sardar Patel strongly opposing it due to a concern that such a reorganization could lead to the destabilization of the Indian Union itself. Guha (2007) captures both sentiments by noting that, 'When it began, the movement for linguistic states generated deep apprehensions among the nationalist elite. They feared it would lead to the Balkanization of India, to the creation of many more Pakistans,' and then also noting that: 'In retrospect, however, linguistic reorganization seems rather to have consolidated the unity of India. On the whole the creation of linguistic states has acted as a largely constructive channel for provincial pride. It has proved quite feasible to be peaceably Kannadiga, or Tamil, or Oriya—as well as contentedly Indian.'

8   For instance, the linguistic reorganization of Indian states in 1956 improved the alignment between citizen needs and education policy. Prior to 1956, many children lacked access to a school that taught in their native language. Jain (2017) shows that educational achievement in linguistically mismatched districts

significantly increased after the 1956 reorganization of Indian states on linguistic lines.

9   See Pritchett and Pande (2006) for a more detailed discussion.

10   See Khosla (2022) for a recent discussion of these issues in the Indian context.

11   See Khera (2011b), Anderson et al. (2015), Jenkins and Manor (2017) and Veeraraghavan (2021) for an illustrative set of discussion and evidence on this point.

12   Urban local bodies are classified by size into municipal corporations (population over 1 million), municipalities (population over 1,00,000) and *nagarpalikas* (population over 20,000).

13   Specifically, it provides special powers to the Central government to take over the entire administration of a state in case the elected government is not able to function according to constitutional provisions, such as a total breakdown of law and order.

14   Historically, this practice was a feature of Congress governments. However, it is increasingly also seen in the BJP, which has started developing the 'high command' culture of the Congress and we have seen multiple changes of chief ministers in BJP-governed states, including Gujarat, Karnataka, and Uttarakhand (which saw three chief ministers in 2021).

15   This reflects a combination of two factors. The first is the increased importance of regional political parties in an era of coalition governments (which India had during 1989–2014). The second is the Supreme Court's 1994 judgment in the Bommai case, which made it more difficult to arbitrarily dismiss elected state governments.

16   Prior to 2000, the divisible pool of tax revenue included only income tax and union excise taxes from a few commodities. Thus, while the states' share of income taxes was high (ranging between 77 and 85 per cent), the divisible pool itself excluded major components of revenue. Following the 80th Amendment to the Constitution, the divisible pool included Central taxes on all goods and services, except cesses and surcharges. The claim

that the states' share of divisible pool revenues has been below one-third is based on the expanded definition of the divisible pool after the 80th Amendment. See Table 1.1 in Panda et al. (2019). Data on states' shares of all shareable taxes is reported from 2000 onwards.

17 See Chakraborty (2019).

18 The Central government contributes larger amounts, up to 90 per cent, for 'special category' states.

19 See Bordoloi et al. (2020).

20 See Aiyar and Kapur (2019) for an extensive discussion of fiscal federalism for social policy in India.

21 See Nilakantan (2022) for additional examples of the costs and limitations of the one-size-fits-all model adopted by several of our centrally sponsored schemes.

22 I thank Alok Kumar for pointing this fact out to me (when he was health adviser at NITI Aayog).

23 In practice, the main beneficiaries of these rules appear to be the armies of consultants employed by state governments to prepare the PIPs and by the Central government to review them!

24 This point has been mentioned to me by several senior officials.

25 In 2015, the Centre constituted a committee of chief ministers through NITI Aayog to suggest reforms to CSSs. Consistent with the issues outlined above, this committee recommended significantly reducing the number of CSSs. However, in practice, Central ministries responded by bundling existing schemes under larger umbrella schemes, rather than reducing the number of CSSs. As a result, this promising effort failed to bring about meaningful reforms.

26 See Amarnath and Singh (2019).

27 Note that obtaining comparable numbers for local government spending as a share of total government spending is not easy because different datasets classify local government differently. Thus, the original source for the numbers cited in Ren (2015) is from Shah (2006), which uses numbers from 2003. However, the broad patterns highlighted in Figure 8.2 are likely to still be true,

with India being among the least fiscally decentralized countries in the world.

28 Prepared from data presented in Ren (2015).

29 Prepared from data presented in Kapur (2020).

30 See Guha (2007) for several evocative quotes from multiple sources to this effect.

31 See Zubrzycki (2023) for an illustrative discussion.

32 See Figure 1 in Keay (2000).

33 See Austin (1999).

34 See Khosla (2020) for an expansive discussion of this point.

35 See Guha (2007) for a discussion of Ambedkar's opposition to instituting villages as the basic unit for governance. Based on Constituent Assembly Debates, vol. 7, p. 39.

36 In a recent podcast with Amit Varma, retired IAS officer K.P. Krishnan reinforces this point using the example of land reform, where a key policy goal was to redistribute land from large landlords to landless tillers. Enforcing these laws in practice required a powerful centralized civil service that could implement policies that would be resisted by local elites (see Episode 355 of the *Seen and the Unseen* podcast).

37 The practice, referred to as 'sarpanch patis/putra/pita (husband, son or father)', has been documented by Palanithurai (2002), Mathew (2003) and several researchers. Even Prime Minister Narendra Modi has identified it as a hurdle to women's progress in his remarks on National Panchayati Raj Day 2015: https://www.narendramodi.in/pms-remarks-on-national-panchayati-raj-day-7464, accessed January 2021.

38 Evidence suggests that greater political participation by women does lead to policy choices more attuned to women's needs and concerns (Chattopadhyay and Duflo 2004), broader societal benefits such as better infant mortality rates (Bhalotra and Clots-Figueras 2014) and better education outcomes in urban areas (Clots-Figueras 2012).

39 As with women's reservations, studies have also found that mandated political representation for disadvantaged castes have benefited them. See Pande (2003) for an illustrative study.

40 The debate centres on whether election processes are constitutionally under state control, versus the argument that the 'Equal Protection' Clause of the 14th Amendment to the US Constitution (passed in 1868 to codify abolishing of slavery) allows Federal oversight on state actions that undermine equality. Such disputes are regularly argued before the US Supreme Court including as recently as 2023.

41 These terms were coined by political scientist and federalism scholar William Riker in Riker (1964) and have been widely adopted in political science literature since then.

42 Interestingly, this is partly why the US Constitution is so short (because most powers were with states), whereas the Indian Constitution is one of the world's longest documents.

43 See Asher and Novosad (2015) and Dhillon et al. (2016).

44 See Goyal (2023), who uses data from Telangana to study the long-term effect of bringing government closer to people by dividing blocks into smaller mandals. On a related note, studies have shown that villages that are farther away from administrative headquarters have weaker public good provision across India (Asher et al. 2018).

45 See Narasimhan and Weaver (2022). The study methodology uses the delimitation rules that say that villages with over 1000 people should have their own GP, whereas those below this threshold can be combined with other villages as part of a larger GP. So, the study compares outcomes for villages with just over 1000 people (who get their own GP), versus those with just below 1000 people (who do not, and are instead grouped with other villages in a larger GP).

46 See Mokyr (2016).

47 See Vogel (2011).

48 See Fernandez and Rodrik (1991) for a classic example of how uncertainty on the distribution of the impacts of a reform can create political opposition even to reforms that will benefit a majority. A key insight of their framework is that reforms that may not receive majority support *before* they are implemented can receive support *after* they are implemented, because the

distributional uncertainty is resolved. This insight may apply to many reform ideas in India, which is why doing them at small scale can generate political support after the fact in pilot areas, and thereby make it easier to scale up.

49 For instance, teacher and doctor absence rates (which are a good measure of leakage of public funds) are higher in poorer Indian states and in lower-income countries. See Chaudhury et al. (2006).

50 See Mbiti et al. (2019).

51 See Burnside and Dollar (2000).

52 See Nilakantan (2022) for data on this point.

53 The sectoral condition makes sense since the goal of the CSS is to ensure minimal spending on key development sectors.

54 Note that federal systems like the US, which give primacy to states, require professionals like doctors and lawyers to be licensed in each state that they practice in. In such a case, even an exam like the NExT would be a considered an overreach by the Central (federal) government. However, the Indian Constitution does provide the Centre the authority to set national standards in medical education.

55 See the recent podcast interview by Amit Varma of retired IAS officer K.P. Krishnan, who served as Secretary in the Ministry of Skill Development when the NCVET was created, for further details on this point (see Episode 355 of the *Seen and the Unseen* podcast).

56 The case is *Union of India vs. Rajendra Shah* (decided in 2021). The Court judgment reflected the principles in the text by allowing the components of the central law that affected multistate cooperatives to stand, but disallowing those that would affect cooperatives operating within one state. As noted in the judgment by Justice RF Nariman: 'There can be no doubt that our Constitution has been described as quasi-federal in that, so far as legislative powers are concerned, though there is a tilt in favour of the Centre vis-à-vis the States given the federal supremacy principle outlined hereinabove, yet within their own

sphere, the States have <u>exclusive</u> power to legislate on topics reserved <u>exclusively</u> to them (the underscore is included in the actual judgment).'

57 For instance, such an interpretation should make it easier for states to reform land use and labour laws within the state without waiting for approval from the Centre for doing so.

58 For instance, making welfare benefits like the PDS nationally portable will help both workers and economic growth (see Chapters 15 and 16). This effort is best led by the Centre.

59 This oversight is exercised in two ways. First, the Centre imposes a ceiling on states' debt-to-GDP ratio to keep interest payments under control. Second, Central fiscal transfers to states are made via the RBI, which ensures that creditors are paid first before transferring the remaining funds to states.

60 Alternatively, since future pension liabilities are akin to borrowing today with a commitment to future payment, the Centre could require states to calculate the implicit debt incurred by reverting to the OPS and include this in states' borrowing limits. This issue also affects the Centre, as seen in the acceptance of the 'One Rank, One Pension' demand by the military, which created large future liabilities. However, the Centre, unlike states, is never at risk of default on domestic debt since it can issue new currency (i.e. print money). While this may cause inflation, the debt will be paid back. States do not control currency, and hence do not have this option. This makes central oversight useful to limit state borrowing and thereby reduce risks of bankruptcy or debt traps. Central government debt is scrutinized by bond market analysts, who can lower sovereign credit ratings based on perceived sustainability of borrowing and interest burdens. In principle, state governments could also borrow more and be disciplined by bond markets. But, India has chosen to not allow states this option, to limit the risk of state fiscal crises, bankruptcy, and default.

61 For instance, at an average monthly salary cost of Rs 35,000–Rs 40,000, the salary cost of a two-teacher school would account for 85–95 per cent of the total budget of Rs 10 lakh/year.

62 This structure would also allow salaries to reflect differences in cost of living, especially if local bodies raise funds through property taxes, which will be higher in high cost-of-living areas since these tend to have higher property prices as well. Another option that combines the two approaches in the text could be for the government to directly pay 80 per cent of the government salary to teacher accounts, and transfer the balance to local body accounts for flexible spending including performance-based salary top-ups.

63 The exact nature of decentralization could vary based on the sector, and the balance between the need for qualifications, local accountability, and accountability to higher levels of government.

64 See Beteille and Ramachandran (2016) as well as Sharma and Ramachandran (2009).

65 See Chapters 5 and 11 for details and references.

66 A similar approach has been suggested by senior government officials experienced in service delivery. For instance, Sinha (2013) suggests an approach where communities nominate a set of candidates for teacher positions, followed by final selection by block and district-level officials. This is another way of combining local agency in hiring with administrative safeguards to limit local elite capture.

67 The lack of direct authority on personnel and budgets is partly why MLAs often try to influence postings and transfers. This lets them work with officials who are more likely to respond to them and transfer out those who are not responsive to them.

68 A typical example is the case of urban roads getting dug for laying pipes or cables and remaining unusable for much longer than needed because of poor coordination across the departments responsible for different aspects of the task.

69 See Vaishnav and Hinston (2019) for a detailed analysis of the likely changes in states' relative representation after delimitation.

70 There are already signs of such resistance in statements by leaders from states such as Tamil Nadu and Telangana. For instance, see

the *Deccan Chronicle* story on 25 September 2023 titled 'KTR Warns of Southern Uprising if Delimitation Cuts Lok Sabha seats'.

71 Note however, that the net result of such an arrangement is that smaller states have a disproportionate voice in national policies relative to their population. This is also true in the European Parliament.

72 See Rajagopalan (2023) for additional ideas on how to proceed.

73 In 1950, adult literacy rates were below 20 per cent, and information access was limited. Seventy-five years later, literacy rates are over 75 per cent and access to smartphones and television is widespread. Thus, India has seen a sharp increase in both access to information and people's ability to process it.

74 The ten countries with the highest per capita income in 2019 (measured on a purchasing power parity basis) in descending order were Luxembourg, Singapore, Qatar, Ireland, Switzerland, the UAE, Norway, the US, Brunei and San Marino. All these countries except the US have fewer than 10 million people. Estimates from the World Bank, World Development Indicators. Data accessed: December 2020.

75 The next ten countries in descending order of per capita income are Iceland, Denmark, the Netherlands, Austria, Germany, Sweden, Belgium, Australia, Kuwait and Canada. Of these, only Germany has a population over 50 million and Canada and Australia have populations between 20–50 million.

76 The quote comes from his website: https://www.ashwinmahesh. in/, accessed February 2021. The value of designing governance systems that encourage more decentralized innovations, rather than imposing top-down 'one size fits all' mandates is also underscored by Pritchett (2013) in the context of education systems. Specifically, he coins the terms 'spider' and 'starfish' systems to denote the difference between top-down and decentralized systems and argues that the latter are much better suited to solving problems of governance and service delivery because of the need for contextualized initiatives and solutions.

Chapter 9:   The State and the Market

1   Source: Economic Survey of India (2023), p. 148.

2   See Aiyar (2020), p. 216. In addition to health and education, Aiyar (2020) discusses how citizens are also exiting to private solutions in sectors such as water, electricity, and security.

3   A classic reference of this view is Drèze and Sen (2013). This view is echoed in the writings of senior officials who have worked on public service delivery (see Sinha 2013, Saxena 2019 for examples).

4   See Bhagwati and Panagariya (2012) for a broad articulation of this view and Tooley (2009) for a detailed discussion of these concepts in the context of education.

5   Of course, each of these sectors have unique features. In particular, a key dimension in which sectors vary is the extent of fixed and variable costs. Sectors with high fixed costs have features of a 'natural monopoly' and need to be regulated accordingly.

6   The government school enrolment rate in rural India was around 65 per cent between 2014 to 2018, but increased to 72.9 per cent in 2022, likely reflecting the closing of many private schools during the pandemic, as well as reduced household income due to the pandemic (based on annual ASER reports). See Ernst & Young-FICCI (2014) for statistics on the market share of private schools in India.

7   See Muralidharan and Kremer (2008) and Muralidharan and Sundararaman (2015) for summary statistics on the characteristics of public and private schools and the demographics of those who use them. Kingdon (2020) discusses private school prevalence in urban and rural areas, broken down by state. She also provides private school fee benchmarks to give context regarding who can afford them.

8   Based on data from the 2017–18 National Sample Survey.

9   See Das et al. (2016).

10   See Subramanian (2017) for an excellent in-depth discussion of the role of private water-tanker operators in providing water in Bangalore. Also, see Chapter 1 of Aiyar (2020).

11 Bureau of Police Research and Development (BPRD) (2019).

12 See Muralidharan and Kremer (2008) for all-India data from 2003, Muralidharan and Sundararaman (2015) for data from Andhra Pradesh during 2008–12. Kingdon (2020) presents data on private versus government school teacher salaries from other states and time periods and finds that private school teacher salaries are one-twelfth to one-thirtieth the salaries of government school teachers.

13 A recent study finds that private schools in rural India had much higher management scores on the globally standardized World Management Survey (WMS), compared to government schools. This difference was especially pronounced for personnel management (see Lemos et al. 2023).

14 See Muralidharan and Sundararaman (2015) for detailed data from (unified) Andhra Pradesh and Kremer and Muralidharan (2008) for all-India data.

15 Das et al. 2011.

16 As per the 2017–18 NSS data, 70 per cent of households sought primary care from private health providers. Das et al. (2022) find that around 70 per cent of private health providers are unqualified. Multiplying these figures, around half of the health-seeking interactions of households in India are with unqualified health providers.

17 One legitimate reason for absence could be that doctors were making field visits. In practice, this is unlikely to account for the large absence rates. For instance, Banerjee et al. (2004) use detailed data from Rajasthan and report that only 12 per cent of absent providers who claimed to have been on a site visit, had in fact done so.

18 See (Banerjee et al. 2004) for evidence on the unpredictability of doctor absences.

19 See Das and Hammer (2005), Das et al. (2012), and Das et al. (2016).

20 The study was conducted in partnership with the Azim Premji Foundation and the Government of Andhra Pradesh, and the

findings are reported in Muralidharan and Sundararaman (2015).

21 The finding that private schools do not add significantly more value than government schools is also seen in evidence using non-experimental longitudinal data from Andhra Pradesh (Singh 2015).

22 These larger gains partly reflect the fact that Hindi was not taught in AP government schools.

23 The use of actors as fake patients to measure the quality of healthcare provided (and adherence to care protocols) is common in many medical schools as part of student training and evaluation. The method is known as assessment based on 'standardized patients'.

24 See ASER (2023).

25 Das et al. 2022.

26 See Miranda (2013) for a discussion on the social costs of private school closures due to RTE.

27 In the case of higher education, one striking metric of this shortage of quality options within India is the staggering size of expenditure undertaken by Indian citizens for education overseas. Recent estimates suggest that it is nearly $3 billion per year (Nanda and Mishra 2018).

28 See Das (2015).

29 This partly reflects the prevalence of low-quality training institutes that sell certifications without much actual training (see Chapters 5 and 11).

30 See India Institute (2015), and Ramnani (2017) for examples of school closures, and PTI (2018) for an example of state government-issued notices to show cause (for unrecognized private schools to explain why action should not be pursued against them).

31 Multiple studies in South Asia show that private schools pay higher salaries to more effective teachers, whereas there is no relationship between pay and effectiveness in government

schools (see Bau and Das 2020 and Lemos et al. 2023). Thus, if teacher-training programmes are in fact effective, their graduates would command a pay premium, and such programmes would be more likely to be in demand.

32 See Andrabi et al. (2017) for the Pakistan study, and Afridi et al. (2020) for the Rajasthan study.

33 For instance, a recent study on private schools in Chhattisgarh finds that the fees in private schools that students apply to for RTE lotteries is under Rs 12,000/year (Romero and Singh 2023).

34 The main difference between vouchers and charter schools is that vouchers provide access to typical private schools, which may be aspirational, but whose pedagogy may be optimized for higher SES students and may not be as effective for lower SES students who are first-generation learners (see Bau 2022 for evidence on this point). In contrast, charter schools are often set up explicitly to provide high-quality education to low SES students and include additional instructional and homework support to help them succeed. This may explain why more studies seem to find positive impacts of charter schools on learning outcomes than of vouchers. See Muralidharan (2019c) for a review of the evidence.

35 See Hirschman (1972).

36 See Sanin (2022) for recent evidence on this point from Rwanda and Bhattacharya (2021) for an extensive discussion of this issue in the Indian context.

37 See Kingdon (2020).

38 See Hoxby (2003).

39 See Hart, Shleifer, and Vishny (1997), which examines public versus private provision in the context of prisons. See also procurement norms for PPPs by the World Bank (https://ppp. worldbank.org/public-private-partnership/overview/practical-tools/procurement-bidding) and by Gajendra Haldea for the Planning Commission of India (http://www.gajendrahaldea.in/download/03-B-Model-RFP.pdf).

40 Romero et al. (2020).

41 It also may make sense to pilot PPP approaches in densely-populated urban areas that can sustain both public and private providers.

42 For instance, teacher appointments in government-aided schools in UP were often politically driven, with fake trusts acting as fronts for politicians and politically-connected candidates being given lifetime sinecures as teachers in these schools. This model of corruption worked because once a school was recognized and teacher posts sanctioned and filled, they were guaranteed for life even if students attended other schools. However, it is less likely to work if each student gets a fixed voucher and can only use this in one school (public or private) with the school and student ID known to the government.

43 At present, income taxes are progressive, but less than 10 per cent of Indians pay them. Since indirect taxes are less progressive, and many public benefits do *not* go to the poorest (see Chapters 6 and 15), India's tax and transfer system may be regressive in some parts of the income distribution. Creating a composite indicator of deprivation, and introducing a sliding scale of vouchers for essential services can therefore make the overall tax and transfer system more progressive (also see Chapter 15).

44 For an overview of the research on framing, nudges and simplicity, see World Bank (2015).

45 For examples of court cases involving controversial fine print, see Ayres and Schwartz (2014).

46 Mullainathan and Shafir (2013).

47 See Benartzi and Thaler (2001).

48 Campbell et al. (2014).

49 Sen (1999).

50 See Schilbach (2019) for evidence in the context of studying self-control problems for alcohol use.

51 See, for example, Bhagwati and Panagariya (2012), and Swarup (2019).

Chapter 10: Shifting the Preston Curve for Development

1   Data source: World Bank.
2   The graphs in the text show health outcomes. Similar patterns hold for other development outcomes.
3   See Schoellman (2012) for instance. PISA is the 'Program for International Student Assessment'.
4   This is why countries like Finland and Singapore are less relevant as role models for Indian education (despite their strong performance) than countries like Vietnam. The per capita income of Vietnam is similar to that of India, whereas those of Finland and Singapore are over *twenty times higher*. Further, their populations are under 6 million compared to nearly 100 million for Vietnam. Thus, the Finnish and Singaporean education systems can implement ideas that are unlikely to be practical at scale in India, whereas there are likely to be many more practical ideas for us to learn from Vietnam.
5   Sen (1999).
6   It also reflects the facts that GDP and HDI are mechanically correlated since GDP has a one-third weight in the HDI.
7   See Bhagwati and Panagariya (2014).
8   Consistent with this view, economists Mark Rosenzweig and Andrew Foster have shown in a set of influential papers that education attainment in the 1960s and 1970s went up more in areas that had early exposure to the Green Revolution. They argue that this was because the returns (and hence value) of education increased in the context of needing better education to reap the benefits of more advanced agricultural technologies. See Foster and Rosenzweig (1995) and (1996). More recently Oster and Steinberg (2013) show that the introduction of IT-enabled service centres in India led to a significant increase in demand for English-medium schools in nearby areas, which is also consistent with increased demand being a key factor in increasing education levels.

9   See Drèze and Sen (2013). In general, a policy focus on equity
    is key for improving average outcomes because averages are
    brought down substantially by large numbers of people in the
    'left tail' of outcomes.

10 In 2021, US GDP per capita was over US$70,000, which is over
    fifteen times higher than that of Sri Lanka (around US$ 4000)
    and Kerala (under US$ 4000) that year. However, Sri Lanka's life
    expectancy in 2021 was 77.2 and Kerala's was 77.0, which are slightly
    higher than the US life expectancy of 76.4. Consistent with the point
    above, this striking result likely reflects the much higher inequality
    in the US health system compared to those of Sri Lanka and Kerala.

11 See Banerjee, Niehaus, and Suri (2019) for a review.

12 Examples include Chetty et al. (2011) and Hoddinott et al.
    (2013).

13 In 1924, exactly a hundred years ago, the son of US President
    Calvin Coolidge (Calvin Jr) died from getting a blister on his
    foot while playing tennis that developed into a bacterial blood
    infection. Historical accounts note that 'there was little that
    the Coolidges could have done to save Calvin Jr', though his
    condition would have been easily cured with antibiotics available
    a few decades later (see Rhoads 2014). I thank Lant Pritchett for
    bringing this incident to my attention.

14 See Preston (1975).

15 The estimates are quite similar, indicating that higher incomes
    are correlated with better development outcomes both across
    states at any given time (cross-section estimate), and for
    population-weighted averages across states over time (time-
    series estimate). However, they are different because cross-
    sectional elasticities also reflect differences in governance quality
    and spending priorities across states, while time-series estimates
    include technological improvements over time that can boost the
    translation of income into outcomes. These confounding factors
    are also why these income elasticities are *not* the *causal* effect of
    income on development. They are correlations, which show the
    average rate at which income gains have yielded development

gains across states and over time. Interestingly, the cross-state income elasticities in Table 10.1 are very similar to the cross-country estimates for comparable outcomes.

16 Note that the time-series income elasticity of mathematics learning outcomes is slightly negative, suggesting that these have deteriorated over time. So, the projections for mathematics learning use the more optimistic cross-sectional elasticity estimates, which are positive.

17 Prior to 2020, India's population grew at roughly 1 per cent per annum. So, a GDP per capita growth rate of 6 per cent would require a GDP growth rate of 7 per cent.

18 This multiplier can be calculated for each outcome by considering the improvement between 2047 and the starting point in Figure 10.5 as the 'base case', and then taking the improvement under each of the more optimistic cases and dividing it by the 'base case' to calculate an improvement multiplier.

19 A concrete example of a policy that can contribute to such a doubling of income elasticity would be to limit the use of funds for unconditional pay increases of anganwadi workers, and instead use these funds to hire a million additional anganwadi workers to add an extra worker to every anganwadi centre in India. Such an investment would improve student learning, reduce stunting, mainly benefit the poor, and have an estimated RoI of 1200 to 2000 per cent (twelve to twenty times the cost). The benefits could be higher if the extra workers are also used for home visitations to train mothers on evidence-based home techniques to improve early-childhood development (see Chapter 12).

20 Each year's cohort size is estimated using demographic projections, and the fraction of children who cannot read in each year from 2022–47 are taken from the data used to create Figure 10.5. These are multiplied to calculate how many children will complete primary school without being able to read for each year from 2022 to 2047. The figure of 200 million adds these annual numbers for twenty-five years.

21 Hsieh and Klenow (2010).

22 To be more precise, the growth accounting literature examines the output of the entire economy, whereas I am referring to the output of public spending. So, the argument in the text requires the assumption that the relative importance of TFP in the output from public spending is the same as in the production of output more generally. In practice, the returns to improving TFP of public spending may be even higher because management quality in the public sector has been found to be significantly lower than in the private sector, and the variation of management quality has been found to be higher within the public sector (see Lemos, Muralidharan, and Scur 2023).

23 See Sen (1999) for an illustrative synthesis of this view, Deaton (2015), and Banerjee and Duflo (2011) for more on these contributions.

24 See Deaton (2015). Notable advances in medical knowledge he highlights include the germ theory of disease, and the discovery of oral rehydration therapy for diarrhoea. The main government action he credits for shifting of the Preston curve is investments in better public health and sanitation. He also notes that the main source of variation across countries in health outcomes is not medical knowledge or even cost, but the extent to which governments choose to act on available knowledge.

25 See Banerjee and Duflo (2011) for an illustrative synthesis of this work. Also see Muralidharan (2019a).

26 See Pritchett (2009) and Muralidharan and Singh (2023) for illustrative examples.

27 For instance, many external donor-driven development projects in LMICs create their own Project Management Unit (PMU) with dedicated staff or consultants to ensure that *their* programme is implemented better than what their government counterparts would otherwise be able to do. However, while this approach may improve implementation of those projects, it is unlikely to deliver national 'development' because external loans and grants are typically only a small fraction of national budgets. This challenge is consistent with the findings of Vivalt (2020), who reviews several impact evaluations in development economics

and shows that government-implemented programmes have a smaller effect than those implemented by academic researchers or non-government organizations.

28 The first approach is typified by the debate between Bhagwati and Sen on *what* the state should focus on, and the second by Banerjee, Duflo, and Kremer who have argued that research (ideally based on RCTs), should be used to identify effective interventions that states should scale up. Deaton does highlight the importance of state capacity for actions such as investing in better measurement systems and public health systems. However, none of them deeply examine the question of *how* the state itself should be made more effective or the practical challenges of doing so.

29 Epistemically, analysing a complex topic like state capacity requires a broad approach to synthesizing research and evidence that spans methods and disciplines. Overall, my arguments in this book aim to build on a body of credible causal studies of impact, often but not always using RCTs, and to connect the *principles* from this body of micro evidence to macro questions of how we can understand and improve state functioning. While my broader claims are necessarily more subjective, they are not only informed by quantitative empirical evidence and my own field research, but also by engaging with research in other disciplines, and years of interactions with practitioners in and outside the government.

30 This message is relevant for any government, even beyond India. It is also consistent with the results reported in Pritchett (2022).

31 Joseph (2023) estimates that remittances account for 15 per cent of Kerala's GDP, compared to an all-India average of 3 per cent, and discusses the high dependence of Kerala's economy on remittances.

32 While recipients of remittances benefit directly, the overall economy benefits from the demand created by remittances, and the government benefits from higher GST revenue from taxing this consumption.

33 Khandelwal (2023) shows that Vietnam has been one of the
    main beneficiaries of companies choosing to diversify their
    production locations by moving out of China.
34 Friedman (2005).
35 In this sense, my approach reflects the 'hard heads, soft hearts'
    terminology coined by Princeton economist Alan Blinder in his
    book with the same title (Blinder 1998).

Chapter 11: Education and Skills

1   These include being able to make better health decisions, manage
    personal finances, provide home inputs into the education of
    their children, and being more informed citizens. This is why
    education is a key component of the 'capabilities' framework
    developed by Amartya Sen (as discussed in Chapter 10).
2   Of course, India's lack of competitiveness in low-skilled labour-
    intensive manufacturing has also been driven by many other
    factors such as regulatory barriers to scale, underinvestment in
    logistics, and high cost of credit (as discussed in Chapter 16).
    However, the pattern of education investments have also played
    a role in shaping India's relative areas of comparative advantage
    and disadvantage.
3   Notable schemes include Operation Blackboard in 1987, District
    Primary Education Programme (DPEP) in 1994, and Sarva
    Shikhsa Abhiyan (SSA) in 2000.
4   See ASER (2023).
5   See ASER (2023). These figures include private schools. Learning
    levels in government schools are even lower, with only 44.2 per
    cent of Class 5 students being able to read at a Class 2 level in
    2018, and only 38.5 per cent in 2022.
6   Source: Economic Survey of India 2022–23, p. 148.
7   See the UN (2019). This figure is likely to underestimate average
    years of schooling in younger cohorts who would have benefited
    from the expansion of schooling access in the 1991–2018 period.
8   See Hnatkovska, Hou, and Lahiri (2021) for evidence of such
    convergence across castes.

9 Based on Pratham's ASER reports, that have been produced nearly every year from 2005 to 2023.

10 For cross-country evidence on the importance of the quality of education, see Hanushek and Woessmann (2008). For micro evidence on the impact of the quality of schooling on labour market outcomes, see Schoellman (2012).

11 There are very few randomized evaluations on school infrastructure, but high-quality longitudinal studies find very little correlation between improving infrastructure and better student learning. For instance, see Table 6 (column 3) of Muralidharan and Sundararaman (2011a).

12 See Waldinger (2016).

13 Using matched data between households and schools in Andhra Pradesh, collected in 2006–10, we found that over 70 per cent of primary school children reported relieving themselves in the open even when their school had a toilet. This specific finding has not been reported in any of my prior published work and is based on a simple cross-tabulation of the data we collected as part of this project.

14 See Rivkin, Hanushek, and Kain (2005) for US evidence, and Bau and Das (2020) for South Asia.

15 See Muralidharan and Sundararaman (2011a), Muralidharan (2012), and Azam and Kingdon (2015) for evidence from India, and Glewwe and Muralidharan (2016) for a broader review of the evidence.

16 Banerjee et al. (2007), Muralidharan and Sundararaman (2013), and Ganimian, Muralidharan, and Walters (2023), and Singh, Romero, and Muralidharan (2022).

17 See Ramachandran et al. (2017).

18 We see evidence of the last point in multiple studies where trained teachers are no more effective than untrained teachers under typical conditions, but are more effective when there are performance-based bonuses. Further, high-quality training materials that were valued by private schools (as seen by their willingness to pay for them) had no impact in government schools.

See Muralidharan and Sundararaman (2010), Muralidharan and Sundararaman (2011a and 2011b), and Muralidharan (2012).

19 See Banerjee et al. (2007).

20 See Kaushik and Muralidharan (2022).

21 See Lazear (2001).

22 See Muralidharan and Sundararaman (2013), Duflo et al. (2015), and Muralidharan et al. (2017).

23 See Kingdon (2020).

24 See Malamud and Pop-Eleches (2011).

25 See Das et al. (2013). Of course, publicly provided inputs can make households better off because they have to spend less, but a reduction in household spending on items provided by the government is an important channel by which school inputs may not translate into improved student outcomes.

26 For instance, a well-known study by Nobel Prize-winner Michael Kremer and co-authors showed that the provision of free textbooks to middle-school students in Kenya improved learning outcomes for students who were high-performing to begin with, but had no effect on average learning outcomes because the average student was not able to read the English-language textbook (Kremer et al. 2009).

27 See Beuermann et al. (2015) and Cristia et al. (2017).

28 Girls' age-appropriate secondary school enrolment increased by 5.2 percentage points on a base rate of 16.3 per cent (an increase of 32 per cent), and gender gaps fell by 5.2 percentage points on a base gap of 13 per cent (a reduction of 40 per cent). See Muralidharan and Prakash (2017).

29 See Muralidharan et al. (2017). These averages mask enormous variation across states. Teacher absence rates in the 2010 measurement round were below 16 per cent in better-governed states such as Tamil Nadu, Kerala, and Maharashtra, but exceeded 30 per cent in states like UP and Jharkhand. While the two rounds of all-India teacher absence data are from 2003 and 2010, more recent data from Madhya Pradesh reveal teacher absence rates of over 30 per cent even in 2017 (Muralidharan and Singh 2023).

30 See Muralidharan et al. (2017). Also, see Duflo et al. (2012) for related evidence.

31 See Muralidharan and Sundararaman (2013), and Muralidharan (2013) for a review of other studies.

32 For evidence from India on the positive effects on performance pay for teachers, see Duflo, Hanna, and Ryan (2012), Muralidharan and Sundararaman (2011a), and Muralidharan (2012). Muralidharan and Sundararaman (2011a) also find no correlation between the level of teacher pay and their effectiveness.

33 See de Ree et al. (2018).

34 See Giridhar (2022) for a collection of vignettes of extraordinary government schoolteachers in India.

35 This figure is reproduced from Muralidharan (2019b).

36 See Muralidharan, Singh, and Ganimian (2019). This finding is consistent with students being so far behind curricular standards that textbook-based classroom instruction is essentially useless.

37 See Paglayan (2022) for evidence on the role of education as 'indoctrination' in explaining why *non-democratic* governments often expanded mass education.

38 The specific CEOs are Satya Nadella, Sundar Pichai, Arvind Krishna, Indra Nooyi, Ajay Banga, Rajesh Subramaniam, and Lakshman Narasimhan.

39 Aiyar (2020), p. 101.

40 Even as per egalitarian liberal philosophers like John Rawls, inequality is justified if it helps improve outcomes for the most disadvantaged—as noted by the 'difference principle' in Rawls (1971). Thus, an element of sorting to identify the most talented citizens for positions of leadership and innovation can be justified even on egalitarian ethical grounds because these positions affect the welfare of others.

41 This is why well-intentioned ideas, such as scrapping the Class 10 board exam, are counterproductive in practice. Scrapping the signal does not remove the need for one, and ends up disproportionately hurting disadvantaged students who do not have other options for signalling their talent.

42 Competence refers to the ability to do a task. Fluency is measured by speed, such as words read or problems solved in a given time.

43 In other words, the mission has focused on the substance of FLN, but not enough on the governance improvements needed to deliver it.

44 Muralidharan and Singh (2023). The paper also provides an extended discussion on the points in the next two paragraphs.

45 The only 'losers' under this proposal may be the owners of low-quality teacher training institutes, but their numbers should be small enough to be countered by a combination of political and public support for a proposal that will generate widespread visible benefits,

46 See Kingdon (2020).

47 See Kochar (2008).

48 Based on calculations in Kingdon (2020) and ongoing work in several states.

49 School integration across communities is seen as important for social progress globally as seen in the demands for school integration by the US civil rights movement. In the Indian context, Rao (2019) shows that increasing exposure to socioeconomically disadvantaged students in elite private schools in Delhi led to greater intergroup empathy and willingness to socially engage across SES divides.

50 See Bordoloi and Shukla (2019).

51 She is also responsible for a large amount of administrative work and is only supported by a helper for cooking and cleaning.

52 In our field studies, 20–25 per cent of AWW time is spent on paperwork. See Ganimian et al. (2023). The results discussed in the section are mainly based on this multi-year study.

53 The facilitators worked half time and were paid a stipend of Rs 4000 per month. Thus, adding an extra worker would make sense even at the full salary of an anganwadi worker of Rs 8000. However, hiring an extra staff member may not be very cost-effective at the salary of a regular government teacher, which ranges from Rs 30,000 to Rs 50,0000 a month.

54 While the stipend was modest, it was Rs 1000 for around thirty
    hours of work (ninety minutes a day for twenty days per month)
    or a daily wage of over Rs 250, which is comparable to the NREGS
    daily wage.

55 See Singh, Romero, and Muralidharan (2022) for details on the
    evaluation. See Agrawal (2022) for a detailed description of the
    programme based on field experiences.

56 See Ho, Jalota, and Karandikar (2023) for evidence on the
    importance of flexible work arrangements for raising female
    labour force participation.

57 These positive findings were confirmed in a study conducted by
    the Tamil Nadu State Planning Commission (see Kandavel 2023).

58 See Beuermann et al. (2015) and Cristia et al. (2017).

59 See Malamud and Pop-Eleches (2011).

60 See Banerjee et al. (2007), and Muralidharan et al. (2019) for
    examples from India, and Escueta et al. (2020) for a synthesis of
    global evidence on technology in education.

61 Singh (2020).

62 Note that exam marks are only one component of doctor
    effectiveness. Studies show that traits such as demographic
    similarity with patients also matter because of enhanced patient
    trust in doctors who share common traits with them (see Alsan
    et al. 2019). So, reservations in medical education not only help
    candidates from underrepresented groups, but can also improve
    healthcare at the population level by increasing the number of
    doctors who share traits with their patients. This is especially
    important in settings like India, where underprivileged groups
    comprise a large fraction of the population.

63 See Alon (2019).

64 See Swarup (2019).

65 While ASER reports have mainly focused on measuring basic
    literacy and numeracy skills, ASER (2018) also examines student
    performance on very simply 'beyond basic' skills and finds that
    over 50 per cent of Class 8 students are not able to answer these
    questions.

66 Many of the ideas in this chapter are also presented in Muralidharan (2019b), which in turn is based on my written inputs to the committee that drafted the NEP.

67 This estimate is based on the same methods used for the projections in Chapter 10, but is calculated for the cohorts who would have completed primary school between 2013 and 2022.

Chapter 12: Health and Nutrition

1 The idea of a nutrition-based poverty trap is one of the oldest analytic models of a poverty trap in development economics. See Leibenstein (1957), and Dasgupta and Ray (1986).

2 Arrow (1963).

3 Consider a scenario with average life expectancy of seventy years. Then for every child who dies under age one, we need seventy people to live one year longer to maintain the same average. So, improving outcomes in the 'left tail' of the distribution (reducing infant mortality) can significantly boost life expectancy.

4 See Almond and Currie (2011), and Currie and Vogl (2013).

5 Source: World Bank indicators (to enable comparison across regions). India's National Health Accounts report current health expenditure as a percentage of GDP as 3.8 per cent and government health expenditure as 1.2 per cent of GDP for the year 2016–17. The World Bank reports these as 3.53 per cent and 0.96 per cent respectively for 2017.

6 Private out-of-pocket spending made up 58.7 per cent, private health insurance expenditure another 4.7 per cent, and the remaining 4.6 per cent came from domestic and international donors. The figures for government spending are from India's National Health Accounts. As per World Bank figures, India's public health expenditure is 27 per cent of total spending (as opposed to 32 per cent). 2017 figures are presented since that is when the comparative World Bank figures are from.

7 It is also not easy to compare this figure over time, because the government started including spending on nutrition and sanitation as health spending in 2021 (see Bhatia and Singh 2021).

While this is conceptually reasonable, it makes comparisons over time and across countries more difficult.

8 Mohanty and Behera (2020) look at correlations between government health expenditure and health outcomes across states in India. Farahani, Subramanian, and Canning (2009) do the same across ninety-nine countries and over a forty-year period. Both studies find these to be positively correlated.

9 The breakdown of the 85.8 per cent spending on curative care was: outpatient care (17.1 per cent), inpatient care (35.3 per cent), pharmaceuticals (29 per cent), and labs and imaging (4.4 per cent). The 6.8 per cent spent on preventive care was allocated to: information, education and counselling (IEC) (0.7 per cent); immunization (1.25 per cent); early disease detection (0.12 per cent); healthy condition monitoring (2.4 per cent); epidemiological surveillance; risk and disease control (2.3 per cent); and preparing for disaster and emergency response (0.02 per cent). The remaining categories include transport (4.3 per cent), administration (3.4 per cent), and other functions (1.5 per cent).

10 Rajasthan data collected in 2002–03, see Banerjee, Deaton and Duflo (2004); Madhya Pradesh data collected in 2010–11, see Das et al. (2016); Delhi data collected in 2001–02, see Das et al. (2012).

11 Krishna (2013) provides an excellent discussion of how health shocks are a key reason for people descending into and getting stuck in poverty, in his aptly title book *One Illness Away*.

12 Staffing norms reported here are based on the Indian Public Health Standards (IPHS) 2012 published by the Union Ministry of Health and Family Welfare.

13 See Rao, Shahrawat, and Bhatnagar (2016).

14 Rural Health Statistics 2018–19.

15 Muralidharan et al. (2011).

16 Banerjee, Deaton, and Duflo (2004).

17 These absences were not explained by nurses doing field visits. The study tracked all villages served by the sub-centre, and only found the nurse in one of these villages only 12 per cent of the time.

18 Dhaliwal and Hanna (2017).
19 See Das et al. (2022). The study covered nineteen states at the time of the fieldwork (2010), but included representative samples across socio-economic regions of undivided Andhra Pradesh, and therefore provides representative estimates across the current states of Telangana and Andhra Pradesh.
20 Das and Hammer (2007).
21 Das and Mohpal (2016).
22 See Das and Hammer (2005), Das, Hammer, and Leonard (2008), and Das and Hammer (2014) for further details on the methodology of fieldwork and measurement.
23 See Das et al. (2022).
24 These figures are based on the Appendix to Das et al. (2022), available online.
25 Mohanan et al. (2016). This paper uses the method of standardized patients (SPs) discussed below. Note that of the 72.4 percent who said they would offer ORS, over 90 per cent of them also said they would offer other unnecessary drugs.
26 The SP method combines the strengths of vignettes and participant observations, where researchers or enumerators sit in a clinic and observe the doctor. Unlike a participant observation, the SP allows researchers to code the quality of the diagnostic effort as well as treatment quality (because the underlying ailment is *known*). It also controls the case mix by presenting the *same* case across providers. However, unlike a vignette that only measures provider knowledge, the SP method allows us to also measure provider effort. The main limitation of the SP method is the greater cost and effort of implementation, which yields a smaller sample size for a given research budget.
27 See Das et al. (2012) for additional details on how the SP method was contextualized for this setting.
28 SPs were coached to accurately and consistently present one of three cases: unstable angina in a forty-five-year-old male, asthma in a twenty-five-year-old female or male, and dysentery in a child who was at home presented by the father of the child.

29 The same case was presented by different SPs with a reasonable time lag to avoid detection.

30 See Mahal and Mohanan (2006).

31 Women's empowerment in the household influences several determinants of child health and nutrition, including age of marriage and fertility, birth spacing, intra-household food allocation, and even the ability to leave the home to seek care for unwell and malnourished children. See Alexander (2023) for an example of vivid field-level descriptions of these issues.

32 For instance, see Hoddinot et al. (2013). Reducing child stunting and malnutrition is also likely to have inter-generational benefits, since poorly nourished women are more likely to have low birth weight children, who are then more likely to be stunted.

33 See IQAir World Air Quality Report (2020).

34 See Greenstone et al, (2015).

35 For instance, see Adhvaryu et al. (2022) for a firm-level study in India showing links between pollution and reduced productivity, and Pandey et al. (2021) for an estimate of the total economic burden of pollution across Indian states.

36 See Dupas (2011), and Dupas and Miguel (2017) for illustrative summaries.

37 Weaver, Sukhtankar, Niehaus, and Muralidharan (2023).

38 Effectively improving environmental quality requires attention to several practical details. These include (a) choice of policy instruments such as taxes and subsidies, quantity restrictions on emissions, creating an emissions trading system, setting emission standards for highly polluting sectors such as power plants and cars, charging levies on pollution, and several other options, (b) choice of enforcement mechanisms such as fines, bans, blacklisting, etc., and (c) state capacity for effective enforcement including staff, budgets, technical support, and well-defined legal authority. This is a specialized area of academic and policy research, and covering these details is beyond the scope of this book.

39 See Aggarwal (2018). To isolate the effect of PMGSY, the study compared health outcomes in villages with populations just

above and below 500, which was the population threshold for PMGSY eligibility.

40 For instance, Kelkar and Shah (2019) make the same point and expand on the example of road safety.

41 The programme roll-out can be staggered to admit a new cohort every three to four months to optimize capacity utilization in the training institutes, and provide the first module of theory before a round of practicum. It may also make sense for the initial theoretical modules to last longer (say six months) to provide a minimum level of knowledge before embarking on practical work.

42 The same approach is used in medical training, which involves a considerable practical component.

43 The minimum qualification for an ASHA worker is Class Seven, and many have also passed Class 10. So, the government could encourage ASHA workers to take the Class 12 exam through an open-school system as private candidates, and give them priority for admission into the nurse training programme.

44 See Banerjee (2019).

45 See Sundararaman and Parmar (2019) for more details on the limitations of medical doctors as public health providers.

46 See the report on 'Assessment of State Public Health Cadre' by the Thakur Family Foundation, with an excellent collection of individual studies on different matters related to public health in India.

47 See Balabanova et al. (2013).

48 See Institute of Medicine (2012), Johnson and Rehavi (2016), and Allen (2018) for studies that show evidence of unnecessary tests, treatments, and procedures.

49 One way of inferring that over-prescription by informal providers in rural India is not driven only by misaligned provider incentives is that our work in MP finds that such over-prescription is common in public clinics as well, where there is no financial incentive to do so. Our field interviews suggest that patient demand for symptomatic relief is a key consideration in public clinics as well. See Lopez, Sautmann, and Schaner (2022) for experimental evidence on patient-induced demand for unnecessary medication.

50 Das et al. (2016).

51 The ABHA number is the Ayushman Bharat Health Account number.

52 This may reflect the political reality that citizens may care about government support when they have serious illnesses and large associated expenses than when they need to take preventive actions.

53 See Ganimian, Muralidharan, and Walters (2023).

54 Rao (2014) compares high-focus states that hired ASHA workers a few years before with low-focus states, and finds a significant increase in vaccination rates in the high-focus states.

55 See Mbiti et al. (2019).

56 See Alexander (2023) for an insightful description of the importance of field-level coordination across what the 3 As— ANM, ASHA worker, and anganwadi worker; and of ensuring that supply side initiatives by the government are complemented with community engagement to better understand and alleviate the binding constraint to action for *each* vulnerable household.

57 Based on my work in several states, state and national nutrition missions often create parallel programme implementation and reporting structures. This is inefficient and even counterproductive (see the example of data systems in Chapter 8). Similarly, there is still too much siloing of initiatives across concerned departments without effective convergence on the ground. These are both areas where there is considerable scope for improvement.

58 The 150 million figure is calculated using projections in Chapter 10 under Scenario 1 (the base case).

59 Such an integrated strategy helped Peru, a middle-income country with 35 million people, to reduce stunting from 28 to 13 percent between 2005 and 2016, as detailed in a World Bank Report by Marini, Rokx, and Gallagher (2017). Of course, as with any composite intervention, it is difficult for researchers to pinpoint the specific component that drove impacts. But this intervention was consistent with a core principle highlighted in several chapters of this book, which is the importance of

combining resources with incentives to use them better. In
particular, it combined resources to communities and parents
(see Chapter 4 of the report), *and* elements of performance-
based financing (see Chapter 5 of the report).

Chapter 13: Police and Public Safety

1   FICCI and BDO India LLP 2019 Study on the Private Security
     Industry in India discusses the emergence of this new industry
     from the perspective of employment generation and the
     increasing demand for security services. The growth in demand
     for private security could also reflect growing economic
     inequality that increases the demand for 'guard labour' (as
     documented by Jayadev and Bowles 2006).
2   For instance, see Wilkinson (2004) and (2005) for an extended
     discussion. One way of seeing this is that even though states
     like UP and Bihar have lower state capacity on most measures
     than states like Gujarat and Maharashtra, there was much less
     communal rioting in UP and Bihar under the chief ministerships
     of Mulayam Singh Yadav and Lalu Prasad Yadav because
     minimizing communal violence was a top political priority and
     the police were directed to ensure this.
3   See Ahuja and Kapur (2023), Chapter 1.
4   However, they note that most of these investments have come
     from the Central government through a sharp expansion in
     various Central Armed Police Forces (CAPF) and not from state
     governments. The essay by Shakti Sinha in the same volume
     argues that this was less because of over-reach from the Central
     government and more a case of 'filling the void' left by state
     governments (Sinha 2023).
5   The crime index is defined as the rate of reported crime per
     1,00,000 population. This metric could suffer from under-
     reporting, which is likely worse in poorer countries, which
     would make the slope even steeper.

6   This is a problem that all societies struggle with, including the US as seen in the summer of 2020 with the large-scale 'Black Lives Matter' protests against the widely documented problem of excessive use of force by police—especially against racial minorities.

7   NHRC case statistics can be found on their website at https:// nhrc.nic.in/complaints/human-right-case-statistics.

8   See Human Rights Watch (2020), Joseph (2021), and Bhadra (2023) for several examples of human rights violations conducted by India's *de facto* security state.

9   The official term for an 'encounter' killing is 'officer-involved fatalities', which is a euphemism for extra-judicial executions of suspected criminals by the police to avoid the costs, uncertainties, and delays associated with formal trials. Officers known to be 'encounter specialists' are often viewed favourably by the public and have also been favourably portrayed in movies like *Ab Tak Chhappan*. Movies with memorable scenes of police brutality include *Ardh Satya*, and *Gangaajal*. Recent TV serials depicting police violence include *Sacred Games*, *Paatal Lok*, *Jai Bhim*, and even an episode of *Made in Heaven* (which is not even a show about police per se).

10 Most recently, this point is made by several authors across multiple chapters of Ahuja and Kapur (2023) including Vakil (2023), Bhonsle (2023), and Sinha (2023).

11 As quoted by Prakash Singh on *Satyamev Jayate* (Season 2, Episode 2 on Indian Police). Prakash Singh was the former director general of police (DGP) of India's largest state (Uttar Pradesh), and was also the director general of India's Border Security Force (with over 2,50,000 personnel), and has been a staunch advocate for police reforms in India. Also see his recent book *The Struggle for Police Reforms in India* (Singh 2022) for more details of the history of the Indian police and its functioning.

12 See Rakshit (1999) for further details.

13 As quoted on the TV show *Satyamev Jayate*.

14 The report is from the Bureau of Police Research and Development (BPRD). See BPRD (2019).

15 See BPRD (2020) for data on sanctioned posts and vacancies. The armed reserve battalions are primarily deployed to maintain law and order in parts of the country facing challenges such as internal insurgency or Naxal violence. This does not include Central paramilitary forces such as the CRPF, CISF, etc.

16 See BPRD (2020).

17 I am not aware of formal analysis to document the extent of spatial skew in police staffing. However, it is commonly acknowledged that higher-quality security is provided to areas with more affluent residents.

18 3.39 police personnel per VIP relative to 195 police personnel per 1,00,000 ordinary citizens translates to a ratio of 1738.

19 Source for training budget is the India Justice Report, 2020. Since over 90 per cent of the police budget is spent on salaries, there are very limited funds left for equipment or training. This is true at both the national level (Joy 2015), and the state level (Sane and Sinha 2017; the *New Indian Express* 2021).

20 See Faleiro (2021) for a vivid description of the poor conditions of post-mortem analysis even in a high-profile case that received media attention.

21 As observed by S.R. Darapuri, retired inspector general of police, on *Satyamev Jayate*.

22 See Page 207 of Status of Policing in India Report, 2018 by Common Cause and CSDS. This fact is also commonly spoofed in Indian movies, where the police usually reach the crime scene only after the hero has defeated the villain(s) personally.

23 There are 10,021 rural police stations (as per BPRD 2019), 6,49,481 revenue villages and 2,38,054 gram panchayats (as per Census 2011). This implies around sixty-five villages and twenty-five panchayats per station.

24 Colloquially, this is referred to as 'kissing up' and 'kicking down' or 'lick up' and 'kick down'.

25 See Jauregui (2013), who in turn quotes from Viswanathan and Sethi (1998).
26 The FIR reporting rates for theft ranged from 5.9 to 8.4 per cent across the 4 cities (Duranti et al. 2017).
27 Bhattacharya and Kundu (2018).
28 As per the 2019 NCRB report, there were 49,66,118 total FIR registrations compared to 1,96,52,660 complaints, which is around a 25 per cent conversion rate.
29 See Lokniti and CSDS (2018).
30 Indiaspend, 7 March 2017.
31 See Saxena (2019).
32 The work of Arvind Verma is especially insightful on this point since he is a former IPS officer (Bihar cadre) who served in the IPS for seventeen years, then resigned from the IPS to pursue an academic research career, and is now a professor of criminology. An illustrative article on the organizational culture of corruption in the Indian police is Verma (1999).
33 *Satyamev Jayate*, Season 2, Episode 2.
34 Notable commissions and committees include: (a) National Police Commission (1978–82), (b) the Padmanabhaiah Committee on Police Reforms (2000), and (c) the Malimath Committee on reforming the criminal justice system (2002–03). The key points from each of them are documented at http://dfs.nic.in/pdfs/PoliceReforms(E)181013.pdf.
35 The Ribeiro Committee was set up by the Supreme Court in 1998 to assess the implementation of police reforms proposed by prior committees. In its verdict in *Prakash Singh v Union of India*, the Supreme Court directed state governments to report on the implementation of the Padmanabhaiah Committee recommendations and the Model Police Act, 2006, resulting from the Malimath Committee. Yet, progress on implementing the recommendations and submitting related reports remains incomplete.
36 See Borker (2021).
37 See Holmstrom and Milgrom (1991).

38 These could include tasks such as driving, delivering challans, and filling out routine paperwork. In some cases, the younger trainees may be more technology savvy and may be better positioned to digitize records and help with data entry.

39 Brooks (2008) examines Business Improvement Districts (BID), a collective institution established by neighbourhood property owners in Los Angeles to provide for local public goods to reduce crime and vandalism. She finds that BIDs are strongly associated with a 6–10 per cent decline in crime. These institutes turned out to be highly cost-effective with $21,000 expenditure on averting crime compared to $57,000 in social cost of crime. In a recent multisite RCT across low-income countries, Blair et al. (2021) find that community policing did not have any positive impact on reducing crime or improving citizens' perception of safety. However, these programmes did not augment overall policing capacity, which may have been a key constraint to the effectiveness of the approach. In contrast, the proposal above would add considerable capacity to the police system by using the candidates of practicum-based training programmes to perform the community policing tasks.

40 Sukhtankar, Kruks-Wisner, and Mangla (2022).

41 See Aiyar (2020). He also notes that another private company, Tops Securities, had over 1,40,000 employees in 2019.

42 The stipend was Rs 7500/month, which was considerably lower than the salary of a regular constable (which was around Rs 25,000–Rs 30,000/month at the entry level at that time).

43 There are also some parallels with the military's Agniveer scheme, including a four-year tour of duty with regularization of the top 25 per cent of cadets. However, I think that the proposed approach works better for civilian policing, and for non-combat military roles for the reasons explained in the notes to Chapter 5.

44 The scale of these weaknesses is so large that a book on the Indian police by a former IPS officer was titled *The Crumbling Edifice* (Kapur 2003). Also, see Verma (2005) for another account of the Indian police by a former IPS officer.

Chapter 14: Courts and Justice

1   The total number of pending cases is over 50 million. However, that figure includes cases that have just been filed, which is not a fair indicator of delay. Focusing attention on cases pending for over a year is a more relevant metric for assessing judicial efficiency.

2   Data accessed from https://njdg.ecourts.gov.in on 26 April 2022.

3   Data accessed from https://njdg.ecourts.gov.in on 26 April 2022. At High Courts, this distribution is flipped, with civil cases and appeals forming over 70 per cent of the trials.

4   See Narasappa and Vidhyasagar (2016).

5   Data accessed from https://njdg.ecourts.gov.in on 1 March 2021. NJDG and Daksh.

6   See Narasappa and Vidyasagar (2016), State of the Indian Judiciary.

7   Data from Ash et al. 2021, accessed via Dev Data Lab Judicial Data Portal.

8   India number accessed from Bloomberg Quint news report from 6 February 2019. Judge population ratio for the UK and the US from DNA India report from 22 December 2018.

9   Supreme Court of India, 2023 (https://main.sci.gov.in/pdf/Collegium/31012023_131717.pdf) for Supreme Court data; India Justice Report, 2022 (for district and high courts).

10 Daksh India (2016), 'Time-and-Motion-Study of Four District and Sessions Courts in Karnataka'.

11 Vidhi Centre for Legal Policy, 2017, 'Inefficiency and Judicial Delay'.

12 Based on National Crime Records Bureau (NCRB) statistics for 2022.

13 See the report on 'Criminal Justice in the Shadow of Caste'; Singh (2018).

14 Bothra, 2019, the *New Indian Express*.

15 Jain, 2020, the *Times of India*, 10 March 2020.

16 See Chen and Shapiro (2007) who study whether harsher prison conditions reduce recidivism rates. In fact, they find the opposite—that is, harsher prisons *increase* recidivism rates,

suggesting plausible peer effects of more 'seasoned' criminals in harsher prisons.

17 See Gupta (2020) for a summary of the problem of undertrial incarceration in India. She points towards operational inefficiencies of courts and police as among key reasons behind the situation, in addition to poor infrastructure and outdated laws that do not provide for subsidiary jails to implement segregation of undertrials from convicts.

18 Jails in India are also highly understaffed and jail guards (who are a separate cadre from district police) are often much more poorly trained and equipped than the district police (India Justice Report 2019).

19 These include shows such as *Made in Heaven* (2019), and in Hindi films like *Gangaajal* (2003), and Tamil films like *Visaranai* (2015).

20 See Chemin (2018) and Visaria (2009).

21 See Rao (2022). This finding is consistent with the fact that many disputes before district courts involve non-payment of loans. Thus, resolving these disputes sooner, likely allowed banks to recover unpaid loans and lend to other firms, and thereby boost credit circulation and firm economic activity.

22 See Rao (2022) for these calculations.

23 The control of the recruitment process for district and subordinate judges is under respective state High Courts. Writing in *Business Standard*, Ghosal (2020) describes an instance of recruitment by the Delhi High Court in 2014 where out of 1000 applicants, only 115 applicants qualified for 85 available posts. Further, among those that failed, 68 were judges in other states and even among the 115 that initially qualified, many were related to previously appointed judges.

24 Each judge would have two clerks, with one clerk joining and leaving each year. Thus, at any given point in time, there will be a senior second-year clerk and a junior first-year clerk.

25 See Singhvi (2021) where senior advocate Abhishek Singhvi discusses the weaknesses of law colleges in India, and notes that only a handful of national law universities produce well-trained law graduates.

26 This assumes compensation of Rs 3.5 lakh per year; and recruitment, training, and administrative costs of Rs 1.5 lakh per year.

27 For comparison, the annual cost of a district judge is around Rs 25 lakh. So, if having two clerks can increase productivity by even 50 per cent, hiring clerks will be cost-effective. Note also that finding enough good district judge candidates may be more challenging than hiring good young judicial clerks.

28 The reasons are the same as noted in the text: a system of judicial clerks boosts the productivity of existing judges, and improves the training of younger lawyers. Indeed, clerking for district, appellate, and Supreme Court justices is considered a very prestigious opportunity for graduates of top law schools.

29 See Chapter 5 in the 2018–19 Economic Survey of India for a more detailed discussion of some of these possibilities.

30 This would be an efficient reform even if court hours were to be reduced by say an hour a day, to account for time spent by the judge in reviewing adjournment requests outside court hours. The efficiency gains will come from listing only, say, ten cases as opposed to 100 on the daily court docket, but with a much higher probability that listed cases will, in fact, be heard on that day.

31 The numbers are based on personal experience. I recall waiting in line for a darshan at Tirupati temple for ten to twelve hours when I was a young boy in the 1980s. The time had come down to an hour when I visited again in 2004.

32 As noted in Narasappa and Vidhyasagar (2016).

33 See Boserup (1993) for further discussion of how bringing formal institutions and technology from outside can *weaken* informal property rights that are recognized by the community.

34 Examples include harmonizing the jurisdictions and decision-making authority on urban land use, recognizing the claims of landless labourers and sharecroppers to having some use rights on agricultural land based on historical considerations (and accounting for their welfare), and suitably protecting community use rights in areas designated for common use such as forests.

35 Under Section 138 of The Negotiable Instruments Act of 1881.

36 See Thomas (2021). Cases filed under the Negotiable Instruments
    Sec. 138 category are those of a bounced cheque.

37 See Bharadwaj, Lakdawala, and Li (2020).

38 See Basu (2018) for a deeper discussion of how laws can have
    positive effects even without being fully enforced by changing
    the social 'focal point' of acceptable behaviour. However, most
    models of laws acting as 'focal points' require enforcement above
    a threshold to change population-level behaviour. If enforcement
    is below a threshold, the laws are often ineffective or can even be
    counterproductive.

39 See Calvi and Keskar (2023) on how anti-dowry laws in India
    reduced female decision-making power and *increased* domestic
    violence, and Cameron et al. (2021) on how criminalizing
    commercial sex work in Indonesia led affected women to have
    an *increase* in sexually-transmitted infections, lower incomes,
    lower ability to meet educational expenses for their children,
    and an increase in child labour.

40 The value of academic research and expertise to inform the work
    of the commission is well illustrated by works like Chandra,
    Kalantry, and Hubbard (2023), and the work of Ajay Shah,
    Susan Thomas and colleagues at the XKDR from conducting a
    wide variety of data-driven analyses of court functioning.

41 As reported by many TV channels during the news hour on 24
    April 2016. An illustrative example is the story titled: 'CJI TS Thakur
    Breaks Down in front of PM Modi, Appeals to Protect Judiciary',
    available at: https://www.youtube.com/watch?v=vGPON9dDgbw.

42 See Chandra et al. (2023) for evidence on the last point.

Chapter 15: Social Protection and Welfare

1   Summary information on state budgets is obtained from the PRS
    (Parliamentary Research Service) Budget Briefs. Information on
    welfare spending by scheme was collected for a few states by
    going through state budget documents and speeches.

2   For instance, Nobel Prize-winning economist Thomas Sargent
    has noted that one of the twelve key principles of economics is

that there are 'tradeoffs between equality and efficiency'. See Tabarrok (2014) for the full set of twelve economics principles highlighted by Sargent.

3   The intellectual tradition of development economics provides many other examples of 'poverty traps' that make it possible for policy interventions to improve both equity and efficiency. Other examples include improving the bargaining power of peasants and landless labourers vis-à-vis landlords with market power (see Banerjee, Gertler, and Ghatak 2002 and Muralidharan, Niehaus, and Sukhtankar 2023a).

4   This is a very old, classic idea in development economics dating back to at least Rosenstein-Rodan (1943) and Nurkse (1953). See Murphy, Shleifer, and Vishny (1989) for a modern theoretical treatment; and Muralidharan, Niehaus, and Sukhtankar (2023) for empirical evidence on this point.

5   See Barnwal and Ryan (2023) for a more detailed explanation of these issues.

6   Note that stopping free electricity for farmers would change crop mix more than it would stop cultivation itself. However, a sharp increase in fertilizer prices could stop cultivation itself.

7   In practice, this requires the bank to write off the loan *and* for the government to recapitalize the bank with fresh equity. This equity is financed by tax revenues, which is why it is a giveaway to big businesses. These examples are consistent with the points made in Chapter 2 and 18 that large fractions of India's tax revenues are captured by big businesses and large landowners.

8   One plausible explanation is that landlords often lend to workers in the lean season, and deduct high interest payments from peak season wages. By boosting wages and incomes in the lean season, NREGS may reduce workers' need to borrow from landlords, thus keeping wages higher in the peak season as well. See Muralidharan, Niehaus, and Sukhtankar (2023). This example also illustrates the point made in Chapter 9 that improving public options can have far-reaching positive effects, even at low market shares, by also forcing private options to improve for *all*—including those who do not use the public option.

9 See Muralidharan et al. (2023), and Cook and Shah (2021), for illustrative studies and Sukhtankar (2017) for a review of the evidence. The results in my work suggest that the most important mechanisms were NREGS's value in counteracting employer monopsony power, and the increase in local demand for non-agricultural output enabled by higher labour incomes.

10 See Chakraborty and Jayaraman (2019).

11 See Dutta, Howes, and Murgai (2010) for evidence on the targeting and delivery efficiency of social security pensions in Karnataka and Rajasthan.

12 Thus, NYAY featured similar design flaws as India's policies to help small and medium enterprises. The goal should have been to help these firms improve efficiency by growing and reaching scale. But, in practice, policies designed to help small firms often encouraged them to stay small and inefficient (see Chapter 16). See the symposium on NYAY with inputs from several researchers including myself at: https://www.ideasforindia.in/topics/poverty-inequality/introduction-to-e-symposium-decoding-congress-nyay.html.

13 See Basu (2011) for an in-depth discussion of the challenges caused by such a structure.

14 See Romero and Singh (2023).

15 See Murgai and Ravallion (2005) for an illustrative discussion of the concerns about NREGS. On a personal note, I consider my recently published paper on the 'general equilibrium' effects of improving NREGS implementation to be my most important research paper to date (see Muralidharan, Niehaus, and Sukhtankar 2023). This is partly because of the importance of NREGS, and the illustration of many classic ideas in development economics in this paper. But a key reason is that our findings from a large-scale RCT *changed my prior views* regarding the impact of NREGS. The last point highlights the broader social value of research based on high-quality empirical designs, to inform both theory and policy.

16 This evidence can include both descriptive analysis of the economic incidence of programmes to inform impacts on equity, as well as causal evidence on their impacts on outcomes of interest.

17 Jaitly and Shah (2022).

18 See Dvara Research (2022).

19 See Narayanan, Dhorajiwala, and Golani (2018), who report that only 21 per cent of NREGS payments were made on time in 2016–17, even a decade after NREGS was launched.

20 As observed in this interview: https://www.youtube.com/watch?v=hpwPciW74b8.

21 See Yadav (2023).

22 See Muralidharan, Niehaus, and Sukhtankar (2016), and Muralidharan, Niehaus, Sukhtankar, and Weaver (2021) for examples across NREGS and farmer welfare payments respectively.

23 See Sharan and Kumar (2021).

24 This is based on joint work with Paul Niehaus, Sandip Sukhtankar, and Jeff Weaver. Our pilots of DBT choice in the PDS were conducted in Bihar in 2012–13, Rajasthan in 2015–17, and Maharashtra in 2019–20. We have also conducted extensive process documentation of beneficiary experiences of switching from PDS to DBT in the union territories of Chandigarh, Puducherry, and Dadra and Nagar Haveli.

25 The biggest practical challenge in implementing the choice-based architecture in the PDS is to set up systems so that beneficiaries cannot access *both* cash and in-kind benefits. When we ran our first pilots of this approach in Bihar, beneficiaries were provided with barcoded coupons that they needed to hand over to the PDS dealer to collect their monthly entitlements. The choice-based pilot required beneficiaries to hand over the coupon to the business correspondent, if they chose to avail of the cash option. However, implementing the system at scale would have been much more difficult using this system. This is why the Aadhaar-based backend of the PDS is key to implementing the choice-based architecture at scale.

26 This pilot is being evaluated by JPAL South Asia led by Nicholas Ryan and Anant Sudarshan. See Barnwal and Ryan (2023) for more details on the design of such reform pilots and preliminary findings.

27 See Bardhan (2011), Joshi (2016), Mundle (2016), and Ray (2016). The 2016–17 Economic Survey, whose writing was led by Arvind Subramanian, made a prominent call for a UBI in India.

28 See Banerjee, Niehaus, and Suri (2019) for a review of the global evidence on universal basic income, and Davala, Jhabvala, Mehta, and Standing (2015) for evidence on a UBI pilot in Madhya Pradesh.

29 See Muralidharan, Niehaus, and Sukhtankar (2018) and Muralidharan (2020) for op-ed length discussions of the idea of an 'Inclusive Growth Dividend', and see Ghatak and Muralidharan (2021) for a more detailed policy paper on the idea.

30 See Ghatak and Muralidharan (2020) for a detailed discussion of the evidence that informs the claims in this paragraph.

31 See Egger et al. (2022).

32 See Glaeser (2011) for an excellent discussion of the centrality of cities in improving human welfare.

33 See Bryan et al. (2014).

34 See Kansikas, Mani, and Niehaus (2023) for evidence that people prefer to receive such transfers.

35 See Khilnani (2010) and Ray (2016). A similar argument has been made in the context of the US by Nobel Prize-winning economist Robert Shiller (Shiller 2009).

36 This point was confirmed by analysis of the CMIE Consumer Pyramids Household Survey (CPHS) survey data by one of my PhD students, who found that the correlation between income and consumption is significantly higher in urban areas than in rural areas. This is a classic test of the extent of insurance and consumption smoothing, and suggests that these are weaker in urban areas of India.

37 See Drèze (2020), Drèze (2021), and Basole et al. (2020) for more
    details. Also see the 'Ideas for India' symposium on DUET for
    commentary on the idea by several leading economists, including
    Ashok Kotwal, Dilip Mookherjee, Martin Ravallion, and Debraj
    Ray.

Chapter 16: Jobs, Productivity, and Economic Growth

1   Given that only around 5 per cent of Indians pay income tax, the
    fraction who can live off their capital income (without working)
    is almost certainly below 5 per cent.
2   The substantially lower monthly earnings of casual wage workers
    reflects the fact that they often do not find a paying job on all
    days of the month.
3   Men's total earnings are 35 per cent higher than women among
    salaried workers, but 75 per cent higher among casual wage
    earners, and nearly 400 per cent higher among the self-employed.
    The much greater difference in the latter two categories likely
    also reflects differences in hours worked.
4   See Kumar (2022).
5   67 per cent of the total population is of working age (fifteen to
    sixty-four) and 56 per cent of this population is in the workforce,
    implying around 2.7 dependants for every member in the
    workforce.
6   Intuitively, it makes sense to think of education as increasing
    productivity of labour. However, the academic economics
    literature treats education as an input because it can be measured
    (typically by the average years of schooling), and estimates TFP
    as the 'residual' of output differences across countries (or firms)
    that cannot be explained by differences in *measured* inputs.
7   See Adhvaryu et al. (2023) for this evidence. They find that the
    elasticity of emoluments (comprising wages and benefits) to
    sales per worker is nearly one, implying that a 1 per cent increase

in worker productivity translates to a 1 per cent increase in emoluments. Of course, this does not imply that workers obtain *all* the benefits of increased productivity. But it does mean that their emoluments increase proportionately with increases in productivity.

8　This is why economists distinguish between TFP in quantity produced (TFPQ) and TFP in revenue (TFPR). TFPQ measures productivity in terms of output produced per unit of inputs, whereas TFPR also accounts for changes in prices and measures the revenue produced per unit of inputs.

9　In practice, the downward pressure on prices creates political pressure for governments to both increase the minimum support price for rice and to procure surplus rice. However, this puts severe pressure on public finances, and is unsustainable over time.

10　Such views have been widespread in history. For instance, the term 'Luddites' (used to describe those who refuse to use and adapt to new technologies), originates from the nineteenth-century groups of English textile workers who used to destroy textile machinery that they felt would put weavers out of jobs.

11　See the collection of essays on the 'economics of new goods' in Bresnahan and Gordon (1997) for an excellent overview of the relevant theory and empirics of estimating the welfare gains from new goods.

12　A 2017 article in 'Forbes tracked the US top fifty firms in 2017, 1967, and 1917, and finds only nine firms common between the 2017 top fifty and the 1967 top fifty, and only two that are common between the 2017 and the 1917 top fifty (Kauflin and Noer 2017).

13　See, for example, Lewis (1954), Murphy, Shleifer, and Vishny (1989), Rodriguez-Clare (1996), Alvarez-Caudrado and Poschke (2011).

14　This was memorably documented by Adam Smith using the example of the pin factory to show how division of labour allowed a team of specialized workers to be dramatically more productive than a situation where workers made a full pin by themselves Smith (1776).

15 Exports of manufactured goods played a crucial role in the rapid growth of East Asian tiger economies such as South Korea and Taiwan, and even for a country like China with a very large domestic population. See the discussion in Chapter 15 of the role of market size in development.

16 See DeLong (2022) for an excellent recent synthesis of the economic history of 1870 to 2010, where he argues that the combination of three factors—full globalization, the industrial research lab, and the modern corporation—played a transformative role in increasing global productivity and output per capita.

17 This was similar to the role played by companies like Walmart in accelerating China's progress in low-cost manufacturing by sourcing thousands of products and teaching local firms to meet global quality standards, and rewarding successful firms with progressively larger contracts.

18 See Aiyar (2022a).

19 Thus, it has delivered the first two benefits of manufacturing-led growth noted earlier, but not the third.

20 See Krishna (2018) and Avdiu et al. (2022).

21 From the PLFS 2022–23.

22 Classic references documenting misallocation in India and comparing with other countries include Hall and Jones (1999), Banerjee and Duflo (2005), Restuccia and Rogerson (2008), Bartelsman et al., (2013), and Hsieh and Klenow (2009).

23 See Foster and Rosenzweig (2011) and (2022). More generally, Gollin, Lagakos, and Waugh (2014) estimate that the agricultural output per worker in rich countries is thirty to fifty times higher than in poor countries.

24 In addition to agriculture, this is also true in jobs like running small retail shops, where someone may be minding a store all day, but spending large amounts of time idle waiting for customers.

25 Fan, Peters, and Zilibotti (2023) show that even non-traded consumer services are produced much more efficiently in urban areas as compared to rural areas.

26 See Moretti (2004) for empirical evidence on this point.

27 Diamond (2016) shows that the geographic sorting of high skilled workers (college graduates) in the US is partly attributable to the quality and quantity of amenities and services available in urban areas.

28 Urban India has 34 per cent of India's population and 63 per cent of GDP, while rural India accounts for 66 per cent and 37 per cent, implying that GDP per capita is over three times higher in urban India.

29 See Glaeser (2011).

30 This anti-urban bias partly reflects a political delimitation process that is biased towards rural areas because it does not adjust quickly enough to reflect increasing urbanization, and because many migrants are still registered to vote in their villages (see Gaikwad and Nellis, 2020). It also reflects a common belief among Indian elites that urbanization is bad because cities can barely keep up with the needs of existing residents, and because of the squalid and poor living conditions in urban slums.

31 See Lagakos (2020). It is well documented that there are differences in average productivity across rural and urban areas (for example, Restuccia et al. 2008; Lagakos and Waugh 2013, Emerick 2018) but it isn't clear whether this is driven by selection. For example, Hicks et al. (2021) show that accounting for individual fixed unobservable factors using individual level panel data from Indonesia and Kenya leads to a much smaller labour productivity gap between agricultural and non-agricultural sectors, at least within five years since their transition. Thus, the gains from migration may be less than that suggested by average wage differences, but they are still likely to be positive as argued by Lagakos (2020).

32 Although the SSI reservation policy has now been dismantled, there are several continuing policies favouring small and medium enterprises, including preferential treatment of MSMEs

for loans from public-sector banks, and preferential public procurement from MSMEs. While businesses often start small and need an enabling environment to grow, states should be wary of distortionary policies that can inhibit growth. A large body of research has studied the effect of SSI policies using the de-reservation reform, showing that such reservations led to large productivity losses within the manufacturing sector as well as in the aggregate. See for example, Garcia-Santana and Pijoan-Mas (2014); Martin et al., (2017).

33 For empirical evidence of the barriers posed by red tape on firm entry, see Djankov et al. (2002), and Klapper et al. (2006).

34 These figures are based on personal interviews with industry experts. Unfortunately, there is no good comparable data on firm size distributions across India and comparator countries like Vietnam and Bangladesh because of differences in sampling methodologies.

35 There are many reasons why larger scale is a key driver of higher productivity. These include: (a) scale allows greater specialization and division of labour among workers, (b) it enables investing in better management practices because the returns to even minor productivity gains are multiplied by a much larger volume of output, (c) it helps to lower costs of inputs and credit, (d) scale makes it possible to cover the fixed costs of marketing and market access, and (e) scale enables faster learning: several studies have shown the existence of a 'learning curve' whereby the unit cost of production falls as a function of the total amount of past production.

36 See Sabharwal and Arora (2016).

37 The 'financial development' of an economy has two main components. The first is mobilizing savings into the formal financial system and away from assets like cash and gold, which can *store* value but do not typically produce additional value since these are *not productive* assets. The second is directing these savings to the most productive investment opportunities. Rajan and Zingales (1998) find that financial development facilitates economic growth by reducing firms' cost of accessing

external finance. Within India, Breza and Kinnan (2021) show that a contraction in credit supply in the aftermath of the 2008 MFI crisis in Andhra Pradesh is associated with lower wages, household earnings, and consumption.

38 Literature documenting credit constraints include Banerjee and Duflo (2014), and Kapoor et al. (2017) among Indian firms; and de Mel et al. (2008), and Fafchamps et al. (2014) on constraints faced by small and medium enterprises in Sri Lanka and Ghana, respectively. In all these studies, the returns on capital far exceeded the going interest rate on loans.

39 This is a long-standing problem: in 2002, banks held 39 per cent of their assets in government securities against an SLR of 25 per cent. Seventeen years later, in 2019, banks still held 36 per cent of their assets in government securities even though the SLR has been reduced to 19 per cent (Source: RBI's fortnightly data on banks' statement of position from 17 July 2020).

40 See Shah (2020) for details of the number of no-objection certificates (NOCs) needed to start a business on his own land, and how many of these steps seemed to be explicitly designed for extortion.

41 See Foster and Rosenzweig (2022) for agriculture and Adamopoulos and Restuccia (2020) for industry.

42 See Goldberg, Khandelwal, Pavcnik, and Topalova (2008) for a classic paper that shows large gains to Indian industry from lower tariffs (through increasing access and affordability of intermediate inputs).

43 This is consistent with a long tradition in development economics, which has discussed how the presence of multiple binding constraints can keep individuals and countries in a 'poverty trap'. The key policy implication of these models is that there are likely to be 'complementarities' across reforms whereby the benefits of alleviating multiple constraints at the same time are greater than the sum of the benefits of relaxing constraints individually. Montek Singh Ahluwalia has noted that

a key feature of the 1991 economic reforms was the alleviation of multiple constraints together (see Ahluwalia 2020).

44 As seen at https://mahatextile.maharashtra.gov.in/ (accessed 25 November 2022, though the emphasis on power subsidies has been there for several years). Interestingly though, these subsidies may be economically justified as undoing the burden of cross-subsidies on the textile industry. The larger point, however, is that of the large invisible burden imposed by cross-subsidies that hurt the economy.

45 This could also be the development commissioner, or the principal secretary to the chief minister. The key is for the concerned officer to have enough seniority, convening power, and coordinating authority.

46 A detailed discussion of the comparative experiences with SEZs is beyond the scope of this chapter. See Aggarwal (2012) for a detailed analysis of SEZs in India including comparative insights.

47 In other words, such an approach would aim to encourage 'rules-based' capitalism rather than the 'deal-based' capitalism that occurs when states use incentive-based strategies to attract investments.

48 The private partner's equity in the SEZ should correspond to their investment volume, with their returns tied to the SEZ's overall success, to align their incentives with managing the SEZ well. The government's equity reflects its provision of public goods, like law and contract enforcement, and crucially, land acquisition. This model allows the government to lease land from farmers, using its annual SEZ revenue to pay them a growing dividend, in line with the park's success and rising commercial rents. This approach could offer a politically viable method for land acquisition for the SEZ.

49 See Rajan and Lamba (2023) for a detailed critique of the PLI scheme. They argue that the subsidy per job is too high, and that these funds could be better used to invest in education, skills, and research.

50 See Muralidharan (2019d) for some of these calculations. Also
    see Foster and Rosenzweig (2011) for additional calculations on
    the relationship between farm size and profitability.

51 See Chapter 9 of the 2016–17 Economic Survey for a discussion
    of India's fertilizer subsidies and their challenges. One way to
    reform fertilizer subsidies would be to phase them out at 5 per
    cent per year gradually over the next twenty years, and augment
    the PM-KISAN transfer by a similar amount each year.

52 See Porzio, Rossi, and Santangelo (2022) for this global evidence.
    Interestingly, Jayant Sinha, the MP from Hazaribagh, a coal-
    producing area, said something very similar in the context of
    balancing livelihoods of coal miners and accelerating a green
    energy transition (at a conference where I heard him speak). He
    said that the goal should be to ensure that the *children* of today's
    coal miners are not dependent on coal mining twenty-five years
    from now.

53 More generally, there is a deep tension between the productivity-
    enhancing benefits of scale and the potential for exploiting
    market power by scale operators. This is a central issue in
    antitrust/competition policy. The experience from more
    developed countries suggest that the benefits to scale in terms
    of lower costs are large enough that regulators have permitted
    substantial consolidation in industries as long as there are at
    least three or four viable providers. The implication for India
    is that scale should be encouraged, and antitrust concerns may
    be better addressed through having at least one high-quality
    public option. This is consistent with the principles discussed in
    Chapter 9 on the State and the Market.

54 See Patel, Byahut, and Bhatha (2018) for an illustrative study.
    They analyse the effects of building regulations on the supply
    of two-room homes in Ahmedabad and show that 'rationalizing
    regulations can reduce housing costs by 34 per cent and increase
    supply by as much as 75 per cent, without significantly lowering
    quality or compromising safety'.

55 See Mangal (2023) and Chapter 5.

56 See Muralidharan, Niehaus, and Sukhtankar (2023a).

57 See Carranza et al. (2022).

58 As per a 2022 report by Global Alliance for Mass Entrepreneurship (GAME) and Dun & Bradstreet

59 See Burns and Zhiren (2010).

60 As quoted by former chief economist of the UK Department for International Development, Stefan Dercon in Dercon (2022), p. 129.

61 In practice, some of this aligning of incentives also took place through corruption, with local officials often acquiring land or purchasing/obtaining shares in local companies. However, this form of corruption does not seem to have been deleterious to the public interest, because it helped to provide adequate incentives for officials to enlarge the overall size of the economic pie. See Ang (2016) for an extensive discussion of how corruption per se need not deter development if it is structured in ways that align the private incentives of officials with higher economic growth.

62 See Adhvaryu, Kala, and Nyshadam (2022), and Somanathan et al. (2021).

63 For instance, by turning off production facilities or running them at low capacity prior to inspection to ensure that measured emissions on the day of inspection are low.

64 See Greenstone, Pande, Sudarshan, and Ryan (2022).

Chapter 17: Reimagining Institutions

1   This is a widely used framework among scholars of public policy and has been used to study and explain a wide variety of topics ranging from international trade to health policy. See Bhagwati (1988) for an illustrative use of this framework to explain trade policy choices.

2   The framing of institutions as setting the 'rules of the game' follows that of Nobel laureate Douglass North. Multiple Nobel Prizes have been awarded for scholarly work on institutions,

including to Douglass North, Elinor Ostrom, Ronald Coase and Oliver Williamson (the latter two are known for their work on the central role of transaction costs in economic interactions, and have indirectly worked on institutions by showing the importance of institutions for boosting trust and thereby reducing transaction costs). See North (1990, 1991) and Ostrom (1990) for influential syntheses of scholarly research on institutions.

3   However, it is important to recognize that agents of the state as well as citizens also function against a backdrop of social norms and values such as the social respect accorded to honesty, probity, and public service, and the social costs (or lack thereof) of deviating from these values. These in turn are shaped by families, religious organizations, communities, and the media, and are beyond the scope of this book.

4   See North (1990) for a synthesis of the early literature on institutions and development. More recent quantitative studies that have been highly influential include Acemoglu, Johnson, and Robinson (2001) and (2002). See Acemoglu, Johnson, and Robinson (2005) for an updated synthesis of the literature. Engermann and Sokoloff (2012) provide an excellent overview of this literature focused on the Americas. Finally, Banerjee and Iyer (2005) show how differences in colonial land tenure institutions in India have had a long and persistent effect on the development trajectory and outcomes of different parts of India.

5   See Acemoglu and Robinson (2012).

6   See Kapur and Mehta (2005) and Kapur, Mehta, and Vaishnav (2017) for prominent scholarly works on this subject. See Bhadra (2023) for a more recent treatment.

7   See Austin (1999), De (2018), Bhatia (2019), and Khosla (2020) for book-length treatments of the process of crafting the Indian Constitution, the major debates among the founders, how and why it built a set of 'inclusive institutions', and its broader impact on Indian society.

8   See Kapur and Mehta (2005), and Kapur, Mehta, and Vaishnav (2017). My summary of the decline of Indian institutions and their causes largely relies on the essays in these two volumes.

9   Since the executive is typically made up of senior leaders of the *same* party that has a majority in the legislature, holding the executive accountable would involve MPs and MLAs criticizing their own government, which explains why unfavourable CAG reports are often just buried by the legislature. In recent years, CAG reports have only had an impact when the findings are so startling that the media takes an interest in them (as happened in the 2G case). However, this kind of accountability is ad hoc and unpredictable and is far from the ideals of routine institutional effectiveness.

10 See Somanathan and Natarajan (2022).

11 The analysis of liabilities should include provisioning for the cost of implicit government guarantees for borrowing by state-linked special purpose vehicles (such as for urban infrastructure projects).

12 In particular, we urgently need to build the capacity of local bodies for revenue mobilization. However, this requires careful attention to the fiscal devolution formula to make sure that local bodies both have the funds needed to provide minimum levels of services, and have the right incentives to raise their own revenue. This will require continuous iteration and tweaking of devolution formulae. Such an ongoing process will be better done under a permanent PFC than an episodic SFC.

13 States would also do well to set up institutions like a Judicial Process Reforms Commission as suggested in Chapter 14.

14 As reported by the Forum for State Studies: https://forumforstatestudies.in/ (accessed 18 July 2023).

15 This insight applies to a wide range of behaviours ranging from healthy eating (which is made easier by not keeping unhealthy foods nearby) to reducing procrastination (which is made easier by keeping distractions like electronics away). See Clear (2018) for more examples and research evidence.

16 See, for instance, endorsements by Nobel Prize-winning economists Eric Maskin and Amartya Sen in two *New York Times* columns (2016 and 2018). There is extensive academic literature on voting systems and their properties. Illustrative examples include Taagepera and Shugart (1991), and Cox (1997). In the Indian context, RCV has been recommended among others by legal scholar Tarunabh Khaitan (see Khaitan 2019).

17 Two striking examples of how spoiler candidates can alter the trajectory of elections and subsequent national policies are the 2000 and 2016 US elections. In both cases, voters who chose Ralph Nader (2000) and Jill Stein (2016) would likely have preferred the Democratic candidate for President (Al Gore and Hillary Clinton, respectively). However, their votes for Nader and Stein were likely responsible for the victories of George W. Bush and Donald Trump, respectively, because the winning margin in key states was less than the number of votes obtained by Nader and Stein.

18 See the large set of studies summarized by Drutman and Strano (2022).

19 Khaitan (2019) recommends starting RCV pilots in India by allowing up to three choices since this will be much easier to communicate to voters and reduces the risk of wasted votes due to incorrect ballots.

20 See Kapur and Vaishnav (2019).

21 As per the judgment in the *Citizens United versus Federal Election Commission* case.

22 See Landemore (2020).

23 See Guerrero (2014). The political science literature also refers to this idea as 'sortition'. Bhadra (2023) briefly mentions it for consideration in the Indian context, but does not develop the idea in further detail.

24 Of course, there is no guarantee that corruption will be eliminated since members of the assembly could still be bribed by contractors. However, there is considerable potential for this structure to reduce corruption since no money will be needed

to fight elections, which reduces both the need for bribes and *removes the internal moral justification* for corruption that many leaders use—which is that they need to be corrupt to raise money to contest elections. Further, random selection of average citizens increases the chances of having at least a few honest members on the assembly who refuse to be bribed. Finally, the regular rotation of members may make it more difficult to *institutionalize* corrupt arrangements.

25 Several studies have found that reservations for scheduled castes and women in elected office have led to improved outcomes for those groups and have also contributed to improved public perception of the suitability of these groups for leadership roles. See Pande (2003), Chattopadhyay and Duflo (2004), and Beaman et al. (2009) for examples.

26 This is because accounting for different dimensions of deprivation increases the number of categories multiplicatively and would result in very large numbers of categories. Given finite numbers of seats, it would often be mathematically impossible to ensure fine-grained quotas without some aggregation.

27 An intersectional category of deprivation refers to individuals who are disadvantaged on *multiple* (two or more) dimensions, such as caste, gender, disability, income, wealth, etc. Existing quota systems do a poor job of ensuring adequate representation of people of intersectional disadvantage. For instance, reservations for scheduled castes and tribes tend to benefit the economically better-off within these groups, and reservations for women tend to benefit those from advantaged caste and income groups.

28 See Varshney (2003) for a classic study on the contributions of institutions where different religious groups interact to maintain peace in times of conflict. More recently, Rao (2019) and Lowe (2021) present experimental evidence on the 'contact hypothesis' and show that increasing engagement across caste groups builds greater inter-group trust and willingness to engage more in the future.

29 See Rao and Sanyal (2018) for a detailed scholarly account of the functioning of gram sabhas in Karnataka.

30 This comment was made by Prof. Jean-Paul Faguet of the London School of Economics (a scholar of decentralization) at a conference on decentralization organized by the World Bank that I had attended.

Chapter 18: State, Citizens, and Civil Society

1   This is also partly why assessments of Indian democracy by scholars and commentators like Ramachandra Guha and Ashutosh Varshney describe it as 50–50 (Guha 2007) or 'Battles Half Won' (Varshney 2013).

2   Bardhan (1984). These classes can also be roughly mapped into those that are endowed with financial capital (businesses), physical capital (land owners), and human capital (government employees).

3   This quote is originally attributed to economist Joan Robinson, but has also been widely used by others.

4   I use 'elite' as a composite term to identify privileged groups. This privilege can reflect a combination of wealth, income, caste, gender, education, occupation, and/or other axes of identity. Decomposing the dimensions of privilege and deprivation and their relative importance is beyond the scope of this chapter. This is because my focus here is not on parsing dimensions of disadvantage, but on making the case for forming broad coalitions *across* multiple disadvantaged social groups to create the political pressure to build a more effective Indian state.

5   While *Kendriya Vidyalayas* and *Navodaya Vidyalayas* are examples of high-quality government schools, both sets of schools are atypical. The former cater to children of government employees, and their strong performance also reflects the considerable benefits from the higher education levels, incomes, and cultural capital of their parents. The latter have an exam-based selection process after primary school and while they do

provide access to quality education, the selectivity makes them atypical.

6 See Das and Zajonc (2010). Note that this does *not* imply that the investment in tertiary education was a mistake for the country. However, it has skewed our development towards high-skill-intensive sectors as opposed to low-skill-intensive ones, which would have created many more higher-quality jobs and likely further accelerated Indian economic growth (as noted in Chapters 11 and 16).

7 During the Russian invasion of Ukraine in 2022, the initial focus in India was on safely evacuating Indian medical students. Only later did the media start asking why 15,000 Indian medical students were in Ukraine in the first place! As per Hossain (2022) the high fees of Indian medical colleges, which reflect restricted supply, was a key reason. Also, many private medical colleges are owned by politicians (a point made publicly by Arvind Kejriwal), giving them an incentive to restrict supply to preserve their profits.

8 While doctors may know best about *curative* care, health *policy* has many other considerations including understanding of market failures, incentives, externalities, and cost-effectiveness. So, doctors need not make the best health policy advisers. Ajay Shah makes this point in Episode 223 of *The Seen and the Unseen* podcast with Amit Varma. I expand on these issues in Episode 225 of the same podcast.

9 See Krishnan (2015) for an extensive feature documenting the outsized role of a few super-specialist doctors on health policy in India by virtue of their role as personal physicians of politicians. Also see Kumbhar (2022) for an exploration of the long-standing elite bias in the practice of medicine in India.

10 These benefits accrue to lawyers on *both* sides of the dispute, as depicted memorably in the movie *Mohan Joshi Hazir Ho!*.

11 See Saxena (2021) for statistics and a more detailed discussion.

12 Consistent with these facts, several scholars and commentators on India have argued that India in its current form mainly

works for its elites but is failing the vast majority of its citizens. See Krishna (2018) and Mody (2023) for illustrative examples.

13 See Shah (2004) for a review of the academic literature on social movements in India, and the essays in Katzenstein and Ray (2005) for a discussion of Indian social movements in the context of poverty.

14 While the state has the power to acquire land for national development, it is also incumbent upon a modern democracy to use these powers sparingly and to adequately compensate those affected by such displacement. When it does not do so (as has often been the case), civil society has actively resisted the state. As one well-known example, the Narmada Bachao Andolan (NBA) led by Medha Patkar brought public attention to the problem of displacement of tribal populations by the Sardar Sarovar dam. Other civil-society organizations like Action Research in Community Health and Development (ARCH) then worked with tribals and the government to design and implement an effective rehabilitation package. See Aiyar (2022b and 2022c) for further details.

15 This is because elections can hold leaders accountable for widespread violations of individual rights (like under the Emergency), but are not frequent or granular enough to secure the rights of individuals or small groups against overreach by the state.

16 The case of child development provides a powerful example. Multiple policy documents over the past two decades, including the 2009 Right to Education Act, the 2020 National Education Policy and even the 86th Constitutional Amendment of 2002 call for the state to provide early childhood education to all children under six. However, these policy aspirations have not been achieved due to constraints in funding and underinvestment in state capacity for implementation (Prasad and Sinha 2015). This is an illustration of the much more general phenomenon of India having large gaps between the aspirations set out in

well-crafted policy documents and the quality of delivery in practice (Pritchett 2009).

17 For instance, a recent book by Oxford economist Stefan Dercon (who served as chief economist of the UK Department for International Development) notes how a shared commitment among 'those with the power to shape politics, the economy, and society to striving for growth and development is what, above all, more successful countries appear to have in common, despite disagreement on important details, including those on economic policy-making' (Dercon, 2022, p. 57).

18 Indeed, it is not an accident that the NREGS was launched after over a decade of rapid economic growth when it was more fiscally feasible to do so.

19 An example of this is the UPA government's experience of regular disagreement on social policy questions between members of the National Advisory Council (NAC) comprised mainly of activists, and the Planning Commission, led by Montek Ahluwalia, who was an economist.

20 See the introductory essay in Drèze (2017).

21 My op-ed on the 2019 economics Nobel Prize expands on this point (Muralidharan 2019a).

22 See Engermann and Sokoloff (2012). Also see Piketty (2014). See Sinha and Varshney (2011) for similar concerns of business capture of politicians and policy in the Indian context.

23 For instance, the idea of continuous and comprehensive assessment, which was a progressive and good idea in theory, has been found to have no impact in practice (Berry et al. 2020); extensive school construction to promote access has created tens of thousands of sub-scale schools and may have been counterproductive on multiple dimensions including pedagogy, governance, cost-effectiveness, and social integration (see Chapter 11); and finally, the no-detention policy—which was again well-intentioned as a way of reducing dropouts—has contributed to the enormous variation in learning levels within the same grade in higher grades, which makes it very difficult

for teachers to teach effectively (see Chapter 11). Reflecting on some of these issues, even one of the leaders of the rights-based movement in India has mentioned (in correspondence with me in 2012) that the RTE was in practice a 'Right to Education Facilities' Act and not a 'Right to Education' Act.

24 Specifically, free markets with choice and competition use prices as an incredibly efficient tool for aggregating information from millions of producers and consumers regarding their valuation of various goods and services, and using this signal to allocate scarce factors of production to their highest-value use. These prices also serve as a signal to reward both consumers and producers for being as efficient as possible, and to constantly innovate to either reduce costs or increase the value of production.

25 See Kapur, Babu, and Prasad (2014).

26 There are other important weaknesses, including market failures, such as externalities and coordination failures (with pollution and climate change being the most salient example). However, economists usually agree that correcting these market failures requires either societal or government intervention, and so this is not as much of a 'blind spot' for them as matters of equity and justice.

27 See the open letter on this point signed by Jean Drèze and several other economists at https://countercurrents.org/2022/12/open-letter-to-finance-minister-from-51-eminent-economists/.

28 This is why legislative guarantees may be needed for such reforms to be feasible (see Chapter 15). Given the centrality of these reforms for national welfare (especially phasing out electricity subsidies to solve our water crisis), it may even make sense to have an all-party consensus followed by a Constitutional Amendment to guarantee payments to farmers in lieu of subsidies for ten to fifteen years.

29 The importance of rulers keeping their word is also enshrined in Indian traditions, including in epics like the Ramayana, where one of its well-known sayings is '*Raghukul reet sada chali aayee; praan jaaye par vachan na jaaye*', which translates

to 'The long-standing tradition of the family of Raghu (that Rama was born into) is that one may lose one's life, but should never break one's word.'

30 The importance of 'public reasoning' for a healthy democracy has been highlighted in several newspaper columns by Pratap Bhanu Mehta.

31 Note that middle classes in India, comprising the salaried and professional classes, are actually in the top 10 per cent and not in the middle of the income distribution. Thus, the term 'middle class' does not represent the middle of the income distribution. Rather, it represents classes who occupy positions in the 'middle' between elites who control land and capital, and occupy the top tiers of the government (and comprise less than 1 per cent of the population), and the working classes who mainly rely on their physical labour for income (and comprise around 90 per cent of the population). This is a class that is usually better educated than the working classes and has a salaried job. One measure of India's small middle class is the small fraction of Indians who have a salaried job (seen in Chapter 16).

32 The Aam Aadmi Party's victories in Delhi elections are based in large part on building such a coalition.

33 The terminology above is inspired by the words of Dr Martin Luther King Jr, who noted that 'the arc of the moral universe is long, but it bends towards justice.'

34 This is a quote attributed to Mario Cuomo, a former governor of New York state.

35 Of course, the practical problem is that opposition parties often cynically try to limit the successes that the government can claim, and often oppose ideas that even they have supported when in government (or in their manifesto). In this case, they may short-sightedly prefer to have a weaker car so that the ruling party cannot drive it very far. But this is where broader public awareness and support for a constructive reform agenda can help, because such support can limit the social cost of a cynical Opposition.

36 A well-known result in game theory (an important branch of economic theory) is that private knowledge (even when known to many people) may not be enough to induce changes in settings requiring *coordinated* action, because people do not know who else has that knowledge. In contrast, common knowledge implies not only that everyone has the information, but everyone *knows* that everyone else has the same information. This makes it much more likely for coordinated action to take place.

37 See Drèze and Sen (2013).

38 It may also reflect the fact that teacher unions have been much more politically powerful in democratic India (see Kingdon and Muzammil 2001) than in communist China or Vietnam. This is consistent with the outsized influence of concentrated interest groups in a democracy (Chapter 2). An interesting parallel is seen in Indonesia, which transitioned to more democracy after Suharto in the early 2000s, and passed a 2003 education law stipulating spending a minimum 20 per cent of the budget on education. However, the increased influence of teacher unions after the democratic transition contributed to most of this higher budget being spent on a *doubling* of teacher pay. A large-scale RCT that I helped conduct found that this unconditional teacher pay increase had no impact on learning (de Ree et al. 2018).

39 While anganwadi workers are not as overpaid relative to market norms as government teachers, they are still paid well by the cost of living standards of the communities they work in (especially in rural areas). The best way of seeing this is the fact that there are multiple applicants for every job, and the positions are seen as attractive enough that the hiring is often politically influenced.

40 See, for instance, Sinha (2006) and the 2012 report of the Working Group for Children Under Six of the Right to Food Campaign.

41 See Debroy and Sinha (2023).

42 For instance, Rocket Learning, a non-profit focused on early childhood development (ECD) held a nationwide conference in

Delhi in March 2023 to build salience for more investment in ECD, and prominently featured some of this evidence in their discussions.

43 Specifically, they segment the Indian market into three groups: India One—comprising the top 10 to 15 per cent with disposable income at the level that they can demand the products of many start-ups; India Two—comprising the next 30 per cent who provide services to India One and benefit from the 'trickle down' of income growth in India One; and India Three—comprising the remaining 55 to 60 per cent who are mostly left out of India's economic growth and depend on government welfare programmes financed through increasing taxes to benefit from India's growth story. See Chawla (2016) and Pai (2021).

44 For example, the discussion in Chapter 9 highlights the value of better information on price and quality across service providers to make markets work better. It also explained the challenges with existing business models. Social entrepreneurs can make an important contribution to public welfare by figuring out answers to such questions and designing practical solutions to make markets work better.

45 These two questions reflect my own approach to research and policy, influenced in part by advice that I received many years ago from Montek Ahluwalia. As a researcher, my choice of topics is based on asking if the research question is important enough that the answer can meaningfully matter for policy. As a policy adviser, my focus is on synthesizing knowledge that we already have but are not acting upon.

46 They could be in the government full-time during summer breaks when students are away and for a day a week during the academic year. The time spent by researchers on these assignments could be either pro bono/honorary, paid for by the government, or covered by CSR/philanthropy.

47 For instance, I learnt recently at a joint conference on education organized by FLAME University, Pune and the non-profit

organization Leadership for Equity (LFE) that faculty at FLAME were working with LFE exactly along these lines. Thus, the model is likely to work and is worth considering by others as well.

48 A project team comprising faculty members and motivated students can be a cost-effective way for government agencies who do not have budgets to procure consultants to obtain local technical expertise.

49 As an example, Prof. Arjun Jayadev of Azim Premji University (APU) has shared X (Twitter) threads summarizing the master's theses of APU students. One such project entailed students analysing the spatial distribution of public facilities along the lines suggested in Chapter 6. Thus, even if a state government takes time to set up a unit that can do such analysis, motivated faculty and students can access publicly available data on budgets and facilities and conduct such analysis on their own, and share it with the public and the media—including in local languages.

50 Obviously, this reasoning does not apply as much to topics like defence, international trade, and foreign policy that are in the domain of the national government.

51 For instance, commercial pressures to cut costs have led to the reduction in the number of field-level beat journalists employed by media houses. It is cheaper to fill airtime with opinions and debates and printed pages with syndicated stories from news aggregators, than with well-researched original stories. Even worse, the economics of the media industry combined with the psychology of viewership creates commercial incentives to prioritize sensational headlines over nuanced discussion of facts, conspiracy theories over scientific evidence, fear over hope, and polarization over civic engagement.

52 I thank Manasi Narasimhan for pointing me to this example.

53 Nilekani (2022), p. 149.

54 As noted in Iyer (2021).

55 See Giridharadas (2018) for a cautionary tale on the limits of 'philanthrocapitalism'.

56 Sharan (2021). For additional illustrative examples of citizen engagement, see Balasubramaniam (2015), titled *I the Citizen: Unraveling the Power of Citizen Engagement.*

57 This is a variant of the quote: 'Showing up is 80 per cent of life', which is attributed to Woody Allen.

58 This frustration extends to people in positions of power! In one of my field visits to a school in rural Madhya Pradesh, the government-school teachers were absent, and children were loitering around with no instruction during school hours. I proceeded to find and interview the *pradhan* (village head) and found out that his own child was in a private school. On asking him how the village school would improve when his own child was not there, he memorably said to me: *'Jab tak main yeh school ko sudhaar sakoon, tab tak mere bachche ka bhavishya bigad jaayega'* (By the time I can improve this school, my child's future will have been spoilt). His words still resonate many years later.

59 For instance, many elites and middle classes in India are probably unaware of the facts in Section 1.1 of this chapter that highlight how much of India's public spending is skewed towards elites.

60 Of course, most Indians are very busy and may not have time for civic engagement. However, increased civic participation may be especially worthwhile for those who have retired from full-time jobs, have children who are settled, and still have a good ten to fifteen years (say between ages sixty and seventy-five) when they have the knowledge, experience, time, and energy to be productively engaged in local government, and be able to augment and support its capacity with their skills. Such activity can also contribute to improved mental health and happiness since many studies show that these are boosted by increasing social connections and feeling like one is able to make a positive impact on others.

61 This quote is attributed to feminist Gloria Steinem, but it has also been used by many other leaders of social reform movements.

62 The idea of 'isomorphism' has been one of the most influential ideas in organizational sociology in the last fifty years, and posits that organizations often copy the practices of more successful organizations to improve their *appearance* of legitimacy even though the practices may not actually be effective. See DiMaggio and Powell (1983) for the original reference in the context of organizations, and Andrews, Pritchett, and Woolcock (2017) for an adaptation to the context of development policy and practice.

63 Placed in the context of the global discourse on state capacity, both points above are consistent with the problem-driven iterative adaptation (PDIA) framework proposed in Andrews, Pritchett, and Woolcock (2017). The goal of the book is to present a set of ideas to improve governance and state capacity in India that reflect contextualized understanding and evidence. These are, however, only a starting point, and will require ongoing iteration to improve their performance in practice.

64 See www.indiastack.org.

65 See Aiyar (2017) for a well-researched account of the Aadhaar project and its evolution.

66 See Muralidharan, Niehaus, and Sukhtankar (2022).

67 See State of Aadhaar Report 2018 and 2019. The 2019 report finds that 92 per cent of survey respondents (in a nationwide sample of over 1,65,000 households) report being satisfied with Aadhaar, and that 80 per cent feel that it has made PDS, NREGS, and social pensions more reliable.

68 See Nye (2004) for the classic reference on the idea of soft power and its contrasts with hard power.

69 Specifically, hard power enables a country to achieve national goals by threatening adverse consequences, with actions ranging from economic sanctions, trade embargoes, and even war.

70 While India has always harboured ambitions of being respected as a global leader, these ambitions have been limited by our low GDP per capita, and correspondingly limited economic and military power. See Sagar (2022) for an excellent discussion of

the various strands of thought regarding Indian foreign policy and India's role in the world.

71 See Kotasthane, Kanisetti, and Pai (2020), and Tellis, Debroy, and Mohan (2022) for recent collections of essays on how India can strengthen its place in the global order.

72 See Krishna (2018). More recently, Mody (2023) has made a similar point.

73 See Singh, Romero, and Muralidharan (2022).

74 The meeting was organized by the World Bank and included ministers of education from several countries. My co-authors and I were invited to present our paper evaluating ITK at this meeting by the World Bank global director for education.

75 See Forbes (2022) for an illustrative discussion of why Indian leadership is important for the world.

76 This is a point that is being realized and acted upon even by countries like Germany and Japan that renounced seeking hard power after World War II but now see no option but to bolster their hard power in response to the increased risk of wars of aggression as seen in the recent Russia-Ukraine War.

77 While India ranks in the top five countries in the world by total GDP, this mainly reflects our large population. The stark reality is that our GDP per capita is only 5 to 10 per cent that of other Quad countries like the US, Japan or Australia. The political pressure and moral imperative of catering to the basic needs of a large low-income population in turn limits our ability to accumulate hard power.

78 Numerically, if India grows at 8 per cent on a base of $100, it adds $8 to GDP; whereas if China grows at 4 per cent on a base of $400, it adds $16 to GDP. So, China's total GDP will increase by double that of India even if India grows twice as fast.

79 Military budgets are driven by total tax revenue, which reflects total GDP. So, the annual increase in China's military budget will be higher even if India grows faster because China adds more to total GDP each year. Of course, military salaries are

also higher in China and so they also have higher costs. But the cost of military hardware is the same since these are traded on global markets, implying a greater annual increase in China's military hardware budget, assuming staff costs increase proportionately.

80 Concrete ways of doing so include seeking both technology and financing for innovations that can benefit India and the world. Beyond multilateral development agencies, such financing can also be obtained from private capital and global philanthropy.

81 Clear (2018), p. 27.

References

Accenture-NSDC. (2013). *Overcoming India's Skills Challenge: Transforming India into a High Performance Nation.* Accenture-National Skill Development Corporation.

Accountability Initiative (2012). PAISA Report. Centre for Policy Research, New Delhi.

Acemoglu, Daron; Johnson, Simon; and Robinson, James A. (2001). The Colonial Origins of Comparative Development: An Empirical Investigation. *American Economic Review, 91*(5), 1369–401.

Acemoglu, Daron; Johnson, Simon; and Robinson, James A. (2002). Reversal of Fortune: Geography and Institutions in the Making of the Modern World Income Distribution. *The Quarterly Journal of Economics, 117*(4), 1231–94.

Acemoglu, Daron; Johnson, Simon; and Robinson, James A. (2005). Institutions as a Fundamental Cause of Long-Run Growth. In Phillipe Aghion and Steven Durlauf (Eds.), *Handbook of Economic Growth;* (Vol. 1, 6) North-Holland.

Acemoglu, Daron; Naidu, Suresh; Restrepo, Pascual; and Robinson, James A. (2019). Democracy Does Cause Growth. *Journal of Political Economy, 127*(1).

Acemoglu, Daron; and Robinson, James A. (2012). *Why Nations Fail: The Origins of Power, Prosperity, and Poverty;* Crown Business. New York.

Adamopoulos, Tasso; and Restuccia, Diego. (2020). Land Reform and Productivity: A Quantitative Analysis with Micro Data. *American Economic Journal: Macroeconomics, 12*(3), 1–39.

Adhvaryu, Achyuta; Gade, Smit; Gauthier, Jean Francois; Nyshadham, Anant; and Srinivas, Sandhya. (2023). Workers, Managers, and Productivity: How Investments in Workers Can Fuel India's Productivity Growth. *India Policy Forum NCAER.*

Adhvaryu, Achyuta; Kala, Namrata; and Nyshadham, Anant. (2022). Management and Shocks to Worker Productivity. *Journal of Political Economy, 130*(1), 1–47.

Afridi, Farzana; Barooah, Bidisha; and Somanathan, Rohini. (2020). Improving Learning Outcomes through Information Provision: Experimental Evidence from Indian Villages. *Journal of Development Economics, 146*(C).

Agarwal, Ananay; Agrawal, Neelesh; Bhogale, Saloni; Hangal, Sudheendra; Jensenius, Francesca Refsum; Kumar, Mohit, . . . Verniers, Gilles. (2021). TCPD Indian Elections Data v2.0. In: Trivedi Centre for Political Data, Ashoka University.

Agarwal, Aradhna. (2012). *The Social and Economic Impact of SEZs in India;* Oxford University Press. New Delhi.

Aggarwal, Shilpa. (2018). Do Rural Roads Create Pathways out of Poverty? Evidence from India. *Journal of Development Economics, 133,* 375–95.

Agrawal, Sarthak. (2022, 05.09.2022). Illam Thedi Kalvi: A Booster Shot for Post-Covid Education. *Ideas For India.*

Ahluwalia, Montek Singh. (2020). *Backstage: The Story behind India's High Growth Years;* Rupa Publications India. New Delhi.

Ahluwalia, Montek Singh; and Rajagopalan, Shruti (2023) *Mapping the Journey of Policy Reform with a Policy Reformer/Interviewer: Shruti Rajagopalan.* Mercatus.

Ahuja, Amit. (2019). *Mobilizing the Marginalized: Ethnic Parties without Ethnic Movement;* Oxford University Press, USA. New York.

Ahuja, Amit; and Kapur, Devesh. (2023). *Internal Security in India: Violence, Order, and the State;* Oxford University Press. New York.

Ahuja, Amit; and Mehta, Aashish. (2023). How Does Growth Affect Everyday Corruption? *Heidelberg Papers in South Asian and Comparative Politics* (81).

Aiyar, Shankkar. (2017). *Aadhaar: A Biometric History of India's 12-Digit Revolution;* Westland.

Aiyar, Shankkar. (2020). *The Gated Republic: India's Public Policy Failures and Private Solutions;* HarperCollins. Noida.

Aiyar, Swaminathan. (2022a, 09.07.2022). The $20b Business with 20 lakh Indians People Don't Know of. *Times of India.*

Aiyar, Swaminathan. (2022b, 04.09.2022). Medha Patkar Was Wrong on Narmada Project. *Times of India.*

Aiyar, Swaminathan. (2022c, 11.09.2022). The Real Story of How Narmada Dam Oustees Became Crorepatis. *Times of India.*

Aiyar, Yamini; and Kapur, Avani. (2019). The Centralization vs Decentralization Tug of War and the Emerging Narrative of Fiscal Federalism for Social Policy in India. *Journal of Regional and Federal Studies, 29*(2), 187–217.

Aiyar, Yamini; and Bhattacharya, Shrayana. (2016). The Post Office Paradox: A Case Study of the Block Level Education Bureaucracy. *Economic and Political Weekly, LI*(11), 61–69.

Alagh, Yoginder K. (1961). Case for an Agricultural Income Tax. *Economic and Political Weekly, 13*(39).

Alcazar, Lorena; Rogers, Halsey; Chaudhary, Nazmul; Hammer, Jeffrey; Kremer, Michael; and Muralidharan, Karthik. (2006). Why Are Teachers Absent? Probing Service Delivery in Peruvian Primary Schools. *International Journal of Educational Research, 45*(3), 117–36.

Alesina, Alberto; and Ferrara, Eliana La. (2005). Ethnic Diversity and Economic Performance. *Journal of Economic Literature, 43*(3), 762–800.

Alesina, Alberto; and Glaeser, Edward. (2004). *Fighting Poverty in the US and Europe: A World of Difference;* Oxford University Press.

Alesina, Alberto; and Spolaore, Enrico. (1997). On the Number and Size of Nations. *The Quarterly Journal of Economics 112*(4), 1027–56.

Alesina, Alberto; and Spolaore, Enrico. (2003). *The Size of Nations;* MIT Press.

Alexander, Sneha; and Padmanabhan, Vishnu. (2019a, 04.03.2019). How NDA 2 and UPA 2 compare on MNREGS performance. *Mint.*

Alexander, Sneha; and Padmanabhan, Vishnu. (2019b, 28.07.2019). The Roots of India's Deepening Rural Water Crisis. *Mint.*

Alexander, Ashok. (2023). *How the Light Gets In: A Journey through the Struggles and Hopes of India's Poorest Mothers;* Penguin.

Allen, Marshall. (2018, 01.02.2018). Unnecessary Medical Care: More Common Than You Might Imagine. *National Public Radio.*

Almond, Douglas; and Currie, Janet. (2011). Human Capital Development before Age Five. In David Card and Orley Ashenfelter (Eds.), *Handbook of Labour Economics* (Vol. 4B, 15) North-Holland.

Alon, Titon. (2019). Earning More by Doing Less: Human Capital Specialization and the College Wage Premium. *UC, San Diego.*

Alsan, Marcella; Garrick, Owen; and Graziani, Grant. (2019). Does Diversity Matter for Health? Experimental Evidence from Oakland. *American Economic Review 109*(12), 4071–111.

Alvarez-Cuadrao, Francisco; and Poschke, Markus. (2011). Structural Change Out of Agriculture: Labor Push Versus Labor Pull. *American Economic Journal: Macroeconomics, 3*(3), 127–58.

Amarnath, H.K.; and Singh, Alka. (2019). Impact of Changes in Fiscal Federalism and Fourteenth Finance Commission Recommendations: Scenarios on States Autonomy and Social Sector Priorities. *NIPFP Working Paper Series*(257).

Ambedkar, Bhim Rao. (1936). *Annihilation of Caste.*

Anderson, Siwan; Francois, Patrick; Kotwal, Ashok; and Kulkarni, Ashwini. (2015). 'One Kind of Democracy' Implementing MGNREGS. *Economic and Political Weekly, 26, 27,* 44–48.

Andrabi, Tahir; Das, Jishnu; and Khwaja, Asim Ijaz. (2017). Report Cards: The Impact of Providing School and Child Test Scores on Educational Markets. *American Economic Review 107*(6), 1535–63.

Andrews, Matt; Pritchett, Lant; and Woolcock, Michael (2017). *Building State Capability: Evidence, Analysis, Action;* Oxford University Press. New York.

Ang, Yuen Yuen. (2019, 04.10.2019). China's Corrupt Meritocracy. *Project Syndicate.*

Ang, Yuen Yuen (2016). *How China Escaped the Poverty Trap;* Cornell University Press. Ithaca.

Arrow, Kenneth. (1963). Uncertainty and the Welfare Economics of Medical Care. *American Economic Review, 53*(5), 941–73.

ASER. (2018). *Annual Status of Education Report 2018.* Pratham.

ASER. (2023). *Annual Status of Education Report 2023.* Pratham.

Ash, Elliot; Asher, Sam; Bhowmick, Aditi; Bhupatiraju, Sandeep; Chen, Daniel; Devi, Tanaya, . . . Siddiqi, Bilal. (2021). In-Group Bias in the Indian Judiciary: Evidence from 5 million Criminal Cases.

Asher, Sam; Nagpal, Karan; and Novosad, Paul. (2018). The Cost of Distance: Geography and Governance in Rural India. *World Bank Working Paper Series.*

Asher, Sam; and Novosad, Paul. (2015). The Impacts of Local Control over Political Institutions: Evidence from State Splitting in India.

Athar, Shoaib; White, Roland; and Goyal, Harsh. (2022). *Financing India's Urban Infrastructure Needs.* World Bank Group.

Austin, Granville. (1999). *The Indian Constitution: Cornerstone of a Nation;* Oxford University Press.

Avdiu, Besart; Bagavathinathan, Karan Singh; Chaurey, Ritam; and Nayyar, Gaurav. (2022). India's Services Sector Growth: The Impact of Services Trade on Non-Tradable Services. *NCAER Working Paper Series*(142).

Ayres, Ian; and Schwartz, Alan. (2014). The No-Reading Problem in Consumer Contract Law. *Stanford Law Review, 66*(3), 545–609.

Azam, Mehtabul; and Kingdon, Geeta Gandhi. (2015). Assessing Teacher Quality in India. *Journal of Development Economics,* 117(C), 74–83.

Baker, George.; and Hubbard, Thomas. (2004). Contractibility and Asset Ownership: On-Board Computers and Governance in U.S. Trucking. *The Quarterly Journal of Economics, 119*(4), 1443–79.

Balabanova, Dina; Mills, Anne; Conteh, Lesong; Akkazieva, Baktygul; Banteyerga, Hailom; Dash, Umakant, . . . Mckee, Martin. (2013). Good Health at Low Cost 25 years on: lessons for the future of health systems strengthening. *Lancet, 381,* 2118–33.

Balasubramaniam, Ramaswami (2015). *I, the Citizen: Unraveling the Power of Citizen Engagement;* Grassroots Research and Advocacy Movement (GRAAM).

Bandiera, Oriana; Prat, Andrea; Best, Michael Carlos; and Valleti, Tommasso. (2021). The Allocation of Authority in Organizations: a Field Experiment with Bureaucrats. *The Quarterly Journal of Economics, 136*(4), 2195–242.

Bandiera, Oriana; Prat, Andrea; and Valleti, Tommasso. (2009). Active and Passive Waste in Government Spending: Evidence from a Policy Experiment. *American Economic Review, 99*(4), 1278–308.

Banerjee, Abhijit V. (1997). A Theory of Misgovernance. *The Quarterly Journal of Economics 112*(4), 1289–332.

Banerjee, Abhijit V. (2019). A Note on Healthcare. In Abhijit V. Banerjee, Raghuram G. Rajan, Gita Gopinath, and Mihir S. Sharma (Eds.), *What the Economy Needs Now;* (1) Juggernaut Books. New Delhi.

Banerjee, Abhijit V.; Chattopadhyay, Raghabendra; Duflo, Esther; Keniston, Daniel; and Singh, Nina. (2021). Improving Police Performance in Rajasthan, India: Experimental Evidence on Incentives, Managerial Autonomy, and Training. *American Economic Journal: Economic Policy, 13*(1), 36–66.

Banerjee, Abhijit V.; Cole, Shawn; Duflo, Esther; and Linden, Leigh. (2007). Remedying Education: Evidence from Two Randomized Experiments in India. *The Quarterly Journal of Economics, 122*(3), 1235–64.

Banerjee, Abhijit V.; Deaton, Angus; and Duflo, Esther. (2004). Wealth, Health, and Health Services in Rural Rajasthan. *American Economic Review, 94*(2), 326–30.

Banerjee, Abhijit V.; and Duflo, Esther. (2005). Growth Theory Through the Lens of Development Economics. In Phillipe

Aghion and Steven Durlauf (Eds.), *Handbook of Economic Growth*; (Vol. 1A, 7) North-Holland.

Banerjee, Abhijit V.; and Duflo, Esther. (2011). *Poor Economics: A Radical Rethinking of the Way to Fight Global Poverty*; PublicAffairs. New York.

Banerjee, Abhijit V.; and Duflo, Esther. (2014). Do Firms Want to Borrow More? Testing Credit Constraints Using a Directed Lending Program. *The Review of Economic Studies 81*(2), 572–607.

Banerjee, Abhijit V.; Gertler, Paul; and Ghatak, Maitreesh. (2002). Empowerment and Efficiency: Tenancy Reform in West Bengal. *Journal of Political Economy, 110*(2), 239–80.

Banerjee, Abhijit V.; and Iyer, Lakshmi. (2005). History, Institutions, and Economic Performance: The Legacy of Colonial Land Tenure Systems in India. *American Economic Review 95*(4), 1190–213.

Banerjee, Abhijit V.; Niehaus, Paul; and Suri, Tavneet. (2019). Universal Basic Income in a Developing World. *Annual Review of Economics, 11*, 959–83.

Bang, Abhay; Bang, Rani; Baitule, Sanjay; Reddy, Hanimi; and Deshmukh, Mahesh. (1999). Effect of Home-Based Neonatal Care and Management of Sepsis on Neonatal Mortality: Field Trial in Rural India. *Lancet, 354*(9194), 1955–61.

Bansal, Samarth. (2021). #1: Inside a fictional education revolution. https://medium.com/the-interval/1-inside-a-fictional-education-revolution-7ee500d175dc.

Bardhan, Pranab K. (1984). *The Political Economy of Development in India*; Basil Blackwell, Oxford University Press. New Delhi.

Bardhan, Pranab K. (2004). *Scarcity, Conflicts, and Cooperation: Essays in the Political and Institutional Economics of Development*; MIT Press.

Bardhan, Pranab K. (2011). Challenges for a Minimum Social Democracy in India. *Economic and Political Weekly, 46*(10), 39–43.

Barnwal, Prabhat. (2023). Curbing Leakage in Public Programs: Evidence from India's Direct Benefit Transfer Policy. Michigan State University.

Barnwal, Prabhat; and Ryan, Nicholas. (2023). Is Electrification in India Fiscally Sustainable? *India Policy Forum. NCAER.*

Bartelsman, Eric; Haltiwanger, John; and Scarepetta, Stefano (2013). Cross-Country Differences in Productivity: The Role of Allocation and Selection. *American Economic Review, 103*(1), 305–34.

Baru, Sanjaya (2016). *1991: How P.V. Narasimha Rao Made History;* Aleph Book Company. New Delhi.

Basole, Amit; Shrivastava, Anand; Narayanan, Rajendran; and Swamy, Rakshita. (2020, 24.11.2020). The Time Is Right for an Urban Employment Guarantee Programme. *Ideas for India.*

Basri, Chatib M.; Felix, Mayara; Hanna, Rema; and Olken, Benjamin A. (2021). Tax Administration versus Tax Rates: Evidence from Corporate Taxation in Indonesia. *American Economic Review, 111*(12), 3827–71.

Bassiri, Dina. (2015). *Statistical Properties of School Value-Added Scores Based on Assessments of College Readiness.* ACT.

Basu, Kaushik. (2011). India's Foodgrains Policy: An Economic Theory Perspective. *Economic and Political Weekly, 46*(5), 37–45.

Basu, Kaushik. (2018). *The Republic of Beliefs: A New Approach to Law and Economics;* Princeton University Press. Princeton.

Basu, Susanto; and Bundick, Brent. (2017). Uncertainty Shocks in a Model of Effective Demand. *Econometrica, 85*(3), 937–58.

Bau, Natalie. (2022). Estimating an Equilibrium Model of Horizontal Competition in Education. *Journal of Political Economy, 130*(7), 1717–64.

Bau, Natalie; and Das, Jishnu. (2020). Teacher Value-Added in a Low-Income Country. *American Economic Journal: Economic Policy, 12*(1), 62–96.

Beaman, Lori; Chattopadhyay, Raghabendra; Duflo, Esther; Pande, Rohini; and Topalova, Petia. (2009). Powerful Woman: Does exposure reduce bias? *The Quarterly Journal of Economics, 124*(4), 1497–540.

Benartzi, Shlomo; and Thaler, Richard A. (2001). Naive Diversification Strategies in Defined Contribution Saving Plans. *American Economic Review, 91*(1), 79–98.

Berman, Evan; Bowman, James; West, Johnathan; and Van Wart, Montgomery. (2016). *Human Resource Management in Public Service: Paradoxes, Processes and Problems;* SAGE Publications.

Berry, James; Kannan, Harini; Mukherji, Shobini; and Shotland, Marc. (2020). Failure of Frequent Assessment: An Evaluation of India's Continuous and Comprehensive Evaluation Program. *Journal of Development Economics, 143.*

Besley, Timothy; and Persson, Torsten. (2009). The Origins of State Capacity: Property Rights, Taxation, and Politics. *American Economic Review, 99*(4), 1218–44.

Beteille, Tara. (2009). Absenteeism, Transfers and Patronage: The Political Economy of Teacher Labor Markets in India. *Stanford University.*

Beteille, Tara; and Ramachandran, Vimala. (2016). Contract Teachers in India. *Economic and Political Weekly, 51*(25), 40–47.

Beuermann, Diether; Cristia, Julian; Cueto, Santiago; Malamud, Ofer; and Cruz-Aguayo, Yyannu. (2015). One Laptop per Child at Home: Short-Term Impacts from a Randomized Experiment in Peru. *American Economic Journal: Applied Economics, 7*(2), 53–80.

Bhadra, Subhashish. (2023). *Caged Tiger: How Too Much Government Is Holding Indians Back;* Bloomsbury Publishing. New Delhi.

Bhagwati, Jagdish. (1988). *Protectionism;* MIT Press.

Bhagwati, Jagdish; and Desai, Padma. (1970). *Planning for Industrialization, Industrialization and Trade Policies since 1951;* Oxford University Press. London.

Bhagwati, Jagdish; and Panagariya, Arvind. (2012). *India's Tryst with Destiny: Debunking Myths that Undermine Progress and Addressing New Challenges;* HarperCollins Publishers. Noida.

Bhagwati, Jagdish; and Panagariya, Arvind. (2014). *Why Growth Matters: How Economic Growth in India Reduced Poverty and the Lessons for Other Developing Countries;* PublicAffairs.

Bhalotra, Sonia; and Clot-Figureas, Irma. (2014). Health and the Political Agency of Women. *American Economic Journal: Economic Policy, 6*(2), 164–97.

Bharadwaj, Prashanth; Lakdawala, Leah K.; and Li, Nicholas (2019). Perverse Consequences of Well Intentioned Regulation: Evidence from India's Child Labor Ban. *Journal of the European Economic Association, 18*(3), 1158–195.

Bhargava, Anjuli. (2022, 20.05.2023). India's Govt Jobs: Telangana's Experiment Can Make Bureaucracy More Accountable. *The Quint.*

Bhatia, Gautam. (2019). *The Transformative Constitution: A Radical Biography in Nine Acts*; HarperCollins Publishers India.

Bhatia, Mrigesh; and Singh, D.P. (2021). Health Sector Allocation in India's Budget (2021–2022): A Trick or Treat? *The International Journal of Community and Social Development, 3*(2), 177–80.

Bhattacharya, Anindita. (2022). 'The Day I Die Is The Day I Will Find My Peace': Narratives of Family, Marriage, and Violence Among Women Living With Serious Mental Illness in India. *Violence Against Women, 28*(3-4), 966–990.

Bhattacharya, Pramit. (2019, 07.05.2019). How India's Statistical System was Crippled. *Mint.*

Bhattacharya, Pramit. (2023). *India's Statistical System: Past, Present, Future.* Carnegie Endowment for International Peace.

Bhattacharya, Pramit; and Kundu, Tadit. (2018, 24.04.2018). 99% Cases of Sexual Assaults go Unreported, Govt Data Shows. *Mint.*

Bhattacharya, Shrayana (2021). *Desperately Seeking Shah Rukh: India's Lonely Young Women and the Search for Intimacy and Independence*; HarperCollins.

Bhonsle, Anubha. (2023). The Persistence of AFSPA. In Devesh Kapur and Amit Ahuja (Eds.), *Internal Security in India: Violence, Order, and the State*; (3) Oxford University Press. New York.

Blair, Graeme; Weinstein, Jeremy M.; Christia, Fotini; Arias, Eric; Badran, Emile; Blaire, Robert A., . . . Wilke, Anna M. (2021). Community policing does not build citizen trust in police or reduce crime in the Global South. *Science, 374*(6571).

Blinder, Alan. (1988). *Hard Heads, Soft Hearts: Tough-minded Economics For A Just Society*; Basic Books.

Bloom, David E.; Kuhn, Michael; and Prettner, Klaus. (2018). Health and Economic Growth. *IZA Discussion Paper Series* (11939).

Bloom, Nicholas. (2009). Impact of Uncertainty Shocks *Econometrica*, *77*(3), 623–85.

Bloom, Nicholas; Eifert, Benn; Mahajan, Aprajit; Mckenzie, David; and Roberts, John. (2013). Does Management Matter: Evidence from India. *The Quarterly Journal of Economics, 128*(1), 1–51.

Bloom, Nicholas; Genakos, Christos; Sadun, Rafaella; and Reenen, John Van. (2012). Management Practices Across Firms and Countries. *Academy of Management Perspectives, 26*(1).

Bloom, Nicholas; Lemos, Renata; Sadun, Raffella; and Van Reenen, John. (2015). Does Management Matter in Schools? *Economic Journal, 125*(584), 647–74.

Bloom, Nicholas; and Van Reenen, John. (2007). Measuring and Explaining Management Practices across Firms and Countries. *The Quarterly Journal of Economics, 122*(4), 1351–408.

Bloom, Nicholas; and Van Reenen, John. (2009). Human Resource Management and Productivity. *Handbook of Labour Economics, 4B*, 1697–767.

Bloom, Nicholas; and Van Reenen, John. (2010). Why Do Management Practices Differ across Firms and Countries? Journal of Economic Perspectives. *Journal of Economic Perspectives 24*(1), 203–24.

Bloomberg Quint (2019) (06.02.2019). India Has 20 Judges For Every 10 Lakh People: Law Ministry. *Bloomberg Quint.*

Bordoloi, Mridusmrita; Pandey, Sharad; Irava, Vastav; and Junnarkar, Ruchi. (2020). *State Education Finances: A Deep-Dive into School Education Finances in Eight States.* Accountability Initiative.

Bordoloi, Mridusmrita; and Shukla, Ritviz. (2019). *School Consolidation in Rajasthan: Implementation and Short Term Effects.* Accountability Initiative.

Borker, Girija. (2021). Safety First: Perceived Risk of Street Harassment and Educational Choices of Women. *World Bank Working Paper Series*(9731).

Boserup, Ester. (1993). *The Conditions of Agricultural Growth: The Economics of Agrarian Change Under Population Pressure;* Routledge.

Bothra, Arun. (2019, 21.02.2019). Why is Our Conviction Rate so Low? *New Indian Express.*

BPRD. (2019). *Data on Police Organizations (as January 1, 2019).* Bureau of Police Research and Development.

BPRD. (2020). *Data on Police Organizations (as of January 1, 2020).* Bureau of Police Research and Development.

Braun, Martin. (2021, 04.11.2021). Cannabis Taxes May Generate $12 Billion for U.S. States by 2030, According to Barclays Strategists. *Fortune.*

Bresnahan, Timothy F.; and Gordon, Robert J. (1997). *The Economics of New Goods;* University of Chicago Press. Chicago.

Breza, Emily; and Kinnan, Cynthia. (2021). Measuring the Equilibrium Impacts of Credit: Evidence from the Indian Microfinance Crisis. *The Quarterly Journal of Economics, 136*(3), 1447–497.

Brooks, Leah. (2008). Volunteering to Be Taxed: Business Improvement Districts and the Extra-Governmental Provision of Public Safety. *Journal of Public Economics, 92*(1), 388–406.

Bryan, Gharad; Chowdhury, Shyamlal.; and Mobarak, Ahmed Mushfiq. (2014). Underinvestment in a Profitable Technology: The Case of Seasonal Migration in Bangladesh. *Econometrica, 82*(5), 1671–748.

Bureau, The Hindu. (2023, 08.05.2023). Govt. Warns Striking Junior Panchayat Secretaries of Dismissal. *The Hindu.*

Burns, John; and Zhiren, Zhou. (2010). Performance Management in the Government of the People's Republic of China: Accountability and Control in the Implementation of Public Policy. *OECD Journal on Budgeting, 10*(2), 1–28.

Burnside, Craig; and Dollar, David (2000). Aid, Policies, and Growth. *The American Economic Review, 90*(4), 847–68.

Bussell, Jennifer (2018). Whose Money, Whose Influence? Multilevel Politics and Campaign Finance in India. In Devesh Kapur and Milan Vaishnav (Eds.), *Costs of Democracy: Political Finance in India;* Oxford University Press.

CAG. (2018). *Report on Accelerated India Benefits Program.*

Cai, Weiyi; Byrd, Aaron; Buckley, Chris; and Robles, Pablo. (2023, 02.09.2023). How Xi Returned China to One-Man Rule. *New York Times*.

Calvi, Rosella; and Keskar, Ajinkya. (2023). Til Dowry Do Us Part: Bargaining and Violence in Indian Families. *Review of Economics and Statistics*.

Cameron, Lisa; Seager, Jennifer; and Shah, Manisha. (2021). Crimes Against Morality: Unintended Consequences of Criminalizing Sex Work. *The Quarterly Journal of Economics, 136*(1), 427–69.

Campbell, John.Y; Ramadorai, Tarun; and Ranish, Benjamin. (2014). Getting Better or Feeling Better? How Equity Investors Respond to Investment Experiences. *NBER Working Paper Series* (20000).

Carranza, Eliana; Garlick, Robert; Orkin, Kate; and Rankin, Neil. (2023). Job Search and Hiring with Limited Information about Workseekers' Skills. *American Economic Review, 112*(11), 3547–583.

Cellini, Stephanie Riegg; Ferreira, Fernando; and Rothstein, Jesse. (2010). The Value of School Facility Investments: Evidence from a Dynamic Regression Discontinuity Design. *The Quarterly Journal of Economics, 125*(1).

Chakraborty, Lekha. (2019). Indian Fiscal Federalism at the Crossroads: Some Reflections. *NIPFP Working Paper Series*(260).

Chakraborty, Tanika; and Jayaraman, Rajshri. (2019). School feeding and learning achievement: Evidence from India's midday meal program. *Journal of Development Economics, 139*, 249–65.

Chakravorty, Sanjoy; Kapur, Devesh; and Singh, Nirvikar. (2017). *The Other One Percent: Indians in America;* Oxford University Press, USA. New York.

Chandra, Aparna; Kalantry, Sital; and Hubbard, William H.J. (2023). *Court on Trial: A Data-Driven Account of the Supreme Court of India;* Penguin Random House India.

Chandrasekhar C.P.; and Ghosh, Jayati. (2019, 29.07.2019). The Withering Trend of Public Employment in India. *Hindu BusinessLine*.

Chandrasekharan, N.; and Purushotthaman, Roopa. (2019). *Bridgital Nation: Solving Technology's People Problem;* Penguin Allen Lane.

Chang, Alfredo lee; Dym, Andrew. A.; Venegas-Borsellino, Carla; Bangar, Maneesha; Kazzi, Massoud; Lisenenkov, Dmitry, . . . Eisen, Lewis Ari. (2017). Comparison between Simulation-based Training and Lecture-based Education in Teaching Situation Awareness. A Randomized Controlled Study. *Annals of the American Thoracic Society, 14*(4).

Chattopadhyay, Raghabendra; and Duflo, Esther. (2004). Women as Policy Makers: Evidence from a Randomized Policy Experiment in India. *Econometrica, 72*(5), 1409–43.

Chauchard, Simon. (2018). What Costs so Much in Indian Elections? Intuitions from Recent Electoral Campaigns in Mumbai. In Devesh Kapur and Milan Vaishnav (Eds.), *Costs of Democracy: Political Finance in India;* Oxford University Press.

Chaudhury, Nazmul; Hammer, Jeffrey; Kremer, Michael; Muralidharan, Karthik; and Rogers, F. Halsey. (2006). Missing in Action: Teacher and Health Worker Absence in Developing Countries. [2006]. *Journal of Economic Perspectives, 20*(1), 91–116.

Chawla, Haresh. (2016, 30.08.2016). How India's digital economy can rediscover its mojo. *Founding Fuel.*

Chemin, Matthieu. (2018). Judicial Efficiency and Firm Productivity: Evidence from a World Database of Judicial Reforms. *Review of Economics and Statistics, 102*(1), 49–64.

Chen, Keith; and Shapiro, Jesse. (2007). Do Harsher Prison Conditions Reduce Recidivism? A Discontinuity-based Approach. *American Law and Economics Review, 9*(1), 1–29.

Chetty, Raj; Friedman, John. N; Hilger, Nathaniel; Saez, Emmanual; Schanzenbach, Diane Whitmore; and Yagan, Danny (2011). How Does Your Kindergarten Classroom Affect Your Earnings? Evidence from Project Star. *The Quarterly Journal of Economics, 126*(4), 1593–660.

Chetty, Raj; Friedman, John N; and Rockoff, Jonah E. (2014a). Measuring the Impact of Teachers I: Evaluating Bias in Teacher

Value-Added Estimates. *American Economic Review, 104*(9), 2593–632.

Chetty, Raj; Friedman, John N.; and Rockoff, Jonah E. (2014b). Measuring the Impact of Teachers II: Teacher Value-Added and Student Outcomes in Adulthood. *American Economic Review, 104*(9), 2633–79.

Chhibber, Ajay; and Soz, Salman Anees. (2022). *Unshackling India: Hard Truths and Clear Choices for Economic Revival.* HarperCollins.

Chhibber, Pradeep K. (2001). *Democracy without Associations: Transformation of the Party System and Social Cleavages in India (Interests, Identities, And Institutions In Comparative Politics).* University of Michigan Press.

Chokkakula, Srinivas; Kapur, Avani; and Singh, Arkaja. (2021). *Water and Federalism: Working with States for Water Security.* Accountability Initiative.

Choudhary, Mita; and Dubey, Jay dev. (2020). Equity in Intra-State Distribution of Public Spending on Health: The Case of Bihar and Tamil Nadu. NIPFP working paper series (315).

Choudhary, Mita; and Mohanty, Ranjan Kumar. (2018). Utilisation, Fund Flows and Public Financial Management under the National Health Mission. NIPFP Working Paper Series (227).

Citizens United v. FEC, No. 08-205 (Supreme Court of the United States 2010).

Clark, Gregory (2007). *A Farewell to Alms: A Brief Economic History of the World;* Princeton University Press. Princeton.

Clear, James. (2018). *Atomic Habits;* Random House Business Books.

Clot-Figureas, Irma. (2012). Are Female Leaders Good for Education? Evidence from India. *American Economic Journal: Applied Economics 4*(1), 212–44.

Cook, Justin C.; and Shah, Manisha. (2022). Aggregate Effects from Public Works: Evidence from India. *Review of Economics and Statistics, 104*(4), 797–806.

Cox, Gary W. (1997). *Making Votes Count;* Cambridge University Press. Cambridge, MA.

Cristia, Julian; Ibarraran, Pablo; Cueto, Santiago; Santiago, Ana; and Severin, Eugenio. (2017). Technology and Child Development: Evidence from the One Laptop per Child Program. *American Economic Journal: Applied Economics, 9*(3), 295–320.

Cuberes, David; and Jerzmanowski, Michal. (2009). Democracy, Diversification and Growth Reversals. *The Economic Journal, 119*(540), 1270–302.

Cullen, Julie Berry; Turner, Nicolas; and Washington, Ebonya. (2021). Political Alignment, Attitudes toward Government, and Tax Evasion. *American Economic Journal: Economic Policy, 13*(3), 135–66.

Currie, Janet; and Vogl, Tom. (2013). Early-Life Health and Adult Circumstance in Developing Countries. *Annual Review of Economics, 5*, 1–36.

DAKSH. (2016). *Time and Motion Study of Four District and Sessions Court in Bangalore, Karnataka.*

Dalberg. (2018). *State of Aadhar Report 2018.*

Dalberg. (2019). *State of Aadhar Report 2019.*

Daly, John (2010). *Human Resource Management in the Public Sector: Policies and Practices;* Routledge.

Daniyal, Shoaib. (2022, 08.08.2022). Why do Such a Small Number of Indians Pay Income Tax. *Scroll.*

Dar, Aaditya; and Sahay, Abhilasha (2018). Designing Policy in Weak States: Unintended Consequences of Alcohol Prohibition in Bihar. *Indian School of Business.*

Das, Gurcharan. (2021, 10.10.2021). AI: Branding and Billion Dollars—Tatas Will Have to Infuse Substantial Equity and Run Two Brands to Optimise the Air India Acquisition. *Times of India.*

Das, Jishnu; Chowdhury, Abhijit; Hussam, Reshmaan; and Banerjee, Abhijit V. (2016). The Impact of Training Informal Health Care Providers in India: A Randomized Controlled Trial. *Science, 7*(354).

Das, Jishnu; Daniels, Benjamin; Ashok, Monisha; Shim, Eun Young; and Muralidharan, Karthik. (2022). Two Indias: The Structure of Primary Health Care Markets in Rural Indian Villages with Implications for Policy. *Social Science and Medicine, 301.*

Das, Jishnu; Dercon, Stefan; Habyarimana, James; Krishnan, Pramila; Muralidharan, Karthik; and Sundararaman, Venkatesh. (2013). School Inputs, Household Substitution, and Test Scores. *American Economic Journal: Applied Economics,* 5(2), 29–57.

Das, Jishnu; and Hammer, Jeffrey. (2005). Which doctor? Combining vignettes and item response to measure clinical competence. *Journal of Development Economics,* 78(2), 348–83.

Das, Jishnu; and Hammer, Jeffrey. (2007). Money for Nothing: The Dire Straits of Medical Practice in Delhi, India. *Journal of Development Economics,* 83(1), 1–36.

Das, Jishnu; and Hammer, Jeffrey. (2014). Quality of Primary Care in Low-Income Countries: Facts and Economics. *Annual Review of Economics,* 6(1), 525–53.

Das, Jishnu; Hammer, Jeffrey; and Leonard, Kenneth. (2008). The Quality of Medical Care in Low Income Countries. *Journal of Economic Perspectives,* 22(2), 93–114.

Das, Jishnu; Holla, Alaka; Das, Veena; Mohanan, Manoj; Tabak, Diana; and Chan, Brian. (2012). In Urban and Rural India, a Standardized Patient Study Showed Low Levels of Provider Training and Huge Quality Gaps. *Health Affairs, 31*(12), 2774–84.

Das, Jishnu; Holla, Alaka; Mohpal, Aakash; and Muralidharan, Karthik. (2016). Quality and Accountability in Health Care Delivery: Audit-Study Evidence from Primary Care in India. *American Economic Review, 106*(12), 3765–99.

Das, Jishnu; Kremer, Michael; Holla, Alaka; and Muralidharan, Karthik. (2011). *Mapping Medical Providers in Rural India: Four Key Trends.* Centre for Policy Research.

Das, Jishnu; and Zajonc, Tristan. (2010). India Shining and Bharat Drowning: Comparing two Indian states to the worldwide distribution in mathematics achievement. *Journal of Development Economics, 92*(2), 175–87.

Das, Monalisa (2015, 29.01.2015). Are Good Low Cost Private Schools Bearing the Brunt of a Faulty RTE Act? *The News Minute.*

Dasgupta, Aditya; and Kapur, Devesh. (2020). The Political Economy of Bureaucratic Overload: Evidence from Rural Development Officials in India. *American Political Science Review, 114*(4), 1316–34.

Dasgupta, Partha; and Ray, Debraj. (1986). Inequality as a Determinant of Malnutrition and Unemployment: Theory. *The Economic Journal, 96*(384), 1011–34.

Dasgupta, Sravasti (2021, 24.03.2021). Over 42,000 posts reserved for SC, ST & OBC Vacant in Union Ministries, Govt Tells Lok Sabha. *ThePrint.*

Davala, Sarath; Jhabval, Renana; Standing, Guy; and Mehta, Saumya Kapoor. (2015). *Basic Income: A Transformative Policy for India;* Bloomsbury.

Dayaram. (2002). *Parateachers in Primary Education: A Status Report.*

DeLong, Bradford J. (2022). *Slouching Towards Utopia: An Economic History of the Twentieth Century;* Basic Books.

de Mel, Suresh; McKenzie, David; and Woodruff, Christopher. (2008). Returns to Capital in Microenterprises: Evidence from a Field Experiment*. *The Quarterly Journal of Economics, 123*(4), 1329–72.

de Ree, Joppe; Muralidharan, Karthik; Pradhan, Menno; and Rogers, Halsey. (2018). Double or Nothing? The Impact of Doubling Teacher Salary on Student Performance in Indonesia. *The Quarterly Journal of Economics, 133*(2), 993–1039.

De, Rohit. (2018). *A People's Constitution: The Everyday Life of Law in the Indian Republic;* Princeton University Press. New Jersey.

Deaton, Angus. (2015). *The Great Escape: Health, Wealth, and the Origins of Inequality;* Princeton University Press. New Jersey.

Debroy, Bibek. (2020, 03.01.2020). Indian Railways Reforms: A Single Cadre for Railways Management. *Financial Express.*

Debroy, Bibek (2022, 09.07.2022) *PM Modi's Economic Adviser Bibek Debroy Calls For Single GST Rate/Interviewer: Siddarth Zarabhi. Business Today.*

Debroy, Bibek; and Sinha, Aditya (2023, 15.06.2023). Strengthening the Integrated Child Development Services scheme. *The Hindu.*

Deccan Chronicle. (2023, 25.09.2023). KTR Warns of Southern Uprising if Delimitation Cuts LS Seats. *Deccan Chronicle.*

Department of Economic Affairs, Government of India (2014). *Tax Administration in India: Spirit, Purpose and Empowerment.*

DePillis, Lydia (2019, 13.03.2019). Amazon Gets an Edge with its Secret Squad of PhD Economists. *CNN.*

Dercon, Stefan. (2022). *Gambling on Development. How some countries win and others lose;* Hurst Publishers.

Desai, Sonalde; Dubey, Amaresh; Joshi, Brij Lal; Sen, Mitali; Sheriff, Abusaleh; and Vannerman, Shariff Reeve. (2010). *Human Development in India: Challenges for a Society in Action;* Oxford University Press. New Delhi.

Deshpande, Ashwini (2011). *The Grammar of Caste: Economic Discrimination in Contemporary India;* Oxford University Press. New Delhi.

Deshmukh, Yashwant; and Guru, Sutanu. (2023). *The Pro-Incumbency Century: How Leaders Are Fashioning Repeat Mandates in India;* Prabhat Prakashan.

Devlin, Kat; and Johnson, Courtney. (2019, 25.03.2019). Indian Elections Nearing Amid Frustration With Politics, Concerns About Misinformation. *Pew.*

Dhaliwal, Iqbal; and Hanna, Rema. (2017). The Devil is in the Details: The Successes and Limitations of Bureaucratic Reform in India. *Journal of Development Economics, 124,* 1–21.

Dhillon, Amrita; Krishnan, Pramila; Patnam, Manasa; and Perroni, Carlo. (2016, 02.03.2016). How are India's New States Faring? *Ideas for India.*

Dhingra, Sanya. (2019, 23.04.2019). Modi govt has reduced recruitment of IRS officers by over 70% since 2014. *The Print.*

Diamond, Rebecca. (2016). The Determinants and Welfare Implications of US Workers' Diverging Location Choices by Skill: 1980–2000. *American Economic Review 106*(3), 479–524.

Diamond, Rebecca; McQuade, Tim; and Qian, Franklin. (2019). The Effects of Rent Control Expansion on Tenants, Landlords, and

Inequality: Evidence from San Francisco. *American Economic Review, 109*(9), 3365–94.

DiMaggio, Paul J.; and Powell, Walter W. (1983). The Iron Cage Revisited: Institutional Isomorphism and Collective Rationality in Organizational Fields. *American Sociological Review, 48*(2), 147–60.

Dixit, Avinash; and Pindyck, Robert. (1994). *Investment under Uncertainity;* Princeton University Press. Princeton.

Djankov, Simon; La Porta, Rafael; Lopez-De-Silanes, Florencio; and Shleifer, Andrei. (2002). The Regulation of Entry. *The Quarterly Journal of Economics, 118*(1).

Donthi, Praveen. (2011, 01.12.11). Tailspin: Praful Patel and the Fall of Air India. *Caravan.*

Doucouliagos, Hristos; and Ulubasoglu, Mehmet Ali. (2008). Democracy and Economic Growth: A Meta-Analysis. *American Journal of Political Science, 52*(1), 61–83.

Drèze, Jean. (2017). *Sense And Solidarity: Jholawala Economics for Everyone;* Oxford University Press.

Drèze, Jean. (2020, 09.09.2020). DUET: A Proposal for an Urban Work Programme. *Ideas for India.*

Drèze, Jean. (2021, 09.03.2021). DUET Re-Examined. *Ideas for India.*

Drèze, Jean; Gupta, Prankur; Khera, Reetika; and Pimenta, Isabel. (2019). Casting the Net: India's Public Distribution System after the Food Security Act. *Economic and Political Weekly, 54*(6).

Drèze, Jean; and Sen, Amartya. (2013). *An Uncertain Glory: India and its Contradictions;* Princeton University Press. Princeton.

Drutman, Lee; and Strano, Maresa. (2022). *Evaluating the effects of Ranked Choice Voting.* New America.

Dubbudu, Rakesh. (2018, 20.06.2018). How Many Times is the President's Rule imposed so far? *Factly.*

Duflo, Esther; Greenstone, Michael; and Pande, Rohini. (2018). The Value of Discretion in the Enforcement of Regulation: Experimental Evidence and Structural Estimates from Environmental Inspections in India. *Econometrica, 86*(6), 2123–60.

Duflo, Esther; Dupas, Pascaline; and Kremer, Michael. (2015). School Governance, Teacher Incentives and Pupil-Teacher

Ratios: Experimental Evidence from Kenyan Primary Schools. *Journal of Public Economics, 123*, 92–110.

Duflo, Esther; Hanna, Rema; and Ryan, Stephen. (2012). Incentives Work: Getting Teachers to Come to School. *American Economic Review, 102*(4), 1241–78.

Dupas, Pascaline. (2011). Health Behavior in Developing Countries. *Annual Review of Economics 3*(1), 425–49.

Dupas, Pascaline; and Miguel, Edwards. (2017). Impacts and Determinants of Health Levels in Low-Income Countries. In Abhijit V. Banerjee and Esther Duflo (Eds.), *Handbook of Economic Field Experiments;* (Vol. 2, 1) North-Holland.

Duranti, Avani; Kumar, Rithikia; Sane, Renuka; and Sinha, Neha. (2017). *Safety Trends and Reporting of Crime.* IDFC Institute.

Dutta, Puja; Howes, Stephen; and Murgai, Rinku. (2010). Small But Effective: India's Targeted Unconditional Cash Transfers. *Economic and Political Weekly, 45*(52).

Dvara Research. (2022). *State of Exclusion: Delivery of Government-to-Citizen Cash Transfers in India.*

Economic Times (2012). (07.12.2012). Income Tax Department Manpower Shortfall at 29.47%. *Economic Times.*

Egger, Dennis; Haushofer, Johannes; Miguel, Edward; Niehaus, Paul; and Walker, Michael (2022). General Equilibrium Effects of Cash Transfers: Experimental Evidence From Kenya. *Econometrica, 90*(6), 2603–43.

Elkins, Zachary; Ginsburg, Tom; and Melton, James. (2009). *The Endurance of National Constitutions;* Cambridge University Press.

Emerick, Kyle (2018). Agricultural Productivity and the Sectoral Reallocation of Labor in Rural India. *Journal of Development Economics, 135*, 488–503.

Engerman, Stanley; and Sokoloff, Kenneth. (2012). *Economic Development in the Americas since 1500: Endowments and Institutions;* Cambridge University Press.

Escueta, Maya; Nickow, Andre Joshua; Oreopoulos, Philip; and Quan, Vincent (2020). Upgrading Education with Technology:

Insights from Experimental Research. *Journal of Economic Literature, 58*(4), 897–996.

EY-FICCI. (2013). *Reaping India's Promised Demographic Dividend—Industry in Driving Seat.*

EY-FICCI. (2014). *Private Sector's Contribution to K-12 Education in India: Current Impact, Challenges and Way Forward.*

Fafchamps, Marcel; Mckenzie, David; Quinn, Simon; and Woodruff, Christopher. (2014). Microenterprise growth and the flypaper effect: Evidence from a randomized experiment in Ghana. *Journal of Development Economics, 106,* 211–26.

Falerio, Sonia. (2021). *The Good Girls: An Ordinary Killing;* Grove Press.

Fan, Tianyu; Peters, Michael; and Zilibotti, Fabrizio. (2023). Growing Like India—the Unequal Effects of Service-Led Growth. *Econometrica, 91*(4), 1457–94.

Farahani, Mansour; Subramanian, S.V.; and Canning, David (2009). Effects of state-level public spending on health on the mortality probability in India. *PGDA Working Paper Series.*

Fernandez, Raquel; and Rodrik, Dani. (1991). Resistance to Reform: Status Quo Bias in the Presence of Individual-Specific Uncertainty. *American Economic Review, 81*(5), 1146–55.

FICCI; and LLP, BDO India. (2018). *PRIVATE SECURITY INDUSTRY: Job Creation and Skill Development.*

Finan, Frederico; Olken, Benjamin A.; and Pande, Rohini. (2017). The Personnel Economics of the Developing State. In *Handbook of Field Experiments;* (Vol. 2, 6).

Forbes, Naushad. (2022). *The Struggle And The Promise: Restoring India's Potential;* HarperBusiness.

Foster, Andrew D.; and Rosenzweig, Mark R. (1995). Learning by Doing and Learning from Others: Human Capital and Technical Change in Agriculture. *Journal of Political Economy, 103*(6), 1176–209.

Foster, Andrew D.; and Rosenzweig, Mark R. (1996). Technical Change and Human-Capital Returns and Investments: Evidence from the Green Revolution. *American Economic Review, 86*(4), 931–53.

Foster, Andrew D.; and Rosenzweig, Mark R. (2011). Are Indian Farms Too Small? Mechanization, Agency Costs, and Farm Efficiency.

Foster, Andrew D.; and Rosenzweig, Mark R. (2022). Are There Too Many Farms in the World? Labor-Market Transaction Costs, Machine Capacities and Optimal Farm Size. *Journal of Political Economy, 130*(3), 636–80.

Friedman, Benjamin. (2005). *The Moral Consequences of Economic Growth;* Vintage.

Fujiwara, Thomas. (2015). Voting Technology, Political Responsiveness, and Infant Health: Evidence From Brazil. *Econometrica, 83*(2), 423–64.

Fukuyama, Francis. (2005). 'Stateness' first. *Journal of Democracy, 16*(1), 88–84.

Gaikwad, Nikhar; and Nellis, Gareth. (2020). Overcoming the Political Exclusion of Migrants: Theory and Experimental Evidence from India. *American Journal of Political Science 65*(4).

GAME; and Dun and Bradstreet. (2022). *Unlocking the Full Potential of India's MSMEs Through Prompt Payments.*

Ganimian, Alejandro J.; Mbiti, Issac; and Mishra, A. (2022). Improving STEM Learning: Experimental Evidence from Urban Primary Schools in India.

Ganimian, Alejandro J.; Muralidharan, Karthik; and Walters, Christopher R. (2023). Augmenting State Capacity for Child Development: Experimental Evidence from India. *NBER Working Paper Series*(28780).

Ganjapure, Vaibhav. (2020, 20.12.2020). Over 70,000 posts vacant at govt's CBDT, CBIC depts: RTI query. *Times of India.*

Garcia-Santana, Manuel; and Pijoan-Mas, Josep. (2014). The Reservation Laws in India and the Misallocation of Production Factors. *Journal of Monetary Economics 66*, 193–209.

George, Siddharth; and Subramanian, Arvind. (2015, 22.07.2015). Transforming the Fight Against Poverty in India. *New York Times.*

Ghatak, Maitreesh; and Muralidharan, Karthik. (2020). An Inclusive Growth Dividend: Reframing the Role of Income

Transfers in India's Anti-Poverty Strategy. *India Policy Forum,* *16*(1), 109–68.

Ghosal, Sayan. (2020, 08.01.2020). Why India's Courts Are Struggling to Find Judges. *Business Standard.*

Giddens, Anthony (1985). *The Nation-State and Violence;* University of California Press. Berkeley.

Giridhar, S. (2022). *Ordinary People, Extraordinary Teachers: The Heroes of Real India;* Westland Books.

Giridharadas, Anand (2018). *Winners Take All: The Elite Charade of Changing the World;* Alfred A. Knopf.

Glaeser, Edward. (2011). *Triumph of the City: How Urban Spaces Make Us Human;* Macmillan.

Glaeser, Edward; and Luttmer, Erzo. (2003). The Misallocation of Housing Under Rent Control. *American Economic Review,* *93(4),* 1027–46.

Glewwe, Paul; Kremer, Michael; and Moulin, Sylvie. (2009). Many Children Left Behind? Textbooks and Test Scores in Kenya. *American Economic Journal: Applied Economics, 1*(1), 112–35.

Glewwe, Paul; and Muralidharan, Karthik. (2016). Improving Education Outcomes in Developing Countries: Evidence, Knowledge Gaps, and Policy Implications. In Eric A. Hanushek, Steven Machin, and Ludger Woessman (Eds.), *Handbook of the Economics of Education;* (Vol. 5, 10).

Goldberg, Pinelopi K.; Khandelwal, Amit Kumar; Topalova, Petia; and Pavcnik, Nina. (2008). Imported Intermediate Inputs and Domestic Product Growth: Evidence From India. *The Quarterly Journal of Economics, 125*(4), 1727–67.

Gollin, Douglas; Lagakos, David; and Waugh, Michael E. (2014). The Agricultural Productivity Gap. *The Quarterly Journal of Economics, 129*(2), 939–94.

Govinda, R.; and Josephine, Y. (2005). Para-Teachers in India: A Review. *Education Dialogue 2*(2), 193–224.

Goyal, Radhika. (2023). Does Distance Matter: Building State Capacity by Reducing Remoteness. *UC, San Diego, PhD Dissertation 2023.*

Greenstone, Michael; Nilekani, Janhavi; Pande, Rohini; Ryan, Nicholas; Sudarshan, Anant; and Sugathan, Anish. (2015). Lower Pollution, Longer Lives: Life Expectancy Gains if India Reduced Particulate Matter Pollution. *Economic and Political Weekly, 50*(8), 40–46.

Greenstone, Michael; and Pande, Rohini. (2014, 09.02.2014). India's Particulate Problem. *New York Times.*

Greenstone, Michael; Pande, Rohini; Sudarshan, Anant; and Ryan, Nicholas. (2022). The Benefits and Costs of Emissions Trading: Experimental Evidence from a New Market for Industrial Particulate Emissions.

Grove, Andrew S. (1983). *High Output Management;* Vintage.

Guerrero, Alexander. (2014). Against Elections: The Lottocratic Alternative. *Philosophy and Public Affairs, 42,* 135–78.

Guha, Ramachandra. (2007). *India After Gandhi: The History of the World's Largest Democracy;* Harper Collins.

Gupta, Aashish; and Spears, Dean. (2017). Health externalities of India's expansion of coal plants: Evidence from a national panel of 40,000 households. *Journal of Environmental Economics and Management 86,* 262–76.

Gupta, Akhil. (2012). *Red Tape;* Duke University Press.

Gupta, Dipankar. (2013). *Revolution from Above: India's Future and the Citizen Elite;* RainLight.

Gupta, Monika. (2016). Willingness to Pay for Carbon Tax: A Study of Indian Road Passenger Transport. *Transport Policy, 45,* 46–54.

Gupta, Poonam; and Panagariya, Arvind. (2014). Growth and Election Outcomes in a Developing Country. *Economics and Politics, 26*(2), 332–54.

Gupta, Shekhar. (2019, 23.05.2019). 12 reasons why Modi-Shah's BJP Got the Better of Congress and Everyone Else. *ThePrint.*

Gupta, Shekhar. (2023, 13.05.2023). Limits to Modi Magic, Liability of Lightweight CMs and Perils of Polarisation—10 Lessons from Karnataka. *ThePrint.*

Gupta, Vidushi. (2020). The State of Undertrial Incarceration in India. https://criminallawstudiesnluj.wordpress.com/2020/10/25/the-state-of-undertrial-incarceration-in-india/.

Haggard, Stephen; and Kaufman, Robert. (2008). *Development, Democracy, and Welfare States: Latin America, East Asia, and Eastern Europe;* Princeton University Press. Princeton.

Haines, Andy; Sanders, David; Lehmann, Uta; Rowe, Alexander K.; Lawn, Joy E.; Jan, Steve, . . . Bhutta, Zulfiqar. (2007). Achieving child survival goals: potential contribution of community health workers. *Lancet,* 2121–31.

Hall, Robert E.; and Jones, Charles I. (1999). Why Do Some Countries Produce So Much More Output Per Worker Than Others? *The Quarterly Journal of Economics, 114*(1), 83–116.

Hanna, Rema; and Wang, Shing-Yi. (2017). Dishonesty and Selection into Public Service: Evidence from India. *American Economic Journal: Economic Policy, 9*(3), 262–90.

Hanushek, Eric A.; and Woessman, Ludger. (2008). The Role of Cognitive Skills in Economic Development. *Journal of Economic Literature, 46*(3), 607–68.

Hart, Oliver; Shleifer, Andrei; and Vishny, Robert. (1997). The Proper Scope of Government: Theory and an Application to Prisons. *The Quarterly Journal of Economics, 112*(4), 1127–61.

Hemrajani, Nikhil. (2018). The Jobs in India that Attract Thousands of Applicants. *BBC.*

Hicks, John Hamory; Kleemans, Marieke; Li, Nicholas Y.; and Miguel, Edward. (2021). Reevaluating Agricultural Productivity Gaps with Longitudinal Microdata. *Journal of the European Economic Association, 19*(3), 1522–55.

Himanshu; and Sen, Abhijit. (2011). Why Not a Universal Food Security Legislation? *Economic and Political Weekly, 46(12),* 38–47.

Hingorani, Pritika; Tandel, Vaidehi; Pachisa, Harsh Vardhan; Shah, Kadambari; Agrawal, Harshita; Srinivasan, Sharmadha; and Das, Mehul. (2019). *Reforming Urban India/* IDFC Institute.

Hirschman, Albert. (1972). *Exit, Voice, and Loyalty: Responses to Decline in Firms, Organizations, and States;* Harvard University Press.

Hnatkovska, Viktoria; Hou, Chenyu; and Lahiri, Amartya. (2021). Convergence Across Castes. *MPRA Paper.*

Ho, Lisa; Jalota, Suhani; and Karandikar, Anahita. (2023). Bringing Work Home: Flexible Arrangements as Gateway Jobs for Women in West Bengal.

Hobbes, Thomas. (1651). *Leviathan.*

Hoddinott, John; Alderman, Harold; Behrman, Jere R.; Haddad, Lawrence; and Horton, Susan. (2013). The economic rationale for investing in stunting reduction. *Maternal and Child Nutrition, 9,* 69–82.

Holmstrom, Bengt; and Milgrom, Paul. (1991). Multitask Principal-Agent Analyses: Incentive Contracts, Asset Ownership, and Job Design. *Journal of Law, Economics, & Organization, 7,* 24–52.

Hornbeck, Richard. (2012). The Enduring Impact of the American Dust Bowl: Short- and Long-Run Adjustments to Environmental Catastrophe. *American Economic Review, 102*(4), 1477–507.

Hossain, Zoya. (2022, 09.07.2022). Explained: Why Ukraine Remains A Preferred Education Destination of Indian Medical Students. *Indiatimes.*

Hoxby, Caroline (2003). School choice and school competition: Evidence from the United States. *Swedish Economy Policy Review 10.*

Hsieh, Chang Tai; and Klenow, Peter J. (2009). Misallocation and Manufacturing TFP in China and India. *The Quarterly Journal of Economics, 124*(4), 1403–48.

Hsieh, Chang Tai; and Klenow, Peter J. (2010). Development Accounting. *American Economic Journal: Macroeconomics, 2*(1), 207–23.

Huntington, Samuel. (1968). *Political order in changing societies;* Yale University Press. Palo Alto.

Husted, Thomas A.; and Kenny, Lawrence. (1997). The Effect of the Expansion of the Voting Franchise on the Size of the Government. *Journal of Political Economy, 105*(1), 54–82.

IANS. (2019). Ajay Chautala Walks Out of Tihar on Two-Week Furlough. *Economic Times.*

India Institute. (2015). #Save Deepalaya School: Don't shut down Deepalaya School in Sanjay Colony! Retrieved from https://

www.change.org/p/government-of-delhi-savedeepalayaschool-don-t-shut-down-deepalaya-school-in-sanjay-colony.

India Justice Report (2019). TATA Trusts.

India Justice Report (2020). TATA Trusts.

India Justice Report (2022). TATA Trusts.

IndiaSpend. (2017, 07.03.2017). UP's IPS Officers Transferred At Four Times The Indian Average. IndiaSpend.

Institute of Medicine (2012). *Roundtable on Value & Science-Driven Health Care.* National Academies.

IQAir. (2020). *World Air Quality Report.*

Iyer, Kavitha. (2019, 28.11.2019). Explained: Maharashtra's Irrigation Scam, and how NCP Leader Ajit Pawar Figures in it. *Indian Express.*

Iyer, Lakshmi; and Mani, Anandi. (2012). Traveling Agents: Political Change and Bureaucratic Turnover in India. *Review of Economics and Statistics, 94*(3), 723–39.

Iyer, Parameshwaran. (2021). *Method in the Madness: Insights from My Career as an Insider-Outsider-Insider;* HarperCollins.

Jadeja, Asha. (2023, 13.01.2023). Gujarat is Anything But a Dry State. Decriminalise liquor, Use Tax Revenue for Development. *ThePrint.*

Jain, Bharthi. (2020, 03.10.2020). Conviction Rate for Crimes Under IPC Improved Marginally in 2019. *Times of India.*

Jain, Tarun. (2017). Common Tongue: The Impact of Language on Educational Outcomes. *Journal of Economic History, 77*(2), 473–510.

Jaitly, Akshay; and Shah, Ajay. (2022, 16.05.2022). Root Cause Analysis for the Electricity Crisis. *Business Standard.*

Jauregui, Beatrice. (2013). Beatings, Beacons, and Big Men: Police Disempowerment and Delegitimation in India. *Law and Social Inquiry, 38*(3), 643–69.

Jayadev, Arjun; and Bowles, Samuel. (2006). Guard Labour. *Journal of Development Economics, 79*(2), 328–48.

Jeffrey, Craig. (2010). *Timepass: Youth, Class, and the Politics of Waiting in India;* Stanford University Press. Palo Alto.

Jenkins, Rob; and Manor, James. (2017). *Politics and the Right to Work: India's National Rural Employment Guarantee Act;* Hurst and Company.

Jensen, Anders. (2022). Employment Structure and the Rise of the Modern Tax System. *American Economic Review, 112*(1), 213–34.

Jensen, Robert. (2012). Do Labor Market Opportunities Affect Young Women's Work and Family Decisions? Experimental Evidence from India. *The Quarterly Journal of Economics, 127*(2), 753–92.

Jesudasan, Dennis S. (2018, 26.10.2018). No Sensitive Posts for 'Tainted' Officers. *The Hindu.*

Jha, Prashant. (2017). *How the BJP Wins: Inside India's Greatest Election Machine;* Juggernaut Books.

Jha, Ramanath. (2022, 15.11.2022). Bihar Prohibition: An Unmitigated Disaster. *Observers Research Foundation.*

Jodhka, Surinder S. (2015). *Caste in Contemporary India;* Routledge.

Johnson, Doug; and Parrado, Andres. (2021). Assessing the Assessments: Taking Stock of Learning Outcomes Data in India. *International Journal of Educational Development, 84.*

Johnson, Erin; and Rehavi, Marit. (2016). Physicians Treating Physicians: Information and Incentives in Childbirth. *American Economic Journal: Economic Policy, 8*(1), 115–41.

Joseph, Josy. (2016). *A Feast of Vultures: The Hidden Business of Democracy in India;* HarperCollins India.

Joseph, Josy. (2021). *The Silent Coup: A History of India's Deep State;* Context.

Joseph, K.V. (2023, 10.06.2023). GDP growth, high remittances and fragile Kerala economy. *New Indian Express.*

Joshi, Ruchika; McManus, Jeffrey; Nagpal, Karan; and Fraker, Andrew. (2022). Are Voter Rolls Suitable Sampling Frames for Household Surveys? Evidence from India. *Field Methods 35*(4), 333–48.

Joshi, Vijay. (2016). *India's Long Road: The Search For Prosperity;* Penguin Books.

Joy, Shemin. (2015, 28.04.2015). 90 pc of Police Funds Spent on Salaries, Ration. *Deccan Herald.*

Juyal, Shikha; Saxena, Abhishek; Sharma, Shweta; and Srivastava, Anil. (2018). *Transforming India's Mobility*. NITI Aayog.

Kala, Namrata. (2022). The Impacts of Managerial Autonomy on Firm Outcomes.

Kalaiyarasan, A. (2014). A Comparison of Developmental Outcomes in Gujarat and Tamil Nadu. *Economic and Political Weekly, 49*(15), 55–63.

Kandavel, Sangeeta. (2023, 12.02.2023). State Planning Commission Study Concludes 'Illam Thedi Kalvi' Scheme Should Continue. *The Hindu*.

Kansikas, Carolina; Mani, Anandi; and Niehaus, Paul. (2023). Customized Cash Transfers: Financial Lives and Cash-flow Preferences in Rural Kenya. *NBER Working Paper Series*(30930).

Kapoor, Mudit; Ranjan, Priya; and Raychaudhari, Jibonayan. (2017). The impact of credit constraints on exporting firms: Evidence from the provision and subsequent removal of subsidised credit. *The World Economy, 40*(12), 2854–74.

Kapur, Devesh. (2020). Why Does the Indian State Both Fail and Succeed? *Journal of Economic Perspectives, 34*(1), 31–54.

Kapur, Devesh; Babu, Shyam D.; and Prasad, Chandra Bhan. (2014). *Defying the Odds: The Rise of Dalit Entrepreneurs;* Vintage Books.

Kapur, Devesh; and Mehta, Pratap Bhanu. (2005). *Public Institutions in India: Performance and Design;* Oxford University Press.

Kapur, Devesh; Mehta, Pratap Bhanu; and Vaishnav, Milan. (2017). *Rethinking Public Institutions in India;* Oxford University Press. London.

Kapur, Devesh; Somanathan, T.V.; and Subramanian, Arvind. (2014, 21.07.2014). Land Shackled-1. *Business Standard*.

Kapur, Devesh; and Vaishnav, Milan. (2018). *Costs of Democracy: Political Finance in India;* Oxford University Press. New Delhi.

Kapur, V.P. (2003). *The Crumbling Edifice: Experiences and Thoughts of a Police Officer;* Rupa.

Katzenstein, Mary Fainsod; and Ray, Raka. (2005). *Social Movements in India: Poverty, Power, and Politics;* Rowman and Littlefield Publishers.

Kauflin, Jeff; and Noer, Michael (2017, 27.07.2017). America's Top 50 Companies 1917–2017. *Forbes*.

Kaushik, Arushi; and Muralidharan, Karthik. (2022). Class-Size Effects in Developing Countries: Longitudinal Evidence from India. *UC San Diego, PhD Dissertation 2022*.

Keay, John. (2000). *India: A History*; Avalon Travel Publishing.

Kelkar, Vijay; and Shah, Ajay. (2019). *In Service of the Republic: The Art and Science of Economic Policy*; Penguin Allen Lane.

Kelsall, Tim; Schulz, Nicolai; Ferguson, William D.; Vom Hau, Matthias; Hickey, Sam; and Levy, Brian. (2022). *Political Settlement and Developments: Theory, Implications, evidence*; Oxford University Press.

Keyssar, Alexander. (2000). *The Right to Vote: The Contested History of Democracy in the United States* Basic Books. New York.

Khaitan, Nitika; Seetharam, Shalini; and Chandrashekharan, Sumathi. (2017). *Inefficiency and Judicial Delay: New Insights from the Delhi High Court*. Vidhi Centre for Legal Policy.

Khaitan, Tarunabh. (2019). Ranked-Choice Voting System Could Deepen Democracy, Prevent Polarisation. *Indian Express*.

Khan, Adnan Q.; Khwaja, Asim I.; and Olken, Benjamin A. (2016). Tax Farming Redux: Experimental Evidence on Performance Pay for Tax Collectors. *The Quarterly Journal of Economics, 131*(1), 219–71.

Khan, Adnan Q.; Khwaja, Asim I.; and Olken, Benjamin A. (2019). Making Moves Matter: Experimental Evidence on Incentivizing Bureaucrats through Performance-Based Postings. *American Economic Review, 109*(1), 237–70.

Khan, Mushtaq H. (2010). Political Settlements and the Governance of Growth-Enhancing Institutions.

Khandelwal, Amit. (2023). The US-China Trade War and India's Exports. *India Policy Forum. NCAER*.

Khera, Reetika. (2011a). Trends in Diversion of Grain from the Public Distribution System. *Economic and Political Weekly, 46*(21), 106–14.

Khera, Reetika. (2011b). *The Battle for Employment Guarantee*; Oxford University Press.

Khilnani, Sunil. (2010, 19.11.2010). An Idea for India. *Mint.*

Khosla, Madhav. (2020). *India's Founding Moment: The Constitution of a Most Surprising Democracy;* Harvard University Press.

Khosla, Madhav. (2022). The Future of Indian Federalism. *Seminar.*

Kingdon, Geeta Gandhi. (2020). The Private Schooling Phenomenon in India: A Review. *Journal of Development Studies, 56*(10), 1795–817.

Kingdon, Geeta Gandhi; and Muzzamil, Mohd. (2001). A Political Economy of Education in India: I: The Case of UP. *Economic and Political Weekly, 36*(32), 3052–63

Kingdon, Geeta Gandhi; and Muzzamil, Mohd. (2009). A Political Economy of Education in India: The Case of Uttar Pradesh. *Oxford Development Studies 37*(2), 123–44.

Klapper, Leora; Laeven, Luc; and Rajan, Raghuram G. (2006). Entry Regulation as a Barrier to Entrepreneurship. *Journal of Financial Economics, 82*(3), 591–629.

Kochar, Anjini. (2008). Can Schooling Policies Affect Schooling Inequality? An Empirical Evaluation of School Location Policies in India. *India Policy Forum, 4*(1), 53–99.

Kondepati, Rajendra. (2013). A Comparative Study of Nutritional Programmes in Andhra Pradesh.

Kotasthane, Pranay; Kanisetti, Anirudh; and Pai, Nitin. (2020). *India's Marathon: Reshaping the Post-Pandemic World Order.* Takshashila Institution.

Kothari, Rajni. (1964). The Congress 'System' in India. *Asian Survey, 4*(12), 1161–73.

Kothari, Rajni. (1970). *Caste in Indian Politics;* Orient Longman.

Kotwal, Ashok. (2019, 01.05.2019). Introduction to e-Symposium: Decoding Congress' NYAY. *Ideas For India.*

Kremer, Michael; Nazmul Chaudhury; F. Halsey Rogers; Muralidharan, Karthik; and Hammer, Jeffrey. (2005). Teacher Absence in India: A Snapshot. *Journal of the European Economic Association, 3*(2/3), 658–67.

Krishna, Anirudh. (2002). Enhancing Political Participation in Democracies: What is the Role of Social Capital? *Comparative Political Studies, 35*(4), 437–60.

Krishna, Anirudh. (2013a, 18.06.2023). Between Government and Citizen. *Indian Express.*

Krishna, Anirudh. (2013b). *One Illness Away: Why People Become Poor and How They Escape Poverty*; Oxford University Press.

Krishna, Anirudh. (2018). *Broken Ladder: The Paradox and Potential of India's One Billion*; Penguin Random House India.

Krishna, Rama S. (2020, 04.01.2020). Telangana Gets New Chief Secretary, 13 IAS Officers Refuse to Work Under Him. *Sunday Guardian Live.*

Krishnan, Vidya. (2015, 01.02.2015). Private Practice: How Naresh Trehan Became One of India's Most Influential Doctor-Businessmen. *Caravan.*

Kruks-Wisner, Gabrielle. (2018). *Claiming the State: Active Citizenship and Social Welfare in Rural India*; Cambridge University Press. Cambridge, U.K.

Kumar. (2001, 27.10.2001). The Trouble with 'Para-Teachers'. *The Hindu.*

Kumar, Raksha. (2022, 16.03.2022). This Burning Train is a Symbol of the Anger of India's Out-of-Work Youth. *National Public Radio.*

Kumar, Sanjay. (2017). *Attitudes, Anxieties and Aspirations of India's Youth: Changing Patterns.* CSDS-Lokniti.

Kumar, Sanjay; and Gupta, Pranav. (2018, 22.08.2018). What Young India Wants: 'Sarkari Naukri'. *Mint.*

Kumbhar, Kiran. (2022, 19.08.2022). Distrust of Indian Doctors Isn't New. Class-Caste Bias Always Ruled Medical Profession. *ThePrint.*

Kumbhar, Sitaram. (2009, 23.05.2009). Has the Congress Earned Dividend from the NREGA? *Mainstream.*

Lagakos, David. (2020). Urban-Rural Gaps in the Developing World: Does Internal Migration Offer Opportunities? *Journal of Economic Perspectives, 34*(3), 174–92.

Lagakos, David; and Waugh, Michael E. (2013). Selection, Agriculture, and Cross-Country Productivity Differences. *American Economic Review, 103*(2), 948–80.

Lahiri, Ashok. (2023). *India in Search of Glory: Political Calculus and Economy*; Penguin Business.

Lall, Rajiv B. (2023). *The State, Democracy and Markets: Global Perspectives and Learning*; Artha Global.

Lamba, Rohit; and Subramanian, Arvind. (2020). Dynamism with Incommensurate Development: The Distinctive Indian Model. *Journal of Economic Perspectives, 34*(1), 3–30.

Landemore, Hélène. (2020). *Open Democracy: Reinventing Popular Rule for the Twenty-First Century*; Princeton University Press.

Landes, David S. (1998). *Revolution in time: Clocks and the Making of the Modern World*; Viking.

Landes, David S. (1999). *The Wealth and Poverty of Nations: Why Some Are So Rich and Others*; W. W. Norton and Company. New York.

Lazear, Edward P. (2001). Educational Production. *The Quarterly Journal of Economics, 116*(3), 777–803.

Leibenstein, Harvey. (1957). *Economic Backwardness and Economic Growth*; Wiley.

Lemos, Renata; Muralidharan, Karthik; and Scur, Daniela. (2023). Personnel Management and School Productivity: Evidence from India. *Economic Journal* (forthcoming).

Levy, Brain; Hirsch, Alan; and Woolard, Ingrid (2014). South Africa's Evolving Political Settlement In Comparative Perspective. *A Southern Africa Labour and Development Research Unit Working Paper, 138*.

Levine, Ruth. (2017). The Moral Case for Evidence in Policymaking. https://hewlett.org/moral-case-evidence-policymaking/

Lewis, Arthur W. (1954). Economic Development with Unlimited Supplies of Labour. *The Manchester School, 22*(2), 139–91.

Liebman, Jeffrey; and Mahoney, Neale. (2017). Do Expiring Budgets Lead to Wasteful Year-End Spending? Evidence from Federal Procurement. *American Economic Review, 107*(11), 3510–49.

Lizzeri, Alessandro; and Persico, Niccola. (2001). The Provision of Public Goods under Alternative Electoral Incentives. *American Economic Review, 91*(1), 225–39.

Lokniti-CSDS. (2018). *Status of Policing in India Report*.

Lokniti-CSDS; and APU. (2018). *Politics and Society between Election*.

Lopez, Carolina; Sautmann, Anja; and Schaner, Simon. (2022). Does Patient Demand Contribute to the Overuse of Prescription Drugs? *American Economic Journal: Applied Economics, 14*(1), 225–60.

Lowe, Matt. (2021). Types of Contact: A Field Experiment on Collaborative and Adversarial Caste Integration. *American Economic Review, 111*(6), 1807–44.

Luttmer, Erzo; and Singhal, Monica. (2014). Tax Morale. *28*(4), 149–68.

Mahadevan-Dasgupta, Uma. (2020, 11.01.2020). 'What Ails the IAS and Why It Fails to Deliver' Review: Handing out Band-aid, Not Permanent Solutions. *The Hindu.*

Mahal, Ajay; and Mohanan, Manoj. (2006). Growth of Private Medical Education in India. *Medical Education, 40*(10), 1009–11.

Malamud, Ofer; and Pop-Eleches, Christian. (2011). Home Computer Use and the Development of Human Capital. *The Quarterly Journal of Economics, 126*(2), 987–1027.

Malhotra, Sarika. (2022, 08.03.2022). Why Bihar's Liquor Ban is Bad. *Mint.*

Mangal, Kunal. (2023). *The Indian Labour Market Through the Lens of Public Sector Recruitment.* Azim Premji University.

Mangla, Akshay. (2015). Bureaucratic Norms and State Capacity in India: Implementing Primary Education in the Himalayan Region. *Asian Survey, 55*(5), 882–908.

Mani, Anandi; and Mukand, Sharun. (2007). Democracy, Visibility and Public Good Provision. *Journal of Development Economics, 83*(2), 506–29.

Mankiw, Gregory N. (2006). The Macroeconomist as Scientist and Engineer. *Journal of Economic Perspectives, 20*(4), 29–46.

Manur, Anupam. (2018, 28.10.2018). The Addictive Nature of Bad Policies. *Mint.*

Marini, Alessanda; Rokx, Claudia; and Gallagher, Paul. (2016). *Standing Tall: Peru's Success in Overcoming its Stunting Crisis.* World Bank Group.

Martin, Leslie A.; Nataraj, Shanthi; and Harrison, Ann. (2017). In With the Big, Out with the Small: Removing Small Scale Reservations in India. *American Economic Review, 107*(2), 354–86.

Martinez-Bravo; Monica, Gerad; Miquel, Gerard; Qian, Nancy; and Yao, Yang. (2012). The Effects of Democratization on Public Goods and Redistribution: Evidence from China. *CEPR Discussion Paper Series.*

Maskin, Eric; and Sen, Amartya (2016, 28.04.2016). How Majority Rule Might Have Stopped Donald Trump. *New York Times.*

Maskin, Eric; and Sen, Amartya. (2018, June 10, 2018). A Better Electoral System in Maine. *New York Times.*

Mathew, George. (2003). Panchayati Raj Institutions and Human Rights in India. *Economic and Political Weekly, 38*(2), 155–62.

Mathew, Santhosh; and Moore, Mick. (2011). State Incapacity by Design: Understanding the Bihar Story. *IDS Working Papers,* 1–31.

Mathur, Nayanika. (2015). *Paper Tiger: Law, Bureaucracy and the Developmental State in Himalayan India;* Cambridge University Press.

Mathew, A. Santosh, Bhumi Purohit and Devesh Sharma. (2024). Public Financial Management, State Capacity, and Public Services in India. Oxford University Press (forthcoming).

Mayshar, Joram; Moav, Omer; and Pascali, Luigi. (2022). The Origin of the State: Land Productivity or Appropriability? *Journal of Political Economy, 130*(4).

Mazzucato, Mariana; and Collingtone, Rosie (2023). *The Big Con: How the Consulting Industry Weakens our Businesses, Infantilizes our Governments and Warps our Economies;* Allen Lane.

Mbiti, Isaac; Muralidharan, Karthik; Romero, Mauricio; Schipper, Youdi; Manda, Constantine; and Rajani, Rakesh. (2019). Inputs, Incentives, and Complementarities in Education: Experimental Evidence from Tanzania. *The Quarterly Journal of Economics, 134*(3), 1627–73.

Mehta, Nalin. (2022). *The New BJP: Modi and the Making of the World's Largest Political Party;* Westland Non Fiction.

Mehta, Pratap Bhanu. (2003). *The Burden of Democracy;* Penguin.

Menon, Nikhil. (2022). *Planning Democracy: How A Professor, An Institute, And An Idea Shaped India;* Penguin Viking.

Ministry of Finance. (2017). *Economic Survey of India 2016–17.*

Ministry of Finance. (2018). *Economic Survey of India 2017–18.*

Ministry of Finance. (2019a). *Economic Survey of India 2018–19.*

Ministry of Finance. (2019b). *Receipts of the Government of India.*

Ministry of Finance. (2023). *Economic Survey of India 2022–23.*

Mint. (2019, 22.04.2019). The Good and Bad News in Bureaucrat Transfers. *Mint.*

Miranda, Luis (2013, 20.11.2013). Impact of the RTE Shutdown of Schools. *Forbes.*

Mitra, Arup; and Mehta, Barjor. (2011). Cities as the Engine of Growth: Evidence from India. *Journal of Urban Planning and Development 137*(2).

Mitra, Punya Priya; and Tomar, Shruti. (2018, 01.11.2018). 5 years on, Vyapam Scam Returns to Haunt Madhya Pradesh. *Hindustan Times.*

Mobarak, Ahmed Mushfiq. (2005). Democracy, Volatility, and Economic Development. *Review of Economics and Statistics, 87*(2), 348–61.

Modi, Narendra. (2015). PM Modis remarks on National Panchayat Day [Press release].

Mody, Ashoka. (2023). *India is Broken: A People Betrayed, 1947 to Today;* Juggernaut Books.

Mohan, Archis. (2022, 09.01.2022). The Great Indian Outflow Sets off Another Brain Drain Debate. *Deccan Herald.*

Mohan, Rakesh. (2018). *India Transformed: Twenty-Five Years of Economic Reforms;* Brookings Institution Press.

Mohan, Rakesh. (2019). *Moving India to a New Growth Trajectory: Need for a Comprehensive Big Push.* Brookings India.

Mohanan, Manoj; Donato, Katherine; Miller, Grant; Truskinovsky, Yulya; and Vera-Hernández, Marcos. (2021). Different Strokes for Different Folks? Experimental Evidence on the Effectiveness of Input and Output Incentive Contracts for Health Care Providers with Varying Skills. *American Economic Journal: Applied Economics, 13*(4), 34–69.

Mohanan, Manoj; Hay, Katherine; and Mor, Nachiket. (2016). Quality Of Health Care In India: Challenges, Priorities, And The Road Ahead. *Health Affairs (Millman), 35*(10), 1753–58.

Mohanan, P.C. (2019, May 25). Sample Surveys are Important to Validate Administrative Databases. *Indian Express.*

Mohanty, Prasanna. (2020, 27.03.2020). Taxing the Untaxed I: Why Govt Should Tax Agricultural Income. *Business Today.*

Mohanty, Ranjan Kumar; and Behera, Deepak Kumar. (2020). How Effective is Public Health Care Expenditure in Improving Health Outcome? An Empirical Evidence from the Indian States. *NIPFP Working Paper Series*(300).

MoHFW. (2019). *Rural Health Statistics 2018–19.*

MoHRD. (2011). *Sarva Shiksha Abhiyan: Thirteenth Joint Review Mission.*

Mokyr, Joel. (2016). *A Culture of Growth—The Origins of the Modern Economy;* Princeton University Press. Princeton.

Ministry of Personnel, Public Grievances and Pensions. (2010). *Civil Services Survey: A Report.*

Moretti, Enrico. (2004). Workers' Education, Spillovers, and Productivity: Evidence from Plant-Level Production Functions. *American Economic Review, 94*(3), 656–90.

MoSPI. (2019). *Periodic Labour Force Survey 2017–18.*

MoSPI. (2023). *Periodic Labour Force Survey 2022–23.*

Mullainathan, Sendhil; and Shafir, Eldar. (2013). *Scarcity: Why having too little means so much;* Times Books/Henry Holt and Company. New York.

Mundle, Sudipto. (2016, 16.09.2016). Universal Basic Income: An Idea Whose Time Has Come? *Mint.*

Muralidharan, Karthik. (2012). Long-Term Effects of Teacher Performance Pay: Experimental Evidence from India. *UC, San Diego.*

Muralidharan, Karthik. (2013). Priorities for Primary Education Policy in India's 12th Five-year Plan. *India Policy Forum, 9*(1), 1–61.

Muralidharan, Karthik. (2016). A New Approach to Public Sector Hiring in India for Improved Service Delivery. *India Policy Forum, 12*(1), 187–236.

Muralidharan, Karthik. (2019a, 15.10.2019). A Prize for Evidence Based Policy | Analysis. *Hindustan Times.*

Muralidharan, Karthik. (2019b). Reforming the Indian School Education System. In Abhijit Banerjee, Raghuram Rajan, Gita Gopinath, and Mihir S. Sharma (Eds.), *What the Economy Needs Now;* (10) Juggernaut Books. New Delhi.

Muralidharan, Karthik. (2019c). The State and the Market in Education Provision: Evidence and the Way Ahead. *UC, San Diego.*

Muralidharan, Karthik. (2019d, 23.03.2019). With Rural Economy as Leading Theme of Polls, the Policy Options to Address Farm Crisis. *Hindustan Times.*

Muralidharan, Karthik. (2020a, 11.06.2020). A Post-Covid-19 Social Protection Architecture for India. *Hindustan Times.*

Muralidharan, Karthik. (2020b, 24.02.2020) To an Extent, Both Supporters and Critics of Aadhaar for Service Delivery are Correct/Interviewer: Udit Misra. *Indian Express.*

Muralidharan, Karthik; Chaudhury, Nazmul; Hammer, Jeffrey; Kremer, Michael; and Rogers, Halsey. (2011). Is there a Doctor in the House? Medical Worker Absence in India. *UC, San Diego.*

Muralidharan, Karthik; Das, Jishnu; Holla, Alaka; and Mohpal, Aakash. (2017). The Fiscal Cost of Weak Governance: Evidence from Teacher Absence in India. *Journal of Public Economics, 145,* 116–35.

Muralidharan, Karthik; and Kremer, Michael (2008). Public and Private Schools in Rural India. *School Choice International.*

Muralidharan, Karthik; Niehaus, Paul; and Sukhtankar, Sandip. (2016). Building State Capacity: Evidence from Biometric Smartcards in India. *American Economic Review, 106*(10), 2895–929.

Muralidharan, Karthik; Niehaus, Paul; and Sukhtankar, Sandip. (2017). *Direct Benefits Transfer in Food: Results from One Year of Process Monitoring in Union Territories. UC, San Diego.*

Muralidharan, Karthik; Niehaus, Paul; and Sukhtankar, Sandip. (2018). Go for an 'Inclusive Growth Dividend' in India. In *Hindustan Times.*

Muralidharan, Karthik; Niehaus, Paul; and Sukhtankar, Sandip. (2022). Integrating Biometric Authentication in India's Welfare Programs: Lessons from a Decade of Reforms. *India Policy Forum, 18*(1), 139–72.

Muralidharan, Karthik; Niehaus, Paul; and Sukhtankar, Sandip. (2023a). General Equilibrium Effects of Improving Public Employment Programs: Experimental Evidence from India. *Econometrica, 91*(4), 1261–95.

Muralidharan, Karthik; Niehaus, Paul; and Sukhtankar, Sandip. (2023b). Identity Verification Standards in Welfare Programs: Experimental Evidence from India. *Review of Economics and Statistics,* 1–46.

Muralidharan, Karthik; Niehaus, Paul; Sukhtankar, Sandip; and Weaver, Jeffrey. (2021). Improving Last-Mile Service Delivery Using Phone-Based Monitoring. *American Economic Journal: Applied Economics, 13*(2), 52–82.

Muralidharan, Karthik; and Prakash, Nishith. (2017). Cycling to School: Increasing Secondary School Enrollment for Girls in India. *American Economic Journal: Applied Economics, 9*(3), 321–50.

Muralidharan, Karthik; and Sheth, Ketki. (2016). Bridging Education Gender Gaps in Developing Countries: The Role of Female Teachers. *Journal of Human Resources, 51*(2), 269–97.

Muralidharan, Karthik; and Singh, Abhijeet. (2021). India's New National Education Policy: Evidence and challenges. *Science, 372*(6537), 36–38.

Muralidharan, Karthik; and Singh, Abhijeet. (2023). Improving Public Sector Management at Scale? Experimental Evidence on School Governance in India. UC San Diego.

Muralidharan, Karthik; Singh, Abhijeet; and Ganimian, Alejandro J. (2019). Disrupting Education? Experimental Evidence on Technology-Aided Instruction in India. *American Economic Review, 109*(4), 1426–60.

Muralidharan, Karthik; and Subramanian, Arvind. (2015, 05.08.2015). Charting a Course for the Indian Economy. *Ideas For India.*

Muralidharan, Karthik; and Sundararaman, Venkatesh. (2010). The Impact of Diagnostic Feedback to Teachers on Student Learning: Experimental Evidence from India. *Economic Journal, 120*(546), 187–203.

Muralidharan, Karthik; and Sundararaman, Venkatesh. (2011). Teacher Performance Pay: Experimental Evidence from India. *Journal of Political Economy, 119*(1), 39–77.

Muralidharan, Karthik; and Sundararaman, Venkatesh (2011b). Teacher Opinions on Performance Pay: Evidence from India. *Economics of Education Review, 30*(3), 394–403.

Muralidharan, Karthik; and Sundararaman, Venkatesh. (2013). Contract Teachers: Experimental Evidence from India. *NBER Working Paper Series*(19440).

Muralidharan, Karthik; and Sundararaman, Venkatesh. (2015). The Aggregate Effect of School Choice: Evidence from a Two-Stage Experiment in India. *The Quarterly Journal of Economics, 130*(3), 1011–66.

Murgai, Rinku; and Ravallion, Martin. (2005). Employment Guarantee in Rural India: What Would It Cost and How Much Would It Reduce Poverty? *Economic and Political Weekly, 40*(31), 3450–55.

Murphy, Kevin M.; Shleifer, Andrei; and Vishny, Robert W. (1989). Industrialization and the Big Push. *Journal of Political Economy, 97*(5), 1003–26.

Namboodiri, Vijay Mohan. K; Stefan, Mihalas.; and Hussain Shuler, Marshall G. (2014). A Temporal Basis for Weber's law in Value Perception. *Frontiers in Integrative Neuroscience, 8*, 1–11.

Nanda, Prashant K.; and Mishra, Asit R. (2018). More Indians Going Abroad for Studies, but Foreign Students aren't Coming in. *Mint*.

Narayanan, Rajendran; Dhorajiwala, Sakina; and Golani, Rajesh. (2018). Analysis of Payment Delays and Delay Compensation in NREGA. *CSE Working Paper* (5).

Narasappa, Harish; and Vidyasagar, Shruti. (2016). *State of the Indian Judiciary*; Eastern Book Company.

Narasimhan, Veda; and Weaver, Jeffrey. (2022). Polity Size and Local Government Performance: Evidence From India. University of Southern California.

NCRB. (2019). *Crime In India*.

NCRB. (2022). *Crime in India*.

Newell, Richard G.; Jaffe, Adam B.; and Stavins, Robert N. (1999). The Induced Innovation Hypothesis and Energy-Saving Technological Change. *The Quarterly Journal of Economics, 114*(3), 941–75.

Nichter, Simeon. (2018). *Votes for Survival: Relational Clientelism in Latin America;* Cambridge University Press.

Niehaus, Paul; and Sukhtankar, Sandip. (2013). The Marginal Rate of Corruption in Public Programs: Evidence from India. *Journal of Public Economics, 104,* 52–64.

Nilakantan, R.S. (2022). *South vs North: India's Great Divide;* Juggernaut Books.

Nilekani, Rohini. (2022). *Samaaj, Sarkaar, Bazaar: a Citizen-First Approach;* Notion Press.

Nooruddin, Irfan. (2011). *Coalition Politics and Economic Development: Credibility and the Strength of Weak Governments;* Cambridge University Press.

North, Douglass C. (1990). *Institutions, Institutional Change and Economic Performance (Political Economy of Institutions and Decisions);* Cambridge University Press.

North, Douglass C. (1991). Institutions. *Journal of Economic Perspectives* 5(1), 97–112.

Nurske, Ragnar. (1953). *Problems of Capital Formation in Underdeveloped Countries;* Oxford University Press.

Nye, Joseph. (2004). *Soft Power: The Means to Success in World Politics;* PublicAffairs.

Oates, Wallace. (1972). *Fiscal Federalism;* Elgar Publishing.

Olson, Mancur. (1965). *The Logic of Collective Action;* Harvard University Press. Cambridge, Massachusetts.

Open letter to Finance Minister from 51 Eminent Economists. (2022, 05.12.2022). *CounterCurrents.*

Oster, Emily; and Steinberg, Bryce Millet. (2013). Do IT service centers promote school enrollment? Evidence from India. *Journal of Development Economics, 104,* 123–35.

Ostrom, Elinor. (1990). *Governing the Commons;* Cambridge University Press.

Padmanabhan, Vishnu. (2018, 29.08.2018). Will a Coalition Govt in 2019 Harm the Indian Economy? *Mint.*

Paglayan, Agustina. (2022). Education or Indoctrination? The Violent Origins of Public School Systems in an Era of State-Building. *American Political Science Review 116*(4), 1242–57.

Pai, Sajith (2021). The Indus Valley Playbook.

Palanithurai, Ganesh. (2002). *Dynamics of New Panchayati Raj System in India: Select States;* Concept Publishing Company.

Panda, Manoj; Joe, William; Dasgupta, Purnamita; and Murty, M.N. (2019). Resource Sharing between Centre and States and Allocation across States: Some Issues in Balancing Equity and Efficiency. *Institute of Economic Growth.*

Pande, Rohini. (2003). Can Mandated Political Representation Increase Policy Influence for Disadvantaged Minorities? Theory and Evidence from India. *American Economic Review,* 93(4), 1132–51.

Pandey, Anamika et al. (2021). Health and Economic Impact of Air Pollution in the states of India: the Global Burden of Disease Study 2019. *The Lancet Planetary Health,* 5(1).

Parth, MN. (2020, 04.11.2020). A Parallel Economy: Bootleggers Flourish in Bihar's Liquor Crackdown. *Business Standard.*

Patel, Bimal; Byahut, Sweta; and Bhatha, Brijesh. (2018). Building Regulations are a barrier to Affordable Housing in Indian Cities: the Case of Ahmedabad. *Journal of Housing and Built Environment,* 33(1), 175–95.

Piketty, Thomas (2014). *Capital in the Twenty-First Century;* Harvard Business School Press India Limited.

Pincus, Steve; and Robinson, James A. (2016). Wars and State-Making Reconsidered: The Rise of the Developmental State. *Annales, Histoire, Sciences Sociales—English Edition,* 71(1), 9–34.

Plumber, Mustafa; and Chindarkar, Pranali Lotlikar. (2018). Dismal: 19.49 judges Per Million People, Shows Data. *DNA India.*

Pomeranz, Dina. (2015). No Taxation without Information: Deterrence and Self-Enforcement in the Value Added Tax. *American Economic Review,* 105(8), 2539–69.

Pomeranz, Dina; and Vila-Belda, Jose. (2019). Taking State-Capacity Research to the Field: Insights from Collaborations with Tax Authorities. *Annual Review of Economics,* 11(1), 755–81.

Poonam, Snigdha (2018). *Dreamers: How Young Indians Are Changing Their World;* Viking.

Porzio, Tomasso; Rossi, Federico; and Santangelo, Gabriella. (2022). The Human Side of Structural Transformation. *American Economic Review, 112*(8), 2774–814.

Prakash Singh vs Union of India. (Supreme Court 2006).

Prasad, Vandana; and Sinha, Dipa. (2015). The Reluctant State: Lacunae in Current Child Health and Nutrition Policies and Programmes in India. In (Challenges of Public Health) Oxford University Press.

Preston, Samuel H. (1975). The Changing Relationship Between Mortality and Level of Economic Development. *Population Studies, 29*(2), 231–48.

Pritchett, Lant. (2008). Battling the Babu Raj. *The Economist.*

Pritchett, Lant. (2009). Is India a Flailing State?: Detours on the Four Lane Highway to Modernization. *HKS Faculty Research Working Paper Series, RWP09-013.*

Pritchett, Lant. (2013). *The Rebirth of Education: Schooling Ain't Learning;* Center for Global Development. Washington, D.C.

Pritchett, Lant. (2022). National development delivers: And how! And how? *Economic Modelling 107.*

Pritchett, Lant; and Pande, Varad. (2006). Making Primary Education Work for India's Rural Poor: A Proposal for Effective Decentralization.

PTI. (2018, 21.03.2018). Kerala Govt Poser to Unrecognised schools over RTE Norms. *Business Standard.*

Rajagopalan, Shruti. (2023). Demography, Delimitation, and Democracy. https://srajagopalan.substack.com/p/demography-delimitation-and-democracy.

Rajagopalan, Shruti; and Tabarrok, Alexander. (2019). Premature Imitation and India's Flailing State. *The Independent Review, 24*(2), 165–86.

Rajan, Raghuram G.; and Lamba, Rohit. (2023). *Breaking the Mould: Reimagining India's Economic Future;* Penguin Business.

Rajan, Raghuram G.; and Zingales, Luigi. (1998). Financial Dependence and Growth. *American Economic Review, 88*(3), 559–86.

Rajshekhar, M. (2021). *Despite the State: Why India Lets Its People Down and How They Cope;* Context-Westland. Chennai.

Rakshit, Nirmalendu Bikash. (1999). Right to Constitutional Remedy: Significance of Article 32. *Economic and Political Weekly, 34*(34/35), 2379–81.

Ramachandran, Vimala. (2016). The Misunderstood Schoolteacher. *Seminar.* Retrieved from http://www.india-seminar.com/2016/677/677_vimala_ramachandran.htm.

Ramachandran, Vimala; Beteille, Tara; Linden, Tobias; Dey, Sangeeta; Goyal, Sangeeta; and Chatterjee, Prerna Goel. (2016). *Teachers in the Indian Education System: Synthesis of a 9-state study.* National University of Educational Planning and Administration.

Ramachandran, Vimala; Beteille, Tara; Linden, Tobias; Dey, Sangeeta; Goyal, Sangeeta; and Chatterjee, Prerna Goel. (2017). *Getting the Right Teachers into the Right Schools: Managing India's Teacher Workforce.* World Bank Group.

Ramnani, Meeta. (2017, 07.06.2017). Students Left in the Lurch, as ZP, PMC Shut Schools. *Pune Mirror.*

Rao, Gautam. (2019). Familiarity Does Not Breed Contempt: Generosity, Discrimination, and Diversity in Delhi Schools. *American Economic Review, 109*(3), 774–809.

Rao, Krishna D.; Shahrawat, Renu; and Bhatnagar, Aarushi (2016). Composition and Distribution of the Health Workforce in India: Estimates Based on Data from the National Sample Survey. *WHO South East Asia J Public Health, 5*(2), 133–40.

Rao, Manaswini. (2022). Front-line Courts As State Capacity: Evidence From India. *University of Delaware.*

Rao, Tanvi. (2014). The Impact of a Community Health Worker Program on Childhood Immunization: Evidence from India's 'ASHA' Workers. *SSRN electronic journal.*

Rao, Vijayendra; and Sanyal, Paromita (2018). *Oral Democracy: Deliberation in Indian Village Assemblies;* Cambridge University Press.

Rasul, Imran; and Rogger, Daniel. (2018). Management of Bureaucrats and Public Service Delivery: Evidence from the Nigerian Civil Service. *Economic Journal, 128*(608), 413–46.

Rawls, John. (1971). *A Theory of Justice: Original Edition;* Harvard University Press.

Ray, Debraj. (2016, 29.09.2016). The Universal Basic Share. *Mint*.

Ren, Xuefei. (2015). City Power and Urban Fiscal Crises: The USA, China, and India. *International Journal of Urban Sciences, 19*(1), 73–81.

Research, PRS Legislative. (2022). *Tamil Nadu Budget Analysis 2021–22*.

Restuccia, Diego; and Rogerson, Richard. (2008). Policy Distortions and Aggregate Productivity with Heterogeneous Establishments. *Review of Economic Dynamics, 11*(4), 707–20.

Restuccia, Diego; Yang, Dennis Tao; and Zhu, Xiaodong. (2008). Agriculture and Aggregate Productivity: A Quantitative Cross-Country Analysis. *Journal of Monetary Economics, 55*(2), 234–50.

Rhoads, Jared (2014). The Medical Context of Calvin Jr's Untimely Death. https://coolidgefoundation.org/blog/the-medical-context-of-calvin-jr-s-untimely-death/.

Right To Food. (2012). Working Group for Children Under Six of the Right to Food Campaign. Retrieved from http://www.righttofoodindia.org/data/campaign/primers/July_2012_strategies_children_under_six_12th_plan_april_2012.pdf.

Riker, William. (1964). *Federalism: Origin, Operation, Significance*; Little, Brown and Company.

Rivkin, Steven G.; Hanushek, Eric A.; and Kain, John F. (2005). Teachers, Schools and Academic Achievement. *Econometrica, 73*(2), 417–58.

Rodriguez-Clare, Andres. (1996). Multinationals, Linkages, and Economic Development. *American Economic Review, 86*(4), 852–73.

Romero, Mauricio; Sandefur, Justin; and Sandholtz, Wayne Aaron. (2020). Outsourcing Education: Experimental Evidence from Liberia. *American Economic Review, 110*(2), 364–400.

Romero, Mauricio; and Singh, Abhijeet. (2023). The Incidence of Affirmative Action: Evidence from Quotas in Private Schools in India.

Rosenstein-Rodan, P.N. (1943). Problems of Industrialisation of Eastern and South-Eastern Europe. *The Economic Journal, 53*(10/11), 202–11.

Rukmini S. (2019, 23.09.2019). Cracks in Our Healthcare System. *Mint.*

Rukmini S. (2014, 02.02.2014). Question Mark Over Data on Learning. *The Hindu.*

Rukmini S. (2021). *Whole Numbers and Half Truths: What Data Can and Cannot Tell Us about Modern India;* Context.

Sabharwal, Manish; and Arora, Sonal. (2016). Enabling India's Job Renaissance: Not More Cooks But a Different Recipe. In *Economy of Jobs;* (17) FICCI.

Sagar, Rahul. (2022). *To Raise a Fallen People: The Nineteenth-Century Origins of Indian Views on International Politics;* Columbia University Press.

Sane, Renuka; and Sinha, Neha. (2017, 11.04.2017). Budgeting for the Police. *Mint.*

Sanghera, Tish. (2018, 21.11.2018). As India Becomes Wealthier, More Indians Leave Its Shores. *IndiaSpend.*

Sanin, Deniz. (2022). Do Domestic Violence Laws Protect Women From Domestic Violence? Evidence From Rwanda.

Saxena, Namit. (2021, 23.05.2021). Disproportionate Representation at the Supreme Court: A Perspective Based on Caste and Religion of judges. *Bar and Bench.*

Saxena, Naresh Chandra. (2019). *What Ails the IAS and Why it Fails to Deliver;* SAGE Publications New Delhi.

Schilbach, Frank. (2019). Alcohol and Self-Control: A Field Experiment in India. *American Economic Review, 109*(4), 1290–322.

Schoellman, Todd. (2012). Education Quality and Development Accounting. *Review of Economic Studies, 79*(1), 388–417.

Scott, James C. (2017). *Against the Grain: A Deep History of the Earliest States;* Yale University Press.

Sen, Amartya. (1999). *Development as Freedom;* Alfred Knopf.

Service, Express News. (2021). 90% of TN Police Budget Sanctioned for Cops' Salary. *New Indian Express.*

Seth, Dilasha. (2021, 14.07.2021). Over 400 Top-Level Posts Lie Vacant in the Income Tax Department. *Business Standard.*

Shah, Ajay. (2016). Marginal Cost of Public Funds: A Valuable Tool for Thinking About Taxation and Expenditure in India. https://

blog.theleapjournal.org/2016/08/marginal-cost-of-public-funds-valuable.html#gsc.tab=0.

Shah, Anwar. (2006). *Local Governance in Developing Countries;* World Bank Publications.

Shah, Ghanshyam. (2004). *Social Movements in India: A Review of Literature;* Sage India.

Shah, Rohan. (2020). I Tried Starting a Manufacturing Unit in India ... https://superr.in/economy/i-tried-starting-a-manufacturing-unit-in-india/.

Sharan, M.R.; and Kumar, Chinmaya (2021). Something to Complain About: How Minority Representatives Overcome Ethnic Differences.

Sharan, M.R. (2021). *Last Among Equals: Power, Caste and Politics in Bihar's Villages;* Context.

Sharma, Rashmi; and Ramachandran, Vimala. (2009). *The Elementary Education System in India: Exploring Institutional Structures, Processes, and Dynamics;* Routledge India. New Delhi.

Shiller, Robert J. (2009, 27.12.2009). A Way to Share in a Nation's Growth. *New York Times.*

Shultz, George P. (2020, 11.12.2020). The 10 Most Important Things I've Learned About Trust Over My 100 years. *Washington Post.*

Singh, Abhijeet. (2015). The Private School Premium: Size and Sources of the Private School Advantage in Test Scores in India. *Journal of Development Economics, 113,* 16–32.

Singh, Abhijeet. (2020). The Myths of Official Measurement: Auditing and Improving Administrative Data in Developing Countries. *RISE Working Paper Series, 20/042.*

Singh, Abhijeet. (2023). Improving Administrative Data at Scale: Experimental Evidence on Digital Testing in Indian Schools. *Stockholm School of Economics.*

Singh, Abhijeet; Romero, Mauricio; and Muralidharan, Karthik (2022). Covid-19 Learning Loss and Recovery: Panel Data Evidence from India. *NBER Working Paper Series*(30552).

Singh, Prakash. (2022). *The Struggle for Police Reforms in India: Ruler's Police to People's Police;* Rupa Publications India.

Singh, Prerna. (2016). *How Solidarity Works for Welfare: Subnationalism and Social Development in India;* Cambridge University Press.

Singh, Rahul. (2018). *Criminal Justice in the Shadow of Caste.* National Dalit Movement for Justice.

Singh, Shivam Shankar. (2019). *How to Win an Indian Election: What Political Parties Don't Want You to Know;* Penguin Ebury Press.

Singhvi, Abhishek. (2021, 10.01.2021). A New Vision For Legal Education in India. *Hindustan Times.*

Sinha, Amarjeet. (2013). *An India for Everyone: A Path to Inclusive Development;* HarperCollins Publishers India.

Sinha, Dipa. (2006). Rethinking ICDS: A Rights Based Perspective. *Economic and Political Weekly, 41*(34), 3689–94.

Sinha, Jayant; and Varshney, Ashutosh. (2011, 07.01.2011). It is Time for India to Rein in its Robber Barons. *Financial Times.*

Sinha, Neha; and Duranti, Avani. (2017). *Why 92% Thefts in Indian Metros Are not Reported.* IDFC Institute.

Sinha, Shakti. (2023). Role of MHA in Internal Security. In Devesh Kapur and Amit Ahuja (Eds.), *Internal Security in India: Violence, Order and the State;* (4) Oxford University Press. New York.

Sinha, Shishir. (2023, 02.07.2023). Central GST Authority Found Fake Invoices Amounting ₹63K crore, Collected ₹3k crore. *Hindu BusinessLine.*

Sitapati, Vinay. (2018). *The Man Who Remade India: A Biography of P. V. Narasimha Rao;* Oxford University Press. London.

Smith, Adam. (1776). *An Inquiry into the Nature and Causes of the Wealth of Nations.*

Sneha, P.; Sinha, Neha; Varghese, Ashwin; Durani, Avanti; and Patel, Ayush. (2021). Bureaucratic Indecision and Risk Aversion in India. *Indian Public Policy Review, 2*(6).

Somanathan, E; Somanathan, Rohini; and Tewari, Meenu. (2021). The Impact of Temperature on Productivity and Labor Supply: Evidence from Indian Manufacturing. *Journal of Political Economy, 129*(6), 1797–827.

Somanathan, TV; and Natarajan, Gulzar. (2022). *State Capability in India;* Oxford University Press.

Srivastava, Amitabh. (2017, 17.04.2017). Bihar's Sobering Statistics: 1 year of Prohibition, Rs 5,000 crore Short, but Laurels Galore for Nitish. *India Today.*

Subramanian, Arvind. (2009). The India Vote. *Wall Street Journal.*

Subramanian, Samanth. (2017, 02.05.2017). India's Silicon Valley Is Dying of Thirst. Your City May Be Next. *Wired.*

Sukhtankar, Sandip. (2017). India's National Rural Employment Guarantee Scheme: What Do We Really Know about the World's Largest Workfare Program? *India Policy Forum, 13*(1), 231–85.

Sukhtankar, Sandip; and Vaishnav, Milan. (2015). Corruption in India: Bridging Academic Evidence and Policy Options. *India Policy Forum, 11*(1), 193–276.

Sukhtankar, Sandip; Kruks-Wisner, Gabrielle; and Mangla, Akshay. (2022). Policing in Patriarchy: An Experimental Evaluation of Reforms to Improve Police Responsiveness to Women in India. *Science 377,* 191–98.

Sundararaman, T; and Parmar, Daksha. (2019). Professionalizing public health management. *Mandate for Health, Seminar Journal*(714).

Swarup, Anil. (2019). *Not Just a Civil Servant;* Unicorn Books. New Delhi.

Taagepera, Rein; and Shugart, Matthew Soberg. (1991). *Seats and Votes: The Effects and Determinants of Electoral Systems;* Yale University Press. New Haven, CT.

Tabarrok, Alexander. (2014). Tom Sargent Summarizes Economics. https://marginalrevolution.com/marginalrevolution/2014/04/tom-sargent-summarizes-economics.html

Tanwar, Sangeeta. (2019, 07.10.2019). Modi's UDAY Scheme Hasn't Helped Indian Power Firms, Instead It's Wrecking State Finances. *Quartz.*

Tarlo, Emma. (2000). *Paper Truths: The Emergency and Slum Clearance through Forgotten Files.*

Tellis, Ashley J.; Debroy, Bibek; and Mohan, Raja C. (2022). *Grasping Greatness: Making India a Leading Power;* Viking India.

Thakur, Sankarshan. (2000). *Making of Laloo Yadav: The Unmaking of Bihar;* HarperCollins India.

Thakur Family Foundation. 2022. Assessment of State Public Health Cadre.

Thomas, Abraham. (2021, 10.03.2021). Centre Agrees to Set Up More Courts to Clear Backlog of Cheque Bounce Cases. *Hindustan Times.*

Tiebout, Charles. (1956). A Pure Theory of Local Expenditures. *Journal of Political Economy, 64*(5), 416–24.

Tilly, Charles. (1975). Reflections on the History of European State Making. In Charles Tilly (Ed.), *The Formation of National States in Western Europe;* Princeton University Press. Princeton.

Tooley, James. (2009). *The Beautiful Tree: A personal journey into how the world's poorest people are educating themselves;* Cato Institute. Washington D.C.

Trusts, TATA. (2022). *India Justice Report.* TATA Trusts.

UN-Habitat. (2022). *World Cities Report.*

UNESCO. (2021). *No Teacher, No Class: State of the Education Report for India.*

Union of India vs Rajendra Shah (Supreme Court of India 2021).

Usmani, Azman. (2019, 04 Jun 2019). In Charts: India's Election Becomes The World's Most Expensive. *BloombergQuint.*

Vaishnav, Milan; and Hinston, Jamie. (2019). *India's Emerging Crisis of Representation.* Carnegie Endowment for International Peace.

Vaishnav, Milan. (2017). *When Crime Pays: Money and Muscle in Indian Politics;* Yale University Press. New Haven, CT.

Vaishnav, Milan. (2019). *Electoral Bonds: The Safeguards Of Indian Democracy Are Crumbling.* Carnegie Endowment for International Peace.

Vaishnav, Milan. (2015). *Understanding the Indian Voter.* Carnegie Endowment for International Peace.

Vaishnav, Milan; and Swanson, Reedy. (2015). Does Good Economics Make for Good Politics? Evidence from Indian States. *India Review, 14*(3), 279–311.

Vakil, Raeesa. (2023). Internal Security and India's Constitution. In Devesh Kapur and Amit Ahuja (Eds.), *Internal Security in India: Violence, Order, and the State;* (2) Oxford University Press.

Varma, Amit (2021a, 7 February 2021). [The Seen and the Unseen] *Episode 211: The Tragedy of Our Farm Bills (with Ajay Shah).*

Varma, Amit. (2021b). [The Seen and the Unseen] *Episode 223: The Economics and Politics of Vaccines (with Ajay Shah)*.

Varma, Amit. (2021c). [The Seen and the Unseen] *Episode 225: Understanding Indian Health Care (with Karthik Muralidharan)*.

Varma, Amit. (2022). [The Seen and the Unseen] *Episode 293: Womaning in India (with Mahima Vashisht)*.

Varma, Amit. (2023a). [The Seen and the Unseen] *Episode 347: India's Massive Pensions Crisis (with Ajay Shah and Renuka Sane)*.

Varma, Amit. (2023b). [The Seen and the Unseen] *Episode 355: The Life and Times of KP Krishnan (with KP Krishnan)*.

Varshney, Ashutosh. (2003). Ethnic Conflict and Civic Life (2nd Edition: Hindus and Muslims in India ed.) Yale University Press.

Varshney, Ashutosh. (2013). *Battles Half Won: India's Improbable Democracy;* Penguin Random House India.

Veeraraghavan, Rajesh. (2021). *Patching Development: Information Politics and Social Change in India;* Oxford University Press, USA.

Venkatachalam, L. (2015). Informal Water Markets and Willingness to Pay for Water: a Case Study of the Urban Poor in Chennai City, India. *International Journal of Water Resources Development, 31*(1), 134–45

Venkataramakrishnan, Rohit. (2021). The Political Fix: Why is India Still Pursuing 'Tax Terrorism' Cases Against Cairn and Vodafone? *Scroll.*

Verma, Arvind. (1999). Cultural Roots of Police Corruption in India. *Policing: An International Journal, 22*(3), 264–79.

Verma, Arvind. (2005). The Police in India: Design, Performance and Adaptability. In Devesh Kapur and Pratap Bhanu Mehta (Eds.), *Public Institutions in India: Performance and Design;* Oxford University Press.

Verma, Lalmani. (2015, 17.09.2015). Around 250 PhD Holders in Line For Peon's Job in UP. *Indian Express.*

Verma, Rahul; and Barthwal, Ankita. (2022, 13.03.2022). Why More Women Voted for the BJP in 2022 Elections | Analysis *India Today.*

Vij-Aurora, Bhavna; and Jolly, Asit. (2013, 20.05.2013). The Million-Dollar Nephew: Arrest of Vijay Singla by the CBI uncovers a jobs-for-cash scandal that has blown the lid off rampant corruption in railways. *India Today.*

Visaria, Sujata. (2009). Legal Reform and Loan Repayment: The Microeconomic Impact of Debt Recovery Tribunals in India. *American Economic Journal: Applied Economics, 1*(3), 59–81.

Visvanathan, Shiv; and Sethi, Harsh. (1998). *Play: Chronicles of Corruption, 1947–97; Banyan Books.* New Delhi.

Vivalt, Eva (2020). How Much Can We Generalize From Impact Evaluations? *Journal of the European Economic Association 18*(6), 3045–89.

Vivek, S. (2014). *Delivering Public Services Effectively: Tamil Nadu and Beyond;* Oxford University Press. New Delhi

Vogel, Ezra. (2011). *Deng Xiaoping and the Transformation of China;* Harvard University Press.

Wade, Robert. (1985). The Market for Public Office: Why the Indian State is not Better at Development. *World Development, 13,* 467–97.

Waldinger, Fabian. (2016). Bombs, Brains, and Science: The Role of Human and Physical Capital for the Creation of Scientific Knowledge. *Review of Economics and Statistics, 98*(5), 811–31.

Watch, Human Rights. (2020). *Human Rights Watch World Report.*

Weaver, Jeffrey; Sukhtankar, Sandip; Niehaus, Paul; and Muralidharan, Karthik. (2023). Cash Transfers for Child Development: Experimental Evidence from India.

Weber, Max. (1968). *Economy and Society: An Outline of Interpretative Sociology;* Bedminster Press. New York.

WIDER, UNU. Government Revenue Dataset. In.

Wilkinson, Steven. (2004). *Votes and Violence: Electoral Competition and Ethnic Riots in India;* Cambridge University Press. Cambridge, U.K.

Wilkinson, Steven. (2005). Communal Riots in India. *Economic and Political Weekly, 40*(44/45), 4768–70.

World Bank. (2015). *World Development Report 2015: Mind, Society, and Behavior.*

World Bank. (2020). *Poverty and Equity Brief.* India. April 2020.

Wrong, Michela. (2010). *It's Our Turn to Eat: The Story of a Kenyan Whistle-Blower;* Harper Perennial.

Yadav, Yogendra. (2023, 17.05.2023). Karnataka Has Told The Opposition Where to Focus on for 2024—the Base of the Social Pyramid. *The Print.*

Yang, Benhua. (2008). Does Democracy Lower Growth Volatility? A Dynamic Panel Analysis. *Journal of Macroeconomics, 30*(1), 562–74.

Zendejas, Benjamin; Brydges, Ryan; Wang, Amy T.; and Cook, David A. (2013). Patient Outcomes in Simulation-Based Medical Education: a Systematic Review. *Journal of General Internal Medicine, 28*(8)

Zubrzycki, John. (2023). *Dethroned: Patel, Menon and the Integration of Princely India;* Juggernaut Books.

Acknowledgements

This is my first book and reflects a lifelong journey of learning from many scholars, teachers, analysts, and practitioners. It would also not have been possible without contributions and support from several organizations, colleagues, and well-wishers. I aim to acknowledge and thank both sets of enablers of this book.

For my PhD training in economics, I am deeply grateful to my advisers Michael Kremer, Caroline Hoxby, and Martin Feldstein, and acknowledge the intellectual influences of Alberto Alesina, Josh Angrist, Abhijit Banerjee, Esther Duflo, Edward Glaeser, Oliver Hart, Lawrence Katz, and Greg Mankiw. Key intellectual influences in my undergraduate years include Andrew Metrick, Jonathan Morduch, Dwight Perkins, Sanjay Reddy, Jeff Sachs, Amartya Sen, Peter Timmer, Martin Weitzman, and Jeffrey Williamson; and my journey into economics was kindled by an amazing high-school economics teacher—James Reeves at Raffles Junior College in Singapore.

I have learned much over the years from the scholarship of, and interactions with, Pranab Bardhan, Tim Besley, Angus Deaton, Stefan Dercon, Shanta Devarajan, Andrew Foster, Maitreesh Ghatak, Jeffrey Hammer, Asim Khwaja, Ashok Kotwal, Amartya Lahiri, Edward Miguel, Dilip Mookherjee, Ben Olken, Rohini Pande, Lant Pritchett, Debraj Ray, and Mark Rosenzweig. My most important source of ongoing learning has been the deep intellectual engagement with my frequent co-authors Jishnu Das, Paul Niehaus, Halsey Rogers, Mauricio Romero, Abhijeet Singh, Sandip Sukhtankar, and Venkatesh Sundararaman, and colleagues at UC San Diego (UCSD) including Sam Bazzi, Prashant Bharadwaj, Gordon Dahl, Roger Gordon, Gordon Hanson, Sara Lowes, Craig McIntosh, and Tom Vogl.

For insights into political science and India's political economy, I am especially grateful to Devesh Kapur, Pratap Bhanu Mehta, and Ashutosh Varshney. I have also learned from the work of Amit Ahuja, Pradeep Chhibber, Ramachandra Guha, Madhav Khosla, Anirudh Krishna, Vinay Sitapati, Milan Vaishnav, and Steven Wilkinson. My thinking on ethics and justice has been influenced by the works of Elizabeth Anderson, Robert Nozick, John Rawls, Michael Sandel, and Amartya Sen.

On the Indian economy and Indian economic policy, I have learned much from the writings of, and interactions with, Reuben Abraham, Shankar Acharya, Viral Acharya, Isher Judge Ahluwalia, Montek Singh Ahluwalia, Junaid Ahmad, Shankkar Aiyar, Swami Aiyar, Yamini Aiyar, Sanjaya Baru, Kaushik Basu, Suman Bery, Surjit Bhalla, Jagdish Bhagwati, Laveesh Bhandari, Pranjul Bhandari, Pramit Bhattacharya, Ajay Chhibber, Sajjid Chinoy, Gurcharan Das, Bibek Debroy, Jean Drèze, Subir Gokarn, Poonam Gupta, Shaibal Gupta, Ashok Gulati, Himanshu, Sunil Jain, Vijay Joshi, Radhicka Kapoor, Vijay Kelkar, Reetika Khera, Anne Krueger, Ashok Lahiri, Rajiv Lall, Puja Mehra, Santosh Mehrotra, Neelkanth Mishra, Prachi Mishra, Rakesh Mohan, Sudipto Mundle, Rinku Murgai, V. Anantha Nageswaran, Nandan Nilekani, T.N. Ninan, Arvind Panagariya, Ila Patnaik, Suyash Rai, Niranjan Rajadhyaksha, Raghuram Rajan, Jairam Ramesh, Indira Rajaraman, M. Govinda Rao, Y.V. Reddy, Rathin Roy, S. Rukmini, Renuka Sane, Mohit Satyanand, Pronab Sen, Ajay Shah, Shekhar Shah, Mihir Sharma, N.K. Singh, Jayant Sinha, T.N. Srinivasan, Arvind Subramanian, Amit Varma, and Arvind Virmani.

My understanding of governance and public administration in India has greatly benefited from interactions over the years with senior officers in Central and state governments, including Manoj Ahuja, Arti Ahuja, Surendra Bagde, Tarun Bajaj, Sunil Barnwal, Mukhmeet Bhatia, Sekhar Bonu, Sumit Bose, Arunish Chawla, Keshav Desiraju, Param Iyer, D.K. Jain, Amitabh Kant, K.P. Krishnan, S. Krishnan, Srivatsa Krishna, Alok Kumar, Amod Kumar, Dhanendra Kumar, Vini Mahajan, Santhosh Mathew, Deepti Gaur Mukerjee, Anup Mukherjee, Gulzar Natarajan, M. Raghunandan Rao, K. Ramakrishna Rao, Vrinda Sarup, Ajay Seth, Tripurari Sharan, Rajiv Sharma, Rohit Singh, Tejveer Singh, Amarjeet

Sinha, T.V. Somanathan, I.V. Subbarao, Reddy Subrahmanyam, Anil Swarup, Girija Vaidyanathan, and Anup Wadhawan.

My understanding of education research, policy, and practice has benefited greatly from interactions with Rukmini Banerji, Rachel Glennerster, Eric Hanushek, Rachel Hinton, Narendra Jadhav, Pranav Kothari, Ben Piper, Lant Pritchett, Sridhar Rajagopalan, Vimala Ramachandran, Jaime Saavedra, and Ludger Woessman; through participation in multiple global research and policy efforts, including RISE (Research on Improving Systems of Education) and the GEEAP (Global Education Evidence Advisory Panel); and from serving as the global education co-chair of J-PAL (Abdul Latif Jameel Poverty Action Lab). My learnings from trying to implement research-based ideas to improve education in India and other countries have crucially shaped my intellectual evolution, reinforcing the view that weak governance and state capacity are critical binding constraints to delivering better human development at scale in nearly every sector.

I would also like to thank the organizations and individuals who have generously funded the research conducted by me and other scholars cited in this book through several competitive research funding initiatives. Basic research is a public good with very long-term returns, and research funders are often under pressure to show short-term impacts, which can be difficult. However, as noted in Chapter 10, most human progress has resulted from creating new knowledge, disseminating it, and then acting on it. This book, drawing on over two decades of primary research, aims to contribute to dissemination and action by synthesizing key insights, and providing an evidence-informed roadmap for policymakers to act on to accelerate development in India and globally.

Doing large-scale field-based research requires not only funding but also organizational capacity to carry it out. I am grateful to J-PAL South Asia for building the high-quality research infrastructure that has enabled much of my work, and especially to Iqbal Dhaliwal, John Floretta, Ruben Menon, Shobhini Mukherjee, Tithee Mukhopadhyay, Sripada Ramamurthy, and Shagun Sabharwal for their support over the years. I also thank the many research assistants and managers over the years whose work has contributed to the research reflected in this book. Finally, I thank A.V. Surya and the IMRB team; and

Dileep Ranjekar, S. Giridhar, D.D. Karopady, M. Srinivasa Rao and the staff of the Azim Premji Foundation for their partnership and support in carrying out field research in the years before J-PAL South Asia existed.

This research would have been mostly confined to academic papers in peer-reviewed journals and not translated into this book without the encouragement and support of many people. The person most responsible for my writing this book is K. Ramakrishna Rao, who heard lecture recordings of my course on the Indian economy at UCSD and strongly urged me to write a book based on those ideas, saying that it was the best way I could contribute to India's development. Devesh Kapur (a long-term mentor and friend) and Abhijeet Singh (my frequent co-author) agreed that the timing was right and encouraged me to take it on.

The timing was also perfect since I had accumulated enough sabbatical credits at UCSD to take on this project, and I am grateful to my department chairs (Graham Elliott, Julie Cullen, Marc Muendler) and Dean (Carol Padden) for their support that has enabled this project. I am also grateful for the support of UCSD Chancellor Pradeep Khosla, and Executive Vice Chancellors Suresh Subramani and Elizabeth Simmons for their support over the years to enable my field-intensive research work.

I am especially grateful to Burak Eskici, who manages my research portfolio and has been a key intellectual and organizational partner in taking this book from conception to completion over nearly five years. Vishnu Padmanabhan has been another critical partner in the process, helping me brainstorm the outlines and structure of both the entire book and individual chapters, and also doing the heavy lifting of the early rounds of editing. He warned me that a book like this would take around twenty drafts to get right and that he'd be able to help me accelerate the process from draft one to ten, after which I should send chapters to others for comments. This is exactly what we did!

I thank the PhD students and postdoctoral fellows who have helped me with literature reviews, analysis, and fact-checks on various chapters. I received invaluable help from Manaswini Rao (Chapters 10, 13, 14, and 16), Radhika Goyal (Chapters 6, 7, and 8), Naveen Kumar (Chapters 11 and 15), Vikram Jambulapati (Chapters 3 and 5), Shah Bano Ijaz (Chapter 2), and Sabareesh Ramachandran (Chapter 12). Hannah Blackburn, Michelle Galvez, Pankhuri Prasad, and Ophira Shalev at UCSD provided research and writing support in the early stages of the book, and Arshad Azad at the Centre for Effective Governance for Indian States (CEGIS) helped to update figures in 2023. Finally, I am deeply grateful to Sravan Pallapothu at CEGIS for organizing all the references, tables, and figures, along with the data needed to replicate them provided on the book website.

I am immensely grateful to Prashant Bharadwaj, Burak Eskici, Vikas Gothalwal, Devesh Kapur, Gaurav Khanna, Aprajit Mahajan, Vishnu Padmanabhan, Vijay Pingale, Mathu Shalini, and Sandip Sukhtankar for reading and commenting on the *entire* book! I am also very grateful for the comments provided on several chapters by Ronald Abraham, Rahul Ahluwalia, Mukhmeet Bhatia, Hari Menon, Paul Niehaus, Lant Pritchett, K. Ramakrishna Rao, Rakesh Rajani, and Rajiv Sharma.

The book has greatly benefited from my parallel efforts at setting up CEGIS, a non-profit organization launched in late 2019 to support Indian state governments in implementing reforms based on some of the ideas in this book. My original plan was to first finish the book, and *then* think about ways of helping governments to act on its ideas. However, after an extended meeting with Ashish Dhawan in late 2018, we were both convinced that time was precious and that it made sense to start immediately. While building CEGIS in parallel has partly contributed to the delay in completing this book, it has also greatly enriched it—especially by increasing my understanding of government functioning, and giving me the confidence that many of the ideas in this book can be implemented by motivated leaders and officials.

I am deeply grateful to Ashish Dhawan for the financial support to write this book and to build CEGIS, and for his intellectual engagement in this journey. I am also incredibly grateful to the entire CEGIS team led by Vijay Pingale, who are dedicating their careers to improving government functioning to accelerate India's development. CEGIS and its work have become an essential part of my continuing education by enabling an iterative cycle of thinking, doing, learning, rethinking, and doing again! I would like to especially thank Parul Agarwal, Ankit Kumar Chatri, Devashish Deshpande, Ziaul Hoda, Sriharini Narayanan, Siddharth Pandit, Ganesh Rao, Praveen Ravi, and Mathu Shalini for leading workstreams based on some of the ideas in this book and iteratively contributing to strengthening our thinking on them. I also thank Shantanu Bhanja, Matangi Jayaram, Praveen Khanghta, and Vikas Srivastava for their contributions to CEGIS and the book, and Rajendra Kondepati and Kartik Akileswaran for comments on draft book chapters while at CEGIS. Finally, the support of, and discussions with, Vikrant Bhargava, Sekhar Bonu, Govind Iyer, Santhosh Mathew, Jayaprakash Narayan, Rakesh Rajani, Murugan Vasudevan, and Ireena Vittal have benefited both CEGIS and the book.

I am also grateful to Amit Varma and to listeners of *The Seen and Unseen* podcast, for the affirmation during this book project. Single-authored book writing can be a very lonely enterprise, and I have greatly benefited from doing three extended podcast episodes with Amit covering different chapters (11, 12, and 1 and 8) over the past three and a half years. The positive reactions to these episodes have helped sustain my momentum on this project. I also thank Shruti Rajagopalan and Milan Vaishnav for their India-focused podcasts, which have been an effective way of staying abreast of new books and authors while focused on writing my own.

I thank Penguin Random House India and my editors Premanka Goswami (at the start) and Karthik Venkatesh (at the finish) for their patience, support, and multiple rounds of editorial feedback, as the scope of the project expanded from a proposal of a 1,20,000-word book to be finished in three years to a 2,25,000-word book (including notes) that has taken nearly five years! One unintended benefit of this delay is that I was able to use suggestions from ChatGPT to further tighten the writing and cut 5 to 10 per cent of the text during the final round of editing in late 2023, and I acknowledge this technological support. I also thank Ralph Rebello for shepherding the manuscript through the copy-editing and proofreading process, Aakriti Khurana for designing the cover and bearing with my many iteration requests, and Nabajit Malakar for inputs and iterations on the cover design.

Finally, this book would simply not have been possible without the rock-solid support of my family. My wife, Srinithya, has been a bedrock of love, support, and encouragement for over twenty years of married life. My children (Tejas and Tapasya) have provided joy, motivation, and much-needed diversions throughout this process. My parents (Girija and R. Muralidharan), parents-in-law (Lalitha and Srinivasa Ramasubramanian), brother (Vinayak Muralidharan), sister-in-law (Srividya Ramasubramanian), uncle (Rajagopalan Ravi), and extended family have all contributed in various ways to this book, especially by stepping in as needed on the family front to minimize my distractions while writing.

The one tinge of sadness in these years has been that my father's deteriorating health has made it impossible for him to read, engage with, and enjoy this book. He has been the most important source of guidance and advice in my professional life, and has pointed me in the right direction at every key juncture, starting with the pivotal decision and sacrifice my parents made in letting me leave home in Ahmedabad at sixteen to go to Singapore on a scholarship. I vividly recall my father's words in my farewell card where he wrote: 'You have a solid foundation, on which you can build a monument. A monument of your choice, and one that we can all be proud of.' Those words have been a source of motivation and inspiration ever since, and I hope that this book adequately pays back my parents and all those who have supported and enabled my life's journey, and pays it forward by helping accelerate India's development and thereby benefiting many more in the years to come.

Additional Resources

This book aims to both be simple enough to be accessible to general readers, and comprehensive enough for academic readers, researchers, students, and practitioners to use as a ready reference on key topics of relevance to India's future. Two sets of additional resources are provided to support the latter users.

I. Book Website

This book has a dedicated website at:
www.acceleratingindiasdevelopment.in

The website includes the data and code needed to produce the Figures in this book, and links to the data used in the Tables.

It also includes links to the references cited in this book, with links to open access variants wherever possible.

Finally, the website will aim to be interactive and list all upcoming talks and public lectures based on ideas in the book to allow readers to stay engaged with the ideas in the book and continue the conversation.

II. Expanded Table of Contents

This section includes an expanded table of contents up to two sub-sections of each chapter, to help readers navigate the book. This may be especially useful for those who have read the book once and seek to quickly revisit specific topics or refresh their understanding of an argument's narrative and evidentiary arc.

However, it has been placed at the end of the book and not at the beginning, since expanded tables of contents are more common for textbooks than for books meant for a general readership. This structure aims to make the book easier to read for general readers (who can focus on the main text), while also being comprehensive for academic readers, students, and practitioners (who will benefit from the detailed notes, references, and the extended table of contents, located after the main text). The index at the end of the book focuses on names and places referred to in the book, with the expanded table of contents being provided in lieu of a 'subject index.'

Expanded Table of Contents

Contents .... **ix**

Preface .... **xi**

Chapter 1: India@75: The Imperative of State Capacity **1**

1. Framing the Problem.. 1

2. Characterizing India's Crisis of State Capacity 6

3. Why Is the Indian State Ineffective at Core Service Delivery? 10

    3.1 From nation-building to election-winning *11*

    3.2 Systemic overload *12*

    3.3 Trust deficits *13*

    3.4 An ineffective bureaucracy.. *14*

    3.5 Elite exit *15*

    3.6 A highly stratified, fragmented, and unequal society................ *15*

    3.7 Institutional stasis *17*

    3.8 Fixing the problem is really difficult...................................... *18*

4. Why Should Investing in State Capacity Be a Top
Priority for India? 19

    4.1 It offers a 10x+ Return on Investment (RoI) opportunity........... *19*

    4.2 An effective state is essential for accelerating India's development *21*

    4.3 All Indians will benefit from a more effective state *22*

    *4.4 We also need state capacity to secure democratic freedoms
for individuals*... *23*

    4.5 The COVID-19 crisis highlights the importance of state capacity.......... *24*

5. How Do We Build a More Effective State and Accelerate
India's Development? 25

    5.1 The key actors 26

    5.2 Building an effective state 27

    5.3 Accelerating India's development 29

    5.4 Making it happen 30

6. Why States and Chief Ministers Should Lead the Way 30

7. Conclusion 33

Section I: The Key Actors

Chapter 2: The Politicians' Predicament 39

1. Indian Democracy in a Global Historical Perspective 41

    1.1 The evolution of the modern state 41

    1.2 Indian exceptionalism and its consequences 44

2. Understanding Political Incentives and Constraints 47

    2.1 The status quo incentivizes vote-bank politics and polarization 47

    2.2 Concentrated benefits and diffused costs of bad policies 50

    2.3 Strategic underinvestment in state capacity 52

    2.4 Politicians value visible and short-term measures of effectiveness 53

    2.5 Political financing and the 'democracy tax' 54

    2.6 Disproportionate influence of elites on politics and the state 55

3. Making the Political Case for Investments in
State Capacity 56

    3.1 Voters increasingly reward good governance 58

    *3.2 Winning political narratives increasingly rely on a record
of good governance* 59

    3.3 Data-driven governance reforms can work—and work fast 62

    *3.4 A politics of service delivery can reduce the need for
political fundraising* 63

3.5 Intrinsic and legacy motivations... 64

3.6 Preserving faith in democracy itself.. 65

4. Conclusion 67

Chapter 3: The Bureaucracy's Burden.......................................**69**

1. The Indian Bureaucracy: Key Facts and Challenges 71

1.1 Severe staff shortages... 72

1.2 Limited and misdirected accountability 74

1.3 Inadequate autonomy... 76

1.4 Lack of local embeddedness of government employees........................... 77

1.5 Limited opportunities and incentives for skill upgradation..................... 78

1.6 A paperwork state... 79

1.7 Lack of tenure and managerial stability 80

2. Understanding the Status Quo...82

2.1 Colonial legacy... 82

2.2 Political factors 84

2.3 Economic factors... 85

2.4 Judicial factors 86

2.5 Institutionalized risk aversion 87

2.6 The bureaucracy's work can be inherently more challenging................. 89

2.7 Premature load bearing: Trying to do much with too little..................... 90

2.8 Bureaucratic self-interest 91

3. How Can We Ease the Bureaucracy's Burden and Make
It More Effective? 93

*3.1 Make it a political priority to invest in strengthening
the bureaucracy* 93

3.2 Eliminate corruption in hiring, postings, and transfers........................ 94

3.3 Ensure stability of tenure of government staff................................. 97

3.4 Increase autonomy on process and accountability for outcomes........... 97

3.5 Invest in data-driven governance at all levels of the government........... 99

3.6 Communicate the rationale for reforms both
    internally and externally.. *100*
4. Conclusion 101

Section II: Building an Effective State

Chapter 4: Data and Outcome Measurement.................... 105
1. Understanding the Status Quo and Its Limitations 107
  1.1 A snapshot of the Indian statistical system........................... *107*
  1.2 There is little actionable data on fundamental
      development outcomes *108*
  1.3 The government lacks visibility on citizen experiences with
      public services... *108*
  1.4 The government's own administrative data is often unreliable *109*
  1.5 Why is there no systematic, actionable measurement
      system in India? *112*
2. Building a New Measurement Architecture for Better
  Governance 113
  2.1 Who should lead measurement?.. *114*
  2.2. Conduct regular field-based surveys to measure key
      development outcomes *116*
  2.3 Use phone-based surveys to capture real-time beneficiary experience.. *119*
  2.4 Implement nested supervision to improve administrative
      data integrity... *123*
  2.5 Institutional safeguards for data quality, privacy, and transparency......... *125*
3. Conclusion 127

Chapter 5: Personnel Management 129
1. Key Facts on Public Sector Personnel Management in India.........130
  1.1 Government salaries (on average) are too high.......................... *30*
  1.2 High public sector pay may hurt recruitment quality,
      and the broader economy... *132*

1.3 There is no link between pay and productivity in the public-sector *135*

1.4 Credentialing and training systems for public employees are weak *137*

1.5 Public sector personnel management is also weak *138*

1.6 Lifetime employment *139*

1.7 Geographic mismatch *141*

2. Some Implementable Ideas for Improving Public Personnel
Management 141

*2.1 Invest in a digital human resource management
information system (HRMIS)* *141*

*2.2 Institutionalize capacity-building and competence-based
career progression* *143*

*2.3 Design and implement apprenticeship-based models
for skilling and hiring* *145*

*2.4 Augment state capacity by hiring staff on fixed-term
renewable contracts* *152*

2.5 Improve time use and task allocation of staff *156*

*2.6 Implement data-driven performance measurement
and management* *157*

2.7 Case Study: Junior Panchayat secretaries in Telangana *160*

2.8 Key implementation principles *161*

3. Conclusion 163

Chapter 6: Public Finance—Expenditure **165**

1. Key Facts and Themes on Public Spending in India 166

1.1 Expenditure by level of government and sectors *166*

1.2 Expenditure by major spending categories *168*

1.3 Investment versus welfare spending *170*

2. Quality of Expenditure Is Weak across All Categories
of Spending 172

2.1 Quality of welfare spending *172*

2.2 Quality of capital spending *177*

2.3 Quality of salary spending *180*

2.4 Weak fund flow processes hurt quality of expenditure *180*

3. Improving Quality of Expenditure—Key Principles 181

3.1 Improving effectiveness of budget allocation *182*

3.2 Improving effectiveness of expenditure *187*

3.3 Improving timing and process of fund flows *191*

4. Improving Quality of Expenditure—An Action Roadmap 192

*4.1 Invest in technical and analytical capacity in state
finance departments* *192*

*4.2 Institutionalize a focus on quality of expenditure in
budget processes* *193*

4.3 Use strategic budgeting analysis for better public communication *194*

4.4 Pay Commission reforms *195*

4.5 An innovation fund for improving expenditure quality *196*

5. Conclusion 197

Chapter 7: Public Finance—Revenue **199**

1. Key Facts on Government Revenue in India 200

1.1 India's tax-to-GDP ratio in global perspective *200*

1.2 Volume and composition of tax collection by level of government *203*

1.3 Key challenges in the status quo *205*

2. Key Principles and Evidence on Effective Revenue Collection 208

2.1 Economic principles for revenue collection *208*

2.2 Political principles for revenue collection *212*

2.3 Empirical evidence on effective revenue collection *214*

3. Some Implementable Reform Ideas 215

3.1 Improve strength, skills, and utilization of staff *215*

3.2 Strengthen investments in data analytics and forensics *216*

3.3 Pay special attention to revenue collection in urban areas *217*

*3.4 Use 'sin' taxes to the extent possible and undo the
folly of prohibition* *222*

3.5 Tax agricultural incomes above a high threshold.................................. 225

3.6 Support a uniform GST rate 226

4. Conclusion 227

Chapter 8: Federalism and Decentralization 229

1. Key Concepts 230

1.1 How does country size affect the quality of governance?...................... 230

1.2 The promise of federalism 233

1.3 Key tensions in federal governance systems 234

1.4 Summary... 236

2. Federalism: The Indian Experience 236

2.1 India's federal structure of government 236

2.2. Governance in India is highly centralized.. 238

2.3 Why is governance in India so centralized?.. 244

3. Implementable Reform Ideas 247

*3.1 Consider creating smaller states, districts, sub-districts,
and local bodies* 248

*3.2 Encourage greater state- and district-level policy
experimentation*... 249

*3.3 Increase both autonomy and accountability in centrally
sponsored schemes* 251

*3.4 Use principles of federalism to clarify jurisdiction across
government tiers* 254

3.5 Accelerate decentralization within states... 258

3.6 The delimitation challenge and opportunity 262

4. Conclusion 264

Chapter 9: The State and the Market 267

1. Key Facts and Insights on State and Market Provision
of Services in India.. 270

*1.1 Private options are increasingly popular even when
the public option is free* 270

1.2 Private providers (in health and education) have fewer credentials but are better managed and work harder 270

1.3 Private providers deliver comparable quality—at a significantly lower cost 272

1.4 Quality of public and private providers within a market are highly correlated 275

2. Conceptualizing State and Market 276

3. Making Markets Work Better for Overall Welfare 278

3.1 Regulate with a light touch, based on disclosures rather than mandates 279

3.2 Invest in providing information to allow for informed decision-making 281

4. Leveraging Markets to Better Serve the Poor 284

4.1 Vouchers and public-private partnerships (PPP) 285

4.2 Exit and voice 286

4.3 Designing vouchers and PPPs for equity 288

4.4 Procurement and contracting 289

4.5 Targeting and fiscal implications 291

4.6 Importance of investing in a robust public option 291

4.7 Some practical examples 293

Example 1: Choice-based DBT in the PDS 293

Example 2: Charter Schools 295

5. Conclusion 296

Section III: Accelerating India's Development

Chapter 10: Shifting the Preston Curve for Development 301

1. Benchmarking India's Performance 302

2. The Growth versus Development Debate 304

3. Accelerating Development *and* Growth 307

3.1. The case for optimism: shifting of the Preston curve for life expectancy 307

3.2. Shifting the Preston curve for all development sectors *309*

3.3 Shifting India's Preston curve for development
between now and 2047 .... *310*

3.4. Bringing 'state capacity' to the centre of the development discourse *317*

3.5. Jumpstarting a virtuous cycle of faster development and growth *319*

3.6. The importance of jobs, productivity, and economic growth *320*

4. Conclusion *322*

Chapter 11: Education and Skills.. **325**

1. Understanding the Indian School Education System *327*

1.1 Key facts and trends *327*

1.2 Our default approach is not working *327*

1.3 Does anything work? *332*

1.4 Putting it together.. *336*

2. Evidence-Based Reform Ideas *338*

2.1 Foundational literacy and numeracy mission *338*

2.2 Implement a practicum-based teacher training and
selection programme... *342*

2.3 School size optimization... *343*

2.4 Invest in strengthening public pre-school education *346*

2.5 Consider implementing volunteer-led after-school programmes........... *348*

2.6 Leveraging technology for improving pedagogy and governance........... *349*

2.7 Exam reform *352*

2.8 Take skilling and vocational education seriously..................... *354*

2.9 Leverage private schools for the public good *357*

3. Conclusion *359*

Chapter 12: Health and Nutrition **361**

1. Key Facts...*362*

1.1 India's performance on health outcomes *362*

1.2 Health expenditure: public and private *365*

1.3 Access to healthcare in India *367*

1.4 Quality of healthcare across public and private providers.................... 372

1.5 Cost-effectiveness 378

1.6 Putting it together: access, quality, and cost 379

1.7 The nutrition challenge.. 379

1.8 The pollution challenge 380

2. Principles and Policy Ideas 381

2.1 Prioritize preventive public health over curative private health............ 381

2.2 Consider health impacts of actions outside the health ministry............ 383

2.3 Invest strategically in medical education 386

2.4 Strengthen public health systems for both curative and
   preventive care.. 389

2.5 Improve the functioning of healthcare markets................................... 393

2.6 Improve child nutrition in mission mode 399

3. Conclusion 402

Chapter 13: Police and Public Safety **403**

1. Key Facts on Policing in India.. 404

1.1 The big picture 404

1.2 Colonial origins.. 407

1.3 Police in India are underfunded, understaffed, and overworked.......... 408

1.4 Police are also poorly trained and underequipped 409

1.5 Police are not representative, and have limited
   connection to communities 411

1.6 Poor public perception and low public trust in the police.................... 412

1.7 Chronic under-reporting of crime.. 413

1.8 Limited professional autonomy and institutionalized corruption 414

2. Implementable Reform Ideas 415

2.1 Improve measurement of public safety... 416

2.2 Competency-based career management for existing staff...................... 419

2.3 Create a practicum-based diploma and degree in public safety............ 422

3. Conclusion 428

Chapter 14: Courts and Justice 431

1. Key Facts on Courts in India 432

1.1 Structure of the Indian justice system 432

1.2 Delays and backlog in courts 433

1.3 Understaffed and under-resourced courts 434

1.4 High procedural inefficiencies 435

*1.5 Costs of weak judicial processes, and returns to
augmenting judicial capacity 436*

2. Implementable Reform Ideas 439

2.1 Fill district court vacancies and sanction more posts 439

*2.2 Create a judicial clerkship programme to boost
productivity of district judges 440*

2.3 Improve operational efficiency of courts 443

2.4 Executive actions to reduce the need for litigation 444

2.5 Legislative actions to improve judicial capacity 445

2.6 Making it happen 448

3. Conclusion 450

Chapter 15: Social Protection and Welfare 453

1. Key Facts on Welfare Programmes in India 454

2. Principles for Effective Social Protection and Welfare
Programmes 456

*2.1 Analyse welfare programmes through the lens of
equity and efficiency 456*

2.2 Help the poor through income support rather than price subsidies 464

2.3 Make social protection programmes systematic and reliable 465

2.4 Build social safety trampolines rather than social safety nets 466

3. Implementable Reform Ideas 467

3.1 Harmonize and simplify welfare schemes 467

*3.2 Create a dedicated implementation quality cell for all
welfare programmes 468*

3.3 Empower citizens with choices regarding accessing welfare programmes 469

3.4 Replace agriculture subsidies with income-based support 471

3.5 Consider implementing an inclusive growth dividend 474

3.6 Consider piloting and evaluating an urban employment guarantee programme 479

4. Conclusion 480

Chapter 16: Jobs, Productivity, and Economic Growth 483

1. Key Facts on Employment and Wages in India 485

2. Key Concepts 489

2.1 Some basic economics of growth, productivity, jobs, and wages 489

2.2. Structural transformation and Indian exceptionalism 491

2.3 Factor misallocation 493

2.4 Multiple binding constraints 500

3. An Action Agenda for State Governments 501

3.1 Assign responsibility for jobs, productivity, and economic growth 501

3.2 Focus less on concessions to specific investors and more on providing high-quality public goods, which benefits all actors in the economy 502

3.3 Launch a structural transformation mission 506

3.4 Reform public-sector hiring to create more jobs both directly and indirectly 510

3.5 Measure and monitor key indicators of productivity and misallocation 512

3.6 Improve alignment of incentives within the government 514

3.7 Balancing economic dynamism with worker protection 516

3.8 Balancing economic growth with environmental protection 517

4. Conclusion 519

Section VI: Making It Happen

Chapter 17: Reimagining Institutions.................................... **523**

1. India's Institutions: A Brief Overview......................................526

   1.1 The state-level opportunity *530*

2. Institutional Reforms to Strengthen State Capacity.........................531

   2.1 State Statistics Commission *533*

   2.2 State Public Human Resources Commission *535*

   2.3 State Public Finance Commission *537*

   2.4 Summary and common themes *539*

3. Institutional Reforms to Make Indian Democracy
Work Better...541

   3.1 Replace 'first past the post' with 'ranked choice voting'. *541*

   3.2 Pilot 'citizen assemblies' with randomly chosen citizens as members *546*

   3.3 Some practical considerations. *553*

4. Conclusion 554

Chapter 18: State, Citizen, and Society.................................. **557**

1. A Framework for Constructive Civic Engagement.........................559

   1.1 Understanding how class structure has shaped the status quo *559*

   1.2 From class conflict to collective action. *561*

   1.3 Economists, activists, and finding common ground *563*

   1.4 Building trust between the state and civil society *567*

   1.5 Building a broad social coalition to improve public service delivery *570*

   1.6 Section summary *571*

2. How Can We All Contribute to Accelerating India's
Development?...572

   2.1 Government *572*

   2.2 Civil society *575*

   2.3 Entrepreneurs and business leaders. *579*

2.4 Academia and think tanks.. *581*

2.5 Media *583*

2.6 Philanthropy *584*

2.7 Individual citizens *588*

3. Strengthening India, and Leading the World 592

3.1 Finding solutions that are 'made for India' *592*

3.2 Strengthening India's position in the world *594*

4. Conclusion 598

Notes... **601**

References.. **729**

Acknowledgements **783**

Additional Resources **791**

Expanded Table of Contents **793**

Index.. **807**

Index

Acemoglu, Daron 525, 617, 712
Acharya, Shankar 624
Adityanath, Yogi 60, 64
Ahluwalia, Montek 606, 623,
    708, 719, 723
Ahuja, Amit 405, 428
Aiyar, Shankkar 267, 337, 426
Aiyar, Yamini 80
Allen, Woody 618, 725
Ambedkar, Bhimrao (Babasaheb)
    16, 44, 66, 246, 571, 618, 662
Andhra Pradesh, AP 20, 59, 61,
    65, 75, 111, 121, 131, 135,
    136, 137, 173, 193, 238, 248,
    271, 273, 275, 327 351, 352,
    369, 378, 395, 624, 626, 632,
    633, 634, 644, 648,
    669, 670, 679, 708
Andrews, Matt 90
Appleby, Humphrey 622, 647
Arrow, Kenneth 362
Assam 52, 205, 238

Bajari, Pat 630
Banerjee, Abhijit V. 89, 317,
    318, 335, 369, 392, 396, 632
Banerjee, Mamata 61
Banerji, Rukmini 113

Bang, Abhay 147, 388
Bang, Rani 147, 388
Banga, Ajay 681
Bangladesh 304, 363, 364, 365,
    496, 504, 707
Bardhan, Pranab 55, 57,
    474, 559, 612
Basu, Kaushik 14
Bhagwati, Jagdish 33, 268,
    305, 606, 677
Bharadwaj, Prashant 446
Bhatia, Mukhmeet 605
Bhattacharya, Shrayana 80
Bhattacharya, Pramit 625
Bihar 49, 61, 65, 73, 74, 140,
    173, 175, 181, 184, 193,
    205, 208, 223, 224, 237,
    241, 248, 263, 275, 331,
    344, 365, 370, 374, 375,
    386, 411, 446, 461, 469,
    470, 589, 612, 652, 653,
    657, 690, 693, 701
Blinder, Alan 678
Bloom, David 308
Botswana 601
Brazil 8, 218, 233, 237, 243,
    265, 493, 610
Bush, George W. 714

Canada 238, 667
Chawla, Haresh 476, 580
Chelliah, Raja 258
Chhattisgarh 61, 173, 248, 365,
   369, 479, 671
China 8, 10, 65, 66, 72, 99, 130,
   201, 213, 217, 218, 230, 233,
   243, 244, 247, 250, 265, 304,
   305, 306, 311, 322, 363, 364,
   365, 381, 484, 493, 504,
   514, 515, 566, 576, 597, 598,
   601, 606, 618, 650, 678, 705,
   722, 727, 728
Chiplunkar, Gaurav 632
Chouhan, Shivraj Singh 61, 65
Clear, James 600
Coase, Ronald 712
Congo, Democratic Republic
   of (DRC) 237
Cuba 320, 321
Cuomo, Mario 721

Darapuri, S.R. 408, 692
Das, Chittaranjan 262
Das, Jishnu 396
Dasgupta, Aditya 73
Deaton, Angus 317,
   318, 369, 677
Debroy, Bibek 447,
   577, 622, 658
Dercon, Stefan 711, 719
Desai, Padma 606
Dixit, Sheila 64
Drèze, Jean 33, 130, 268, 306,
   480, 563, 720
Duflo, Esther 317, 318,
   335, 369, 677

Egypt 237
Ethiopia 237

Faguet, Jean-Paul 716
Finland 673
Foster, Andrew D. 673
France 201, 218, 237, 608
Friedman, Benjamin 322
Friedman, Milton 287

Gandhi, Indira 84, 262
Gandhi, Mohandas (Mahatma)
   44, 184, 322, 490, 561, 659
Germany 237, 328, 355,
   667, 727
Ghatak, Maitreesh 475
Glaeser, Edward 495
Greenstone, Michael 381
Grove, Andy 157
Guerrero, Alexander 548
Guha, Ramachandra 716
Gujarat 48, 60, 61, 65, 205, 224,
   237, 304, 374, 375, 502, 503,
   519, 531, 657, 690,
Gupta, Akhil 79
Gupta, Shekhar 617

Haldea, Gajendra 671
Haryana 183, 205, 304, 459,
   472, 622, 631, 635
Himachal Pradesh 225,
   392, 620
Hirschman, Albert 286
Hobbes, Thomas 609
Holmstrom, Bengt 419, 693
Hong Kong 306, 601
Huntington, Samuel 602

Indonesia 136, 214, 233, 333,
    648, 698, 706, 722
Iyer, Param 153

Jaitly, Akshay 464
Jammu and Kashmir 205
Japan 237, 727
Jayadev, Arjun 724
Jharkhand 73, 121, 173, 205,
    238, 248, 369, 370, 374, 375,
    383, 386, 479, 629. 680
Jinping, Xi 66, 597
Joshi, Vijay 474

Kamaraj, K. 65
Kapur, Devesh 2, 73, 244, 405,
    428, 528, 603
Karnataka 61, 193, 237, 369,
    370, 378, 386, 479, 502, 617,
    635, 660, 695, 700, 716
Kejriwal, Arvind 64, 259, 717
Kelkar, Vijay 209, 457
Kenya 238, 477, 612, 680, 706
Kerala 16, 52, 175, 193, 238,
    241, 263, 275, 304, 306, 320,
    321, 365, 369, 370, 374, 375,
    378, 674, 677, 680
Keynes, John Maynard 172
Khaitan, Tarunabh 714
Khan, Aamir 583
King, Martin Luther Jr. 721
Kingdon, Geeta Gandhi 343
Kondepati, Rajendra 629
Kornai, Janos 85
Kotwal, Ashok 703
Kremer, Michael 317,
    318, 677, 680

Krishna, Anirudh 53, 595
Krishna, Arvind 681
Krishnan, K.P. 662, 664
Kumar, Alok 661
Kumar, Nitish 61, 65

Lahiri, Ashok 606
Landemore, Helene 548
Landes, David 35

Madhya Pradesh, MP 65, 74,
    79, 110, 136, 173, 205, 237,
    248, 271, 273, 334, 365, 367,
    371, 424, 479, 626, 680,
    685, 702, 725
Mahalanobis, P.C. 107, 625
Maharashtra 16, 138, 147, 173,
    174, 178, 181, 205, 207, 223,
    237, 341, 388, 392, 414, 470,
    479, 498, 501, 502, 644, 645,
    652, 680, 690, 701
Mahesh, Ashwin 265
Maskin, Eric 714
Mathew, Santhosh 59,
    616, 629, 636
Mathur, Nayanika 612
Mehta, Pratap Bhanu
    528, 612, 721
Milgrom, Paul 419, 693
Modi, Narendra 60, 61, 64, 65,
    478, 569, 617, 662, 698
Mohan, Rakesh 5, 602, 624
Mohanan, P.C. 629
Mokyr, Joel 250
Mookherjee, Dilip 703
Morocco 238
Mundle, Sudipto 474

Nadella, Satya 681
Nader, Ralph 714
Naidu, Chandrababu 65
Narasimhan, Lakshman 681
Narasimhan, Manasi 724
Natarajan, Gulzar 87, 607
Nehru, Jawaharlal 44,
    178, 262, 659
Niehaus, Paul 475, 701
Nilekani, Nandan 593
Nilekani, Rohini 586
Nooyi, Indra 681
North, Douglass 711, 712
Norway 8, 72, 667

Odisha 61, 121, 173, 238, 455,
    479, 507, 646
Olson, Mancur 613
Ostrom, Elinor 712

Pai, Sajith 580
Pakistan 76, 237, 245, 275, 282,
    633, 659, 671
Panagariya, Arvind 33, 268, 305
Pande, Rohini 130, 380
Patel, Sardar Vallabhbhai
    71, 262, 659
Patkar, Medha 718
Patnaik, Naveen 64
Penalosa, Enrique 220
Pichchai, Sundar 681
Portugal 250
Prakash, Nishith 331
Prasad, Rajendra 262
Preston, Samuel 308

Pritchett, Lant 3, 12,
    90, 602, 674
Punjab 172, 174, 183,
    459, 472, 644

Rajagopalachari, C. 262
Rajasthan 143, 207, 237, 282, 327,
    333, 334, 345, 367,369, 411,
    626, 669, 671, 685, 700, 701
Rao, Chandrasekhar
    Kalvakuntala 61
Rao, Narasimha 25
Rao, Rama N.T. 248
Ravallion, Martin 703
Rawls, John 647, 681
Ray, Debraj 474, 703
Reddy, Rajasekhar Y.S. 65
Riker, William 663
Robinson, James 525
Rosenzweig, Mark 673
Roy, Rathin 476, 496
Rukmini, S. 64
Russia 65, 608, 717, 727
Ryan, Nicholas 702

Sabharwal, Manish 296, 355, 496
Sahni, Sanjay 589
Sane, Renuka 643
Sargent, Thomas 698
Saudi Arabia 238
Saxena, Naresh
    Chandra 92, 414
Schumpeter, Joseph 491
Sen, Amartya 33, 130, 268, 292,
    305, 306, 317, 678, 714

Shah, Ajay 209, 457, 464, 604,
    643, 698, 717
Shanmugaratnam, Tharman 466
Sharan, M.R. 589
Shiller, Robert 702
Shilton, Peter 623
Shultz, George 3
Singapore 65, 220, 277, 306,
    355, 466, 601, 667, 673
Singh, Abhijeet 110, 341, 351
Singh, Chaudhary Charan 48
Singh, Manmohan 25
Singh, Param Bir 414
Singh, Prakash 407, 415,
    560, 691, 693
Singh, Raman 61
Singhvi, Abhishek 696
Sinha, Jayant 710
Sinha, Shakti 690
Smith, Adam 704
Solanki, Madhav Singh 48
Somanathan, T.V. 87,
    219, 607, 623
South Africa 218, 512
South Korea 65, 238,
    306, 601, 705
Soviet Union 232
Spain 238, 250
Sri Lanka 304, 306, 674, 708
Stein, Jill 714
Steinem, Gloria 725
Subramaniam, Rajesh 681
Subramanian, Arvind 45, 192,
    193, 219, 474, 615, 702
Sudarshan, Anant 702

Sukhtankar, Sandip 475, 701
Sundararaman, Venkatesh
    135, 272
Sunstein, Cass 293
Swarup, Anil 359, 634
Sweden 201, 667
Switzerland 355, 667

Taiwan 65, 306, 601, 705
Tamil Nadu 16, 21, 51, 52, 65,
    73, 74, 111, 132, 134, 136,
    143, 149, 184, 193, 197, 205,
    224, 237, 241, 254, 263, 275,
    334, 335, 346, 348, 349, 365,
    374, 375, 378, 392, 393, 400,
    427, 479, 502, 576, 596, 611,
    657, 659, 666, 680, 683
Tanzania 237, 252
Telangana 19, 61, 73, 119, 120,
    160, 161, 205, 238, 248, 327,
    334, 386, 395, 455, 479, 531,
    622, 644, 645, 663, 666
Thaler, Richard 292, 293
Thomas, Susan 698
Tilly, Charles 41, 201, 602
Trump, Donald 714

Uganda 238
Ukraine 717, 727
United Kingdom, UK, Britain
    9, 41, 44, 45, 201, 218,
    237, 434, 609, 615, 650,
    695, 711, 719
United States, USA, US 8, 9,
    13, 44, 45, 46, 72, 172, 201,

209, 212, 221, 224, 225, 230,
233, 243, 246, 247, 263,
264, 265, 306, 308, 355, 408,
434, 442, 491, 493 539, 545,
547, 609, 610, 614, 645, 646,
650, 654, 655, 659, 663, 664,
674, 679, 682, 691, 695, 702,
706, 714, 727
Uttar Pradesh, UP 48, 49, 60,
61, 72, 74, 117, 132, 134,
207, 208, 237, 248, 263, 275,
304, 337, 365, 375, 378, 411,
414, 488, 502, 615, 652, 653,
672, 680, 690, 691
Uttarakhand 248, 304,
620, 660
Uzbekistan 238

Vaishnav, Milan 52, 528
Vajpayee, Atal Bihari 226
Varma, Amit 583, 604, 630,
639, 643, 662, 664, 717

Varshney, Ashutosh 716
Vashisht, Mahima 639
Verma, Arvind 693
Vietnam 201, 237, 304, 306,
321, 322, 363, 364, 365, 496,
576, 673, 678, 707, 722
Virmani, Arvind 624

Weaver, Jeff 701
Weber, Max 602
West Bengal 52, 61, 74, 173,
205, 237, 370, 396, 479
Williamson, Oliver 712
Woolcock, Michael 90

Xiaoping, Deng 66, 99, 514

Yadav, Lalu Prasad
49, 612, 690
Yadav, Mulayam Singh 49, 690
Yadav, Yogendra 466
Yugoslavia 232

Scan QR code to access the
Penguin Random House India website